THE LIFE, WORK AND LEGACY OF FRIEDRICH ENGELS

THE LIFE, WORK AND LEGACY OF FRIEDRICH ENGELS

EMERGING FROM MARX'S SHADOW

Edited by
Eberhard Illner, Hans A. Frambach and Norbert Koubek

Translated by
Joseph Swann and Mícheál Úa Séaghdha

BLOOMSBURY ACADEMIC
LONDON • NEW YORK • OXFORD • NEW DELHI • SYDNEY

BLOOMSBURY ACADEMIC
Bloomsbury Publishing Plc
50 Bedford Square, London, WC1B 3DP, UK
1385 Broadway, New York, NY 10018, USA
29 Earlsfort Terrace, Dublin 2, Ireland

BLOOMSBURY, BLOOMSBURY ACADEMIC and the Diana logo are trademarks of
Bloomsbury Publishing Plc

First published in English in Great Britain 2023

Copyright © Eberhard Illner, Hans A. Frambach and Norbert Koubek, 2023

Eberhard Illner, Hans A. Frambach and Norbert Koubek have asserted their right under the
Copyright, Designs and Patents Act, 1988, to be identified as Editors of this work.

Translated by Joseph Swann and Mícheál Úa Séaghdha

The original edition was published in 2020 under the title *Friedrich Engels. Das rot-schwarze
Chamäleon* by WBG Academic, Darmstadt (Germany)

Series design by Tjaša Krivec
Cover Image: Engels, Friedrich Politician and socialist theoretician,
Barmen 28.11.1820 – London 5.8.1895. Portrait, c. 1850. (© AKG Images)

All rights reserved. No part of this publication may be reproduced or transmitted
in any form or by any means, electronic or mechanical, including photocopying,
recording, or any information storage or retrieval system, without prior
permission in writing from the publishers.

Bloomsbury Publishing Plc does not have any control over, or responsibility for,
any third-party websites referred to in this book. All internet addresses given in
this book were correct at the time of going to press. The author and publisher
regret any inconvenience caused if addresses have changed or sites have ceased
to exist, but can accept no responsibility for any such changes.

Every effort has been made to trace the copyright holders and obtain permission
to reproduce the copyright material. Please do get in touch with any enquiries or
any information relating to such material or the rights holder. We would be pleased
to rectify any omissions in subsequent editions of this publication should they
be drawn to our attention.

A catalogue record for this book is available from the British Library.

A catalog record for this book is available from the Library of Congress.

ISBN HB: 978-1-3502-7268-2
PB: 978-1-3502-7267-5
ePDF: 978-1-3502-7269-9
eBook: 978-1-3502-7270-5

Typeset by Newgen KnowledgeWorks Pvt. Ltd., Chennai, India
Printed and bound in Great Britain

To find out more about our authors and books visit www.bloomsbury.com
and sign up for our newsletters.

CONTENTS

List of Plates vii
List of Figures ix
List of Contributors xi
Preface xiv

Introduction 1

1 'My Immortal Works': Friedrich Engels as Journalist and
   Publicist – An Overview 7
   Jürgen Herres

2 Engels on Marx: Biography as Politics 27
   Wilfried Nippel

3 Friedrich Engels, Victor Adler and Austromarxism 43
   Günther Chaloupek

4 Man and Machine: Conceptions of Technology in the Writings
   of Friedrich Engels, Karl Marx and Ernst Kapp 63
   Eberhard Illner

5 'The General' as Admiral: Friedrich Engels and the Naval Warfare Debate 85
   Kurt Möser

6 The 'Promised Land'? Friedrich Engels, the United States and
   the Future of Capitalism 101
   James M. Brophy

7 The Transformation of the World: Friedrich Engels and
   the Development of Productive Forces in the Second Half
   of the Nineteenth Century 119
   Werner Plumpe

8 The Revolutionizing of Labour: Friedrich Engels and the Changing
   Face of Work in Manchester and London 137
   Margrit Schulte Beerbühl

Contents

9 The Economic Thought of His Age: Friedrich Engels and the Tension between Creation and Destruction 165
Hans A. Frambach

10 'This Frederick! This Frederick! A Naughty Wicked Boy Was He …': Engels, Marx and the Critique of Political Economy 199
Heinz D. Kurz

11 Repairing *Das Kapital*?: Friedrich Engels and the Publication of *Das Kapital II* and *III* 223
Regina Roth

12 Work and 'The Company': Historical and Current Trends 241
Norbert Koubek

13 Overview: Engels in His Time 249
Jürgen Kocka

14 Annex: Note on the Editorial History of Marx's and Engels' Writings 255

Notes 257
Bibliography 319
Index 337

PLATES

1 Friedrich Engels, c. 1864
2 Adolph Menzel, *Iron Rolling Mill*, 1872/5
3 Francois Bonhemmé, *Casting in Le Creusot*, 1864
4 Paul Friedrich Meyerheim, *Borsig's Locomotive Assembly Hall*, 1873
5 Carl Eduard Biermann, *Borsig's Engineering Works in Berlin*, 1847
6 Carl Wilhelm Hübner, *The Silesian Weavers*, 1846
7 V. Poljakov, *Karl Marx and Friedrich Engels at Work on the Communist Manifesto*, 1961
8 *Capital and Labour*, 1843
9 Pyotr Beloussov, *Lenin with Delegates to the Third Komsomol Congress 1920*, 1949
10 Viktor Adler (1852–1918), c. 1910
11 Joan Planella i Rodriguez, *The Working Girl* or *The Weaver*, 1882
12 Karl Marx, sketch of a simple-acting atmospheric steam engine after Thomas Newcomen, c. 1851
13 Charles Babbage, c. 1850
14 Jean Veber (1864–1928), *Dynamis*
15 Edward Moran, *The Commerce of Nations Rendering Homage to Liberty*, 1875
16 C. Parsons, *City of New York*, 1856
17 National Cotton Mule Spinners Association of America
18 Robert Köhler, *The Strike*, 1886
19 Paul Friedrich Meyerheim, *Railway Bridge over the Rhine at Ehrenbreitstein*, 1875
20 Francois Bonhommé, *Forging of the Elbow Shaft of a 60 hp Frigate at the Indret Works*, 1865
21 Ludwig Dettman, *Golden Sunday*, 1893
22 Augustus Edwin Mulready, *Uncared For*, 1871
23 Paul Friedrich Meyerheim, *Wheel Production at Borsig's Locomotive Factory*, 1873
24 George Cruikshank, *The Tax on Property*

Plates

25 *Pyramide a Renverser*, c. 1900
26 David Ricardo, 1839
27 Thomas Malthus, 1833
28 Justus von Liebig, 1856
29 Heinrich Kley, *The Krupp Devils*, 1914
30 Isaak Israilovich Brodsky, *Lenin in Smolny*, 1930

FIGURES

1.1	Friedrich Engels, 'My Immortal Works', 1892	8
1.2	Draft of the *Manifesto of the Communist Party*	13
1.3	Friedrich Engels' membership card of the International Working Men's Association	23
2.1	*World History: The Communists*, 1848	28
2.2	David Levi Elkan, *Karl Marx as Prometheus*, 1843	31
2.3	Karl Marx (1818–1883), 1875	33
2.4	Mikhail Alexandrovich Bakunin (1814–1876), c. 1863	35
4.1	Karl Marx, 1861	69
4.2	Andrew Ure	71
4.3	Ernst Kapp	76
4.4	Franz Reuleaux, 1879	80
5.1	Sailors of HMS *Eclipse*	86
5.2	HMS *Warrior*	88
5.3	USS *Monitor* in James River, Virginia, 1862	92
5.4	The capture of CSS *Atlanta*	97
5.5	Types of armoured ships	99
6.1	Friedrich Engels in Brighton, 1877	102
6.2	Corliss Steam Engine at the Philadelphia World's Fair, 1876	112
8.1	George Cruikshank, *The British Bee Hive*, 1840 (reprint 1867)	155
8.2	*London: A Pilgrimage*, 1872	156
9.1	Friedrich List, 1845	168
9.2	*Das Zollvereinsblatt*, 1843	172
9.3	Carl Menger	176
9.4	Robert Owen	185
9.5	Lorenz von Stein	188
9.6	Joseph Alois Schumpeter, c. 1920	191
10.1	Friedrich Engels, 1845	201
10.2	Adam Smith, *Wealth of Nations*, 1828	207

Figures

10.3	Pierre-Joseph Proudhon, *c.* 1855	212
10.4	John Stuart Mill, 1870	215
10.5	Justus Liebig's chemical laboratory, 1842	219
11.1	Friedrich Engels, 1888	225
11.2	Karl Marx, *c.* 1868	226
11.3	Karl Marx, *Das Kapital*, 1867	229
11.4	*A Sisyphean Task* – editing the manuscripts of *Das Kapital*	233
13.1	Forward to the XI SED Party Congress, 1986	249

CONTRIBUTORS

James M. Brophy is Francis H. Squire Professor of European History at the Department of History of the University of Delaware, USA, since 2008; as assistant professor of history he worked at the University of Delaware since 1992; Chair of the Central European History Society in 2019–20. His research focuses on the social, economic, and political history of nineteenth-century Germany.

Günther Chaloupek, former head and director of the Department of Economic Research, Chamber of Labour, Vienna, Austria (1986–2013); he has held leading positions in numerous commissions of Austrian organizations; author of publications on issues of economic policy and economic history, and co-author of an Austrian industrial history and an economic history of Vienna.

Hans A. Frambach, Professor of Economics at the Faculty of Economics, Schumpeter School of Business and Economics, University of Wuppertal, Germany, since 2003 and the Head of Department of Microeconomics and History of Economic Thought since 2014; research focuses on the history of economic thought, New Institutional Economics, economic theory of the nineteenth century and the theory of social and economic change.

Jürgen Herres, historian at Berlin-Brandenburg Academy of Sciences and Humanities on the Marx-Engels-Gesamtausgabe since 1994. He has researched widely on the history of capitalism, the life and works of Marx and Engels. He published *Marx und Engels. Porträt einer intellektuellen Freundschaft* (Marx and Engels: Portrait of an Intellectual Friendship, 2018).

Eberhard Illner is a historian and director of Friedrich Engels House – Museum of Early Industrialization, Wuppertal, Germany (2008–18); archivist at the Federal Archives Koblenz 1984–6 and Historical Archives City of Cologne 1986–2008. He organized many exhibitions and published books and articles on social and cultural history of the nineteenth and twentieth centuries, as well as on Marx and Engels and their environment.

Jürgen Kocka, German social historian and professor emeritus at the Free University of Berlin; Permanent Fellow at International Center for Advanced Study in the Humanities, Humboldt University Berlin, Germany, and Senior Fellow at the Center for Contemporary Historical Research Potsdam, since 2009. His main research interests include German and European history of modernity, history of workers and labour, history of the European bourgeoisie, social history of the GDR, and comparative history.

Contributors

Norbert Koubek is professor emeritus of Economics at the Faculty of Economics – Schumpeter School of Business and Economics, University of Wuppertal; Chair of Business Administration, especially production and innovation (1994–2010); his research focuses on the theory of entrepreneurship, international corporate strategies, management of innovations, and strategic production management.

Heinz D. Kurz is professor emeritus of the University of Graz, Austria, and Director of the Graz Schumpeter Centre, since 2006; visiting fellow at Wolfson College, University of Cambridge (UK) (1977–8), Theodor Heuss Professor at Graduate Faculty of New School for Social Research, New York (1990–1) etc.; numerous visiting professorships all over the world. His research interests in economic theory comprise production, growth, income distribution, technological change and natural resources; he also works on the history of theory in economics and is General Editor of the unpublished works of Piero Sraffa.

Kurt Möser, professor at the Institute of History at Karlsruhe Institute of Technology, Karlsruhe, Germany, since 2011; he is one of the leading German-speaking mobility historians; many teaching positions, e.g., DAAD lectureships in Oxford (1984–6) and New Delhi (1991–3); he was curator of the State Museum of Technology and Labour Mannheim 1989–2006; research interests are on cultural history of technology, history of mobility and military history in the industrial age.

Wilfried Nippel is a senior professor at the Humboldt University of Berlin since 2015, after holding professorships in ancient history at the University of Bielefeld and the Humboldt University of Berlin (1992–2015); full member of the Berlin-Brandenburg Academy of Sciences and Humanities since 1997; visiting scholar at the Swedish Collegium for Advanced Study in Uppsala (2008–9), Fellow at the Max Weber Kolleg of the University of Erfurt (2011–12); recipient of the Karl Christ Prize of the University of Frankfurt; research in the history and social sciences, constitutional and social history of antiquity, ancient political theory and its modern reception, history of antiquity, Max Weber, Marxism.

Werner Plumpe is professor of Economic and Social History at the Goethe-University, Frankfurt am Main since 1999; Director of the Department of History at Goethe University; visiting professorship at Keio University, Tokyo 1998; member of the Historical Commission of Bavarian Academy of Sciences; Chairman of the Association of Historians of Germany, 2008–12. His research is on history of business and industry in the nineteenth and twentieth centuries, history of industrial relations, history of economic thought and economic theories.

Regina Roth is a historian at the University of Heidelberg, research assistant Free University of Berlin; research associate Marx-Engels-Gesamtausgabe (MEGA), Berlin-Brandenburg Academy of Sciences and Humanities since 1995: editor of manuscripts of Karl Marx's *Das Kapital* (1871–94) and letters of the late Engels, currently editing early works of Friedrich Engels (1844–6); since 2006, she has coordinated the digital edition of MEGA.

Margrit Schulte Beerbühl, temporary professorships at the Institute of History at Heinrich Heine University of Düsseldorf since 2012, Great Britain Center Berlin 2015; board member Society for Overseas History; Visiting Research Fellow University of Hertfordshire 2018–20; Research Fellow Historical College Munich spring 2020. Research focuses: British history of seventeenth to twentieth centuries, international trade history in the First Global Age and history of industrialization, migration history, history of the lower classes and trade unions, and the history of the family.

PREFACE

> Labour is the source of all wealth, the political economists assert. And it really is the source – next to nature, which supplies it with the material that it converts into wealth. But it is even infinitely more than this. It is the prime basic condition for all human existence, and this to such an extent that, in a sense, we have to say that labour created man himself.[1]

Friedrich Engels wrote this short note in 1876. He was living at the time in London and for some years had been deeply concerned with questions of science. The three sentences shed light on the conceptual world of one of the nineteenth century's last universal theoreticians. The specialization of the sciences, each with its own logic, was by the late 1870s a long-established fact, and it is against this background that Engels raises the category of work into a prime mover not only of the economy but of society and, indeed, of life itself. This was the basis on which he and Marx developed their theories, and the breadth of insight informing his perspective demands that any critical-historical approach to Friedrich Engels' writings be interdisciplinary. Engels had early freed himself from the confines of his upbringing and surroundings, and with advancing years, he increasingly saw himself as a citizen of the world and its concerns.

The critical-historical analysis of the writings of these two great nineteenth-century figures must take an overall account of the (often neglected) fact that many of these works were published posthumously, and hence without original authority. One thinks, for example, of the collection of disparate fragments, notes and manuscripts from 1845 later published as *The German Ideology* or of the body of writings in various stages of development assembled and edited as Engels' *Dialectics of Nature*. The uniform interpretation imposed on the works of Marx and Engels in the course of the twentieth century – partly under the ideologically charged influence of such sources, resurrected and abstracted from their historical context – has inevitably created false impressions about the completeness and coherence of an 'oeuvre', and this, in turn, has complicated the reception history of the ideas and theorems in question.

The instrumentalizing of the no more than seemingly consistent 'works' of Marx and Engels for political purposes was a highly significant aspect of twentieth-century history. All the more surprising, then, some thirty years after the end of political block-building and the breakdown of its ideologies, to still find in the academic literature historically uncritical 'head in the air' excursions that treat the works of these two writers – the philosophically minded theorist Marx and the empirically interested entrepreneur and commentator Engels – as if they expressed universal truths abstracted from time and place. On the other hand, an increasing body of well-sourced research is currently engaged in elucidating the historical development of the works and their themes rather than simply expounding their content. Here, it is not so much a matter of adding interpretation to interpretation, but of contextualizing Marx's and Engels' writings for present-day readers.

The idea of a longitudinal project reflecting this concern came into being some years ago - initially in Manchester, a city intimately associated with Engels' work and its impact. As both a merchant and an entrepreneur, he had observed the close connection between the Industrial Revolution and its technological presuppositions and social consequences - perspectives highlighted both in Manchester's Museum of Science and Industry and at Quarry Bank Mill in the Cheshire village of Styal. But a third dimension, the history of economic thought, was clearly also of importance in this context, and it seemed appropriate to broach this by outlining the importance of Engels' early *Outlines of a Critique of Political Economy* (1844) and the impact it had on Marx.

To set the questions Engels raised in their historical context, and to analyse the history of their impact, is a far-ranging but at the same time fascinating undertaking. The ball had begun to roll, but it would not have made it over the first hill if it had not been urged on by colleagues willing to invest energy and empathy transcending the line of duty. Wuppertal's Schumpeter School Foundation offered a framework within which a wide range of experts could collaborate in truly interdisciplinary dialogue, and our thanks are due in this respect above all to the authors who have contributed to this volume and to those who have provided help and support to the project.

This includes in the first place the board, advisory council and benefactors of the Foundation, in particular Dr Dr h.c. Jörg Mittelsten Scheid, who provided generous funds both for the originally planned conference - which unfortunately had to be cancelled as a result of the Covid-19 pandemic - and for the publication of the present volume. His lively interest in new approaches to Friedrich Engels - with whom his own family is related - was a great encouragement to the project: without him, the undertaking would have remained enshrined in a desk drawer.

Our thanks are also due to the University of Wuppertal - especially to the Faculty of Economics and the Schumpeter School of Business and Economics - for the organizational support they have given to our research and to the many other individuals and institutions who have contributed to the success of the project. Among these, the archives, museums and private collectors who provided access to their holdings and allowed us to use their photographs and artworks deserve special mention: for the expert, these add valuable atmosphere, and for the general reader, they bring the historical sources closer.

Many questions have been raised, and many, both old and new, remain unanswered. In future, indefatigable research will still be necessary. There is no final wisdom; the task of science and scholarship endures, and truth must be gained afresh every day. This applies in full measure to the findings presented here. Far from being definitive, they claim only to be facets in a wide and complex field of research.

Wuppertal and Düsseldorf (April 2020)

INTRODUCTION

Ever since the Industrial Revolution, 200 years ago, technology, labour and capital have been seen as key determinants of a society's economic and social progress. Technology has been a factor in the history of civilization at least since humans developed tools and learnt the use of fire. And work has been an invariable constituent of human survival in interaction with nature. Every age in which humans have met and exchanged goods has also known some form of accumulation of capital. At the end of this long evolutionary, dynamic and indeed irreversible development stands what today we call 'capitalism', understood in the general sense of a universal socioeconomic system using the profits of productive and speculative investment for reinvestment and consumption. From this perspective, capitalism has had a greater impact on almost all the world's societies in the past 200 years than any earlier socioeconomic order. Whether, and to what extent, it can meet present and future challenges depends on its ability to change and adapt. Already in 1848, when this order of production was still young, Marx and Engels saw no future in it – a perspective they sought to theoretically underpin. But it is an open question whether they maintained their notion of the inevitable collapse of capitalism through to the end.

This book offers – with a view to a better understanding of problems both past and present – a critical analysis not only of the historical course of the capitalist system but also of its theoretical patterns of explication. It takes account, too, of significant insights of contemporaries whose positions not infrequently contrasted with those of Marx and Engels. The questions asked in these pages address the emergence of technology, labour and capital as central categories of economic thought, particularly on the threshold of European capitalism in the 'long 19th century', which stretched from *c.* 1780 to 1914. They focus, too, on the growth of real relations among these factors and the terms in which their interactions were perceived by astute contemporary observers. New problems of uneven development and massive economic fluctuation accompanying the incipient Industrial Revolution in the first half of the nineteenth century presented immense challenges and, in the search for answers, many – following the usage of the day – had recourse to theories derived from traditional cameralism (state fiscal administration), political science or the philosophies of Hume and Hegel.

On these central issues of global development, the journalist and later textile merchant Friedrich Engels (1820–1895) had strong opinions and the ability to express them eloquently. He was a practical man, an autodidact; not a good public speaker, but a powerful writer whose knowledge of foreign languages quickly brought him international respect as a journalist. His writings – to this day under the long shadow of Karl Marx – range encyclopaedically from *belles lettres* to history, from military science to technology, from anthropology to the natural sciences and from politics to economics.

At the centre of Jürgen Herres's overview of these texts stands an unremarkable sheet of paper, ironically headed 'My Immortal Works', on which the 70-year-old Engels listed his numerous, wide-ranging publications. His career as a writer had begun with poems and reports in his early years as a business apprentice, before his 1845 book *The Condition of the Working Class in England* ignited discussion of the social issue and its economic roots. For half a century, Engels was extraordinarily productive: in UNESCO's *Index Translationum* (Index of Translations), he ranks among the world's 50 best-selling authors. Nevertheless, his published writings, along with the unpublished manuscripts – for example, the sketches later collected under the heading *Dialectics of Nature* – should not be treated as a body of unified and coherent 'works'.

Much research over recent decades has been dedicated to the 'Marx–Engels problem', in other words, the question to what extent Engels, as the trusted custodian of Marx's thought, was responsible – through popular writings like *Socialism Utopian and Scientific* and, especially after Marx's death on 14 March 1883, through the publication of Volumes II and III of *Das Kapital* – for the spread and reception of an emphatically modified and hence no longer authorized version of theoretical elements which Marx himself had left indeterminate. In view of the fact that some of the writings we have today were unpublished and generally unknown at the end of the nineteenth century, the first generation of Marxist theoreticians and politicians relied heavily on what Engels transmitted to them. Wilfried Nippel's critical approach to the sources opens perspectives on this question – crucial for a modern understanding of the works of Marx and Engels – aspects that may come as a surprise to not a few 'Marxologists' of our own day.

From late 1849, Friedrich Engels had been living in England, from where he had repeatedly sought – with mixed success – to influence the socialist and social-democratic parties of the European mainland. In the 1880s and 1890s he was particularly interested in the path taken by Victor Adler's Austrian social-democratic movement. Günther Chaloupek's essay sheds light on the arguments and reasoning adduced by Engels in pursuit of a programmatic, but at the same time pragmatic, approach by the Social-Democratic Workers' Party, founded in 1889, towards a socialist Austria.

In the thought of the day, the industrialization of the early nineteenth century represented an unquestionable 'revolution' based on technological invention, although on closer scrutiny it was driven rather by the updating and innovation of pre-existing inventions. The widespread changes, on the one hand, in energy provision and raw materials extraction and, on the other hand, in material processing and production methods, as well as in transportation, mobility and communications and in the ancillary fields of chemistry and pharmacy, were welcomed by the majority as the 'triumphal progress of technology'. With it came a readjustment of the relation between the human and the machine. Engineering became a fundamental scientific discipline, with the resultant development in England of early principles of a theory of technology. Based on empirical and positivist ideas derived from contemporary philosophy of science, Engels outlined a technological anthropology quite different from anything the Hegelian Karl Marx ever conceived. On his own admission unversed in technology, Marx nevertheless, in *Das Kapital*, undertook a new theoretical definition of the human–machine interface to explain the historical development of productive forces in light of contemporary technology. Against this background, Eberhard Illner compares the technological concepts of Friedrich Engels, Karl Marx and Ernst Kapp – the founder of the philosophy of technology in Germany – whom neither Marx nor Engels knew.

Virtually forgotten today, Engels' articles on military science and technology were an important aspect of his output – and he judged them so. War, in its varied forms and changing instrumentation, was for him never an isolated phenomenon of history: he always saw it in its political, economic and technological contexts. As such, it granted him insights not only into the social structure of the combatant parties but also into the close connection between military technology and constitutional provisions – a field in which the autodidact gained recognition as a perceptive analyst with an eye for detail. Kurt Möser sets 'the General's' (as the Marx family called him) talent for naval conflict in the context of radical innovation between 1860 and 1890 in the Great Powers' conception of the role of the fleet, strikingly exemplified in the armament of American warships during the Civil War.

Not only through its defence industry but above all in the mass production of capital goods and the opening up of the immense spaces of the country through rationalized, large-scale agricultural production, the United States leaped in the last quarter of the nineteenth century into the front rank of industrial nations. Both Marx and Engels realized the potential of this 'awakening giant' at an early stage, chronicling with care America's economic heartbeat and its impact on Europe; Engels went so far as to visit the United States himself to gain an immediate impression. James M. Brophy examines Engels' analyses of the American economy and the situation and outlook of labour, which differed so markedly from those in Germany or France.

In contrast with the many contemporary observers fascinated by the sheer abundance of goods and changing consumption patterns of the age, Engels saw the gap opening between those patterns and opportunities and the 'misery' of the working classes whose labour ultimately created them. Werner Plumpe analyses Engels' answer to this social question. The explicatory historical model he worked out with Marx postulated a developmental dynamic in capitalism rooted in the antagonism between productive forces and conditions of production that would necessarily lead to the collapse of the system. What he largely overlooked was the energy latent within prevailing conditions, whose cyclical crises can be seen as fluctuations in an upward trend borne above all by relatively constant growth in productivity rather than as the inevitable death knell of capitalism. The centripetal tendencies of the last third of the nineteenth century were not, as Engels supposed, signs of an inevitable monopolization and consolidation; most of the major corporations of the period were eventually brought down by radical discontinuities in technology. Nor did temporary technological bottlenecks lead to the demise of capitalism as such. Engels' conception of productive forces was as naïve as it was rigid: naïve in the automatisms to which he considered it subject, rigid inasmuch as he admitted no change in the penal conditions of production he had observed and recorded since the 1840s.

Margrit Schulte Beerbühl sets Engels' admonitory observations in *The Condition of the Working Class in England* in the context of contemporary source material relating to the exploitation of labour, particularly in Manchester and London. The widespread mechanization of production processes and the transition to factory environments and modern business forms caused, albeit haltingly and unevenly, the dissolution of traditional work structures. Early losers in this process were spinners, weavers and women, who worked by hand at home, many of whom were forced into the low-wage sector of untrained casual labour, where they competed with Irish immigrants. As the capital city, London had a significantly different demand structure from other urban centres, with a requirement, on the one hand, for high-end luxury articles, many of which could not yet be industrially produced, and on the other, for cheap mass-produced goods to satisfy an exploding populace. Land and energy prices, as well as wages, were too high for the city to become a hive of factory-based industry, but developments were no less dramatic for that. Economies of scale introduced here immediately affected people rather than machines, reducing the manual work of tailors, seamstresses and shoemakers, for example, to a dreary mechanical routine. Many in the world's biggest city were condemned as a result to a level of miserable existence.

Staking out central elements of what later became known as 'scientific socialism', Engels' well-known early economic studies, *Outlines of a Critique of Political Economy* (1844) and *The Condition of the Working Class in England* (1845), did much to stimulate Marx's interest in political economy. Engels clashed head-on with the economic theories of the day and was not shy in stating his own counter-positions. From the viewpoint of the history of economic thought, Hans Frambach asks to what extent these writings met contemporary critical and scientific standards: Did they take account of existing perspectives and approaches? How disinterested were they in what they recorded, how prejudiced in choosing what they observed? Did Engels prefer sources that suited his own opinions to those judged at the time scientifically sound? The question of the overall significance of political economics – the discipline he so scorned – for life in the burgeoning industrial nations is touched upon, as also are the many contemporary positions critical of that approach, some of them issuing from classical economists, some from representatives of other theoretical trends. Background analyses are broached as to how Engels arrived at some of his convictions – for example his vehement rejection of Malthusian population theory – and reasons given for his inattention to the writings of Lorenz Stein, whose contribution to the dissemination of socialism in Germany was anything but negligible. Finally, the concept of creative destruction – established in economic theory above all by Joseph Schumpeter in the twentieth century but already known in the nineteenth – is seen to play a role in Engels' thought and actions alike.

On the basis of the *Outlines of a Critique of Political Economy*, Heinz D. Kurz provides a systematic analysis of Engels' perception of that field. Castigating the industrial conditions prevailing in the mid-1840s, and attacking the national economy that in his view supported them, the young textile merchant sketched his vision of a better future society. More faithfully than most contemporaries, he records the pulse of the time: his observations on science, technology and work resound with the beat of the first machine age, the thunder of mechanical hammers, the din of factories. As never before, the new industrial world enslaved men and women in a social order of privately owned production facilities, but with more equitable distribution the massive increase in productive forces could, he maintained, afford a future in morally acceptable circumstances. Engels' assault on 'the economists' landed the occasional telling blow, but not everything he aimed at actually existed. From Adam Smith to David Ricardo, he repeatedly misunderstood classical political economics or credited it with notions it had never held. Moreover, his envisioned future society remained pale and undefined. He addressed the information problem but underestimated its consequences for the organization of a pre- or non-market society, and the idea that an acceptably functioning society could dispense with humanly created institutions seems somewhat bizarre. So far as Engels was concerned, the national economy was an embodiment of error to be combated with every available means.

While *Outlines* marks the beginning of Engels' concern with political economics, Volumes II and III of Marx's *Das Kapital*, which he edited after the author's death, established Engels as that work's prime interpreter. Regina Roth's detailed analysis of the genesis of the manuscript and its far-reaching editorial emendations confirm Engels' claim to interpretive authority over Marx's economic theory and with it over the direction of the socialist movement and its political issues and implications. On the other hand, Engels left to posterity the Pythian saying, 'Our theory is not a dogma but the exposition of a process of evolution', a statement which in every sense invites interpretation. Chameleon-like, he slipped into the role of the Delphic oracle, launching a still ongoing worldwide discussion as to the right way to exit from capitalism.

How, then, did capitalism develop after Engels? In a brief overview, Norbert Koubek details the shift in the conditions of commercial activity resulting from technological developments, changing needs and aspirations of the workforce and changes in economic, political and societal structures – displacements in the universe of corporate work expressed in such keywords as Taylorism, Fordism, lean management, participative management, globalization, digitization and sustainability. These developments, however, have affected different regions of today's networked and globalized world very differently. The processes of change evident in the Western parliamentary democracies, where industrialization began and whence it spread across the world, call for a different developmental model from that applicable to countries at the initial stage of development, where the conditions described by Engels to some extent still obtain. Between these two model regions lie the so-called emerging nations, with aspects and options in both directions. Against this broad backdrop, certain issues remain as relevant today as they were for Engels, among them population growth, the distribution of wealth and the changing technological and social nature of work processes.

In his concluding summary, Jürgen Kocka notes the rising appreciation accorded to Engels in recent years relative to Marx – a result, among other things, of a more nuanced historical approach to his person. On the one hand, it has become repeatedly clear how decisively Engels' notions of capitalism and its crises derived from his first-hand experience in the West German and English textile (and in particular cotton) industry.

On the other hand, Engels can be seen – despite the Bohemian traits and other non-bourgeois elements of his lifestyle and despite the sharp critique of bourgeois culture that informs his writings – as a striking example of the European bourgeoisie. He is a product of bourgeois culture in its nineteenth-century West European dress. The Friedrich Engels of this volume, then, is an unequivocally nineteenth-century figure – a historical distance that seems entirely appropriate for his reception today.

CHAPTER 1
'MY IMMORTAL WORKS': FRIEDRICH ENGELS AS JOURNALIST AND PUBLICIST – AN OVERVIEW

Jürgen Herres

Amid the handwritten documentation in the estate of Friedrich Engels lies an unremarkable sheet of paper dated 1891. On it Engels lists his numerous publications. Although the list was meant seriously, he revealed a distance to it, in his own way, by giving it the ironic title *My Immortal Works*.

The 70-year-old had been asked by the German national economist Ludwig Elster, one of the editors of the recently established *Handwörterbuch der Staatswissenschaften* (Concise Dictionary of Political Science), for a list of his writings along with 'absolutely reliable' autobiographical information.[1] Engels apparently sent both to Elster immediately. Neither the letter of reply nor the materials sent to Germany have survived, but at least the sheet of paper mentioned has. A year later, a short biographical encyclopaedia entry about him appeared – accompanied by a more detailed list of his writings. The *Handwörterbuch*, which was published by Gustav Fischer Verlag in Jena, quickly gained in circulation and reputation as an encyclopaedia of the social sciences; it went through several editions and was updated in the 1950s first as the *Handwörterbuch der Sozialwissenschaften* (Concise Dictionary of the Social Sciences) and then as the *Handwörterbuch der Wirtschaftswissenschaften* (Concise Dictionary of Economics).[2] Engels thus availed himself of the opportunity to be introduced to the German-speaking academic world. A year later he did the same for Karl Marx, whose death had occurred some ten years earlier in 1883.[3]

The piece of paper with the list is at first glance unspectacular. Engels lists his work for newspapers as well as independent publications, along with books and pamphlets based on magazine articles. And yet, even though the list includes over thirty entries, important texts and projects – not only from a modern point of view – remain absent. It contains – presumably in keeping with the origin of the request – almost exclusively German-language publications; Engels' numerous English and French publications are left out, as are his activities as a correspondent for the *New York Tribune*, which extended over a decade, and his commentary on the Franco-Prussian War of 1870–1 in the London evening newspaper *The Pall Mall Gazette*. From our modern perspective, there is no reference to his participation in the drafting of *The German Ideology* or to his own manuscripts treating the *History of Ireland* or the *Dialectics of Nature*.

While Engels might speak of his 'works' with delicate irony, both his and Marx's writings and theories were ideologized in the twentieth century to an extent and with an earnestness that is hardly comprehensible today. Their writings and the manuscripts

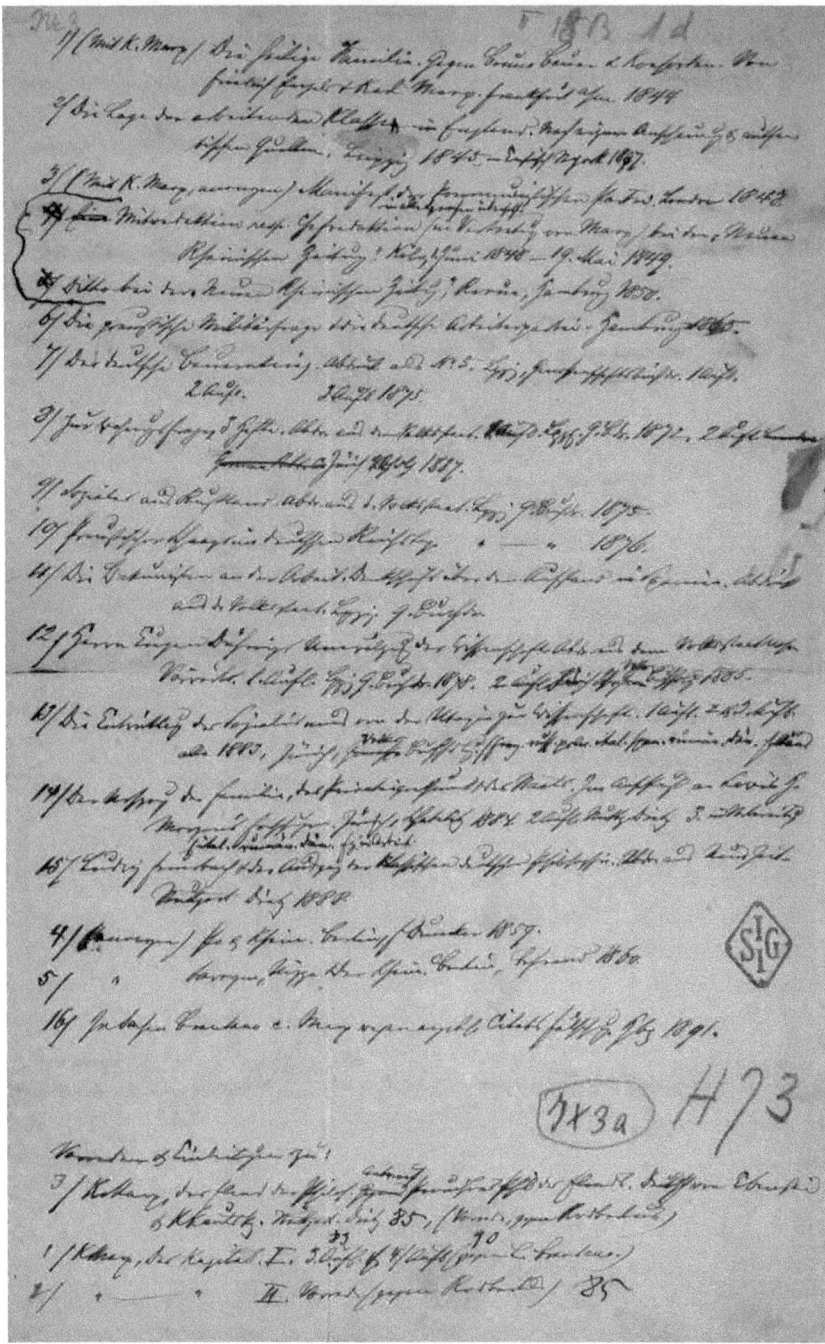

Figure 1.1 Friedrich Engels, 'My Immortal Works', 1892. Handwritten draft of a list of his publications, written in April 1891. In 1892, a printed version of the list with a biographical sketch of Engels appeared in the *Handwörterbuch der Staatswissenschaften*. © IISG Amsterdam Marx-Engels Archive.

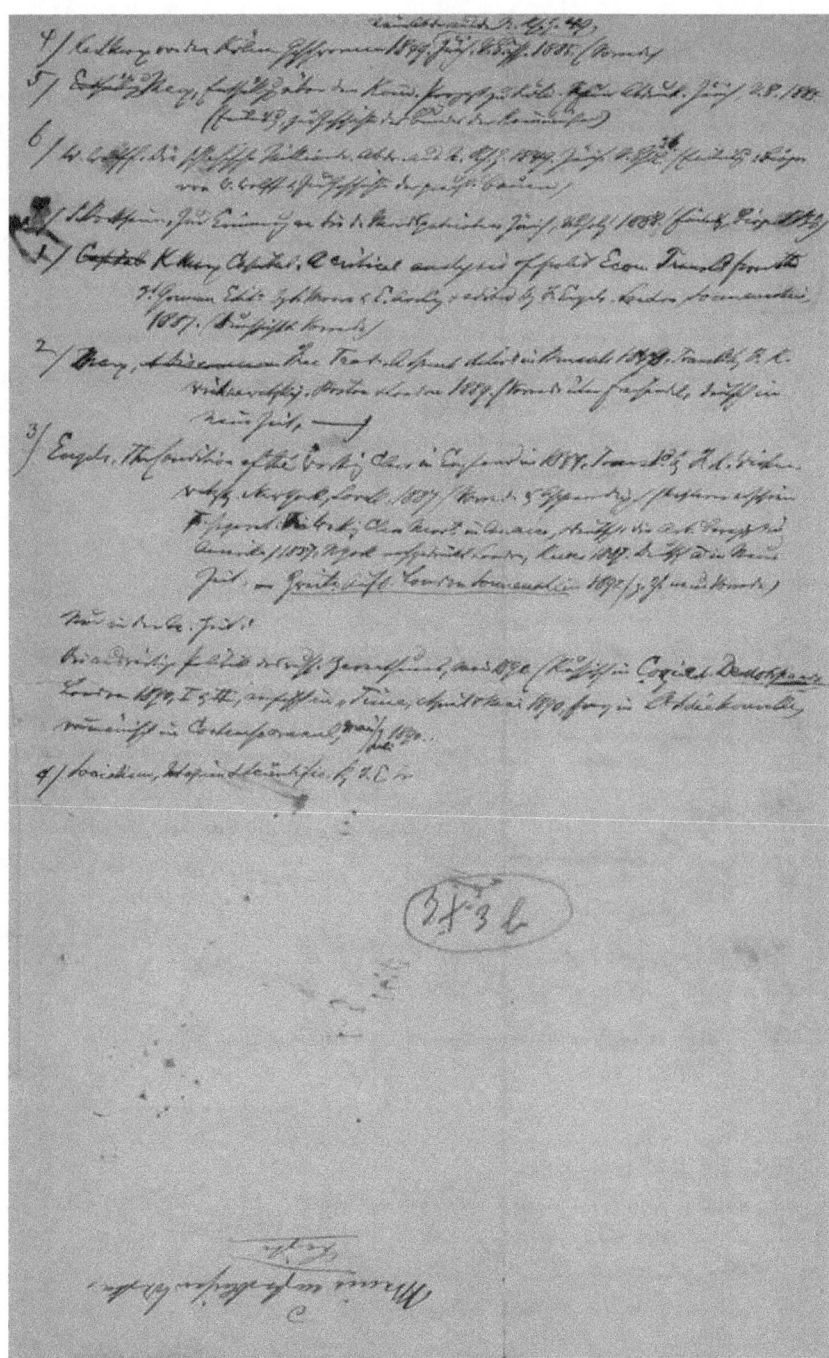

Figure 1.1 continued

unpublished during their lifetimes were taken out of the context of contemporary debate and intellectual trends in which they belonged, thus effectively reinterpreting many of the terms they had used and coined. Equally important was the uniform interpretation (*Vereindeutigung*) to which their manuscripts and writings were subjected: their reading as coherent 'works' – I deliberately use the term *Vereindeutigung* here in the sense of 'loss of complexity' recently made prominent by the Islamic scholar Thomas Bauer.[4]

Engels and Marx were in no way the founders of a self-contained theory nor indeed of a political worldview that provided a language of power and protest. Their *oeuvre* has a far more fragmentary character. Neither as revolutionaries nor as analysts of capitalism did they leave behind a single finished or even self-contained work. Marx's *Economic and Philosophic Manuscripts of 1844*,[5] for example, is a mixture of verbatim book excerpts and his own notes, not the first draft of a planned book. Marx's and Engels' 1845–6 manuscripts of *The German Ideology*[6] were indeed drafts, not, however, for a book, but for articles in a planned magazine. They never conceived such a book. And the first volume of *Das Kapital*, the only one to appear in Marx's lifetime, represents only a fragment of Marx's economic writings. The books now known as Volumes II and III of *Das Kapital* were compiled by Engels from the unfinished manuscripts – and that, we know, with great difficulty – after Marx's death.[7] Marx's original texts, which have now been deciphered and published, show that one can speak neither of a completed work nor of a complete theory.

With regard to Marx, this is now largely the consensus, though not for Engels, although it also to some extent applies to him. Engels' manuscripts of the *Dialectics of Nature*, which he wrote between 1873 and 1882,[8] present only fragments of consistent textual material, some of which are mnemonic aids with keywords intended for later elaboration and some of which are first drafts, with only a small proportion truly ready for print. Even his *Anti-Dühring*,[9] his attempt at an encyclopaedic summary of his and Marx's theories and reflections, was ultimately only a polemically slanted pamphlet. Engels' letters in the last decade of his life, the so-called *Altersbriefe*, can also be read as an attempt to recapture spirits summoned long ago.

Engels worked as a journalist and publicist throughout his life. Even as a trainee merchant at a Bremen cigar and coffee wholesaler's, the 18-year-old began publishing poems and reports, first in the *Telegraph für Deutschland* edited by Karl Gutzkow and then in newspapers published by the Cotta publishing house. In his first major series of articles, *Briefe aus dem Wuppertal* (Letters from Wuppertal), which provides us with one of the earliest descriptions of a German industrial area, he criticized the 'terrible poverty [that] prevails among … the factory workers' of his hometown.[10] The writer Gutzkow, however, claims to have regularly reworked Engels' beginner texts: 'If every rookie were to eject critical vomitings like this, who would ever print the greeny-yellow stuff in a decent paper?'[11] As a correspondent for the *Augsburger Allgemeine Zeitung* (Augsburg General News), Engels reported on the beginnings of 'screw steam navigation'[12] and, in a piece of reportage, described his trip to Bremerhaven, where he visited an emigrant ship.[13] In Manchester in 1842–4 and in Paris in 1847, he wrote about European social movements for German, English and French newspapers. Only once, during the revolution of 1848–9, was he employed as an editor; otherwise he worked until his death as a correspondent (alongside Marx from 1851 to 1862 for the *New York Tribune*) and as a freelance journalist and political activist for numerous socialist and social-democratic magazines and newspapers. Again and again, he proclaimed that he wanted 'to put the very narrowest limits to his journalistic activity', so as not to be forever the 'milk cow' – today we might say 'one-stop shop' – for all the needs of the social-democratic party and its press.[14] The range of topics he dealt with during his life was remarkably broad, ranging from politics, economics and contemporary history to philology, philosophy and natural history. For him Europe was a theatre of events, perceptions and thoughts.

If we take a closer look at Engels' list, we see a Western European social critic who dealt intensively with the dramatic upheavals of his time. As a young republican and communist who observed the process of industrialization with his own eyes, he sought to perceive and explain the changing world in a new way. He used the term *revolution* as a descriptive category for the tangible economic and social processes of change, but at the same time to express both his political concept of *acceleration* and his perspective on the future. The revolution of 1848–9 was the only truly European revolution that Engels witnessed, and its failure left a deep mark on him and his contemporaries. A '48er refugee, he worked in the 1850s and 1860s as an employee and then as a partner in a textile company in Manchester, able to publish only in his rather limited spare time. With his retirement from professional life in 1869, a second spring as a publicist and private scholar began. After Marx's death in 1883, he became the spin-doctor of European social democracy, successfully keeping alive the expectation that Marx (and he) had decoded the DNA of modern society. Today, we can see in him a social and societal critic more complex than his twentieth-century portrayal allowed, but also more self-contradictory.

In anticipation of a 'revolution'

Engels, the eldest son of an energetic textile industrialist of the same name from Barmen in the Wupper Valley – the 'German Manchester' – knew the Industrial Revolution and its consequences first-hand. In the British Manchester, one of the world's first industrial centres, where steam power and machinery had long since revolutionized production, he completed his commercial training between 1842 and 1844, radicalizing from a democratic republican to a fully-fledged communist. With his essay *Outlines of a Critique of Political Economy* – which appeared in 1844 in the Franco-German Yearbook,[15] edited jointly by Arnold Ruge and Karl Marx in Paris, and which strongly influenced Marx – he became the first representative of the German philosophical Left to enter the field of political economy and to draw attention to the contradictions associated with the concept of private property.[16]

Of all things, *this* essay is missing from Engels' list. Instead, the list begins with the book *The Holy Family* (1845), the first work he published together with Marx, but in which he himself had only a small share. The list of writings printed in the *Handwörterbuch*, which contains a number of additions to the handwritten list, does, however, refer to the reprint of the essay in the social-democratic journal *Die Neue Zeit* (The New Age) published shortly before the *Handwörterbuch* on the occasion of Engels' seventieth birthday.[17]

Engels in Manchester and Marx in Paris underwent similar intellectual transformations. When they first contacted each other by letter in 1844, and then met for ten summer days in Paris, they both saw socialism and communism as their socially transformative perspective. The focus of their thinking turned to 'modern bourgeois society, the society of industry, of universal competition, of private interest freely pursuing its aims, of anarchy, of self-estranged natural and spiritual individuality ... itself', as Marx wrote in *The Holy Family*. The French Revolution of 1789 was by no means to be regarded as an eighteenth-century experiment; on the contrary, as Marx succinctly put it, they jointly regarded the 'communist idea' that had emerged from it as 'the *idea of the new world order*'.[18]

The second publication Engels lists is his book *The Condition of the Working Class in England*. Written between autumn 1844 and March 1845 after his return to his native Wuppertal and published in May 1845, it made him famous throughout German-speaking central Europe.[19] For the English translation, which did not come until much later (1885–7), he wrote a preface and an appendix which also feature in his list of publications.[20] Using the example of cotton processing in England, he traces the development of large-scale industry and the formation of an impoverished industrial and agricultural proletariat. He examines the housing, health, nutritional and educational situation in the ghettoized slums of the big cities, where a brutal social war was raging. His book is a sociological monograph but at the same time a moral indictment. As late as 2007, Pope Benedict XVI cited Engels in his encyclical *Spe salvi* as a key witness to the 'horrific living conditions' of industrial workers, which he had described 'in a deeply shocking way'.[21] Third on the handwritten list is the *Manifesto of the Communist Party* (aka *The Communist Manifesto*), written in Brussels in the winter of 1847–8 and delivered in London in March 1848.[22]

Throughout his life, Marx always referred to Engels as his co-author, although he himself probably wrote at least sections one and two of the text alone in a single sitting, as is indicated by the only surviving sheet of manuscript, which is now on the UNESCO World Documentary Heritage list.[23] The unfinished sections three and four, which were obviously written in an even greater hurry, polemicizing against contemporary socialist and communist literature and outlining the next tasks of the communists in various countries, were possibly completed with the direct collaboration of Engels, who, expelled from Paris, had returned to Brussels at the end of January 1848.[24] Marx and he had received the commission in December 1847 in London at the founding congress of the Communist League, a secret society of émigré intellectuals and craftsmen activists.[25]

In the *Manifesto*, Marx and Engels summarized the materialist views of history and society which they had been developing since 1844. Political movements, institutions and ideas are described as historically and class-based, ultimately conditioned by basic macro-societal processes such as the unleashing of productive forces which began

Friedrich Engels as Journalist and Publicist

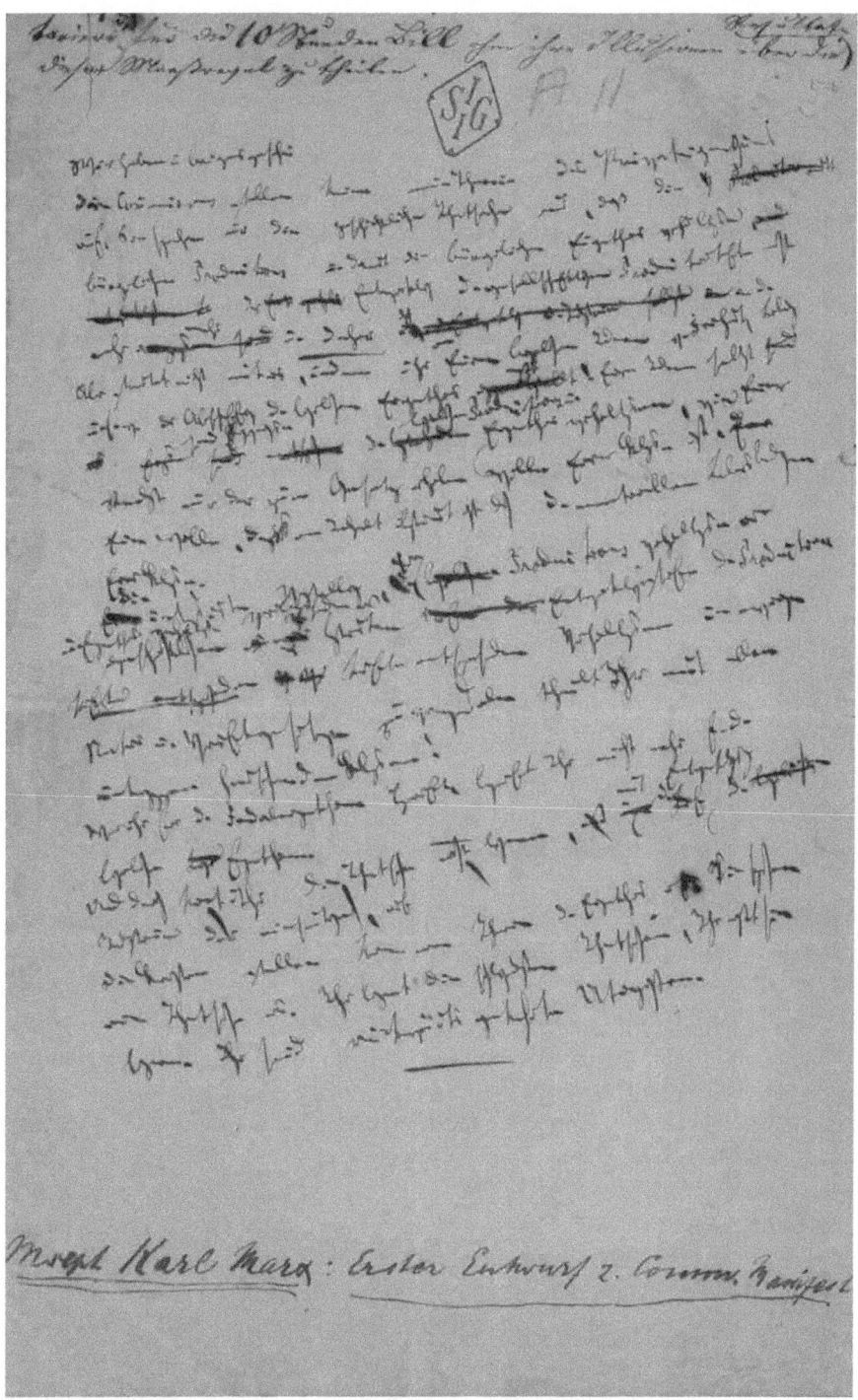

Figure 1.2 Draft of the *Manifesto of the Communist Party*. Marx's manuscript. © IISG Amsterdam Marx–Engels Archive.

with the Industrial Revolution, first in Britain and then in the early nineteenth century in western continental Europe. The upper middle class, the 'bourgeoisie', is itself 'the product of ... a series of revolutions in the modes of production and of exchange', in which each step was 'accompanied by a corresponding political advance of that class'.[26] In a type of dialectic of progress, the possibility of collective liberation of the revolutionary 'proletariat' was linked to the immanent contradictions of capitalism. In the spring of 1848, presumably one or two thousand copies of the *Manifesto* were distributed throughout the European continent,[27] but it had little effect on the revolution of 1848–9. Its real impact did not come until 1872 and above all in the twentieth century, when it was read primarily as a communist party programme,[28] only to be seen in 1998, on its 150th birthday, as a far-sighted account of capitalist globalization. The British historian Eric Hobsbawm was 'struck by the acuteness of the Manifesto's vision of the then remote future of a massively globalized capitalism'.[29]

The four publications mentioned above cannot adequately capture these formative years for Engels and Marx in Manchester, Brussels and Paris. Writing from Manchester, Engels described British political and social conditions in numerous correspondent reports in German opposition newspapers and continental European conditions in English newspapers. In the *New Moral World*, edited by Robert Owen, he claimed that England, France and Germany, the three great civilized countries of Europe, had recognized that a thoroughgoing revolution of social relations on the basis of common property had now become an urgent and unavoidable necessity.[30]

In 1844, in a series of articles published prior to his book *The Condition of the Working Class in England*, Engels described the 'revolution through which British industry has passed' as a process with its own internal dynamics that could not be stopped by anything and that was 'the foundation of every aspect of modern English life'.[31] He saw the 'creation of the proletariat by the industrial revolution' as 'the most important effect of the eighteenth century for England'.[32] The term 'proletariat' had begun to circulate only since the beginning of the nineteenth century. When Marx, writing at the end of 1843, interpreted the 'proletariat' politically as the subject of revolution, he was not yet thinking of industrial workers. For him, the term referred rather to a product of social dissolution and decay, to 'human masses ... resulting from the drastic dissolution of society, mainly of the middle estate'.[33]

In 1845–6, Engels and Marx came together with other communists in Brussels in a 'small German colony' (Jenny Marx).[34] Living next door to each other, they wrote the manuscripts that have become known as *The German Ideology*.[35] In them, we can see how Engels and Marx, coming from a background of criticism of religion and philosophy, discussing French and English social sciences and socialists, began to develop their 'materialist conception of history'. From 1890 onwards, Engels also began speaking of 'historical materialism'.[36] Their goal was to see the world differently, to recognize connections and developments, but also to renew the foundations of perception. As '*practical* materialists, i.e. *Communists*', they first wanted to impart basic awareness to the Germans – a people 'without presuppositions' – so that they could understand the sensual world surrounding them as a 'product of industry'.

From their point of view, the systems of thought of the time were not prepared for the processes of social transformation currently being driven by tensions and conflicts between relations of production (structures of ownership, class and distribution) and productive forces. Among these forces they subsumed the growing abilities and skills of men and women, which they saw as the driving force of social change as well as technological inventions and the development of new materials. In their view, 'the productive forces and the relations of exchange' had already 'developed so far ... that they had now, under the rule of private property, turned destructive',[37] a view that the 74-year-old Engels was to correct self-critically in 1895 in his last major text.[38] The fundamental considerations outlined above were originally formulated by Marx and Engels together. In January 1847 Engels expressly authorized Marx to use their joint findings in his *Anti-Proudhon* – a critique of the French socialist Pierre-Joseph Proudhon.[39]

In the Belgian capital, Engels and Marx also took the step into active politics. In 1847 they became co-founders of the Communist League, on whose behalf they wrote the *Communist Manifesto*. In the run-up to this, Engels was involved in the formulation of a *Draft of a Communist Confession of Faith* in June 1847[40] and wrote *The Principles of Communism* in October–November of that year. The future 'community of property', the draft states, will be based 'on the mass of productive forces and means of subsistence resulting from the development of industry, agriculture, trade and colonisation, and on the possibility inherent in machinery, chemical and other resources of their infinite extension'.[41] Engels went on to explain in the *Principles* that 'the Proletariat originated in the industrial revolution', and this in turn 'was precipitated by the discovery of the steam engine, various spinning machines, the mechanical loom, and a whole series of other mechanical devices'. On the proletarian revolution, he states that it will, above all, 'establish a democratic constitution, and through this, the direct or indirect dominance of the proletariat'. But 'democracy would be wholly valueless to the proletariat if it were not immediately used as a means for putting through measures directed against private property and ensuring the livelihood of the proletariat'.[42]

In 2019 the hitherto completely unknown *Circular of the First Congress to the Communist League* (co-authored by Engels as secretary of that congress in November–December 1847) appeared at an auction for the insane sum of €450,000. The document (dated 15 December 1847) stated that in the shadow of the 'significant movements ... in all the countries of Europe, ... the decisive struggle between the bourgeoisie and the absolute monarchy with its appendages of nobles, civil servants, soldiers and clergy is finally imminent in Germany, too'.[43] Previously, speaking to German workers at the London-based German Workers Educational Association on 30 November 1847, Engels had outlined the development of world history since the discovery of America. Since the 'advent of machines ... the barbaric condition' of all countries has been ruinously disturbed. The 'whole of human society, which formerly consisted of 4–6 different classes, has divided into two mutually hostile classes. ... The workers of the whole world have everywhere the same interests, everywhere different classes are disappearing and different interests coincide'.[44]

In the European Revolution of 1848–9

On 24 February 1848, after a brief, fierce barricade fight in Paris, the throne of the French King Louis Philippe was publicly burned and a republic proclaimed. Engels, expelled from Paris at the end of January, followed the news of the successful uprising at the Brussels railway station on the night of 25–26 February.[45] 'We confess that we had not dared hope for this brilliant success of the Paris proletariat,' Engels wrote in the *Deutsche-Brüsseler-Zeitung* (Brussels German News). 'Three members of the provisional government belong to the decisive Democratic Party. ... The fourth is a worker[46] – for the first time in any country in the world.' He could see 'the age of democracy' dawning.[47]

Together with Marx, he hurried via Paris to Cologne, where Marx succeeded in launching the *Neue Rheinische Zeitung* (New Rhenish Newspaper) with the support of Rhineland Democrats. The daily appeared for just under a year, from 1 June 1848 to 19 May 1849, as an 'organ of democracy'. In the brief moment when freedom of the press existed in Germany, the paper, financed by a limited partnership under French law, achieved a circulation of 5,000 to 6,000 copies. In the concert of German-language newspapers, it was a republican voice of its own, on the French model.

For the first and only time, Engels was an editor of a daily newspaper, writing commentaries and editorials and doing daily news reporting. In order to avoid – possibly prolonged – pretrial imprisonment for his republican sentiments, he fled Cologne at the end of September 1848 and stayed in Switzerland from October 1848 to January 1849. As a foreign correspondent in Bern, he reported on the creation of a federal state in Switzerland. In his list of publications, he expressly records his function as an editor and emphasizes that he deputized for Marx as an editor-in-chief whenever Marx was travelling, which was the case in August–September 1848 and April–May 1849.

In 1846–7, using England and France as examples, Engels and Marx had developed the idea of a multiphase political revolution inaugurating a transformation of society. In the manuscript for *Der Status quo in Deutschland* (The Status Quo in Germany) of 1847,[48] Engels formulated the political consequences that resulted from Germany's economic and political backwardness. In Prussia and other individual German states, he perceived late-absolutist rule yielding to bureaucracy. A class of government and administrative officials was concentrating all power in its own hands. While in 1848 the Paris February Revolution had proclaimed a republic, the German March Revolution stopped short at the foot of their princely rulers' thrones. Engels and Marx hoped that the liberal 'national and constitutional revolution' would also establish a democratic republic in Germany and that the 'half' German Revolution would become a 'full' republican revolution as quickly as possible. They had, in fact, always been convinced that revolutionary upheaval must be preceded by a legal and constitutional bourgeois revolution. In 1848, the republic they were aiming for should, according to their vision, enable initial social interventions in civil law and private property rights, as seemed at first to be happening in Paris. However, it remained unclear how this could be realized under the complex and heterogeneous conditions of Central Europe, not least because at that time (1848–9) so many overly ambitious sociopolitical objectives were being linked with the idea of a republic.[49]

Engels covered an impressively broad range of topics in the *Neue Rheinische Zeitung*, ranging from the First Schleswig War, through revolutionary events and wars in Italy and Hungary to debates in the German National Assembly in Frankfurt and the Prussian National Assembly in Berlin. Working in tandem with Marx, he dissected important legislative projects. When the Berlin government tightened the penalties for 'libelling' state officials in a draft press law, Engels foresaw the danger that the press, 'the only effective control', would 'no longer *report*' but would be allowed 'merely to *speak* in general *phrases*'.[50] He analysed and evaluated the complex national, social and agrarian problems of Central, Eastern and Southern Europe from the perspective and experience of a Rhenish radical, for whom the abolition of feudal rights and privileges in France on the night of 4–5 August 1789 was exemplary. For the *Neue Rheinische Zeitung*, he claimed to have 'from the very first moment sided with the Poles in Posen [Poznań], with the Italians in Italy and the Czechs in Bohemia'.[51] However, he did not grant (from his point of view) the non-revolutionary peoples – thus the majority of the Slav nationalities – the right to their own independent state, not even the Czechs.

When Engels returned to Cologne from Berne at the end of January 1849, he saw the development of the revolution still in flux, but his and Marx's hopes for a new impetus were directed towards developments in France, Hungary and Italy, not towards those in Germany. 'The defeat of the Piedmontese is more important than all the German imperial tricks taken together,' Engels commented at the end of March 1849 on the renewed failure of the Italians to push Austria back from northern Italy. 'But unless all the signs are deceptive, precisely this defeat of the Italian revolution will be the signal for the outbreak of the European revolution. … Paris is ripe for a new revolution.'[52] After initial successes by the Habsburg troops, the Hungarians gradually began to advance at the beginning of 1849. As soon as the border river between Hungary and German-speaking Austria was crossed, Engels predicted, a 'fifth revolution' would take place in Vienna, 'a revolution which will not be simply an Austrian, but simultaneously a European one'.[53] When in the last week of April 1849 a new (third) insurrectionary movement broke out in Germany with the aim of installing an Imperial Constitution for the whole country, Engels, who was deputizing for Marx as editor-in-chief, was taken by surprise. On 19 May 1849, the last issue of the *Neue Rheinische Zeitung* appeared, all in red.

Political refugee and 'cotton-lord' in Manchester

After fighting against Prussian troops in southern Germany for the Imperial Constitution adopted by the Frankfurt National Assembly, Engels managed to escape to Switzerland, from where he arrived in London aboard an English ship on 12 November 1849. Britain was one of the few European countries that offered protection to political refugees. At first he tried to make a living as a political journalist, but in October 1850 he joined his father's textile company, Ermen & Engels, in Manchester – manufacturers of sewing thread and knitting yarn. He worked there, first as an employee, then as a partner, for two decades, managing the multilingual correspondence of the company, which had extensive trade connections. From 1854 he was admitted to the Manchester Stock Exchange, which ran the British cotton market. He could pursue his political writing only in the evenings and on Sundays. He was 'at the office by 10 o'clock in the morning at the very latest', as he wrote to Marx in March 1857, where he had to 'slave away ... until 8 o'clock'.[54]

In his handwritten list, Engels named his 'co-editing' of the *Neue Rheinische Zeitung. Politisch-ökonomische Revue* – the 'political-economic review' of that newspaper – which he published together with Marx from London in 1850 in six issues. Of his extensive essays there, he listed only the account of the failed German peasant uprising of 1525, *Der deutsche Bauernkrieg* (The German Peasants' War)[55] – probably because it was reprinted as a separate pamphlet in 1870 and went through three editions by 1875[56] – but not his contemporary historical memoirs of *Die deutsche Reichsverfassungskampagne* (The Campaign for the German Imperial Constitution)[57] or the overviews of political and economic developments in Europe, which he wrote together with Marx and called simply 'Reviews'. In the *Revue* for May–October 1850, which appeared with the final issue of the *Neue Rheinische Zeitung*, Engels and Marx came to the realization that 'everywhere the revolutionary party has been forced off the stage' and that, in view of the general economic prosperity, there could 'be no talk of a real revolution'. Such a revolution is only possible in periods when *both these factors,* the *modern* productive *forces* and the *bourgeois forms of production, come in collision* with each other'. 'A new revolution', they summarily stated, *'is possible only in the consequence of a new crisis'*.[58]

Also unmentioned on Engels' list was his collaboration with various organs of the British Chartists in the form of 'spurious' (i.e. fictitious) correspondent reports titled *Letter from Germany* and *Letter from France*. However, he did mention three current pamphlets. In *Po and Rhine* (1859)[59] and *Savoy, Nice and the Rhine* (1860),[60] both published anonymously in Berlin, he discussed the military-strategic and national political impact on political movements in Germany of the Second Italian War of Independence of 1859. And in the 1865 essay *Die preussische Militärfrage und die deutsche Arbeiterpartei* (The Prussian Military Question and the German Worker's Party),[61] he took a stand on the constitutional conflict arising from reform of the Prussian army, calling on the workers' movement to continue 'its campaign for bourgeois freedom, freedom of the press and rights of assembly and association which the bourgeoisie had betrayed. Without these freedoms', he commented, the Worker's Party 'will be unable to move freely itself'.[62]

Engels also omitted any reference to his work as a correspondent for the *New York Tribune* from 1851 to 1862. Founded in 1841, the US newspaper was the mouthpiece of a rallying movement against the expansion of slavery, from which the Republican Party was to emerge later (1854). It comprised a daily, a semi-weekly and a weekly edition and had a total circulation of just under 150,000 (1854); by 1861, with 287,000 copies, it was the highest-circulation newspaper in the world. Officially, Marx was its correspondent, but in fact, Engels was the author and co-author of many reports and analyses for which Marx was credited. Engels' involvement remained a carefully guarded secret for a considerable time – not least from the New York editors themselves; only in 1892 was it revealed. In the biographical sketch on Marx for the *Handwörterbuch* mentioned at the beginning of this chapter, Engels wrote that the 'military' *Tribune* correspondence, 'on the Crimean War, Indian Rebellion etc.', had come from him.[63] The full extent of his collaboration first became clear with the publication of the Marx–Engels correspondence in 1913. Of the more than five hundred articles and article series published by the *New York Tribune*, Engels wrote at least seventy-one. He also contributed – again with Marx – to the sixteen-volume *New American Cyclopaedia*.[64] In contrast to Marx, Engels found the lexicon work a 'very useful … encyclopaedic course', through which he expanded his knowledge in particular of military history.[65]

Engels' series of articles *Revolution and Counter-Revolution in Germany* – which in a way continued his 1850 text *The Campaign for the German Imperial Constitution* – appeared in 1851–2 as the first Marxian text in the *Tribune*. Subsequently, he wrote on the military conflicts in Europe and in the colonies as well as on questions connected with Russia. 'Since arriving in Manchester I have been swotting up military affairs,' Engels reported to a former artillery-lieutenant friend in June 1851.[66] Through intensive reading he acquired the tools for a more systematic analysis of military warfare. In addition, he learned other languages, including Russian, which enabled him to consult a wide variety of newspapers and other information sources. Engels discussed the Crimean War – which developed from a Turko-Russian conflict into a European war in which all the major European powers except Prussia intervened – on the basis of British newspaper reports and the maps in front of him. He also discussed the Indian uprising of 1857–8 and the Italian War of Independence of 1859. He wrote about the American Civil War in 1861–2 in the Viennese daily newspaper *Die Presse*. At the same time he intended to write a history of the revolutionary wars of 1848–9 in Italy and Hungary.

Independent intellectual and political journalist in London

In 1869, Engels retired from professional life at the age of not yet forty-nine and from then on lived off the proceeds of his share deals. Nothing much is known about Engels the entrepreneur or about the Engels who acted as his own fund manager. As a partner in a company and via commissions business, which he received on the side, he had acquired a handsome fortune, which he invested to a large extent in shares, 'mostly gas, waterworks and railway shares, all English companies', as he wrote to his brother Hermann in 1869.[67] He was even able to finance an annual pension for Marx and his family. Surviving account statements show that he continued to pursue his share and commission business later on.[68] In September 1870 he moved from Manchester with his partner Lizzie Burns and her niece Mary Ellen Burns to a terraced house in London's Regent's Park Road, where he lived only ten minutes' walk from Marx and his family until Marx's death in 1883. 'Every day … Engels came to see my father; often they went for a walk together', wrote Marx's youngest daughter, Eleanor, in 1890, 'and just as often they stayed at home and walked up and down my father's room'.[69]

Engels now developed a range of multifaceted political, journalistic and scientific activities. His handwritten list of publications provides only partial information about this, although the majority of the writings he listed were produced during this phase of his life. These included numerous articles for German, but also French, English and Italian socialist newspapers and magazines. In his list, however, he records only texts that appeared either in social-democratic newspapers and magazines or that were reprinted as independent pamphlets, sometimes running to several editions. At considerable length and with broad strokes, he expounded on contemporary historical developments and options for socialist action. However, his texts repeatedly met with rejection due to their sharp, often hurtful attacks and all-too-brash assertions.

In a polemical series of articles *Zur Wohnungsfrage* (On the Housing Question) of 1872 in the social-democratic Leipzig newspaper *Der Volksstaat* (The People's State), Engels criticized as insufficient the measures taken by the 'bourgeoisie' to solve the housing shortage. 'As long as the capitalist mode of production continues to exist', he concluded, 'it is folly to hope for an isolated settlement of the housing question or of any other social question affecting the lot of the workers. The solution lies in the abolition of the capitalist mode of production and the appropriation of all the means of subsistence and instruments of labour by the working class itself'.[70] In 1876, in another series of articles in the same newspaper, *Preussischer Schnaps im deutschen Reichstag* (Prussian Schnapps in the German Reichstag), he claimed that Prussia would be doomed if the large-scale agricultural potato spirits industry lost its dominance of the world market to its Russian competitors. 'With the collapse of schnapps distilling, Prussian militarism collapses, and without it Prussia is nothing.' There was no use to 'complaining and moaning', the 'laws of capitalist production' also applied inexorably to 'Junkers' and large landowners.[71]

Even during Marx's lifetime, Engels considerably boosted the circulation and recognition of their theories through an almost encyclopaedic summary of his and Marx's works. In the early 1870s, the Berlin scholar and university teacher Eugen Dühring, claiming to be renewing the received doctrine of both society and revolution, gained considerable influence on the inchoate German Social Democratic movement. Together with Marx, the social democrat Wilhelm Liebknecht, editor of *Der Volksstaat*, urged Engels to write a comprehensive critique of Dühring's writings. Known as *Anti-Dühring*, this was published in 1877–8, first as a series of articles and then in a book form. In Engels' view, 'socialism had become a science'. Because of their haughty tone, his articles initially met with vehement criticism; leading social democrats even demanded that they cease printing. Engels published the introduction to this text, and the final chapters dealing with socialism, in a revised edition under the title *Die Entwicklung des Sozialismus von der Utopie zur Wissenschaft* (Socialism: Utopian and Scientific), first in French, then in German and English.[72] This became one of the most influential texts of 'Marxism'.

After Marx's death in 1883, Engels found in his friend and colleague's estate extensive commentated excerpts noted in summer 1880 from the American anthropologist Lewis Henry Morgan's book *Ancient Society* (1877). 'There's a definitive book – as definitive as Darwin's was in the case of biology – on the primitive states of society', Engels reported in February 1884 to the social democrat Karl Kautsky, editor of the theoretical journal *Neue Zeit* (New Age): 'Morgan rediscovers for himself Marx's materialist view of history, and concludes with what are, for modern society, downright communist postulates.' Eduard Bernstein, editor of the weekly *Der Sozialdemokrat* (The Social Democrat), who was in London in February–March 1884, recalled later (in 1918) that Engels had read to him 'evening after evening until deep in the night' from Marx's manuscripts and 'the draft of a book he was basing on Marx's extracts from the American Lewis Morgan's *Ancient Society*'.⁷³ Despite lack of time, Engels wrote *Der Ursprung der Familie, des Privateigentums und des Staats* (The Origin of the Family, Private Property and the State) in April–May 1884.⁷⁴ His first major publication after Marx's death became the 'fulfilment of a behest'. It ends, quoting Morgan, to the effect that future society, no longer hunting for wealth, would be '*a revival, in a higher form, of the liberty, equality and fraternity of the ancient gentes*'.⁷⁵ In the last third of the nineteenth century, the need grew among the emerging European workers' movements for education, orientation and legitimacy. Having Marx's literary legacy at his disposal increased the pressure on Engels to provide his own contributions and at the same time to make it possible for earlier texts by him and Marx to be translated and reprinted. In *Die auswärtige Politik des russischen Zarentums* (Foreign Policy of Russian Tsardom), written around the turn of the year 1889–90 – a text whose republication in the Soviet Union was forbidden by Stalin in 1934 – Engels thematized two centuries of Russian history. It was published in German in the social-democratic journal *Die Neue Zeit*, but also in English, French, Romanian and partly in Russian translation. In Engels' eyes, the Russian Empire was preventing any reform and reorganization of Europe. He characterized the Russian 'Empire of the Tsar', as in the revolution of 1848 and in the 1850s, as 'the mainstay of European reaction',⁷⁶ which threatened the progress of Europe with its expansive foreign policy and therefore had to be fought with every available means. Engels' 1886 work *Ludwig Feuerbach und der Ausgang der klassischen deutschen Philosophie* (Ludwig Feuerbach and the End of Classical German Philosophy) was also a special reprint from *Die Neue Zeit*. In it he gave a detailed account of what he called the 'materialist world outlook' and concluded by calling the German working-class movement 'the heir to German classical philosophy'.⁷⁷ – Personal acerbity and disproportionate length characterized his polemic *In Sachen Brentano kontra Marx wegen angeblicher Zitatsfälschung* (In the Case of Brentano vs. Marx Regarding Alleged Falsification of a Quotation) of 1891, in which he responded to the accusation of the social reformer Lujo Brentano that Marx had falsely reproduced a quotation from the 1863 budget speech of Gladstone, then the British chancellor of the exchequer.⁷⁸

Parallel to these works, numerous of Marx's writings were also reprinted – provided by Engels with new introductions, which were usually also published separately. Engels showed himself to be a 'genius of a preface writer', as the historian Wilfried Nippel has recently observed. He succeeded in giving new meaning to forgotten or completely lost texts by Marx as 'handouts on current problems as well as fundamental programmatic statements'.⁷⁹ In his list of publications, Engels listed ten prefaces and introductions that he had added to new editions of his own or Marx's writings between 1885 and 1891.

He listed his prefaces or introductions to the translation of Marx's 1847 *Das Elend der Philosophie* (The Poverty of Philosophy), originally written in French (1885),[80] to the republication of Marx's 1852 *Revelations Concerning the Communist Trial in Cologne* (1885),[81] to the third edition of Volume I of *Das Kapital* (1883)[82] and to the English translation of that work (1887),[83] as well as to the first edition of Volume II of *Das Kapital* (1885), which Engels had compiled from Marx's estate.[84] But Engels also listed his biographical-historical introductions to Sigismund Borkheim's *Zur Erinnerung für die deutschen Mordspatrioten 1806–1807* (In Memory of the German Blood-and-Thunder Patriots 1806–1807) (1888)[85] and to Wilhelm Wolff's series of articles *Die schlesische Milliarde* (The Silesian Billion) (1886 and 1890).[86] The latter sequence originally appeared in the *Neue Rheinische Zeitung* in 1849, where it took up the demand of French republicans and socialists for compensation. 'Wilhelm Wolff reminded the Silesian peasants', Engels wrote, 'how they had been cheated out of money and land by the landowners with the help of the government when the feudal dues were abolished, and demanded one billion *thaler* in compensation'.[87]

After the victory against Bismarck's Anti-Socialist Laws, which between 1878 and 1890 had banned social-democratic organizations and their press throughout the German Empire, Engels believed in the last decade of his life that he had finally found in German social democracy the instrument for victory over capitalism. He had a close political and personal relationship with the social democrat August Bebel in particular, describing 'how our lines and mode of thought have coincided' in this regard as 'literally miraculous'.[88] Engels was actively involved in the preparation of the International Workers' Congress held in Paris in July 1889 on the occasion of the 100th anniversary of the French Revolution, at which, amid considerable argument, the Second International was founded. In the Social Democratic programme deliberations, in 1875 at the Gotha and in 1891 at the Erfurt Party Congress, Engels argued from London that the Workers' Party should not avoid confrontation with the German state. If it was not possible to draw up 'a republican party programme openly', Engels said in 1891, then one must at least demand the '*concentration of all political power in the hands of the people's representatives*'.[89] Inside the European workers' movements, he demanded 'complete freedom of debate'. A critical attitude was, in his view, the 'breath of life' of every political movement.[90]

In the list of his *immortal works*, Engels left out unfinished book projects just as he did some important published texts. Thus, he also mentions only in passing the compilation and publication of the second and third volumes of Marx's *Das Kapital*, with which he was intensively occupied for years despite eye disease (probably chronic conjunctivitis). In this context, his first political and academic project after leaving Ermen & Engels was to write a German-language history of Ireland, an undertaking he set about with great enthusiasm but never completed. In 1869–70 he worked through an extensive body of literature on the subject and numerous historical sources, from which he produced excerpts – unpublished to this day – amounting to over six hundred printed pages. He did, however, manage to write the first two of a total of three chapters.[91] Then, when the Franco-Prussian War broke out in July 1870, he wrote commentaries on it for several

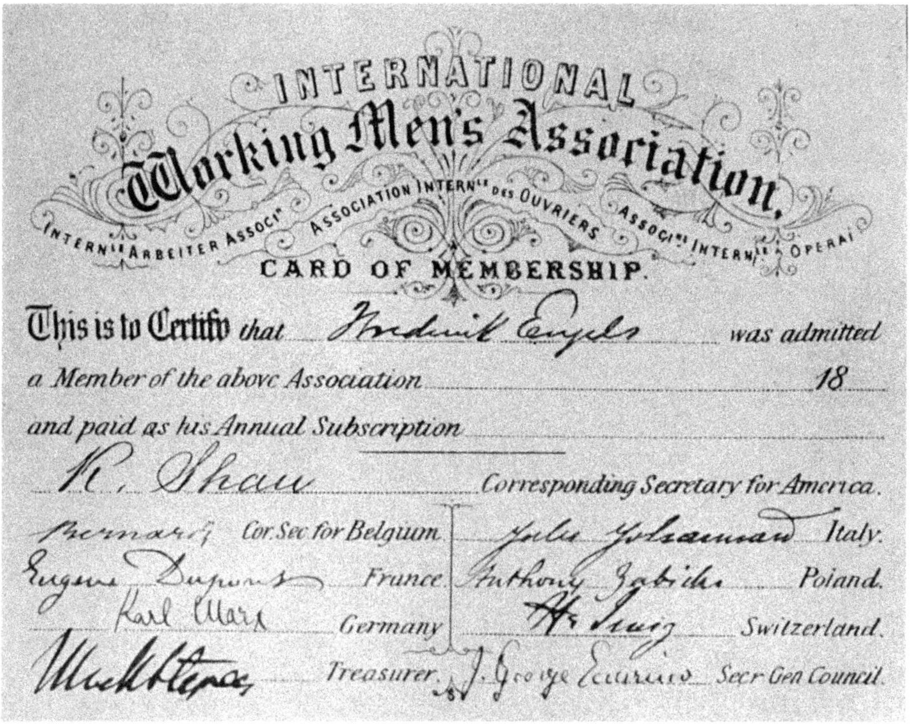
INTERNATIONAL
Working Men's Association,
INTERN.LE ARBEITER ASSOC.N ASSOCIATION INTERN.LE DES OUVRIERS ASSOCI.NE INTERN.LE OPERAI
CARD OF MEMBERSHIP.
This is to Certify that … was admitted
a Member of the above Association 18
and paid as his Annual Subscription
R. Shaw Corresponding Secretary for America.
Cor. Sec for Belgium. Italy.
Eugene Dupont France. Poland.
Karl Marx Germany. Switzerland.
Treasurer. Secr Gen Council.

Figure 1.3 Friedrich Engels' membership card of the International Working Men's Association. © Karl Marx and Friedrich Engels Museum of the Institute of Marxism-Leninism of the Central Committee of the CPSU, Moscow/AKG.

months in the liberal-conservative London evening paper *The Pall Mall Gazette*.[92] These were based on the official telegrams of both warring parties, which he analysed in a balanced and critical manner.

Engels had followed scientific progress throughout his life, but he began to study the natural sciences in depth in 1873. He planned a 'work of natural philosophy' in which he wanted to combine the common characteristics of all the natural sciences of his time into a comprehensive theory of nature. The almost two hundred fragmentary texts he had assembled for this purpose were summarized in the twentieth century under the title *Dialectics of* Nature,[93] a collection which was regarded as a fundamental philosophical work of Marxism–Leninism. Engels himself was more sceptical. 'Perhaps, however, the progress of theoretical natural science makes my work largely or entirely superfluous', he wrote in 1885.[94] Asked for an expert opinion in 1924, Albert Einstein thought that Engels' notes could at least provide important insights into the enthusiasm for science and its reception at that time.[95]

In the first half of the 1870s, Engels and Marx – partly on behalf of the General Council of the International Workingmen's Association – wrote several articles against the Russian anarchist Mikhail Bakunin. In his list of publications, Engels mentions only his 1873 series

The Bakuninists at Work,⁹⁶ in which he attributed the setbacks of the socialist movements after the proclamation of the Spanish Republic to the machinations of Bakunin and his followers there. However, he left out *Les prétendues scissions dans l'Internationale* (Fictitious Splits in the International) of 1872⁹⁷ and *L'Alliance de la Démocratie Socialiste et l'Association Internationale des Travailleurs* (A Plot against the International Workingmen's Association) of 1873–4,⁹⁸ both written jointly with Marx. The first paper was read in March 1872 in the General Council of the International Workers' Association, of which Engels had been a member since 1870, and two thousand copies were sent out. It has been called a 'conglomeration of errors',⁹⁹ with no understanding of political connections and developments within revolutionary movements. The second pamphlet was – according to Engels' biographer Gustav Mayer – 'the passionate plea of a public prosecutor firmly convinced of the rightness of his point of view, who misses no argument that might contribute to the conviction of the accused'.¹⁰⁰ If we are to believe Engels and Marx, there seems to have been nothing but intrigue under Bakunin's leadership.

'History has ... proved us wrong' (Engels, 1895)

In his last major published text, dated 1895, the now famous introduction to the reissue of Marx's 1850 series of articles *The Class Struggle in France 1848–1850,* the 74-year-old Engels was critical of his and Marx's political revolutionary ideas of 1848–9. 'The time of surprise attacks, of revolutions carried through by small conscious minorities at the head of masses lacking consciousness is past.' Instead, universal (male) suffrage, political enlightenment and 'parliamentary activity' would do their 'slow ... work'.¹⁰¹

After Engels' death, this text provoked furious controversy. Eduard Bernstein, who had been appointed by Engels (together with August Bebel) as a literary executor of his estate and who initiated the revisionist dispute in German social democracy, saw it as Engels' 'political testament'. At the founding congress of the German Communist Party (Kommunistische Partei Deutschlands [KPD]) at the end of December 1918, Rosa Luxemburg, on the other hand, distanced herself from Engels' remarks, which she held 'partly responsible' for the fact that a policy of 'pure parliamentarianism' had triumphed in social democracy. On the occasion of Engels' 100th birthday in 1920 and the 30th anniversary of his death in 1925, the Soviet communists accused Social Democracy of having made deletions from Engels' original manuscript, thus deliberately falsifying Marxism. In the official Engels biographies of the German Democratic Republic (GDR) and the Soviet Union, Bernstein was singled out as the 'spokesman behind this forgery'.¹⁰²

In fact, Engels himself had agreed to omissions from and weakening of the printed version of his article in order not to provide the Berlin government with an additional pretext for a planned successor to the Anti-Socialist Law, which had expired in 1890. If one delves deeper into the text, it becomes clear, in fact, that his self-critical words were neither lip service nor temporary tactical concessions, but were meant seriously. For Engels, history had 'shown us to have been wrong' and 'revealed our point of view at that time as an illusion'. It had 'made it clear' that 'the state of economic development on the continent' in 1848 as in 1870 was 'not, by a long way, ripe for the elimination of capitalist production'. It was only in recent times that the 'economic revolution' had really established 'big industry' throughout Europe and 'produced … a genuine large-scale industrial proletariat'. And with it, 'it has also completely transformed the conditions under which the proletariat has to fight'.[103]

With these 'revisionist' reflections, Engels tried to take into account the growth of industry and the expansion of cities as well as military and technological developments. Remaining true to his basic 'materialist' considerations, he saw these processes as products of the interaction of a multitude of conditions, developments and moments, ultimately as a consequence of changing productive forces. These developments had changed 'everything in favour of the military' in terms of any violent uprising of the proletariat. But the growth of the workers' movement was proceeding 'as spontaneously, as steadily, as inexorably and at the same time as calmly as a natural process'.[104] This growth towards social and political supremacy should not, as far as possible, be jeopardized by provoking the state into action. 'As for us, our policy should be', he explained to Marx's son-in-law Paul Lafague in February 1895, 'not to let ourselves be provoked at this point; … in two or three years we will have on our side the peasants and the petty-bourgeois crushed by taxation'.[105]

Engels' growing concern that the 'system of mutual outbidding in armaments carried to extremes' could result in 'a world war of a hitherto unimagined extent and ferocity', with 'the devastation of the Thirty Years' War compressed into three or four years', should also be seen in this context.[106] Engels always saw war as a social phenomenon mediated by economic conditions and attached great importance to military-technological developments, but despite several attempts, he did not succeed, as the political scientist Herfried Münkler has noted, in developing a theory of war that could function as a parallel to Marx's theory of capital.[107] In the last decade of his life, he considered the development of weapons technology to have been perfected. 'We are … sitting upon a live mine', he wrote to August Bebel in January 1890, 'and a spark would be enough to set it off'.[108] In the series of articles *Kann Europa abrüsten?* (Can Europe Disarm?), which also appeared as a separate publication, he therefore pleaded in 1893 for a 'general transition from a standing army to the arming of the people organized as a militia' as an important step towards general disarmament. From a 'purely military point of view', he asserted, there was 'nothing whatever to prevent the gradual abolition of standing armies'.[109]

This admittedly idiosyncratic discussion of Engels' 'immortal works' has taken into account not only works listed by Engels but also his unmentioned publications and projects. As such, it reveals him as a European social and societal critic who was more multifaceted and complex, but also more self-contradictory, than the twentieth century usually reckoned him. Faced with an unparalleled upheaval in society and the economy, he sought rational explanations that would at the same time open up political perspectives. Yet he refused to see the dangers of political violence and revolutionary self-empowerment, though he could have done this very well on the basis of the experiences of the French Revolution of 1789. We should, then, see Engels as a participant in important discussions on serious questions and major problems, as a nineteenth-century radical who tried to understand globalization and industrialization as preconditions for human self-liberation. However, which of his texts and manuscripts will actually become *immortal* only time will show.

CHAPTER 2
ENGELS ON MARX: BIOGRAPHY AS POLITICS
Wilfried Nippel

After Marx's death, Friedrich Engels explained what Marx had called their 'partnership'[1] in various terms. He had, he said, always been happy to play 'second fiddle' to Marx, but when 'in matters of theory' he had been called upon to deputize for Marx, he had – he admitted in a private letter[2] – 'inevitably made blunders'. In a later publication he saw his role as that of 'representing our views in the periodical press, specifically against our opponents, so that Marx had time to complete his major work. Thus it fell to me to present our approach for the most part … in polemical form'.[3]

In a celebratory piece for Engels' birthday in 1887, his 'pupil' Karl Kautsky wrote – in close collusion with his friend and master – that Marx 'had systematically elaborated the jointly developed theory for the learned world', while Engels had defended it polemically against all comers, addressing 'the great questions of the present day … and the attitude to these issues taken by the proletariat'. At the same time he emphasized that, with *Anti-Dühring* (published in 1877–8, i.e. during Marx's lifetime), Engels had composed 'the foundational work of modern socialism', in which 'the most important insights of the whole of modern knowledge are presented from the standpoint of the Marx-Engelsian materialist dialectic'.[4] In an obituary, Eduard Bernstein, Engels' other 'master pupil', called him 'the interpreter and transmitter of the major aspects of our movement'. History will see him as 'the co-founder of modern scientific socialism' and grant him 'the appropriate place beside Karl Marx that he had always modestly declined to assume'.[5]

Without Engels there would have been no 'Marxism',[6] inasmuch as the publication by Engels of Volumes II and III of *Das Kapital* from the manuscripts left in Marx's estate completed the latter's work[7] and the reissue of various earlier writings established an initial corpus of Marxian texts[8] which Engels duly furnished with prefaces, putting them in their historical context and at the same time bringing them up to date. Endowed with interpretive authenticity, these introductory pieces had a decisive impact on the reception of Marx's oeuvre.[9] Engels also spent several months at this time composing a seventy-five-page booklet, *In the Case of Brentano vs. Marx Regarding Alleged Falsification of a Quotation* (1891), in painstaking response to the objection – rehashed for transparently political reasons after almost twenty years by the national economist Lujo Brentano – that Marx's *Kapital* contained a misquotation.[10]

Whether in his own writings Engels had really 'committed blunders', whether his extension of Marxian theory in principle to all branches of knowledge (*Anti-Dühring*) or his application of the 'materialist conception of history' (Engels' phrase) to the entire

Figure 2.1 *World History: The Communists*, 1848, Fliegende Blätter, Munich. © In the public domain.

course of human history (*The Origin of the Family, Private Property and the State*, 1884), was still Marxian or not rather specifically Engelsian, is an extremely difficult question that cannot be pursued any further here. The focus of this chapter is on Engels' biographical sketches and the particular image of Marx he presented there – an image which, for well-known political reasons, gained canonical status in the course of the twentieth century. Here, too, Engels showed himself in the dual role of public communicator and polemicist.

An essay in public relations

After the appearance of Volume I of *Das Kapital* in 1867, Marx's friend and admirer Ludwig (Louis) Kugelmann, together with Engels' remote relative Carl Siebel, undertook every conceivable measure, by submitting reviews to daily newspapers, to counter the concerted silence which had greeted the work. As this at first proved fruitless, Engels sprang into the breach and, presenting himself as a bourgeois critic, succeeded in having reviews printed anonymously in nine German newspapers.[11] These consistently propagated the idea that Marx had given the socialist movement the theoretical basis which predecessors like Proudhon or Lassalle had been unable to provide and, in his analysis of capitalism, had achieved something of which bourgeois economists had shown themselves incapable. In both these respects, Marx had confirmed the leading position of German scholarship.

In continuation of this campaign, Engels published in mid-1869 – again anonymously – an initial biographical sketch of Karl Marx.[12] This had a rather complex prehistory. In January 1868, Kugelmann had written to Marx that a Hanover author wanted to publish an article about him in a popular magazine, whereupon Marx provided a list of his publications and the salient features of his life.[13] At first nothing happened, and then in July 1868, Kugelmann informed Engels that *Gartenlaube* (The Bower) – a highly respected cultural journal with a wide readership – might be interested in an article along these lines. Engels responded by taking on the task himself; his authorship, however, was not to be made public.[14] Marx read Engels' text and added a few points,[15] but no response came from *Gartenlaube*, so Kugelmann turned to its competitor, *Daheim* (At Home), which, however, wanted to see the article first, under the pretext that 'Dr. Marx's standing as a national economist' was difficult to determine.[16] Marx was predictably annoyed at having committed himself to something that was beneath his scholarly dignity.[17] But Kugelmann did not give up, and the following summer he negotiated a contact with the leftish-liberal Berlin paper *Die Zukunft* (The Future). Engels revised his article, and it appeared (anonymously) on 11 August 1869; Wilhelm Liebknecht reprinted it, slightly shortened, in his *Demokratisches Wochenblatt* (Democratic Weekly) three weeks later, with the explicit assurance that it derived from 'a most competent source'.

Under the title 'Karl Marx', the article nevertheless begins with a different figure: 'One has become used, in Germany, to seeing Ferdinand Lassalle as the originator of the German workers' movement. Nothing, however, could be less correct.' Lassalle, according to Engels, had won the plaudits of the masses only with 'triumphal appearances … that might awaken the envy of a ruling prince' because the ideas he propagated had long been familiar to the 'thinkers' among the working classes. The younger generation knew almost nothing of the Revolution of 1848-9 and its reactionary aftermath up to 1852 and had to be reminded that 'before and during the 1848 Revolution a well-organized socialist party was active among the workers, particularly of Western Germany; and although this collapsed after the Cologne Communist trial (November 1852), its individual members continued quietly to prepare the ground of which Lassalle later took possession'. With his immense energy, Lassalle had played a major political role, 'but he was neither the initiator of the German workers' movement, nor an original thinker. The entire content of his writings was borrowed – and borrowed not without misunderstanding. He had a predecessor and intellectual master of whose existence he remained silent while he vulgarized his writings. This intellectual predecessor was Karl Marx.'[18]

Marx and Engels had watched with suspicion – mounting in their private correspondence to vitriolic outbursts – Lassalle's earlier efforts to establish the *Allgemeine Deutsche Arbeiterverein* (General German Workers' Association) founded at the end of May 1863. In recognition of his achievement as an organizer and inspirational mover, their public utterances, however – until Lassalle's death on 31 August 1864 – were remarkably restrained. Even three years later, the accusation of plagiarism Marx publicly levelled against Lassalle in the Preface to *Das Kapital* (1867) remained relatively mild. Engels repeated the charge with considerably greater force in order to counter the 'cult of personality'[19] which had arisen after Lassalle's early death and was still flourishing. But Liebknecht – who both earlier[20] and later repeatedly begged Marx and Engels for texts to combat Lassalle's influence – cut this passage as inopportune in light of the recent foundation in Eisenach (7–9 August 1869) of the *Sozialdemokratische Arbeiterpartei* (Social Democratic Workers' Party), which had already been joined by a splinter group of the General German Workers' Association and which hoped for further gains from that quarter.[21] Engels was peeved: instead of 'castrating' his text, Liebknecht would have done better to dispense with it altogether.[22]

Even taking into account the popular nature of Engels' text, it remains decidedly vague as to the exact nature of Marx's 'outstanding theoretical achievement'. Marx's *Kapital*, Engels writes, describes 'the political economy of the ruling class, reduced to strictly scientific terms' by 'rigorous scholarly deduction' as opposed to Lassalle's 'provocative phrases'.[23] The work, he argues, is also important for its presentation of actual working conditions in England, including the Factory Acts concerning children's, women's and night work – rulings that 'are of crucial interest to every industrialist'.[24] More instructive are Engels' biographical comments,[25] which depict Marx as a champion of the freedom of the press and one repeatedly subjected to repressive measures, namely the prohibition of the *Rheinische Zeitung* (Rhenish News) in 1843, expulsion from France in 1845 and from Belgium in 1848 (followed by an invitation from the French Provisional Government to return to France[26]) and then the actions of the Prussian authorities, who, after Marx had been entrusted with editorship of the *Neue Rheinische Zeitung* (New Rhenish News) in 1848-9, found themselves – after repeated attempts to press criminal charges – unable to prevent him from exploiting the new laws governing the freedom of the press and had as a consequence reverted to the measure of expulsion. A particularly loaded assertion by Engels is that Marx remained aloof from 'the disputes and quarrels of every kind' rampant among the political refugees in London. This raises the question why he should nevertheless have earned the reputation of being the 'best calumniated' of German

Figure 2.2 David Levi Elkan, *Karl Marx as Prometheus*, 1843. It was probably the Cologne graphic artist David Levi Elkan who, in connection with the banning of the *Rheinische Zeitung*, placed Prometheus, the god of ancient mythology favoured by Marx, on the stage of an ancient tragedy. Marx, chained to the newspaper's printing press, has his liver eaten by the 'Prussian' eagle Aethon, led from the background by a squirrel (German *Eichhörnchen*) – an allusion to the Prussian Minister of Culture Friedrich von Eichhorn. In the foreground, the wailing chorus of Rhenish cities have lost their political medium with the banning of the newspaper. © Public Archives of Nordrhein-Westfalen, Duisburg.

writers, forced in self-defence into such extensive polemics that he had been long delayed – by this and his indefatigable scholarly conscientiousness – from presenting the results of his economic investigations to the public.[27] Finally, Engels presents Marx as 'one of the founders' of the *Internationale Arbeiter-Assoziation* (International Working Men's Association), which had inaugurated a new epoch in the history of the workers' movement.

Creating a conception of history

International interest in the person of Karl Marx had rocketed since he had become known as the author of the International Working Men's Association's reaction to the Paris Commune (*The Civil War in France*, 1871; German version by Engels). His combination there of apotheosis and burial speech had led governments and press alike to assume that he headed an international organization with considerable political and financial clout. Against this background, Engels continued to collect biographical material on Marx, some of which he used in an extended French version of his 1869 portrait sketch, published (again anonymously) in a French periodical in November 1871.[28] Marx's role in the International Working Men's Association was emphasized even more strongly in a second French version of the same sketch, published under a pseudonym in autumn 1873.[29]

The last biographical piece published by Engels during Marx's lifetime[30] appeared – this time under Engels' own name – in August 1877, in the *Volks-Kalender* (People's Calendar) for 1878, a widely read product of the Braunschweig publisher Wilhelm Bracke. Bracke was a leading representative of the Social Democratic Workers' Party and one of the few social-democratic politicians who had taken a serious interest in Marx's *Das Kapital*. He had been in correspondence with Marx and Engels since 1869 and had asked Engels for an article that would provide an outline of Marx's life and present his political and academic work in a readily understandable way. A comparison with the 1869 text shows that Engels, on the one hand, dispensed with the polemics against Lassalle and his followers and, on the other, laid more emphasis on Marx's scientific insights. The biographical part is somewhat fuller, with an account, for example, of how Marx tricked the censors at the *Rheinische Zeitung* – a detail that must have come from Marx himself.[31]

Marx's political and scholarly activities are on the whole more fully represented in the *Volks-Kalender* article, although the 'facts' tend here to be somewhat value laden.[32] Focusing, for instance, on the passages in which Engels highlights Marx's historical significance, one sees Marx and 'his political friends' in 1847 creating the '*first* organized body of the German Social-Democratic Party' with their transformation of the Communist League from a 'more or less conspiratorial grouping' into a 'by pure force of circumstance secret communist propaganda organization'.[33] The Communist League, one learns, effectively dominated the German workers' associations in England, Belgium, France and Switzerland and, with membership drawn from various nations, was the first

Figure 2.3 Karl Marx (1818–1883), 1875. © Mayall, London/AKG.

organization 'to emphasize and demonstrably practise the international character of the workers' movement as a whole'.[34] Indirectly, this makes it the model for the International Working Men's Association. In the same vein the *Neue Rheinische Zeitung* was declared 'the only organ … within the democratic movement of the time to present the viewpoint of the proletariat, as it did with its unconditional support for the Parisian insurgents of June 1848, which lost it almost the entire body of its shareholders'[35] – a statement which, read conversely, suggests that the paper had taken little interest in the earlier stages of the German workers' movement.

Engels did not hesitate, for instance, to portray Marx as the real founder of the International Working Men's Association. However, he formulated the matter so skilfully that it was suggested rather than counterfactually asserted: 'The foundation of a workers' association, covering the most progressive countries of Europe and America, that will physically embody, as it were, … the international character of the socialist movement' was the 'longstanding desire' of Marx to which the foundational London assembly of 28 September 1864 responded with enthusiasm.[36] That the initiative for the assembly came (originally in 1862) from French and English associations and trade unions and that Marx received an invitation only later in the day and did not address the assembly is passed over in resounding silence. That Marx was the 'soul' of the General Council, inasmuch as he had composed all its important documents, is somewhat exaggerated; that the history of the International Working Men's Association begins and ends with his activities there is grossly so.[37]

Engels further defends the – 'oft criticized, both at the time and later' – resolutions of the (early September 1872) Hague Congress of the International Working Men's Association as deriving from 'a heroic decision' by Marx to transfer the organization's General Council to New York and to exclude the Bakuninists.[38] In view of the repressive measures taken after the suppression of the Paris Commune – intensified on account of Bakuninist insurgent activities – this had been the only way to avoid unnecessary bloodshed and to maintain the international solidarity of the proletariat while dispensing with an organizational form rendered obsolete by current circumstances. That Engels does not enlarge on the dubious methods he and Marx used to bring about these decisions is hardly surprising.

A new element in Engels' *Volks-Kalender* portrait was his tribute to the 'discoveries with which Marx had established his name in the annals of scientific history', founding 'modern scientific socialism'. Marx had not only 'accomplished a revolution in the overall understanding of world history' as a sequence of class struggles but also provided the first explanation of capitalism as an exploitative system based on the absorption of added value derived from the workers' sale of their labour.[39] These facets of Marx's system closely reflect the presentation given in *Anti-Dühring* – a series of articles on which Engels was currently working.

Publication in the *Volks-Kalender* proved highly successful, on the one hand, because of the popularity of the medium – Bracke announced sales of twenty thousand by October 1877 – and, on the other, because of its long-term impact. On Marx's death in 1883, many obituary notices took their cue from Engels' text, not least (albeit with

Figure 2.4 Mikhail Alexandrovich Bakunin (1814–1876), c. 1863. © AKG.

enrichment from personal memories) those of Marx's daughter Eleanor, his son-in-law Paul Lafargue and fellow socialists like Wilhelm Liebknecht and Friedrich Lessner. That Lenin also used the *Volks-Kalender* portrait accounts for its canonical status in later Marxist orthodoxy.[40]

In his funeral oration for Marx, published on 22 March 1883 in *Der Sozialdemokrat* (The Social Democrat) – the party newspaper, printed in Switzerland and (illegally) distributed in Germany[41] – Engels emphasized Marx's dual role as a scholar and revolutionary. He compared Marx's 'discovery ... of the evolutionary law of human history' as of seminal standing equal to Darwin's 'law of the evolution of organic nature',[42] and in a piece published in the same organ on May 3 to counter false rumours circulating in the press, he gave an account of Marx's last months, his terminal illness and the circumstances of his death.[43] At the same time, he announced that the manuscript of Volume II of *Das Kapital* had been preserved in full, although he could not yet say whether it could be printed as it stood. Finally, Engels confirmed that Marx had 'orally determined his youngest daughter Eleanor and myself as his literary executors'.[44] In a continuation of this piece two weeks later, he changed course and attacked the 'small-minded people' who saw fit to draw 'political, literary and, indeed, financial capital ... from the death of a great man'.[45] That was directed primarily against Johann Most, a former social-democrat member of the German Parliament who had converted to the cause of violent anarchism and claimed, at a memorial service for Marx in New York, to have published a widely read abbreviated version of *Das Kapital*.[46] A second target of Engels' wrath was the young Italian academic Achille Loria, who had not only accused Marx of misquoting but also gone on to suggest that he had never intended to publish any further parts of *Das Kapital*.

Looking back on the 1848 revolution under the anti-socialist law

Engels wanted to write either a biography of Marx or a history of the International Working Men's Association – both projects belonged, from his point of view, together, inasmuch as he saw Marx's activities in the Association as the high point of his political influence; moreover, he considered himself the only one who could, with his personal knowledge, counter the calumnious rumours being noised abroad.[47] In the event, neither project was realized. All Engels managed to publish in 1884-5 was some texts on Marx's stance during the 1848-9 Revolution. This he did at the request of Eduard Bernstein at the weekly *Sozialdemokrat*, with whom he exchanged a lively correspondence, and of Hermann Schlüter at the *Volksbuchhandlung* (People's Bookshop) in Hottingen, near Zurich. Their intention was to mobilize their readers to concerted resistance against the Anti-Socialist Law and against those elements in the party[48] – notably the members of the *Reichstag* (German Parliament) – who in the face of mounting persecution were prepared to make concessions to the government.

To mark the first anniversary of Marx's death on 14 March 1884, Bernstein had asked Engels for an article on 'Marx and the Revolution' and suggested either 1848 or the Paris Commune of 1871 as appropriate subjects. Engels chose the former and titled 'Marx and the *Neue Rheinische Zeitung* 1848–49',[49] presumably intending to present that paper as an exemplarily militant news organ. He sketched the history of the paper, including its lightning takeover by Marx; the print run; the problems with shareholders, many of whom abandoned ship because of its radicalism; and Marx's authoritarian leadership – 'the editorial staff were simply subdued by Marx's dictatorship'[50] – which was, however, generally accepted as necessary for a daily paper. At some length he explained the protection afforded to freedom of the press by the French law still pertaining in the Rhineland.[51] A particularly lurid detail was the reluctance of the military authorities in Cologne who, 'with a garrison of 8000 men', declined to take measures against the newspaper 'in view of the eight rifles fitted with bayonets and the 250 loaded pistols stacked in the editorial office, not to mention the red Jacobin caps of the typesetters'.[52]

Claiming a readership throughout Germany, the *Neue Rheinische Zeitung*, Engels argued, far from being a 'street corner huckster' for communism, was a major organ representing the far left of the democratic movement.[53] Its programme had two 'cardinal points': 'a single, indivisible, democratic German republic, and war with Russia, including the restoration of Poland'.[54] The first point entailed an end to the 'parliamentary cretinism'[55] of the national assemblies in Frankfurt and Berlin, from the former of which nothing had ever been expected, while the latter (especially its left wing) had been criticized in the paper's columns as insufficiently radical. The second point involved the propagation of a revolutionary war, without which it would be impossible to dismantle the Habsburg Empire or Prussia. These points are a concise résumé of the political line followed by Marx and Engels in their editorials – albeit with a vigour with regard to war that at the time would probably have eluded the perceptions of their readers.[56] The early months of 1849 had seen the paper pushing ever more intensely contemporary hopes for this great war and for parallel uprisings in Germany and at the same time focusing more closely on 'the social objectives of our policies', as evidenced in a series of articles by Wilhelm Wolff on 'The Silesian Billion',[57] by Marx on 'Wages and Capital' and a final issue (dated 19 May) proclaiming the 'Emancipation of the Working Class'.[58] In sum, Engels made bold to claim, 'No German paper before or since has ever had the power and influence, or has understood so well how to electrify the proletarian masses, as the *Neue Rheinische*.'[59]

While Bernstein in *Der Sozialdemokrat* reprinted a number of small pieces from the *Neue Rheinische Zeitung*,[60] whose current relevance, he considered, would be self-evident, Schlüter sought to republish some longer older articles in a special series of his *Volksbuchhandlung*, the 'Social-Democratic Library'. He began with Marx's defence in Cologne on 8 February 1849 against the charge of inciting the local committee of the Rhenish Democrats on 15 September 1848 to withhold taxes.[61] Engels, at Schlüter's request, composed a preface,[62] and the booklet appeared in October 1885 under the title *Karl Marx before the Cologne Jury*. In the trial – which ended with the acquittal of the accused – Marx had rhetorically turned the charge against the Prussian government, whose actions against the Prussian National Assembly had been illegal. Engels confined himself to highlighting the current reasons for remembering this trial: there was something 'utterly comical', he observed, in demanding a commitment to legality from a party proscribed under special law.[63]

Parallel to this, Schlüter planned to reprint Marx's *Revelations Concerning the Communist Trial in Cologne*, an event which had ended – to general, as well as Marx's own surprise – with the conviction in November 1852 of seven of the eleven accused,[64] all of them actual or suspected members of the Communist League. Marx had denounced the illegal actions of the Prussian police and in the same breath intimated that the rival wing of the League – led since the split of September 1850 by August Willich and Karl Schapper – had been colluding with the police. Printed in Basel and Boston in 1853, Marx's text – long unobtainable in Germany because of confiscation – had been reissued in 1874–5 in view of the repressive measures enacted against both social-democratic parties even before the Anti-Socialist Law itself came into force (in 1878). For Schlüter's new edition, Engels was again to write a preface, which – composed in late September and early October 1885 – was pre-released in three instalments of the October *Sozialdemokrat* before duly prefacing the Marx book early in 1886.

There would have been little sense in again drawing obvious parallels with the present situation, so Engels focused here on 'The History of the Communist League',[65] beginning with its prior organization, the 'League of the Just'. He described the pioneering role (and later excommunication) of Wilhelm Weitling and laid particular emphasis on the new London-based leadership of Karl Schapper, Heinrich Bauer and Joseph Moll – 'the first revolutionary proletarians I had known [in 1843]'[66] – and their negotiations with Marx and himself in 1847, which had ended with the refounding of their organization in the Communist League. This was the first such grouping to realize the internationalist principle. Translated 'into almost every language', its manifesto, 'still serves today in widely different countries as the handbook of the proletarian movement'.[67] Engels went on to mention the transfer of the leadership of the League to Paris in March 1848 and quoted in full the seventeen 'demands of the German Communist Party'[68] published at the end of that month. He also gave a more detailed account as to why, in Paris, they had opposed Georg Herwegh's establishment of a German Legion[69] and described how, negotiating with the provisional French government, they had gained support for the repatriation of 'three-to-four-hundred workers to Germany, most of them members of the Communist League'.[70] After this point, the League had been unable to play any further part as an organization. Nevertheless, it had proven to be 'an excellent school of revolutionary activity', its members assuming 'leading roles in the radically democratic movement'[71] in various regions[72] (see below for the ensuing attack on Stephan Born).

On the other hand, Engels maintained that, beginning in late 1849, the London-based reorganization of the Communist League in Germany had been highly successful, quickly establishing it as 'the only revolutionary organization of any significance' in that country. Marx and Engels had, however, realized that hopes of revolution in the near future were illusory, a standpoint that led to a split in the League, with the remaining revolutionary group, led by Willich and Schapper, finding established allies in European émigré circles in London. Willich, a 'natural Communist' and 'thoroughgoing prophet', was 'convinced of his personal mission as predestined liberator of the German proletariat' and saw himself as 'direct pretender to both political and military dictatorship'.[73] Schapper had simply followed his 'inveterate revolutionary drive'.[74] All that ended, however, with the arrests of early 1851 and the Cologne trial of November 1852: 'Immediately after sentence had been passed', Engels wrote, 'we dissolved our League, and a few months later the Willich-Schapper splinter group also passed into eternal rest.'[75]

Engels' pettiness here is breathtaking and calls at least in some aspects for commentary. He emphasizes the 'demands of the Communist Party in Germany' but fails to note that Marx and he had no interest in propagating the party after their return to Germany, as this would have meant the cessation of the newspaper project, for which they needed shareholders.[76] Furthermore, the reorganization of the Communist League in Germany, in which Marx had taken no interest since his return,[77] had already begun (against his will) in November 1848.[78] Finally, whatever Willich may have thought about his own role as leader, the letter he received early in 1851 urging him as military dictator to instigate an uprising among the Rhenish reserves was a forgery commissioned by none other than Marx himself and sent with the evident intention of exposing Willich.[79] But that, and a great deal more, remained hidden from the public at the time.

The sardonic remarks about Willich are not surprising, but why should Engels have turned against Stephan Born, who from 1846 to 1848 had energetically supported him and Marx in Brussels and Paris? Following his remarks on the activities of League members in 1848, Engels enlarges on the *Allgemeine Deutsche Arbeiterverbrüderung* (General Workers' Brotherhood), a movement initiated by Born: 'Born, a very talented young man, albeit bent on rising rather too fast in the political world, "fraternized" with the most diverse rag-tag-and-bobtail with the sole purpose of getting a crowd together.' His organization, Engels argued, propagated a crude spectrum of theoretical notions – drawn from such disparate sources as the *Communist Manifesto*, Proudhon and Louis Blanc – and practical demands, yet in the decisive phase of spring 1849, it had failed. That the reactionary forces had thought it necessary to proscribe it only in 1850 was due to the fact that it 'for the most part only existed on paper'.

Born (who was only twenty-three at the time) had initially (since April 1848) built up a workers' movement in Berlin and then (since the autumn of that year) turned his energies to the General German Workers' Brotherhood, a supra-regional body of trade and workers' organizations voicing political as well as social demands and keeping a distinct distance to bourgeois circles. Marx, at the *Neue Rheinische Zeitung*, had neither supported nor opposed Born's activities and evidently received him cordially at the editorial office and at his family home at the end of January 1849 on his (Born's) way back from a congress in Heidelberg, where he had won over a number of South German associations to his Brotherhood.[80] When in mid-April 1849 Marx executed an about-turn and – along with Schapper and others – resigned from the Union of Rhenish Democratic Associations, the Cologne Workers' Association immediately joined the Workers' Brotherhood and prepared to send delegates to its planned (but in the event unrealized) congress.[81] By then (1849–50) the Brotherhood had some 15,000–18,000 members,[82] whereas the Communist League had never counted more than a few hundred,[83] many of whom were also active in the Brotherhood, but none of whom, *pace* Engels,[84] formed any sort of centrally directed cadre. On the contrary, they pursued exactly the type of ideological and pragmatic eclecticism for which Engels had reproved the Brotherhood as a whole.[85] Moreover, networks were established at that time, which allowed the workers' associations to survive the post-1850 decade of repression and would later provide the

General German Workers' Association with an indispensable body of activists socialized in the ranks of the Brotherhood or the Communist League.

What, then, for Engels, was Born's political crime – his independence?[86] Why Engels should descend to this caricature, and indeed spice it with personal invective,[87] calls for some explanation. Born's public role in 1848–9 had by then (autumn 1885) been largely forgotten, and Born himself had long since ceased to be of interest to either Marx or Engels.[88] To Schlüter's initial request, Engels had replied that he wanted to show 'the old Lassalleans' one final time that 'there had been something going on' in Germany 'even before the great Ferdinand'.[89] That the aggressiveness in the published text was directed not at Lassalle but at Born seems to derive from the fact that Engels had in the meantime read Georg Adler's recent book on the origins of the German workers' movement in the 1840s–50s. For Adler, Born was 'the most important of the Berliners and, indeed, of the general workers' movement: … a gifted speaker, and endowed with personal courage and energy'.[90] Of the leaders of the early workers' movement in general, Adler's judgement was equally inclusive: 'Alongside a creative thinker of the first water like Karl Marx, we find significant talents like Friedrich Engels, Wilhelm Weitling, Karl Grün and Born.'[91] Engels surmised that Adler's information came from Born, and for that, Born must feel the lash.[92]

As also, of course, must Adler. Engels gave his annotated copy of Adler's book to Karl Kautsky, who duly wrote a review reeking of petty criticism[93] – correction of dates and the like,[94] which Engels, incidentally, had also cited incorrectly[95] – with the aim of demonstrating Adler's ignorance of the matters in question. Kautsky had relied entirely on Engels' notes and directions,[96] which led both of them into embarrassing errors.[97] Kautsky was right inasmuch as Adler had often quoted his sources uncritically, but the material they presented – which to a great extent reflected Adler's reading of no longer available newspaper articles and other documents[98] – was by the standards of the day overwhelming. If Engels had ever been able to realize his hope of 'working up the large body of material collected by Marx and myself on the history of the glorious youth of the international workers' movement [1836-52]', he would inevitably have had to draw on Adler's book.[99] But Adler had already disqualified himself in the eyes of Engels and Kautsky by joining the party of those who considered Karl Rodbertus the founder of 'scientific socialism'.[100]

Engels' attack on Born had the unintended effect of drawing renewed attention to the long-forgotten Workers' Brotherhood, a theme Franz Mehring later (1897) took up in his book on the history of German Social Democracy. Here, Mehring profoundly relativized Engels' criticism of Born[101] and motivated the latter, shortly before his death in 1898, to write his own memoirs. These, in turn, became a source of (partly false) information on Marx and Engels' years in Brussels and Paris – which leads one to wonder if Born's memory was failing or if he was having the last laugh, a sort of revenge foul.[102]

A sober balance sheet – with errors

Engels' final biographical sketch of Karl Marx was written towards the end of 1892 for the *Handwörterbuch der Staatswissenschaften* (Concise Dictionary of Political Science) at the request of the editor, Ludwig Elster.[103] Engels compiled a bibliography[104] and wrote a broadly sober preface.[105] He seems to have thought Elster would merely use his material for its biographical data, as had happened with his own entry in a previous volume of the dictionary.[106] In the event, he was surprised that his text – composed 'wholly from our own position' – was printed in full, apart from 'some simply too unbourgeois passages',[107] which unfortunately have not been recorded.

Reprinted in the party organ *Vorwärts* (Forwards) and soon afterwards in various translations to mark the tenth anniversary of Marx's death (14 March 1893), Engels' text contained some new items of information. On the one hand, he revealed the until then closely guarded secret that he had, in the 1850s, ghostwritten a number of Marx's articles for the *New York Tribune*, 'among them the military essays on the Crimean War, the Indian Rebellion etc.'[108] Other points derived from his work on Marx's literary estate: first, that immediately after publication of *A Contribution to the Critique of Political Economy* (1859), Marx, realizing the inadequacy of his treatment, set himself to rewrite the book rather than simply continue it; secondly, that in preparation for Volume III of *Das Kapital* – whose publication Engels announced for 1893 – Marx had immersed himself in the study of 'prehistory, agronomy, Russian and American land ownership, and geology'.[109] Engels went on to relativize Marx's role as the founder of the International Working Men's Association: 'Many, in particular the French, have claimed the honour of founding this Association, but it must be obvious that this cannot be the achievement of just one person.' Marx alone, however, 'realized with clarity what it was they were founding and what had to be done to achieve it'.[110] Marx had succeeded in bringing French Proudhonists, German Communists and English trade unionists together; only 'Bakunin's anarchists' disrupted this 'harmony'. Engels' preface concluded with the remark that most biographical portraits of Marx were riddled with errors;[111] the only 'authentic' account was the one he himself had published in Bracke's *Volks-Kalender*. This, however, proved an 'own goal' with respect to his present text, which also contained some obvious errors: that Marx had, for example, taken his doctorate in Berlin (rather than in Jena *in absentia* – but the thesis Engels names here was on natural philosophy),[112] or that the *Rheinische Zeitung* was subjected to a triple (rather than double) censorship; further, that the date of its prohibition (with effect from 31 March 1843) was 1 January (rather than 20 or 24 January) 1843 and that Marx ceased to work as an editor on that day (rather than on 17 March). Engels was evidently writing from memory,[113] and either did not have his own 1877 text to hand[114] or did not consult it. In that text the censors' measures against the *Rheinische Zeitung* had been communicated by Marx himself and had been depicted correctly.[115]

Résumé

The Engels texts presented here were generally written quickly, their factual basis often quoted from memory, which inevitably generated mistakes that were then carried forward into later literature. Engels wrote with his eye on current circumstances, with the clear political intent and polemical verve against opponents old and new that marked his entire output as a political commentator. One cannot often tell whether the mention or omission of details was done with intent, by chance or as mere embellishment, but the overall purpose is always clear: Marx is to be portrayed as the founder not just of 'scientific socialism' (an Engels phrase) but of the entire modern German and international workers' movement. His political decisions, including the initiation and dissolution of institutions, were invariably geared to the requirements of the particular historical juncture – a fact frequently misunderstood by his contemporaries but vindicated by history.

As is evident from his various memoirs and obituaries for colleagues and contemporaries, Engels claimed an interpretive monopoly not only over Marx but over the history of the socialist movement as such. These pieces tend to draw a selective picture, embodying loaded judgements or glossing over earlier differences in the interests of overall control.[116] The ignorance of the younger generation about the early days of the workers' movement, so often lamented by Engels, had the advantage, when these texts were published, that there was hardly anyone who could check his statements – although neither was he often a first-hand witness of the events he related (not in itself a guarantee of authenticity either) nor could he have been directly informed about them.[117] Engels had, however, also called on old socialists to write their memoirs and/or to secure for posterity any relevant materials in their possession,[118] which eventually – in the (very) long term – had the effect that his own interpretive sovereignty could be broken.

Engels' disposition that his correspondence with Marx should be published had the effect of making known much that contradicted his 'official' image of Marx. Post-1910, when, after years of personal and political squabbling, the correspondence – bequeathed by Engels to Bernstein and Bebel – gradually became known, everyone who opened it was horrified at the vulgarity of the language, the intemperance of the attacks on 'party friends' (Liebknecht and Lassalle) and the disturbing exposure of mud-slinging in émigré milieus, from which Marx by no means remained aloof. Such was its impact that the question arose of foregoing publication altogether. Finally, it was decided to present a 'purged' edition (published 1913).[119] The decisive point came with the *Marx–Engels Gesamtausgabe* (the 'new MEGA': *Marx–Engels Complete Edition*, launched in 1975), which included letters to Marx and Engels preserved largely in the 'party archive'[120] Engels had established during his time in Manchester. So long as the MEGA edition was in the hands of Communist Party institutes in Moscow and East Berlin, its introductions faithfully reproduced Engels' (and Marx's) judgements, above all when these had been approved by Lenin. Nevertheless, even in the volumes issued before 1990, the subversive potential of the sources was – to varying degrees – apparent from the annotations and references.[121]

CHAPTER 3
FRIEDRICH ENGELS, VICTOR ADLER AND AUSTROMARXISM
Günther Chaloupek

Engels and European social democracy

In the twelve years by which he outlived Karl Marx, Friedrich Engels saw his role as that of a guardian and authentic interpreter of Marx's theoretical and political legacy. In addition to editing the unpublished parts of *Das Kapital*, Engels saw to the republication of both older Marxian and his own writings, providing them with new prefaces in which he commented on the changes that had occurred since their first appearance and also on any misconceptions that had subsequently become apparent. It was at the same time a period of vigorous growth of social democratic parties on the European continent. While the initial organization of the socialist movement in the form of the first International Working Men's Association had failed in 1876, the movement reconstituted itself in the form of nationally organized workers' parties, which became a powerful political factor and were increasingly perceived as a threat by the bourgeoisie.

Engels' importance to the growth of European social democracy at this time can hardly be overestimated. He maintained an extensive correspondence with party functionaries in almost every country in Europe, many of whom he also received for visits to his home in London. He became more involved – apart from England, which to his disappointment had long lagged behind the continent in building a Marxist-oriented Workers' Party – in the affairs of the French socialists and German social democrats. Avoiding overly forceful interventions, he nevertheless tried to set the parties on what he believed to be the right course. In the process, it was inevitable that he would also be drawn into conflicts both between and within the parties, especially those of France and Germany. In Germany in particular, he repeatedly intervened in intraparty discussions between the party leadership and reformist 'dissenters'.

Engels turned his attention to Austrian social democracy relatively late. It can be assumed that he was informed about conditions there by his closest political comrade-in-arms, the Austrian Karl Kautsky, who had been actively involved during the period of internal dissension in the movement prior to the 'Unification Party Congress' of 1888–9. Intensive contact was established after the re-establishment of the party by Victor Adler, whom Engels soon came to value extraordinarily and with whom he was bound by a deep friendship that was as much personal as political. Engels took an intense interest in the rapid development of the party and also provided the party and its chairman with considerable financial support. Their relationship remained unclouded until the end: Engels had full confidence in the party leadership and saw the party on the right 'road to socialism'.

The road to socialism

In the understanding of 'scientific' – as opposed to 'Utopian' – socialism, the overcoming of capitalism is an ineluctable consequence of its inherent development, seen as a long-term process. The progressive unfolding of the productive forces gives rise to internal contradictions in capitalism, which 'press forward … to the abolition of their quality as capital, *to the practical recognition of their character as social productive forces*'.[1] The sociopolitical force that carries out this transformation is the proletariat which, as a result of capitalist development, comprises the majority of the population and, as an organized political movement, is able to take over power within the capitalist state. Whether this takeover was an expression of democratic will or the outcome of a final 'crisis' remained open.

The *Communist Manifesto* speaks of 'the first step in the revolution by the working class [being] to raise the proletariat to the position of ruling class to win the battle of democracy'.[2] The widespread failure of the bourgeois revolution of 1848 was initially a setback to this effort. With the increasing spread of universal suffrage among the male population and its extension to ever larger segments, a promising perspective opened for the social democratic parties to take over power in the state within a few generations and, on the way to this, to achieve core demands such as the introduction of the eight-hour day. This was the focus of Engels' political-strategic considerations, on which his recommendations to the social democratic parties were based.

The socialists cannot achieve victory 'in one stroke' but can only 'slowly … press forward from position to position in a hard, tenacious struggle'.[3] 'The time of surprise attacks, of revolutions carried through by small conscious minorities … is past. Where it is a question of the complete transformation of the social organization, the masses themselves must be in on it.'[4] Engels regarded German social democracy as exemplary 'as the strongest, most disciplined, and most rapidly growing socialist party' that showed sister parties in other countries 'how to make use of universal suffrage'.[5] Engels extrapolated into the future the increase in the German Socialist Party (SPD)'s share of votes and seats in the Reichstag elections, which had risen to a quarter by 1894, and saw the attainment of a parliamentary majority no longer as a distant prospect but well within reach. The steady increase in the share of the vote was not an end in itself, but a means to strengthen the class consciousness of the working class and thus increase its fighting strength, always directed towards the approaching ultimate goal of a socialist society.

Therefore, any form of 'anarchist' terror merited the strictest condemnation from Engels as counterproductive. Assassinations and conspiracies would only give the bourgeoisie a reason for police measures or even for putsch-like actions.[6] Engels especially warned against relying on violent rebellion and street fighting in the struggle for power.

If 'rebellion in the old style' seemed obsolete to him as early as 1848, the advancement of weapons technology and military logistics had since made 'all the conditions of the insurgents' side ... worse'. The proletariat should not allow itself to be provoked by a bourgeoisie fearful of losing power into 'tak[ing] without more ado to the streets, where we are certain of defeat in advance'.[7]

In the parliamentary debates on individual questions of economic and social policy, the social democrats should support, or at least not hinder, any measures that might accelerate the liquidation of feudal structures and the diminution of the independent petty bourgeois or peasant strata of the population, such as the abolition of protective agrarian tariffs. The faster capitalism developed to its pure form, the faster would the share of the proletariat increase, and with it the political power base of social democracy. Energetically, Engels therefore opposed all reformist and 'state socialist' tendencies in the SPD.

The increasing instability of the capitalist economy and society would play an important role in triggering the takeover of power by the proletariat. Marx assumed the periodic recurrence of intensifying economic crises as a 'historical tendency of capitalist accumulation'.[8] And, with increasing capital accumulation, ever broader strata of the population and ever more countries would feel its consequences. There would be a growing polarization between power and wealth on the side of capital and misery and insecurity on the side of the workers: 'the mass of misery, oppression, slavery, degradation, exploitation', would grow, 'but with this too grows the revolt of the working class, a class always increasing in numbers, and disciplined, united, organized by the very mechanism of the process of capitalist production itself'. This process would be driven by falling profits. Large parts of the third volume of *Das Kapital* are devoted to proving the existence of a 'law expressing the tendency of the rate of profit to fall, without Marx ever being able to provide such proof'.[9]

With Engels, the thesis of the intensification of periodically recurring crises appears only in weakened form in his *Anti-Dühring* (first published in 1878). At intervals of about ten years, the point is repeatedly reached at which 'the whole mechanism of the capitalist mode of production breaks down under the pressure of the productive forces, its own creations. It is no longer able to turn all this mass of means of production into capital. ... But 'abundance becomes the source of distress and want' (Fourier)'.[10] While this situation is presented as revolutionary in Marx – without, however, using the word revolution – in Engels 'the crises demonstrate the incapacity of the bourgeoisie for managing any longer modern productive forces'. The joint stock company will increasingly take over the function of the private owner – a form of entity created by the state, which will itself increasingly take on the function of the organizer of the capitalist economy and thus become the 'ideal ... national capitalist'. This is the point at which the proletariat must seize control of the state. Engels had little interest in analytical-theoretical questions of the process of accumulation and the mechanism of crisis, with which Marx dealt intensely in the volumes of *Das Kapital* edited by Engels after his death. Engels was more concerned with the strategic-political question of the takeover of state power by the proletariat.

A brief history of the socialist movement in Austria up to the Unification Party Congress of 1888–9

In Austria, the first initiatives to establish a Social Democratic Party organization took place only a little later than in Germany. After 1867, a variety of workers' educational associations formed in rapid succession. Repression set in much earlier in Austria than it did in Germany with Bismarck's Anti-Socialist Act of 1878. After a mass demonstration in December 1869, the leading functionaries were imprisoned and the workers' educational associations were banned, a devastating blow that set the movement back twenty years compared to that in Germany. While in Germany the two distinct currents of the Lassallians and Eisenachers came together at the Gotha Party Congress in 1875 and appeared as a united party in parliament, the scattered Austrian factions fought fiercely over their political objectives, dividing broadly between 'moderates' and 'radicals'. In this muddled situation, Victor Adler joined the Social Democratic Movement in 1886 and devoted his personal energies to overcoming those policy struggles. In barely three years, Adler succeeded in uniting the conflicting wings at the Unification Party Congress at the turn of the year 1888–9 ('Hainfeld Party Congress') on the basis of the new 'Hainfeld Programme', which was adopted almost unanimously.

Victor Adler (1852–1918)[11] came from a middle-class Jewish family originally based in Prague. After moving to Vienna in the mid-1850s, Adler's father acquired a considerable fortune through real estate and financial transactions. Victor spent his childhood and school years in the capital. At university he graduated in medicine in 1876 and then trained in psychiatry, establishing himself as a psychiatrist and neurologist with a practice at Berggasse 19.[12] His choice of specialization in the medical field indicates his strong interest in the social implications of his profession.

Adler's first political involvement was with the liberal *Deutsche Fortschrittspartei* (German Progress Party). He first came into contact with the Social Democratic labour movement in 1881 through the mediation of Karl Kautsky (also originally from Prague), who, however, had shifted his field of activity to Germany and Switzerland in view of the desolate state of the Austrian party's organization. Kautsky, who had been in contact with Engels since 1881, was also the one who arranged Adler's visit to Engels: 'He is not an actual party comrade, but very close to us and, as far as I know him, an honest philanthropist.'[13]

In 1883, a works (or factory) inspectorate was introduced in Austria with the task of checking compliance with prescribed protective measures against accidents at work, the employment of non-adult workers, compliance with working hours and systems of wage payment in factories with more than twenty employees. Adler immediately applied for the position of factory inspector and, in preparation, undertook a study trip to England, Germany and Switzerland, whose results he summarized in an extensive treatise.[14] The most important finding of this study was that the effectiveness of this institution was considerably diminished by deficiencies in the implementation of the regulations, mainly due to inadequate staffing and a lack of sanctions for violations of the law, which were frequent. Economic and political power structures were proving stronger than the – in any case modest – attempts at social reform.

For Adler's turn to Marxist socialism, the starting point was not the philosophy or political economy of the English classics, but, on the one hand, his unsparing analysis of the social situation of large sections of the working class, for whose poverty and misery he felt a deep sympathy, and, on the other, the urgent need for political action. It was the search for deeper causes that led him to the theories of Marx and Engels. After the failure of his application to become a factory inspector, he devoted all his energies to bringing together the different policy orientations and fragmented workers' organizations into a Marxist-oriented Social Democratic Party. As an engine of agitation, he used the considerable private financial resources inherited from his father to found the weekly newspaper *Die Gleichheit* (Equality), whose first number appeared in December 1886.

Adler's agitation met with immediate success when, in December 1888, he sneaked undetected into the brickworks of the *Wienerberger Gesellschaft* on the outskirts of Vienna and denounced the appalling conditions there in detail in several articles in *Die Gleichheit*. This led to a demand in the *Reichsrat* (Imperial Council – the Austrian parliament) by the democratic deputies Engelbert Pernerstorfer and Ferdinand Kronawetter for information about the unlawful inactivity of the authorities, immediately after which the trade inspector appeared at the factory. At last, wages were to be paid in cash and not in tin tokens which could be redeemed only in the company store at inflated prices. Against it, tough measures were taken by the police against Adler's helpers.[15]

The impression Engels received of Adler's personality during his visit in 1883 was so positive that he wrote to Kautsky immediately afterwards: 'he is a man of some promise'.[16] Direct contact did not initially result from the visit, but there was indirect contact via Karl Kautsky, who was living in London at the time and who reported to Adler as late as 1886 that *Gleichheit* '[pleases] Engels greatly'.[17]

Adler's efforts to unify the Social Democratic movement made considerable progress, especially through mass meetings at which resolutions were passed largely unanimously. In the process, Adler aroused Kautsky's suspicions by being overly willing to compromise with the 'radicals'. 'I fear', Kautsky wrote to Engels, 'Adler is too much possessed by the addiction to see success, to make the party great at any price. Instead of promoting existing capable elements, he has, in order to win over highly doubtful elements, repelled and embittered capable people.'[18] Kautsky's reservations quickly disappeared, however, when he was called in by Adler to help prepare the Unification Party Congress, especially the draft programme, at first called only a 'Declaration of Principles'.[19] At the party congress, held from 30 December 1888 to 1 January 1889 at an inn in Hainfeld, a small town in the Lower Austrian foothills of the Alps, Kautsky was chosen as a deputy speaker by the overwhelming majority of those in favour of the draft.

In theoretical terms, this Declaration of Principles of the (now united) Austrian Social Democratic Workers' Party stands clearly on the footing of Marxian socialism. Among its demands – after that of the abolition of all prerogatives of nationality, birth and property, and freedom of organization and agitation – the third place was already taken by universal, equal and direct suffrage without distinction of gender for all representative bodies, this being seen 'as one of the most important means of agitation and organization'. Adler's willingness to compromise with the radicals found expression in the fact that universal suffrage was to be sought 'without our being in any way mistaken about the value of parliamentarianism as a form of modern class rule'.[20] Kautsky also accepted this concession, which secured for the declaration a nearly unanimous vote of all delegates.

The re-establishment of Austrian social democracy occurred almost simultaneously with that of the Socialist International. The 'Second International' constituted itself at its founding congress in Paris in July 1889 as an international association of the national party organizations now existing in most European countries. As a delegate of the Austrian party, Adler attended the congress and was able to report there on the notable progress of the movement in his country, to enthusiastic applause from the participants. It was at this congress that Adler met Engels for the second time, and from this encounter sprang 'the intimate friendship that linked them until the end of Engels' life'.[21]

Friedrich Engels' friendship with Victor Adler

From 1889 on, a continuous correspondence began until Engels' death in 1895.[22] Adler sometimes apologized for late replies because of his heavy workload with party work and the party newspaper. He found time for longer letters several times while serving prison sentences, which police harassment measures earned him even after the end of the Anti-Socialist Law. During one such imprisonment, Adler read the second and the just-published third volumes of *Das Kapital*. Engels gave him detailed reading instructions for this by letter.

A not inconsiderable part of their correspondence is more or less of a private nature. The physician Victor Adler gave Engels advice several times on which doctors he should consult in Vienna and in London for the treatment of his illnesses, amid cautious exhortations to a healthier lifestyle. The Adler family also played the role of mediator in the relocation of Luise Kautsky (Mrs Freyberger after 1894) to London after her divorce from Karl Kautsky. There, she took over the management of Engels' household after the death of Helene Demuth in 1891.

Engels provided substantial financial support to the Austrian party by having the German Dietz publishing house remit fees for his publications directly to Austria. He similarly helped Victor Adler over a difficult personal situation when his wife Emma was stricken with depression and urgently needed spa treatment. Adler no longer had the financial means for this, as he had made over his inherited fortune to the party. He accepted the support on the condition that he would later repay the money to the party.

Adler invited Engels to visit Vienna several times, but Engels did not visit until 1893, when on 15 September he addressed a crowded gathering of workers in Vienna's 3rd district. However, Engels declined Adler's renewed invitation to the 1894 party congress there. The deep friendship between the two men proved itself in the last year of Engels' life, when Adler, informed in confidence by the physician Dr Freyberger of Engels' rapidly spreading cancer, announced in his last-ever letter to Engels a visit at short notice to Eastbourne in order to obtain his 'advice, in more detail than is possible in writing'. Adler extended his absence and remained at Engels' side as long as he could. Immediately after his return to Vienna, a telegram arrived that Friedrich Engels had died on 5 August.[23]

The politics of the Austrian party during Engels' lifetime

If Engels had high hopes for Austrian social democracy, they were based on his great confidence in Victor Adler, the party's undisputed leader. Adler had the merit of having unified the party on the basis of a Marxist programme and of having decisively pushed back the opponents of such an orientation. Adhering to the revolutionary perspective of overcoming capitalism, he consistently stood for a path to power that reflected Engels' strategy and initially pursued the struggle for universal suffrage as his prime political goal.

The first May Day

The party was able to achieve considerable organizational and political successes soon after its founding. Engels' correspondence with Adler and Kautsky bears witness to 'the joy with which Engels followed the rise of the Austrian party and how he rejoiced at the growing respect it instilled in the bourgeoisie and the government'.[24] Only a year old, the party made a spectacular debut in 1890 with the first May Day celebration ever in Austria. At the Paris Congress in 1889, it had been decided to organize a mass rally on 1 May for the introduction of the eight-hour working day. A difference of opinion emerged, however, on the question of whether this rally should be held on 1 May, even if it fell on a working day (advocated by the French and Austrian parties), or on the following Sunday (advocated by the Germans and the English). Agreement was finally reached that it should be on 1 May, but with an exemption clause. When, in 1890, the year the decision was first to be implemented, the SPD – under severe pressure from the employers – moved the rally to the following Sunday, thus angering the French, Victor Adler risked calling the workers to rally on 1 May (a Thursday). And, in fact, work stopped in most of Vienna's factories, as many thousands of workers 'strolled' across the Ringstrasse to the Prater (Vienna's fairground) as part of what was still an officially sanctioned event, even with emergency security regulations still in force. Despite the strong reactions and great anxiety on the part of the bourgeoisie, the well-organized rally passed off calmly. For Victor Adler it was particularly painful that he could not take part in the celebrations, as he was then serving time in prison.

For Engels, 'the May Day celebration of the proletariat was epoch-making not only by its universal character which made it the first international *action* of the militant working class'. 'Friend and foe agree,' he wrote in a subsequent article in the *Arbeiter-Zeitung*,[25] '*that on the whole Continent it was Austria, and in Austria Vienna, that celebrated the holiday of the proletariat in the most brilliant and dignified manner*, and that the Austrian, above all the Viennese, workers thereby won themselves an entirely different standing in the movement'.[26] Despite this, Engels's position in the international debate over May

Day was thoroughly ambivalent. In the conflict between the Germans and the French, he regretted 'the bad impression it must make everywhere "when the strongest party in the world suddenly sounds the retreat."' Ultimately, however, he defended the SPD's decision to postpone the May Day celebration until the Sunday (4 May 1890), because 'the "non-interruption of the victorious run of the German party is now the main thing", and "it is nonsense to want to make the movement uniform in all countries."'[27]

The suffrage movement

In this sense, it was consistent for Engels to fully support Victor Adler's controversial course in the Austrian party in the dispute over universal suffrage. Shortly before his resignation, the conservative prime minister, Count Taaffe, had introduced a draft for electoral law reform, according to which two-thirds of the *Reichsrat* deputies were to be elected by a third *curia* (franchise), for which a significant expansion of voting rights for male citizens was envisaged.[28] Taaffe's goal was to strengthen imperial cohesion, but he also feared that the Austrian workers might 'speak Belgian' – that is follow the example of their Belgian comrades, who had fought for universal suffrage in 1893 with mass strike actions. The draft was rejected by the *Reichsrat* with a large majority. Victor Adler resolutely opposed all efforts to support Taaffe's electoral reform through extra-parliamentary action, which earned him some criticism within the party and also from left-liberal quarters. He even stopped a campaign for Taaffe's bill launched by the other members of the Executive Committee during his absence at the Zurich Congress of the International.[29] The decisive factor, as Adler said in a report to the Party Congress a little later, was that 'we could not possibly jeopardize our programme for the sake of a one-off gain. ... [We] could not pull the chestnuts out of the fire for a government which had the state of emergency in Vienna and Prague on its conscience. ... That would have thoroughly misled the proletariat'.[30]

Engels assured Adler of his full support on the matter, that there should be an end 'to folly' (meaning mass strike actions).[31] Kautsky wrote to Engels that without Adler's intervention, 'the hot-blooded Austrians would probably have achieved a second instalment of the state of emergency in Vienna'.[32] Engels also justified his cautionary position by saying that 'a political strike must either score an immediate victory ... or else end in a colossal fiasco or, finally, *lead direct to barricades*'[33] and that in any case the risk was far too high.

With his expectation of an early introduction of a new, broader electoral law, however, Engels was overly optimistic. The electoral law reform of 1897 clearly fell short of Taaffe's draft, and the election results were disappointing, especially in Vienna, where the social democrats did not win a single seat in the general *curia*. It took until 1907 for the *Reichsrat* to be elected for the first time under universal, equal suffrage for men. The party won eighty-seven seats (equivalent to a 17 per cent share), but from the beginning it was severely weakened by its ethnic heterogeneity into being a mere umbrella organization in parliament. In 1911, the number of seats declined to eighty-four – and there could be no talk of a 'victory run', as in Germany, during Engels' lifetime.

The nationalities question

Despite some cautionary indications,[34] Engels – and initially Adler with him – adhered to what Otto Bauer later called the attitude of 'naive cosmopolitanism'[35] in this question, which was equally important for the Habsburg monarchy as it was for Austrian social democracy: national affiliation was seen as a 'bourgeois prejudice' that would disappear of its own accord in the victorious class struggle. In a greeting to the Czech comrades on the occasion of their May Day celebration in 1893, Engels reiterated his view 'that all national strife is only possible under the rule of the big landed feudal lords and capitalists; that it serves solely to perpetuate this rule; that Czech and German workers have the same common interests and that as soon as the working class attains political power all causes for national strife will be removed'.[36]

If in the Hainfeld party programme the nationality problem was referred to only in the sweeping statement that the social democrats as an international party condemned 'the prerogatives of nationality'[37] – albeit mentioned in first place – 'birth etc.', it was recognized soon afterwards that 'naïve cosmopolitanism' did not offer a viable basis for a solution to the problem. As early as 1896, a year after Engels' death, Kautsky had to admit 'that the old Marxian attitude had become untenable – as had also his attitude towards the Czechs. It would be quite un-Marxist to close one's eyes to the facts and persist in the old Marxian standpoint'.[38]

The nationality problem became most virulent in the highly industrialized mixed-language areas of Bohemia and Moravia, but also in the southern Crown Lands with Slovenian and Italian populations. Conflicts arose particularly in the area of trade unions, where local Czech trade unions rebelled against the centralism of the industry-based associations controlled by German-speaking workers' representatives and the Central Trade Union Commission. Czech social democrats often felt that 'the desire to maintain a unified movement was not always an expression of internationalism, but could also serve the tendencies of a certain Great Power nationalism'.[39]

A fundamental discussion of the nationality problem took place at the party congress in Brno in 1899. The so-called Brno Nationalities Programme envisaged the dissolution of the historical Crown Lands and the formation in their place of democratically organized 'nationally delimited self-governing bodies' (Engels' 'territorial principle'); this was, however, unrealistic from the outset because a practical territorial disentanglement of Germans and Czechs was hardly possible. In his pamphlet *Nation und Staat* (Nation and State),[40] published shortly before the congress, Karl Renner had proposed the 'principle of personality' as an alternative solution in the area of constitutional law. The Brno Programme was an expression of 'a far-reaching integration and identification of Social Democracy with the state'.[41] The solution of the nationality question was to inspire the younger generation of social democratic theorists to the first *chefs d'oeuvre* of what has since 1907 been called Austromarxism: Renner's *Der Kampf der österreichischen Nationen um den Staat* (The Austrian Nations' Struggle for the State, 1902)[42] and Otto Bauer's *Die Nationalitätenfrage und die Sozialdemokratie* (The Nationalites Question and Social Democracy, 1907).[43]

Engels' liking for Austrian social democracy

With no other party did Engels have such a trouble-free relationship as with the Austrian Social Democratic Workers' Party. In the correspondence, there is no hint of differences of opinion either on fundamental theoretical issues or on everyday strategy in political debate. The contrast is striking, especially with the German party, to whose development Engels devoted the greatest attention. On the one hand, the political strategy of the SPD since the Unification Party Congress of 1875 corresponded in its fundamental orientation to his ideas of the right path to socialism, and the party's subsequent successes confirmed his views and presented a model for other continental European parties and ultimately also for laggard England. On the other hand, Engels repeatedly ran into trouble with internal conflicts in the party, in which he supported his like-minded friends – first and foremost August Bebel – in the fight against 'petty-bourgeois' attitudes.

For example, Engels repeatedly criticized Wilhelm Liebknecht (1826–1900), his comrade-in-arms from emigrant days who, as the editor of *Vorwärts*, in his view reported too leniently on the parties in France and England that were overly willing to compromise[44] and of whose tendency towards 'vulgar democratic and vulgar socialist catchwords'[45] he also disapproved. If these were merely old quarrels *en passant*, another source of conflict touched on a more serious problem. In various legislative matters before the *Reichstag*, such as the agricultural question, the Bavarian deputy Georg von Vollmar argued in favour of supporting protective measures for farmers. For electoral success in the rural constituencies, the party 'could not possibly win many supporters if it only preached to the farmers that their downfall was inevitable'.[46] Discord of a similar kind was evident in the question of subsidizing shipyards (the so-called steamer subsidy question).[47] For Bebel, it became more difficult over time to commit the party to the line laid down by Engels.

In Austria, the party had been represented in the parliament only since 1897 (i.e. after Engels' death) and – until the introduction of universal suffrage – with only a small number of deputies. Under such conditions of powerlessness compared to the German party, such questions did not arise for the time being. Clearly, the top priority as a political objective was universal suffrage.[48] Improvements in the area of labour protection and working hours were achieved, thanks to direct action by the trade unions, which had developed strongly since the founding of the party. The first Congress of Austrian trade unions, at which sixty-nine associations were represented, took place in 1893.[49]

The late establishment of the party organization also meant that, although the party newspapers offered the opportunity to publish longer treatises, intellectual discussion of theoretical and strategic issues developed late in Austria.[50] Victor Adler did not consider himself a theoretician but published several essays on fundamental questions in *Neue Zeit*, edited by Kautsky and published in Germany. It was not until 1907 that the party had its own theoretical publication in the form of the monthly journal *Der Kampf*. If there were differences of opinion, such as over tactics in the electoral law dispute, it was not least the outstanding authority of Victor Adler that was able to bridge differences and provide compromise formulations.

Engels expected great successes of the Austrian party to have positive effects, in particular on the development of German social democracy. Referring to the then current political dispute over the reform of electoral law, he wrote to Karl Kautsky on 3 November 1893: 'Austria is now the most important country in Europe, at any rate for the moment. It is here that the initiative lies, which in a year or two will have its repercussions in Germany and other countries.'[51] From the early success of the Austrian party, he expected an impetus for the SPD to take up the struggle for universal suffrage in Prussia, where a three-class suffrage system was still in force.

In Engels' view, a revolution – with or without violence – had to take place more or less simultaneously in all advanced states, but the impetus for it could well come from revolutions in backward countries. 'The fall of tsarist despotism – revolution in Russia', he wrote in 1894, 'will also give the labour movement of the West fresh impetus and create new, better conditions in which to carry on the struggle, thus hastening the victory of the modern industrial proletariat.'[52] In Austria, the final push for universal suffrage came, in fact, from the 1905 Russian Revolution. This time, unlike in 1893, Victor Adler decided to use the general strike as a 'last resort', and in 1906, when the reform threatened to fail in the *Reichsrat*, preparations were made for mass strike action. Pressure from the streets played a major role in ensuring that the reform was passed at the end of 1906.

Reformism and revisionism

After two decades of parliamentary activity, there were increasing signs in the SPD that the relationship between everyday political work and the ultimate revolutionary goal could not be resolved as easily as Engels had presented it in his strategy for the road to socialism. The Erfurt programme attempted to resolve this tension by appending to a Marxist theoretical section, in which the party was committed to a – not necessarily revolutionary – overcoming of capitalism (its 'future programme'), a catalogue of reformist 'present demands', with no statement of how the struggle for these present demands was to contribute concretely to achieving the ultimate goal. That this tension persisted is shown by the fact that deep debates developed on some questions of principle: on the agrarian question, on which Engels again commented in detail in a protracted essay in the *Neue Zeit*,[53] and on the concept of 'state socialism'. If for Bismarck 'state socialism was only a means for the even more effective fettering of the people', what mattered to Georg von Vollmar was 'the use the state made of the rights to which it was entitled, i.e. in what sense and by whom the state was to be directed'. For him it was clear that 'as the democratization of state power progressed', this role would be assumed by the social democrats, so he saw 'no reason to fight the idea of state socialism *per se* with particular zeal'.[54]

Internal party conflicts of a similar nature did not develop in Austria, although the structure and list of demands of the Hainfeld Programme were similar to those of the Erfurt Programme. Unlike in Germany, in Austria it was a group of radicals, a 'Bakuninist-anarchist' current rather than a Lassallian state-socialist one, that was committed to a Marxist programme. The difference between state socialism and Marxist socialism was initially of little relevance in the Austrian party. In Germany, the temptation to slide into reformism came from the parliamentary work that had now been going on for decades. The Austrian party had only relevant representation in the parliament since 1907; until then, it was mainly the trade unions that had provided a certain breeding ground for reformism. In addition, the nationality problem increasingly preoccupied the party.

An internal conflict of far greater intensity developed in the SPD when, after the death of Engels, Eduard Bernstein published his revisionist theses in individual articles, systematically elaborated in his book *Die Voraussetzungen des Sozialismus und die Aufgaben der Sozialdemokratie* (The Preconditions for Socialism and the Role of Social Democracy, 1899). Unlike the reformist quarrels, Bernstein's revisionism concerned the core areas of socialist theory and political strategy on the road to socialism. At issue was nothing less than the 'historical tendency of capitalist accumulation': the ever-advancing concentration and centralization of capital under pressure of the law of falling profit rates, the elimination of the propertied petty bourgeois and peasant strata of society, the increasing exploitation and impoverishment of the proletarian workers, the increase in severity of the periodic economic crises and so on – all of which tendencies would in concert culminate in a final crisis in which the proletariat, united in class consciousness, would put an end to the capitalist system in a momentous revolutionary act. This analysis could not but nullify the quasi-natural certainty of victory of the social democratic movement.

That Victor Adler's authority also radiated to Germany is shown by the fact that he was involved from the beginning in the fierce controversy triggered by Bernstein's theses. Adler's attitude in the conflict shows a certain ambivalence. Again and again he emphasizes that he considers Bernstein's theses incorrect, but in the same breath, in his first public response, he says that he does not understand Kautsky's reaction, that he takes 'Ede's [Eduard Bernstein's] opinions to be half garbage ... [but] I am grateful to him for every nudge in the ribs and have learned immeasurably from it'.[55] Adler tried to persuade Kautsky and Bebel to greater moderation and understanding of Bernstein's criticism. In a letter, he advised Bebel to 'avoid anything that might prove that a man like Ede had no place in the party'[56] – a warning against Bernstein's expulsion.

Bernstein turned to Adler immediately before publication of his book with a request for a review, citing Kautsky's opinion that 'it would be good if you were the first in the party press to give your dictum on my book'. Bernstein counted on Adler's 'love of reconciliation. ... I believe I can count on understanding from you, which the reviewers now setting the tone in the German party press lack'.[57] Adler, for his part, took pains to downplay the significance of the antagonisms. The dispute, he said, was about 'where we stand, ... not about where we should go'.[58] Despite repeatedly professing his orthodoxy, he expressed clear scepticism about both the theory of increasing immiserization of the proletariat (*Verelendungstheorie*) and the catastrophe theory.[59] But ultimately Adler subordinated theory to political activity (*Gegenwartsarbeit* – 'work in the present'). For 'the proletarian movement [is] by no means primarily dependent on its theory; far rather the reverse. ... Socialist theory is, in a certain sense, the superstructure which is overturned with the progress of the development of the proletariat'. Theory will 'always be able only to illuminate the way for the movement, not to prescribe its trajectories'.[60]

The Bernstein debate also spread to the Austrian social democrats, but without 'leading to a reaction with the power and far-reaching consequence of German revisionism'[61]. For all his scepticism about too much theory, Adler did see the need for some changes in the programme. Thirteen years after Hainfeld, it seemed to him that the time had come to revise the programme at the 1901 Party Congress, at which there was also a fundamental debate on Bernstein's theses. The passage concerning universal suffrage – 'without allowing any misconceptions about the value of parliamentarism: a form of modern class rule' – was left out. In essence, the Marxist orientation was retained. Revisionism was reflected in the new programme by the elimination of the immiserization thesis, which was replaced by a more differentiated formulation. Kautsky, who like Bebel attended the Party Congress as a guest, had reservations about the new text but ultimately gave his approval. His misgivings, shared by Bebel, centred on the replacement of the term 'common property' in the transition of ownership with 'new forms of cooperative production based on social ownership',[62] in which they saw a concession to Bernstein's terminology. Equally, however, the change reflects the influence of state-socialist ideas. The reformist tendency is evident in the elimination of the statement that 'workers' insurance does not touch the core of the social problem at all' in favour of a demand that 'workers' insurance be subjected to a thoroughgoing reform ... and [be] uniformly organized under universal self-administration by the insured'.

Engelbert Pernerstorfer, Adler's friend since youth and comrade-in-arms in resistance to the Anti-Socialist Law of 1886, emerged as a pronounced defender of Bernstein's views, a position shared, albeit more moderately, by Wilhelm Ellenbogen.[63] If Adler largely represented Marxist orthodoxy on theoretical issues, he did so within an emphatically pluralist orientation for the party as a whole, which explicitly recognized the positions of those who deviated from the orthodox mainstream as productive contributions to the progress of the movement.[64] The fact that the divergences between orthodoxy and revisionism did not solidify into party wings in Austria is due not least to Adler's pre-eminent position. Although he repeatedly emphasized that he did not see his role in those terms, he was *de facto* also the party's 'chief theorist'.[65]

Intellectually, he sought to resolve the conflict between reformist practice, which increasingly characterized the party's activities up to the First World War, and revolutionary theory by describing disputes over reform or revolution as 'disputes over words'.

> We Social Democrats have never known ourselves as anything else but reformists, and we have never known ourselves as anything else but at the same time revolutionaries. Every reform is important and worth every effort, but every reform is only worth as much as the revolution contained in it! When we are asked: revolution or reform? We say revolution and reform![66]

The more the organizations within the workers' movement – party, trade unions, consumer cooperatives – consolidated up to 1914 and achieved tangible improvements in the social conditions of the workers, the stronger the reformist traits of Austrian social democracy became. Nowhere did this tendency appear with greater clarity than in the nationality problem. This seemed on the surface a matter of party unity. For although the explosive power of the problem for the Habsburg monarchy could have been used along Engels' strategic-political lines to generate pressure for the dissolution of the pre-bourgeois, feudal structures of the Austro-Hungarian state – above all by demanding the right of secession for individual entities within it – the social democratic reform proposals actually sought the preservation of the state as a whole, albeit with altered internal structures, but without a thought of how much revolution such a reform involved.

The final crisis of capitalism

As already observed, Adler subordinated the further development of socialist theory to the requirements of political practice. He had repeatedly referred to Marx's thesis of the final crisis of capitalism in the years after the Hainfeld Party Congress,[67] but cautiously relativized it ten years later in the course of the revisionist debate. There will 'always be discussion ... as to whether the capitalist economy could endure the rapidity of technical development arising from market expansion, or whether, having reached the limit of its elasticity, it would drift towards catastrophe'.[68] For the time being, he did not seek to go further in his scepticism, so as not to irritate core groups and functionary strata of the party whose faith in Marx's forecasts had remained unshaken.

The younger generation of Marxist theoreticians found this approach to theoretical problems unsatisfactory. The historical tendency of capital accumulation is the central issue of what is probably the most famous treatise of Austromarxist economics, Rudolf Hilferding's *Das Finanzkapital* (Finance Capital, 1910), a topic which Otto Bauer also addressed from a different angle in an article in the *Neue Zeit*. Published as Volume 3 of *Marx-Studien*,[69] Hilferding's work was elevated by Kautsky to the highest echelons of Marxist literature as 'Volume IV of *Das Kapital*'. Hilferding analysed the development of capitalism under the conditions of the progressive concentration and centralization of capital predicted by Marx and its mobilization through joint stock companies, banks, and stock exchanges. He saw the process as driven by Marx's law of falling profit rates in the wake of an increase in the organic composition of capital.[70] The most important structural changes in capitalism occurring under the rule of finance capital were, he argued, the restriction of competition by cartels, ultimately culminating in a universal cartel, the emergent gap between profit and investment – compensated by capital exports to parts of the world still largely or wholly untouched by capitalism (imperialism theory) – and an increasing utilization of the state and its services by organized capital.

The consequence for the question of the susceptibility of the capitalist system to crises is ambivalent. On the one hand, 'capital appears to be a unitary force governing the development of society' in such a way that 'the question of how the economy is organized is increasingly resolved through the development of finance capital itself'. This form of organization is nothing less than the 'conscious regulation of society in antagonistic form – an antagonism of distribution'.[71] Finance capital 'creates the final organizational conditions for socialism' and at the same time 'makes the political transition easier'. This transition is not non-violent; the end of capitalism will not be the result of an economic collapse, but of a final political-economic catastrophe:

> [Finance capital] completes the dictatorship of the capital magnates. At the same time, it makes the dictatorship of the rulers of capital in one country increasingly incompatible with the capitalist interests of another country, and the rule of capital within a country increasingly incompatible with the interests of the masses exploited by finance capital, who are also called upon to engage in the struggle. In the violent clash of hostile interests, the dictatorship of the capital magnates will finally turn into the dictatorship of the proletariat.[72]

Otto Bauer developed an original version of the cyclical crisis theory of capitalism in the context of his critique of Rosa Luxemburg's *Die Akkumulation des Kapitals* (The Accumulation of Capital).[73] Bauer contrasted Luxemburg's mechanical theory of collapse with a crisis theory based on *Das Kapital*. In this crisis theory, there is an adjustment mechanism that enables capitalism to repeatedly re-establish the conditions for balanced capital accumulation. The decisive determinants of the crisis cycle are the growth of the population – and thus the potential labour force – on the one hand, and the long-term tendency towards an increasing organic composition of capital (cf. the ratio of constant to variable capital), on the other. Accumulation will 'take place without hindrance, provided that it remains within a certain proportion of magnitude on the one hand to the growth of the population and on the other to the development of productive forces – a development expressed in progress towards a higher organic composition of capital'. Bauer foresaw an 'objective limit to accumulation' when the population and potential labour force cease to grow. 'Accumulation will then be possible only to the extent that the development of the means of production requires additional constant capital for the employment of an unchanging mass of workers.' However, capitalism will be 'felled earlier', not by the impossibility of realizing greater value, but as a result of 'growing working class indignation'.[74] If these theories of crisis differ fundamentally in their argumentation from Karl Marx's version, they both nevertheless have a strikingly anti-revisionist tendency in that they both forecast a final crisis.

Austromarxism – theory and politics

'Austromarxism'[75] was originally a collective term used of the Austrian 'scientific socialist' writers. With the publications of Rudolf Hilferding, Karl Renner, Otto Bauer and Max Adler, all appearing between the turn of the century and the First World War, the theoretical output of Austrian social democracy, until then hardly existent, gained a high international reputation in a relatively short time. On the basis of orthodox Marxist, non-revisionist political economy, the Austromarxists strove to position scientific socialism in the context of contemporary sociological and philosophical currents (Austrian School of Economics, neo-Kantianism), taking into account economic and societal developments since Marx.

In his essay *Kausalität und Teleologie im Streite um die Wissenschaft* (Causality and Teleology in the Debate on Science) in Volume I of *Marx-Studien*, the philosopher Max Adler (1873–1937) attempted a synthesis between Kantian epistemology and the Marxian theory of society.[76] However, the postulated Kantian foundation for Marxism foundered on the rocks of the dialectical-materialist theory of knowledge. The lack of formal coherence in the theoretical approaches of scientific Austromarxism can be seen, for example, in Renner's naïve-positivist position in epistemology and in the fact that his political-economic views owed more to Lassalle than to Marx or Engels. Moreover, on the question of the relationship between theory and practice, there were considerable differences of opinion between the active politicians Renner and Bauer and Max Adler, whom Renner described as a 'Marxist scholastic'.[77]

Reflecting the relationship formulated by Victor Adler between reform and revolution, the combination of Marxist class struggle and revolutionary objectives with practical reform work was the defining characteristic of interwar political Austromarxism,[78] which remained anti-revisionist and avoided all criticism of individual theorems of Marx and Engels.[79] Its difference from Bolshevik Communism[80] was clearly marked by its adherence to democratic parliamentarism and consistent rejection of violence – even on the left wing of the party – as a means of attaining political power. Victor Adler's legacy was also visible in a strong concern for unity between right-wing and left-wing currents within the party, even during the Republic, in order to avoid a split in the labour movement of the kind that happened in Germany after the First World War.

When, at the end of the war, what is now Austria was constituted as a democratic republic,[81] the social democrats, who in Renner supplied the first chancellor and provided numerous other ministers, suddenly found themselves in possession of governmental power, albeit in coalition and without a parliamentary majority of their own. In this phase of extreme political instability, the party pursued an anti-revolutionary policy. In contrast to Germany, it succeeded in preventing violent action by the so-called Red Guards and, above all, in gaining control over the Workers' Councils, thus removing the likelihood of any communist rebellion. Equally important was the social reform policy of the immediate post-war years. Supported by pressure from the workplace and the streets, the social democrats were able to push through the parliament a large number of social laws that tangibly improved the short-term social and economic situation of the workers, contributing decisively to calming the political situation.[82] Viewed in the long term, these laws still form the basis of the modern welfare state. All calls from the contemporary Hungarian Soviet Republic to follow its example were rejected out of hand by the Austrian social democrats.

The 1920 parliamentary elections, however, made the Christian socialists the strongest party. Confined to the role of opposition in the state as a whole, the social democrats retained unchallenged political control over the federal capital, Vienna, where far-reaching social reform measures were implemented (so-called Red Vienna). A realignment of the party's political strategy was decisively shaped by its role in opposition, with Otto Bauer determining the political course. In his book *Die Österreichische Revolution* (The Austrian Revolution, 1923), he had made participation in a governing coalition with one of the bourgeois parties conditional on 'whether the coalition government can be an expedient and effective means in the class struggle'.[83] To achieve an absolute majority in parliamentary elections, however, the party would have had to win the votes of considerable sections of the peasant and petty bourgeois population groups. This meant reformist policy proposals, largely without revolutionary potential, in special programmes (e.g. Social Democratic Agrarian Programme of 1925, Employment Policy) and in the new party programme (Linz Programme) of 1926.

The goal of becoming electable to non-proletarian working-class strata was thwarted by the programme's revolutionary Marxist terminology. This reaffirmed social democracy's goal of 'gathering the majority of the people under the leadership of the working class ... and winning power for the working class in the Democratic Republic'. The statement that 'the working class would be forced to break the resistance of the bourgeoisie by means of dictatorship'[84] should they attempt to sabotage the restructuring of society after a social democratic electoral victory aroused fierce opposition among the other parties and the general public and even caused concern within the party itself. At this point in particular, a glaring misjudgement of the real balance of power took place. That this had deteriorated massively to the disadvantage of the social democrats became evident when in February 1934 the attempt by the party's armed organization, the Republican Protection League, to defend the Republic against the assault of the authoritarian-fascist forces ended in complete defeat.

Some retrospective conclusions about the road to socialism

Two issues are of particular interest here: the political strategy conceived by Engels to achieve the ultimate goal of a socialist economic and social order and the question of a synthesis of revolutionary goals and reformism.

Engels' political strategy was based on the long-term perspective of the development of capitalism in accordance with economic law, as depicted by Marx in the first volume of *Das Kapital*. However, Engels evaluated the individual determinants of that development quite differently in light of changes that had occurred since Marx's time. He held steadfastly to the expectation of an elimination of the petty bourgeois and agrarian middle classes through an ineluctable process of concentration and centralization of capital. Driven by competition and technological development, this would bring about an ever-widening polarization of society, in which in the end a socially homogeneous, levelled working class constituting the overwhelming mass of the population would face a small number of capitalists holding state power. Engels barely held on to the thesis of the increasing misery of the proletarian masses, which lacked empirical confirmation; his expectations were directed to the development of a class consciousness within the proletariat. Imbued with a revolutionary certainty of victory based on Marx's scientific theory, and politically organized in party and trade unions, the workers' movement would continue to grow towards that goal. For Engels it was not a question of 'whether' but only of 'when' the proletariat would acquire such a preponderance within the population that it dominated the parliament of the capitalist state – which is why he consistently backed the struggle for universal suffrage and advocated the use of every political opportunity this offered for the representatives of the proletariat.

If the inherent dynamics of capitalism produced of itself forms of economic and social organization that promoted the transition to socialism, Engels nevertheless always resisted the notion of a peaceful, unbroken growth into socialism. For him, this transformation remained a revolutionary act, accomplished after the proletariat had taken over political power, with or without the use of force. Engels emphasized the function and effects of crisis in the development of capitalism, especially in relation to the concentration and centralization of capital. Of relatively little importance in his political strategy, on the other hand, was Marx's thesis of an increasing intensity of periodically recurring crises.

Already in Engels' lifetime, and more and more clearly in the following decades up to the beginning of the First World War, there were increasing signs that the development of capitalism did not fit the picture sketched by Marx and Engels. The ups and downs of the business cycle corresponded to the notion of periodically recurring crises, but showed no tendency to aggravate. The projected tendency towards a concentration and centralization of capital found confirmation in real developments, but the consequences were not, in fact, as Marx and Engel had expected. On the one hand, the property-owning petty bourgeois strata proved much more capable of adaptation and survival, especially in agriculture, as well as in the crafts, trade and commerce. Even more important in the long run was the strong growth of a new white-collar and civil service class. In the labour force there was no sign of the expected polarization between a small number of capitalists, on the one hand, and a homogeneous proletarian mass of (typically industrial) workers, on the other. The structure of society changed, but its social differentiation increased rather than decreased. The proletariat did not become the majority, and the foundation of Engels's political strategy, the development of an irresistibly revolutionary proletariat increasingly marked by class consciousness, became less realistic every day.

It was impossible to overlook the fact that the propertied petty bourgeois and agrarian class would for the foreseeable future continue to hold a considerable stake in the social structure; nor could this be relativized by the argument that these strata were economically dependent on large capitalist enterprises and/or banks and had thus lost their independence and become virtually proletarian.[85] In order to further increase their share of seats in parliamentary elections, social democratic parties had to either court votes from the petty bourgeoisie and peasant farmers or seek coalition with other parties. Both alternatives encouraged the reformism that Engels had always opposed.

Paradoxically, it was precisely the problematic element of Marx and Engels' theory of capitalist development – that it would lead to socialism with quasi-natural necessity – that contributed significantly to the successes of social democracy before the First World War.[86] Invoked and affirmed in countless pamphlets, songs and poems, the sense of belonging to a victorious movement, of the historical mission of the proletariat to liberate humanity from oppression and exploitation and lead it into a happier future, formed an indispensable basis for more and more people originally living in miserable conditions to place their hopes in, and to join, an organized workers' movement. Extending far beyond the political sphere, the movement, even if it remained excluded from formal political power, had to be taken seriously by the ruling classes as a political and social force.

The increasingly reformist character of Austrian social democracy before the First World War was expressed in practice above all in the growing organizational strength of the trade union movement, which achieved tangible improvements in the living standards and social situation of large groups of workers. In the sphere of politics, the Social Democratic Party made the preservation of the Habsburg monarchy through democratic reforms – of which the traditionalist monarchy was itself no longer capable – one of its central concerns. Admittedly, without success, the party opposed the policy of obstruction pursued by representatives of nationalist groupings in the *Reichsrat*, which had paralyzed the parliament since 1911.

In the extremely difficult transitional phase from the Great Power of the Habsburg monarchy to the residual state of the Republic of (German-speaking) Austria, social democracy suddenly found itself in possession of political power, albeit shared with bourgeois parties. The party achieved its greatest successes during this period with reformist anti-revolutionary policies embracing a broad wave of sociopolitical reforms. The failure of its socialization programme – also reformist in conception – was due, however, not only to opposition from the bourgeois parties, and the party's participation in government came to an end again after two years, characterized by Otto Bauer as a period of 'balance of class forces'. Thereafter, the party pursued a political strategy of revolutionary reformism, intended by Bauer as a continuation of the class struggle by democratic means in order to achieve the ultimate revolutionary goal. The theory of the final crisis of capitalism experienced a temporary renaissance as a result of the Great Depression of the 1930s. In fact, however, it was not the socialist alternative that received a political boost from the economic depression, but fascism which put a violent end to social democratic hopes in Austria as well.

Already during the First World War, Karl Renner – in contrast to Bauer – had conceived a Lassallian model of state socialism oriented towards the long-term expansion of a 'state democratic economy'.[87] Renner retained the word 'class struggle' but gave it a different, non-revolutionary meaning in the sense of a permanent conflict of interests between labour and capital, negotiated within a legal framework by legal means. Whether this concept would have had a chance in view of the profound hostility of significant sections of the bourgeoisie in the First Austrian Republic seems highly doubtful. In 1945, Renner became the new founder of the Second Republic and his programme became its unofficial philosophy.

Engels was to be proved right in one point of his political strategy for Austria. He resolutely warned the social democrats against toying with the idea of armed rebellion, which, given the advanced state of military technology, would end in defeat for the insurgents and set the movement back by decades. At the same time he warned the German social democrats against being provoked by reaction into rebellion or even into a rhetoric of readiness for violence. It was provocative action by the fascist *Heimwehr* (Homeland Defence) that triggered an armed uprising by the Republican Protection League in February 1934, which ended in a catastrophic defeat and gave the Christian social government the reason it had long sought to transform Austria into an authoritarian state based on the traditional estates of society.

CHAPTER 4
MAN AND MACHINE: CONCEPTIONS OF TECHNOLOGY IN THE WRITINGS OF FRIEDRICH ENGELS, KARL MARX AND ERNST KAPP

Eberhard Illner

Introduction

For more than 150 years, economists, sociologists and historians have been talking about the Industrial Revolution, which fundamentally changed living conditions as hardly ever before in history and which continues to have a formative effect right into the twenty-first century. The term is predominantly used to describe the technological, economic and social changes that shaped Britain into a modern industrialized country in the late eighteenth and nineteenth centuries. The main sites were the rapidly growing industrial centres of London, Manchester, Sheffield and Glasgow and the seaports of Liverpool, Hull, Southampton and Portsmouth, as well as the London docks at Woolwich. This unique growth was caused by a complex of changes in agricultural production, trade, commerce, and coastal and ocean transport, with far-reaching demographic effects and structural changes in the extraction of raw materials and the production of goods.[1] The textile and iron industries kicked off around 1750, followed by mining, chemical processing, engineering and communications. Heavy industry, with shipbuilding and railway construction, as well as mechanical engineering and later the electrical industry, then marked the transition to the high industrialization of the second half of the nineteenth century.[2] To this day, new questions are continually being raised as to where, when and how industry developed into such a powerful agent of change that a veritable revolution – a radical upheaval of (mainly) economic-technological structures – came about.[3]

From the very beginning, the discussion around the character and scope of industrial revolution(s) gained additional momentum through being embedded in developmental theories of modern industrial capitalism, as was the case – with the model of the French Revolution of 1789 clearly in mind – in the writings of Karl Marx and Friedrich Engels. These saw the Industrial Revolution, and in particular mechanization, as a necessary precondition for the establishment of capitalist forms of production. While, on the one hand, the dynamic of high productivity and enhanced efficiency was indispensable, especially for a future socialist society, it would, they argued, under the conditions of capitalism, inevitably lead to a crisis-ridden phase culminating in self-destruction. The negative side effects of mechanization were constitutive components of capitalist commodity production whose potential for alienation and exploitation in a bourgeois society built on private property could only result in social antagonism and political revolution. Marx adopted this central argument, derived from Engels' critique of industrial conditions in Britain in the 1840s, during his period in Brussels and especially after his visit to Manchester in the summer of 1845.[4]

At the time, the question of the impact of machine technology was linked to the search for a coherent way of embedding 'the technology factor' within a socioeconomic frame of reference. Some contemporaries, impressed by spectacular innovations such as the steam engine or mechanical spinning and weaving devices, had sought a plausible explanation under the heading 'industrial revolution'. In Britain, in-depth technical analyses 'on machinery' had been published as early as the 1830s, while the first beginnings of a philosophy of technology appeared in continental Europe only in the 1870s and 1880s.

Which arguments, then, in this long-lasting discussion between engineers and economists did Engels address? How thoroughly did he concern himself with the specific forms of industrial, factory-centred production and in particular with the technology used in them? A glance at Marx and his fragmentary theory of machines reveals an understanding of technology markedly different from that of Engels, whose later writings are quite open to the notion of technological development. The question arises in this context whether the human–machine relationship, which Engels and Marx understood as a disturbed antagonism in the form of alienated labour set up to achieve profit from human capital, can in the final analysis be traced back to nothing more than a limited, idiosyncratic interpretation by Marx of Hegel's utterances on technology.

But what would happen if the Utopia came true, and, after eliminating the bourgeois world of private ownership, the exploitation and the relationships it had created were abolished? Would humankind then, thanks to a change of legal dispensation, find itself overnight in harmony with technology – especially since technology, as Marx himself said, would have to develop to a far higher level of complexity if it would achieve the productivity necessary to satisfy society's needs? Fishing, hunting and criticizing alone would hardly be enough, even in a Communist paradise, for there, too, production facilities – plant, machines and expertise – would have to be kept on course.

Another relevant question is whether between 1830 and 1890 alternative concepts for remedying the unintended social consequences of the Machine Age did not exist, unknown to Marx and Engels, despite their widely vaunted comprehensive examination of both historical and contemporary economic and social theories. A comparison with the anthropological philosophy of technology published in 1877 by the geographer Ernst Kapp will show that quite different conclusions could be drawn from the problems of an economy in the throes of rapid technological change. Kapp – reflecting both Aristotle and Hegel – developed his philosophy on the basis of practical experience in America. Even in societies marked by social inequality, technological innovations can bring about new structures of production and create new opportunities for workers. Social structures that have temporarily gone awry can, he argued, be revitalized on a higher level. Precisely where the conflict between capital and labour started, namely with the capital-intensive use of large-scale industrial technology like the steam engine, lay the solution in the form of decentralized, low-cost engines that would make small businesses competitive again and in doing so open up new potential for innovation. With his advocacy of creative technological and business innovation, Kapp foreshadowed Joseph Schumpeter's (1883–1950) notion of 'creative destruction' provided to a later generation of entrepreneurs addressing the challenge of a continuously self-reinventing capitalism.

The human–machine interface in Friedrich Engels' early writings

> The history of the proletariat in England begins with the second half of the last century, with the invention of the steam-engine and of machinery for working cotton. These inventions gave rise, as is well known, to an industrial revolution, a revolution which altered the whole civil society; one, the historical importance of which is only now beginning to be recognised.[5]

With this minimalist reduction of his main thesis, the 24-year-old commercial clerk (as he was then) from Barmen introduced his first major work, *The Condition of the Working Class in England from Personal Observation and Authentic Sources*, in 1845.[6] As a result of the use of steam engines and autonomous spinning machines and looms – the advanced technologies of the day which had replaced traditional trades with factory production – 'the human being, the worker, is regarded in manufacture simply as a piece of capital for the use of which the manufacturer pays interest under the name of wages'.[7] The new relationship of dependency had produced the proletariat and at the same time transformed bourgeois society in its entirety. The working class had created Britain's greatness and was now demanding its share, which, however, was denied to it in multiple ways by domineering factory owners. With his empirical investigation, Engels sought to substantiate his critique of the neglect of the social question by classical British national economists – a critique which had been formulated for some time, from Sismonde de Sismondi (1773–1842), through Charles Fourier (1772–1837) to Adolphe Blanqui (1798–1854). Moreover, Engels declared, this was by now no longer a question for Britain alone, but a central issue for the entire 'civilized world'.

Adolphe Blanqui, since 1833 successor to the famous economist Jean Baptiste Say (1767–1832) in the *chaire d'économie industrielle* at the *Conservatoire des arts et métiers* in Paris, had been the first to speak, in his *Cours d'Économie industrielle* (1837)[8] – after a detailed exposition of the effects of the French Revolution on the liberalization of commercial activity – on 'the economic revolution brought about in England by the discoveries of Watt and Arkwright':

> Two machines, henceforth immortal, the steam-engine and the spinning-machine, overturned the old commercial system and gave birth almost simultaneously to material products and social questions unknown to our fathers. The small workers were about to become tributary to the great capitalists; the spinning-frame replaced the wheel, and the steam-cylinder succeeded … horse-power.[9]

From today's perspective, the thesis of an economic revolution reduced to two inventions seems overly dramatic. However, this narrowing of the focus was due more to the didactic goals of Blanqui's lecture on the history of political economic theory. While Blanqui was content to treat the impact of machines on employment, wages and competition among workers in general as 'the social question', Engels' empirical analysis – primarily of textile processing but also of other industries – amounted to practical causal research. As the scion of a family of textile manufacturers, he was familiar with the machines and apparatus used in spinning and weaving and dealt in detail[10] with the various steps in their technological development, their function within the work processes and their impact on the intensity of the work.[11] According to the young entrepreneur, the three levers of industry were the division of labour, the importance of water and steam power, and the 'mechanism of machinery'. Industrial work in factories, he argued, required high levels of capital and large numbers of workers familiar with the operation of machinery. Engels was interested in the effects of expanded machine use on wage dumping and of improved technology on job differentiation as well as in the growth of lower-value work and the elimination of occupations. In short, he identified a displacement effect, especially among male adult workers, without adequate distribution of the benefits deriving from the wider utility brought about by the constantly spreading use of machines.

Engels had grown up within the traditional patriarchal structures of a relatively profitable, decentralized textile manufactory in Barmen. In 1842–3 he witnessed a wave of redundancies as a result of the introduction of the self-acting mule, a powerful spinning machine with automatic functions, both at Ermen & Engels' Victoria Mill in Salford, Manchester, and at numerous larger competitors in Lancashire like the Greg family, with whose Quarry Bank Mill, his father, Friedrich Engels Senior, conducted business. The effects of this rationalization drive were exacerbated by an economic downturn and a wave of immigration of unskilled workers to Lancashire triggered by the famine in Ireland, which led to wage dumping and mass lay-offs of previously well-paid English workers. At best, highly qualified fine spinners and experienced machine operators could still make a living of 30–40 shillings a week. Engels' assessment was that 'in a well-ordered state of society, such [technological] improvements could only be a source of rejoicing; in a war of all against all, individuals seize the benefit for themselves, and so deprive the majority of the means of subsistence'.[12] He also took issue with the argument that lower product prices would lead to increased demand and thus to the expansion of production and additional jobs, so that workers would quickly return to waged employment.[13] He objected that this could apply only to products with low raw material prices and that the time lag of the increase in demand would be too great for workers to bridge. Wage labour in factory towns had robbed them of their former part-time agricultural subsistence. Now, for better or worse, they were at the mercy of the volatile industrial cycle.

In place of theoretical conjecture, Engels sought to support his theses with concrete facts. He attended the highly regarded lectures of John Watts, secretary of the Mechanics' Institute in Manchester, and adopted some of the arguments from his pamphlet *Facts and Fictions*. Engels' source for the workers' view of things was the leader of the Chartist

Movement in Manchester, James Leach, who ran a bookshop not far from the city offices of Ermen & Engels on St Mary's, off Deansgate in Manchester. Leach provided the young merchant, whose grammatically impeccable English and German accent had attracted his attention, with profound factual knowledge and detailed statistics on working conditions in factories, the development of labour wages and productivity, and the social consequences of technological innovations. With this material, Leach was able, time and again, to counter the statistics presented and often manipulated by the factory owners. In 1844 – just before Engels' departure from Manchester – his compendium of facts and figures appeared as *Stubborn Facts from the Factories*, so that Engels was able to draw on it when writing up the situation in Barmen in the winter of 1844–5. Engels also made use of the factory inspectors' reports on violations by factory owners of working hours and the unauthorized employment of children and young people. The 'poor doctor' of Manchester, James Phillips Kay, wrote harrowing reports, especially on the cholera epidemics in the slum district of Little Ireland. Georg Weerth, a merchant in Bradford and close friend of Engels, took a similar approach. As an assistant to the local doctor for the poor, Weerth gained direct insights into the unhygienic living conditions of the workers and recorded these impressions in reports. Engels also made a point of experiencing local poverty on the spot. The rage that repeatedly flares up in his book seems to have reached boiling point thanks to the woman at his side, the 20-year-old Irish worker Mary Burns, who almost certainly introduced the ever elegantly dressed Mr Engels to the horrors of Little Ireland, for without her he would scarcely have remained unmolested there.

Let us summarize Engels' findings, even if the result, as he later freely admitted,[14] turned out to be incomplete and, owing to his youthful *furor*, even in parts erroneous. On the basis of a hitherto unique collection of empirical data, Engels developed the first explanatory approaches to the impact of far-reaching technological innovation on a bourgeois society of competing private interests and growing social inequality. Technological change in itself did not necessarily lead to social dislocation: such progress was rather to be welcomed if it was followed by fair distribution of the benefits derived from concomitant advances in productivity. However, in the prevailing state of 'dissolution of mankind into monads' through 'the unfeeling isolation of each in his private interest', distribution to all those involved in production was not envisaged. Social warfare, Engels asserted, reigns in Britain and 'capital … is the weapon with which this social warfare is pursued'. This included the systemic crises that ran in five- to six-year cycles. According to Malthus, the 'surplus' population of Britain, with its puny levels of existence, was nothing but a reserve of workers potentially needed in a boom. For three-quarters of the cycle, however, this reserve had neither work nor bread. The labour market reacted with them 'quite as with any other article of commerce'.

For Engels, technological progress was always linked to specific economic, political and social structures.[15] That these structures were influenced and changed by the advance of technology and that they would in future dominate all other societal influences had from the beginning been the basis of his concept of 'industrial revolution'. But where exactly was the lever to be applied in order to break the vicious circle of increasing social stratification caused by inequitable distribution of the gains achieved by such progress? This is where Marx came into play, a thinker who had been philosophically committed to the goal of radical political and social change since around 1842. To the mind of that time – which Marx shared – the answer could only be a revolution along the classical lines of the French Revolution of 1789. *Les Trois Glorieuses*, the July Revolution of 1830 in Paris, had confirmed this model and helped the bourgeoisie to power. The energy necessary for a revolution could now only come from the newly created social class, the proletariat, for the wage workers had 'nothing but their chains' to lose. As a journalist of Young Hegelian orientation, Marx saw himself in the role of an analyst and enlightener on the issue of the inhumane consequences of capitalist commodity production and also as a strategist in the organization of a proletarian rallying movement of international outreach.[16] Engels offered himself as *Spannmann*, or 'philosopher's mate', and confronted Marx, his master in matters of theory, for the first time in Manchester in the summer of 1845 with the intricacies of modern textile factories and the working and living conditions of their employees. Marx failed at his first audacious attempt to formulate a critique of political economy in a few weeks. Volume I of *Das Kapital*, his economic analysis of the capitalist mode of production, did not appear for another two decades, and the *magnum opus* remained forever incomplete. There were many reasons for this. The decisive factor was that Marx could never actually prove his assumption that increasing crises leading to a final collapse of the capitalist mode of production were the result of a tendency of the rate of profit to fall. Until the end of his life, he was concerned with how and why capitalism had always been able to overcome such crises.

Karl Marx's failed attempt at a philosophy of technology

It is curious that Marx initially showed relatively little interest in the actual technology used in industry, which – following the British example – had since the 1840s been undergoing a process of innovation, both on the continent and in the United States, that could no longer be overlooked.[17] No critique of classical political economy could be formulated without an analysis of the modes and methods of creating added value and increasing productivity. This presupposed an in-depth knowledge of the technology used in industry, which Marx – a layman in the field – had to painstakingly acquire without any training or prior knowledge. In 1845-6, as yet unpractised in English, he drew initially on the French translation of Andrew Ure's overview of the 1820s English textile industry. Ure, a controversially narrow-minded figure, was a conservative partisan of the factory owners and, as such, a sitting target for Marx who, like Engels before him, could work off his biting irony and typically roughhouse criticism on him without having to deal with technology in the narrower sense.

Marx completed a kind of autodidactic course in technology by reading historical works on mills and on Mathew Boulton's (1728–1809) and James Watt's (1736–1819) onwards development of the steam engine.[18] He also used, albeit cursorily, Charles Babbage's seminal and widely read *On the Economy of Machinery and Manufactures* (1832)

Figure 4.1 Karl Marx (1818–1883), May 1861. © Mayall, London / AKG.

in its French edition of 1834 – indeed, as late as the 1860s, Marx referred to this text in his preparatory work for *Das Kapital*.[19] He remained unaware that a German translation, produced by the Prussian Trade Association, had been available since 1833. In other words, Marx knew nothing of the analyses of industrial developments in Britain conducted in Germany since the 1820s. Inspection trips and observation of British technological and industrial exhibitions had been recorded in German-language polytechnical journals, and the relevant English literature had been translated and disseminated as soon as it appeared.[20] A visit to Klosterstrasse 36 in Berlin, the headquarters of the *Gewerbeverein* (Trade Association) – either during his trips to Germany or through agents – would have saved the philosopher a lot of trouble and many blind alleys.

Marx was probably unaware that his reading presented him with obsolete technology. With a view to his critique of political economy, he was interested solely in the economic and social effects of factory technology, and these he could describe with examples of the transition from domestic to factory operation, thus laying the ground for his thesis of an intact production relationship before and disturbed antagonism after that watershed. However, the machinery used in Marx's time was completely different from the simple steam engine made by John Smeaton in 1770, which Marx, with a view to explaining its functioning, still sketched as 'Watt's steam engine' at the beginning of the 1850s.[21] Not until 1861 did he finally grasp the fact that the steam engine – already important early on and for Engels in 1845 still decisively so – had been the cornerstone of the Industrial Revolution. But Marx also had only a vague idea at first of the central significance of machine tools for self-reproducing industrial development – at the time advancing both quantitatively and qualitatively into new dimensions.[22] Among engineers, that realization was by 1840 no longer news, and in economics, too, machine tools had been identified as a significant factor. Indeed, in the 1820s, the rapid improvement of such tools, starting with the automatic lathe or slide rest, had already led to the construction of powerful machines of higher precision and quality with greatly increased efficiency.[23] Mass use of efficient motor and machine tools in combination with completely new sales and marketing strategies, such as those pursued by American manufacturers since the 1850s, led to a further intensification and spread of industrial production. This owed much to the reorientation of producers towards the actual needs and purses of their consumers, with new modes of distribution, supplies of spare parts and credit purchase. In the medium to long term, despite occasional cyclical fluctuations – still the norm rather than the exception in such rapid developments – far from bringing about the predicted internal collapse of the capitalist economy, production stabilized, due to gigantic market expansion, with an almost insatiable demand for products for use in agriculture, the household, transport and communications.

If a camera had been pointed at Marx in London around 1860, much as Nadar photographed Paris from a balloon, a bizarre picture would have emerged: Marx, living in the largest city in the world at that time with hundreds of state-of-the-art industrial plants and famous engineers, spent weeks and months at his reading desk in the British Museum hunched over outdated technical literature, when he could have easily exchanged views on questions of modern machine technology with, for example,

Figure 4.2 Andrew Ure (1778–1857). The Glasgow physician and chemist became a professor of natural history and chemistry at the Andersonian Institution in 1805 and was involved in physical experiments as well as the application of chemical processes in industry. In 1814 he invented the alkalimeter, and he was admitted as a Fellow of the Royal Society in 1822. From 1830 onwards he lived in London and published, among other things, a study *On the Cotton Manufacture of Great Britain* (1836) and the reference work *Dictionary of Arts, Manufactures and Mines* (1839), from whose German translation Karl Marx drew much of his technological knowledge. © AKG.

Charles Babbage, who lived not far away and was an idiosyncratic but thoroughly sociable personality. All the then important machine tools had been presented at the 1851 and 1862 World's Fairs in London. The basic motor and processing technologies had matured and British mechanical engineering was at its peak.[24] American and German producers were catching up and already entering into direct competition – keenly followed by the public – in specialized products such as weapons technology. But Marx had nothing but scorn for such events,[25] although a tour of the world's most advanced technological products might have considerably updated his own studies.[26] A few years later at Millwall Docks, the engineer Isambard Kingdom Brunel (1806–1859), famous for railways and bridges as well as for the first tunnel under the Thames, had begun construction of *The Great Eastern*, the largest and most innovative ship the world had ever seen, built with the most modern techniques. In 1858, a Sunday stroll to the docks would have brought Marx more practical knowledge than any notebook filled with quotations from the history of past technological epochs over which several tides of innovation had meantime passed.

But Marx was a theorist, a bookworm who drew his knowledge selectively from the works of others[27] and only years later, after futile effort, came to the conclusion that he lacked the necessary certainty. He evidently had considerable problems distinguishing tools from machines, which was an important analytical question for the spread of the capitalist production mode he sought to fathom.[28] In January 1863, he wrote to Engels:

> I am inserting certain things into the section on machinery. There are some curious questions which I originally failed to deal with. To elucidate these, I have re-read all my note-books (excerpts) on technology and am also attending a practical (purely experimental) course for working men given by Prof. Willis (in Jermyn Street, the Institute of Geology, where Huxley also lectured). For me, mechanics presents much the same problem as languages. I understand the mathematical laws, but the simplest technical reality that calls for ocular knowledge is more difficult for me than the most complicated combinations.[29]

The result of Marx's attempts to understand the technology used since the 1850s in industrial production processes can be found in *Das Kapital* (Vol. I, Cap. 5).[30] As a Hegelian, he understood labour as a human activity of reciprocal self-production, a source of movement in and influence upon nature, changing both object and agent.[31] He described the means of labour – that is tools and machines – as 'a thing, or a complex of things, which the labourer interposes between himself and the subject of his labour, and which serves as the conductor of his activity'.[32] He referred to Benjamin Franklin's formula of man as a 'tool making animal'. But the ideal – the freely determined use of tools – applied, for him, only until the beginning of the division of labour, at best to a limited extent into the manufactory epoch. Since the emergence of the capitalist mode of production, a stark contradiction had come about between the liberating function of labour – which Hegel had still postulated in an ideal sense by taking the means as having a higher purpose than the end[33] – and actual social conditions. Production itself was now the engine driving the perfecting of work through technology.

Technology increases the productivity of labour – that is the ratio of input to output – but simultaneously replaces human labour with machines; it throws the freed workers back into 'barbaric forms of labour and turns the other part into a machine'.[34] Marx envisioned this process as a classical tragedy in the struggle of flesh and blood with iron:

> Here too past labour – in the automaton and the machinery moved by it – steps forth as acting apparently in independence of [living] labour, it subordinates labour instead of being subordinate to it, it is the iron man confronting the man of flesh and blood. The subsumption of his labour under capital – the absorption of his labour by capital – which lies in the nature of capitalist production, appears here as a technological fact.[35]

From this it followed: 'With machinery – and the mechanical workshop based on it – the domination of past labour over living labour assumes not only a social validity – expressed in the relation of capitalist and worker – but so to speak a technological validity.'[36] Marx thus charged the inner logic of machine technology with co-responsibility for the alienation of labour. He developed the concept of the ambivalence of factory work on the basis of Andrew Ure's *Philosophy of Manufactures*. Ure foresaw in the factory a new form of cooperation in which workers supervised machines and thus remained agents in the process. In fact, however, the modern factory, according to Marx, resembles a 'vast automaton ... a system of connected productive mechanisms, receiving their motive power from a self-acting central motor'.[37] Here, the machine itself becomes the agent and the worker the object of its agency. The human is forced to submit to the inner logic of the machine and can perceive the work itself only as 'an alien [*fremd*], overbearing object'[38] – at which point Marx jumped abruptly from tool to process and product: the activity itself can no longer be seen as *my* work or *my* reality, nor can any joy or pleasure be taken in it or what it makes; instead, in bourgeois society, the owners of the means of production are the beneficiaries, appropriating the goods produced as their own. Marx's use of the adjective *fremd*, meaning both *foreign in nature* and *belonging to someone else*, deftly achieves in a single word the discursive switch from technology to economics – a sleight of semantics that is logical only under his own premises, but with which he bypasses the crucial point of working with machines.

Marx's further deliberations in this area no longer have technology as their main subject but revolve around such matters as how to represent technology in economic terms or around incidental details such as the internal accounting of assets and the annual depreciation of machines.[39] Engels repeatedly served Marx as a competent adviser in questions of business administration, and his knowledge and know-how in the field of textile processing and its machinery and equipment was extensive. His father and brothers were happy enough to draw on his expertise in connection with the transfer of technology from Manchester to Engelskirchen,[40] yet Marx considered such knowledge superfluous. He was convinced of his own project with technology.

At the beginning of the long Chapter 15 of *Das Kapital* on 'Machinery and Modern Industry', Marx distinguishes between three types or 'parts' of all 'fully developed machinery':[41] 'the motor mechanism, the transmitting mechanism, and finally the tool or working machine'.[42] Even this simple distinction, made not neatly according to technical functionality but probably according to a classification commonly used in steam boiler test statistics,[43] reveals serious terminological problems.[44] Marx made it difficult for himself to recognize a qualitative difference between a work-machine (*Arbeitsmaschine*) and a machine tool (*Werkzeugmaschine*). Only after circumstantial descriptions of examples – clearly drawn from a reading of encyclopaedias, catalogues and newspaper articles – did he begin to grasp the significance, already important from the beginning of the nineteenth century, of self-operating or automated machine tools in processes of industrialization.[45] For lack of an appropriate terminology, he remained unable to understand the full significance of these constructs, whose design represented an ongoing process of improvement in terms of function, performance and energy efficiency. In particular, Marx failed to grasp the processes of analytical breakdown and creative restructuring that went into an integrated system meeting contemporary developmental parameters. He could capture only the end result of such a system under the generalized abstraction of the constitutive 'nature' of its components: 'The co-operative character of the labour process is', he affirmed, 'a technical necessity dictated by [the *nature* of] the instrument of labour itself'[46] – that instrument being a machine.

Marx also sidestepped the need to provide any technological explanation of automation by simply referring the automatic device ('automaton') back to its archetype, the human being, defining the degree of automation negatively by the amount of human input not needed to operate it.[47] At crucial points in his argumentation, wherever he lacked adequate terminology (and thus a plausible explanation), he abruptly plunged into the world of metaphor, in which he felt at home both as a Hegelian and as an adept of ancient myth. 'Along with the tool, the skill and power (*Virtuosität*) of the workman in handling it passes over to the machine'.[48] Marx breathed into the machine a kind of autonomous techno-soul, a notion quite common in the eighteenth and nineteenth centuries and one he could readily invoke. The machine both confused and fascinated many contemporaries, as it seemed to move by itself and thus gave the impression of life. But similarity did not mean identity, and philosophical mechanism was by no means yet machine theory. Marx used the widespread ignorance (or was it his own uncertainty?) about the actual functioning of machines. He oscillated between the worlds of the dead and the living and added a further conundrum by extracting the 'soul' of an 'animate' machine and degrading it to a 'dead mechanism' while, conversely, the workman caught up in this complex became 'part of the detail-machine' within a 'lifeless mechanism'. 'Human material' was 'incorporated'[49] into the structured machine system of the factory, where work became 'endless drudgery … like the work of Sisyphus'.[50]

Marx struggled almost painfully to grasp the logical relationship of machine, with or without a life of its own, to human labour, dead or alive.[51] Larger units of single machines 'to which motion is communicated by the transmitting mechanism from a central automaton' – and these could be found in thousands of cotton mills in England alone – seemed to overwhelm his technological understanding. He took refuge in a metaphor still invoked by the literature critical of technology today: 'Here we have, in the place of the isolated machine, a mechanical monster whose body fills whole factories, and whose demon power, at first veiled under the slow and measured motions of his giant limbs, at length breaks out into the fast and furious whirl of his countless working organs.'[52] Marx recoded the apocalyptic horsemen of the Middle Ages into 'cyclopean machines'[53] and 'mechanical monsters' whose quasi-organic 'liveliness' had 'feverish' and 'mad' (i.e. pathological) features. For Marx the machinery in capitalist commodity production was sick and dominated human beings like a demon. Raised to frenzy in the 'automatic workshop', the villain ultimately devoured the human entirely, replacing factory workers and depriving them of their livelihood.

With this mindset, which – in combination with a sweeping postulate of alienation – relegated central questions of the philosophy of technology to the realm of fictional dystopias, Marx effectively denied himself any way of adequately analysing the rapidly changing structures of industry in the 1860s and 1870s.[54] By contrast, Engels, freed from his professional duties, developed in the course of the 1870s an intense interest in scientific and technological questions and broached new perspectives. A comparison with Ernst Kapp's philosophy of technology will not only illustrate Engels' thinking in contemporary terms, on the basis of similar philosophical assumptions, but also show him in the 1880s to have been an astute commentator on technological change who had recognized the signs of the times and was capable of adapting to them.

Technology in Friedrich Engels' later writings compared to Ernst Kapp's philosophy of technology

Since the beginning of the nineteenth century, much had been written in Britain on machinery, manufactures and engineering,[55] but the first German publication devoted solely to the *Philosophy of Technology* appeared only in 1877. Its author was the geographer and historian Ernst Kapp, who, after studying in Bonn, taught in a high school in Minden (Westphalia) from 1830 to 1849. His *Vergleichende allgemeine Erdkunde* (Comparative General Geography, 1845) laid the foundations for a discipline of anthropo- and biogeography. However, as a left-wing Hegelian with democratic convictions, he affiliated himself during the 1848 Revolution with a constitutional political association and fell out of favour with his Prussian employer. Thereupon he emigrated to Texas, where he ran a cotton farm in Kendall County. As a freethinker and opponent of slavery, conflicts again arose between Kapp and the Texan Confederates during the Civil War, so he returned to Germany with his family in 1865 and settled in Düsseldorf as a private scholar.

Kapp was concerned to 'explain the origin and perfecting of artefacts originating from human hands as the prime condition of development towards reflective consciousness'.[56] The emancipatory achievement of the human race was based on a striving for freedom, demonstrated in overcoming the barriers set by nature, as well as in improvement to the

Figure 4.3 Ernst Kapp (1808–1896). Kapp is one of the founders of the modern philosophy of technology. © Alamy Stock Photos.

circumstances of life with the help of tools and technical inventions.[57] The reason for this can be discerned in the tools themselves:

> Because tools and machines neither grow on trees nor fall ready-made from heaven as gifts from the gods, but *because we have made them ourselves*, they bear as products of this self the clear imprint of our sometimes unconsciously discovering, sometimes consciously inventive mind. Hence, traced back to the site of their creation, they may yield both explanation and rationale of the particular organic activity to which they owe their origin, like a copy reproducing a mould, and must thus be seen as one of the most important impulses both towards a theory of knowledge in general and for the development of our self-awareness in particular.[58]

In contrast to Marx's interpretation of Hegel, which emphasized the antagonism of ideal and reality,[59] Ernst Kapp understood the human interface with nature in a broader anthropological sense as progress and as a locus of reconciliation with the harsh reality of natural forces. He saw tools and machines in an Aristotelian light as human artefacts (*technai*) in confrontation with nature (*physis*). The standard governing this could only be human because there was no other on which we might orient ourselves. Progress, for Kapp – especially technological progress – had to meet human needs and should not be transposed to some theoretically ideal but unattainable Utopia. Work and society were two poles of a dialectical process in which tools and technology played a mediating role, as they did, too, in the reciprocal process of our journey to self-knowledge.[60]

Kapp's anthropological perspective led him – in line with Aristotle – to see the origin and measure of all tools in the human body, especially the hand. As a highly developed tool, the hand is also a complex organ of perception and serves both as the model for artificial tools and as the instrument of their production. In this process, the human being, consciously as well as unconsciously, applies so-called organ projection. Starting from a cultural-historical perspective, from the first tools up to more complex devices, instruments and machines, Kapp provided numerous examples. His comparative analysis of the American axe has become famous: its construction, functionally reflecting the physiology of the human arm and continuing projectively in the tool itself, shows a two- to threefold increase in efficiency compared to the German axe.[61] Organ projection also becomes clear in the weights and measures systems based on the hand and foot, which even in the decimal system remain recognizable, like a palimpsest on a codex.

Kapp's anthropogenesis included the adoption of construction principles from nature, such as the similarity of the tension and compression lines of the cancellous bone of the upper part of the human femur to constructional solutions in bridge building, or the parallelism of the morphology of nerves and telegraph wires. Kapp was convinced that progress in the recognition of the inner relationship between organic model and mechanical copy increased our self-awareness.[62] At higher stages of development, the outward similarity between human model and tool or machine decreases or is no longer present at all. Nevertheless, projection, in the form of measurement ratios taken from the human body – *Inzahl* (in-count) as the natural counting measure internal to the human and *Anzahl* (tally) as the external counting measure – remains, even attaining a higher quality, for these ratios 'present themselves as all the purer and more transparent to the mind, the less our attention is distracted by too great a fidelity of plastic form'.[63] The gradual accumulation of experiential knowledge led earlier generations to the production of tools for making other tools and from there to the systematic construction of machines.[64] However, Kapp criticized a rampant mixing of terms that 'has, as it were, transferred the idea of the organic involuntarily and unnoticed from the model to its mechanical reproduction'[65]:

> A striking confusion of the terms 'mechanical' and 'organic' has arisen, and the production of the machinery necessary for large-scale industry and global communication uses such a volume of scientific technology that – as is evident on closer and more informed examination – the mechanical transmission of force eludes our perception, and steam engines and telegraph apparatus take on the appearance of self-determined motion.[66]

Kapp explained the fundamental difference between appearance and actual effectiveness in tool development using the example of Götz von Berlichingen's iron hand. As a prosthetic device, this was only a 'mechanical shell' made for an individual purpose, with no lasting effect on technological progress. In contrast, a hammer is an item in a long reproductive line of tools. A hammer 'helps forge new hammers, builds entire hammer mills, and makes world history. ... How imposing is the organic analogy of a tool making tools in comparison with the barren machinations of artificial limbs and [even] entire automata afflicted with the uncanniness of wax cabinet figures'!'[67] With reference to the interaction of natural forces described by Hermann Helmholtz (1821–1894), it was clear that the effect of intelligence in the work of the machine can be traced back to its builder. 'The wheel train of the clock therefore does not add any energy not already communicated to it, but only distributes that communicated to it evenly over a longer period of time.'[68] And referring to the philosopher Otto Liebmann (1840–1912), Kapp clarified: 'The *hegemonicon* of the locomotive does not belong to it, does not reside in it; stoker and train driver sit aboard it and steer it, just as the rider steers his steed.'[69] The steam engine was for him 'the machine of machines' because of its versatility[70]: 'Many machine parts, originally isolated implements, are outwardly united in the steam engine into an overall mechanical effect'; its complexity was based on a long chain of incremental mechanical advances.[71]

At this point, let us take a look at Friedrich Engels, who – living in London since 1870 – was, without knowledge of Ernst Kapp's publications, likewise concerned with the emergence of tools in early anthropological history and, like Kapp, took the human hand as his starting point.[72] With an anthropologist's eye, Engels traced the roots of humanity on the way to socialization[73] and posited these in an improved food supply:

Food became increasingly varied, and with it the substances entering the body, substances that were the chemical premises for the transition to man. But all that was not yet labour in the proper sense of the word. Labour begins with the making of tools. And what are the most ancient tools that we find? ... hunting and fishing implements, the former at the same time serving as weapons.[74]

There is a feedback loop of specialization in play here:[75]

> Thus the hand is not only the organ of labour, *it is also the product of labour*. Only by labour, by adaptation to ever new operations, through the inheritance of muscles, ligaments, and, over longer periods of time, bones that [have] undergone special development and the ever-renewed employment of this inherited finesse in new, more and more complicated operations, [has] the human hand [gained] the high degree of perfection required to conjure into being the pictures of a Raphael, the statues of a Thorwaldsen, the music of a Paganini.[76]

Engels identified an interrelationship of brain and hand as the product of the experience of practical utility over long periods of time.[77] However, this process would always also be 'subject to the interplay of unintended effects from uncontrolled forces', so that it 'achieves its desired end only by way of exception, but much more frequently the exact opposite'. What Charles Darwin had described as the 'struggle for existence' in the animal kingdom is to be found again in the current free competition economy, but this cannot be the final human condition. 'Only conscious organisation of social production, in which production and distribution are carried on in a planned way, can lift mankind above the rest of the animal world as regards the social aspect, in the same way that production in general has done this for mankind in the specifically biological aspect.'[78] In other words, as late as the 1870s, Engels saw the solution to this technologically induced dilemma primarily in the reorganization of property structures in the economy – that is in a system of controlling economic variables and sociopolitical influences that was alien to technology.

Kapp, on the other hand, sought to embed the universal employment of complex machines and apparatus, now possible due to their already advanced level of development, in an overall technological-social system. With its ability to transfer symbol and thought at the speed of sound, the electromagnetic telegraph, a prime example of organ projection in physical analogy to the human nervous system, had opened the door to a universal telegraphy. In describing developments in the machine sciences, Ernst Kapp basically oriented himself on Franz Reuleaux, the founder of theoretical kinematics and an internationally recognized engineer from the Rhineland.[79] With his theory, Reuleaux had created an original and independent basis for mechanical engineering, without looking to source it either in mathematics or in mechanics, as did, for example, his colleagues at the *École Polytechnique* in Paris.[80] To determine the level of perfection of machines, Reuleaux first analysed the relationships of motion and force at the nodal points of *kinesis* (active movement) and *kinema* (passive movement). On the

Figure 4.4 Franz Reuleaux (1829–1905), 1879. © BPK.

one hand, the transmission of force could be achieved via a frictional connection with an unenclosed housing, such as an open bearing, while, on the other hand, increased reliability and performance could be achieved with a paired connection – exemplified in a nut enclosing a screw – creating a 'kinematic chain'. Progress consisted 'in the decreasing use of the frictional connection and its increasing replacement by the paired connection, with the completion of the kinematic chain thereby formed'.[81]

Based on Charles Babbage's attempt to develop a specific code to simplify design development, Reuleaux analysed the structural elements of machines and initially classified them into rigid elements, flexible elements and gears distinguished by their frictional connections. While the three assemblies, *receptor* (power drive), *transmission* and *tool*, which until then had been distinguished according to common, but purely external considerations – Marx had also followed this practice – might indeed occur, these should be seen as 'accidental assemblages' that could not logically be called essential parts. Thus, for example, a steam engine cannot be classified as a tool, and in general machines that are not set up as tools are mostly used to change location. In contrast, machines serving as tools, such as lathes, milling machines and band saws, change the shape of materials. Accordingly, for Reuleaux, powered engines and work tools constitute the two main groups of machines, which, though they do not differ fundamentally, can be distinguished by degree. In this way, he also succeeded in providing a precise definition of a machine – one that placed man at the centre in two distinct ways, as a designer, 'setting the machine up' according to a conscious plan, and in his role as *rector agitandi*, 'compelling' and using natural forces (e.g. thermal or hydromechanical force) by means of the machine. Kapp's definition runs: 'A machine is a combination of resistant bodies set up in such a way that, by means of it, mechanical natural forces can be compelled to perform certain movements.'[82]

Franz Reuleaux and, with him, Ernst Kapp saw the reason for the concentration of 'massed work in colossal factory buildings', with its ambivalent consequences, not in the machine as such, but in the increased performance of steam engines, along with corresponding adaptations of the work machines driven by them. They contrasted the cheapening of consumer goods with the devaluation of family life, the rise in the cost of living necessities and the 'conspicuous decline in manual dexterity' of workers. Referring to Reuleaux, Kapp saw here the solution to 'the workers' question':

> *Thus this one prime mover, the steam engine, becomes the mother of a legion of work machines and mistress of the situation.* … Reuleaux calls small engines the true power machines of the people and asserts that air and gas engines, since they now already work considerably more cheaply, can successfully compete with the steam engine. He counts them among the most important of all new machines and finds in them *the seeds of a transformation of a whole industrial sector.*[83]

And Kapp continues:

> It follows from this that the remedy lies precisely at the point from which the conflict between capital and labour started. If the large machine is under the

warranty of capital, small work machines, on the other hand, are procurable at relatively low cost. The prospect opens that small craftsmen will revive rewardingly and that cottage industry will find new nourishment.[84]

Such was Ernst Kapp's prognosis, based on an understanding of the overall techno-social system.

By 1900 the central steam engine had in fact become obsolete in the vast majority of production facilities: at a stroke, some forty thousand steam engines in Germany alone became unprofitable. Their iron was smelted down into new, higher quality products. They were replaced in power plants by high-performance turbines, and in production workshops the electric motor established itself: it was not only cheap to procure but could be used decentrally and controlled without complex transmission. As a result, small and medium-sized companies were once again able to hold their own in competition and to mobilize and develop the technological potential present in their specializations. The typical structure of small and medium-sized enterprises still found in German industry, especially in Saxony, Baden and the Rhineland, took shape and was consolidated.

While, according to Marx, money and capital were responsible for converting the dimension of space into that of time, for Kapp it was the tool and the technological artefact – the ocean liner or automobile – that were responsible. According to Kapp, the dimension of time fed back to the human dimension via advances in communication – in contemporary terms by means of the telegraph – in such a way that, building on these technological advances, continuous progress was being made to higher levels in a basically endless process. Although these steps were also connected with changes in the variety of professions and occupations and required some adaptation, the issues raised were basically solvable, so long as the state, as in a natural organism, kept the interests of the whole at heart and given an overall orientation towards growth based on human measure and reason.[85] Calling on the Aristotelian concept of energy as unifying the bodily sensual and intellectual-mental basis of the state, Kapp drew a sharp dividing line between an executive bureaucracy acting like a machine and the central state as an overall organism mediating and balancing the interests of free, responsible individuals with those of the whole, providing the conditions necessary for the exercise of freedom. In this way Kapp formulated the outline of an organic constitutional state founded on technological progress and individual freedom in accordance with the 'principle of humanity', to which the human–machine interface must also be subordinated.[86] Of itself, Kapp argued, technology engenders not discord but self-knowledge.

Friedrich Engels, for his part, was interested in the social consequences of technological innovation on the level of both scientific research and practical implementation. This interest was already inherent in his contributions to military theory, in which he repeatedly pursued the question of the influence of industrial innovations – for example the construction of armoured turret ships or the rifled barrel of guns – and their effects on equipment, strategic and tactical command, and logistics. After retiring from company operations, he was able to devote more time to scientific questions and was especially impressed by the rapid development of electrical engineering.[87] With it the way seemed free, all at once, to penetrate a world of almost unlimited possibilities. Between 1880 and 1910, electricity was all the rage in journalism and at major exhibitions and congresses. It was now storable, transportable and seemingly clean, of limitless power and yet so finely measurable that every small household could benefit from it. The prerequisite, however, was complex distribution systems that could only be built if science, technology, industry, capital and politics all worked together.

The innovations in the field of weak-current technology accompanying the Morse telegraph from 1835 onwards had initially been quite modest in Germany and were limited to military and railroad traffic. In contrast, the use of weak current for message transmission was far more important in Britain and the United States, where cable and telegraph companies were booming. Dividends of up to 25 per cent were paid on capital employed, which – encouraged by the British Companies Act – triggered a run on shares. The most daring of plans, as long as they were electric, were accepted without criticism and funded with capital. In France, there was talk of *l'électromanie en Angleterre*, though this soon turned into a hangover after bankruptcies and the Electric Lighting Act of 1882.

Electrification with high-voltage technology, which began in the 1880s, was a process accompanied by lively propaganda campaigns, as public opinion was instrumentalized in the competition between direct-current (DC) and alternating-current (AC) systems.[88] Soon after the invention of the dynamo by Werner von Siemens (1816–1892) in 1866, it became possible to build an industrially usable machine that supplied continuous DC. Bright arc lamps could now be used as practical substitutes for moonlight, and around 1880 several demonstrations of spectacular illuminations took place in public squares in London, Paris and Detroit. In 1882, with investors in mind, Thomas Edison (1847–1931) built the first DC power station in Manhattan, then already the financial district of New York. When the French physicist Marcel Deprez (1848–1908) successfully commissioned the first experimental power line for DC electricity transmission between Munich and Miesbach at the International Electrotechnical Exhibition in Munich in 1882,[89] Friedrich Engels, who took a lively interest in the experiments, commented on the effects of this practical test:

> In fact, however, it's a tremendously revolutionary affair. The steam engine taught us to transform heat into mechanical motion, but the exploitation of electricity has opened up the way to transforming all forms of energy – heat, mechanical motion, electricity, magnetism, light – one into the other and back again, and to their industrial exploitation. The circle is complete. And Deprez's latest discovery, namely that electric currents of very high voltage can, with a comparatively small loss of energy, be conveyed by simple telegraph wire over hitherto undreamed of distances and be harnessed at the place of destination – the thing is still in embryo – this discovery frees industry for good from virtually all local limitations, makes possible the harnessing of even the most remote hydraulic power and, though it may benefit the towns at the outset, will in the end inevitably prove the most powerful of levers in eliminating the antithesis between town and country.

> Again, it is obvious that the productive forces will thereby acquire a range such that they will, with increasing rapidity, outstrip the control of the bourgeoisie.[90]

Engels was to be fundamentally correct in his prediction of the industrial use of remote water forces. In practice, however, the AC system of Nikola Tesla (1856–1943), who had initially worked for Edison, prevailed over the DC system in certain areas of application. Two decades later, a hydroelectric power plant was built at Niagara Falls in New York State. It provided large amounts of power over long distances for the states of New York, Connecticut and Massachusetts, where industrial sites diversified. Broad industrial development, with a variety of medium-sized ventures with innovative potential, permeated the East Coast states.

Engels' prediction that with the availability of the all-important means of power independent of place and time, productive forces would 'outstrip the control of the bourgeoisie' seems comparatively low key. If in 1848 the potential of capitalist production had been underestimated, in the meantime 'large-scale industry ... has really taken root, and has made Germany into an industrial country of the first rank'.[91] Ever new inventions had triggered technological upheavals and innovations, as had the steam engine a hundred years before. Social and political conflicts would, Engels argued, now take on new forms, for example the parliamentary route made possible by the increase in votes for the SPD in the *Reichstag*.[92] There is no longer any mention of revolution.

Following this line of argumentation, we can see a certain convergence of causal reasoning between Engels' prediction and Kapp's forecast. In a developed, all-embracing technological system, innovations might well lead to the defusing, by quasi-technological and parliamentary means, of the sharp social antagonisms characteristic of the first phase of the industrial revolution, without any radical political revolution. Advanced technology, which (*pace* Marx) by no means always leads to the destruction of jobs, can certainly establish new structures of industrial production. In other words, the dilemma of the unintended negative consequences harboured by positive technological developments was softened by Engels in the early 1890s and seen as an opportunity for a not yet precisely determinable shift in industrial production. Thus, indirectly, an essential element of Marx's postulated law of the tendency of the profit rate to fall – based on the assumption that in capitalism rationalization is always connected with the displacement of labour by mechanization and automation – was also shaken. In the last years of his life, the death of capitalism as a consequence of technological advance[93] appeared increasingly unlikely to the 'inventor of Marxism' – a role Engels is still assigned today.

CHAPTER 5
'THE GENERAL' AS ADMIRAL: FRIEDRICH ENGELS AND THE NAVAL WARFARE DEBATE
Kurt Möser

Friedrich Engels had served from October 1841 as a one-year volunteer with the rank of bombardier in the 12th company of the Guards Artillery Brigade in Berlin and had undergone his baptism of fire in 1849 as an adjutant in the volunteer corps of the rebel Colonel August Willich (1810–1878) during the Palatinate campaign for the German Imperial Constitution. According to Wilhelm Liebknecht (1826–1900), who had close contact with Engels in England in the 1850s, he was 'as if made for the military, with a clear eye, rapid overview and evaluation of even the smallest detail, quick power of decision, and imperturbable sangfroid'. Equipped with a specialist library, Engels pursued his military studies throughout that decade with great energy and, self-taught, became quite an expert, 'so that at least one civilian', as he put it, 'can hold his own with them on theory. At all events I want to get to the point where these asses can't talk me down'.[1] He published fundamental articles on specialist military topics in the *New American Cyclopædia*[2] and wrote analyses of military events for the international press as well as contributed anonymously to military journals. These won him recognition in the specialist world,[3] and after his forecast in the London evening paper *Pall Mall Gazette* of the French defeat at Sedan (1–2 September 1870) in the Franco-Prussian War, the Marx family affectionately referred to him as 'the General', the word – according to August Bebel, who got to know Marx and Engels personally in 1880 – being pronounced, even when they were speaking German, in the English way, with a soft 'g'.[4] That Engels also published in various formats on naval issues justifies our titling him here 'the Admiral', especially as there were – as we shall see – considerable technological overlaps at the time between marine and land-based weapons.

Engels' military analyses came at a time of extraordinary upheaval in almost all departments of warfare and most particularly in naval matters. The period between the decade preceding the Crimean War (1853–6) and the 1880s was conceptually and technologically open-ended in all that concerned ship construction, propulsion and weaponry, on the one hand, and naval engagement strategy and tactics, on the other. Typically for such phases, elements of tried-and-tested old ways coexisted with untried – and/or not yet conceptually integrated – innovations, problematic adaptations and new learning processes. Accordingly, it was a time of intense debate – far more so than the later phase of consolidation and closure. And these debates were conducted not only by those professionally involved in the development and implementation of naval technology and tactics but also by politicians, journalists, writers and experts from other

Figure 5.1 Sailors of HMS *Eclipse*, a wooden sailing vessel commissioned in 1860 for the Royal Navy, which was equipped with a 200 hp steam engine and four Armstrong guns for land bombardment but was decommissioned as early as 1867 after missions in Australia and New Zealand. © Bridgeman Images.

areas. It is difficult, in retrospect, to distinguish between 1850 and 1890 firm schools of thought in these technological-tactical debates or of practice in the vessels to which they gave rise. Only the beginning and end points of the transformation are clear: on the one hand, the wooden fighting ship under sail firing solid-shot broadsides from smooth-bore, muzzle-loaded cannon – if at all, then these vessels were equipped only with an auxiliary steam engine for manoeuvring in harbour and battle; on the other hand, the purely steam-powered iron-hulled ship, its gun turrets armed with rifled, breech-loaded cannon firing explosive armour-piercing shells – ships that represented the temporary culmination of the forty years' development in question.

Between these two points, from the perspective of technological history – and to the confusion of the historian – a number of highways and byways branch off, not seldom backwards. All the more remarkable, then, is Engels' anticipation of that dramatic change in naval strategy at an early juncture and in connection with a relatively minor engagement of the American Civil War (1861–5), which initially attracted little notice in Europe: 'About three-and-a-half months ago', he wrote, 'on March 8, 1862, the battle between the *Merrimac* and the frigates *Cumberland* and *Congress* in Hampton Roads closed the long era of the wooden fighting ship. On March 9, 1862 the encounter between the *Merrimac* and the *Monitor* in the same waters inaugurated the era of the ironclad vessel'.[5] What sources, what insights, we may well ask, led Engels to this far-reaching statement? Where did he stand in the contemporary debate on naval warfare? What conclusions and forecasts did he draw from his observations?

The phase of naval development Engels observed and commented from the early 1850s is marked above all by changes in the technological equipment of fighting ships in the areas of propulsion, armaments, defence and construction. But the changes did not stop there: tactics, deployment organization of bases, training, servicing and repair – these and many other aspects were caught up in the same whirlwind. Ships, after all, do not exist on their own: they are embedded in an overall military system, and in this context, the concept of technological revolution is, as the American military historian Max Boot has argued, 'only a shorthand way of referring to more sweeping changes that occurred at the organizational and doctrinal level'.[6] These changes, he suggests, are summed up in the broader NATO term 'Revolution in Military Affairs' (RMA). Among the aspects concerned, then as now, are, first of all, the technological developments that lead to a functioning artefact; secondly, their concrete military application and utility; thirdly, their integration in organizational structures; fourthly, the development of a doctrine of military use; fifthly, their deployment in specific minor (in traditional terms non-decisive) engagements; only then, sixthly, can a new weapons system be judged effective on the wider military scale. To this list of categories, one more factor might be added: identification of the future potentialities of a new military technology.

Ironclads – a twofold pedigree

The development of armour-plated ships was the direct result of difficulties repeatedly experienced in sea-land engagements. During the Crimean War the French hurriedly built three ironclad *batteries flottantes* armed with eleven heavy guns with which they besieged the Russian fortress of Kinburn in October 1855. Hardly seaworthy in any real sense, these single-use combat machines were the pioneers and predecessors of the American Confederate and Unionist vessels mentioned above and, further down the line, the germ cell of the armoured ships that determined naval warfare until the onset of the Second World War.

The second major influence evolved from the replacement of solid iron ammunition with explosive shells. Built of two-foot-thick 'heart of oak' – the tough core of the oak tree – the sidewalls of ships of the line were nearly proof against conventional twenty-four- and thirty-six-pound cannonballs but not against the innovative explosive charges of the artillery shell[7] invented by Henri-Joseph Paixhans (1783–1854). The lethal effectiveness of this weapon was demonstrated in a rather untypical confrontation on 30 November 1853, on the eve of the Crimean War, when a Russian fleet armed with Paixhans' cannon inflicted the 'Bloodbath of Sinop' on Ottoman vessels sheltering in the harbour of that Black Sea port.[8] It became a proven fact that, without armour, wooden ships were no longer viable against the new naval artillery, and in 1859–60 the French

Figure 5.2 HMS *Warrior* – the first ironclad. © Eberhard Illner.

and the British, with two ocean-going, steam-powered, armoured ships, the frigate *La Gloire* and HMS *Warrior*, launched a new age in naval architecture and by the same token an arms race.[9]

Armour, artillery and placement

The armour-plating of ships – whether French wooden-hulled or British iron-hulled – initiated inevitable competition between attack and defence, weaponry and armour, one aspect of which was decidedly reactionary. This concerned the explosive shell, an extremely effective weapon on land, but far less so against armoured ships, as it burst on impact with the armour before it could wreak its damage in the ship's interior. In this respect, solid cannonballs were better: they were heavy enough to break or penetrate any contemporary armour. On the other hand, their weight and that of the cannon required to fire them was a problem. Only a few such weapons could be carried if the ship's displacement was not to exceed ocean-going and manoeuvring limits. This was seen as one element of compromise. Partial armouring was another.

Thus developed the modern ship of the line, whose main armament was restricted to a few heavy cannon, no longer distributed broadside along the decks but concentrated in a citadel or casemate and so placed that the ship could fire ahead, astern and to each side.

Only the casemate and other vital parts of the ship were armoured; bows and stern had only rudimentary protection because, given contemporary changes in combat tactics, they were hardly threatened. Alongside the casemate, revolving turrets armed with one or two heavy guns were introduced; these widened the arc of fire but also created new problems for high-seas vessels.

The list of available armaments was even more complicated. Muzzle loaders and breech loaders, smooth-bored and rifled barrels, all had their protagonists. The variety of shell types and breech constructions, on the one hand, and a rapidly evolving technology of rifling and projectile shapes, on the other, led to confusing competition with no clear winner. In this situation, promising future developments were at times rescinded and innovations thereby blocked. Thus, in the Royal Navy, breech loaders – *ex post* definitively modern – temporarily yielded ground to the older muzzle loaders. Opposing lines of argument and parameters often failed to meet, and views on vessels built in accordance with different concepts diverged radically. Not even the British Admiralty was of one mind: almost every ship built between 1860 and 1880 was a one-off item, and many were already obsolete on commissioning.

Naval engagements in a time of transition

The complexities of contemporary naval construction and armament clearly required a fundamental revision of operational and tactical concepts. Was the main function of the navy to engage in battle on the high seas or to defend the national coast? And if the latter, how close to one's defences did one allow enemy ships to come? What, indeed, was the optimum combat distance for maritime warfare? The fleets of the great naval powers around 1850 were still – with the Napoleonic Wars as predominant model – geared to militarily and politically decisive confrontation on the high seas: 'Wooden man o'war against wooden man o'war' was the supreme art of the admiral. But doubts were growing, new concepts arising and practical experience leading to new perspectives.

The main naval engagements of the nineteenth century had, in fact, gradually become directed against land fortifications, a purpose for which traditional ship types had proven not particularly suitable. Most engagements of this kind had ended badly for high-seas vessels, the disastrous confrontation between the Danish fleet and a single Prussian sixteen-gun shore battery at Eckernförde in April 1849 being a case in point: a wooden sailing ship was captured and the battleship *Christian VIII* exploded. Later, the ironclad *Rolf Krake*, a new-style gun-turret ship built in Glasgow in 1862 for the Danish navy, had small success against the combined Austrian–Prussian land forces in the decisive Siege of Dybbøl in the Second Schleswig War (18 April 1864). Finally, both French and British ships of the line suffered heavy losses and inflicted little damage in the sieges of Sevastopol, Odessa and Kronstadt (off St Petersburg) during the Crimean War.[10] A series of engagements between ships and land batteries during the American Civil War had also seen the ironclads on the losing side, even disastrously so, as in the case of the USS *Mound City* against a Confederate shore battery in the Battle of St Charles (27

June 1862). Armour-plated ships provided no guarantee of success against land-based artillery firing from a secure position.

Lessons of experience – the artillery debate

'The revolution in artillery currently brought about by the rifled gun barrel seems considerably more significant for naval warfare than anything that can be achieved by armour-plated vessels.'[11] Already in 1860, Engels saw the offensive argument as conclusive purely in terms of cost-effectiveness: 'we can say with assurance that to develop rifled artillery heavy enough to penetrate iron and steel plates and to set it up on board ship is a great deal simpler than to build ships whose armour-plating is thick enough to withstand the shot or shell from such a gun'.[12] Opinions, however, differed on how artillery could get the better of armour. Armour-piercing shells with delayed-action fuses which detonate only a split second after penetrating a ship's defensive plating had not yet been developed. In view of the engagement between the armoured vessels of the Confederates (CSS *Atlanta*) and Unionists (USS *Weehawken* and *Nahant*) in Wassaw Sound, Georgia, on 17 June 1863, in which five 350-pound solid shots brought victory to the Unionists within a few minutes, Engels therefore, given the ineffectiveness of available explosive shells, came down on the side of the maximum calibre solid shot fired from fifteen-inch muzzle-loaded guns. However, because of their relatively low muzzle velocity (v_0), the function of such projectiles was not primarily to penetrate armour but to impact it with such force that both the plate and the wood holding it in place would be shattered – which was, conversely, the reason for the wooden backing layers still being used to absorb that impact. The outcome of the duel between armoured vessels in Hampton Roads on 9 March 1862, in which CSS *Virginia* was hit by several large-calibre shots, demonstrated that, despite their low velocity, such projectiles could be devastatingly effective.[13]

The issue was complicated by the breech loader/muzzle loader problem – 'one of the most hotly debated questions in the whole of artillery, but above all in naval artillery'[14] – for muzzle-loaded guns could be either smooth-bored or rifled and could fire either solid shot or explosive shells, but breech loaders (always rifled) could as a rule fire only the latter. The history of technology is full of cases where the way from the old to the new is unclear, and this was one of them. In this instance, the Royal Navy, after introducing breech loaders, went back for a whole decade to muzzle loaders – an outcome based not only on the experience of the American Civil War but also on the as-yet-imperfect, and indeed unsafe, construction of gun breeches. Thus, in the bombardment of the Japanese port of Kagoshima on 15–17 August 1863, the Royal Navy recorded 'in the course of 365 salvos of its 21 Armstrong breech loaders 128 accidents, some fatal'.[15] No wonder it was decided to return to proven ways, especially given well-founded doubts about the effectiveness of the new guns: tests had shown that the old sixty-eight-pounder muzzle-loaded[16] smooth-bore gun was more effective against armour plating than Armstrong's 110-pounder rifle gun. To solve the immediate problem, the admiralty returned to the smooth-bored front loader in the form of the Somerset cannon.[17] Engels' position in the debate had two aspects: he saw the plate-bursting theory as paving the way to future armour-breaking ammunition but considered the modified older system currently more effective against armoured vessels.

Gun placement – the alternatives

The first engagement between armour-plated vessels took place during the American Civil War, on 8–9 March 1862, in Hampton Roads, Virginia. It aroused extraordinary interest in specialist circles and served as a catalyst in the military debate. On the previous day, the Confederate ship CSS *Virginia* had experienced a major success in sinking the Unionist frigate *Cumberland*, demonstrating the superiority of a relatively small armoured vessel against a much larger wooden ship. The ensuing confrontation with USS *Monitor* was between the two types that would determine naval warfare over the next twenty years: the *Monitor*'s two-gun turret versus the *Virginia*'s ten-gun casemate – competing designs that would cause heated controversy, not just from the standpoint of artillery but also from that of the respective vessels' overall usefulness as fighting ships.

Engels' position on future warship design was determined not so much by the British 'high seas' debate but by the ostensibly peripheral but in fact paradigmatic (and as such widely noticed) boarding and capture on 17 June 1863 of the Confederate casemate ramship *Atlanta* in Wassaw Sound, Georgia, by the Monitor-class USS *Weehawken*. Engels concluded from this encounter: 'Gun-turret ships armed with heavy 10–15″ cannon are out of all proportion the strongest vessels, whether for defence of one's own shores, or for attack against neighbouring coasts.'[18] And he combined his plea for this (typically US Navy) vessel with a precise description of the deployment he envisaged for it: in rivers or coastal waters as a blockade breaker engaging with vulnerable wooden vessels or as a floating battery besieging coastal emplacements. This latter function he saw – as later research has confirmed[19] – as the determining factor in the development of ships' armour. In a bold transference of the American Civil War experience to the strategic situation on the German North Sea and Baltic coasts, he wrote: 'Learn to cast cannon of American calibre and to build gun-turret ships. Two such vessels in the Elbe and Weser will protect the entire northern coast. Four in the Baltic will secure that sea for us and compel Copenhagen, if needs be, to capitulate. No one will speak of today's Danish fleet any more.'[20]

The conception of the gun-turret ship as a game changer shows Engels as a creative, forward-looking strategist. And in this he was not alone: in the 1860s the combat advantages of gun turrets were in the air, and smaller naval powers saw in them a chance to draw closer to the major fleets. Both Denmark and the Netherlands – otherwise not exactly known for rapid take-up of marine innovations – ordered such vessels: Denmark in 1862: the three-masted schooner *Rolf Krake* (with a 700 hp steam engine) from the Glasgow shipyard of Robert Napier & Sons,[21] and the Netherlands in 1865, 1867 and

1868: the ram-and-turret ships *Prins Hendrik der Nederlanden*, *Schorpioen* and *Buffel* from French and Scottish yards.²² Designed for coastal defence, these vessels were the result of lessons learnt from the American Civil War – and, in Denmark's case, probably also from the 1849 disaster against the Prussian shore batteries at Eckernförde. Engels' advice anticipated this development, which very soon took effect in the Danish commission and only a few years later in the Dutch.²³

At the same time Engels was aware of the problems associated with the instability of contemporary turret ships on the high seas. We can presume, given his interest in the subject, that he knew of two typical and widely commented marine incidents involving such vessels. The USS *Monitor* – famed from the Battle of Hampton Roads²⁴ – sank in January 1862 in stormy weather near Cape Hatteras (Outer Banks), and a sister ship of the Passaic class, the USS *Nahant*, narrowly missed the same fate. Equally (or even more) devastating was the loss of the battleship HMS *Captain*. Designed by Captain Cowper Coles (1819–1870), a competitor of *Monitor* architect John Ericsson (1803–1889), the

Figure 5.3 USS *Monitor* in James River, Virginia, 1862. View on deck, starboard side towards the bow of the ship, showing the gun turret with the muzzle of one of the two 11-inch Dahlgren guns. Crewmen in the turret above and damage below caused by Confederate heavy guns in the engagement with CSS *Virginia*. Officers (left to right): third engineer Robinson W. Hands, Captain Louis N. Stodder, second engineer Albert B. Campbell (seated) and lieutenant William Flye (with binoculars). © U.S. Naval History and Heritage Command.

Captain – a three-masted, twin-turreted, steam-powered vessel[25] – was, despite her very low freeboard, commissioned on 30 April 1870 for the high-seas fleet. Her loss discredited for some time the idea of seagoing turret ships – all the more so as the designer went down with his work.

Preceding this disaster, a lively debate had been conducted in both military and civilian circles in Britain between supporters of the innovative turret ship as endowed with superior future potential and the admiralty, in whose opinion gun turrets were not yet suitable for seaborne use. Coles, a particularly vocal supporter of the turret solution, propagated his ideas in a press campaign against an allegedly backward-looking naval high command and its obsolete ships. In the face of explicit warnings from the Chief Naval Constructor, Edward Reed (1830–1906), he urged the completion of a prototype. Conceived and built against this agitated political and cultural background,[26] HMS *Captain* sank on her maiden voyage in a storm off Cape Finisterre with the loss of almost five hundred men.[27] From this point until the late 1880s – influenced above all by the concepts, designs and experience of the admiralty's naval architectural team under Edward Reed – the casemate or 'box battery' was considered the only practicable artillery placement for high-seas vessels.[28]

The difficulties of ship design in this transitional period are apparent in the many judgements whose priorities sharply diverged from or even contradicted each other. So complex were the parameters that compromises had to be found among virtually incompatible elements.[29] Each vessel amounted to a new prognostication, and the lead time was so long that developments in artillery and its placement, as well as in armour and propulsion, might well outstrip it: technology was always a step ahead. Engels took a pragmatic line in these debates. In the technological context of 1863, his judgement was sound: a warship should carry few cannon, but they should be heavy enough to destroy armour from any angle. This was possible only with turret-mounted muzzle loaders; in the mid-1860s, breech-loading systems were reliable only for lighter projectiles and smaller bores, quite apart from the ineffectiveness of current shells against armour. Engels's ideal ship, then, was a 'Super-Monitor' equipped with all these items – plus good seaworthiness. In hindsight, one can say that his vision pinpointed the vector of development that would lead to the standard warship of the 1890s.[30]

Naval engagement strategy – close combat and ramming

A further controversy arose around the question of the optimum distance for a naval engagement. Naval artillery specialists were often sceptical not only about their ability to shatter or penetrate an opposing ship's armour but also about the overall accuracy of the new guns. This depended on the aiming process, ballistic performance, stability of the ship in high seas, preferred combat range and the rate of fire of the few artillery pieces on board. However, softer aspects relating to tradition, military doctrine and even personal preferences of the commanders also played a role in artillery tactics. The widely held belief in point blank range in the tradition of Admiral Horatio Nelson (1758–1805) led almost inevitably, as it had in the Battle of Trafalgar (21 October 1805), to a confused melee when ships closed in on an enemy. Nevertheless, in this situation, ramming the enemy was, with wooden men o'war, both dangerous and – especially on a windless day – ineffective.

Steam tactics changed this radically, and ramming an enemy vessel in a melee suddenly became a relevant tactical option. But the extent to which actual engagements – always the acid test – should be allowed to determine either tactical doctrine or issues of technology and its deployment was another hotly debated matter at the time.[31] That the Austrian commander, Rear Admiral Wilhelm von Tegetthoff, could decide the *Battle of Lissa* in the Adriatic on 20 July 1866 by ramming Italian vessels led to a lengthy period of equipping new warships with rams. Whatever maritime historians say, this was by no means absurd in the contemporary context, where artillery confrontations among ironclads were often inconclusive – historians, too, enjoy playing the prophet in retrospect. Moreover, the appalling losses resulting from accidental collisions between ironclads in peacetime proved beyond doubt the effectiveness of ramming as an offensive tactic. On 31 May 1878 the SMS *Grosser Kurfürst* was rammed and sunk, with a loss of 289 men, by the German flagship SMS *König Wilhelm* during manoeuvres in the English Channel outside Folkestone. Another spectacular incident of the same kind occurred near Tripoli in the Lebanon on 22 June 1893, when the British battleship HMS *Camperdown*, in a manoeuvre mistakenly signalled by Vice Admiral Sir George Tryon, rammed and sank HMS *Victoria*, with the loss of the admiral and 358 crew members.

In peace as in war, ramming was, for the vessel on the receiving end, a dangerous and rapidly lethal procedure. In 1878 the ram was rated 'a ship's most powerful offensive weapon, [which] in future maritime warfare will play the primary role'.[32] The dictum of American Admiral Louis M. Goldsborough (1805–1877), 'The vessel must be the projectile, the steam-power the gunpowder',[33] indicates that ramming was conceived as the logical development of heavy artillery. In this respect it should be interpreted not necessarily as a blind alley, a short-lived fashion after the Battle of Lissa (1866), but as a response to the limitations of contemporary naval artillery, which amounted to more than just the problem of overcoming enemy armour: the crucial weaknesses lay rather in the guns' restricted range and lengthy loading processes. The bigger the calibre and the heavier the shell, the longer it took to load the weapon, and given the lack of accuracy at any distance beyond point blank or pistol range, slow-firing, armour-breaking heavy artillery had little chance of success. Ramming was more effective. Ex post it is always easy to identify dead ends, but recourse to an ancient technique was not in this case mere conservatism on the part of naval high command but an answer to deficiencies in a technology that later swept all before it. The ineffectiveness of shells and solid shot even against older wooden vessels – notable in the success of the screw-driven Austrian ship of the line SMS *Kaiser* against modern Italian ironclads in the Battle of Lissa – only ended with the development of armour-piercing shells in the 1890s. Until then, ramming brought better results.

Naval engagement strategy – long-range combat

Engels was first and foremost an artilleryman, not a naval specialist, and he judged ships as artillery platforms rather than in their complexity as integral technological-tactical wholes. Thus, in his comments on the engagement in Wassaw Sound, it was not the ram tactics, or even the combination of the vessels' gunfire with their manoeuvring and other capabilities, that interested him; he noted that ram ships armed only with marksmen were also used but did not comment on this;[34] his focus was solely on the artillery. And in this respect he came to the conclusion: 'Every rifle-bored gun that deserves the name ensures such long-range precision that the earlier inadequacy of naval gunnery at such distances will soon be a thing of the past.'[35]

It was a clear-sighted view, for from the 1880s at the latest, naval doctrine favoured longer-range engagement, and faster ships at greater distances made for faster manoeuvring irrespective of wind conditions: 'Rifled cannon will assuredly soon put an end to the close combat in which carronades [heavy, short-barrelled, short-range guns KM] might be useful. Manoeuvring will again gain the upper hand, and as steam power makes fighting vessels independent of wind and current, naval warfare will in future approximate more closely the methods and tactical movements of land engagements.'[36] Engels rightly perceived the Royal Navy's new 'steam tactics'[37] – the manoeuvring of a formation of vessels under their own power, much like that of a formation of troops on land – as the beginning of a new tactical era.[38] Given the complexities and reverses of the 'hectic '60s and '70s'[39] in matters of naval strategy, weapons technology and battle tactics, this could by no means be taken for granted. *In nuce*, then, Engels foresaw the ship of the line that came into being in the 1890s – albeit under transformed technological and tactical premises, industrial capabilities and deployment doctrine – as the standard vessel of the fleet.

Lessons of experience – precision versus contingency

In all the controversies about artillery versus armour, smooth versus rifled gun barrels, breech versus muzzle loaders – as in the related aspects of artillery placement, firing charge and loading procedure – the question arises as to the adequacy and reliability of the sources from which the disputants drew their data. Here, armament trials played a central role. The qualities of both guns and armour were tested at the time under reproducible conditions in numerous, for the most part publicly accessible, experiment series – a culture of empirical verification that, in an era of technological development and transition, took on unique significance. Engels could, then – as he did in a series of 1860 articles in the *New York Tribune* 'On Rifled Cannon'[40] – call on a wealth of published reports: in this instance, concerning not only armaments trials but also the problems arising from faults in artillery design and manufacture experienced by the French during the 1859 Sardinian War.

Engels had followed the specialist discussion for several years[41] and had gone to the trouble of checking the capability of various gun types against his own calculations. His conclusions took account of both military and non-military opinions, and he underpinned his arguments with precise figures on thickness of armour, ballistic performance, shell and charge types, and penetrating power of the projectiles in question. Moreover, he took account of the inevitable difference between experiments under laboratory conditions and the realities of military use. Test reports often lacked information about the structure and metallurgy of armour plating or the impact angle of projectiles, nor could they account for the contingencies of rolling and yawing ships as artillery platforms – with resultant wide discrepancies in impact angles – let alone the conditions of actual combat. Under stress, errors are made like those of the Italian naval gunners in the Battle of Lissa who fired practice shells by mistake, enabling the Austrian navy's old wooden SMS *Kaiser* to survive bombardment from the latest type of cannon.

In his judgement on the performance of ironclads in the American Civil War, Engels tacitly assumed that the vessels were adequately developed and battle-ready and interpreted their encounter as paradigmatic for turret and casemate ships rather than as a complex containing many contingent elements. On the basis of the (not always disinterested) press reports that were his sole source of information, he could know nothing of aspects like shallows and currents, the draught of the ships concerned or the training level of the crews. Thus, he took no account of the fact that in the Battle of Wassaw Sound (17 June 1863) the Confederate ram ship CSS *Atlanta* ran aground on a sandbank,[42] or that, like most Confederate ironclads, its armour – made of flattened railway-line steel mounted on a wooden frame – was entirely inadequate, and above all, that its overall condition could only be described as jerry-built.[43] Any conclusions about 'systems' of weapons or armour drawn from available information about the encounter would have to be hedged around with considerable reservations. Here too, Engels judged as an artilleryman, not as an expert on naval warfare.

Engels and the ideas of the *jeune école*

The second half of the nineteenth century saw the genesis of two virtually incompatible schools of naval strategy, known as the 'blue water' and 'white water' schools. For the first group, dominance of the high seas in a decisive naval battle was the strategic and operational goal; for the second, the goal was coastal defence, providing temporary local dominance, in combination with blockading, blockade-breaking and camouflaged 'commerce raids' to capture enemy merchant shipping. The blue water school concentrated (albeit not exclusively) on building up a fleet of high-seas vessels; the white water school, generally conceived as an option for smaller naval powers, invested in coastal fortifications (so-called brick and mortar tactics) and ships suitable for offensive as well as defensive operations in coastal waters – including fast corvettes and frigates with high-seas capability and endurance for individual missions. The book that formulated this doctrine, *The Influence of Sea Power Upon History* by U.S. Rear Admiral

Figure 5.4 The capture of CSS *Atlanta* – CSS *Atlanta* (left) bombarded by USS *Weehawken* in Wassaw Sound, Georgia, 17 June 1863. © U.S. Naval History and Heritage Command.

Alfred Thayer Mahan (1840–1914, aka 'the naval Clausewitz'), was not, however, published until 1890,[44] and the small-ship and raiding tactics propagated by the French *jeune école*[45] were first advocated by Vice Admiral Philippe-Victor Touchard in 1873, well after Engels' articles on naval subjects.

What might seem an unambiguous conceptual dichotomy was in practice, however, complicated by a number of supervening factors, questions and alternatives. During the whole ironclad era, for example, there was not a single decisive battle on the high seas[46] – even the famous Battle of Lissa was arguably, from the Austrian point of view, a coastal defence action of the island of Lissa. And then – What ships should one build? What capabilities should they have? How far from home coasts should they operate? The initial result was the 'brick-and-mortar' defence ship for coastal waters, built in the first place by lesser naval powers with geographically complex maritime interests, like those of Prussia before 1870. The type of vessel appropriate for these functions, complementing and extending existing fortifications and shore batteries, was nonetheless still open to debate,[47] and here, the distinctions and classifications were less a matter of armour and armament than of deployment. This could vary from coastal protection duties (also heavily armed and armoured), through port and battery defence (which might also call for offensive capabilities), to overt attacking sorties (also outside coastal waters). In a revealing terminological transference from land warfare, vessels designed for this latter purpose – for example the four Saxon-class frigates built for the German Navy from 1878 onwards – were known in Prussia as 'sortie corvettes'; the Austro-Hungarian Navy's three similar Vienna-class vessels bore the more straightforward title 'coastal defenders'. The next level up was the high-seas warship. These different functional classes required structurally different vessel types, although the most important criterion, enduring seaworthiness in adverse conditions, was common to all. Moreover, a general caveat applicable to this period is that not only the predominant doctrine but also the technological limitations of the ships must be borne in mind.[48]

Coast versus capital – the defence of Britain

Historically speaking, the defence of the coasts was seen as the central task of the world's navies until well into the second half of the nineteenth century, when the blue water school – at least in the strategic thinking of the chief naval powers – finally gained dominance. In the 1860s, reinforced by the experiences of the Crimean and the American Civil War, the naval doctrine – even of a major power like Britain with her traditional high-seas focus – began to turn in the direction of coastal defence as a counterweight to the battle fleet.[49] Again, other factors supervened: notably, the higher troop-carrying capacity of steam-powered vessels for potential invading forces as well as their greater speed and independence of weather conditions, all of which increased the vulnerability of the long British coastline to a mass surprise attack. The response was to enhance fortification of the country's arsenals and strengthen its coastal defences,[50] a policy also applied to Britain's many overseas bases,[51] whose significance as military, technological and logistic centres grew in direct proportion to the technological sophistication of the fleet. In an age of floating steam-and-steel machines,[52] coaling stations, docks and technical support were eminently important, and they, in turn, required large numbers of professional personnel and extensive quasi-industrial facilities for service and storage.[53] Moreover, it was the era of high imperialism, when naval bases served as nodes of global influence. Against this background, steam-powered armoured warships can be seen as the technological presupposition for – and driving force of – change at the interface of naval policy, infrastructure and imperialism.

Where, then, within this complex matrix did Friedrich Engels stand? The issue of coastal defence versus the high-seas fleet interested him only in the context of Prussia's Baltic coastline, where there was no reasonable alternative to protection of the kingdom's 'wet flank' from Kiel to Königsberg. For the mutual antagonists France and Britain, caught up in an intense (qualitative as well as quantitative) arms race, the problem was different. France's commissioning of the first seagoing ironclad, the frigate *La Gloire*, in August 1860 had sent shockwaves through the British navy and led in return to the construction of HMS *Warrior*, the first fully iron-hulled high-seas vessel.[54] In such circumstances, coastal defences seemed an urgent necessity. Engels, however, writing in 1860[55] against the background of possible invasion, took a line quite different from either of the two main alternatives and subjected the fortification plans for fleet bases and arsenals to critical scrutiny. Staff engineers, he objected, seemed 'to veritably wallow in an abundance of fortifications' such that England 'is threatened by a vegetation of forts and batteries that shoot up like mushrooms from the ground and grow with the luxuriance of vines in a tropical forest'.

'The General' as Admiral

Figure 5.5 Types of armoured ships of the most important navies, Meyers Grosses Konversations-Lexikon, vol. 15 (Leipzig 1908). © In the public domain.

This by no means meant that Engels was an adherent of the blue water school, for he accepted the much-heard British plea 'that the country's "wooden walls", its ships, no longer protect it and national defence requires funds to be allocated for fortifications'.[56] What he criticized was the distribution and positioning of the defences. Instead of investing massively in strengthening harbours and arsenals, as naval high command planned, the government should, he argued, construct a ring of fortresses around London, as the French had around Paris. That might well be 'more complicated and expensive' than a full-scale fortification of individual harbours, but London must be defended with a powerful army: 'Where is this army to come from if Portsmouth, Plymouth, Chatham and Sheerness, and perhaps even Pembroke, are to be transformed into fortresses of the first rank like Cherbourg, Genua, Koblenz or Cologne, which have garrisons of 15,000 to 20,000 men to defend them?'[57] Engels came to this conclusion simply by observing the discrepancy between those figures and the number of Britain's professional army units actually available for mobilization. 'Shipyards should, of course, be properly fortified,' he conceded, but that 'only needs half the money being squandered on it today.' So, he concluded, 'if you want a national defence plan, then set about fortifying London'.[58]

This represented an interesting position oblique to the main disputants. On the one hand, Engels' suggested strategy for defending the southern English coastline anticipated the ideas of the brick-and-mortar school as well as the later *jeune école*. On the other hand, he – 'the General' trained in land warfare and with his personal competencies and interests in this field – grasped the options open to invading forces more clearly than did the planners of the British senior service. A quick assault on the 'heart of empire' seemed to him a more plausible strategy than spreading the attack over a number of fortified coastal bases, even if the support facilities of the British fleet remained thereby in the hands of the defenders. Engels' argumentation took balanced account of both positions, that of the navy and that of the army, and his overall plan for the defence of the United Kingdom was well thought through. In that sense, 'the General' is to be counted neither amongst the supporters of the high-seas fleet – even if he once called for a 'Super-Monitor' – nor as a member of the navy's brick-and-mortar faction. Schooled in land warfare, Engels reacted in that perspective to the conceptual challenges of defending the British Isles.

CHAPTER 6
THE 'PROMISED LAND'? FRIEDRICH ENGELS, THE UNITED STATES AND THE FUTURE OF CAPITALISM

James M. Brophy

'Whatever happens, it's essential that you should also go on the American tour.' With these words, Friedrich Engels exhorted his friend August Bebel (1840–1913), the Reichstag deputy for the Social Democratic Party, to participate in his party's upcoming informational tour of the United States in 1886. Bebel should 'not miss the opportunity' of seeing with his own eyes 'the most progressive country in the world',[1] he commented, especially as it 'coincides with the first formation of a real American working men's party'.[2] Characterizing the trip as a breath of fresh air, Engels declared to Bebel, 'Life in Germany exerts an oppressive and constricting influence on anyone, even the best, as I know from my own experience, and one ought to get out of the place – from time to time at any rate.'[3] Engels' ringing endorsement to visit the United States, even if it went unfulfilled, was not a casual remark but, rather, an informed opinion that reflected Engels' decades-long engagement with the emerging industrial nation.

Since the 1840s, Friedrich Engels and Karl Marx set their sights on grasping the importance of the United States. Both perceived the young republic as an important engine of global capitalism, whose bright economic prospects and whose role in global affairs had not yet fully made its mark. Like many economists and journalists of their time, Engels and Marx initially perceived non-European territories as colonial appendages to Europe's industrial base. By the late 1840s, however, they grasped American industrialization as an economy that exceeded the function of a colonial outpost. In their evolving interpretive framework, America's role as a transatlantic bridge for European wealth created its own industrial independence, which also reconfigured the tempo, pattern and future of global capitalism. An unbridled capitalist economy in the 'land of unlimited possibilities' could magnify the contradictions of capitalist production, heighten social distress, galvanize the workers' movement and thereby ripen the conditions for social and political upheaval. In the 1850s and 1860s, evolving economic conditions challenged the two thinkers to adapt and recast their theories of economic and political change. The United States was neither a mere supplier of raw materials to European metropoles nor a simple replication of conditions that mirrored European paths of development. On the one hand, the waves of migration and its technological bases linked American development to European civilization and thus permitted Engels and Marx to assume that class conflict would drive the American workers' movement in the same way that it did in Europe. On the other, they recognized

Figure 6.1 Friedrich Engels in Brighton, 1877. Engels enjoyed travelling and did so regularly to the English coast at Eastbourne or Brighton, but also to Ireland or – as in 1888 – to the United States. © In the public domain.

The 'Promised Land'

the exceptional elements of North America that resisted comparison to the old world. The geographical and material dimensions transcended European proportions. Its vast natural resources – ores, minerals, forests and arable land – and spatial dimensions tokened a scale of agricultural and industrial production that reconfigured the cycles and competitive pressures of global capitalism.[4] In a polemic against the French socialist Pierre-Joseph Proudhon in 1847, Marx anticipated such tensions when interpreting the United States as both an offshoot of European capitalism and a vanguard of global capitalism: 'Wipe North America off the map of the world, and you will have anarchy – the complete decay of modern commerce and civilization.'[5] Indeed, successive waves of gold rush, railroad construction and electrification only strengthened the claim of America as a pacemaker.

Marx's concern for modelling the future of capitalism made the vagaries of American development a persistent problem for conceptualizing capitalism's transitional phases. America loomed as a large, open question for Marx during the critical decades of the 1860s and 1870s. For Engels, America's Civil War of 1861–5 reoriented his viewpoints and spurred him to deepen his knowledge of America's economy, politics and military affairs. He followed its industrial and labour developments with the keen eye of a businessman, journalist and socialist. Less fazed by theoretical inconsistencies than Marx, Engels approached America's leadership in labour politics more pragmatically, favouring a hands-on approach. As he noted in 1888, 'It is a place one really must have seen with one's own eyes, this country whose history goes back no farther than commodity production and which is the promised land of capitalist production. People's usual conceptions of it are as false as those a German schoolboy has of France.'[6] In view of his own trip to the United States in 1888 and four decades of information-gathering through reportage and personal contacts, this essay traces Engel's perceptions of the United States. It reviews his early writings, his travel diary and his extensive correspondence, especially his letters to Friedrich Adolph Sorge (1828–1906), the former general secretary of the First International and the founder of the Socialist Party of America, to reconstruct Engels' evolving perception of the United States and its role in the workers' movement. While underscoring Engels' impressive knowledge of American conditions, the essay also reveals blind spots. America's patterns of social mobility, its absence of a corporatist caste system, its deep-seated ethos of individualism and, finally, its ethnic and racial differences all contributed to significant anomalies that undermined Engels' expectation that socialist parties could mobilize and win the allegiance of workers. He situated his optimism for a breakthrough in American labour politics within the broader framework of a long-awaited global crisis in capitalism, a mode of deductive reasoning that characterized his political thinking.

Giant steps and civil war

Soon after arriving at Ermen & Engels, the family enterprise in Manchester, the 'workshop of the world' for textile production, Engels first articulated his vision of America's 'giant steps' and the significance of transatlantic industry and commerce. In *The Condition of the Working Class in England* (1845), Engels' scathing reportage of Manchester's social misery, he sketched the economic potential of the United States: 'America, with its inexhaustible resources', was destined for supremacy, 'with its unmeasured coal and iron fields, with its unexampled wealth of water-power and its navigable rivers, but especially with its energetic, active population'. By comparison, he quipped, the 'English are phlegmatic dawdlers'. With the water-driven mills in New England, such as those in Lowell and Lawrence (Massachusetts) or in Pawtucket (Rhode Island), 'America has in less than ten years created a manufacture which already competes with England in the coarser cotton goods, has excluded the English from the markets of North and South America, and holds its own in China, side by side with England.' On the basis of his personal experience with Manchester's trade and stock reports, whose accuracy at the time was unparalleled, he hazarded the prediction: 'If any country is adapted to holding a monopoly of manufacture, it is America.'[7]

The young Karl Marx was also informed about the United States, although he turned more readily to social and political questions. Because Thomas Paine's *Rights of Man* (1792) stood in his father's library, one can assume that Marx read the classic early in his life.[8] A side remark in 'The Jewish Question' (1845) further reveals that he was acquainted with Alexis de Tocqueville's *De la démocratie en Amérique* (1835), the era's seminal work for explaining American government and society.[9] In 1846, Marx co-authored a polemic against Hermann Kriege, a German journalist in New York, who advocated the 'free soil movement'. In this pamphlet, Marx rejected Krieg's assertion that the cost-free distribution of land to workers amounted to a communist reform.[10] Marx furthermore acquainted himself with the American ideals of republicanism, which celebrated a citizen's economic independence and political freedom. For craftsmen and workers, the early introduction of universal (manhood) suffrage in the 1830s played a central, if not decisive, role in their political development. As a jurist versed in constitutional history, Marx saw the importance of civic rights that guaranteed claims of liberty and freedom. In the 'German Ideology' (1845–6), he noted: 'the workers attach so much importance to citizenship, i.e., to active citizenship, that where they have it, for instance in America, they "make good use" of it, and where they do not have it, they strive to obtain it'.[11] Such constitutional rights shaped the political behaviour of American workers over the course of the entire nineteenth century.[12] Forged in the early republic, the credo of political individualism endured, even when large-scale industrialization and mass politics arguably called for collectivist strategies within the workers' movement.

The unearthing of gold in California in 1849 reframed the American question for Marx and Engels, who were still processing the painful setbacks of the German Revolution of 1848–9. They labelled the discovery as 'the most important thing to have occurred here, more important even than the February Revolution … one may predict that this discovery will have much more impressive consequences than the discovery of America itself'. For them, the wheel of world history had turned, with global trade taking a new direction. With a panoramic historical survey, they declared:

The role played by Tyre, Carthage and Alexandria in antiquity, and Genoa and Venice in the Middle Ages, the role of London and Liverpool until now – that of the emporia of world trade – is now being assumed by New York and San Francisco, San Juan de Nicaragua, and Leon, Chagres and Panama. The centre of gravity of world commerce, Italy in the Middle Ages, England in modern times, is now the southern half of the North American peninsula. The industry and trade of old Europe will have to make huge exertions if they are not to fall into the same decay as the industry and trade of Italy since the sixteenth century, if England and France are not to become what Venice, Genoa and Holland are today.[13]

In the wake of political defeat in Europe's mid-century revolutions, Marx and Engels welcomed the gold rush as a leavening agent for socioeconomic upheaval.

Even with its vast undeveloped spaces, America's economic potential emerged over the 1850s, thus adumbrating its future leadership role for global trends.[14] In this context, the economic and financial crisis of 1857–9 confirmed Marx's thesis that the productive forces had already shifted to the new world. The overheated speculation with banks and railroad stocks brought turmoil to stock exchanges and initiated a worldwide financial panic, which demonstrated that business cycles on both sides of the Atlantic were synchronized. The instability of capitalism that Friedrich Engels observed on the Manchester stock exchange in 1844, and what Marx predicted in 1848 in the *Communist Manifesto*, now arose in Ohio and New York with full force. For both authors, the systematic overproduction of business cycles and the resulting recessions augured the collapse of capitalism – a mantra that repeatedly arose throughout their lives. In October 1857, Marx only saw their theory confirmed and wrote to Engels: 'The American crisis – its outbreak in New York was forecast by us in the November 1850 Revue – is beautiful.'[15] The prognosis that the United States would set the tone for the future development of crisis-ridden capitalism took on persuasive materialist dimensions in the 1850s.

But slavery stood in the way of capitalism's full development in North America. In the first volume of *Capital*, Marx wrote, 'In the United States of North America, every independent movement of the workers was paralysed so long as slavery disfigured a part of the Republic. Labour cannot emancipate itself in the white skin where in the black it is branded.'[16] Building on that claim, he prophesized, 'As in the eighteenth century, the American War of Independence sounded the tocsin for the European middle class, so in the nineteenth century, the American Civil War sounded it for the European working class'.[17] He further characterized President Abraham Lincoln's Emancipation Proclamation of 1 January 1863 as 'globally ground breaking'. Depriving the Confederate states of the material and human basis for its monoculture cotton production had now injected a revolutionary dimension to the conflict.[18]

In the first years of the Civil War, Engels complained vehemently about the Union's overly moderate position and regretted the absence of actual revolutionary deeds. 'If only there were some evidence', Engels remonstrated to Marx in 1862, 'that the masses in the North were beginning to act as in France in 1792 and 1793, everything would be splendid. But the only revolution to be anticipated seems more likely to be a democratic counter-revolution and a hollow peace'.[19] Two months before Lincoln's proclamation, he wrote, 'unless the North instantly adopts a revolutionary stance, it will get the terrible thrashing it deserves – and that's what seems to be happening'.[20] 'It's too pitiful', he commented a few weeks later to Marx, 'and, in contrast to the spineless goings-on in the North, the chaps in the South, who, at least, know what they want, seem to me like heroes'.[21] In November of the same year, he confessed, 'I feel no enthusiasm for a people who, faced with an issue as colossal as this, allow themselves to be beaten again and again by a force numbering ¼ of their own population and who, after 18 months of war, have gained nothing save the discovery that all their generals are jackasses and their functionaries, crooks and traitors'.[22] His judgement in February 1863 was still more damning:

> Things don't look so good in Yankeeland ... signs of moral prostration are daily more in evidence and the inability to win grows daily greater. ... The people have been cheated, more's the pity, and it's lucky that peace is a physical impossibility or they'd have concluded it long since, if only so that they could again devote themselves to the almighty dollar.[23]

Because of the decisive actions of the Confederate generals, Engels hesitated to predict a victory for the Union. Only at the end of 1864 did Engels find enough evidence to make an argument for a Union victory. He marked his change of heart in a letter to Joseph Weydemeyer in St. Louis, declaring, 'That war of yours over there is really one of the most stupendous things that one can experience. Despite the numerous blunders made by the Northern armies (enough by the South, too), the tide of conquest is rolling slowly but surely onward.' Engels further elaborated on the nature of this world-historical event:

> A people's war of this kind, on both sides, has not taken place since great states have been in existence, and it will, at all events, point the direction for the future of the whole of America for hundreds of years to come. Once slavery, the greatest shackle on the political and social development of the United States, has been broken, the country is bound to receive an impetus from which it will acquire quite a different position in world history within the shortest possible time, and a use will then soon be found for the army and navy with which the war is providing it.[24]

Marx only concurred, declaring that '*never* has such a gigantic revolution occurred with such rapidity. It will have a highly beneficial influence on the whole world'.[25] With slavery abolished, Marx reasoned, the path was clear for the dominance of genuine waged work throughout the entire continent. American workers were now in the position to recognize and respond to the exploitative dimensions of wage labour, thereby setting in motion the mechanisms for acquiring class consciousness. 'The best Yankee writers are loud in proclaiming the stubborn fact that, if the Anti-Slavery war has broken the chains of the black, it has on the other hand enslaved the white producers.'[26] And in *Capital*, he argued, 'The first fruit of the Civil War was the eight hours' agitation, which ran with the seven-leagued boots of the locomotive from the Atlantic to the Pacific, from New England to California.'[27] Despite a deep-seated scepticism about the power of the vote for workers' emancipation, Marx conceded a certain respect for America's electoral culture.[28] Through elections, ordinary people could become heroes, which is how he characterized Abraham Lincoln:

> Lincoln is not the product of a popular revolution. This plebeian, who worked his way up from stone-breaker to Senator in Illinois, without intellectual brilliance, without a particularly outstanding character, without exceptional importance – an average person of good will, was placed at the top by the interplay of the forces of universal suffrage unaware of the great issues at stake. The new world has never achieved a greater triumph than by this demonstration that, given its political and social organisation, ordinary people of good will can accomplish feats which only heroes could accomplish in the old world![29]

Putting the abolition of US chattel slavery with Russia's earlier emancipation of serfs in 1861, Marx and Engels recognized an epochal breakthrough. The radicalization of American politics could only accelerate the dynamic.

Capital and free trade

At Philadelphia's World Fair in 1876, America ostentatiously celebrated its centennial. Its lavish displays of industry, commerce and progress announced to both clients and competitors America's industrial ascendancy. The confidence was justified. In 1869, railroads connected the Atlantic and Pacific oceans, consolidating one of the world's largest domestic markets. During the three decades between the Civil War (1861–5) and the economic crisis of 1894, industrial production and gross national product had increased threefold. In small towns, factories grew by 159 per cent; in cities, by 245 per cent. In this period, America's productivity rose to stand among the world's leaders. And despite the influx of skilled workers from Europe, there was still insufficient labour pools to cover the needs of expanding industrial sectors, thus promising additional prosperity and growth for all economic branches.

Above all, intensified industrialization altered labour relations and redefined workers' political rights.[30] In short supply, labour became more expensive. The extensive mechanization of work, so argued economists and entrepreneurs, would balance out labour costs and still guarantee good returns on investment. With accelerated industrialization in the 1870s, Marx and Engels saw a greater potential for global capitalism to intensify its internal contradictions and hasten its demise. As Marx noted in 1878, 'The most interesting field for the economist is now certainly to be found in the United States, and, above all, during the period of 1873 (since the crash in September) until 1878 – the period of chronic crisis. Transformations – which required *centuries* in England – were here realised *in a few years*.'[31] The concentration of American capital, he continued in another letter, stemmed from 'unprecedented rapid industrial development', whose tempo far outstripped English progress. Moreover, Marx noted, 'the masses are quicker, and have greater political means in their hands'.[32]

Far-reaching consequences for world markets grew out of America's explosive economic growth.[33] On the basis of these observations, Marx sought more accurate information. He assembled statistical reports from Ohio, Pennsylvania, New York, Massachusetts, New Jersey, Iowa and California.[34] He praised the statistical offices that collected the information and saw a model that European states should emulate. In 1880, he wrote to Friedrich Adolph Sorge to request more of these offices' economic data. 'California is of great importance to me because in no other place has revolution by capitalist centralisation been effected with such effrontery at such great speed.'[35] With the rapid transformation of the North American continent, Marx posed the question whether the scale, scope and tempo of industrialization altered the future of global capitalism. In the last third of the century, the United States challenged Britain's industrial supremacy and, with it, its status as a theoretical paradigm.

For completing *Capital*, Marx's major opus, the question of modelling future economic and political development was obviously of paramount importance. In 1880, Marx conceded to a New York newspaper that he needed to rework the third book of *Capital* because of the surprising developments in America's credit system.[36] Despite his declining health, Marx struggled through piles of official US statistical reports, because he recognized developments that economists could not ignore.[37] When appraising Marx's papers after his death in 1883, Engels remarked that these 'detailed studies' detained Marx for years. 'Had it not been for the mass of American and Russian material', noted Engels to Sorge, 'Volume II would have long since been printed'.[38] Such evidence suggests that Marx at the end of his life re-evaluated his theoretical bearings and conceptualized capitalism's future development through a less Eurocentric lens.[39]

Friedrich Engels was no less impressed by the 'colossal speed with which the concentration of capital is taking place in America'.[40] In 1882, Engels dubbed Cornelius Vanderbilt, the shipping and railroad tycoon who amassed more than three hundred million dollars over thirty years, as the 'king' of American capitalists. But 'the number of American money barons is far greater',[41] he stressed, and their concentration of wealth ripened revolutionary conditions. The expropriation of land for railroads and mines, Engels wrote, raised the price of land, which only the well-off farmers could afford, thereby radicalizing the immigrant small-scale farmers in the West.[42] He further saw far-reaching consequences in the pattern of American land settlement for other countries. To contest Karl Kautsky's Malthusian fears regarding the overpopulation of Germany and its meaning for socialism, Engels referred to the successful mechanization of agriculture in the United States. 'Mass production, as yet only in its infancy, and *really* large-scale agriculture', he argued, 'are threatening to all but suffocate us by the sheer volume of the means of subsistence produced … an upheaval of which one of the first consequences must be to *populate the globe*'.[43] With this opposing argument, Engels corrected Kautsky's assumption that American social conditions didn't differ radically from Europe's: 'this holds good only so long as you consider nothing but the larger coastal cities, or even the outward legal forms those conditions assume. There can be no doubt that the vast mass of the American people live in conditions that are exceedingly favourable to demographic growth. The stream of immigrants is proof of this. ... Alarmism doesn't come into it.'[44]

With the cultivation of the American prairie and the mechanization of agriculture, such as with the McCormick reaper, Engels foresaw a new epoch, one characterized by demographic growth, technological progress through concentrated capital and an increasingly radicalized working class. In the fourth edition to the German-language version of the *Communist Manifesto*, Engels took stock of the world's political economy and underscored the reversed role of the United States in relation to Europe. Whereas America's raw materials once stabilized the European order, 'how all of that has changed today!':

> It is the self-same European emigration which has made possible the immense development of North American agriculture which, through its competition, is shaking the very foundations of European landed property – large and small. It has also enabled the United States to make a start on exploiting its tremendous industrial resources, and with such energy and on such a scale that this is bound in a short while to put an end to the industrial monopoly of Western Europe. And these two circumstances react in a revolutionary manner also on America itself. The small and medium landed property of the self-employed farmers, the foundation of America's entire political system, is increasingly succumbing to competition from giant farms, whilst simultaneously in the industrial regions a numerically strong proletariat is taking shape for the first time alongside a fabulous concentration of capital.[45]

Such developments in North America portended repercussions for the workers' movement in Europe, because America no longer acted as the safety valve for Europe.

> In this manner, the stream of emigration, which Europe sends to America annually, only exaggerates the consequences of the capitalist economy, so that a colossal crash will come in the long or short term. Then the emigration flow will stagnate or even recede, which means the moment has come where the European, but especially the German, worker confronts the alternative: starvation or revolution![46]

Convinced of America's role as a driving force for the imminent revolution, Engels increasingly advocated that America give up its protectionist trade policy. After its Civil War, the US government, under Republican leadership, introduced an array of protectionist duties. Export-oriented manufacturers as well as labour leaders argued that duties had increased the prices of goods and unduly enriched the state.[47] When elected as president in 1888, Benjamin Harrison, a Republican, continued the policy and even raised duties for many commodities between 38 and 50 per cent. The rates of return for industry, which stood between 15 and 30 per cent, pleased manufacturers,[48] but this politics of enrichment did not escape the attention of voters, who punished Harrison for raising the price of staples. In the mid-term elections of 1890, the Republicans lost ninety-three seats in the House, providing the Democrats with an impressive majority vote.[49] In practical electoral terms, Engels' hope for less protectionism in American policy had empirical support.

The economic and political changes on both sides of the Atlantic spurred Engels to refine his analysis of global political economy. His correspondence with Florence Kelley-Wischnewetzky, the prominent social worker and the translator of Marx, highlights Engels's efforts to adjust to the current conditions. America, he wrote to her, is not in the position to inherit England's monopoly. Such advantageous conditions, which England enjoyed in the years 1848 to 1870, could not be produced anywhere, 'and even in America the condition of the working class must gradually sink lower and lower'. Instead, Engels emphasized a progressive dynamic brought about by the competitive pressure of world markets:

> For if there are three countries (say England, America, and Germany) competing on comparatively equal terms for the possession of the *Weltmarkt*, there is no chance but chronic overproduction, one of the three being capable of supplying the whole quantity required. That is the reason why I am watching the development of the present crisis with greater interest than ever and why I believe it will mark an epoch in the mental and political history of the American and English working classes.[50]

Not as an enthusiastic free trader but, rather, as a committed socialist, Engels promoted the unrestricted flow of goods in the Atlantic basin and throughout the world. The dovetailing of British, American and European markets would, according to Engels' schema, raise the susceptibility and frequency of business cycles, exert new pressures on the international working class and thereby accentuate more clearly the political goals of the proletariat. Simply put, free trade would stimulate a new revolutionary dynamic. In 1886, using a dubious zero-sum logic, he raised the prospect of economic collapse into a scenario of permanent crisis: 'If one great monopolist industrial country produced a crisis every ten years, what will four such countries produce? Approximately a crisis in 10/4 years, that is to say, practically a crisis without end.'[51] In 1893, he sketched this desideratum with greater care:

> While England is fast losing her industrial monopoly, France and Germany are approaching the industrial level of England, and America bids fair to drive them all out of the world's market both for industrial and for agricultural produce. The introduction of an, at least relative, free-trade policy in America is sure to complete the ruin of England's industrial monopoly, and to destroy, at the same time, the industrial export trade of Germany and France; then the crisis must come, *tout ce qu'il y a de plus fin de siècle*.[52]

Yet Engels reluctantly conceded that other factors and developments confounded short-term predictions. Such new technologies as electricity and telegraphy opened world markets and recalibrated cyclical behaviour, thus postponing the anticipated global crisis to an indefinite future time. As he noted to August Bebel in 1886, 'Apart from destroying Britain's monopoly of the world market, the new methods of communication – the electric telegraph, the railways, the Suez Canal and the supplanting of sail by steam – have gone some way towards breaking down the ten-year industrial cycle. If China is opened up ... overproduction [will] risk losing its last safety-valve.'[53] Although the accelerated race for consolidating world markets conformed with Marx and Engels' notions of capitalism's inherent instability, the developments equally manifested capitalism's capacity for adaptation and realignment.

Engels held onto the belief of socialism's need for competitive world trade for the remainder of his life. He furthermore remained an optimist when it came to America's return to open markets. For a businessman who conducted international trade in raw materials, David Ricardo's thesis of comparative advantage simply possessed a timeless validity. Even American manufactures, Engels reasoned, must come to recognize their own interests: 'Economic facts are stronger than politics, especially if the politics are so much mixed up with corruption as in America.'[54]

The American workers' movement

On 1 May 1886, the Haymarket Riots took place in Chicago, and the events produced consequential reverberations. What started as a rally to demand an eight-hour working day turned into a tragic melee when an unknown participant threw a bomb at police officers, who had been engaged to disperse the crowd. The police shot dead one worker and injured many; gunfire from the crowd killed four policemen and four civilians and wounded numerous others. The violence, along with the state's resolute policy to blame and prosecute anarchists on the thinnest of evidence, set a new political tone for the workers' movement.

The national response to the riots and deaths was galvanic. Approximately 200,000 workers went on strike in Pittsburgh, New York, Louisville, Milwaukee, St Louis, Baltimore and other cities, supported by the Knights of Labour and, after December 1886, the American Federation of Labour.[55] Membership to the Knights of Labour swelled to over 700,000, and the United Labour Party scored success in local city elections. For Engels, it was 'completely unprecedented for a movement to achieve such electoral successes after an existence of barely eight months'.[56] The American proletariat, he wrote in December 1886, 'was moving, and no mistake. ... This appearance of the Americans upon the scene I consider one of the greatest events of the year.'[57] I only wished, sighed Engels, that 'Marx could have lived to see it'![58] He viewed the events through the lens of historical materialism and its developmental stages. On the fortunate soil of America, 'where no feudal ruins block the path, where its history begins in the seventeenth century with already developed elements of modern bourgeois civil society, the working class has reached these stages in only ten months'.[59] With 'giant steps', the 'promised land' of the United States would spring over entire historical epochs, which had required generations in Europe. His visit to America in 1888 only confirmed his faith in the character of average workers to act in their own interest – even the lowest of

Figure 6.2 Corliss Steam Engine presented at the Philadelphia World's Fair, 1876. This gigantic construction was 13.5 metres high, weighed 600 tons and generated 2,500 hp with increased energy efficiency. For the United States, which was celebrating its centenary, this machine became a symbol of its industrial potential and entrepreneurial strength. After the exhibition, George Pullman acquired the machine and used it in his railcar factory. In 1908 it was replaced with a steam turbine and scrapped. © Hagley Museum and Library, Wilmington, Delaware, USA.

social classes. After visiting a prison in Boston, he remarked that the 'chaps, dressed as ordinary workmen, look you straight in the eye with none of the hang-dog look of the usual criminal in gaol – this is something you will see nowhere in Europe. ... I acquired a great respect for the Americans in that place.'[60]

American agitation also affected European politics. The mass strikes of this era undermined bourgeois credos regarding the United States as a safe haven 'that America stood above class antagonisms and struggles'. But that 'delusion has now broken down, the last Bourgeois Paradise on earth is fast changing into a Purgatory, and can only be prevented from becoming, like Europe, an Inferno by the go-ahead pace at which the development of the newly fledged proletariat of America will take place.'[61] Recent events demystified the legend of a classless society:

The absence up till now of a labour movement in England, and more especially in America, has been the great trump card of radical Republicans everywhere, notably in France. Now these chaps are utterly dumbfounded – Mr. Clemenceau in particular who, on 2 November, witnessed the collapse of all that his policy was based on. 'Just look at America', he never tired of saying, 'that's a real republic for you – no poverty and no labour movement!' And it's the same with men of Progress and 'democrats' in Germany and over here, where they are just experiencing an incipient movement of their own. What has completely stunned these people is the fact that the movement is so strongly accentuated as a labour movement, and that it has sprung up so suddenly and with such force.[62]

America's nascent movement, argued Engels elsewhere, would also affect the conservative trade unions in Great Britain. Inspired by transatlantic developments, English workers would politicize themselves, adopt continental socialism and unite themselves with a 'common programme of millions of workers of all countries, from Siberia to California'.[63] At the apex of his euphoria, he declared in 1887: 'But I am absolutely convinced that things are now going ahead over there, and perhaps more rapidly than here.'[64] Engels had good reason to justify his high spirits. Between 1885 and 1890, there was an average of 1,000 strikes per annum; in the early 1890s, the number rose to 1,300.[65] After 1893, however, more sobering trends set in. The workers' movement failed to radicalize in the way that Engels hoped. Although recognizing American differences from European labour conditions, he nonetheless held out the hope that class conflict would fundamentally sharpen and clarify workers' goals in the United States.

Reconciling actual events with desired aims proved difficult, and Engels turned to well-known stereotypes of American politics to justify failed expectations. He emphasized, for example, the baleful influence of anarchists at the Haymarket Riots, which he characterized as 'foolish'. Echoing a common lament about Anglo-American pragmatism, Engels similarly noted that the demonstrations for the eight-hour day remained mired in its 'trade-union stage', when it was necessary for unions and workers to move beyond 'high wages and short hours' and to develop a more 'mixed' program for the American movement.[66] He also mocked the religious piety that so penetrated American culture as well as the sectarian thinking in its political culture: 'it will be years before anything can be done to inhibit sectarianism in America'.[67] The influence of Ferdinand Lassalle, a rival German socialist, and the sway of Karl Heinzen, a transplanted radical democrat, he dismissed as vestigial sectarianism that would soon dissipate.[68] Engels further worried about the political divide between native and immigrant workers as well as the 'theoretical ignorance' of 'all young nations' but waved aside these problems as transitory, stressing instead positive developments. He thus characterized the 'entry of the indigenous working masses into the movement' as one of the 'great events of 1886', for it signalled a unifying process that might bring American labour into the fold of scientific socialism. For this reason, he didn't exempt American praxis from broader theoretical axioms and therefore assigned European workers the role of a patient educator. The 'Germans over there', he advised Sorge, 'will be a step or two ahead of the latter' and thereby constitute the 'nucleus' who 'retain a theoretical grasp of the nature and progress of the movement'. Using abstract metaphors in place of specific facts and trends, Engels averred that assimilated German emigrants 'will keep the process of fermentation going and, eventually, rise to the top again'.[69]

With these reservations, and on the basis of his trip to America in 1888, Engels gradually conceded that American conditions did not align entirely with his analytical forecasts. Although America had 'never known feudalism and has from the outset grown up upon a bourgeois basis', he nonetheless acknowledged that other old-world mentalities and practices did in fact affect American society. Such cultural legacies included common law, religious sectarianism and an Anglo-Saxon pragmatism that held theory in contempt. The widely embraced mindset of expediency and practicality, noted Engels, prevented 'the people to recognize clearly their own social interests'. Regrettably, he observed, American workers were still trapped within 'a wholly bourgeois level of thinking'.[70] 'If America's energy and vitality were backed by Europe's theoretical clarity', wrote Engels in 1883, 'you would get everything fixed up within ten years. But that is, after all, an historical impossibility.'[71] Engels nonetheless remained optimistic through the 1880s and believed that such ideological glitches could be solved. The lack of theoretical knowledge was, he reasoned, a phenomenon of all young cultures. 'True, the Anglo-Americans want to do things their *own* way with a total disregard for reason and science', he noted in 1886, 'nor could one expect anything else, yet they are drawing closer and will end up coming all the way'.[72] A year later, he endorsed the same viewpoint: 'I am absolutely convinced that things are now going ahead over there, and perhaps more rapidly than here, despite the fact that, for the time being, the Americans will have to learn exclusively from practice, and relatively little from theory.'[73] Consequently, he proffered the advice to America's Socialist Labour Party that 'there is no better way to theoretical clearness of comprehension than to learn by one's own mistakes – *durch Schaden klug werden*'.[74] In that same spirit, he added: 'our theory is a theory of evolution, not a dogma to be learnt by heart and to be repeated mechanically. The less it is drummed into the Americans from outside and the more thoroughly they test it – with Germans' assistance – by personal experience, the more deeply will it penetrate their flesh and blood.'[75]

Engels, then, sought to splice together American pragmatism and European socialist theory, but his prescriptive glosses didn't always ring persuasive. While supporting the Socialist Labour Party as the best answer for workers, he recognized that it consisted exclusively of German immigrants. 'If it came from a foreign stock', he asserted, 'it came, at the same time, armed with the experience earned during long years of class-struggle in Europe, and with an insight into the general conditions of working-class emancipation, far superior to that hitherto gained by American workingmen'. It's fortunate for the American workers, he continued, 'who are thus enabled to appropriate, and to take advantage of, the intellectual and moral fruits of the forty years' struggle of their European classmates, and thus to hasten on the time of their own victory'.[76] But that nostrum overlooked the persistent attitude of American workers who didn't wish to be schooled on labour politics. Addressing workers' bourgeois attitudes, Engels argued, 'it is precisely his opposition to a mother country still garbed in feudalism that leads the American working man to suppose the traditional bourgeois economic system he has inherited to be by its nature something immutably superior and progressive, a *non plus ultra*'.[77] Despite poverty and immiseration – 40 per cent of American workers in the 1880s lived in poverty[78] – American workers remained unreceptive to theories of socialism. Engels turned to life-cycle analogies to compare American infancy and youth with European maturity, praising the former as preeminent 'when it comes to practice and still in swaddling clothes as regards theory'[79] or that America is a ' "youthful" country which still can't quite extricate itself from the hobbledehoy stage'.[80] With metaphors of immaturity, Engels justified the dilatory tempo of American radicalization without addressing whether his theoretical premises warranted equal scrutiny.

Four reasons stand out for American workers' reluctance towards a more strident form of political socialism. First and foremost, the analytical fields of political and economic struggle remained discrete arenas of action, which frustrated European socialists. Although factory workers, as well as craftsmen and construction workers, exhibited a pronounced militancy in the 1860s that allowed them to assert their interests through strikes, they perceived their employer as the opponent – and not the state. Whereas European workers regarded state governments and their police forces as long-established adversaries, categorizing them as agents of the bourgeoisie, American workers fundamentally separated political and economic spheres. The impressive strike waves between 1876 and 1900 remained mostly unpolitical – despite the alarmist images of political anarchy from the sensational press. For the overwhelming majority of strikers, the economic stoppages were about a living wage, unjustified dismissals and better work conditions. Approximately 60 per cent of all strikes from this period turned on wages, and a third of them were carried out without a union.[81] Despite organizational deficiencies, many strikes were successful, because their communities – even bourgeois social strata – stood behind them. Manufacturing and mining communities closed ranks against such 'big bosses' as Jay Gould or Andrew Carnegie. Such local support from the bourgeoisie differed considerably from that in Germany or France.[82] In this respect, the assumption that strikes ought to proceed beyond bread-and-butter issues – the so-called trade-union mentality – towards the radical agenda of political strikes never took firm root. For a new era of strikes with political ends, Engels hoped in vain.

Another explanation lies partially in America's republican political culture and the civic rights that it accorded to workers. The myth and reality of the vote loomed large in the American political imagination. In America's decentralized, federated political system, unpropertied workers possessed the franchise and consequently wielded influence in municipal, local, county and state elections. Unions and workers' associations developed political networks in cities and towns – the so-called political machines – and were capable of placing their candidates up for election as mayors, city councillors, sheriffs, police chiefs and local judges. At the national level, diverse social groups and classes formed the Democratic and Republican parties, complex umbrella organizations that mobilized voters into two large camps for national and state elections, thereby undercutting specific labour-oriented issues. To be sure, anarchists, syndicalists, socialists and left-wing populists exerted some influence on the workers' movement, but their long-term impact was minimal.[83] Rather than look to radical political change or even revolution, workers persistently regarded the greed of big businesses as a problem that democracy could resolve, thus viewing the US constitution more as a solution, as a bulwark of political and legal protection, than as a problem. Neither the rudimentary state bureaucracies nor their police forces (notwithstanding particular excesses and riots) emerged as self-evident opponents of organized labour. In this regard, Marx and Engels misjudged the depth and staying power of democratic republicanism. Just as many European socialist movements had moved beyond political republicanism after 1848, so too did Engels and Marx assume that America's infatuation with bourgeois civic culture would eventually erode when confronted with the material inequities of industrialization.

A third factor was the attending question of class consciousness. The clear delineations of class, caste and social privilege that existed in European society did not crystallize in nineteenth-century America. The porous, shifting identity between employee and employer constituted a central element of the century's social fluidity. In 1867, Edwin L. Godwin, the well-known editor of the *Nation*, underscored the blurred distinction between worker and capitalist:

> The social line between the labourer and the capitalist is here very faintly drawn. Most successful employers of labour have begun by being labourers themselves; most labourers hope, and may reasonably hope, to become employers. Moreover, there are ... few barriers of habits, manners, or tradition between the artisan and those for whom he works, so that he does not consider himself the member of an 'order'. ... Strikes, therefore, are in the United States more a matter of business, and less a matter of sentiment, than in Europe.[84]

The mentality of economic independence struck deep roots in the 'producer ideology' of the early republic, when farmers, craftsmen and other producers considered themselves the backbone of the nation. Since the American Revolution, Whig ideology celebrated the 'yeoman producer' as the future of a prosperous America. These modest, preindustrial workers were touted as the essential bearers of the republic's democratic values and constituted the driving force that sustained the inviolable ideal of individual freedom. This form of rights-bearing citizenship saw no contradiction in linking property and equality,[85] a political attitude that persisted well into the twentieth century, if not into the present.

Finally, the long-enduring racist legacy of slavery constituted another essential difference. Prior to the Civil War in the Confederate states, as well as those in the north, white workers assumed greater commonality with employers than with black workers. After the Civil War, the attempt of workers' organizations to absorb and integrate black workers failed because of these cultural and economic legacies. Many craft associations used the pretext of African American workers as unskilled – because they lacked the formal credentials of an apprenticeship – to refuse them membership.

White craftsmen also tenaciously clung to the belief that black union members would bring down wages. Such prejudice was all the more strengthened with the basic division of workers' organizations. In the 1870s and 1880s, closed collective representation of skilled workers (mostly of white European origin) identified themselves as 'trade unions', thus distinguishing themselves from 'labour unions', the open associations of unskilled labourers and factory workers. In 1886, Samuel Gompers founded the American Federation of Labour (AFL), an umbrella organization that effectively represented the economic interests of craftsmen. In doing so, the AFL bracketed out both political issues and unskilled workers, thereby neutralizing the revolutionary potential of organized labour as well as segregating it. In similar fashion, ethnic and religious identities cut across the grain of class consciousness and undermined overarching solidarity among workers. Divisions among European workers – for example Catholic/Protestant and northern/ southern – strengthened fissures in working-class culture; in the western territories, white settlers only saw Mexican and Chinese labourers as constituencies to exclude and exploit.[86] Differences stood out as much as any claim to unity. The intersection of race and class mattered.

Marx and Engels were certainly not oblivious to the segmentation and division of the American workers' movement and engaged the issue with Sorge in the 1870s. With the reconstitution of the 'International Workingmen's Association', or the First International (1865–76), they regarded the recruitment of skilled workers from the northern states as strategically more essential than introducing a broad reform program of American socialists, which primarily promoted the equality of rights for women and African Americans. Convinced of the accuracy and correctness of their 'scientific socialism', Marx and Sorge rejected the ideals of equality that American radicals espoused, even though many elements of Marx's developmental theories accommodated the radicals' platform. Marx and Engels's bruising confrontation with republicanism in the 1840s in Germany and in Europe most likely predisposed them to look askance on the progressive dimensions of American radicalism. At the IWA's conference at the Hague in 1872, the organization's leadership not only excluded Bakunin's anarchists but also distanced itself from 'Section 12', the so-called Yankee International. In this way, Sorge, as general secretary of the First International, reinforced the polarizing divisions of the workers' movement.[87] After Marx's death in 1883, Engels kept to this fateful course of action, a decision that squandered political opportunities.

A few months before his death in 1895, Engels sought to comfort Friedrich Sorge, his important emissary in New Jersey, about socialism's decline in the United States. By wrapping the problem in cultural paradox and emphasizing cultural lags in fashion design, Engels strained to make a persuasive argument:

> I have for some time been aware of the temporary decline of the movement in America and it is not the German socialists who will stem it. Though America is the youngest it is also the oldest country in the world. In the same way as you have, over there, the most antiquated furniture designs alongside your own vernacular ones or, in Boston, cabs such as I last saw in London in 1838 and, in the mountains,

seventeenth-century stage coaches, alongside Pullman cars, so too you continue to sport all the old mental trappings which Europe has already discarded. Everything outmoded here may persist in America for another generation or two.

He also attributed political stagnancy yet again to America's exceptional size and accelerated development, themes that he and Marx had reiterated frequently since the 1840s:

It may also be attributed to the dual nature of America's development, still engaged as it is on the one hand in the primary task of reclaiming the vast area of untamed country, while being already compelled on the other to compete for first place in industrial production. Hence the ups and downs of the movement, according to which point of view takes precedence in the average person's mind – that of the urban working man or that of the peasant engaged in reclamation. In a couple of years' time, all this will change and then we shall witness a great step forward.

Even less convincing was his recourse to racial attributes:

The evolution of the Anglo-Saxon race with its ancient Teutonic freedom happens to be quite exceptionally slow, pursuing as it does a zig-zag course (small zig-zags in England, colossal ones on your side of the Atlantic) and tacking against the wind, but making headway nonetheless.[88]

In other letters, he also drew on general nostrums of scientific socialism to temporize about American peculiarities: 'It is the revolutionising of all time-honoured conditions by the *growth* of industry which likewise revolutionises men's minds.'[89] Engels furthermore resorted to indefinite moments in the future when socialism would avenge itself: '*When* the time comes over there, things will move with tremendous speed and dynamism, but that may not be for some while yet. Miracles never happen.'[90]

With these evasive formulations, laced with subjective impressions and cultural-historical digressions, Engels tacitly acknowledged the failure to provide a clear, substantive prognosis. Such letters suggest that, by the end of his life, he had run into a theoretical cul-de-sac. A persistent belief in an imminent and drastic collapse in capitalist production and in a class consciousness born of European experience did not accord with the American labour movement. Despite Engel's prodigious talents for analysing and schematizing empirical data, and despite his predilection for pragmatic political action, a young country had evaded his analytical grasp.

CHAPTER 7
THE TRANSFORMATION OF THE WORLD: FRIEDRICH ENGELS AND THE DEVELOPMENT OF PRODUCTIVE FORCES IN THE SECOND HALF OF THE NINETEENTH CENTURY

Werner Plumpe

The dawn of modernity

The nineteenth century was the century of the 'transformation of the world'.[1] This transformation was at once both comprehensive and global, a process at the end of which hardly a stone was left unturned in the centres of change. At its core were economic changes: starting in Great Britain, modern production methods conquered the world, changing it by transforming the conditions of production as well as increasing the abundance of products and services on a previously unimaginable scale. The increase in agricultural and industrial productivity was the cause and condition not only of population growth but also of extensive migration processes; it was only through these transformations that urban industrial centres of a kind previously unknown became possible. These increases in productivity were linked to technological innovations that radically changed the face of the world, making it smaller, more manageable and more intelligible. Where a sea voyage from Amsterdam to Southeast Asia in the seventeenth century took two years, Jules Verne's *Around the World in Eighty Days* in 1873 was a bestseller that struck its readers as anything but far-fetched.[2] And telegraph cables that had been connecting different parts of the world since the 1850s accelerated communication to a previously unimaginable extent. Not only were stock prices, along with other market news, now available globally at short notice, increasing the complexity of economic business networks many times over, but news in general could now spread almost in real time, making actual contemporaneity possible – something that had been out of the question before.[3] This was not merely a matter of a 'transforming the world'; it was nothing less than, to quote the title of the book by Christopher Bayly, *The Birth of the Modern World*.[4]

That their world was undergoing a fundamental upheaval was not only clear to contemporaries; they also sensed that this upheaval was primarily related to modern machines and their economic application. Technological progress assumed a central position; the future of mankind seemed to hang on its potential, at least in its material conditions of existence, which now no longer appeared God-given, but were obviously alterable – and were indeed being altered and by no means only for the upper classes, who had long lived in abundance. The change was much more drastic:

It is by no means the rich alone, but all classes, who derive benefit from these industries [i.e. the modern economy, WP]. Things which in former days hardly anyone could afford are now cheap and abundant, and even the lowest classes are much better off in point of comfort. In the Middle Ages, a King of England once borrowed a pair of silk stockings from one of his lords, so that he might wear them in giving an audience to the French ambassador. ... To-day every shopman has them. Fifty years ago ladies wore the kind of calico gowns which servants wear now. If mechanical science continues to progress at the same rate for any length of time, it may end by saving human labour almost entirely, just as horses are even now being largely superseded by machines. For it is possible to conceive that intellectual culture might in some degree become general in the human race; and this would be impossible as long as bodily labour was incumbent on any great part of it.[5]

This observation by Schopenhauer was made only a short time after the publication of the *Communist Manifesto* by Karl Marx and Friedrich Engels,[6] a document which in fact expressed very similar sentiments. The modern economy was the catalyst of a comprehensive process of change with ultimately liberating prospects; an end to material misery and the suffering associated with hard physical labour suddenly seemed not only possible but also probable, the 'realm of freedom' more than an unfounded hope or even illusion. In contrast to Arthur Schopenhauer and many other contemporary observers, however, who were fascinated above all by the abundance of goods and the changing bourgeois consumer habits of the time,[7] not only Marx and Engels but also other attentive contemporaries saw a peculiar contrast between the increasing opportunities for consumption and the misery of the working classes, whose labour made this abundance possible.[8] Far from possessing a fixed conception of modern society and its social structures, many observers were certain that they were witnessing not simply something new but the emergence of hitherto unimagined social extremes that seemed inextricably linked to the use of modern technology.[9] And this new social issue, rooted in the opposition of capital and labour, seemed infused with an incalculable dynamic and, from its very inception, with acute political relevance.[10]

The new contrast between increasing wealth and exploding poverty appeared – not only to the representatives of the emerging labour movement – to constitute a great deal more than a mere phenomenon of the times; it was widely perceived as *the* structural characteristic of the new economic order that was gradually conquering the world from Great Britain outwards. For many observers, then, the poverty crisis of the 1830s and 1840s, which gripped the whole of Europe, was not just an exceptional cyclical event caused by the inclemency of the weather of a type well known from the past; it was perceived as the hallmark par excellence of the new economy, which in this respect could not be reformed but had to be called into question altogether if mass poverty was ever to be overcome. Hunger and misery were particularly visible in the explosively developing industrial housing quarters, which themselves became a symbol of the modern economy. Engels' *Condition of the Working Class in England*, with its bleak descriptions of life in the slums of Irish migrant workers in Manchester,[11] was by no means the only chronicle of scandal of the time. Horror reports on the living conditions in the sometimes extreme density of the cities of the 1840s became virtually a new literary genre, perfectly served by a Charles Dickens[12] or a Eugène Sue.[13] Such works primarily reached a bourgeois reading public which, in turn, was accustomed to seeing social problems represented in literary form as the result of the moral depravity of affluent factory owners.[14] Engels himself, under the pseudonym Friedrich Oswald, had unceremoniously described in his *Letters from Wuppertal* how the pietistic entrepreneurs of Elberfeld had no qualms about letting factory children perish, as long as homage was paid to their bigoted pietism.[15]

Ultimately, in purely phenomenal terms, it seemed irrefutable that the modern economy was not only associated with widespread pauperization; it produced it of its very nature. The sheer headcount of the poor was exploding.[16] A public welfare that could have mastered mass misery did not exist, because the propertied citizens did not want to pay for it, and the few strictly bourgeois attempts at reform seemed pathetic, even mendacious, since they did so little to change the desperate situation of the lower classes.[17] No amount of talk had improved the lot of the Silesian weavers or prevented the mass mortality of the Irish Famine – the result of poor harvests and widespread plant disease. Only emigration seemed to bring relief, but the living conditions of the Irish workers who emigrated to England only worsened. In the 1840s, overseas migration to America alone offered hope and became proof of a sort that, without thorough social reform, the fate of the poor and the working classes of Europe was inescapable. For this reason, perhaps, more than anything else, the prospect of fundamental political upheaval gained increasing currency – the vision of a cataclysm that would finally change the indifference of the upper classes to the lot of the poor or indeed challenge their very existence as a class. In the mid-1840s, in the face of political reaction and mass misery, when economic and climatic conditions were also deteriorating, revolutionary upheaval seemed inevitable and imminent.[18]

Pauperism and the founding era

In the eyes of its protagonists, however, the 1848 Revolution proved a thorough miscarriage; virtually nothing of its political and social goals was achieved. Revolutionary hopes and illusions were shattered by the inertia of an inherited mindset, but above all because they failed to appeal to large sections of the population, for whom active support for the Revolution was clearly out of the question. There was another reason, however, why revolutionary hopes were dashed so quickly. Shortly after the Revolution, an economic upswing began that was to last, albeit with interruptions, for the next twenty years and has gone down in history as the *Gründerzeit* or Founding Era of modern Germany.[19] This industrial boom, additionally fuelled by extensive gold discoveries in Australia and California, dampened expectations that a renewed economic crisis would initiate a second revolutionary environment, a change in circumstances which Friedrich Engels soon suspected: 'One must hope the Australian gold business won't interfere with the trade crisis. At any rate it has momentarily created a new, largely fictitious market,' Engels wrote to Marx in September 1851.[20] And the first world economic crisis of 1857, which originated in the United States, also proved disappointing; it brought at best a brief interruption in a long-lasting boom[21] in which modern industry, extending beyond textiles, became a mass phenomenon. Indeed, with the emergence of chemical and electrotechnical enterprises and the global implementation of new transportation technologies – railways and steamships – a completely new economic dimension became visible. A kind of second Industrial Revolution began to emerge, in which textiles, the leading sector in the first phase of industrialization, waned in importance and industrial progress was increasingly driven by the transformation of scientific discoveries into mass production.[22] As a result, those branches of industry that supplied energy and materials – above all, mining and iron and steel smelting – continued to gain in importance, alongside which, the emergence of new, large industrial districts boosted the construction industry, which provided employment for ever more people. Headlines were now dominated by new industries, electrotechnology, chemicals, mechanical engineering and the manufacture of precision mechanical and optical instruments. Entirely new names appeared: paint manufacturers like BASF and Bayer, suppliers of electricity and electrically powered equipment like Siemens and (later) AEG, machine builders like Borsig and the instrument maker Carl Zeiss in Jena, which rose like a phoenix from the ashes.[23]

With this new industrial dimension, pauperism also gradually disappeared; pre- and early industrial mass poverty slowly came to an end with continuing emigration and, above all, with the rapid growth of industrial jobs. Not that the lot of the now massed industrial workforce was idyllic,[24] but a slow improvement in the situation did set in, counteracted by continued precarious living conditions in the sprawling industrial centres. Yet, here too, a process of urban renewal – indeed of municipal welfare – began, growing from small beginnings but gradually becoming more extensive.[25] And the mere physical growth of the towns gradually yielded to a process of full urbanization, in which the emergence and consolidation of civic living conditions were accompanied by a more or less comprehensive structure of communal services. Poor relief also underwent a fundamental transformation.[26] The modern city gradually lost its character as a combination of premodern centre and proletarian slum, replaced by an urban (or even metropolitan) world that quickly became attractive in its own right.[27]

Thus, within a few years, capitalism fundamentally changed its face, a fact that did not escape the majority of contemporaries. The former revolutionary mood evaporated and made way for a more inclusive realism that did not necessarily betray old democratic, liberal or occasionally even socialist ideals, but which now pursued them in acceptance of given social conditions, which were manifestly more fluid than they had appeared in Germany's *Vormärz* (pre-'48) poverty crisis. Bourgeois *realpolitik* took the place of older revolutionary dreams,[28] and in combination with the rapidly growing technological possibilities for action, a kind of 'pragmatic social eudaemonism' (Hermann Lübbe[29]) gradually established itself in Germany, finding perhaps its clearest expression in Bismarck's social policy and, behind it, in the 'professorial socialism' that advocated what might be called a socially contained capitalism.[30] Although this did little to change the misery of the proletariat in the eyes of the nascent labour movement, it was a mistake to underestimate the level of change in the economy and the social conditions associated with it.

Engels, nevertheless, clung tenaciously to his views, dating back to 1848. In 1872, he emphasized with regard to the tenets of the *Communist Manifesto*: 'However much the state of things may have altered during the last twenty-five years, the general principles laid down in this *Manifesto* are, on the whole, as correct today as ever.'[31] And when, in the mid-1880s, he summed up the past forty years of economic development in England – a period he could survey first-hand – he came to a devastating judgement: although the situation had improved for some groups of workers, 'as to the great mass of the working people, the state of misery and insecurity in which they live now is as low as ever, if not lower'.[32] It was not until after the turn of the century, with the so-called revisionist controversy of the first decades of the twentieth century, that German social democracy, which had always listened to Engels, could no longer escape the challenge of visible change – a challenge Engels had either overlooked or had considered so insignificant that it did not alter his programmatic understanding of the capitalist world. In this respect, he remained a child of the first half of the nineteenth century, often aggressively rejecting any new impressions. For Engels, the shift to *realpolitik* which he had directly witnessed, for example, in German émigré circles of the 1850s–60s, was not a sign of changing conditions, but of impercipience and weakness of character. He could not accept that capitalism was capable of major change, indeed that the productive forces, in particular the working classes *he* had helped to a breakthrough, no longer faced insurmountable barriers to their advancement.

A rebellious nature

What, though, were the roots of this peculiar pessimism, and what did it imply? It is striking how little Engels was personally willing to adapt or develop his own positions as times changed. He actually ascribed an inherent dynamics, amounting almost to a natural law, to what he was later – together with Marx – to call 'the development of the productive forces'. Nor did he regard the obvious social problems associated with their employment to be a consequence of the new technologies, that they could have destructive effects on old industrial practices he accepted as the price of progress, even though the demise of the old world of work as a consequence of the new industrial methods was perfectly clear to him. It was not technology as such, he reasoned, that was responsible for the social misery of the workforce; it was the social mode of its use that had to be changed, and that also meant taking decisive action against the ruling *juste milieu* of the factory owners and their allies, whose addiction to enrichment was both an expression of modern relations of production and of their inherent moral depravity. If the productive forces did not automatically become a blessing for mankind, if they were ever prevented from further development, it was due to these hindrances.

Engels, then, was not pessimistic about the possibilities of future technological development; he simply did not trust prevailing social conditions. And since he justified his distrust doubly, namely both systematically and morally, he saw hardly any chance of achieving change. Under capitalism, he was firmly convinced, technology had reached a dead end. Over the decades he spent in England, he consistently identified the *bourgeoisie* with the dominant group of 'liberal' Manchester-style cotton industrialists of his early years in that city, nor did he see the dire situation of Manchester's workforce in the mid-1840s as an exceptional situation. On the contrary, this was what a world organized on capitalist principles – the moral principles of the cotton magnates – looked like. Behind this stood a deeper notion, which had much to do with Engels' pietistic origins, a conviction that the world was a sinful place, but one that, with correct behaviour, was capable of improvement.

However, because he did not consider the moral indignation inherent in his own religious heritage, with its manifest limits, sufficient to find his way in the world, Engels had sought early further, more convincing explanations of the world and its sinfulness. As the oldest son of a family of factory owners, he was prepared from the beginning for a career in his parents' textile business, although as a schoolboy he displayed strong literary inclinations, which he maintained and cultivated during his mercantile apprenticeship and his subsequent military service as a one-year volunteer in the Prussian army. Throughout his life, he felt the abandonment of his high school education without a school-leaving diploma, and the associated renunciation of university studies, as a great loss, which he tried to compensate with intensive reading, while knowing at the same time that this could hardly succeed on its own. The lack of formal academic training was all the more painful for a young man who, since the late 1830s, had been searching for an alternative to the increasingly unacceptable pietistic world of the Wupper Valley in which he had grown up and whose religious principles he had at first naively adopted. Influenced by his time and a fascination with the literary texts of the *Young Germany* movement, Engels could not simply choose an alternative course at random: his guides must be both world-changing and action-determining, both well founded and – as far as literature was concerned – stylistically demanding. Against this background he began almost manically to devour the influential writings of his day, turning to David Strauss, Schleiermacher and finally Hegel. This led him, during his military service in Berlin in the early 1840s, to link up with the Berlin Young Hegelians.[33] While he had already become aware of his own intellectual inadequacy during his Bremen years as a trainee merchant in foreign trade, in the Berlin academic circles into whose debates on Schelling's philosophy and allied matters he plunged early and uninhibitedly, his dilettantism was all the more conspicuous.

Despite his rebellious nature – which, as his father had already noticed in the pubescent child, would not let him avoid a fight – the knowledge of his own inadequacies and the limits of his autodidactic education finally put a (brief) halt to the flow of polemics from Engels' pen. In July 1842 he informed Arnold Ruge, who published the *Hallische Jahrbücher für deutsche Wissenschaft und Kunst* (The Halle Yearbook of German Science and Art), the most important Young Hegelian organ, that he had decided 'to abandon all literary work for a while in order to devote more time to studying. The reasons for this are fairly plain. I am young and self-taught in philosophy'. He saw his limitations clearly; he had learned enough to form a firm opinion, 'but not enough to be able to work for it with success and in the proper way. All the greater demands will be made on me because I am a "travelling agent" in philosophy and have not earned the right to philosophise by getting a doctor's degree.' When he went back to the public, he said, he wanted to meet these demands. Now, shortly before the end of his military service, and the associated return to Wuppertal and the start of commercial activity in his parents' company, Engels, in his letter to Ruge, took stock:

> Regarded subjectively, my literary activities have so far been mere experiments from the outcome of which I was to be able to learn whether my natural capacities were such as to enable me to work fruitfully and effectively for progress and to participate actively in the movement of the century. I can be satisfied with the results and now regard it as my duty to acquire by study, which I now continue with redoubled zest, also more and more of that which one is not born with.[34]

The aversion to everything autodidactic, to which, however, he had no alternative, had in this respect a paradoxical trait which marked Engels in the years to come – indeed, it may always have provided him with a certain self-distrust even in his later work, for he remained to the last the dilettante who lacked strictly professional expertise. 'Autodidacticism is ... sheer foolishness', he declared programmatically to Joseph Weydemeyer in the early 1850s: only if one pursued 'things' systematically would one arrive at something 'worthwhile'.[35] It is significant that Engels broke his silence only after Moses Hess had opened the door to Communism for him and after his English experiences – he had continued his training in foreign trade in Manchester – had introduced a completely new vista, namely that of the social question against the background of a mounting economic crisis. Now, at last, the will to shape politics could be combined with expertise drawn from immediate experience, a combination that decisively informed Engels' *The Condition of the Working Class in England*.[36] Here, we find a polemic sharpened to the point of irreconcilability, a tone that took up almost verbatim the *Letters from Wuppertal* which, still under a pseudonym and strongly influenced by religious ideas of justice, he had published years earlier: 'It is utterly indifferent to the English bourgeois whether his working-men starve or not, if only he makes money.'[37] Engels' radicalism was eloquently expressed in the general judgement: 'I have never seen a class so deeply demoralised, so incurably debased by selfishness, so corroded within, so incapable of progress, as the English bourgeoisie.'[38]

Engels, however, must also have been aware that this Krummacherian sermonizing[39] would not be sufficient to construct a world that was both scientifically possible and politically attainable. For this, fundamental programmatic work was needed, which Engels, a man of political action, only trusted himself to accomplish in a very limited way. Here, however, his activity as a successful merchant industrialist – an activity he later repeatedly disparaged – offered a possible solution. For the role – or rather all-consuming task – of providing a compelling scientific foundation for his political programme had, from their very first encounters, been assigned by Engels to Karl Marx, a man who appeared intellectually superior to him and who in the field of theory was by no means a dilettante. On the contrary, as a philosopher endowed with impressive acuity as well as a doctorate, he possessed all the prerequisites for presenting his own (and Engels') position in convincing theoretical terms. Marx, however, for all his astuteness, was remarkably unfit for life. He could not make ends meet without Engels' help, and Engels was all the more willing to give this help – made possible by his economic success in Manchester – the more hope Marx inspired in him of substantiating the Communism they jointly espoused. The tug of war over Marx's economic texts, in which Engels pushed, Marx dithered, but at the same time, in order not to offend his patron, continually made new promises, is an educational drama in its own right.[40]

Social protest and communist principles

But what was it that Marx was to substantiate? Engels' communist convictions after the discussions with Moses Hess had remained rather vague, and even the disputes in the first communist associations, specifically in the *League of the Just*, did not suggest any clear programme. Was it to be about moral renewal, was work to be redistributed and better organized, what was the role of private property and economic competition, what might an economically just world look like and in what way could it be achieved? The experiences Engels had gathered from his own observations in England and through conversations with trade unionists, Chartists and workers were anything but clear on this, but in any case, no fundamental opposition to the existing social system could be programmatically derived from them. For the most part, the English workers' representatives wanted to have a say in shaping things; they sought political participation as a means of improving the material situation of the workers. There was little sign of radical rejection of the existing social system, although the social conditions, especially in London and in the dense industrial districts of the Midlands and Northern England, were appalling; above all, the situation of the Irish migrant workers, with whom Friedrich Engels had personal contact, defied description. But the English working class, Engels believed from his observations, was too little educated in matters of theory to be able to grasp its own situation in anything more than a pragmatic way; his hopes lay in German philosophy, which, in the form of left-wing Hegelianism, was in a position to provide both a social diagnosis and a historical blueprint.[41]

And while he admired the English workers' movement for its advanced political character, Engels nevertheless remained convinced that only a fundamental philosophical programme could truly guide the struggle for the improvement of the workers' situation, indeed make possible the design of an entirely different society.[42] The direction in which this programme was to unfold was already clear to him at an early stage, based on the social situation in England, which he saw as characterized by a fundamental contradiction:

> For although industry makes a country rich, it also creates a class of unpropertied, absolutely poor people, a class which lives from hand to mouth, which multiplies rapidly, and which cannot afterwards be abolished, because it can never acquire stable possession of property. And a third, almost a half, of all English people belong to this class.[43]

And yet this class, he had previously conceded, was actually not doing so badly compared to their fellows on the Continent:

> When the English worker is employed, he is satisfied. And he can well be satisfied, at any rate the textile worker, if he compares his lot with the fate of his comrades in Germany and France. The worker there earns just enough to allow him to live on bread and potatoes; he is lucky if he can buy meat once a week. Here he eats beef every day and gets a more nourishing joint for his money than the richest man in Germany. He drinks tea twice a day and still has enough money left over to be able to drink a glass of porter at midday and brandy and water in the evening. This is how most of the Manchester workers live who work a twelve-hour day.[44]

For Engels, then, the means of achieving an adequate living clearly existed under the technological conditions of the time, except that the conditions were anything but stable. And so, after summing up the favourable situation, he asked: 'But how long will it last? The slightest fluctuation in trade leaves thousands of workers destitute; their modest savings are soon used up and then they are in danger of starving to death.' Moreover, 'a crisis of this kind', he wrote in the late autumn of 1842, 'is bound to occur again in a few years' time. The same increased production which is now giving work to "paupers" and is counting on the Chinese market is bound to create a huge mass of commodities and a slump in sales, which will again result in general destitution among the workers.'[45] Only in good times could the working class achieve a certain security; basically, however, capitalism left them little chance:

> What all this boils down to is that England with her industry has burdened herself not only with a large class of the unpropertied, but among these always a considerable class of paupers which she cannot get rid of. These people have to rough it on their own; the state abandons them, even pushes them away. Who can blame them, if the men have recourse to robbery or burglary, the women to theft and prostitution? But the state does not care whether starvation is bitter or sweet; it locks these people up in prison or sends them to penal settlements, and when it releases them it has the satisfaction of having converted people without work into people without morals.[46]

The questions Engels inevitably had to ask himself after this diagnosis provide a key to his further development. Why, if sufficient goods actually existed, did crises and poverty recur? Was it enough to rebel against this? Or was it necessary to find another kind of protest, of political movement, which would not just alleviate but also eliminate the evils of the present root and branch?

Engels made a first attempt to elucidate the misery of his day and pave a way out of it as early as 1844 with his *Outlines of a Critique of Political Economy*.[47] In this text he systematically held the social organization of the economy responsible for the crisis and immiseration of the working class. Private property, on the one hand, and competition, on the other, in no way led to balanced economic development, as claimed in the bourgeois theory of national economy, but served only the desire of the bourgeoisie for enrichment at the price of multiple crises and social catastrophes. Nor was the bourgeois addiction to enrichment, their already noted moral depravity, something that could be changed by simple appeals. The only option was radical upheaval – a course whose theoretical justification therefore had the highest priority.

Marx, who eagerly took up Engels' *Outlines*, was evidently of one mind with him on this point; he willingly took on the task of elaborating the economic programme of Communism and as early as 1844 had signed a contract with the Darmstadt publisher Leske for the preparation of a comprehensive work on the political economy of those times. However, because Marx initially got no further than proclamations and promises, nothing came of the programmatic writing Engels had hoped for,[48] although the worsening economic situation in Europe in the second half of the 1840s made its appearance all the more urgent. Finally, events themselves pushed the theoretical work into the background. And although at the turn of 1847–8 Marx and Engels presented – in the *Communist Manifesto* – an initial draft programme for a future Communist Party in which the assumptions of their historical theory were clearly formulated, this was still a far cry from a differentiated view of the capitalist economy.

Technological progress and revolutionary expectations

The revolution of 1848 and its aftermath put economic studies on the back-burner until the early 1850s. Engels himself, who had been working as an industrial merchant in Manchester since the beginning of the 1850s, confined himself in the coming years almost exclusively to shorter journalistic works, mostly of a military nature, while Marx (in London exile) took a long time to resume and advance his economic studies. Thus, for the time being, the *Manifesto*, although it soon vanished into obscurity, was the only relevant text on the significance of productive forces for contemporary social development. In it Marx – to whose pen, Engels insisted, the work was primarily indebted – had clarified Engels' earlier conception of history as a twofold process: on the one hand, a movement of economic change driven by the progress of productive forces and, on the other, a social and political struggle over the organization of that change. At issue, then, was a history of class struggle whose structure and intensity were closely connected with the respective state of the productive forces. However, since industrial production, emerging out of the will and interests of capital, was not a harmless event, but an expression of the dominance of private property and its exploitative interests, the contradiction of productive forces and relations of production could not be reformed or defused by mere reorganization but would ineluctably pursue its revolutionary sublation (*Aufhebung*) in the Hegelian sense – a step that would fall as a task to the proletariat, which was both the product of private capital and its mortal enemy.[49]

Although in literary terms both eloquently and succinctly described, the actual development of the productive forces, which would later become the pivot of Marx and Engels' entire conception of economic development, remained peculiarly vague. The process seemed to occur almost as a law of nature. Marx's later summary would become canonical:

> In the social production of their existence, men inevitably enter into definite relations, which are independent of their will, namely relations of production appropriate to a given stage in the development of their material forces of production. ... At a certain stage of development, the material productive forces of society come into conflict with the existing relations of production or – this merely expresses the same thing in legal terms – with the property relations within the framework of which they have operated hitherto. From forms of development of the productive forces these relations turn into their fetters. Then begins an era of social revolution.[50]

The moment of this critical clash between the relations of production and productive forces seemed to Marx and Engels to have arrived already in the 1840s, but in its outcome the 1848 Revolution proved a singular disappointment. Even in light of the economic boom of the *Gründerzeit*, however, the two exiles refused to give up their idea that the prevailing opposition between productive forces and relations of production meant the time was ripe for fundamental change. Throughout the first half of the 1850s, they continued to hope that one of the notorious crises of the capitalist economy would result in a social revolution, but each time they were quickly disillusioned. In Marx's introduction to the *Critique of Political Economy* (1859), there was another sentence that could in this context have attracted attention: 'No social formation is ever destroyed before all the productive forces for which it is sufficient have been developed, and new superior relations of production never replace older ones before the material conditions for their existence have matured within the framework of the old society.'[51] What, then, if the developing productive forces had not yet reached the limits of prevailing relations of production?

Neither Marx nor Engels wanted to give space to this obvious thought. They interpreted the social struggles of their time within the paradigm of revolutionary crises and accordingly saw in the Paris Commune of early 1871 a first realization of Communist structures, a clear sign of the possibility of overcoming capitalist relations. Given the burgeoning innovations of those years, this implied a crushing judgement on the implications of technological change within the given order and was probably the reason why the development of the productive forces was so little noted in their contemporary texts: in their world, such change could not exist. After its apotheosis in the *Communist Manifesto* (1848) as the world-transforming instrument par excellence, technological growth of the kind that immediately ensued in the *Gründerzeit* (c. 1850–71) went astonishingly unnoticed. Throughout the global economic developments of those years, which occasionally played a role in the daily journalism and correspondence of Marx and Engels, the massive underlying technological progress seems to have passed them by, for the simple reason that they saw the modern economy as having reached a dead end. Shortly before the end of his life, Engels may have suspected that this was not the case,[52] but in all his previous texts, the cotton industry, and the advances in the iron and steel economy that underpinned it, were for him the measure of all things. In terms of volume, this was not even wrong, for the textile industry at mid-century in Great Britain, the world's leading economy in that sector, encompassed about half of all industrially employed persons. Also, in terms of production and sales, the cotton industry led the field, but by the 1850s, its developmental momentum had already subsided, and newer industries were taking over its earlier pioneering function.[53] Engels, himself a scion of the textile industry, was not alone in overestimating the importance of cotton; it was a popular view then and remains so in some respects to the present day.[54] For him, however, it marked a line of technological development that could not be crossed under capitalist conditions:

> Cotton and iron are the two most important raw materials of our time. Whichever nation is the leading one in the manufacture of cotton and iron articles, that nation heads the list of manufacturing nations generally. And because and as long as this is the case with England, therefore and so long will England be the first manufacturing nation of the world.[55]

Capitalism as a dead end

This was Engels' firm conviction in the early 1880s; he had no eye for newer technological developments, although since the 1870s new industries and new technological applications had come to fruition in many areas of production, albeit not primarily in Britain. There, the textile industry had retained its dominance, and the iron and steel industry on the island also remained a dominant factor, not to mention coal mining, which was traditionally also of crucial importance. Engels obviously expected change less from technological innovation than from shifts in international competition and its increasingly searing consequences for capitalist enterprises. He attentively registered the loss of momentum in British industry. Market dynamics were clear to him, as was the fact that powerful industries were blossoming both on the continent and overseas: 'The fact cannot be longer shirked that England's industrial monopoly is fast on the wane.'[56] In the United States a new industrial region was emerging that threatened British leadership. Convinced of the limited nature of markets under capitalist auspices, Engels saw regional change as a mutually conditioning upward and downward movement; for him, industrial change was a kind of zero-sum game:

> There is no mistake about it, the present generation will see American cotton goods compete with English ones in India and China, and gradually gain ground in those two leading markets; American machinery and hardware compete with the English makes in all parts of the world, England included; and the same implacable necessity which removed Flemish manufactures to Holland, Dutch ones to England, will ere long remove the centre of the world's industry from this country to the United States. And in the restricted field which will then remain to England she will find formidable competitors in several Continental nations.[57]

For Engels, this encapsulated the systemic tendency of capitalism towards self-destruction. For while the bourgeoisie, for reasons of self-enrichment, would expand production without limit, the markets would by no means grow at the same pace. Indeed, the exploitation of the working class would hinder their expansion, and the competitive struggle within the bourgeoisie would assume ever harsher features. Eventually, Engels hoped, this process of intensification would remove from the working class all illusions about the true character of the present economic system:

> But what is to become of the 'hands' when England's immense export trade begins to shrink down every year instead of expanding? If the removal of the iron shipbuilding trade from the Thames to the Clyde was sufficient to reduce the whole East-end of London to chronic pauperism, what will the virtual removal of all the staple trades of England across the Atlantic do for England?[58]

One good thing at least could come from industrial decline, however: the bond between the English bourgeoisie and the proletariat, which had hitherto been stabilized by 'their common working of a national monopoly', would be broken: 'That monopoly once destroyed, the British working class will be compelled to take in hand its own interests, its own salvation, and to make an end of the wages system. Let us hope it will not wait until then.'[59]

It would be completely wrong, at this point, to assume that Engels was generally a technological pessimist, even if his ideas about the future were on the whole not very euphoric. Besides the cotton trade, the area where he was well versed in technology was the military, which he had studied intensively since the beginning of the 1850s. There too, after the Franco-Prussian War, he saw hardly any room for development; everything had been exhausted. Unlike Marx, who already in the last decade of his life had taken less and less note of the structural changes in capitalism, Engels continued to follow economic events in the 1880s and early 1890s. However, he perceived change primarily at the level of corporate organization and financing and was particularly interested in stock corporations and the functioning of stock exchanges, where the separation of ownership from control in large stock corporations led him to speculate about the future role of private ownership.[60] The modern technology used by such industrial giants, he was aware, had its negative sides, namely the displacement of many earlier employment opportunities, as he had long since noted in his essay on *The Condition of the Working Class*.⁶¹ But he saw this as due ultimately not to modern technology, but to the social dimension of its use, which was irremediably defined by the bourgeois desire for enrichment. In this respect, technology itself was innocent, its development not a specific phenomenon of capitalist relations.

Here, in the idea of a virtual law of nature governing the development of human productivity, we find a naïve belief in technology typical of the nineteenth century – one that was also at the heart of the social eudaemonism mentioned above, which Engels rejected only because it questioned the restrictive character of the relations of production for the development of technology. The point, for Engels, was that present-day productive forces were already pushing against the social barrier of capital utilization and that their further development depended on being able to break through that barrier. In this, he was in complete agreement with Marx, whose economic manuscripts he elaborated into further volumes of *Das Kapital* after the latter's death; anything else would have called into question the potentially revolutionary character of the present. Marx had, as we have already seen, proclaimed that 'no social formation is ever destroyed before all the productive forces for which it is sufficient have been developed'.⁶² If Engels had conceded that given conditions still afforded potential for development – an insight obvious enough on closer scrutiny of the technological changes of the age – then he would inevitably have been faced by the question whether the conditions for a revolutionary change in society had actually now been reached. But precisely here, there was hardly any room for manoeuvre.

Socialism as a way out

For Engels, the days of capitalism were numbered. Just as he thought it impossible to stabilize the capitalist order by improving the conditions of the working class, so he considered the economic contradictions of capitalism fatal. In a typically polemical manner he had settled accounts in the late 1870s with Eugen Dühring, whose influence within German social democracy had, in his view, to be countered with a clear socialist programme,⁶³ a position he summarized in 1878 in *Herrn Eugen Dührings Umwälzung der Wissenschaft* (Herr Eugen Dühring's Revolution in Science) – known both in German and in English simply as *Anti-Dühring*. Focusing on topical scientific issues, the work succinctly expressed his and Marx's key ideas. Part of it, excerpted as *Socialism Utopian and Scientific*, became a programmatic text of later Marxism⁶⁴ in which the foundational concepts of the development of productive forces are clearly summarized. From the beginning, this slim volume was designed as a propaganda pamphlet that laid down unmistakably the principles of scientific socialism. Modern socialism, Engels wrote, was 'nothing but the reflection in thought of this conflict in fact' – the conflict, namely, of productive forces and relations of production. 'The new productive forces', he asserted, 'have already outgrown the bourgeois mode of using them', and the manifest tension between these two poles must be made clear.⁶⁵ At the heart of capitalism, Engels saw the contradiction between social production and private appropriation of its produce, with social production being for him the defining characteristic of the age. 'The contradiction between socialised production and capitalistic appropriation now presents itself as *an antagonism between the organisation of production in the individual workshop and the anarchy of production in society generally*.'[66]

If production is geared to the private benefit of capital, it must, in order to enhance the efficiency of the capital employed, become ever cheaper, but the widespread deployment and increased perfection of machine labour means at the same time 'making human labour superfluous'. Hence, it comes about 'that the instruments of labour constantly tear the means of subsistence out of the hands of the labourer; that the very product of the worker is turned into an instrument for his subjugation'.[67] Yet the degradation of the working class is of little help to the capitalist, because sales of the product come to a standstill:

> Thus it comes about that over-work of some becomes the preliminary condition for the idleness of others, and that modern industry, which hunts after new consumers over the whole world, forces the consumption of the masses at home down to a starvation minimum, and in doing thus destroys its own home market.[68]

For Engels there was no way out, and he concludes: 'Accumulation of wealth at one pole is, therefore, at the same time, accumulation of misery, agony of toil, slavery, ignorance, brutality, mental degradation, at the opposite pole.'[69]

Here, Engels saw the core of the cyclical crises of capitalism, for the expansion of production continually comes up against the limits of consumption, and the resultant 'vicious circle' drives capitalism towards its inevitable end: 'The whole mechanism of the capitalist mode of production breaks down under the pressure of the productive forces, its own creations.'[70] Again following Marx's thesis of the concentration and centralization of capital, Engels already saw under current conditions an emerging tendency, given the pressure of crises and competition, towards the abolition of the 'private appropriation' of capital. Monopolization, he argued, led to the transformation of individual branches of industry 'into one gigantic joint-stock company', with the result that 'internal competition ... gives place to the internal monopoly of this one company ... and the production without any definite plan of capitalistic society capitulates to the production upon a definite plan of the invading socialistic society'.[71] Although he did not see the nationalization of monopolies and trusts as actually inaugurating socialism, Engels did see it as an important preliminary stage. In any case, the 'complete development of modern productive forces' would sweep capitalism away – that was clear by now: 'In every crisis, society is suffocated beneath the weight of its own productive forces and products, which it cannot use, and stands helpless, face to face with the absurd contradiction that the producers have nothing to consume, because consumers are wanting.'[72] Against this stood the promise that once the capitalist mode of production was overcome, the development of the productive forces would be free: 'Their deliverance from these bonds is the one precondition for an unbroken, constantly-accelerated development of the productive forces, and therewith for a practically unlimited increase of production itself.'[73]

Conclusion: Belief in technology and hope for progress

In *Anti-Dühring* – and, extracted from it, *Socialism Utopian and Scientific* – Engels had presented a clear conception of the dialectic between productive forces and relations of production, and he further substantiated this scientifically with a series of individual pieces, later published as the *Dialectic of Nature*, which demonstrate that for all his dilettantism and limitations as a specialist, he was awake to the scientific progress of his time, even if he failed to see its economic – or more precisely industrial – implications. Just as at Marx's graveside he had equated his collaborator and friend with Darwin, so socialism should be in harmony with science: Darwin recognizing the laws of natural evolution, Marx those of societal development.[74] And these laws embraced the limiting power of the relations of production vis-à-vis the productive forces, whose dynamics ultimately made a revolutionary solution not only possible but also compelling. What Engels, however, failed to recognize were the opportunities for change that still existed under prevailing conditions – a misjudgement of the internal possibilities for expansion within the capitalist order that was adopted by some later programmatic Marxist theorists, who saw the unbridled struggle for markets as the driving force of imperialism and imperialism as the final stage of capitalism.[75] Although in the Great War they assumed that they had an almost unbeatable empirical argument on their side, they were nonetheless again to be proven wrong.

The pauperization of the labour force did not, in fact, become a permanent central feature of capitalism, nor did the limited nature of markets and the limitless expansion of production prove lethal. Although cyclical crises repeatedly occurred (and have continued do so), they were not a sign of capitalism's demise but fluctuations around an upward trend, supported primarily by relatively continuous growth in productivity. Nor were the centralizing forces of the last third of the nineteenth century, as Engels assumed, signs of an inevitable path to monopolization and agglomeration; most of the large corporations of that time went under in the course of time and technological change. And capitalism did not suffer unduly from technological bottlenecks either. If Engels had looked a little beyond the British horizon, he would have observed as early as the 1880s the upsurge of entirely new branches of industry, whose centre of gravity lay on the other side of the Atlantic and on the European continent, signalling new perspectives for capitalism. Engels certainly took account of electricity,[76] but he failed to recognize the economic potential of this breakthrough, just as his brief remarks on organic chemistry show that he had no real conception, at least in pragmatic industrial terms, of its emerging potential. His notion of productive forces remained as naïve as it was rigid: naïve inasmuch as he assumed a kind of automatism – virtually a law of nature – in their unfolding; rigid because he considered the fetters of the relations of production, as he had known them since the 1840s, to be unchangeable.

Engels' reflections in this regard were certainly momentous, determining the self-image of historical state socialism, which never tired of claiming for itself the liberation of technology from the constraints of capitalist exploitation. But that self-image also failed spectacularly: at the latest since the 1960s, 'real socialism' was no longer able to keep pace technologically with the capitalist competition. Engels' conception of the development of productive forces has also been criticized, however, from a completely different point of view and one that is still influential in the popular critique of economic growth. It was Max Horkheimer, in his preliminary studies on negative dialectics, who broke fundamentally with the notion of an 'innocent' development of productive forces.[77] According to Horkheimer, capitalist relations of production are not just an external fetter imposed on a per se neutral development of those forces. On the contrary, the productive forces themselves are in form and structure the expression of a potentially destructive capitalist escalation, their modern development by no means simply a liberating path into the 'realm of freedom', but itself a prison from which there may be no clear exit. One might add that the naïve 'subject-as-substance' status of Engels' productive forces – and this was precisely Horkheimer's critique – does not do justice to their meaning in real terms. How far this reproach is true can be left open here. What is decisive is that Engels, in his relationship with modern technology, was a child of the nineteenth century who relied on socially better organized technological progress as the means of liberating humankind.

CHAPTER 8
THE REVOLUTIONIZING OF LABOUR: FRIEDRICH ENGELS AND THE CHANGING FACE OF WORK IN MANCHESTER AND LONDON

Margrit Schulte Beerbühl

Introduction

In November 1842 Friedrich Engels left Barmen to complete his apprenticeship in Manchester as a merchant in the spinning mill of Ermen & Engels, of which his father was co-owner. Many non-Mancunians visiting the city were shocked by its appearance at the time. It was the prototype of a rapidly expanding modern industrial centre, with all the consequences, both positive and negative. The extent of the misery Engels encountered in the slums of Manchester famously prompted him to write *The Condition of the Working Class in England*.

The first negative social consequences of the onset of industrialization were also evident in Engels' hometown although not to the same extent as in Manchester. Already three years before he went to Manchester, he wrote about the appalling conditions prevailing in the textile factories of the Wupper Valley and the adjacent Bergische Land:

> Work in low rooms where people breathe in more coal fumes and dust than oxygen – and in the majority of cases beginning already at the age of six – is bound to deprive them of all strength and joy in life. The weavers, who have individual looms in their homes, sit bent over them from morning till night, and desiccate their spinal marrow in front of a hot stove.[1]

On approaching or leaving Elberfeld or Barmen, one did not anticipate – or soon forgot – the vision of the coming industrial age. Engels described his hometown as nestled in a 'rather attractive' area where 'not very high mountains, rising sometimes gently, sometimes steeply, and heavily wooded, march boldly into green meadows'.[2] The traveller approaching Manchester, on the other hand, saw the gloomy harbingers of the industrial city from afar. Even from a distance, wrote the investigative journalist Angus Bethune Reach (1821–1856), 'the tall chimneys begin to figure conspicuously in the landscape; the country loses its fresh rurality of appearance, grass looks brown and dry, and foliage stunted and smutty. The roads, and even the footpaths across the fields, are black'.[3] The closer one came, the thicker the smoke billowed. Large textile factories, foundries, chemical plants, breweries and sugar mills lined up next to residential buildings. As early as 1808, a contemporary remarked, 'the town is abominably filthy ...

the Steam Engine is pestiferous, the Dyehouses noisome and offensive, and the water of the river as black as ink'.[4] In this respect, Wuppertal was not that different, with textile works causing considerable pollution, though the Wupper ran not black but red from the effluent of the many 'Turkish red' dye works along the river.[5]

Engels' famous work presents a comprehensive report on working and living conditions in England at the beginning of the 1840s. That is not the purpose of the present essay. Here, no more than a few aspects will be taken up – from a perspective almost two hundred years later and against the background of more recent research – and the focus will fall on conditions in Manchester and London. Manchester was the city in which Engels earned his living, London his preferred place of residence, where he spent the last decades of his life. The two cities reveal the complexity of working conditions in the age of industrialization, conditions Engels experienced first-hand.

The chapter is divided into two parts. It begins with a brief overview of labour conditions in the early years of the Manchester cotton industry. In this context, the recent debate on women's work and the issue of wage and gender discrimination will be discussed in some detail. A separate section will be devoted to the Irish in Manchester, and more generally in Britain, as Engels is known to have dealt intensively with Ireland and Irish migrants, not only from a theoretical but also from a personal point of view. Moreover, a number of publications have contributed in recent decades to a more multifaceted picture of the Irish in Britain. But they were not the only immigrants who met with reservations and xenophobia from the native population. England was a country of immigration in the nineteenth century though overshadowed in this respect by emigration to America. As a rich and liberal world power, it attracted many Europeans, for economic as well as political reasons. Thus, after the mass immigration of the Irish in the first half of the century, the country experienced in the second half an influx of destitute Eastern European Jews, which occasioned numerous xenophobic attacks and eventually led the British government in 1905 to pass the first modern immigration law in the country's history. In the wake of these population movements, many impoverished migrants also arrived from other countries, including Germans and Italians.

The second part of the essay will examine working conditions in London. The economic structures of the capital were very different from those of Manchester. When Engels first set foot in London, the city already had over 2 million inhabitants. As the largest city in the world at the time, the leading financial and trading centre of the global economy, it held enormous appeal for migrants in search of a better life. And it was expanding rapidly, yet its industrial structure was considered relatively backward compared to the newly established factory towns of the Midlands and North. Countless medium and small businesses in London produced goods for the luxury market of the country's economic and political elite but also for the broad masses of the middle and lower classes. Here, semi-skilled and unskilled immigrants could readily find work. Drawing on some of Engels' remarks in his *Condition of the Working Class*, this section will look at changes in selected London trades.

The cotton city of Manchester

Manchester was *the* hotbed of industrialization. Its rise was directly linked to cotton. The inventions of the waterframe by Richard Arkwright, the spinning mule by Samuel Crompton and the power loom and wool-combing machine by Edmund Cartwright ushered in the machine and factory age in textiles in the late eighteenth century. By 1815, 44 per cent of Manchester's industrial population worked in cotton mills employing more than five hundred people. However, these firms accounted for only 7.8 per cent of all firms in and around Manchester.[6] The number of cotton-spinning machines increased from 82 in 1816 to 185 by 1841.[7] By 1830 at the latest, hand spinning by women and children working at home had given way to industrial work, except in some peripheral regions.

But the process of mechanization in the textile industry was by no means uniform. On the one hand, it depended on the type of fabric: mechanization began at very different times for cotton, wool, worsted wool, linen and silk. At first, the use of machines influenced only individual steps or specific branches of production but not the entire process. Secondly, the technological changes took place at different speeds between one town and the next and between town and country. In Manchester, for example, industrialization spread earlier and faster than in the old textile centres of East Anglia and Yorkshire. Each region also had its specific economic structural characteristics and practices that influenced the degree and timing of mechanization. This disparity allowed domestic and 'put-out' work to coexist for a long time in tandem with factory work. In 1842, for example, the textile industry still needed 250,000 hand weavers to complement its machine weavers. The handloom remained essential for finer, high-quality fabrics and was only very gradually displaced by machines.[8]

According to Hans J. Teuteberg, this overmanning of the handcrafts prolonged and exacerbated the misery of the handloom weavers and at the same time delayed implementation of mechanization.[9] The overstaffing of the trade was certainly reinforced by the mass immigration of the Irish in the 'hungry forties', though Duncan Bythell does not attribute the long survival of handloom weaving and the growing poverty of handloom weavers exclusively to over-occupation in the craft. He sees the extreme nature of the cyclical fluctuations in the cotton trade as the main cause. As a result of the rapid growth of cotton production, as well as speculation, extremely high peaks in demand alternated with sharp economic slumps. In boom years like the early 1820s and 1834–6, when entrepreneurs could not meet the demand with their own labour, handloom weavers earned good money.[10] This sustained handloom weaving but at the same time pushed weavers into the precariat, as they were the first to become unemployed during economic downturns.[11] The violently alternating situation was described by Georg Weerth, whose time in England coincided with Engels': 'The workers, therefore, may twist and turn as they please – after a short period of prosperity they will always fall back into misery, a misery which, for example, after every commercial crisis, … snatches away thousands in the prime of life.'[12]

Working conditions were in a constant state of flux during the period of industrialization. Technological inventions and improvements not only contributed to the expansion of the factories but also changed company structures and organization, and thus everyday working conditions. For example, women also worked on spinning Jennies, but with the introduction of the mule, this became men's work, as its operation required considerable physical strength. This changed again after 1830, when the self-acting mule was introduced, a machine whose operation no longer required as much strength. By 1856, 80 per cent of the workers on self-acting mules were women.[13]

Apart from changes in the structure of the workforce, the spinning mills expanded and enlarged their product ranges by combining spinning, weaving, dyeing and finishing processes under one roof or by integrating the production of different qualities of yarn and fabric. Thus, in the spinning mills, depending on the fineness of the yarn, a distinction was made between *fine* spinning mills, which produced high-quality yarns such as for lace; *coarse* spinning mills, which produced coarser yarn; and *medium* mills, which produced various medium quality yarns. In 1840, for example, a large factory like Ermen & Engels produced a wide range of both basic and higher quality yarns. According to a submission by Friedrich Engels Sr. to the Prussian Ministry of Finance, the Manchester firm produced 'cotton sewing and knitting yarns of acknowledged excellent quality' and simple yarns for the company's own use in doubling.[14] In the absence of sources, this latter point must remain open. According to a spinning mill owner from Manchester, the coarse yarns were used for the production of basic fabrics, exported especially to non-European regions.[15]

Depending on the quality of the yarn and the size of the machines, there were numerous wage levels. For example, spinners received higher or lower wages depending on the number of spindles in a mule. A spinner who had previously worked on a mule with 712 spindles and received between twenty-eight and thirty shillings (s) a week earned only 25s a week on a smaller mule with 528 spindles.[16] Since the tendency of the factory owners was towards ever-larger mules, the spinners on the smaller spinning machines were exposed to wage reductions. Wage differentials also existed between spinners in the coarse spinning mills, who received the lowest wages, and those in the fine spinning mills, who produced higher-quality yarns and received higher wages.[17] Surviving wage data varies widely. Engels, in his *Condition of the Working Class*, gives a weekly wage of 30 to 40s for fine spinners and between 14 and 16s 6d (d for pence) for coarse spinners.[18] Significantly lower wages are reported by Angus Bethune Reach, who visited several spinning mills in Lancashire in the late 1840s to research working conditions. He records an average wage in a fine spinning mill of 11s 3¾d a week and in a coarse spinning mill of 10s 6d.[19]

Wages in many enterprises, such as calico factories or silk-weaving mills, were on the basis of piecework rather than hours worked. Data on weekly wages of pieceworkers are generally calculated on the basis of full employment and should only be considered as indicators. Thus, according to Angus Reach, the weekly earnings of adult calico printers in full employment ranged from 16s to 35s. However, only very few worked full-time, so that they sometimes earned considerably less per week. Women and young people or children also received significantly less. In the calico-printing works, young people earned only 5s a week for a twelve-hour working day. According to Reach's description, they did the most tedious, tiresome and mind-numbing work, turning the wheel that kept the cylinders in the dye vat moving all day.[20] Two boys, each working ten hours a day in a spinning and a weaving mill, earned 5s 6d a week.[21] In the dye works, a 16-year-old boy earned 6s 6d a week. When Reach did his research in the factories of Manchester and the surrounding area in the late 1840s, the ten-hour day had just been introduced, but this law did not apply to calico printers or home workers.

The Working Hours Act of 1847 required women and young people between the ages of thirteen and eighteen to work a maximum of ten hours on weekdays and eight hours on Saturdays. However, it was often circumvented. Some of the children Reach interviewed were younger than thirteen and many worked twelve hours or more. In other jobs, they sometimes earned even less. One 11-year-old boy worked in a foundry from seven in the morning until eight or nine at night for 2s 6d a week.

Women's work

Mechanization changed the gender balance in textile production. As long as textiles were produced by home labour, women sat at the spinning wheels, but men did not. The introduction of the spinning Jenny and the water frame did not initially cause any noticeable gender shift, until the arrival of the mule mentioned above. Traditionally, both sexes had worked at the handloom, with male weavers outnumbering females. That ratio changed with industrialization. The number of women increased in both handloom and machine weaving. In the factories of the 1830s and 1840s, women made up on average from 50–70 per cent of the workforce.[22] In some factories, for example in Courtauld's silk factory, the ratio was much higher, at 89 per cent[23] – as it was in Ermen & Engels' spinning factory, which in 1861 employed 525 female to 150 male workers, that is just under 78 per cent women.[24]

Although it was overwhelmingly women who worked in the textile mills, it is disputed in research whether women's work increased overall as a result of industrialization. Equally controversial is the extent to which factory work was representative of women's work. Nicola Verdon, in any case, argues that factory work was atypical for the female labour force in the nineteenth century. The majority of women, she notes, continued to work in the home, in service industries and smaller workshops, the sweatshops characterized by precarious working conditions and starvation wages.[25] Eric Richards assumes that paid work was more widely available to women in the eighteenth than in the nineteenth century and accordingly assumes a decline in female wage labour.[26] H. M. Boot, on the other hand, points to an increasing demand for women in industry. This grew in the course of the century due, among other things, to legal restrictions on child labour.[27] The extent to which women's wage labour increased or decreased cannot be settled here. But it should be noted that industrialization made wage-earning women more visible than in previous centuries, as the dissolution of the traditional family economy forced them to seek wage-earning activities outside the home.

Contemporary data on women's weekly wages, along with older historical literature, points to clear wage differences between women and men. On average, women's wages were between one-third and 50 per cent lower. In his *Condition of the Working Class*, Engels also points to corresponding wage differences between men and women in the textile mills.[28] His data coincide with those of Angus Reach, according to whom women working as 'throwsters' and 'doublers' in the Macclesfield and Ashton-under-Lyne mills received between 8s and 9s a week, while men earned between 14s and 15s a week for the same work.[29] Given the debates about the still existent wage discrimination against women, recent research has turned to the question of its origins and causes during industrialization. Although the debate has not yet led to uniform results, it has nevertheless highlighted some aspects that have received less attention in the past. Among other things, it has been asked whether and to what extent the wage differences between women and men might reflect different activities and varying working hours.

Parliamentary reports dealing with the situation of textile workers and the censuses of 1841 and 1851 contain extensive data on wages that confirms known wage differences between the two sexes, but no (or no clear) evidence can be found in these files that women did the same work as men.[30] Joyce Burnette and Paul Minoletti do not entirely exclude in their research that women, if they did the same work as men, received the same pay;[31] however, they find no clear evidence for this either. Nevertheless, both authors assume gender discrimination insofar as women were pushed into low-skilled and unskilled wage work and largely excluded from the higher skilled and better paid jobs in the textile industry. Indications of different spheres of activity for women and men can also be found in Engels' *Condition of the Working Class*. He notes there that men worked in the factories as machinists, carpenters and overseers, while 'the actual work … is done by wives and children'.[32] A wage list from Courtauld's silk factory in Halstead (Essex) provides a detailed insight into the different jobs. The men at Courtauld's worked mainly as mechanics and overseers, while the vast majority of women were involved in the actual production of textiles and received much lower wages.[33] According to the payroll, women also worked as overseers but at much lower wages. Minoletti, who has studied women's work as overseers in greater detail, points out that they were employed only as overseers of their own sex, as well as of children and adolescents, and therefore received lower wages. He sees the main reason why women hardly ever did the better paid jobs as overseers in the textile factories in the prevailing gender ideology, namely the aversion to women having authority over men.[34]

Furthermore, in addition to physical differences, the lack of educational opportunities and the policies of the unions kept women out of the better paid jobs. Many unions, including those of the mule spinners or the tailors, not only excluded women from membership but also sought to exclude them from better paid work. Union policy, however, stemmed less specifically from gender bias, since it was equally directed against Irish men and indeed anyone who threatened to jeopardize the hard-won wage agreements with employers.[35]

The question of the extent to which wage differentials were caused by differing working hours has also been taken up in recent research. The fixed working hours in factories made it more difficult for married women to reconcile work and family life. In domestic and 'put-out' work, they could adapt work flexibly to family needs. But what was the situation like for women who worked ten hours a day or more in a factory? Here, Burnette and Boot point to age-specific differences. The proportion of women among factory workers over twenty-one years of age was significantly lower than among younger women between thirteen and twenty. In the cotton mills, the proportion of women over twenty-one fell from 65 to 52.2 per cent, in the flax and silk mills from 77.3 to 59.5 per cent and from 84.3 to 71.3 per cent, respectively.[36] In the mills studied by Burnette, girls under thirteen even received the same wages as boys. From the age of sixteen, the wage gap between men and women grew.[37] The age-specific pattern of working times for women changed little in the second half of the nineteenth century. Boot uses data analysis for the period from 1833 to 1906 to show that the wage gap between the two sexes was the highest in the age bracket over twenty, while under twenty – as well as with older workers – the differences were much smaller.[38] In the second half of the nineteenth century, the wage gap between the sexes narrowed slightly, as women's wages increased more than men's.

In agriculture, according to Burnette, women's lower wages likewise reflected shorter working hours. These were between a third and a half lower than men's, though outside the harvest season, women in any case worked significantly less than men. While men were generally employed six days a week, even in winter, women worked on average only four days outside the harvest season.[39] Their shorter working hours were reflected in correspondingly lower pay. Burnette also notes that when men were not available, women working in agriculture apparently earned as much as or even more than men.[40] Wage differentials, according to both authors, were thus in many cases also lower among factory workers than they appear at first glance on payrolls. Burnette attributes the wage differences primarily to the lower productivity of women as, in order to combine family and work, they worked fewer hours.[41]

English historians quote with pleasure Friedrich Engels' remark of the 1880s that factory work had an emancipatory function for women, since it gave them an income independently of men.[42] In his (forty years earlier) *Condition of the Working Class*, however, he still held the view that women's work in factories meant an 'inversion of the existing social order which, being forced upon them, has the most ruinous consequences'.[43] Social reservations about women working in factories, of the kind expressed here by Engels on behalf of many of his contemporaries,[44] limited their work opportunities, although wage labour was often an economic necessity for both married and unmarried women. Conversely, with the economic boom and the rise of wages in the textile industry after 1860, Burnette notes a withdrawal of married women from factory work whenever men's wages allowed it.[45] Outside the factories, however, women were increasingly relegated to the marginal economies of the sweated trades, as will be further discussed below.

The Irish

Engels is known to have been deeply involved with Ireland and the Irish in Manchester. His interest was also awakened by his partner Mary Burns and her sister Lizzy. The two sisters came from an Irish family who had left their homeland with many others in search of work. He probably met them in his father's cotton factory, Ermen & Engels, in Manchester.[46] Whether they worked as cotton spinners in the factory can no longer be established with certainty.[47]

The immigration of Irish people was not a phenomenon that only began with industrialization and the famine years. Irish men and women had been going to England as seasonal harvest workers in the summer months since time immemorial. The wage gap between their homeland and the harvest country made seasonal work abroad attractive.[48] This did not end with industrialization either, but increased in the nineteenth century, as demand for agricultural products grew with the rapidly growing population. From the 1820s onwards, falling fare prices on ferries between Ireland and England increased the attractiveness of seasonal work on English and Scottish estates.[49] There was, according to Donald MacRaild, virtually no agricultural region in England that did not rely on the regular supply of Irish seasonal workers.[50] They also dominated the brick and lime trades around Liverpool, arriving in the spring to work in the lime and clay pits over the summer and returning home for the winter.[51]

Irish immigration to England and Scotland took on a new dimension after the end of the Napoleonic Wars. The potato crop failure of 1821 already contributed to this. The Irish immigrants came mainly from the agrarian areas of their homeland and had little or no qualifications. They were, as Engels writes in *The Condition of the Working Class*, to be found mainly in occupations demanding only 'simple, less exact work, wherever it is a question more of strength than skill. ... Such occupations are therefore especially overcrowded with Irishmen: hand-weavers, bricklayers, porters, jobbers, and such workers, count hordes of Irishmen among their number.'[52]

Manchester experienced its first wave of Irish immigration at the turn of the nineteenth century, when the city had a shortage of handloom weavers.[53] A significant proportion of those who came were still skilled craftsmen at that time. It was not until the 1820s that the number of unskilled Irish increased considerably.[54] They generally took on the most menial and poorly paid jobs in the blow and carding rooms of the Lancashire cotton mills, with only an absolute minority working as spinners. The situation was different in Scotland: there, they also worked in the higher paid sections of the spinning mills, as the Scots were reluctant to go into the mills at all. In the English silk industry of Cheshire and Macclesfield, the proportion of skilled Irish silk weavers was also higher.[55]

With the onset of the famine years, Irish immigration developed into a mass phenomenon. In Manchester, Irish numbers rose from just under 33,500 in 1841 to over 52,500 in 1851. Liverpool had even higher numbers: there, Irish immigration rose from over 49,640 to over 83,800. The port city acquired the reputation of being the true capital of Ireland.[56] Manchester made a similar impression on foreign visitors. For Jakob Venedey, who visited Engels in Manchester, 'life in the streets was almost more Irish than English'.[57] Data on the percentage of Irish in Manchester's population varies. While Mervyn A. Busteed and Rob I. Hodgson assume a share of 12.5 per cent of the total population of Manchester for the year 1841, Donald

M. MacRaild assumes only 8.5 per cent. Both in absolute numbers and in percentage terms, London, Liverpool and Glasgow had significantly higher numbers of Irish immigrants than Manchester.[58]

The vast majority of Irish newcomers were poor. They found shelter in the slums of the cities, where they lived in damp and dirty flats and basements. However, the disastrous housing conditions in the slums were not due to poverty alone. With rapidly growing populations and mass immigration, cities could not cope with the high demand for housing. Open spaces and backyards were built on, flats and houses were divided into smaller units and basements were converted into flats for an increasing number of needy people. The situation was particularly acute during the famine years in Liverpool. In 1847 alone, around 300,000 Irish arrived in Liverpool, although half of them moved on to America and Canada. Of the 150,000 who remained in Liverpool, 100,000 were described as poor. The number of new arrivals also remained high in subsequent years. By 1853, between 68,000 and 80,000 Irish people were landing in Liverpool each year, more than a third of whom were poor. Housing this large number presented the city with an almost insurmountable problem. Damp basement flats and other slum dwellings often remained the only solution.[59]

Poverty and housing shortages led to social segregation in many large cities in England. In Manchester, three Irish slums developed: Little Ireland near the Oxford Road, Ancoats in the north of the city and Irish Town behind Victoria Station.[60] Little Ireland was for Friedrich Engels 'the most horrible spot' in the city.[61] Jakob Venedey compared the concentration of Irish in these neighbourhoods to a 'kind of barracks'. Other authors attributed ghetto character to the Irish quarters.[62] More recent studies, however, are critical of this characterization as a ghetto. Irish people could be found in other parts of the city, and English, Scottish and Welsh workers lived in the Irish neighbourhoods. There was considerable interaction between the groups, according to Graham Davis and F. J. Williams.[63] The mass immigration of the Irish fuelled the already existing xenophobia and reservations of the English population, who viewed the Catholic Irish as hard-working but irrational, wild and prone to drunkenness, a 'less civilised population' spreading as a 'kind of substratum'.[64] English labour saw them as unwelcome competition for jobs, undermining established wages and working conditions and acting as strike-breakers. In *The Condition of the Working Class*, Engels repeats these contemporary stigmatizations when he describes the Irish as 'dissolute, unsteady' and 'drunken' and as taking jobs away from English workers.[65]

The question whether and to what extent the Irish competed for jobs with the English requires a more detailed analysis. In a case study, the American sociologist Robert Boyd, using the example of the impoverished eastern and south-eastern European immigrants who made inroads into the American retail trade, showed that they did not fundamentally compete with the established small shopkeepers but occupied niches or worked as unskilled labourers for them.[66] In declining trades such as handloom weaving, the Irish certainly contributed to overcrowding and increased the competition. However, this was not necessarily the case in other British trades. MacRaild has used the example of Irish seasonal workers in Scotland to show that for a long time they represented no real competition for the native Scottish cottagers. Only in the course of the Enclosures process from around 1800, and the abolition of the Scottish clan system, which drove many small farmers off their land, did a competitive situation develop between the Irish and the cottagers, who were dispossessed, unemployed and pushed into wage labour.[67]

In other trades, too, it can be assumed that the situation was less one of competition than of supplementary work and niche occupation. According to the testimony of the entrepreneur Samuel Holmes before the Parliamentary Committee of Inquiry in 1836, the Irish worked as 'bricklayers' labourers, plasterers' labourers [and] masons' labourers'.[68] In other trades, such as tanning, they did simple, low-paid work that the English avoided. In the tannery, a far-reaching division of labour had become established by 1850, which led to a disqualification of some of the steps in the processing. There were three stages of processing in a tannery, carried out by different people: the *beam* man, the *yard* (or *job*) man and the *shed* man, of whom only the shed man required a certain qualification. The beam man stripped the hide of hair and flesh and prepared it for the tanning process; the yard man, prepared the tanning pit (the liming), placed the hide in the pit and moved it through the tanning liquid with a long pole. Only then did the tanned hide come to the shed man. The unskilled work of the yard man was done almost exclusively by Irishmen.[69] They also received the lowest wages. Thus, in tanning, the Irish did not compete with the British but took on the simplest and most mindless work.

Examples can also be found in other trades of unskilled migrants taking jobs that the English refused or avoided because the work was considered dirty or disreputable or was particularly hard and poorly paid, such as in sugar refineries. Depending on the season, the sugar boilers would work excessively long hours under conditions of extreme heat in the boiling works while at the same time receiving extremely low wages. As the Scottish sugar manufacturer Thomas Fairie from Greenock remarked:

> The Scotch will not work in sugar houses; the heat drives them away in the first fortnight. If it was not for the Irish, we should be forced to give up trade; and the same applies to every sugar-house in town. This is a well-known fact. Germans would be our only resource, and we could not readily get them.[70]

While in Greenock the Irish largely monopolized work in the sugar houses and Germans were to be found only in isolated cases, numerous German immigrants worked in the Liverpool boiling works, and in London they almost monopolized the trade. The German sugar boilers were also unskilled workers, who came mainly from the agricultural regions of the Elbe-Weser triangle and Hesse.[71] In the building trade, in road, canal and rail construction and in the docks, where they carried out – and partly monopolized – the heaviest jobs, the Irish were also a visible phenomenon. Their numbers were also high among pedlars and small street traders.[72] However, in these latter two occupations, they competed with other destitute immigrants, especially with Eastern European Jews.

London and the East End

London held an almost magnetic attraction for immigrants of all social classes, for economic migrants as well as for the political refugees of Europe, who found asylum here after their failed revolutions. The vast majority of immigrants, Irish and mainland Europeans alike, stayed in the capital. Friedrich Engels, for example, earned his money in Manchester, but he did not like the city. He, like Marx, was drawn to London, where he spent the last decades of his life. When Engels first set foot there, the city's population had already passed the 2 million mark, and by the end of the century it exceeded 6 million.[73] It was an ungovernable city, an 'infernal wen', as Francis Sheppard called it.[74] In terms of size, it was for out-of-town visitors a behemoth; there was, in fact, no bigger city in the world. Weerth spoke of the 'monster city of London'.[75] It was attractive and repulsive at the same time. Engels describes it as 'colossal' and 'impressive', a city in which 'a man may wander for hours together without reaching the beginning of the end', a city in which 'a man cannot collect himself'.[76] The crowds on the streets possessed for him 'something repulsive'; he was shocked by the 'brutal indifference', 'the unfeeling isolation of each in his private interest'. Here ruled 'social war, the war of each against all'. Engels found the immediate juxtaposition of extreme wealth and abject poverty frightening. There were districts in London, Angus Reach observed, whose squalor and misery were far greater than that of the poorest neighbourhoods of Manchester.[77]

London was a city divided in two, with the aristocracy and the wealthy middle classes living in the West End and the poor living in the East End. The geographical separation of rich and poor widened as the century progressed, reflecting sharpening social contrasts. The worst and poorest neighbourhood, described in detail by Engels, was St. Giles in the East End. 'The houses', he wrote, 'are occupied from cellar to garret, filthy within and without, and their appearance is such that no human being could possibly wish to live in them.'[78] St Giles was mainly inhabited by Irish people. Here, between 1841 and 1851, the average population density of a house rose from twenty-four to forty-six people. Some lodgings even housed up to 100 people.[79] From mid-century the housing situation deteriorated in the poor quarters due to the extension of roads and railways, as a result of which entire streets in the East End were demolished.[80] Housing for the poor and small tradesmen became scarce and expensive. According to Gareth Stedman Jones, rents doubled between 1844 and 1887, but wages – for example of shoemakers – increased only by around 20 per cent.[81]

The housing situation also worsened due to the mass immigration of destitute Eastern European Jews and, albeit in smaller numbers, Italians. The East End as a whole developed into a gathering place for poor immigrants who, in order to survive, took on any work that presented itself. German immigrants were generally not viewed in terms of economic migration. Nevertheless, over 50 per cent of German immigrants in London lived in the poor areas of the East End, working in butchers' shops and bakeries, in sugar refineries and tailoring.[82]

Compared to the new industrial areas, the capital's industrial status was long considered backward.[83] It was not an industrial city in the modern sense but littered with a multitude of small and medium-sized businesses and workshops that produced goods for the luxury needs of the economic and political elite as well as for the mass needs of the rapidly expanding middle and lower classes. But the idea that industrialization passed London by, as it were, has been revised. Rather, a different kind of industrialization took place, characterized by high seasonality in demand. This made high investment in large industrial enterprises unprofitable. The ostensibly proto-industrial structure of the capital was in many areas highly efficient and productive; it enabled traders and entrepreneurs to react more quickly and flexibly than any factory to frequent changes in fashion and economic fluctuations.[84] Newly developed machines were certainly used but only those which, like the sewing machine, did not require large capital outlay.

The hallmark of London's industrial structure was the wholesalers and department store owners, who farmed out their orders to small pseudo-self-employed master craftsmen and their workers. This proto-industrial structure gained efficiency through the distinctive division of production processes into small-scale steps, which both simplified and accelerated production. Traditional craft labour was de-skilled in this way, because cheaper unskilled labour, especially that of women, young people and unskilled immigrants, could be hired for many of the individual steps in the production cycle. This intensive division of labour can in principle be characterized as anticipating the assembly line – it constituted a sort of manual assembly line work.

A unique insight into working conditions in the East End is provided by reports published in *The Morning Chronicle* of 1849–50 by Henry Mayhew, as well as by his three-volume work *London, Labour and the Poor*, in which he dealt primarily with the outcast poor: street vendors, itinerant traders, street artists, prostitutes and the like. Mayhew can be considered as an 'English Frederick Engels'. He rebelled against the Victorian virtues and morals of his bourgeois background and strongly denounced the excesses of early capitalism. Unlike Engels, however, he was not a socialist: he wanted to preserve private capital.[85] Mayhew's investigations in the East End were commissioned by the *Morning Chronicle* at a time – the late 1840s – when public interest in the social condition of the poor, high unemployment in much of England and Chartism was intense.[86]

The silk weavers of Spitalfields

The segregation of the city was also reflected in the structure of its trades and employment. In the west of the city, craftsmen worked in the so-called fair trades, producing items for the luxury tastes of the wealthy, and they were unionized. In the east, it was the 'cheap' or 'slop' trades – the sweated trades – which spread and in which excessive working hours and starvation wages were the norm. The East End silk weavers exemplified this graphically. At the beginning of the century, they were considered the aristocracy of the capital's textile craftsmen. Their craft was protected from competition from foreign silk by a ban on imports. In 1773, after years of unrest and violence, they had also ensured the passing of the *Spitalfields Act*, which forbade employers, under penalty, to reduce wages below a minimum set by the city authorities. Moreover, employers were prohibited from contracting work from outside London,[87] though this law also covered the silk industry in Coventry. It was eventually repealed in 1824.

The situation of the silk weavers began to deteriorate with the end of the Napoleonic Wars in 1815, partly due to the rise of the silk industry in Macclesfield and East Anglia. Employers in Macclesfield were the first to implement new work structures. They began to employ so-called half-apprentices, who were not bound by any of the standard periods or regulations of apprenticeship.[88] In order to reduce labour costs, the factory owners gave orders directly to journeymen, bypassing the masters, who in turn hired more half-apprentices who did most of the weaving but received only half a journeyman's wage. These could be dismissed at any time if there was not enough work.

The first mechanical looms for silk were introduced in Lancashire. At first, however, they were suitable for the production of only simple fabrics. Overall, the mechanization of the silk industry was very slow. In Coventry, where silk ribbons were mainly produced, mechanization did not increase until the 1840s. In 1835, the silk trade as a whole still used only 1,750 mechanical looms compared to 40,000 handlooms.[89] Specifically the London silk trade remained mostly small-scale, producing for the upper classes. Of 10,500 handlooms, 97 per cent were owned by families with no more than five looms each.[90] In 1857 there were only eleven mills in Spitalfields.

A strike by silk weavers against wage cuts at the end of the Napoleonic Wars ended in defeat and a 25 per cent cut in their piece rates. Contributing to the further deterioration in the 1820s, apart from the abolition of the *Spitalfields Act* in 1824, was the lifting of the ban on silk imports in 1829 and a reduction in customs tariffs. From then on, weavers had to fight competition from high-quality French silks. The severe recession of the early 1830s caused unemployment to rise acutely. In the winter of 1831, one-third of all looms in Spitalfields and Macclesfield, and as many as two-thirds in Coventry, stood idle.[91] It is estimated that up to 30,000 silk weavers were unemployed at times during the 1830s.[92] Commenting on the dire situation, Engels noted that the silk weavers had 'lived in periodic distress for a long time'.[93]

The London silk weavers complained to Mayhew that their wages had fallen by more than 50 per cent since the repeal of the *Spitalfields Act*, but at the same time working hours had increased by a third.[94] In order not to starve, many silk weavers hired themselves out as casual labourers in the London docks during periods of unemployment, helping out as porters or stevedores.[95] In the face of dramatically worsening working conditions, silk ribbon and crêpe weavers in the country took to a new form of self-help. In order to benefit from technological progress, they set up cottage factories – associations of small workshops that shared a steam engine to meet the energy needs of their looms.[96]

In Lancashire and East Anglia, small independent silk handloom weavers survived for a longer time only because they formed a reserve pool for the factory owners, who fell back on them during short-term peaks in demand.[97] The final decline of the English silk trade began after the complete abolition of import duties in 1860. English silk manufacturers immediately responded to the change in the law by lowering wages. The ensuing two-month strike of the silk weavers ended in defeat. The duty-free import of high-quality silk fabrics from France hit the silk weavers of Spitalfields particularly hard.⁹⁸ By the time of the First World War, silk manufacturing had practically died out in England. The silk trade was not the only industry to go under. Shoemaking and shipbuilding moved to the peripheral regions of the United Kingdom, and English sugar refining collapsed under competition from cheap German beet sugar, which flooded the English market.⁹⁹

Street people: 'The outcast poor'

London's street scene also included a mass of casual labourers, peddlers, thieves, prostitutes and street vendors who mostly eked out an impoverished existence. A characteristic feature of this army of the poor was its sometimes subtle social differentiations. The shoemakers, tailors, silk weavers and many others who tried to earn an honest living in the slop trades were considered the respectable poor. Opposed to these were the outcast poor, who lived more or less on and from the streets and who made a miserable living with the most menial and dirtiest work, such as collecting and recycling rubbish of all kinds.

Among them were the numerous costermongers or street hawkers and vendors – Engels calls them the 'superfluous' – who populated the East End and the London markets, offering food and small everyday items to passers-by for a penny or less. According to Engels, most of them engaged in hawking, the sale of fruit, vegetables and other small goods, such as pairs of braces (suspenders), pencils, pocket knives and so on.¹⁰⁰ The vegetables and fruits offered in baskets on the streets were – according to Engels – 'naturally all bad and hardly fit to use'.¹⁰¹

The costermongers or street vendors supplied the broad population of the middle and lower classes with cheap food and goods of all kinds. Among the fruit and vegetable sellers, and the load and luggage carriers, the Irish, around the middle of the century, formed a conspicuous sub-group. Mayhew estimated the number of Irish who earned their living by street vending and other casual labour in London at more than 10,000.¹⁰² As everywhere, they were regarded by the natives as intruders and a threat to their standard of living, since they were prepared to work below the usual prices and wages. 'I found,' Mayhew remarked, 'among the English costermongers a general dislike of the Irish.'¹⁰³

Many Irish men, however, only occasionally earned their living by selling vegetables, fruits or fish or as luggage porters when they could not find work as day labourers on the building sites or in the docks. In contrast, the livelihood of many Irish women and girls depended on selling vegetables, fruits and food on the streets. According to Mayhew, they were unable to do even the simplest sewing or household chores such as washing or ironing: 'there seems to remain to them but one thing to do … "to sell for a ha'pinny the three apples which cost a faruthing" [sic]'.¹⁰⁴ Both sexes, he notes, are very eloquent and also have a quick wit, but the street vendors rarely prosper; as they limit their activity to goods that can be sold quickly, such as apples, nuts or oranges.¹⁰⁵ Georg Weerth's judgement was harsh: 'unfortunately, an Irishman never knows how to keep house, he lives only for the moment, and the following day is quite indifferent to him. ... Irishmen drink away what they can get their hands on'.[106]

As in most London trades, there was a clear social differentiation among the outcasts between the regular and the irregular street vendors. Fine distinctions and subtle hierarchies existed especially among the lowest strata. For example, several hierarchies existed among the street cleaners, whose prestige and earnings varied accordingly. The street sweepers differed from the dog excrement hunters, who in turn differed from the 'toshers' or sewer hunters, and the latter from the dog excrement and mud collectors. There was also competition from casual pure collectors, such as journeymen tanners, who collected dog excrement and sold it to the tanneries.[107]

Costermongers also distinguished between regular and irregular fruit and vegetable sellers. The majority of the Irish worked in irregular street vending; only a few managed to join the ranks of the regular street traders. Below the layer of costermongers were the refuse-sellers. They were generally women and girls who acquired unsaleable fruits and vegetables to sell to their own social class. Even among the refuse-sellers, fine distinctions existed between the regular refuse-sellers and casual sellers.[108] A regular refuse-seller earned between 4d and, at the very best, up to 1s per day. However, 6d per day was barely enough for the bare necessities, given the irregularity of the income. Some days, an apple seller told Mayhew, she had nothing to eat. The situation was similar for street flower sellers.[109] Among street vendors, child labour was especially widespread.[110] The poorest of all were the orphans – girls aged eleven to fifteen who sold flowers on the street and shared a room and bed with several others in slum accommodation.[111] Among the street boys, Mayhew found some who earned quite as much as the adults.[112]

Before the mass arrival of the Irish in the 1840s, Jews had sold oranges on the streets of London. For a long time, they occupied a niche with orange selling that was shunned by local street vendors. Unlike the Irish, among the Jews only young people up to the age of about twenty-one engaged in orange selling, after which they entered the wholesale trade. According to Mayhew, the Jewish youths were very skilled sellers, offering their wares at stagecoach stations and other profitable places. After the crisis of the 1820s, they increasingly offered other small goods like razor blades, buckles, sealing wax, and so on in addition to oranges. They were later forced out of this hawker trade by the influx of Irish.[113]

The Eastern European Jews

England had already experienced a wave of immigration of destitute Jewish immigrants from Eastern Europe in the late eighteenth century in the wake of the Polish partitions. Their visible presence on London's streets through their traditional dress and begging had, at times, led to violent xenophobic attacks. They had not completely disappeared from the streets of London's East End in the first half of the nineteenth century, but their numbers had decreased significantly. A century later, many of them had integrated into the middle classes. According to Mayhew, there were no more than *c.* 500 to 600 in London, compared to higher numbers in earlier times.[114] Nevertheless, many Jews still worked in the precarious slop trades as pawnbrokers, cigar makers or itinerant traders or dealt in stolen goods. However, the street Jews and old-clothes sellers Mayhew interviewed were not among the poorest. They earned more than the Irish and more than many an English manual labourer.[115] Many had also adapted their appearance, shedding their traditional clothes and beards.

From the 1860s onwards, a new mass immigration of Jews from Poland and Russia began, which Engels witnessed personally. It reached its peak in the last two decades of the century and again caused considerable social unrest and xenophobic attacks. It is estimated that at times in the 1880s between 5,000 and 6,000 Eastern Jews came to England per year.[116] Most of these remained in London. It is estimated that between 1881 and 1901, *c.* 60 per cent lived in London and surrounding areas. The second largest Jewish community was in Manchester with 12 per cent, followed by Leeds, and smaller communities in Liverpool, Birmingham and Glasgow.[117] According to Bill Williams, the integrated Jewish community perceived the newly arriving Jews from Eastern Europe as a threat to their values and Anglo-Jewish image, as they brought a different culture with them, increased the number of petty criminals and peddlers and were a burden, through their poverty, on the local synagogal communities.[118] The mass immigration of Jews also contributed to the cut-throat competition faced by the poor – local manual labourers of Irish, German and other nationalities –in the declining trades of the East End. According to Panikos Panayi, the influx of Jews caused a real ethnic transformation, with originally German neighbourhoods taking on a Jewish character.[119]

The majority of the Eastern Jews were not only poor but also unskilled. Their arrival in London swelled the sweated trades in the East End. Many subsisted in the tailoring and shoemaking trades. Some segments, such as the manufacture of women's coats, developed into typical Jewish immigrant trades. Starvation wages, excessive working hours and extreme seasonal fluctuations due to rapid changes in fashion often characterized their situation. It is estimated that wages ranged from 14s to 21s a week, with women earning significantly less than men. According to Charles Booth's calculations, the subsistence level for a median family in the 1890s was 18s to 21s.[120] Due to the seasonality of many trades, even those earning between 21s and 30s a week often found themselves on the verge of destitution.[121] However, newly arrived immigrants had no choice but to take on the lowest paid jobs.

By now, sewing machines had found their way not only into the shoemaking trade but also into tailoring. They did not require a large investment, especially as they could be bought in instalments. This increased the number of small quasi-self-employed masters who, despite hard work, often lived at a subsistence level and paid their employees only the lowest wages, not only swelling the ranks of the sweaters but at the same time intensifying competition among them.[122] Weerth considered competition among the poor the very worst misfortune.[123] Skilled small masters could, however, leave poverty behind if they found suitable niches in which to trade. Although the Irish of the immigrant generation were said to have no aspirations for social advancement, the following generation certainly succeeded at times in rising into the ranks of the middle class.[124]

Overview

Engels lived in an era of profound change that reshaped not only labour relations and conditions of work but also many areas of daily life not addressed here. Everyday life was revolutionized by the sheer scope of technological change. Railways, steamships and telegraphy transformed our understanding of space and time. Contemporaries such as Heinrich Heine and William Fardely perceived these changes as the annihilation of those dimensions.[125] The relationship of the social classes after the collapse of the old class system had to be redefined. This took place, as Engels, Weerth and others saw it, through the 'war of each against all'. No less dramatic was the change in working conditions that prompted Engels to write the *Condition of the Working Class* and Marx and Engels ultimately to forecast a proletarian revolution; the gap between wealth and poverty in the world power that was Britain was so extremely visible.

The mechanization of many production processes and the transition to factory work and modern forms of operation dissolved traditional labour relations, and new relations had to be fought for.[126] Mechanization also took place in a very uneven – and unevenly timed – process. While it started early in Manchester's cotton industry, in other places and other industries, it came later. On the losing side were the home- and hand-weavers, spinners and women. Many were pushed into the low-wage sector of unskilled day labourers, for whom there was a growing demand. The misery of many manual workers was prolonged and was exacerbated by extreme economic fluctuations caused by speculation, overproduction and foreign, as well as domestic, competition.

Another factor that led to overstaffing and the expansion of precarious working conditions with excessive working hours and starvation wages was Irish mass immigration from the 1820s onwards, which put additional strain on the labour market. However, the immigrants did not compete in all cases for jobs but found shelter in niches not occupied willingly by the locals. There, they worked as labourers for higher skilled craftsmen or took on jobs in construction and many other sectors of the economy. For Donald MacRaild, the Irish were the most important immigrant group during the classic phase of nineteenth-century industrialization, as they played such a significant role in the development of the infrastructure. For him, they were 'at the frontier of industrial expansion: hewing canals, laying railways and blasting docks'.[127]

In London, as has been shown, a different kind of industrialization took place. The capital's demands were different from those of many other cities; on the one hand, there was a growing need for high-end luxury items that could not yet be produced industrially, and, on the other hand, there was also a growing need for cheap mass-produced goods and a low-cost supply of everyday items for the city's overflowing masses. Although the capital did not become a pioneer of the factory age, in part because land and energy costs as well as wages were so high, these developments were no less dramatic. Manufacturing processes were broken down into simple steps that required little or no skill, so that mass production could take place. Economies of scale developed, based not on machines but on manual assembly-line work.

Its global economic importance and size made the capital a magnet for migrants of all kinds – for economic as well as political refugees. The mass immigration of Irish, Jews and other destitute people swelled the marginal economies of the sweated trades. For migrants, however, economic prospects arose, even in these precarious economies, which their homelands did not offer. Competitive situations arose in London in several respects. Firstly, the highly skilled artisans of the West End found themselves in competition with manual workers in the sweated trades of the East End and with foreign imports, as a result of which their wages and working conditions deteriorated. But they were not the only losers. In the sweated trades of the East End, locals and immigrants competed with each other for jobs and a meagre living. In addition to these two competitors, many London trades faced further indigenous competition from the northern counties and the Midlands, where production and labour costs were considerably lower than in the capital. However, there were not only losers. On the one hand, new job opportunities were opening in the expanding service and financial sectors, and, on the other hand, even in the trades affected by decline, skilled master craftsmen and small traders could achieve a modest prosperity.[128]

Figure 8.1 George Cruikshank, *The British Bee Hive*, 1840 (reprint 1867). Cruikshank depicted the large number of professions in their strict divisions and hierarchical social separation in the form of a beehive. The image associated Bernhard Mandeville's bee fable, with the 'Mandeville Paradox' later taken up by Karl Marx: namely that 'Private Vices [may have] Publick Benefits'. The beehive and the bees were common allegories for industriousness, cooperation and prosperity in the nineteenth century. © Alamy Stock Photos.

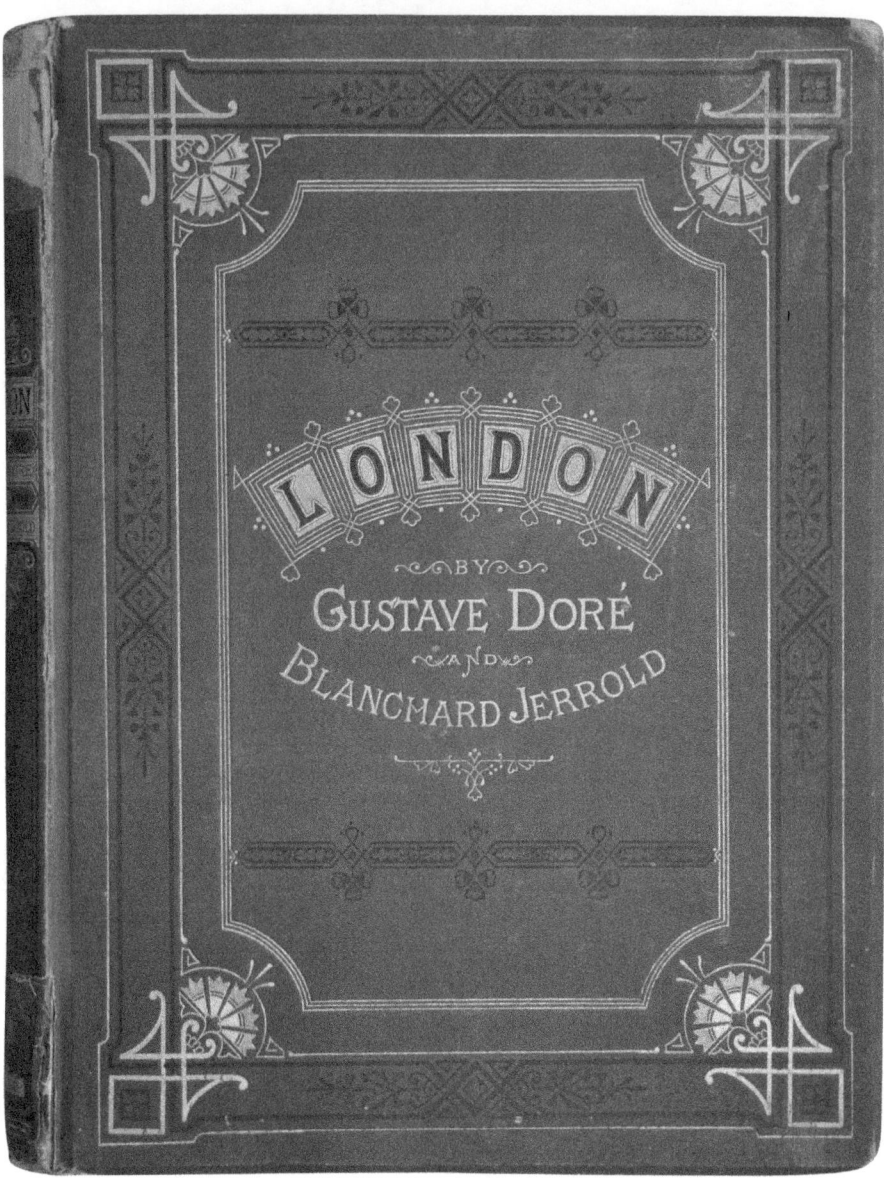

Figure 8.2 *London: A Pilgrimage*, 1872. With illustrations by Gustave Doré, London. Together with the journalist Blanchard Jerrold (1826–1884), Gustave Doré (1832–1883) drew an illustrated picture of both the sunny and shady sides of the British metropolis. He visited the places of the rich as well as those corners where the homeless poor sought refuge. Not everyone liked this unvarnished documentation of the extreme contrasts in what was then the largest city in the world. © Dieter Ante.

Figure 8.2 continued

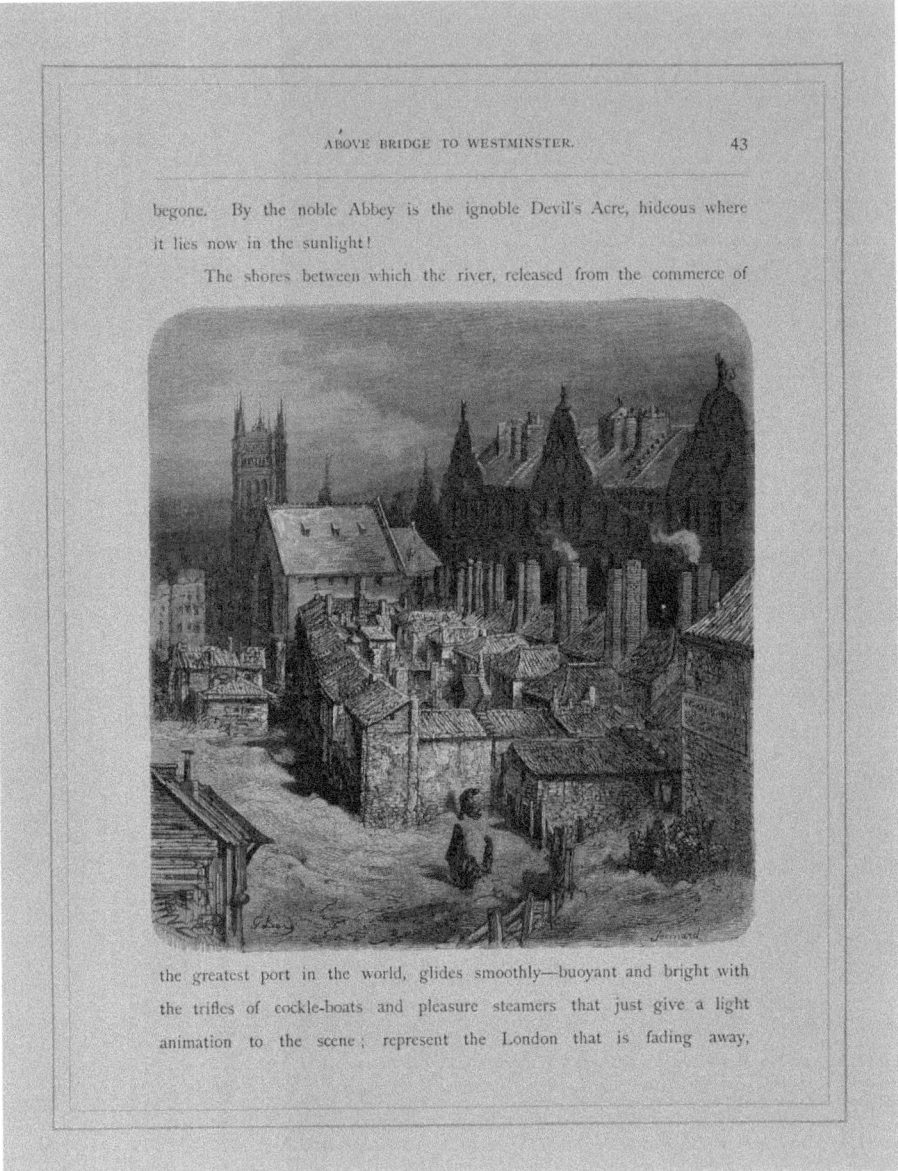

Figure 8.2 continued

Revolutionizing of Labour

Figure 8.2 continued

Figure 8.2 continued

Figure 8.2 continued

Figure 8.2 continued

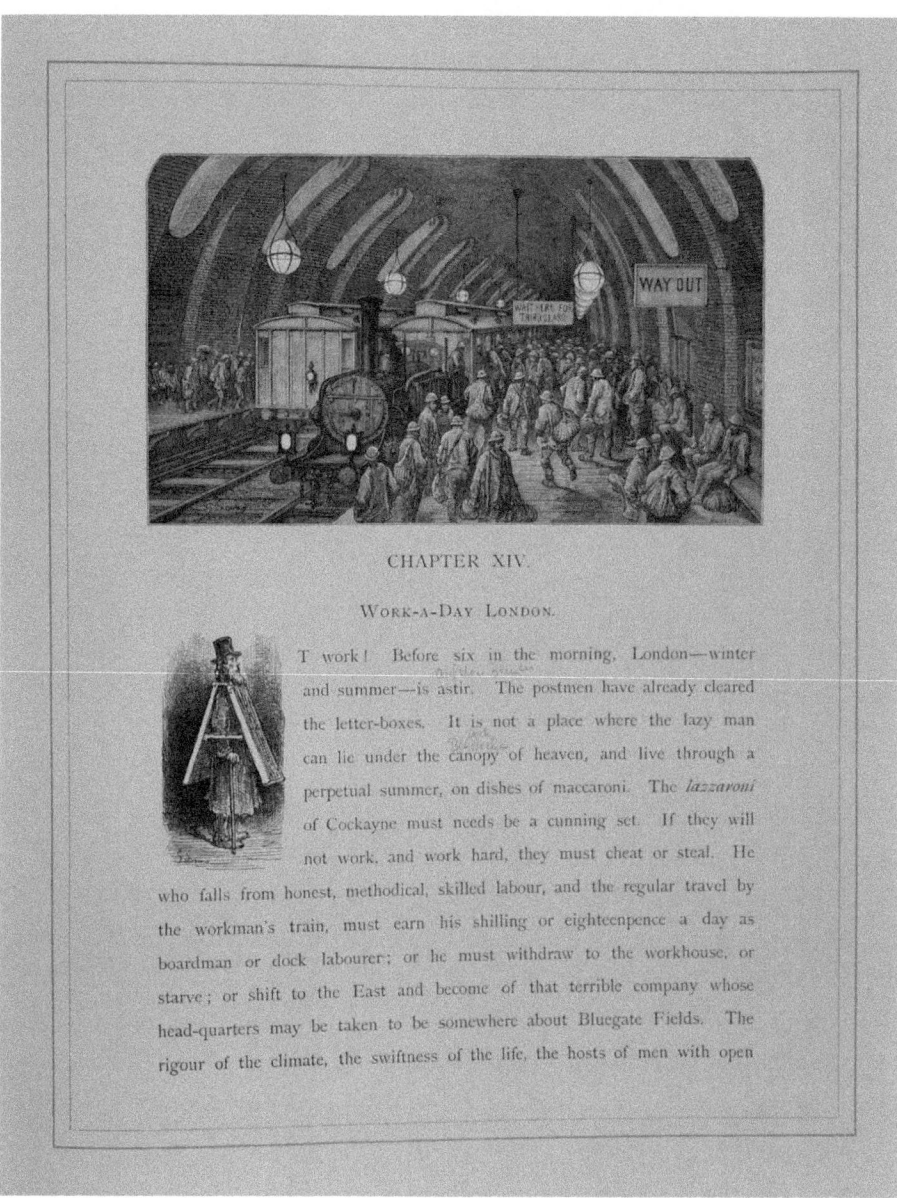

Figure 8.2 continued

Figure 8.2 continued

CHAPTER 9
THE ECONOMIC THOUGHT OF HIS AGE: FRIEDRICH ENGELS AND THE TENSION BETWEEN CREATION AND DESTRUCTION
Hans A. Frambach

Introduction

There are two ways in which Friedrich Engels merits the title 'economist': first of all, as a commercial apprentice in his father's business and then, increasingly, as a vocal critic of prevailing economic doctrine. It was in this second function that he would later, with Karl Marx, lay the foundations of a new theory of society in which the economy played an important role in its own right. Engels had not studied economics: he was an autodidact. As a young man writing the *Outlines of a Critique of Political Economy* (1844) and *The Condition of the Working Class in England* (1845) – two works central to the entire Engels-Marxian theoretical edifice – his knowledge of economic theory was distinctly limited.

From the perspective of the history of economic thought, one may certainly ask whether Engels' statements, even at the time he made them, reflected contemporary economic thought. To what extent did he take account of current scientific approaches and theories? How selective – and how biased – was he in applying what he knew? With what reservations did he choose objects for empirical study, and with what lack of reservation – so long as they suited him – did he select sources for their interpretation? So far as the classical British national economists – Adam Smith, David Ricardo and Thomas Malthus – or the French theorist Jean Baptiste Say are concerned, more recent scholarship has provided extensive answers to these questions.[1] And it was against those thinkers, almost exclusively, that Engels wrote; it was their theories that – like every other theory of the day, apart from socialism – he dismissed as vulgar economics.

In order to avoid repetition and overlapping with existing literature, the present chapter will focus on the economic approaches that flourished around the time when Engels was laying the foundations of his own work (i.e. the years up to 1845) – approaches he could have studied, had he chosen to do so. However, for a faculty member of Wuppertal University's Schumpeter School of Business and Economics, a second line of investigation is almost *de rigeur*: namely the question how far the metaphor of creative destruction propagated in economic theory above all by Joseph A. Schumpeter (1883–1950) is already implicit in the economic thought of Friedrich Engels.

What, then, were the prevailing economic doctrines of the early nineteenth century? What circumstances did they address? What lines of development did they reveal?

The Life, Work and Legacy of Friedrich Engels

Economic theory at the beginning of the nineteenth century

In the early years of the nineteenth century, Europe underwent far-reaching changes in its societal and political systems, and these did not leave economic theory untouched. In the German territories, for example, the reforms imposed after Prussia's defeat at the hands of Napoleon in 1806 were followed by a prolonged period of modernization initiated, in the words of the Prussian chancellor von Hardenberg, as 'revolution from above'.[2] The processes of renewal covered many areas, from public administration and governance, through the organization of agriculture and the military, to cities, customs and taxes, trade and the educational sector, and they inevitably also left their imprint on economic theory and teaching. Two strands can be observed in this development.

On the *societal and political* level, a profound transformation is apparent, above all in the liberation movements that arose in the wake of the French Revolution. A great physical and intellectual productivity was unleashed, whose most notable description in terms of economic theory can be found in the Scottish economist Adam Smith's *The Wealth of Nations* (1776). Smith gave pride of place to the economic growth of the nation and drew together as never before the benefits arising from the abolition of the boundaries and restrictions of the mercantilist epoch. He described the mechanisms responsible for the new type and scale of economic development and, as such, for the national wealth, laying emphasis on the role of newly gained freedoms. The list was long: freedom to choose and exercise one's trade or occupation; the removal of burdens on land, provision of new areas for cultivation and pasture, and the organization of agriculture according to principles of efficiency; industrial inventions and the improvement and extension of the national transport network; the growth of commerce and trade, and the idea of competition as boosting productivity; and finally, the increasing stability Smith had himself observed in food prices, together with a decline in the frequency of periods of inadequate supply.

On the level of *economic thought and training* for public office, these changes were reflected in contemporary society in an intense concern with the question of the direction and administration of public finances. During the early decades of the nineteenth century, the organization of the economy underwent a paradigmatic change, whose beginnings can be seen in criticism, growing over the previous half century, of the funding of the public household. Traditionally, this was a matter for the country's ruling courts, but the demand was increasingly heard that, although the funding could come only from a prince's subjects, the national income should no longer be thought of as the prince's property. On the contrary, the prince's private property should pass to the state, the concept of the 'civil list'[3] being introduced[4] for the upkeep of rulers and their families in accordance with their function and standing.[5] At the same time, the ruling princely courts were subjected to state budgetary discipline, and the guiding principle was established that state income should be calculated to meet the tasks the state was required to perform.

These changes marked the inception of modern state financing and its theory. Financial policy and administration were now, at heart, a matter of planning a budget that fulfilled appropriate political ends, a development clearly discernible in the Napoleonic satellite states of early nineteenth-century Germany. The Grand Duchy of Berg (1806–13), for example (which covered Barmen), introduced the *Code Civil* on 1 January 1810, replacing all prior laws and regulations, some of which derived from local medieval common law; the Kingdom of Westphalia (1807–13) and the Grand Duchy of Frankfurt (1810–13) acted similarly, as did some other states of the Confederation of the Rhine (1806–13). After the Congress of Vienna – when Barmen was allocated to the Prussian province of Jülich-Kleve-Berg – the civil list was adopted into the constitutional law of the German states.

Parallel to the modernizing process in public finance, changes took place in economic theory, although the universities, where future civil servants and administrators were trained, still held fast for many years to elements of late cameralism. The old division of cameralism into the subdisciplines of policy, action (i.e. administration) and finance[6] was by then outdated, and – due not least to ardent disciples of Adam Smith – the broader-based division into the fields of political science, state economy (*Staatswirtschaft*) and political (or national) economy was still in a state of conceptual flux. Thus, Gottlieb Hufeland (1760–1817) advocated the replacement of the concept of *National-Oeconomie* (national economy) coined by Ludwig Heinrich von Jakob (1759–1827) in his *Grundsätze der National-Oekonomie* (Principles of National Economy, 1805) with that of *Volkswirthschaft* (political economy), in order to underline its distinction from state economy.[7] In the same year, however, Count Friedrich Julius von Soden (1754–1831) invoked the concept of national economy in his eponymous treatise *Die Nazional-Oekonomie*. Surprisingly, Engels, too, uses this concept (instead of 'political economy') throughout his *Outlines*, although it was only common in the work of German-speaking authors and (apart from Friedrich List, 1789–1846) he refers there only to English, Scottish and French writers.[8] He was evidently familiar with this term, although he mentions none of the authors closely associated with it.

At least in Germany, cameralism remained important in political and administrative practice,[9] even though in the curricula of the universities, while still taught as part of public budgetary theory, it was being increasingly supplanted by national economics.[10] Cameralism was finally ousted, however, not just by rising liberalism or by competitor theories of national or political economics on the British model, nor should Smith's *Wealth of Nations* be taken without qualification as the only fount of such theories, as Wilhelm Roscher (1817–1894) in particular, and after him even authors like Joseph A. Schumpeter, did.[11] Although still in circulation today, such interpretations were based on careless and selective early reception of *The Wealth of Nations* and are now definitely outdated.[12] Indeed, without relativizing the fundamental differences in their views on the derivation of value and prices or on free trade – in other words the very aspects of central interest to Engels[13] – one must for the sake of completeness note the considerable agreement that existed between cameralists and classical national economists on issues like the promotion of the common good or factors influencing the wealth of the nation.[14] Among the main causes for the decline of cameralism was that it was gradually seen as a more or less random collection of economic, administrative and pragmatic principles,[15]

Figure 9.1 Friedrich List (1789–1846), economist, 1845. © AKG.

with borrowings even from the increasingly diverse field of jurisprudence[16] but without any unified basis in theory.

One cannot hold it against Engels that he ignored many of these aspects, which have in some cases been observed only by more recent historians of ideas. What he might well have noticed, however, was the restricted impact of economic theory on the actual operations of the economy and its underlying political governance and, above all, that economists, entrepreneurs and rulers were generally different individuals with different strategic interests. German advocates of classical national economics were critical in particular of *Wealth of Nations*. Enthusiastic about Smith's ideas of the relation between freedom of action and individual scope for action, they were at the same time sceptical about the practical workings of unrestrained competition. Thus, Karl Heinrich Rau (1792–1870) understood a nation's wealth, and above all its distribution, as the premise on which justice, and hence also social morality, was built – a conjunction from which, following von Soden,[17] he derived the role of the state as 'provider of well-being'.[18] And while in his *Handbuch der Staatswirthschaft* (Manual of State Economy, 1796) Georg Friedrich Sartorius (1765–1828) propagated the ideal of untrammelled freedom, he also admitted that in the prevailing circumstances, given the multiplicity of tasks the state had to perform, the principle of unlimited competition must be restrained.[19] Heinrich Luden (1778–1847), in his *Handbuch der Staatsweisheit oder der Politik* (Manual of State Science or Politics, 1811),[20] took a similar line.

Engels' perception of economic theory: I

Engels ignored classical German national economics and its authors; his critique is directed solely at the British tradition. He begins *Outlines* with the assertion that the national economy is a natural consequence of the growth of trade, replacing 'elementary, unscientific huckstering' with 'a developed system of licensed fraud, an entire science of enrichment'.[21] This idiosyncratic view of economic theory reflects, if anything, the perspective of a businessman concerned to make money with any available means, which in turn may well derive from the young Engels' experience of the factory owners, merchants and wheeler-dealers among whom he grew up and whose morally questionable attitudes confronted him day in, day out in his work.

In his early years Engels had had ample contact with the children of ribbon weavers, cloth dyers, machine workers and other craftsmen. He knew their physical environment and their way of life, and he was aware of the impact of economic downturns on the working conditions and lives of their families. He describes the arduousness of their tasks, the damage to their health from noxious vapours, the stench of bleaching vats, and the smoke from factory chimneys.[22] He notes the rise of alcoholism in the working class and what it meant for their lives, the growing numbers of unemployed wandering the streets and the increase in those with no other recourse than poor relief or the workhouse.

Against his wishes, Engels's father took the young Friedrich out of school at the age of seventeen so that he could begin training in the family business. For a year and more, he was introduced to the production and processing of linen and cotton, spinning and weaving, bleaching and dying. In 1838 Friedrich accompanied his father on a business trip to England; on the return journey, he disembarked in Bremen to continue his commercial apprenticeship with the mercantile house of Heinrich Leupold, linen exporter and consul of the Kingdom of Saxony in that city.[23] There, he learned the ins and outs of the export business, currency trading, import duties and so on and gained deeper insights into the mechanisms of international trade. It was a time of boring routine, dealing with commercial correspondence that brought little satisfaction to him, and Engels began writing articles and reports under the pseudonym 'Friedrich Oswald' for the socially critical *Telegraph für Deutschland* (German Telegraph). His 'Letters from the Wupper Valley', unsparingly describing the lives and surroundings of the workers there in all their need and misery, caused a considerable stir. The 19-year-old Engels is, however, still far removed from any attempt to order what he sees within the framework of existing social, political or economic theories.

What is clear, on the other hand, is the rebellion of the son against the generation of the fathers.[24] Writing from Bremen, a merchant city of international repute, Engels scarcely conceals his scorn for the shabby churches and semi-finished municipal buildings of Elberfeld and Barmen and for the people among whom he grew up – scorn for their overly planned lives, their daytime concern for figures and accounts and their evenings of social merrymaking. He laments the thought that whole generations uncritically pass their way of life on to their offspring, who accept it uncritically in return[25] – a young man, evidently, stung by the nonchalance of his parents and by the innate hypocrisy of the Pietism that dominated his hometown, the bigotry of factory owners who saw themselves as the elect and, far from showing pity for the circumstances in which their employees had to live, felt all the more justified in exploiting them.

Against this biographical background it is easier to understand the young Engels' slanted view of national economic theory as well as of the actual workings of the economy and its agents – to say nothing of his confusion of great economic minds like Smith, Ricardo or Malthus with the merchants and businessmen of his immediate experience. Engels lacked the knowledge and experience to distinguish with any clarity between observers and actors, economic thinkers and businessmen and was in no position to appreciate the achievement of those who sought to grasp and structure the complex economic activities of their time in order to better provide for their countrymen. Moreover, some aspects of Engels' reading of the classical economists were simply mistaken.[26] Thus, he applauds Smith's critique of mercantilism for recognizing the one-sided focus of that philosophy on boosting the balance of trade while imposing profound restrictions on human rights but reduces the progress achieved by the free trade system of *Wealth of Nations* to merely allowing 'the true consequences of private property [to] come to light'[27] – a verdict that can only be called presumptuous. Engels is likewise unaware of the substantial critique of mercantilism present in physiocratic writings and even in the later phases of cameralism.

His main bone of contention with the classical economists is their lack of any critique of individual ownership rights, where the continuation of an economic system based on private property must necessarily lead to the creation of monopolies, which will ultimately lead to the abolition of private property itself – 'just as theology necessarily leads either back to blind faith or forward to free-thinking philosophy'.[28] In other words, Engels sees the factual advantage of classical national economics over mercantilism purely in the light it (unintentionally) sheds on the consequences of an economy based on private property – in his view, the unequivocally negative side of capitalism. It is already clear at this point how far he is from understanding the breadth and diversity of that system, including the critical voices from its own ranks. For Engels, national economics, especially in its British form, is nothing but a stumbling block.

The contemporary critique of classical national economic theory

Engels' rejection of the theory of national economy was motivated above all by his perception of its impact on the working class in terms of unrestrained competition and the general undermining of morals. Leaving aside the British tradition, however, and even the reservations of the classical German school, he could have found similar sentiments in German idealism as well as in the Romantic and historical schools of economic theory. The negative effects of burgeoning economic liberalism were astutely foreseen by German idealists. Johann Gottlieb Fichte (1762–1814), for instance, in his *Der geschlossne Handelsstaat* (The Closed Trading State) called for human activity to be as far as possible a free mastery of nature in which work should not be reduced to joyless drudgery[29] – an ideal scarcely reconcilable with the industrial conditions of the day. Hegel, for his part, saw the increasing fragmentation of work as suppressing all other individual needs;[30] the very concept of work, as he explains it, already to some extent anticipates the negative effects of industrialization.[31]

The materialist direction of economic thought – and with it the reduction of human work to a bare economic activity determined by competition and task-splitting – was vehemently rejected by representatives of the Romantic school like Friedrich von Schlegel (1772–1829), Adam Müller (1779–1829) and Franz Xaver von Baader (1765–1841). Although they agree with Smith and his successors on the principle of economic liberty as boosting productivity, they are outspokenly critical of the meagre attention paid by the British school to the deterioration in the workers' living conditions and the inequitable distribution of the profits of work.[32] As early as 1809, Müller warns in his *Elemente der Staatskunst* (Elements of State Governance) against the excessive prominence given in classical national economics to exchangeable value, its exclusive focus on self-interest and the neglect of cultural and intellectual values as essential sources of progress and well-being. He advocates an 'organic ethical' approach to economics that ranks the commonalty and state higher than individual economic activity.[33] Friedrich List (1789–1846) comments at length on Smith's distinction between productive and unproductive activities and rejects his one-sided focus on the creation of material values. He considers an individual's work performance as crucially dependent on the state of society, which he sees as including the input of art and science, the fostering of intellectual abilities, the securing of law and public order and the maintenance of property laws as well as the safeguarding of morals and existing liberty rights. Acting in consort as 'productive forces', these factors, for List, constitute the real potential for increasing the wealth of a nation.[34]

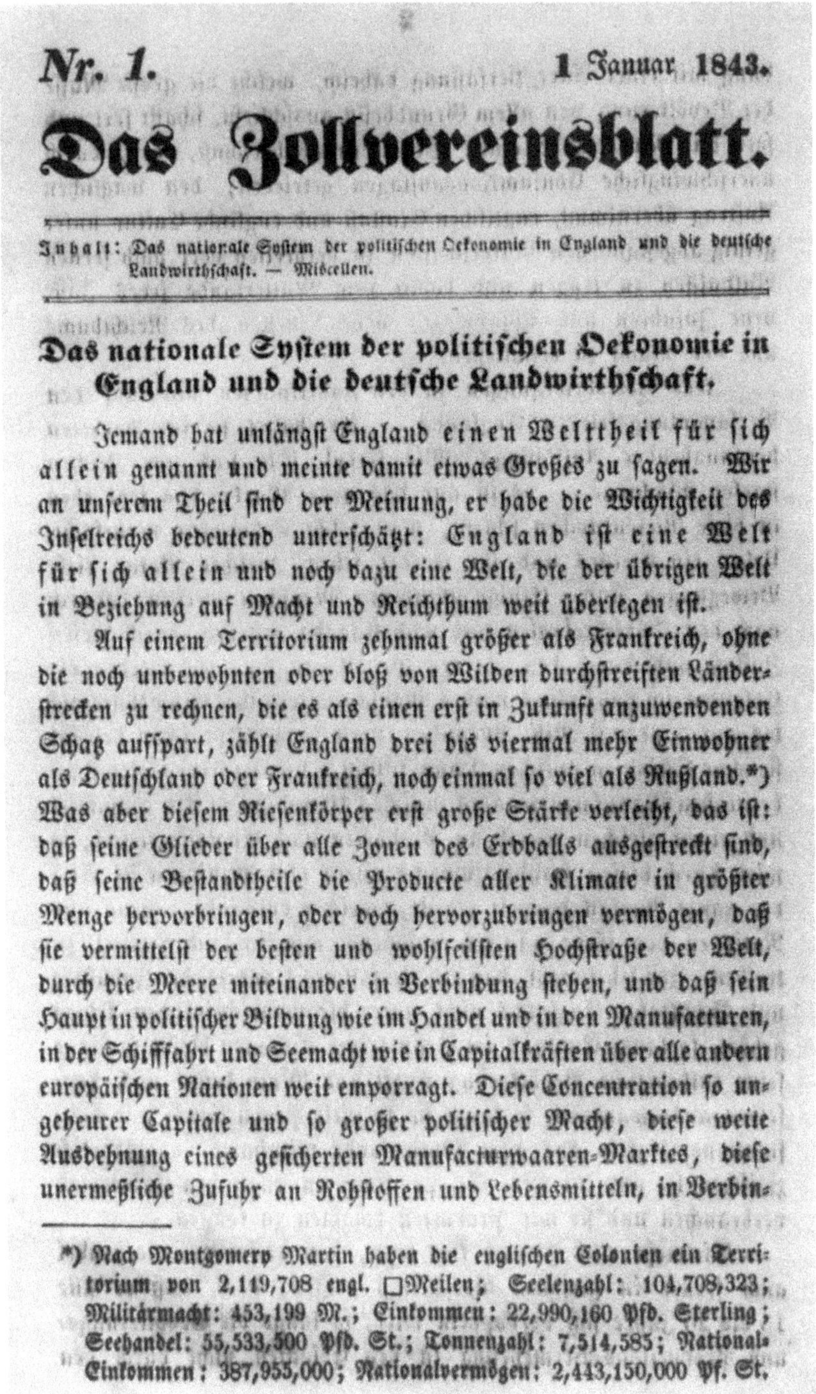

Nr. 1. 1 Januar 1843.

Das Zollvereinsblatt.

Inhalt: Das nationale System der politischen Oekonomie in England und die deutsche Landwirthschaft. — Miscellen.

Das nationale System der politischen Oekonomie in England und die deutsche Landwirthschaft.

Jemand hat unlängst England einen Welttheil für sich allein genannt und meinte damit etwas Großes zu sagen. Wir an unserem Theil sind der Meinung, er habe die Wichtigkeit des Inselreichs bedeutend unterschätzt: England ist eine Welt für sich allein und noch dazu eine Welt, die der übrigen Welt in Beziehung auf Macht und Reichthum weit überlegen ist.

Auf einem Territorium zehnmal größer als Frankreich, ohne die noch unbewohnten oder bloß von Wilden durchstreiften Länderstrecken zu rechnen, die es als einen erst in Zukunft anzuwendenden Schatz aufspart, zählt England drei bis viermal mehr Einwohner als Deutschland oder Frankreich, noch einmal so viel als Rußland.*) Was aber diesem Riesenkörper erst große Stärke verleiht, das ist: daß seine Glieder über alle Zonen des Erdballs ausgestreckt sind, daß seine Bestandtheile die Producte aller Klimate in größter Menge hervorbringen, oder doch hervorzubringen vermögen, daß sie vermittelst der besten und wohlfeilsten Hochstraße der Welt, durch die Meere miteinander in Verbindung stehen, und daß sein Haupt in politischer Bildung wie im Handel und in den Manufacturen, in der Schifffahrt und Seemacht wie in Capitalkräften über alle andern europäischen Nationen weit emporragt. Diese Concentration so ungeheurer Capitale und so großer politischer Macht, diese weite Ausdehnung eines gesicherten Manufacturwaaren-Marktes, diese unermeßliche Zufuhr an Rohstoffen und Lebensmitteln, in Verbin-

*) Nach Montgomery Martin haben die englischen Colonien ein Territorium von 2,119,708 engl. □Meilen; Seelenzahl: 104,708,323; Militärmacht: 453,199 M.; Einkommen: 22,990,160 Pfd. Sterling; Seehandel: 55,533,500 Pfd. St.; Tonnenzahl: 7,514,585; National-Einkommen: 387,955,000; Nationalvermögen: 2,443,150,000 Pf. St.

Figure 9.2 *Das Zollvereinsblatt* (Bulletin of the German Customs Union), edited by Friedrich List, no. 1, 1843. © AKG.

All these aspects of economic theory – especially the critique brought by German authors to issues of classical national economics – were in circulation at the time; they were accessible and in some cases even standard elements of the university curriculum. Yet Engels passes them by, his own critique focusing on specific points in political economic theory, above all its inability to explain fundamental socioeconomic problems like the unequal distribution of incomes and wealth. These problems are common enough in the maelstrom of nineteenth-century development, hovering like dark shadows over every country in which capitalism has taken root, destroying small manufacturing structures, centralizing industries, forcing the various groups involved in the production process into growing competition, giving powerful entrepreneurs influence over government policies, creating ever-greater differences in wealth and driving whole classes of working people into abject poverty. Critics of such outcomes exist in abundance.

Another major nineteenth-century movement unconvinced by classical national economic theory was the historical school, whose key writings, however, began to appear only towards the end of the 1840s, when Engels had largely mapped out his own approach. Despite his contemporaneity with the activities of both the older and younger historical schools, he effectively ignored their contribution to the debate. In fact, apart from the British theory of national economy, he took notice of very little other than socialist writing; moreover, he spent most of his time in England, where the historical school was little known; otherwise he could have availed himself of a whole arsenal of arguments with which to beleaguer the adherents of the classical tradition. British economists were accused, for example, of neglecting the multidimensionality of socioeconomic change: they took inadequate notice of people as social beings and as the products of history.[35]

Thus, Bruno Hildebrand (1812–1878) criticized the classical construct of private interest as the driving force of universal competition, which will always be at the expense of the weakest. That classical theory justified this state of affairs could be seen, it was argued, from the widespread acceptance of activities like playing the stock market, or agio and differential trading, as legitimate economic pursuits.[36] Even the contemporary Brockhaus encyclopaedia remarked critically of the vaunted 'self-healing powers of the market' that unrestricted organizational freedom of labour invited the modern dangers of centralization of capital, creativity and work, with all the structural problems these caused within society. In principle, the free system should be maintained, Brockhaus argued, but it needed substantial ancillary support.[37]

Hermann W. Wagener (1815–1889) observed that unchained economic liberalism brings with it a collapse of moral barriers, legitimizing the amassing of wealth and the quest for artificial satisfactions at the expense of higher aims, while the overwhelming majority still have to work in unworthy conditions.[38] Similarly, Friedrich Albert Lange (1828–1875) rejected the idea of a preordained harmony as absurd in view of the extreme injustices existing in society, of which the inequitable distribution of earnings was in his view the most flagrant.[39]

Gustav Schmoller (1838–1917) even saw the question of distribution as determining the entire future culture of modern states.[40] His essay *Die Arbeiterfrage* (The Worker

Question, 1864) highlights two opposing aspects of capitalism.[41] This question, he argues, is soluble in terms of social reform by establishing the institutions necessary to avoid or cushion social hardship.[42] Before that can be achieved, however, the public must become aware that indigence not only diminishes economic productivity, it jeopardizes the stability and peace of society, sending generation after generation into poverty, unemployment and misery.[43] The state has an important role to play here, intervening in the economic process without disturbing the productive potential of the market. With such considerations, Schmoller opened a middle way between the extremes of an unbridled market economy and strict interventionism.[44]

Wilhelm Roscher's five-volume textbook *System der Volkswirtschaft* (System of National Economics), published over the forty years from 1854 to 1894, dominated university economics teaching in the German cultural area for decades. It set the teachings of the great British economists within a historical context replete with examples and sought to demonstrate the connection between cultural development and the division of labour, pointing out the danger of monotony in work routines and the need to observe moral limits.[45] That Engels does not mention Roscher's work may also be due to Marx's critical dismissal[46] of him as a 'vulgar economist'.[47]

All in all, then, many voices and a wealth of arguments with which to counter the British classical tradition were circulating in German-speaking countries, where they represented the leading academic opinion – a tradition Engels could have taken up, had he cared to.

Engels' perception of economic theory: II

The young moralist of Outlines

In the *Outlines* of 1843–4, Engels is concerned with the elements of national economics. Beginning with private property as the 'economist's principal category',[48] he proceeds to national wealth, trade, questions of value and work and, finally, capital, production costs and competition. He stumbles over the concept of national wealth, objecting that, as used by economists, it is meaningless so long as private property continues to exist.[49] For him, 'national wealth' based on privately owned objects is private wealth, and he suggests replacing the term 'national economy' with 'private economy'[50] – an idea with which, in the sense of an economic theory rooted in private ownership, any modern market economist would probably agree.

Trade is another fundamental economic concept Engels treats on the basis of private ownership rather than as a foundation stone of national welfare. He sees trade, in fact, as an internecine feud between individuals or groups 'with absolutely opposing interests', each of which seeks through buying and selling to get the better of the other.[51] And while he applauds Smith for having expressed the advantages of trade, including its humanitarian side, he qualifies his praise by classifying trade as a mere evolution of medieval highway robbery in which the underlying motives of greed and avarice are concealed beneath a veil of friendship and mutual gain. That regional borders, with all their hindrances for the passage of goods, have lost meaning with the increase in trade – a development culminating in modern globalization – is for Engels synonymous with a dissolution of nationhood which has sown hostility between countries and peoples. In this light, he accuses national economic theory of transforming mankind 'into a horde of ravenous beasts' – for that, he asserts, is what competition really is.[52] Engels did not understand that, at the time of its development, classical economics in Germany aimed in the first place to break up the heritage of small princedoms in favour of a larger national construct which would allow greater freedom of occupation, commerce and trade and that this purpose was motivated above all by the desire to improve the lot of the people. Heinz D. Kurz[53] shows how Engels attacked Smith and other classical authors for opinions they did not hold or, indeed, even opposed. It is as if he superimposed his image of the ruthless entrepreneur on the protagonists of national economic theory, whose work he projects as the root cause of the abuses of capitalism. The most surprising aspect of this perspective is its failure to realize that theory follows reality, not the other way round. In essence, national economic theory described, and then systematized, existing structures. Smith, for example, discovered the principle of the division of labour by observing and describing what actually happened in a pin manufactory.

Engels' next basic economic category was value. Here, he distinguishes between abstract (or real) value and exchange value.[54] Classical (and later neoclassical) national economics, on the other hand, generally – albeit for different reasons – spoke of use and exchange value, the latter being the market price. In economic theory, the complex of issues around value became virtually a discipline in its own right. Almost every work of pre-classical, classical and neoclassical economics contains an extensive treatment of what value is and how it comes to be. The apparent contradiction between exchange value and use value – the so-called paradox of value – was finally resolved when infinitesimal calculus, and with it a marginalist way of thinking, was introduced into economic thought in the early 1870s in the work of William Stanley Jevons (1835–1882), Carl Menger (1840–1921) and Léon Walras (1834–1910), who had been preceded in this respect by Johann Heinrich von Thünen (1783–1850) and Hermann Heinrich Gossen (1810–1858).

Engels' observations on value are fragmentary and generally divorced from the theoretical context established by classical political economists like Ricardo, McCulloch or Say. He himself considers 'the only just basis of exchange' to be the relation between production costs and utility.[55] But this cannot be ascertained, as no one person can determine an object's utility. Moreover, as production costs are 'distorted from the outset by competition', these cannot represent an objective measure of value either.[56] Engels therefore suggests replacing the concept of exchange value with that of trade value (i.e. the equivalent given for a good in trade or in other words its price) in order to distinguish this from its use (or real) value – a distinction no one would be likely to oppose. Why this does not happen is, he asserts, a matter of the motives of the leading economists, who have a vested interest in obscuring the relation between value and price 'lest the immorality of trade become too obvious'.[57] The imputation of such base intentions to

Figure 9.3 Carl Menger (1840–1921), economist and co-founder of the theory of marginal utility, c. 1880. © AKG.

Plate 1 Friedrich Engels, *c.* 1864. © AKG.

Plate 2 Adolph Menzel, *Iron Rolling Mill*, 1872/5. © Alte Nationalgalerie, Berlin/AKG.

Plate 3 Francois Bonhommé, *Casting in Le Creusot*, 1864. © Dépot Academie Francois Bourdon, Le Creusot, France.

Plate 4 Paul Friedrich Meyerheim, *Borsig's Locomotive Assembly Hall*, 1873. © German Museum of Technology, Berlin.

Plate 5 Carl Eduard Biermann, *Borsig's Engineering Works in Berlin*, 1847. © Stadtmuseum Berlin Foundation/Märkisches Museum.

Plate 6 Carl Wilhelm Hübner, *The Silesian Weavers*, 1846. Friedrich Engels wrote about the painting by Hübner exhibited in Berlin, Cologne and Halberstadt in 1844 that 'it has been more effective in propagating Socialism than 100 pamphlets'. © German Historical Museum/AKG.

Plate 7 V. Poljakov, *Karl Marx and Friedrich Engels at Work on the Communist Manifesto*, 1961. © Karl Marx and Friedrich Engels Museum of the Institute of Marxism–Leninism of the Central Committee of the CPSU, Moscow/AKG.

Plate 8 *Capital and Labour*, 1843, *Punch*, vol. 5 (London, 1843). © AKG.

Plate 9 Pyotr Beloussov, *Lenin with Delegates to the Third Komsomol Congress 1920*, 1949. © State Historical Museum, Moscow/AKG.

Plate 10 Viktor Adler (1852–1918), *c.* 1910. Physician and Social Democratic politician. After studying chemistry and medicine in Vienna, he worked as a doctor for the poor and as a neurologist. As a founder and editor of *Gleichheit* and the *Arbeiter-Zeitung* he became the central figure of Austrian social democracy. With his liberal and moderate stance, he struck a balance between the conflicting wings of the party in a humane and winning manner. Dubbed 'Hofrat der Nation' (Court Counsellor of the Nation), he was nominated at the beginning of November 1918 to be Secretary of State for External Affairs in the first government of the Republic of Austria, but he did not live to see the official proclamation of the republic on 12 November 1918. © AKG.

Plate 11 Joan Planella i Rodriguez, *The Working Girl* or *The Weaver*, 1882. The Catalonian trading city of Barcelona was also caught up in industrialization in the second half of the nineteenth century. Children and young people worked in the textile industry. The picture was shown at the World Exhibition in Barcelona in 1888 and elsewhere. © Museum of History of Catalonia, Barcelona.

Plate 12 Karl Marx, sketch of a simple-acting atmospheric steam engine after Thomas Newcomen, *c.* 1720, based on Andrew Ure (1835), *c.* 1851. © IISG Marx Engels Archive.

Plate 13 Charles Babbage (1791–1871), *c.* 1850. The busy mathematician and inventor was Lucasian Professor of Mathematics at Cambridge University and the pioneer of the automatic calculating machine. © BPK/National Portrait Gallery, London.

Plate 14 Jean Veber (1864–1928), *Dynamis*. Known for his incisive socially critical caricatures, the artist took criticism of the effects of modern technology to extremes in this large-scale oil painting. A demonic-looking woman, sitting astride a steam cylinder with a pounding piston, is obviously taking pleasure in the fact that the thermodynamic energy generated is turning men into tumbling dwarfs. Hans Wettich, *Die Maschine in der Karikatur* (Berlin, 1920), 18, gave the picture the title: 'Die Maschine die Menschen verschlingt: The Machine that Eats Men'. © Musée des Beaux-Arts, Tours, France.

Plate 15 Edward Moran, *The Commerce of Nations Rendering Homage to Liberty*, 1875. A monumental painting commissioned by the French artist Frédéric Auguste Bartholdi. Bartholdi's colossal neoclassical statue of the Roman goddess Libertas, Liberty Enlightening the World, was a gift from France to the United States of America on the 100th anniversary of its independence. The painting was used to raise funds to finance the installation and the pedestal. A similar fundraising campaign was organized by Joseph Pulitzer through his newspaper *New York World*. The statue was prefabricated in France, dismantled into individual parts and transported to New York, where it was set up and dedicated on Bedloe's Island in 1886. For millions of immigrants who first set foot on American soil at nearby Ellis Island, it became a symbol of freedom in the New World. © Private Collection, Minnesota Marine Art Museum, Winona, Minnesota, USA.

Plate 16 C. Parsons, *City of New York*, 1856. © Library of Congress.

Plate 17 National Cotton Mule Spinners Association of America, Lowell MASS. © Boott Cotton Mills Museum, Lowell, Massachusetts, USA.

Plate 18 Robert Köhler, *The Strike*, 1886. Shown for the first time at the spring exhibition of the National Academy of Design in New York, it triggered an enormous public response against the backdrop of the mass strike movement in the United States on 1 May, with around 350,000 workers in over 11,000 companies participating. It became an icon of the labour movement. © German Historical Museum/AKG.

Plate 19 Paul Friedrich Meyerheim, *Railway Bridge over the Rhine at Ehrenbreitstein*, 1875. © German Museum of Technology Berlin.

Plate 20 Francois Bonhommé, *Forging of the Elbow Shaft of a 60 hp Frigate at the Indret Works*, 1865. © Dépot Academie Francois Bourdon, Le Creusot, France.

Plate 21 Ludwig Dettman, *Golden Sunday*, 1893. © AKG.

Plate 22 Augustus Edwin Mulready, *Uncared For*, 1871. © Wikimedia Commons (public domain).

Plate 23 Paul Friedrich Meyerheim, *Wheel Production at Borsig's Locomotive Factory*, 1873. © Stiftung Stadtmuseum Berlin Foundation/Märkisches Museum.

Plate 24 George Cruikshank, *The Tax on Property*, that is the costs of being rich, 1835–43. © Alamy Stock Photos.

Plate 25 *Pyramide a Renverser* (A Pyramid to be Overturned), *La Presse Socialiste*, Belgium, c. 1900. © AKG.

Plate 26 David Ricardo (1772–1823), stockbroker and economist, 1839. © AKG.

Plate 27 Thomas Malthus (1766–1834), 1833. The British economist and social philosopher was professor of history and political economy at Haileybury College from 1806. His theory of population, which he developed with 'An Essay on the Principle of Population' (1798) and 'Principles of Economics' (1820), was controversial. © AKG.

Plate 28 Justus von Liebig (1803–1873), 1856. © AKG.

Plate 29 Heinrich Kley, *The Krupp Devils*, 1914. © Westphalian Industrial Museum, Dortmund/AKG.

Plate 30 Isaak Israilovich Brodsky, *Lenin in Smolny*, 1930. ©State Tretyakov Gallery, Moscow/AKG.

economic theorists can at the very least be considered naïve. Prescinding from the fact that he did not himself succeed in constructing a workable notion of value, it must, however, be said in Engels' defence that in the 1840s the economic debate on this issue was by no means finalized and its concepts and phenomena were still in a state of flux. Not till half a century later was the distinction developed between production costs as a measure of objective or real value – as opposed to the subjective judgement of a good's utility – and price as exchange value (also above all an expression of individual utility or significance), and that distinction is still valid today. That Engels could not have been familiar with it may to some extent mitigate his negative conclusion: 'thus everything in economics stands on its head'.[58]

In his treatment of the origin of value, Engels also rejects the classical division of the production factors determining price into land, capital and labour. His critique is twofold: (1) Capital is nothing other than work in a different form: that is 'stored-up labour'; (2) the classical division does not take proper account of science as the expression of human ingenuity and invention.[59] There is some justification in this last point, inasmuch as early national economists propagated some strange classifications in their distinction of productive from non-productive work in areas such as invention, medicine and art as well as government and military activity,[60] but by the 1830s these attributions were of scarcely more than anecdotal interest. Classical authors like Jean Baptiste Say (1767–1832) in *Traité d'économie politique* (1803) or John Stuart Mill (1806–1873) in *Principles of Economics* (1848) argue vigorously against Smith that invention, intellectual work and much that would later be subsumed under the notion of human capital constitute an important aspect of the wealth of a nation.[61] Whatever the case, when the young Engels sits as a 'wise judge' over the classical economists, he overlooks the fact that Smith, for one, never questioned the usefulness of invention and other activities classified as 'unproductive': on the contrary, he valued them highly.

Nor, contrary to Engels' assertion, did classical economics teach that 'what cannot be monopolised has no value'.[62] There is, again, a certain consistency in his position, inasmuch as he *de facto* equates monopolization with privatization – entirely in line with the classical conviction that only a privately owned good can have a price. Engels clearly perceives the impact of private ownership on prices but fails to recognize that this is also the case with goods owned in common, which necessarily also bear a price, but one that is calculated by a central body rather than by the law of supply and demand. Engels makes a common enough mistake, treating as private property whatever can in any way be owned and comparing this class of things with free goods like air, which cannot be priced. The converse impression thereby arises that what is not privately owned cannot have a price: common or collectively owned property must, therefore, be free. But goods owned in common are by no means necessarily free: they may be in short supply, and like private goods, they come at a price. The difference is in the mechanism through which that price is established.

In his analysis of land rent, Engels compares the various definitions of Smith and Ricardo and then gives his own definition: land rent is the relation between the productivity of the land (i.e. what human labour can gain from it) and competition (i.e.

the conditions under which it can be leased or rented).⁶³ He is evidently thinking of the big landowner who leases land to be cultivated by the tenant and profits from its increase in value without having done anything to earn that increase (other than the act of leasing, which is remunerated in rent). Engels goes out of his way to remark that he is not concerned here with the right of the labourer to keep the product of his labour for his own sustenance and that of his family or with the principle that none should reap what they have not sown (which also precludes the inheritance of property), but with the fact that these obvious and elementary principles themselves derive from the institution of private property. He concludes that, in order to reward the sower with the fruit of his labour, one must first abolish private ownership;⁶⁴ this, for him, is the root of all evil, and its abrogation is the first step towards a solution.⁶⁵ What Engels fails to grasp, however, is the role of private property in establishing adequate provision for the population, and that so long as people earn enough and are well enough supplied, they will not rise up against private property but, on the contrary, may even want it – which may be one reason why socialism, with its centrally planned economies, has not yet swept the world. The worldwide revolution of the proletariat has not occurred. Engels sees very clearly, on the other hand, the radically and increasingly inequitable distribution of land ownership and capital assets, a problem from whose solution we are further removed today than ever.

While capital cannot be conceptually divorced from labour, for it is 'stored-up labour'⁶⁶ in practice, Engels argues, the economists have effected just such a separation. And in its wake the allocation of revenue from the production factors of land, capital and labour – and in particular the distribution of interest on capital, which Engels censures as 'the immorality of … receiving without working, merely for making a loan'⁶⁷– is decided, in the absence of any 'inherent standard' common to all three elements, by competition, which he calls 'the cunning right of the stronger'.⁶⁸ Engels finds no answer to what will later be called the question of accountability (the earnings to be ascribed to each production factor) although he locates the problem clearly enough in the 'incommensurability' of the three factors.⁶⁹ (Marx will later, on the basis of Ricardo's treatment of work value, attempt to construct a unified criterion of value for all three production factors, but this attempt, too, will fail.) What Engels does not allow is that the interplay of the production factors, despite the lack of a satisfactory theoretical description of their processes, manifestly works in practice. Market forces undoubtedly play a decisive role here. In lieu of a solution, he generalizes competition – which he perceives solely as the law of the jungle rather than as an economic driving mechanism – into an all-pervading force.⁷⁰ In such negative terms, then, he presents the origin of prices and concludes: 'If we abandon private property, then all these unnatural divisions disappear.'⁷¹

Engels understands competition itself as a consequence of private property, which brings about a 'discord of identical interests' in which 'is consummated the immorality of mankind's condition'.⁷² Passing over the distinction between the positive and negative effects of competition – known since Greek antiquity and familiar also to classical national economists – he emphasizes its destructive impact to the point of exaggeration. That competition exists outside the field of private ownership, that it can enhance motivation and performance, with positive results for teamwork and the sense of sharing and unity, all these he leaves aside.

The counterpart to competition is monopoly: the desire, shared by even the smallest player, to 'get big' on the market. This basic economic instinct Engels unmasks as a 'hollow antithesis', which he calls 'the contradiction of competition'.[73] The individual, he observes, seeks to possess everything, but the common interest is that all should possess equally; the individual 'cannot but desire the monopoly', but the common interest is that monopolies should be removed.[74] Here, too, he provides no evidence for his assertion, which again represents only one aspect of a complex economic discussion. In certain circumstances, monopolies can be beneficial – for example in terms of resource efficiency and cost saving – and, within an appropriate legal framework, they can promote societal welfare, serving both individual and common interests. Modern political economics sometimes speaks in this context of 'temporary monopolies'.

Engels accurately describes how prices rise and fall according to the excess of demand over supply or vice versa,[75] but his conclusion – that stability can never be attained and progress is impossible – is all the more misleading as no explanation is offered for the recurrent trade crises which he prominently mentions.[76] With verve and irony, he accuses the economists of inventing a theory about the workings of the economy without looking at the reality and suggests a way of avoiding such crises. Overproduction will not occur, he argues, if manufacturers ascertain what and how much consumers require and organize and distribute production accordingly: 'then the fluctuations of competition and its tendency to crisis would be impossible'.[77] And he eloquently appeals: 'Carry on production consciously as human beings – not as dispersed atoms without consciousness of your species – and you have overcome all these artificial and untenable antitheses. But as long as you continue to produce in the present unconscious, thoughtless manner, at the mercy of chance – for just so long trade crises will remain,'[78] each more grievous than the last, 'finally causing a social revolution such as has never been dreamt of in the philosophy of the economists'.[79]

One can agree with Engels that to act 'consciously and in the interests of all'[80] in an economy based not on competition but on a deep-rooted individual awareness of the primacy of the common good would be better for all concerned. The problem is that such altruism is an exception, and in the real world, Engels' solution – to abolish private property, and with it competition – would more likely encourage hunger and misery. Moreover, the notion of gearing production to the needs of the species rather than individual interests is conceivable, if at all, in terms of local manufacturers, or a specific industry, agreeing on a common price strategy. There is, in fact, something odd in Engels' appeal to industrialists here, as if the economists were the real enemy determining commercial practice. Otherwise he has no good word for those whose avarice and greed drive turnover and profit to ever greater heights. It is somewhat inconsistent to suddenly expect them to be concerned with the avoidance of crises, let alone social revolution. There is a lot of wishful thinking here. Engels mixes levels of argumentation, moralizing, appealing, evoking Utopias and treating the major complex of questions around economic value as a matter of ethics alone: 'the same [economic] system which appears to attach such importance to value, which confers on the monetary abstraction of value the honour of having an existence of its own – this very system destroys by means of competition the inherent value of all things'.[81] 'Where', he asks, 'does any possibility remain in this whirlpool of exchange based on a moral foundation'?[82] The only way out he can offer is social revolution.

For Engels, 'immorality's culminating point is ... speculation on the Stock Exchange'[83] (although thirty years later he would himself be very successful in that pursuit). Again, one can agree with his denunciation of the greed of speculators and the hypocrisy of reputedly solid merchants, but again he sees only the negative side. That the stock exchange serves to underpin transactions and spread risks in excess of any one individual's capacity and that its ultimate *raison d'être* is to enhance the prosperity of all participants – on this Engels does not waste a word. Setting economic speculation in general within the framework of the relation between production and consumption, he places on the community (understood as an organized body) the onus of calculating 'what it can produce with the means at its disposal'.[84] Here, he refers his readers to the writings of the English socialists as well as of the French philosopher Charles Fourier (1772–1837), whose critique of contemporary economic thought and mercantile practice (capitalist repression of human liberties, trade as fraudulent self-enrichment etc.)[85] is expressed in his major *Théorie des quatre mouvements et des destinées générales* and later writings.[86] Many of Fourier's concepts, as well as his overall attitude to trade, were taken over by Engels. Thus, for Engels, as for Fourier, free trade was a mechanism of 'liberal lies', a 'robber economy, organized and legitimized under the mask of law' and those who engaged in it were the 'biggest of all liars'; accordingly, the economic concepts of trade balance and equilibrium were 'commercial blather'.[87]

With the questions of the 'what, for whom, and how' of production, and the management, distribution and allocation mechanisms of a national economy, Engels raised fundamental economic issues. The answers he offered, however – social revolution, on the one hand, and determination from above (by the community), on the other – have not so far proven practically feasible.

On Malthus and the population question

Engels's economic analysis is based on the economic situation that was so visible in England: the vast production capacity generating gigantic quantities of goods, on the one hand, but leaving large sections of the population in misery and need, on the other. At the same time, he was aware of an economic theory – first and foremost, the Malthusian population theory – that described the sad reality of working-class existence and touched on some fundamental issues but offered no viable solution. Engels rejected the theory as nonsensical,[88] even accusing it of cynicism. He interprets Thomas R. Malthus (1766–1834) as claiming that, in the event of overpopulation, people 'have to be disposed of in one way or another: either they must be killed by violence or they must starve'.[89] With the population theory, the immorality of the economists reached its climax; Malthus's theory was revealed as the 'keystone of the liberal system of free trade, whose fall entails the downfall of the entire edifice'.[90] The root cause of the malaise lay, for Engels, in competition based on private property. But again, he focused only on the dark side of the liberal economic system. The actual results of what he perceived as naked competition in terms of rising productivity, output and per capita consumption remained unmentioned.

Engels' attack on Malthus, especially as expressed in his *Letters from London*[91] – a series of articles on the economic and social situation in England and Ireland published in various issues of the *Schweizerischer Republikaner* (Swiss Republican) in March and June 1843 – is unusually harsh. He writes as an observer acutely concerned at the living conditions he sees and sympathetic to the cause of the workers and the aims of socialism:

> Adam Smith's free trade has been pushed to the insane conclusions of the Malthusian theory of population and has produced nothing but a new, more civilized form of the old monopoly system: a form which finds its representatives among the present-day Tories, and which successfully combated the Malthusian nonsense, but in the end arrived once more at Malthus's conclusions. Everywhere there is inconsistency and hypocrisy, while the striking economic tracts of the Socialists and partly also of the Chartists are thrown aside with contempt and find readers only among the lower classes.[92]

What, then, is the essence of the Malthusian population theory that so aggravated Engels? The economic pessimist Malthus saw the only solution for a supposedly finite food supply in the limitation of population growth. In accordance with his 'population law', rising prosperity leads to increasing population growth. But the population grows in geometric progression, while the means for sustaining its livelihood grows in arithmetic (linear) progression. Population growth is restricted by the availability of means of sustenance. Conversely, the population, and with it the number of workers, will rise wherever intensive tillage, import of agricultural products and changes in the distribution of goods bring an increase in those means. As soon as these conditions cease to apply, the rise in population meets obstacles in the form of bad living conditions, illness, famine, war, late marital age etc. For Malthus, the reason for poverty was simply an excessively high population in relation to what was necessary to sustain it. He considered the amount of food a country could produce or purchase as setting a natural limit to its population growth.[93]

Malthus's population theory was severely criticized for at least two reasons: first, the dubious, axiomatically formulated relation between food supply and population growth in terms of arithmetic and geometric progressions; secondly, the idea of setting the relation between wages and food prices primarily in terms of avoiding overpopulation, this being seen as the only way to really improve the situation of the lower classes.[94] The reception of Malthus' *Essay on the Principle of Population* was further tainted by some formulations (removed from later editions) that were openly and even contemptuously inhumane. Taken together, these circumstances gave rise to rejection of his entire position: Jérôme-Adolphe Blanqui (1798–1854), for instance, cited the passage as follows:

Anyone, he [Malthus] says, born into an already populated world, whose family lacks the means to nourish him or whose society does not need his work, such a person has not the slightest right to demand any portion of nourishment; he is really superfluous on this earth. At the great feast of nature no place has been laid for him. Nature commands him to step down and does not hesitate to execute this command herself.[95]

Leaving aside the prose and concentrating on Malthus's central statement, it becomes clear that he intended to give a description of contemporary reality through a statistical comparison of population growth in different states and regions of the world. It is certainly not the case, as Engels implied – he spoke of 'Malthusian consequences'[96] – that Malthus's theory was responsible for (let alone the cause of) working-class suffering. Confirming his own observations and assumptions, the criticism directed by Blanqui and others against Malthus and the national economists would have been welcome to his ears; at all events, its influence on him was considerable.

Key influences on Engels' thought

In the spring of 1841 Engels left what he considered the stuffy and monotonous mercantile atmosphere of Bremen and returned to the parental business in Barmen. There, however, the situation was no better, so in September of that year he resolved to complete his military service as a one-year volunteer and joined the Royal Prussian Guard artillery in Berlin. As an officer cadet and son of a wealthy factory owner, he could afford to live outside the barracks, and he soon discovered his passion for warfare and laid the foundation for a later career as an artillery expert. At the same time he took the opportunities offered for visits to reading rooms and pubs where philosophical questions were discussed and joined a group of radical young intellectuals including such personalities as Bruno Bauer and Max Stirner, the leading figures of the Berlin Young Hegelians, as well as Bruno's brothers Edgar and Egbert,[97] Karl Friedrich Köppen and Arnold Ruge. They called themselves 'the Freethinkers' and – often in the context of excessive drinking sessions – propagated their contempt for morals, religion and bourgeois decency. Bruno Bauer himself spoke of 'literary tosspots'[98] and a companion and for a while a close friend of Engels, Stephan Born (1824–1898) – founder of the 'General Workers' Brotherhood' – of a 'circle of noisy personalities'.[99]

As a guest student at the Friedrich Wilhelm University, Engels attended lectures by, among others, the Hegel critic Friedrich Wilhelm Schelling (1775–1854), who, in an attempt to combat 'the consequences of Hegelian thought',[100] had (at the age of sixty-six) been appointed to the chair of philosophy. With convictions that set freedom of thought above all else and considered Christianity an obstacle to progress, the Young Hegelians shook the Prussian state to its foundations.[101] If, under Friedrich Wilhelm III, Prussia still met Hegel's criteria of a free, liberal and rational state – although freedom of the press and some other rights had been progressively restricted since 1819 – the accession of Friedrich Wilhelm IV in 1840 brought a return to the old conservative tradition with its monarchist principles and the end of Hegelian ideals. By chance Engels arrived in Berlin at the perfect moment to perceive the practical relevance of philosophy: religion was being radically undermined in critical writings like *The Essence of Christianity* (1841) by Hegel's pupil Ludwig Feuerbach (1804–1872), and practical idealism, in the form of materialism, was in the intellectual ascendant.

In October 1842 Engels completed his military service and again returned to Barmen. His father, displeased with the critical atheistic standpoint of his son and hoping to bring him back to the path of virtue by hard work in the company,[102] sent him to Ermen & Engels in Manchester. In England he was tasked with securing the family interests and familiarizing himself with English trading methods in order to apply these later in the factory in Engelskirchen. On his way to England, Engels visited the office of the *Rheinische Zeitung* in Cologne on 16 November 1842 and met Karl Marx, who only four weeks earlier (15 October 1842) had been appointed leading editor of that paper. It was their first meeting, and it was characterized by mutual caution, as Engels counted himself as one of the Berlin Freethinkers, whose poor reputation, Marx feared, would hinder his own political advancement.[103]

Engels had already made contact with the early German socialist Moses Hess (1812–1875), co-founder of the *Rheinische Zeitung*, whom he later dubbed 'the first communist of the party'.[104] In his book *Die europäische Triarchie* (The European Triarchy, 1841) and the essay 'Sozialismus und Kommunismus' (Socialism and Communism, 1842), Hess, like other advocates of socialism, saw the solution of the social crisis in Germany – which he pointedly blamed on the destruction of medieval institutions and the increasing spread of egoism[105] – as lying in a communist future to be achieved by radical upheaval. The 'principle of modernity', he wrote, was increasingly perceived as 'the absolute unity of all life, manifested in Germany as abstract idealism, in France as abstract communism'.[106] A year later, in November 1843, Engels, reflecting in two articles in *New Moral World* on the 'progress of social reform on the continent' and – with Marx, Hess and Ruge particularly in mind – on the situation perceived in Germany twelve months earlier, wrote:

> Thus, philosophical Communism may be considered for ever established in Germany, notwithstanding the efforts of the governments to keep it down. … And this is the part we have to perform now. Our party has to prove that either all the philosophical efforts of the German nation, from Kant to Hegel, have been useless – worse than useless; or, that they must end in Communism; that the Germans must either reject their great philosophers, whose names they hold up as the glory of their nation, or that they must adopt Communism. And this *will* be proved.[107]

On arriving in England, Engels keenly followed political and economic events, devouring literature on the industrial situation and the condition of the workers, including factory inspectors' reports on the abuse of working hours and the employment of children and adolescents and medical accounts like that of the physician James Phillips Kay on the cholera epidemics in the Manchester slums.[108] At the same time, he closely observed the English socialist workers' movement and took part in many of its meetings. He wrote a number of quick articles on economics and domestic politics, reinforcing with firm reasoning his views on inevitable social revolution.[109] Industry, he argued, has created a class of the absolute poor, a situation which cannot be reversed, because such people are excluded from the stable acquisition of property. Every economic crisis plunges this class, to which almost half the population of Britain belongs, into a human catastrophe, and revolution must necessarily follow once the workers have become conscious of their situation and power. As soon as this has happened, social revolution will take place in the form of a radical and violent change; 'fear of death from starvation ... will be stronger than fear of the law'.[110]

Engels' description of conditions in Manchester and the intellectual rigour of his approach reveal his outstanding gifts as a social commentator. His analyses of economic processes can be ascribed to his entrepreneurial training and experience in international commerce. Where, however, did his theoretical insights come from?

Several aspects of Engels' critique of the classical British economists suggest a substantial debt to the socialist orator John Watts (1818–1887), a thinker in the tradition of Robert Owen (1771–1858), central elements of whose *Facts and Fictions of Political Economy* (1842) recur in Engels' economic theory. Watts had been deputy secretary of the Mechanics' Institute in Coventry and had come to Manchester in July 1841. A frequent public speaker, he became known to Engels principally through his Sunday lectures.[111] His analyses of landed property, land rents and competition, wages and impoverishment, labour and capital cover the same ground as Engels' *Outlines*, and Watts's text also serves as literary reference for the younger man's discussion of Malthus and population theory. Arguments along these lines are not found in any of Engels' writings before June 1843. Moreover, both writers draw on Robert Owen's critique of political economics.[112] The dictum of *Outlines*, for example, that 'elementary, unscientific huckstering' has simply been replaced by 'a developed system of licensed fraud, an entire science of enrichment' which 'bears on its brow the mark of the most detestable selfishness'[113] coincides with Watts's utterances on 'the evil essence' of business. For Watts, too, political economics is a science developed solely in order to grasp the specificities of fraud.[114] Accordingly, one finds in Watts's writing the exclusive causal reduction of national wealth to labour, the rooting of the capitalist value system in force and deceit and the inequitable distribution of the means of production, alongside capitalist greed for profit, rejection of competition and trade etc., as well as widespread criticism of classical economists like Malthus, McCulloch or Mill.[115] Above all, Engels was excited by Watts's views on national economics and religion.[116]

In his critique of the waxing impoverishment of large sectors of the population and their reduction to a proletarian condition, Engels borrows from French socialists like Charles Simonde de Sismondi (1773–1842) and his follower Louis Blanc (1813–1882), whose critique of political economics was indebted to Sismondi's *Principes de l'économie politique, ou de la richesse dans ses rapports avec la population* (1819).[117] Blanc

Figure 9.4 Robert Owen (1771–1858), British philanthropist and socialist, founder of the cooperatives in New Lanark Mills, Scotland (1799), and New Harmony, Indiana, USA (1825). © AKG.

had originally set out his ideas about the organization of work in a series of essays in the *Revue du Progrès politique, social et littéraire*, which he had himself founded; he published them separately in 1839 under the title *Organisation du travail*.[118] The essays spoke of the increasing separation of rich and poor, of those with and without property, of the exploiters and the exploited and of the devastating effects of competition and resultant wage pressure on the living conditions of the workers. Social reform was seen as a general solution for the problems arising from these abuses.[119] Blanc propagated cooperative workshops as an effective means of sweeping aside the results of competition and exploitation and building a society on the socialist premises of justice and equality. Once the state itself, as a 'prime leader of production', entered the competitive process through the cooperative workshops, competition would be abolished:[120] the superior communal life exhibited by the cooperatives would force private industry to follow suit.[121] Blanc did not, however, seek to disturb existing property rights, private ownership of consumer goods or inheritance laws. Engels is more analytic and systematic than his forerunner in his critique of political economics, but he takes over Blanc's combative rhetoric.[122]

Less rhetorically combative but more profoundly anarchistic is Pierre-Joseph Proudhon's (1809–1865) *Qu'est ce que la propriété?* (What Is Property?, 1840), a question to which Proudhon gave the lapidary answer, 'La propriété c'est le vol' (Property is theft).[123] Proudhon finds fault not only with classical economics but also with the various strands of socialism because, like communism, they undermine the freedom of the workers. In fact, he rejects any form of state organization as based on a repressive authoritarian relationship. Proudhon accuses existing societal structures of allowing income to be gained without work, although work alone is productive, and in place of rule by an authoritarian state, he sets organization of the economy through contracts drawn up between individual citizens, social groups, associations and corporations. An ordered society will arise out of the free activity of all its members, the individual field of activity being determined by natural division of labour, freedom of occupation etc. In this system there will be no government, no political parties, no authority: human freedom will be paramount, the liberty of the citizen absolute.[124] No one expressed this ideal of work in perfect freedom more clearly than Charles Fourier.

For Moses Hess, communism would make the ideal actually attainable.[125] Hess saw the capitalist system as the main obstacle to such freedom and the root cause of modern dehumanization. To attain freedom, the basis of capitalism in private property must be abolished: 'No property other than that held in common as a human good can promote my personal freedom. Indeed, only that which is simultaneously a common good can truly be my own inviolate property.'[126] Once private property and capitalism have been abolished, egoism and competition can also be overcome and a new (communist) society created, based on freedom and human togetherness[127] – a view shared by Engels in his postulate of revolution as the way to common ownership: there can, he argued, be no stronger proof that communism necessarily follows from the premises of modern civilization.[128] Engels' observation of actual conditions in the working-class areas of Manchester confirmed his conviction – taken over from Hess – that in capitalism private property and money dehumanize and alienate, degrading human beings to the level of goods, reifying them as economic objects.[129] Political economics, by making such people an object of investigation, simply transforms them back into (now reified) subjects. In Manchester, Engels found the proof he needed of the relevance of communist ideas and the absence of any alternative to social revolution. In *The Condition of the Working Class in England*, he writes: 'The revolution must come; it is already too late to bring about a peaceful solution.'[130]

The various failed attempts of the early socialists – Saint-Simon's fraternity and moral renewal, Fourier's *phalanstère*, Owen's cooperative colony of New Harmony, Indiana – were later dismissed by Marx and Engels as impracticable[131] and contrasted with their own 'scientific socialism'. Looking back on those three predecessors in 1882, Engels wrote: 'The immaturity of capitalist production, the immaturity of the class situation, was met by an immaturity of theory. ... These new socialist systems were doomed from the start as Utopias, and the further they developed in detail, the more they were bound to end in pure fantasy.'[132]

A final question relating to the important influences on Engels' thought is why Lorenz von Stein (1815–1890) is not among them. Engels took little notice of his writings, although his early *Der Sozialismus und Kommunismus des heutigen Frankreich* (French Socialism and Communism Today, 1842) was a major force in the spread of socialism in Germany. Wilhelm Roscher's *bon mot* that, for the German public, socialism was 'a fairytale from a distant land' is scarcely an adequate explanation.[133] It was more the case that Stein's ideas were largely at odds with Engels' own – which by the time Stein's book was published had already attained their basic shape – and simply did not interest him. Various texts written by Marx and Engels in 1845–6 mention Stein, frequently as a source of knowledge among German socialists, and although he is censured for his faulty and superficial account of French socialism[134] – Engels read the French authors in the original – he is credited with at least attempting to 'depict the connection between socialist literature and actual developments in French society'.[135] In his introduction and conclusion to his translation of the first seven chapters of Fourier's *Des trois unités externes*, published as 'A Fragment of Fourier's on Trade', however, Engels accuses Stein of never having familiarized himself to any extent with the central arguments[136] and comments ironically: 'Herr Stein's meagre extracts are quite sufficient to bring about this brilliant victory of German theory over the wretched efforts of foreigners.'[137]

In fact, Stein also ranks work higher than capital, but instead of either a Utopia or a revolution, he propagates 'merely' social reform,[138] not only finding good points in the bourgeoisie but also criticizing the widespread immorality of the proletariat, which he judges is partly responsible for its own condition. This ran utterly counter to Engels' ideas. Moreover, Stein's reform is to be achieved through a harmony of class interests rather than their clash and the subsequent annihilation of the classes as natural enemies. The freedom Stein advocates as the highest principle is the fruit of individuality and self-determination (which includes rather than excludes the acquisition of property and capital),[139] and his final failing is to rate socialism higher than communism – but only as second best. For socialism, too, aims at the abrogation of private ownership, which for Stein remains the foundation and goal of individuality and freedom.[140] Finally, he is critical of Engels' *Outlines of a Critique of Political Economy*, granting only that it is 'the most decisive diatribe against the bourgeoisie that has ever appeared in Germany' and that it 'depicts on a singularly wide canvas the extremes to which industry can proceed in its ruthless exploitation of humanity'.[141]

Figure 9.5 Lorenz von Stein (1815–1890), lawyer, economist and sociologist. © AKG.

Creation and destruction in Engels: I – theory

In Bremen, a shift evidently took place in Engels' outlook and opinions. His creative potential began to unfold, and he rebelled against the petrified structures of the company around him, with its rigid daily routines and the expectations imposed on him by his father. His protest against what he saw as faults in state and society expressed itself in early literary and journalistic work ranging from *Cola di Rienzi* (1840–1), a melodramatic poem possibly conceived as a libretto for an opera, through journalistic descriptions, reports and ironic comments on current events, to social analyses, some of which could claim to be scientific.[142]

At the same time, the young Engels delved into critical theology, in particular Friedrich Schleiermacher's theology of redemption – the reconciliation of intuitive religion of the heart with modern rationality – and David Friedrich Strauss's (1808–1874) *The Life of Jesus Critically Examined* (1835–6), which brought him to the following conclusion: 'When, at the age of 18, you read Strauss, the rationalists and the "Church News", you must either do so unthinkingly or begin to doubt your Wuppertal faith. I cannot understand how orthodox preachers can be so orthodox when the Bible contains obvious contradictions.'[143] Engels struggles to find his personal faith, reading, thinking, doubting and debating in emotional turmoil with himself and others. A few weeks after the letter just cited to Friedrich Graeber, he wrote in July 1839: 'I feel it, I will not be lost, I will come to God, for whom I long with my whole heart.'[144] And in October, after further prolonged heart-searching in the matter of faith, he wrote to Friedrich Graeber's brother Wilhelm, whom he addresses as 'Guillermo':

> Yes, Guillermo, *jacta est alea*, I am a Straussian, a poor poet sheltering beneath the winged genius of David Friedrich Strauss. Just listen to what a fellow that is! There lie the four Gospels, bright and tangled as chaos, before them an adoring Mysticism. Along comes Strauss like a young god and hauls that chaos out into the light of day. *Adios* faith! It is as full of holes as a sieve. Here and there he sees too much myth, but only marginally; otherwise he is brilliant through and through. If you can disprove Strauss – *eh bien*, I'll become a Pietist again.[145]

Via Strauss – who sought not to abolish Christianity but merely to adapt it to the new scientific age[146] – Engels came to Hegel, whose work he studied with his usual enthusiasm, adopting his reflections on mind, history and freedom, his concept of man as sharing God's rationality, his replacement of religious faith with knowledge and culture and his conviction that the functions of the church would henceforth be rendered by education offered at schools and universities. This marked the end of Engels' Christian faith; he turned instead to the materialistic-atheistic philosophy of Feuerbach.

Between the seminal period in Bremen and the socialist awareness and involvement of the Manchester years lies an impressive personal, intellectual and spiritual development: Engels had lost his Christian faith, but he had gained a perspective that drove him to change the world he saw before him. The process of learning and reflection lit in him a flame eager to burn down and renew – a 'new' clearly articulated in *Outlines* and *The Condition of the Working Class*, whose theoretically sketched communism, built on empirical observations in the factories and slums of Manchester, bore within it the ideological framework of 'scientific socialism'. There are many elements of later Marxism: the societal significance of productive forces, class division and conflict, the instability of industrial capitalism, political economics as the ideology of the bourgeoisie, the inevitability of social revolution – all these are present *in nuce*.[147] Only a little later, the 'new' was clearly expressed in two early works written with Marx,

The Holy Family or Critique of Critical Criticism: Against Bruno Bauer and Company (1845) and *The Communist Manifesto* (1848). In the first of these, the authors presented their impressions and experiences of Manchester and Paris, distancing themselves from the Young Hegelians. Philosophical theorizing, they argued, whether Hegelian or Young Hegelian, was ineffective in changing the living conditions of the workers. It must cease, materialist premises must be laid and practical consequences must be drawn: the proletarian revolution is indispensable; the abolition of private property and its replacement with common ownership is an unchallengeable goal.[148]

Creation and destruction in contemporary economic and cultural thought

The education of principles for a better society from a critique of existing structures and the attempt to implement them in practice was not invented by Friedrich Engels: it is a constituent of every political Utopia, beginning with Thomas More's eponymous work in 1516. The idea of breaking down the old in order to make the new was current above all in intellectual circles in the nineteenth century. In the form of the metaphor of 'creative destruction', it reflected the sense of a new dawn in technology, science and organization omnipresent in the industrialized world, from railways and mines, through the physics of heat, light and electricity to breakthroughs in chemistry and biology. It would soon play a key role in the theory of economic development proposed by Joseph A. Schumpeter and is prominent today, for example, in Clayton Christensen's theory of disruptive innovation.[149]

Propagated explicitly in Schumpeter's *Capitalism, Socialism, and Democracy* (1942),[150] the metaphor of the creative destruction of received structures already underlies his pioneering work of evolutionary economics, *Theory of Economic Development* (1912).[151] The idea reflects his notion of economics as a science which, like its object, is a one-way historical process 'in whose course the attempt to understand economic phenomena issues in the construction, extension, and demolition of a never-ending sequence of analytical edifices'.[152] Before Schumpeter promoted the concept, Werner Sombart (1863–1941) had used it in his *Krieg und Kapitalismus* (War and Capitalism, 1913) to explain the immense economic development of the nineteenth century.[153] In essence, it underlay the omnipresent contemporary concept of productive forces, about which Reinert und Reinert[154] remark that in nineteenth-century German economic thought (see especially Friedrich List, 1789–1846), this played a similarly key role in understanding the origins of national wealth as the enhancement of competitiveness does in the growth of the national product today.

The metaphor of creative destruction was not, however, invented by economists; it achieved cultural currency in late nineteenth-century Germany above all in the aphorisms of Friedrich Nietzsche's (1844–1900) *Zarathustra*, for example: 'he that breaks their tablets of values, the breaker, the lawbreaker – he is the maker';[155] 'he that will be a creator must always destroy';[156] 'seek to burn in your own flame; how will you rise anew if you have not first turned to ashes?'[157] and 'he that must be a creator ..., truly he must be first a destroyer and a breaker of values'.[158] Likewise, Nietzsche's *Ecce Homo*

Economic Thought of His Age

Figure 9.6 Joseph Alois Schumpeter (1883–1950), economist, *c.* 1920, © AKG.

declares, 'Within every "Yes" the "No" of destruction is a precondition.'[159] Nietzsche is a key figure of this period, and after his death in 1900, a veritable cult of the philosopher arose, especially among the social elite: between 1890 and 1914 his teachings became an accepted *weltanschauung*[160] that also affected leading economists. Sombart was profoundly influenced by him, [161] and Schumpeter, keenly aware of the elitist theories of his day, would recite Nietzsche's texts by heart.[162] Nietzsche himself, however, was anything but a devotee of capitalism: for the author of *Thoughts out of Season*, 'The conduct of science, when … ever further unleashed in accordance with the motto "the more the better", is as damaging to scholars as the economic doctrine of *laisser faire* to the morals of whole peoples.'[163] Profoundly influenced by the work of Arthur Schopenhauer (1788–1860), he was also acquainted with Hindu thought, in which the process of creation and destruction plays a central role.

The combination of the birth of the new and the destruction of the old is present in Egyptian mythology in the form of the divine bird Benu and in the ancient Greece of Herodotus as the Phoenix, which, at the end of its life cycle, burns in order to rise from its ashes (or its decomposing flesh) as a symbol – in Late Antiquity of immortality; in medieval Christianity of resurrection. With its principle of the endless cycle of life, Hinduism offers a particularly rich version of creative destruction in which the trinity of major gods, Brahma the creator, Vishnu the preserver and Shiva the destroyer, enacts the eternally recurrent cycle of life and decay. In these various cultural forms, the process of creative destruction is not unfamiliar to European intellectual circles of the later nineteenth century.[164]

Through Johann Gottfried Herder (1744–1803), the Indian myth of creative destruction entered German philosophy; his major work *Outlines of a Philosophy of the History of Man* (1784–91) contains similar passages on the need to destroy in order to create, as does the work of his friend Johann Wolfgang von Goethe (1749–1832). The concept passed down to Nietzsche via his 'master' Schopenhauer – or more precisely via the Orientalist Friedrich Majer (1772–1818), himself a pupil of Herder's. One can also discern the influence on Nietzsche of Friedrich Hölderlin (1770–1843) – a favourite poet of his – in the shape of the interplay of creation and destruction, reflecting the Dionysian imagery of Horace:[165] Dionysus as uniting joy and pain, life and death, each arising out of its opposition to the other. Hölderlin viewed the political developments of his day, above all the French Revolution, in this light as the birth of a new world out of the ruins of the old.[166] The revolution had launched a process of dissolution entailing, on the one hand, the passing of the fatherland and, on the other, a new beginning.[167] The underlying notion of life as a constant creative destruction is thematized in his essay 'Das Werden im Vergehen' (Becoming in Dissolution, *c.* 1800):

> The fall of the fatherland, of nature and humanity …: a special, idealized world dissolves in order that out of it, and out of the remnant of families and forces of nature, … a new world may arise. *This dissolution (or transition) of the fatherland* feels within the limbs of the constant world as if in the very moment and degree to which that world dissolves, the newborn, youthful, possible begins to stir.[168]

Although a scientifically minded writer like Goethe was rejected as godless in the Barmen of Engels' schooldays,[169] the young Friedrich still grew up with Goethe's works, along with those of Romantics such as Herder, Schiller, Hölderlin, Schlegel, Klopstock, Wieland, Uhland, Novalis and the Grimm brothers. He developed into an admirer – himself a budding poet – of the heroic German national spirit.[170] But at the same time he was an unflinching observer of life on the Barmen streets who, despite his penchant for the heroic, consciously made the factual and tangible the object of his investigations. In the face of such social misery, graphically expressed (at the latest) in his *Letters from Wuppertal* (1839), Engels rejects the ideal, glorified nationalism of the Romantics.[171] In reviews of popular literature, published under the pseudonym Friedrich Oswald in various issues of the *Telegraph* in November 1839, he calls for a clear focus on present-day concerns – the 'struggle for freedom', 'developing constitutionalism', 'rebellion against pressure from the aristocracy' etc.: 'It should be self-evident', he writes, 'that the usages of former times, whose exercise today would be senseless or even wrong, have no place in popular literature'.[172]

A decade later, in *The Communist Manifesto* (1848), the concept of creative destruction becomes explicit in terms of revolutionary upheaval. This is not just a matter of the one revolution to end capitalism but of the law of creative destruction apparent in history from the most primitive societal organization to socialism itself. The *Manifesto* describes in detail the takeover of power by the bourgeoisie, who have destroyed 'all feudal, patriarchal, idyllic relations' that formerly held sway in society. The proletarians, for their part, in order to take control of society's productive forces, must abolish all previous modes of acquisition, destroying 'all previous securities for, and insurances of, individual property'.[173]

Creation and destruction in Engels: II – action

Engels' activities are not, however, restricted to writing and theorizing; he is active in deed as well as in word in pursuit of his ideals. In the 'year of revolutions' (1848), he supported Marx, he claims, in the effort to make the *Neue Rheinische Zeitung* the public voice of the proletarian movement, travelling to Barmen (albeit without effect) to canvass potential investors for the paper. He wrote about Germany's first National Assembly, recently elected in the Paulskirche (Church of St Paul) in Frankfurt, and, arraigned for high treason, was obliged to flee to Belgium, whence he was immediately deported to France. In May 1849 he appeared again in Elberfeld (Barmen's contiguous sister-town) as a militant revolutionary and advisor against Prussian forces, but when he sought to turn the defence of the city into a communist issue, he was required to leave and proceeded to South Germany to fight with the Baden revolutionary army against the Prussians. Here, he won his spurs as a courageous soldier of the revolution, but again he had to flee, this time to Switzerland. All this time, Engels was also journalistically active for the proletarian cause. After the final failure of the revolution, he joined Marx in England, where he became active in the Communist League.[174]

The 'year of revolutions' did not bring the hoped-for change of systems in the states of Europe, and even Manchester, once projected as *the* ideal city for revolution, had now become a show city, officially visited by Queen Victoria in 1851. The 'great Victorian boom' had broken out and would continue into the mid-1870s, bringing with it a rise in general living standards that was not materially impeded by the minor economic crises of 1857 and 1866. The steel and cotton industries were expanding vastly, and the first World Fair, the Great Exhibition of 1851 in London, underlined the leading role of the British Empire.

Engels stayed for almost twenty years with Ermen & Engels and played a highly successful role in the company. His private income grew, enabling him to live in a manner suited to his position in society and to provide the Marx family with substantial financial support. At the end of June 1869 he was, at his own request, paid off by Gottfried Ermen; he left the company and the following year moved with his companion Lizzy Burns to London, where he was able to live from private means and devote his time to research and organization on behalf of the proletariat. He was elected onto the General Council of the International Working Men's Association (the so-called *Internationale*, founded in 1864) and as a 'corresponding secretary' was instrumental in coordinating the various movements of the left.[175] Engels now devoted himself to the study of science, and after Marx's death in March 1883, he set about systematizing, developing and publicizing his literary and intellectual estate. The impact of Marxism as a political philosophy is undoubtedly to a great extent Engels' work.

Engels was successful not only as an entrepreneur but also in his investments on the stock exchange. He defended himself against the (in his eyes) *petit bourgeois* accusation of making a fortune out of the exploitation of the proletariat, pointing out that the stock exchange alters 'only the distribution of the added value already stolen from the workers' and the concentration of capital that will bring about the fall of the system is, in fact, hastened by that institution.[176] In the logic of capitalism as Engels understood it, his fortune was bringing the revolution closer. That entrepreneurial and speculative activity should be dedicated to the demise and replacement of the system it supports is – argumentatively at least – an eminent example of creative destruction. By his own logic, Engels was bent on establishing the presuppositions for the new dawn of socialism.

In *Anti-Dühring: Herr Eugen Dühring's Revolution in Science* (1878) and the scattered scientific notes and comments of the *Dialectics of Nature* (1873–82), Engels interprets Marx's materialistic premises of historical development as a generalization of the natural dialectic evident in nature and human society, whose processes of change parallel each other: 'It is, therefore, from the history of nature and human society that the laws of dialectics are abstracted. For they are nothing but the most general laws of these two stages of historical development, as well as of thought itself.'[177] The phases of historical progress are determined by their own material. History as we know it is inherent in the evolution of nature through the animal kingdom to humankind. For Engels, the histories of human nature and society are structurally parallel, both governed by the same dialectical principle. Politics is subject to the same deterministic evolution whose supreme laws, Engels states, are the 'most general laws' developed by Hegel, albeit 'in his idealistic way as mere laws of thought'.[178] These are:

1. The law of transition from quantity and quality and vice versa: that cumulative quantitative change over a prolonged period gives rise to a sudden jump, a qualitative change.
2. The law of interpenetration of polar opposites, or the inherent unity-in-opposition of natural and social processes: that contradiction between extremes leads to the development of a new solution (thesis/antithesis/synthesis) – a clear case of destruction creating the new.
3. The law of the negation of negation: that development replaces the old with the new, but not fully; positive elements of the old are as far as possible preserved.

The principle of creative destruction underlies all three laws, and Engels cites in *Anti-Dühring* a number of examples illustrating the process. Thus, a barleycorn sown in the earth decays – is negated – in order to bring forth a plant that represents its negation. A butterfly develops from a chrysalis which is destroyed (negated) in that process; it mates and, after laying its eggs, undergoes the second negation of death.[179] The same principle can be found in mathematics: 'Take any algebraic quantity a; negate it, and we have $-a$ (minus a); negate this negation by multiplying $-a$ with $-a$, and we have $+a^2$: in other words, the original positive quantity on a higher level, namely to the power of 2.'[180] Further examples could be given.

Especially the final third of the nineteenth century is known for its scientific and technological breakthroughs. Progress in classical physics (i.e. pre-relativity and quantum theory) reached a high point and, with similar discoveries in chemistry and biology, launched a frenzy of interest in scientific developments reflected in lecture series, public experiments, educational events etc. at almost every level. An intellectual like Engels could not but be affected by this atmosphere and, with the exception of the marginalist revolution in economics – which he called 'the rotten vulgarized economics of Jevons'[181] and dismissed as 'Jevons's and Menger's theory of use value and marginal utility'[182] – he followed current developments as well as he could, cultivating contacts with leading scientists and reading the work, for example, of the geologist Charles Lyell, the evolutionary biologist Thomas Huxley and Charles Darwin's *On the Origin of Species* (1859). Engels was, however, sceptical about Darwinism, considering 'the whole Darwinian doctrine of the struggle for existence' as no more than an 'application of Hobbes' principle of *bellum omnium contra omnes* [the war of all against all]', a transfer of the principle of competition and 'Malthusian population theory from society onto living nature'. As such, it was, he felt, highly questionable, and the attempt to deduce general laws of nature by projecting insights from natural history onto human social history was utterly naïve.[183]

The transfer of behavioural patterns from the animal to the human already stumbles over the fact that the 'struggle for existence is no longer for bare means of subsistence but for means of enjoyment and advancement'.[184] Capitalist production generates goods in such quantities that they can no longer be consumed, because the population is 'artificially and violently' prevented from accessing them. The result, Engels argued, is that 'every 10 years a crisis re-establishes the balance through destruction not only of the means of subsistence, enjoyment and advancement, but in large part also of the productive forces themselves'.[185] The cyclical mechanism of destruction and creation inherent in the capitalist production method leads inevitably to such crises but then also overcomes them.[186] However, the workers, the ones who actually produce the goods, always lose. Hence, the imperative to break out of that cycle, to abolish once and for all the capitalist social order 'by withdrawing the management of social production and distribution from the incompetent capitalist ruling class, and giving it to the productive masses – that is the socialist revolution'.[187] The revolution revokes all distinctions and differences between the classes and makes the intervention of the state in social relations superfluous. The Darwinian struggle for existence will cease, replaced by planned organization of social production.

The idea of creative destruction is immanent, too, in Marx's explanation (as commonly understood) of the overarching historical development from primitive through slave and feudal societies to capitalism and socialism: a process of epochal change brought about by the opposition of productive forces and relations of production in which each phase builds on the demise of the last – again, the new arises in shedding and overcoming the old. Marx himself illustrates the point in his comment (from *Towards a Critique of Hegel's Philosophy of Right*, 1843–4) that as 'the highest beings for humanity, men and women are called upon to overthrow every circumstance in which their kind is debased, enslaved, abandoned and made contemptible'.[188] Only then can a better situation arise.

Concluding overview

This chapter has aimed the following:

1. To set Friedrich Engels' economic thought in the context of the theories current when he wrote his early treatises. This entails an overview of the economic thought of the age and of its impact (or non-impact) on Engels.
2. To explicate the metaphor of creative destruction as realized in Engels' thought and action.

Engels' critique of economic theory is essentially concerned with the classical principles of national economics, which he sees as sharing responsibility for the misery of working-class living conditions. Given the breadth and diversity of existing critical positions, he concentrates exclusively on the work of socialists and social reformers, ignoring many approaches that might have supported his arguments. Key influences on his reception of economic theory were, for example, the philosopher and writer Moses Hess and the social reformer John Watts, from whom he came to the early French socialists and the idea, on the one hand, of abolishing private property and competition and, on the other, of transforming the socioeconomic system through social revolution. In the shadow of

Hegel's dialectical idealism, Marx and Engels' scrutiny of the early socialists brought them to the materialistic notion of history and ultimately to the 'scientific' theory of socioeconomic transformation, in which the production and exchange of goods are the cornerstones of every societal order:

> For in every society that has appeared in history, the manner in which wealth is distributed and society divided into classes or estates depends upon what is produced, how it is produced, and how the products are exchanged. From this point of view, the final causes of all social changes and political revolutions are to be sought, not in men's minds, not in their increasing insights into eternal truth and justice, but in changes in the modes of production and exchange. They are to be sought, not in the *philosophy*, but in the *economics* of each epoch.[189]

Engels' confidence in technological progress leads him to the (realistic) assumption of ever-changing and adapting productive forces as a fundamental premise for his theory of social transformation, which in turn reflects the metaphor of creative destruction current in the supremely creative and productive nineteenth century. The metaphor informs not only Engels' thought and work but also his personal development and action. The youthful admirer of the German heroic epic becomes a keen observer and reflective theoretician of his world and his own position and thinking within it. The committed Christian becomes an atheist; the student of economic philosophy engages with the fundamentals of socialist economic theory and seeks to realize this step in his own theory as well as in journalistic, political and other activities. Critical of the present, he aims to overthrow it and embrace the new.

Engels certainly succeeds in highlighting faults in the existing economic system, for example the inequitable division of power in a competitive culture between owners of land and capital and workers, or the distribution problem that remains unsolved even in present-day economies. Then as now, however, Engels' clarion call for the abolition of private property bypasses reality. Capitalism has not been revoked by socialism: it would be truer to say that it has developed into a success model with a social face. And competition, as the powerful driver of production, has generated adequate pro-capita income – and hence consumption and living standards – for most people at least in the industrial and service-oriented countries. The major challenge today is to adapt and improve the system in the face of recognized weaknesses. The regulatory policies of national states and groupings seek not to abolish the system altogether but to support competition and control monopolizing tendencies. What remains highly questionable, however – given the limited resources of the planet – is whether the consumption standards of the West can be extended to a surging world population. In that respect, Engels may well be proved wrong in his emphatic rejection, in the context of his refutation of Malthusian population theory and in the shadow of John Watts, of the 'crazy assertion that the earth lacks the power to feed men'.[190]

The young Engels was a visionary driven by an idea. Emotional, moralizing, intuitive and impulsive, he followed his natural sense of justice in situations as he perceived them. He was certainly not the type of the careful academic, the thinker equipped with a profound sense of the ambiguity of each and every situation. It has been often noted that, for all his talent, originality and caustic wit, he constantly (and arbitrarily) shifts from the analytic to the normative level in his critique of political economics, that he misunderstands some situations altogether, that he at times lacks essential knowledge and that his judgements are sometimes overbearing. He occasionally criticizes economists for things they have not said or have explicitly rejected; he draws untenable conclusions and bases arguments on highly – even arbitrarily – selected facts.[191] This was perhaps inevitable, given the breadth of his interests, knowledge and activities, and it becomes especially clear in the intensive scientific studies of his later years. But as a passionate critic of existing social conditions, Engels was undoubtedly a creative spirit, bent on the unremitting acquisition of knowledge and above all on its active and useful application. Friedrich Engels was, more than anything else, a 'destructive creator'.

CHAPTER 10
'THIS FREDERICK! THIS FREDERICK! A NAUGHTY WICKED BOY WAS HE ...': ENGELS, MARX AND THE CRITIQUE OF POLITICAL ECONOMY

Heinz D. Kurz

Introduction

Without Engels, no Marx as we know him; without Marx, no Engels as we know him. In his Marx's biography, Gareth Stedman Jones argues that after Marx's death in 1883, when Engels opened his literary estate, he sought to play down differences in their views – differences of which he had until then been for the most part unaware, as he was largely ignorant of Marx's work from the 1870s.[1] This led to his purveying the notion of 'Marxism' as a theory shared in inviolable unity by both men – a view, according to Stedman Jones, that does not fully represent Marx's position. Instead of *unité de doctrine*, we have major differences at least in three respects: the theory of the collapse of capitalism, the scientific significance of Darwin's teachings and the role of pre-capitalist village economies as primitive societal organizations not based on private property. In the final analysis, for both Marx and Engels, all three questions concerned a right understanding of human nature and history.

When he wrote his biography, Stedman Jones did not know all the material that came to light in the second part of the *Marx Engels Collected Works* (MECW), revealing Engels' editorial intrusions into the texts especially of Volumes II and III of *Das Kapital*.[2] Had he done so, his judgement might have been yet more critical.[3] The question arises, too, whether Engels' influence on the reception of Marx and his work began only after 1883, or was it already there during 'Old Moor's' lifetime – and in that case, why did Marx offer no resistance?[4]

Marx came to 'political economy' only through Engels. The 'brilliant sketch'[5] (Marx's words) by a 23-year-old businessman with neither *Abitur* (higher school-leaving certificate) nor university degree had a track-changing impact, both intellectually and politically, on the life and work of the older man.[6] Without Engels' *Critique* (1844) he might still have taken the step from philosophy to economics. But would he have taken *this* step – one that so strongly bears the imprint of Engels' critique? Engels' influence on Marx goes far beyond just awakening his interest in a new field of study, and Marx accepted this influence ostensibly without demur.

The present chapter is structured as follows: The section 'On the prehistory of Engels' *Critique*' concerns the prehistory of Engels' *Critique*, his commercial and management training and early attempts to prepare the way for a rigorous examination of existing socioeconomic conditions. The section 'Engels' essay and Marx' views the *Critique* in the perspective of Engels' relations with Marx. The section 'Noteworthy features of Engels' essay' discusses some noteworthy features of the work. The section 'Towards a critique of Engels' essay' offers a critical scrutiny of Engels' main objections to political economy and indicates some of his misunderstandings of the classical economists. The section 'Concluding remarks' provides some concluding remarks.

On the prehistory of Engels' *Critique*

Infused with the humanist ideals of his schooling, the young Friedrich found himself increasingly at loggerheads with his father, a cotton manufacturer with leanings towards Pietism. A gifted boy, he was taken out of school against his will a year before his final examinations and employed as a commercial apprentice in the offices of his father's factory in Barmen. He completed his mercantile training in Bremen and was then sent to Manchester, where, from November 1842 to August 1844, he gained further experience and knowledge in a cotton-spinning works in which his father was a partner. By the end of this period Engels knew the modern factory and commercial systems from the shop floor upwards, and he knew the cast and manners of those who operated it. In the *Critique* his rage at the trade system and scorn for the sanctimoniousness of its agents break all bounds.

Both in Bremen and later in Barmen, Engels was on the lookout for critical, analytic works that addressed the appalling socioeconomic conditions of the day. And he soon found what he needed: Charles Fourier's (1772–1837) attack on trade and Pierre-Joseph Proudhon's (1809–1865) identification of private property as the fundamental evil of modern society fascinated him. He acquired a background knowledge of philosophy and economics through his own reading or at lectures like those given by John Watts (1818–1887) every Sunday in Manchester's Hall of Science, a workers' further education institute founded by Robert Owen (1771–1858).[7] In his still very readable, sure-footed biography, Gustav Mayer calls Engels (not unjustifiably) a 'rudderless autodidact'.[8]

On his way to England in the early summer of 1842, Engels had visited Moses Hess in Cologne and metamorphosed from radical to communist. In Manchester he made contact with socialists and Chartists, read their writings and observed, through visits to factories and domestic housing, the condition of the working class in England. His work of that title, a pioneering piece of empirical social research, appeared after his return to Barmen in 1844.[9] On arrival in England, Engels was already acquainted with the work of the early French socialists, especially Henri de Saint-Simon (1760–1825), Fourier, Proudhon and Louis Blanc (1811–1882). Apart from Fourier, however, none of them are mentioned by name in the *Critique*, though some aspects of Engels' argument are clearly indebted to their ideas: for example Saint-Simon's paean of praise for science as the replacement of religion; Fourier's depiction of trade, banking and finance as unproductive, predatory and immoral; Proudhon's famous condemnation of private property as 'theft' and his critique of the value theory of the classical economists Adam

The Critique of Political Economy

Figure 10.1 Friedrich Engels, 1845. © In the public domain.

Smith and David Ricardo; finally, Blanc's attack on competition and his plea for a right to work, together with cooperative organization of the economy and the abolition of markets and the prices they regulate. All of these aspects recur in Engels' essay.[10]

In England, Engels read the work of Robert Owen and his followers. Owen had proved impressively at New Lanark Mill – his cotton spinnery in Scotland – that better working conditions and higher wages do not impede but can even promote productivity.[11] Some observers saw this as indicating that the current socioeconomic system could be successfully reformed without disturbing its foundations in private property. With Proudhon (1840), Engels rejected this opinion. For him, a radical break was necessary: the experience gathered in 'reform laboratories' like Owen's simply underlined the economic, as well as moral, superiority of the type of societal order he had in mind – one based on 'ethical' principles. Why wait, then, when a better world was there in the making?

Full of optimism, Engels reckoned with the dawn of a new era. Even minor social stirrings were for him infallible signs of imminent upheaval. The only question was how to accelerate the process. His answer was: by taking to absurdity the doctrine of the political economists – above all the British school from Smith to Ricardo and a few of their epigones, along with Thomas Malthus and, in France, Jean-Baptiste Say. These, he argued, were the most effective apologists of the present order. Indeed, they not only justified this order, and with it the need and misery of the working class, but were, with their support for private property, competition and the market, also directly responsible for it. With his *Critique*, Engels sought to demonstrate the untenability of that position and thus to remove a crucial obstacle to the advent of the new society. Killing the dragon of 'political economy', he would clear a way to the city gate of a new society. Later, his and Marx's view of society would be spoken of as a new science – as 'scientific socialism'.

Engels' essay and Marx

In its impact on Marx and the relations between the two men, Engels' *Outlines of a Critique of Political Economy* has a number of features that call for brief comment[12]:

First, a young man, graduate of neither high school nor university, makes a lasting impression on a doctor of philosophy two years his elder with a critical essay on the causes of working-class distress and misery. He not only censures an entire academic discipline for failing to provide a credible diagnosis of the situation; he accuses its protagonists of hypocrisy, because in their attempt to cover up their incompetence, they have become rank apologists of prevailing conditions. He, Engels, will do what they could not or would not do: provide an accurate diagnosis of the situation and on that basis a successful therapy. The young Engels does not hesitate in his formulation to broach *the* central issue of humanity: the conditions governing 'the reconciliation of mankind with nature and with itself'.[13] Can one decently reprove such ambition for inadequate differentiation and a penchant for polemics? Engels' goal is revolution, the overthrow of the existing social and political order, and he is convinced that he stands on the very threshold of that cataclysm.

The basic tone of Marx's writings from the 1840s is also strongly polemical, a tendency noticeable throughout the critical literature of the period, especially among émigrés. Only after the suppression of the German Revolution of 1848–9 and, with it the fading of any hope of immediate change, was the need felt for deeper analysis of the situation, subtler debate of the theory of political economy or a precise examination of the 'anatomy' of 'bourgeois society' and its 'law of motion'. Engels' philippic fell manifestly short of what was needed if the great goal of radical societal change envisioned by both authors was to be achieved. It was against this background that Marx undertook to demonstrate with scientific rigour not just the desirability but also the inevitability of the downfall of capitalism: *Das Kapital* set out to inaugurate the era of 'scientific socialism'.

Secondly, and surprisingly, after publication of his *Critique*, Engels left the terrain of political economy increasingly to Marx, who in that field was a novice. After so much respect and recognition from the older man, and given his head start in the matter, one would have expected Engels to pursue his ideas further, with Marx offering active support. But the opposite happened: Marx was soon grappling furiously with political economic theory, while Engels played the role of associate and later merely of onlooker. A few steps in that process may be of interest.[14]

Engels probably authored some of the texts on economic questions written in 1845–6 and published posthumously as *The German Ideology*, and we know that during the first global economic crisis of 1857–8, the two men were also in close contact, exchanging views on the significance of events. Twenty years later, Engels' *Anti-Dühring* (1877–8) still contains a lengthy chapter on the economy.[15] Around the mid-1860s, however, written evidence of discussions between Marx and Engels on the subject of political economics becomes thinner. That Marx sought such communication is apparent from his letters of 1867 and 1868, but his wish left little tangible trace. The same can be said of the conversations they would have had on the occasion of Marx's visit to Engels in Manchester or during their almost daily walks after Engels' move to London in 1869. That Engels, remarkably, read only the first volume of *Das Kapital* when it was already in print – too late for any discussion of its content[16] – also suggests that questions of economic theory played a diminishing role in their intellectual exchanges. Engels' response is confined to redactional comments and – rather unusual – a series of anonymous reviews promoting the book.

In the course of his life, Engels' interests moved away from political economy to other areas of knowledge, and with Marx, the opposite movement occurred. Their political commitment – as their correspondence indicates – remained in each case intense, but Engels turned increasingly to fields in which Marx's interest was fading: materialist movements in philosophy, old and new, general and especially military history with its strategic and tactical issues, science, technological history and a good deal more. Marx shared some of these interests but with varying intensity. His work on *Das Kapital* demanded full concentration and prohibited carefree excursions into otherwise fascinating fields of learning. Only after publication of Volume I of his *magnum opus* did he allow himself such luxuries, as numerous notebooks filled with comments on far-flung disciplinary specialties reveal. But he did this with the clear intention of closing gaps in his knowledge that might hold up his progress on *Das Kapital*. Marx's mathematical exercises, for example, were not, as has sometimes been thought, a matter of mental relaxation but in order to acquire the formal competencies he needed for his work on crises and cyclical economic development. And his study of Justus von Liebig's soil fatigue theory was connected both with his law expressing the tendency of the profit rate to fall and with the perspective opening for socialism after the collapse of capitalism. It may be said without exaggeration that after 1844 a definite shift occurred in Marx's and Engels' respective domains.

Thirdly, so far as political economy is concerned, Engels' withdrawal soon after 1844 into the second line of attack is evident in the style of his support for Marx, which became increasingly less a matter of intellectual debate and more one of financial backing combined with encouragement to complete the great authorial task without delay. Engels would have been well aware how Marx had initially profited from central aspects of his *Critique* and how some of the points made in that essay recur in *Das Kapital* – albeit with correction in detail, especially regarding the evaluation of the classical economists. And we may presume that he would have drawn satisfaction from this awareness and felt himself to have been, as it were, a sleeping partner in the work. Marx alone was acknowledged as author, but Engels could justifiably have heard his own voice speaking in important passages of *Das Kapital*, too – which may in turn explain why he did not hesitate, as editor of Volumes II and III of the work, to undertake textual intrusions beyond what is strictly speaking permissible for an editor.

Fourthly, in the wake of Engels' essay, Marx studied the authors his younger colleague had cited and came to the gradual conclusion that many of the latter's judgements were untenable and some even downright misleading. He proceeded to correct these, most explicitly in the 1861–3 manuscript titled 'A Contribution to the Critique of Political Economy',[17] whose theoretical parts were later published by Karl Kautsky as *Theories of Surplus Value* (1905–10). While working and reworking the field of classical economics, Marx remained uncertain as to the implications of his correction of Engels' *Critique* for his own position. His growth in insight was gradual, and in some respects he never attained full clarity, which is not surprising, given the unusual difficulty of the problems he – like the classical economists before him – were addressing. Be that as it may, Marx could scarcely have avoided the conclusion that Engels' youthful nonchalance towards the classics and his brash treatment of important figures, most especially David Ricardo, propagated a distorted image of their teachings. For Engels, all economists were 'hypocrites'; Marx, however, distinguishes in the manuscript of 'A Contribution' between 'classical bourgeois' and 'vulgar economists'.[18] For the former, he shows considerable respect on account of their worthwhile insights into the 'physiology of bourgeois society'; for the latter, who only 'scratch the surface of phenomena', he has only scorn. The implicit rebuke for Engels is that he does not know the difference and, confusing the two groups, fails to learn from the classics.

Fifthly, what exactly *can* one learn from the classics of political economy, and would this undermine key propositions and postulates in Engels' 'brilliant sketch' – aspects which had guided Marx in what was for him at the time unknown territory? If that were the case, Marx's own work would inevitably have been affected, and how could he have told his patron, close friend and comrade-in-arms that crucial positions they had held in common were, on mature consideration, untenable? In many respects, Marx was indebted to Engels. Would it really be surprising to find that he had hesitated to reveal to his friend and benefactor the reasons for his delay in finishing his monumental project? Is it not understandable that he might have preferred to remain silent, not to reply or to reply evasively – at all events not to put his cards on the table. Engels should not know that he, Marx, had been brought to a halt, that he had begun to doubt the stability of important pillars of his socio-theoretical construct, that the gap was becoming ever clearer between what he knew and what he needed to know if he was to find an answer to the great questions he was asking. And as for Engels – would it have been seemly for him to disturb his friend's eloquent silence? Would this not have been gravely improper? I venture to say that in the later phase of Marx's life, the ebbing correspondence between the two men in the matter of the critique of political economy and the completion of *Das Kapital* was in no small measure due to the circumstances outlined above.

Sixthly, Engels obviously knew little about the exact state of Marx's work on *Das Kapital* at the time of his death in 1883. As his literary executor, he opened the extensive – indeed overwhelming – mass of papers left by Marx with the intention of preparing an edition of Volumes II and III of *Das Kapital* – a Herculean task that could not be accomplished with a single bright idea but demanded years of concentrated hard work. Reading through Marx's preparatory notes and manuscripts, Engels must have come across remarks that confused and irritated him. When he broached the mammoth task, he would have been confident that in all important respects, he and Marx were in agreement. This would above all have been the case with the 'law' of the falling general rate of profit, whose validity Marx had convinced Engels to accept although it had played no part in the latter's *Critique*. For Marx this was the acid test of socialism's claim to be 'scientific': a law even the bourgeois must accept as entailing the transience of the capitalist method of production:

> It comes to the surface here in a *purely economic way* – i. e., from the bourgeois point of view, within the limitations of capitalist understanding, from the standpoint of capitalist production itself – that it has its barrier, that it is *relative*, that it is not an *absolute*, but only a historical *mode of production* corresponding to a definite limited epoch in the development of the material conditions of production.[19]

'From the historical point of view', Marx asserted, 'this is the most important law: a law that for all its simplicity has until now never been understood, let alone consciously expressed'.[20] After the death of his friend, Engels would have discovered to his surprise that Marx had been beset with doubts about the tenability of that law. But if this, the keystone of the arch, did not hold, what would become of the arch? And, most pointedly, what would bring about the hoped and longed-for better society if the 'natural process of history' on which Marx had relied no longer did so? And how should his close political colleague and literary executor react to this revelation of Marx's uncertainty and vacillation? Should he acquaint the reader of it, or should he trust that Marx would eventually have found proof of the law's validity? And is he entitled at some decisive point in the text to add, without informing the reader of the fact, a sentence suggesting that, for Marx, the contraindications cited for the law were a mere mental exercise to which he ascribed no great importance? We know today that Engels answered this last question indirectly in the affirmative when at the crucial point in Volume III of *Das Kapital*, he inserted the words: 'But in reality the rate of profit will, as we have seen, in the long run fall.'[21] We will turn now to some singular features of Engels' essay before addressing, in the section after that, his main objections to classical economic theory.

Noteworthy features of Engels' essay

Engels' *Outlines of a Critique of Political Economy* reveals a number of closely interconnected features that merit special attention:

First, his attack is aimed at 'the economists'. He is, with few exceptions, unconcerned about the frequently substantial differences among them.[22] For him, they are all one. His adversary is the discipline itself, which he calls by its German name, 'national economy', rather than its more usual English one, 'political economy' – although (apart from a brief mention of Friedrich List's criticism of Adam Smith's plea for free trade) German economists play no role in the essay. Engels opens his assault by describing classical economics as 'an entire science of enrichment born of the merchants' mutual envy and greed', which 'bears on its brow the mark of the most detestable selfishness.'[23] Its protagonists, hypocrites to a man, have established the legitimacy of trade as 'legalised fraud' and are busily persuading the world that 'the application of immoral means to attain an immoral end' is ethically unobjectionable and economically superior to any alternative.[24] Everything about this science is anathema to Engels; its very name is misleading, for where private property rules, the wealth in question is not that of the nation but of its private citizens. But the science of economics accepts the institution of private property unquestioningly, as if decreed by nature, although it is in reality made – and can therefore be unmade – by human act.

Engels probably derives the phrase 'science of enrichment' from Adam Smith's definition of the discipline in Book IV of *The Wealth of Nations* – or more precisely, McCulloch's comments on that definition in the introduction to his edition of Smith's work[25] or in his own *Discourse of Political Economy* (1824).[26] Smith sees political economy as 'a branch of the science of a statesman or legislator' whose goal is the enrichment of the population as well as that of the ruler.[27] This reflects the famous dictum of his Glasgow master, Francis Hutcheson (1694–1746), for whom the goal of statescraft was 'the greatest Happiness for the greatest Numbers'. Engels narrows the reference

The Critique of Political Economy

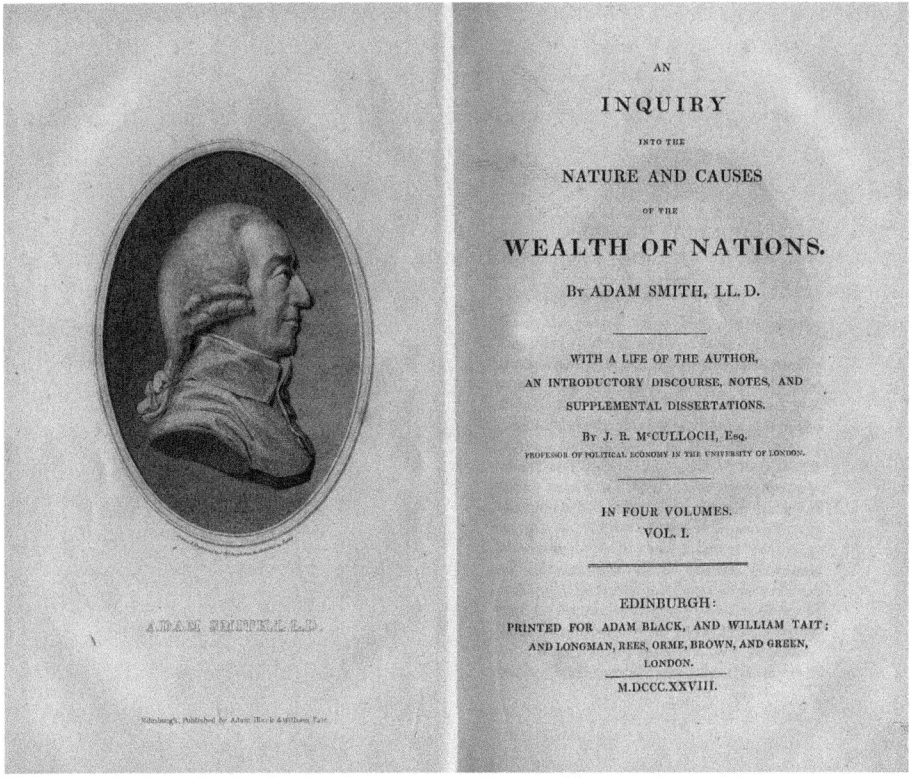

Figure 10.2 Adam Smith, *Wealth of Nations*, 1828. © In the public domain.

of the phrase to the self-serving quest of the individual for material wealth without acknowledging its wide political and societal implications in Smith's usage. These bear primarily on inhibiting the dark, socially damaging aspects of egoism and channelling it into paths that foster the common as well as individual good. Strangely, none of this appears in Engels' *Critique*: neither the goal of increasing public wealth nor the role of the statesman-lawmaker is accorded a mention.

Secondly, Engels projects everything he dislikes about the property-owning classes onto the national economists. He sees the observer here as coincident with the observed, as if the economists' writings and speeches served only to aid and abet the fraudulent purposes of those of whom they wrote: they are manifestly not to be trusted, whose whole work is devoted to the justification of such immoral ends. Engels' attitude suggests that he either did not or would not perceive the difference between positive and normative economics[28] – between analysis of prevailing conditions and their behavioural laws and the mission of improving those conditions towards an ideal. The classical economists were concerned in the first place to understand the dynamics inherent in the conditions of their day. In a second step they asked how these conditions could be improved through economic, societal and political measures. Engels denies their works any contribution to positive economics and rejects them as an underhand attempt to present the status quo as morally acceptable. Whatever emancipatory stirrings their works may have contained are thus denounced as futile and Utopian from the start.

Thirdly, the apologia of the economists for current circumstances is implicitly grounded, Engels argues, in their commitment to the institution of private property. In vain, they have sought explicit justification for this position, from which they derive all further socioeconomic phenomena and relations in modern society – in particular competition, understood as the rivalry of contradictory interests, and the market as the main arena in which that conflict is enacted. From which it follows that a critique of private property is at the same time a critique of competition, the market, wage labour and the factory system. But Engels' essay goes beyond such critique and develops the idea of the ineluctable self-transformation of a property-owning society culminating in its own overthrow. In this 'total transformation of social conditions',[29] private property and its derivatives will collapse and the world will cleanse itself, so to speak, from sin. The historical development whose realization Engels eagerly awaits deprives classical economic theory of its basis, founded as this is on the continuance of private ownership. His expectations are based, in turn, on his prediction of growing antagonism between a small, increasingly wealthy class of possessors and a large, increasingly impoverished class of the dispossessed, a divide exacerbated by the unemployment caused by recurrent trade crises and the introduction of labour-saving technologies.[30] This process inevitably paves the way for the 'social revolution'[31] that will restore the moral order of society – an order that prevailed in earlier tribal and kinship societies. How this might succeed in modern densely populated societies with vastly increased productive capacities and complex national and international divisions of labour is a question Engels left aside. He realized that what holds for small communities cannot necessarily be transferred to larger, inchoately industrial societies, but he bypassed the issue and remained surprisingly confident that – for reasons to be discussed below – revolution was imminent.

Fourthly, the 'hypocrisy' of the economists consists on closer examination, Engels argued, in promising to determine the 'real' or 'intrinsic value' of goods, but producing only a tangle of contradictions. While economists like Ricardo understood value to be determined by the costs of production, others like Say saw the 'utility' of an object as the crucial factor. The dispute was never resolved, but for Engels it was clear that the *real value* of an object could be determined only by abstracting from human institutions like private property, because these influenced the exchange ratios between things – their relative *prices* – which differed from value relations. Real value could be ascertained only within a society free from human institutions,[32] and here, obviously, 'value is the relation of production costs to utility'.[33] At first glance, this looks like a cross between Ricardo and Say, but that is a false assumption, for both those classical economists took the institution of private ownership for granted. Hence, Engels' explanatory comment: 'The production costs of two objects being equal, the deciding factor determining their comparative value will be utility. *This basis is the only just basis of exchange*'[34] – a principle that unmistakably reveals the moral imperative underlying the concept of intrinsic value. For Engels, this concept is *normative*, not positive. In a society not grounded on private ownership, 'there can', he emphatically states, 'no longer be any question of exchange as it exists at present'. And he adds: 'The practical application of the concept of value will then be increasingly confined to the decision about production, and that is its proper sphere.'[35] In such a society, value will be decided directly through the confrontation of production facilities with the needs and wishes of the society's members, not through market transactions and price formation. Again Engels avoids any detailed statement on the question of the allocation of available resources to alternative purposes. This, for him, is a process that can dispense altogether with the guidelines and institutions – and hence, too, with the markets – of current industrial society.

Fifthly, economic theory had its earliest roots in moral philosophy, from which it gradually gained autonomy. John Watts (1842), among others, lamented the discipline's loss of ethical vision – a loss, Engels complained, that the economists had never admitted either to themselves or to others. Their distinction between *use value* – Engels curiously enough speaks of 'abstract value', a concept which to my knowledge occurs in none of the authors he cites – and *exchange value* demonstrates their ongoing pretence of concern with morality. Use value stands for the 'real' or 'intrinsic' value of an object, uncontaminated by institutional interference, whereas exchange value is the price negotiated under the regime of private property. Marx took up this dichotomy between value and price, whereas the economists, unable to establish a way of determining the intrinsic value of an object, had clandestinely reverted to treating its exchange value (alias price) as 'real' – a sleight of hand that sanctified the immorality of private ownership, consummating a monumental swindle.

Engels took it upon himself to unmask that swindle. Exchange value (or price) presupposed markets, which presupposed (more or less intense) competition, which presupposed private ownership. Price could not evade the immorality of its origins, for, as Adam Smith had taught, an object's price is the total sum – made up of 'wages, profit, and rent' – that directly or indirectly flows into its production. But profit and rent (in the sense of unearned income) derive purely from private property, that is from the fountainhead of economic power, advantage and fraud – or as Marx would put it, 'exploitation'. However different the theoretical approaches of Ricardo and Say, they had, Engels maintained, one thing in common: the presupposition of markets and competition and hence *ipso facto* of immorality. How could the true value of a good ever be determined in this way? With each advance in economics, efforts to conceal its failure and justify prevailing conditions were further refined. Engels was willing to grant that the discipline had progressed, but its progress consisted essentially in departing ever further 'from honesty. With every advance of time, sophistry necessarily increases, so as to prevent economics from lagging behind the times. This is why *Ricardo*, for instance, is more guilty than *Adam Smith*, and *McCulloch* and *Mill* more guilty than *Ricardo*.'[36]

Value, according to Engels, should be the fundamental category of economics. Price – a parameter in which prevailing institutional relations are expressed – should be derived from this. But in their inability to establish intrinsic values, the economists take costs of production – presuming the accidental equality of supply and demand – as a surrogate and insist on speaking of 'real' value although such costs merely reflect the price put on the product. This amounts to unmitigated distortion: 'Thus everything in economics stands on its head. Value, the primary factor, the source of price, is made dependent on price, its own product.'[37] The economists' teachings are like a madhouse.

Sixthly, for Engels, Thomas Malthus's population theory capped everything economic theory – the nineteenth-century historian Thomas Carlyle's 'dismal science' – had yet produced. Instead of seeking 'the root of all misery and all vice'[38] in private property, competition and conflicting interests, Malthus made the poor and needy responsible for their own fate. This was not just the height of frivolity; it seemed plain nonsense, and Engels did not hold back: Malthus's 'vile, infamous theory, this hideous blasphemy against nature and mankind' was nothing less than 'the keystone of the liberal system of free trade'. Here, 'the immorality of the economist [is] brought to its highest pitch'.[39] The problem, contrary to Malthus, was not a general lack of means to nourish a growing population. The existing juxtaposition of poverty with riches and need with excess already proved the opposite. 'The productive power at mankind's disposal', Engels was convinced, 'is immeasurable'.[40] The problem was the growing inequality of distribution. In a society governed by private property, wealth and poverty are mutually conditioning factors. 'The population is only too large where the productive power as a whole is too large.'[41] Malthus completely underestimated the exponential growth of productivity made possible by science. Technological progress, Engels argued, outstripped population growth: 'science advances in proportion to the knowledge bequeathed to it by the previous generation, and thus … also in a geometrical progression. And what is impossible to science?'[42] The apocalyptic horseman Thomas Malthus was chasing a mental will-o'-the-wisp.

We come now to Engels' main complaints against the economists. Here, it should be remembered that Engels' *Critique* appeared sixty-eight years after Adam Smith's *Wealth of Nations* and twenty-seven years after David Ricardo's *Principles*. Engels could call on real experience of the Industrial Revolution, including technological and organizational change, economic cycles and crises and a great deal more, which the classical economists lacked. His object of cognition was the object of lived experience.

Towards a critique of Engels' essay

Stedman Jones writes: 'What was novel and arresting about Engels' *Outlines* was its attempt to develop a systematic criticism of the categories of political economy.'[43] Opinions differ, however, as to whether the attempt succeeded: while Stedman Jones gives a hesitantly positive answer, Tribe writes: 'Engels brings clarity into all these confusions by proposing that value is the relationship between the cost of production and utility.' And a little further on: Engels 'presents a robust and systematic critique of political economy'.[44] But Tribe gives no reasons for his judgement, and we shall see that it does not bear serious examination. Engels' essay may well raise important questions and contain interesting reflections, but the very idea that a 23-year-old 'rudderless autodidact' should be in a position to develop a 'robust and systematic critique' of an entire academic discipline is bold, if not foolhardy.

The Critique of Political Economy

The following section summarizes Engels' critique of 'the' economists and their teachings under six main headings and asks a number of questions, for example: Is Engels' reading of the classical teachings accurate and his attack on them justified? To what extent does his essay reflect the approaches and opinions of the literature he consults? Does he conflate what are in fact different perspectives? What are his chief misunderstandings and misinterpretations?[45]

Private property

The *first* objection Engels raises – and one we have already visited in various ways – is that the classical economists never really addressed the issue whether, and if so how, private property is justified at all. The central role of this question for Engels reflects the influence of Proudhon on his thinking and marks perhaps his most significant departure from the position of Robert Owen's followers.[46] Yet the objection, as it stands, is untenable. Private property has been of concern to philosophers and economists from antiquity, the most recent in that line being Thomas Hobbes and John Locke. But even Adam Smith, whom Engels particularly attacked, takes up the issue in his theory of the different stages through which society passes in its development from the 'early and rude' to the 'commercial'. In the first of these, land is not privatized and the deployment of produced means of production is negligible. Whatever one thinks of these historico-philosophical speculations, one cannot deny that the classical authors addressed the underlying question. A widely held view was that a necessary, if not sufficient, condition for the establishment of private property was a scarcity of natural resources like water and tillable (or otherwise usable) land; the resultant problem of distribution led to the introduction of ownership and utilization rights.

But scarcity, and with it the distribution problem, was for Engels a thing of the past. Science was progressing at such a pace, its technological innovations fostering so massive a surge in productivity, that the ethically ordered society loomed closer every day, undermining the individual ownership typical of societies based on private property. In a society without dire material shortages or limitations, private property would be an anachronism.[47] Ironically, Engels' argument implicitly confirms the postulated derivation of private property from a scarcity of natural resources.[48]

Competition

Closely connected with this is Engels' *second* objection: his rejection of the economists' idea of competition, a concept stained with the same odium of contradiction and immorality as the private ownership on which it is based. Competition encourages selfishness and greed, causes unstable prices and trade crises and produces an 'unconscious condition of mankind'.[49] 'So it goes on', Engels writes, 'unendingly – a permanently unhealthy state of affairs – a constant alternation of over-stimulation and flagging which precludes all advance – a state of perpetual fluctuation without ever reaching its goal'.[50] This never-ending switchback, 'this law with its constant adjustment, in which whatever is lost here

Figure 10.3 Pierre-Joseph Proudhon, *c.* 1855, © BPK.

is gained there, is regarded as something excellent by the [liberal] economist'.[51] However, the economist's praise of competition and condemnation of monopoly is based on a serious error, namely that 'the opposite of *competition* is *monopoly*. Monopoly was the war-cry of the Mercantilists; competition the battle-cry of the liberal economists'.[52] This, Engels declares, is 'a quite hollow antithesis': given that private property rests on a 'monopoly of property', 'every competitor *cannot but* desire to have the monopoly'. Hence, 'in short, competition passes over into monopoly';[53] the 'hypocrisy of the liberals' is 'to attack the small monopolies, and to leave untouched the basic monopoly'![54]

The classical economists were well aware that merchants acting in their own interest would seek monopoly positions.[55] The mercantile system – Smith's main target in Book IV of *The Wealth of Nations*[56] – was, according to him, no more than a system of monopolies and privileges. He speaks in a famous phrase of 'the wretched spirit of monopoly'[57] that never rests but is always and everywhere on the lookout for advantage, for opportunities to outdo a competitor and secure monopoly rents. The 'science of a statesman or legislator', which for Smith includes political economy, is called upon to establish instruments and strategies to break up concentrations of economic power and to control the spirit of monopoly that underlies them.[58] In fact, economists from Richard Cantillon (1680–1734) and Anne Robert Jacques Turgot (1727–1781) to Smith and Ricardo have propagated free competition as – with few exceptions – an ideal to be striven for. Not only does it moderate economic power, and with it the distribution of incomes; it entails rivalry, allows unimpeded market entry (and exit), serves to discipline market participants and lends coherence and order to the entire economic system. 'Monopoly,' Smith writes, 'is a great enemy to good management, which can never be universally established, but in consequence of that free and universal competition which forces every body to have recourse to it for the sake of self-defence.'[59] In the same sense, John Stuart Mill would succinctly express the classical view of competition in his *Principles of Political Economy* (1848):

> Only through the principle of competition has political economy any pretension to the character of a science. So far as rents, profits, wages, prices, are determined by competition, laws may be assigned for them. Assume competition to be their exclusive regulator, and principles of broad generality and scientific precision may be laid down, according to which they will be regulated.[60]

Marx himself, in *Das Kapital*, provides a clear echo of this axiom:

> Competition makes the immanent laws of capitalist production to be felt by each individual capitalist, as external coercive laws. It compels him to keep constantly extending his capital, in order to preserve it, but extend it he cannot, except by means of progressive accumulation.[61]

Competition, however, works in two directions. Given a set of technological alternatives, it will seek out the method that minimizes production costs: a centripetal effect. But it will also, as authors like Smith and Marx realized, set in train the development of new, cost-saving methods and their integration in the production system: a centrifugal effect. Innovations of this kind induce a process that Schumpeter would later call 'creative destruction' – a concept implicit in the work of those earlier authors, albeit in less memorable words. Innovation disturbs the balance of production processes and generates turning points, crises, which call for adaptation all round. Finally, imitation of successful innovation communicates and generalizes the new, and the centripetal effect of competition cuts in, forcing the entire system into new paths. What, if anything, Engels perceived of this was confined to the centrifugal working of competition. Its ordering impact on the system – evident in the formation of a general rate of profit and supportive production prices – escaped him. In this respect, Marx would take his lead not from Engels but from the classical economists, first and foremost Ricardo.

'True' value versus price

Engels' *third* objection is that the economists failed to determine not only the true value of goods but also their price as conditioned by competition. But this objection, too, is unsustainable.[62] The value and distribution theory proposed by Adam Smith and then by Ricardo is admittedly not without faults and loose ends, but Engels does not see these. Nor does he understand that those two classical economists, along with others, built up a theory that enabled the determination of value in a profit-free society and price in a society with a tendentially uniform rate of profit. Remarkably enough, Engels' essay is entirely silent on the subject of *general rate of profit*, a concept of central importance to the classical economists and later to Marx. One wonders how carefully he read the authors he so incriminated.

In early societies not based on private property, there was, Smith maintains, neither ground rent nor profit, so the value of a product could be measured only in terms of 'the relation between the amount of labour expended in acquiring different objects'[63] – a succinct statement of the labour-quantity theory of value. Given the heterogeneity of labour, however, different kinds of labour must be reduced to a single kind, so that they are all commensurable and can be added up.[64] What this scale would look like in the ideally moral society Engels does not say. Yet he does make a statement that seems to imply the labour-value theory: '*Labour*,' he writes, 'the main factor in production, the "source of wealth"', is in a society without private property 'its own reward, and the true significance of the wages of labour, hitherto alienated, comes to light – namely, the significance of labour for the determination of the production costs of a thing'.[65] In such a society, we may assume, the labourer will enjoy the entire fruits of his/her labour, although what that means is anything but clear and – without knowing the institutions of that society and how it evaluates different types of work – cannot be decided at all. What is worth of the work of a medicine man, for example (if there is one)? Engels passes over such matters.[66]

And how are relative prices to be determined in the private property society? Here, too, the economists, Engels asserts, have left only a trail of 'confusion',[67] failing even

The Critique of Political Economy

Figure 10.4 John Stuart Mill, 1870. British economist and philosopher. © AKG.

to understand the fundamental role played by competition in this equation. But, here too, his critique is shot through with crucial misunderstandings. In the first place, he ignores the classical distinction between actual (or market) prices and natural (or production) prices. While the former reflect temporary and accidental forces impacting on prices – for example vagaries of the weather in the agricultural sector – the latter express forces exercising a sustained and systematic influence which, due to the mobility of capital across industries, tendentially imply a uniform rate of profit. Natural prices are determined, on the one hand, by cost-minimizing production methods and, on the other, by real wages as the expression of the distribution of economic power among the various social classes.[68] Natural prices change only when technology or wages change; market prices, on the other hand, depend on supply and demand, gravitating over time around their natural levels largely as the expression of movements of capital due to differences in profitability across various sectors. Classical economists – and with them the early Marginalists – believed that generalizable theoretical statements could be made only about natural prices, not about market prices.

Engels ignores the distinction. The instability of market prices stirs him to holy wrath: 'The perpetual fluctuation of prices such as is created by the condition of competition completely deprives trade of its last vestige of morality. It is no longer a question of *value*.' Taking the argument a step further, he adds: 'This very system destroys by means of competition the inherent value of all things, and daily and hourly changes the value-relationship of all things to one another.'[69] But he does not explain how market price fluctuations should destroy the 'true' value of goods: in classical theory they affect neither natural prices nor prices in a profit-free society. As we shall see, Engels is convinced that market prices, by virtue of mutual adjustments of supply and demand, necessarily tend towards a market-clearing level. However – and surprisingly – the idea, familiar from classical natural price theory, of an underlying market price mechanism in the form of the regulatory force of competition is foreign to him – which may explain his impression that the modern economy is adrift with neither anchor nor bed to hold it.

Classical economists understand market price as the price currently prevailing in – and typically clearing – the market. Temporary market clearance, however, and a tendentially uniform rate of profit are not the same thing. The reason for market price shifts is – not solely, but principally – perceived profit and wage rate differentials triggering the migration of capital and labour between economic sectors. This makes itself felt in an oscillating dynamic, of which Smith wrote: 'The natural price, therefore, is, as it were, the central price, to which the prices of all commodities are continually gravitating.'[70] Engels is again silent on the matter.

Price fluctuations

His *fourth* objection follows immediately on the third and maintains that fluctuating prices inevitably promote unethical behaviour: 'Everyone must become a speculator – that is to say, must reap where he has not sown; must enrich himself at the expense of others, must calculate on the misfortune of others.'[71] Smith had spoken of the 'commercial society' in which everyone is a trader operating in interdependent markets; for 'commercial', Engels reads 'speculative'. He sees price fluctuations, interestingly, as resulting from an information problem.[72] In a society structured on private ownership, the plans of producers and consumers are not *ex ante* coordinated; all are in the dark about the world – tomorrow's world for which they must decide today. Seemingly unaware of the fact, Engels thus confirms the principle expressed by Smith and his followers as gravitation, to the effect that, with regard to quantities and prices, commodity markets typically react to the information problem through negative feedback processes. However, where Smith is most concerned with the long-term tendency of prices towards their 'natural' levels, Engels focuses on their short-term tendency towards market-clearing levels. Interpreted by the classical economists as a non-intended result of self-interested human activity, this is, he declares, 'purely a law of nature'[73] which needs no conscious human intervention. But if this essentially speculative activity exercises a stabilizing influence, why does he shower it with such scorn? Smith had already admitted the stabilizing force of speculation in certain markets.[74] Ignoring for a moment the rhetoric of Engels' *Critique*, it seems that in certain respects he unconsciously assumes positions not unlike those of the classical economists.

The brief remarks Engels commits to paper on the subject of the ethical society reveal a naïve conviction that it will know neither dissonance nor discord among its members, information and coordination will no longer present a discernible problem and the question of the distribution of wealth and wages will no longer be disputed. His well-meant admonition, 'Carry on production consciously as human beings – not as dispersed atoms without consciousness of your species',[75] is scarcely enough to solve the crucial issue of the institutional configuration of society. Insecurity and uncertainty mark the human condition, and no society will ever rid itself of them altogether.[76]

Engels lived at a time when the experience of capitalist reality, and the increasingly dire 'Social Question' engendered by it, led to many visions of a better world. But there had as yet been no noteworthy experiences with alternatively structured societies, let alone with really existing socialism. Was there any reason at the time not to look optimistically into the future, not to cultivate the principle of hope?

Instability of the system

Engels' *fifth* objection reads: The economists confused the stability of individual markets with that of the whole system, whereas in fact the system's inherent law – Marx would speak of its 'law of motion' – was to produce revolution[77] and, on the way to revolution, recurrent trade crises. *Pace* the economists, overproduction and a consequent glut of products was not only possible but would 'arrive just as regularly as the great plagues did in the past.'[78] Engels recognized early the cyclical pattern of modern economic development, whereas many economists long thought in terms of progress and crisis. 'Periodic upheavals' in technology and organization, he observed, induced economic cycles, which followed a 'natural law based on the unconsciousness of the participants.'[79]

Engels was doubtless justified in reproaching those many economists who failed to recognize the industrial cycles generated by the rapidly growing manufacturing sector of their day and who therefore denied the possibility of a lack of effectual demand. In this respect, he might actually have found an ally in Thomas Malthus, whom he particularly despised, but who in a well-known controversy with Ricardo had maintained that, in a wealthy society with high savings and a consequent low level of demand, overproduction would be general and recurrent. However, since Malthus, like Ricardo was convinced that every act of saving would be swiftly followed by an equally large act of investment, Ricardo accused Malthus of logical inconsistency. Malthus's perspective corresponded with observable phenomena but failed to explain them; with Ricardo, the case was precisely opposite. Engels, too, expressed what experience seemed to show but could offer no compelling reason for it.[80] His denial of the possibility of crises and cycles in the projected ethical society was, on the other hand, markedly naïve.[81] His unbounded optimism in progress harboured the idea that both nature and human life could be planned and controlled in detail. Engels envisioned a societal order that was no longer 'at the mercy of chance'.

Science and social productive powers

The *sixth* objection was that the economists, and in particular Malthus and his followers, seriously underestimated the potential of science and technology for producing new, economically useful knowledge. This led Malthus to conclude that the distress and misery of the majority of the population must be accepted as the price for falling agricultural productivity. The problem was not private property, but the unbridled drive of the poor to propagate their kind. How, an enraged Engels demanded, was this assertion compatible with 'coexisting wealth and poverty'?[82] Thanks to science, productivity was growing 'immeasurably'; Engels named a dozen important scientists and their inventions. The 'productivity of the soil can be increased *ad infinitum*', he thundered, rendering baseless Malthus's population theory, 'this vile, infamous theory', as we have heard, 'this hideous blasphemy against nature and mankind'[83]. Not the 'propagative instinct of the workers' but competition 'is proved to be the cause of misery, poverty and crime'.[84] But this the economist could not admit, lest he lose the very foundations of his doctrine.

Malthus deserves praise, Engels was ready to admit, inasmuch as through him 'our attention has been drawn to the productive power of the earth and of mankind' and hence to 'the most powerful economic arguments for a social transformation'.[85] This transformation can be undertaken 'straight away', ensuring, through 'the education of the masses', the 'moral restraint of the propagative instinct' and thus ending 'the deepest degradation of mankind', which 'has turned man into a commodity'. In 'the abolition of private property, competition and the opposing interests'[86] Engels saw a key to all-round social improvement. He did not deny that technological progress had been made in the world governed by competition, but the price for the workers – misery and distress – had been too high. He was convinced, moreover, that 'the assistance of science … in present conditions … is directed against labour'[87], where 'present conditions' meant private property and technological advances meant sinking wages and mass dismissals. They might raise social productivity, but from this only the owners profited, while social antagonism remorselessly grew. Only in the ethical society would the 'immeasurable productive capacity, handled consciously and in the interest of all, … soon reduce to a minimum the labour falling to the share of mankind'.[88]

So far as progress – whether scientific or social – was concerned, Engels was an optimist beyond compare. He praised to the heavens such men as Richard Arkwright, Claude-Luis Berthollet, Edmund Cartwright, Samuel Crompton, Humphry Davy, James Hargreaves, Justus von Liebig and James Watt. While the thinking of Malthus and his ilk was riddled with petty bourgeois fears of inadequate harvests and ensuing shortages, the socioeconomic system itself generated an ever-widening stream of new, economically fertile knowledge.

Marx, too, was fascinated by this view and incorporated it into his own writings. Socially productive forces developed 'as if in a hothouse',[89] increasing labour productivity 'in geometrical progression'.[90] Only under such circumstances was socialism even possible: 'The development of the productive forces of labour within society is the historic task and justification of capital, with which it unconsciously creates the material conditions for increased production.'[91]

Engels' reproach that the economists were blind to the force of technological and organizational progress is in many cases justified. But again his judgement is immoderate and undifferentiated. Authors like Charles Babbage (1791–1871), whose *On the Economy*

Figure 10.5 Justus Liebig's chemical laboratory, 1842. © AKG.

of Machinery and Manufactures (1832) – a study of the machine and factory era – was translated into many languages and had wide influence, seem unknown to him. Nor does he mention Ricardo's critique of the automatic re-employment of dismissed workers in the chapter 'On Machinery' in the third edition of *Principles*[92] or the same author's identification of a specific form of technological progress that is particularly detrimental to workers.[93] Marx would use this in *Das Kapital* as the basis for his law governing the tendency of the rate of profit to fall in the form of an increasing 'organic composition of capital'.[94]

Engels describes what he sees (or thinks he sees); he offers little analysis or explanation of observed phenomena. This is not in itself surprising. But the young man from Barmen appears to think that things are different. He has a high opinion of his own achievements and a very low one of the economists he so scathes. And his attack on them carries over into his attitude to Christianity:

> [Malthus's] crazy assertion that the earth lacks the power to feed men ... is the pinnacle of Christian economics – and that our economics is essentially Christian I could have proved from every proposition, from every category, and shall in fact do so in due course. The Malthusian theory is but the economic expression of the religious dogma of the contradiction of spirit and nature and the resulting corruption of both.[95]

All that dogma, Engels avows, is but lies and deception, a protective rampart against any assault on prevailing immoral conditions. In the long run, of this he is certain, 'a total transformation of social conditions, a fusion of opposed interests, an abolition of private property' is unstoppable.[96]

Concluding remarks

Engels' *Outlines of a Critique of Political Economy* is, despite the reservations expressed in the foregoing analysis, a fascinating document. Boldly and eloquently, he castigates prevailing social conditions and attacks the classical economists who allegedly justified them, sketching in outline his notion of a future society in which everything will be better. In his own day, his observations on science, technology and labour were unparalleled in their topicality. His essay echoes with the roar of the First Machine Age, the clangour of steam hammers, the din of the shop floor. The new era of factories has enslaved men and women in a societal order dominated by private ownership, but its surging social productivity promises a better, more ethical future.

In diction and content, the *Critique* breathes a Messianic spirit. The teachers of false doctrine – the economists – are to be cast out of the temple. Engels' diatribe hits the occasional target, but not everything he aims at actually exists. He repeatedly misunderstands the classical political economists from Adam Smith to David Ricardo or attributes opinions to them, which they never held.[97] And he is so convinced of the global justice and urgency of his critique that he cannot indulge in the luxury of differentiating between various authors or schools of thought. His concept of future society is indistinct; he mentions the information problem but underestimates its implications for the organization of a non-market society, and his idea that the ethical society could survive without humanly established institutions is simply bizarre.[98] Political economy is, for Engels, a false doctrine to be combated with every available means; he utterly fails to see that it offers a host of aspects that could help build a better society. It was not for nothing that Adam Smith understood political economy as a key facet of that 'science of a statesman or legislator' which might underpin a political and economic order infused with social theory. Unfortunately, Marx followed Engels in much of this.[99] *Das Kapital* is not a social revolutionary's handbook. Had the two of them only left the world such a work! Given the authority accorded to them in the Socialist movement, they would have been in a position to crucially influence the path taken by history and the behaviour of its principal players.

CHAPTER 11
REPAIRING *DAS KAPITAL*?: FRIEDRICH ENGELS AND THE PUBLICATION OF *DAS KAPITAL II* AND *III*
Regina Roth

Introduction

In the spring of 1883, Friedrich Engels, as executor of Marx's literary estate, sorted through the manuscripts left by his friend and colleague in his house at 41 Maitland Park Road, London, a task in which he was helped by Helene Demuth, who had for forty years kept house for the Marx family. After a brief search, Helene found several bundles of manuscripts destined by Marx for the as-yet-unpublished volumes II and III of *Das Kapital* (henceforth abbreviated as *Kapital II* and *III*). Engels was enthusiastic about the 'scientific revolution' Marx had kept 'in his head' for more than twenty years. He was especially struck by the way in which the most complex questions were simply and directly answered and praised in glowing terms the development of the manuscripts for *Kapital III*: 'It is quite extraordinarily brilliant. This complete reversal of all previous economics is truly astounding.'[1] Above all, this third volume held for Engels the promise that the overriding issues of economics would finally regain their position at the forefront of public discussion,[2] hence his determination to complete editorial work on the books as quickly as possible. He saw this, too, as the best way to erect 'a befitting monument to the memory' of Marx and thus to confirm and propagate his enduring significance.[3]

On closer examination, however, the completion of Marx's 'Critique of Political Economy' from manuscripts compiled by the author over a matter of decades proved more difficult than had appeared in the first flush of discovery. Marx – a chronic improver and reorganizer – had left the manuscripts in various states of incompletion. And there were extraneous reasons, too, like Engels' deteriorating eyesight, which continually impaired his ability to work. The years he devoted to the project, until shortly before his death in 1895, suggest that he may even have doubted privately whether a third volume – for which only 'a first extremely incomplete draft'[4] existed – would ever see the light of day. The question arises, then, as to the nature of Engels' work on *Das Kapital* and its place in his overall output and influence during his last decade. And this, in turn, bears on the judgement of Marx's own achievement, the life's work on which his unparalleled impact, above all on the course of twentieth-century history, rests. The answer to these questions can be found today, if at all, only in the original manuscripts, for later editions of *Das Kapital* have, whether consciously or unconsciously, infused uniform interpretive principles (*Vereindeutigungen*) into the texts.[5] It is a matter, then – as in the deciphering of a medieval palimpsest under quartz light – of revealing the textual layers that tell us of the genesis and composition of the manuscripts by Marx himself and of the emendations undertaken by his later editors, first and foremost Friedrich Engels. Only in this way can the transmission of the text be reliably established as a basis for subsequent philological and historical-critical contextualization and interpretation, without inevitably having recourse to conjecture.

Karl Marx, in his own lifetime, published only *Kapital I*. This dealt with the process by which capital is produced. It fell to Engels to compile *Kapital II* and *III* as soon as possible after Marx's death. For *Kapital II*, he was able in large measure to fulfil his plan: he found in Marx's estate a good dozen manuscripts of differing lengths and completeness with which the philosopher had intended, ever since he had taken up this aspect in 1864, to address the circulation process of capital. The subject was divided into three large sections dealing, respectively, with the 'circuits', the 'turnover' and the 'reproduction process' of capital.[6] The main problem was to decide which of the various versions was 'the last available edited manuscript, compar[ed] … with the preceding ones';[7] only then could the work of connecting and editing the texts for publication begin.

The manuscripts for *Kapital II* had serious gaps, especially in the last of the three sections which, according to Marx's intentions in 1864,[8] were to analyse not just the simple but also the extended reproduction of capital. This was a precondition of the accumulation which he considered to be the central element of capitalist production: 'Accumulate, accumulate!' he had written in *Kapital I*, 'That is Moses and the prophets!'[9] As if under a magnifying glass, the problems of Marx's method of working become apparent here. He set out to analyse the phenomenon of the extended reproduction of capital with arithmetical examples, but he made mistakes in his calculations and, as a result, arrived at an increasing rather than diminishing organic accumulation of capital – or in other words, a higher accession of variable in relation to constant capital – which, as he commented, was 'inconsistent with the capitalist mode of production'.[10] Not finding the mistake,[11] however, Marx dropped the matter and started a new calculation, which he also did not finish, as other matters called him more urgently: a statement in a factory report and a passage from a recent book on European prehistory by James Geikie.[12] The problem was left unresolved as a subject to be tackled later.

What can we conclude from these examples? Marx worked associatively and largely without plan. Rather than proceeding consistently towards a conceptual goal, he digressed, often setting these byways in square brackets so that they would not be lost forever. But procrastination is not a recipe for success – as Marx, critical spirit that he was, well knew. Already in 1858 he commented to Engels about his first essay in economics 'The damnable part of it is that my manuscript (which in print would amount to a hefty volume) is a real hotchpotch, much of it intended for much later sections.'[13] Nevertheless, twenty years later, his procedure in the last extant manuscript for *Das Kapital* – Engels titled it 'Manuscript VIII' – was little changed. Marx composed the manuscript in several phases between 1877 and 1881. At the point in question here, after a number of numerical examples concerned with mechanisms of reproduction, we find a gloss in square brackets, introduced with a simple 'By the by',[14] on educating workers

Figure 11.1 Friedrich Engels, London 1888. He confronts us as the 'typical Engels': upright posture even at an advanced age, his open gaze directed into the distance, well-groomed, in solid businessman's wear, with waistcoat, pocket watch, frock coat and hat. Short haircut, his grey mottled beard is lightly trimmed but still contrasts with the soft facial features and clear eye line. The three volumes of books hint at the task he was about to undertake: editing the third volume of Karl Marx's *Das Kapital*. © In the public domain.

Figure 11.2 Karl Marx, *c.* 1868. Carte de visite. © In the public domain.

to become 'rational' consumers. Or (again in 'Manuscript VIII') he comments on an intended goal of his analysis without pursuing the matter: namely the extended steps of capital reproduction, of which he had already noted in 1864, in the first manuscript passages of *Kapital II*, that it was a subject calling for examination.[15] Even now, *c.* 1880, Marx does not address the matter explicitly, but introduces it with 'Anticipated', as if it really belonged later.[16] That exactly reflects the character of this last received manuscript, which is more a collection of useful materials than a coherent, finished analysis and indeed one that was started not only with *Kapital II* but also with Engels' *Anti-Dühring* in mind – the attack on the German political economist Eugen Dühring on which Engels had already started working. Even after Marx had found a place for these notes in the third chapter of *Kapital II*, they remained a preliminary draft, covering closely written pages with few headings and no room for footnotes. If anything, new topics or approaches were separated with a simple line.[17] Calculations for a consistent analysis of a growing economy never took place.

Marx's associative working method is apparent *par excellence* in *Kapital III*. The manuscript sheet of algebraic equations illustrated here on p. 233 is concerned with the determination of the ratio between 'surplus value' and profit rates and was destined for the beginning of Chapter 1, where it appears in a lengthy footnote. That Engels also considered Marx's subsequent deliberations unsystematic is suggested by the fact that he omitted the first seventy pages of Part 1[18] in the manuscript eventually submitted for publication. A second manuscript (dated 1875)[19] on value-added and profit rates proved no better, and Engels laid it aside, as he did four other attempts by Marx of a few pages each (dated 1867–8) to compose a beginning for *Kapital III*.[20]

Deficiencies of this kind become conspicuous in Part 5, where cash and credit are treated as mechanisms for providing investment capital. Here and elsewhere, Marx compiled many examples of what he saw as a 'confusion of terms in matters concerning capital' in the parliamentary hearings and reports on the British government's monetary policies and the crises of 1848 and 1857.[21] Marx himself, in a letter of 1868 which Engels probably used as a guideline, had called this part of his manuscript 'the CHAPTER on credit',[22] suggesting the considerable significance he ascribed to credit for the functioning of capitalist production. Here, too, however, he failed to achieve clarity; in fact, the section cost Engels – a man known for his ability to get unswervingly to the point – a great deal of time and trouble. That Marx also closely followed American developments in questions of money and credit is evident from an interview of 1880.[23] In the remaining years of his life, he studied the subject intensely and wrote several passages on money, banking and credit, but he neither revised these manuscripts nor prepared them for separate publication – they lack even relevant evidential backing.[24]

Part 6 of *Kapital III*, on the 'Transformation of Surplus Profit into Ground Rent', is in a little better condition. The section is worked out relatively fully,[25] but the final page suddenly presents a different structuring of the whole that is not further pursued in the manuscript;[26] all we have are numerous pieces from Marx's final decade focusing on the relation between ground rent and property ownership.[27] The patchiness of these earlier sections carried over into the concluding Part 7 of *Kapital III*, on 'Revenues and Their

Sources', which is manifestly of a temporary nature, was not even continuously paginated and ends with a disappointing single-page chapter on 'Class'.[28] In short, everything was left as 'work in progress', with many interpretive approaches, many thoughts and re-thoughts, but nothing that could (or would) withstand rigorous criticism.

Engels as 'editor'

Sorting out Marx's literary estate was a time-consuming task. It took Engels until early 1884 to determine which manuscripts in what state of preparation he could use for the remaining two volumes of *Das Kapital*.[29] By the end of March 1884 he had decided to complete work on the second volume, for which he had found a good dozen manuscripts from various phases of Marx's productivity,[30] before going on to the third; he hoped to publish *Kapital II* that same year and *Kapital III* in 1885.[31] Active deciphering of the manuscripts for *Kapital II* began at the end of June 1884 and continued into October of that year. By the following February the editorial work was complete. Then came the proofreading,[32] with the result that the date Engels finally wrote under his foreword was Marx's birthday, 5 May 1885. In February he had also started working on the 'main manuscript' of *Kapital III*, deciphering whatever he could use for dictation.[33] He had been suffering from a back complaint since at least the autumn of 1883 and could sit for only two hours a day, so he employed the typesetter Oscar Eisengarten from Leipzig as an amanuensis. Eisengarten prepared the manuscripts of *Kapital II* and *III* in a good, legible hand for editing.[34]

The story the manuscripts tell is in this way also a tale of London's nineteenth-century *emigré* community, where many banished or otherwise politically persecuted individuals gathered – from Britain, Engels appositely remarked, they could no longer be expelled.[35] Engels himself had taken up residence in Manchester in 1849, where he had represented his father's firm, first in management, then as a business partner. It had been a difficult balancing act for him, as a daytime 'cotton lord' with all the implications he painted in the darkest colours in his 1845 *Condition of the Working Class in England*, while at the same time advocating radical transformation of European society – an act of unstable equilibrium, of which his financial support to the Marx family was more than a symbolic expression. In 1845 he had already found vivid words for his position: 'haggling is too beastly, Barmen is too beastly, the waste of time is too beastly and most beastly of all is the fact of being, not only a bourgeois, but actually a manufacturer, a bourgeois who actively takes sides against the proletariat'.[36] Only in 1869 did Engels finally detach himself from the Manchester factory, and the following year, having secured his financial well-being, he moved to London and settled near Marx. The day of his 'redemption from dogged Commerce' was one of hearty celebration.[37] His financial arrangements proved adequate not only for him and his life's companion Lizzy Burns but also for the Marx family and, indeed, for many emigrants, one of whom was that same Oscar Eisengarten, who as a member of the Social Democratic Working Men's Party in Leipzig had been expelled from Germany in 1882 under the Anti-Socialist Law.[38]

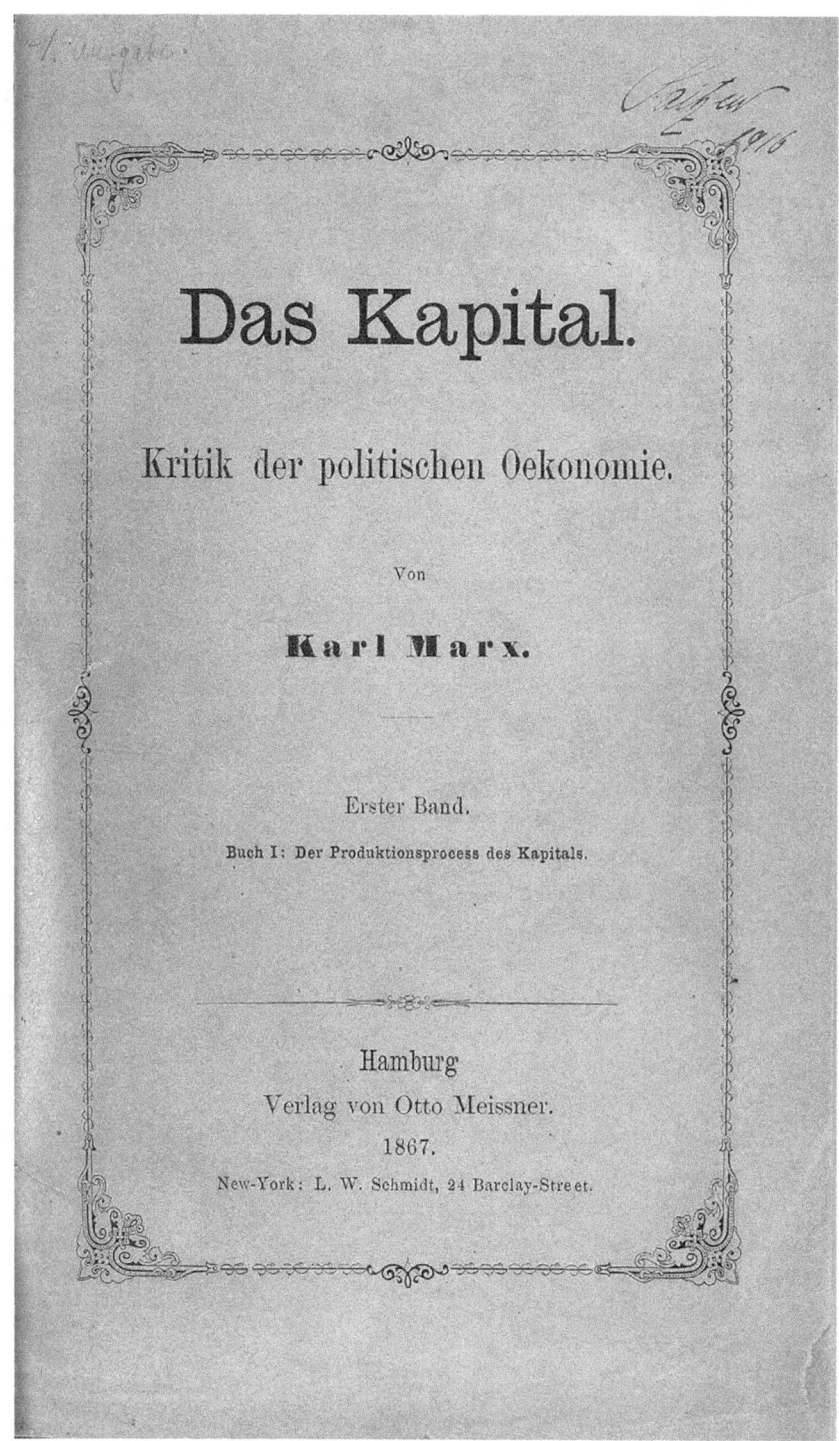

Figure 11.3 Karl Marx, *Das Kapital*, Hamburg 1867. © In the public domain.

By the end of July 1885, Engels wrote that he now had *Kapital III* for the most part in the same sort of readable condition that he had earlier achieved for the second volume.[39] Given that he was the only person – or so he claimed – who could decipher Marx's handwriting with its many and varied abbreviations, this was already a major step.[40] The provisional version could 'if the worst comes to the worst, be printed as it stands, even if I were to kick the bucket in the meantime. Until this had been done I was constantly on tenterhooks'.[41] Autumn 1885 brought further indications of progress with *Kapital III*. As he had, in the dictation phase, skipped the first seventy pages of the 'main manuscript' (his 'Ms. I'), he now returned to the question of how to begin the book. He compared Marx's four subsequent versions, set two aside as 'not used' and marked the other two 'Ms. II' and 'Ms. III'. While Ms I had started its analysis with the rate of profit, the other two started with cost price.[42] Engels welded all three versions into a single text.

On his return from America in autumn 1888, Engels resumed his editorial activities.[43] At the end of March 1886 he had started correcting the English translation of *Kapital I*, an undertaking completed jointly by the cotton manufacturer and lawyer Samuel Moore and the physician Edward Aveling and one for which Eleanor Marx Aveling had checked numerous references to English sources in the British Museum Library.[44] Since early 1887 Engels had also been suffering from health problems: an eye complaint substantially reduced the time he could spend reading and writing every day.[45]

In March 1888, Engels had asked Samuel Moore, who had also studied mathematics, to give his opinion on the last major manuscript Marx had completed for Part 1 of *Kapital III*, a 125-page exercise book he had started in May 1875 with a view to clarifying the relation between value-added and profit rates, a subject he had first tackled in 1864.[46] Engels had marked some potentially useful passages in red but had quickly realized that what Marx had produced was not a new version of the subject but a series of algebraic formulae and numerical examples intended to convincingly illustrate the factors determining rates of profit. However, the series was riddled with errors. Samuel Moore rightly pointed out that Marx's endless numerical calculations could have been accomplished in a few lines simply by recasting the general definitions from which he had started.[47] The upshot was that Engels used only a few passages from this voluminous manuscript – after all it presented hardly any firm evidence and none that was new.[48]

Engels began by compiling an overview of this manuscript and the skipped-over seventy pages of the 'main manuscript' of 1864–5, comparing both versions and marking what he might use. His working method was to summarize Marx's texts in a left-hand column and make his own comments in the corresponding right-hand column.[49] By early 1889, work on the seven chapters of Part 1 was finished, beginning with the difficult Chapters 1–3, compiled as already described. In comparison with Marx's texts, Engels' presentation of the factors determining value-added and profit rates is relatively brief and well-structured. For Chapter 4, Marx had left only the heading 'The Effect of the Turnover on the Rate of Profit'; Engels had to write the chapter himself. Chapters 5 and 6 were comparatively well developed, but Chapter 7 consisted only of 'Supplementary Remarks'.[50] All in all, one can say that Chapters 1–4 of this volume were structured by Engels: he identified potential influences on the relation between value-added and profit rates that had occupied Marx so tenaciously and presented their combinations in a systematic fashion. Moreover, at the end of Chapter 3 he wrote a summary identifying two major determining factors for the rate of profit and sketching out their possible avenues of development. In this respect, Engels acted as de facto author rather than editor.[51]

Parts 2–4 of *Kapital III* needed only revision of the 'main manuscript', but a revision that, despite the speed of its completion, again shows clear editorial intrusions. Among these is the already mentioned Part 3 – 'The Law of the Tendency of the Rate of Profit to Fall' – which, restructured by Engels, noticeably changed the emphasis of Marx's original manuscript without directly offering new interpretations. Ambiguities were smoothed out and chapter headings inserted for ease of orientation – often, though not always, on the basis of Marx's original formulations. The heading of Chapter 15, 'Exposition of the Internal Contradictions of the Law', is a case in point.[52] Here, too, one finds the much-cited passage on the collapse of the capitalist system as a result of centralization processes. In its actual formulation, this is again the work of Engels, as is the added prominence it gains by being set at the end of a section headed 'General'.[53] Also from Engels is the explicit statement, 'But in reality … the rate of profit will fall in the long run',[54] which remains a stone of contradiction to the present day. By spring 1889, six years after Marx's death, approximately a third of *Kapital III* had been put together and edited.[55]

A profound crisis then occurred, caused by Part 5, which was meant to treat the related subjects of interest, profit, money and credit – complex matters which Marx had, however, only fragmentarily addressed. It was unclear not only which of the many factors was central and should be dealt with immediately and which could be left for later but also how these factors impacted the overall capitalist system. In other words, much research must be done; it would in no way suffice to present naked results. Marx had himself observed at the beginning of Chapter 25, on 'Credit and Fictitious Capital', that an 'analysis of the credit system and of the instruments which it creates for its own use (credit money, etc.) lies beyond our plan'.[56] But he had already realized while he was writing that – given the importance of credit instruments in their many forms for the development of the capitalist system of production – he had to include them in his investigation. This is evident in his subsequent reflections and in the copious material he assembled in Part 5, especially in the pages inserted under the heading 'Confusion', with their numerous excerpts from parliamentary reports and tables left with neither commentary nor conclusion. It was this that must have led Engels to insert an adjective to qualify Marx's disclaimer at the beginning of Chapter 25, so that in Engels' version an 'exhaustive analysis' was now announced as being 'beyond our plan'.[57] Marx himself, as we have seen, had in the years after publication of *Kapital I* (1867) shifted the weight allocated to the topic of credit and announced a considerable widening of his approach to the issue, along with a new focus on developments in the United States.

Engels made four attempts in as many years (November 1889,[58] October 1890, November 1891 and October 1892 to March 1893) to prepare Part 5 for publication. As most of his editorial notes are extant, we can reconstruct his approach to mending the gaps and shortfalls in Marx's texts. In order to gain an overall view of the manuscripts and bring them into a 'first order', he first made a conspectus of Marx's topics and argumentation: 'loans' (1889), 'money capital' (1890), 'credit and fictitious capital' (1891) (MEGA² II/14, 228–61). But not everything fell under these headings, so Engels set about organizing Marx's many excerpts in a new system – initially (December 1891) by theme ('second order': MEGA² II/14, 267–73), but then in the winter of 1892–3 by separating Marx's own comments from those of others ('Division of the "Confusion" Material into Marx Texts and Sources': MEGA² II/14, 279–91). This new attempt, however, was no more convincing, so at the end of 1892 Engels tried another thematic approach in which he integrated Marx's identified comments ('third order': MEGA² II/14, 292–304). In this way the collection of excerpts titled 'The Confusion' finally gave rise to Chapters 33–35. It is here in Part 5 that Engels' editorial intrusions are thickest on the ground, where reordering, reformulation and extensive reconnection were needed to create a half-way stringent and legible text.[59] In his preface Engels had described his attempts 'to complete this part ... by filling in the gaps and expanding upon passages that were only indicated', so that it might 'at least approximately' offer 'everything the author had intended'. He had reviewed his work soberly: 'I had no other choice but to more or less cut the Gordian knot by confining myself to as orderly an arrangement of available matter as possible, and to making only the most indispensable additions.'[60] What Engels did as an editor, then, was to provide the first of all interpretations of Marx's fragmentary legacy on the subject of money and credit, but his interventions were arguably often authorial.[61]

In contrast to this detailed story, little information is available about Engels' work on *Kapital III* Part 6 and the relatively short Part 7. Part 6 also needed revision, but Marx's manuscript was in a better state of completion and suggestions had been left for a new structuring. Engels took this up in the first half of 1893 and tackled Part 7 towards the end of that year. Then, without a break, he embarked on the final editing. Further months were spent dealing with printers and proofs, and *Kapital III* was in the bookshops by early December 1894.[62]

Beyond *Das Kapital*

When he started out, Engels had accorded his editorial work the highest priority. He doubtless sought to publicize Marx's literary achievement as a worthy monument to his friend and colleague. That he himself should in doing so re-enter the fray on political economy – his own contribution to that debate lay four decades back – was a welcome side effect.[63] But the sheer length of the editorial process leads one to wonder what became of Engels' initial agenda after the labour of deciphering the manuscripts for *Das Kapital III* was completed in summer of 1885.

Although it was 'absolutely essential' to him 'that a text, both printable and written in a legible hand, be produced of the final volumes of *Capital*',[64] Engels also devoted time to other topics and sometimes gave them pride of place. Developments in Germany

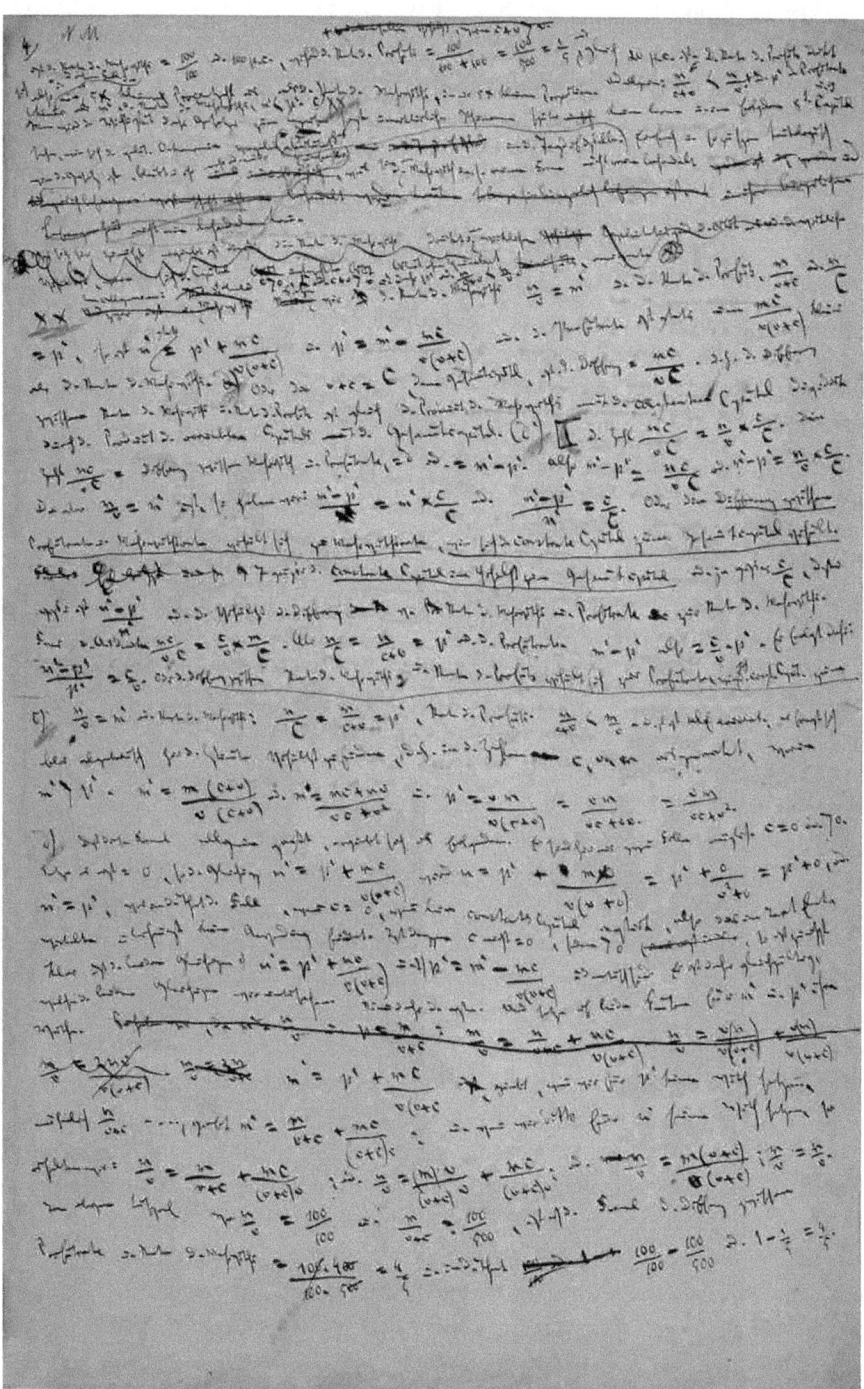

Figure 11.4 *A Sisyphean Task* – editing the manuscripts of *Das Kapital*. © IISG Amsterdam Marx–Engels Archive.

were close to his heart: the impact of Bismarck, the early history of social democracy, the Reformation and Peasant War, indeed revolutions in general. But broader historical processes – the origins of civilization, forms and significance of property ownership, the societal role of women (or, more broadly, questions of gender and power) – also interested him, as did the history of workers and their organizations against the background of capitalist production and its development. Across this whole spectrum, Engels' journalistic activity continued unabated, with views and comments on political movements and events in Britain, France, the United States and above all Germany. This led him in 1889 to become involved in the founding of the Second International, a union of European workers' organizations. And parallel to all of this, he invested much time and energy in debates about the role and historical significance of Marx. Most of these undertakings took the form of articles in newspapers, journals, booklets and so on or of new editions of his and Marx's texts. Rather than substantially revising these, he preferred to add new prefaces in which he commented on their contemporary relevance, generally in terms of specific political developments.

In addition, there was Engels' copious correspondence with socialists of various hues throughout Europe and the United States, with whom he maintained vital contact. Here, too, we find him confirming his intention after Marx's death not to become absorbed in the day-to-day politicking and disputes of the socialist cause, but to concentrate on his primary theoretical commitments.[65] Nevertheless, in the ensuing decade, precisely those controversies claimed a large portion of his time. Engels was too much the political journalist to withdraw from his valued role of commentator as he grew older, and he must have enjoyed his position of elder statesman, above all as evidenced in the respect shown him by younger socialist politicians like Eduard Bernstein and Karl Kautsky.[66]

1883 was taken up with sorting through Marx's estate and preparing the third edition of *Kapital I*, which Marx had already begun; this came out in December of that year.[67] Before starting work (in June 1884) on deciphering and editing the manuscripts for *Kapital II* and *III*, Engels had spent the earlier months of that year composing an essay of some 150 pages on *The Origin of the Family, Private Property and the State*. Among Marx's papers, he had found lengthy excerpts from Henry Lewis Morgan's *Ancient Society* (1877), which had incited him to insert a footnote in the third edition of *Kapital I*. Marx had surmised that at the very origin of civilization, a division of labour had developed between families and then between clans and tribes. Engels now observed that Marx's 'very searching study of the primitive condition of man, led the author to the conclusion, that ... the tribe was the primitive and spontaneously developed form of human association', out of which 'the many and various forms of the family were afterwards developed'.[68] He was fascinated by the idea that human societies may originally have been communistic in nature and that only the growth of private ownership had engendered the family, and with it modern class society with its conflicts and contradictions between bourgeoisie and proletariat. This would at the same time explain the decline in the role and status of women. In the tribe, women would have had a position of equality and respect; only under private ownership and the family had they been degraded into becoming the slaves of men.[69]

Engels' essay may already have been penned on the basis of Marx's excerpts – at the latest, however, once he had received a copy of Morgan's book.[70] He had first thought of circumventing censorship under Bismarck's Anti-Socialist Law by simply writing a review of the excerpts,[71] but then he resolved to expand his text into a booklet. He wrote to Karl Kautsky, for whose Zurich journal *Die Neue Zeit* (The New Age) he had initially intended the piece, that its scope and import exceeded that of any mere evaluative commentary: 'The ... final chapter on private ownership as the source of class antagonisms and also as the detonator that exploded the old communal system I find absolutely *impossible* to couch in such a way as to comply with the Anti-Socialist Law.' Moreover, the text 'will have a particularly important bearing on our general view'.[72] For this reason Engels accepted Hermann Schlüter's offer in July 1884 to have the work printed at his *Volksbuchhandlung* (People's Press) in Zurich, where it appeared at the beginning of October 1884.[73]

Spring 1884 saw Engels engaged in a controversy that paralleled and to some extent complemented his editorial work on *Das Kapital*. Discussions had blossomed in the early 1880s within German social democracy about the socialist theories of Johann Karl Rodbertus (of whom Ferdinand Lassalle was considered to be a pupil) in relation to, or even as replacing, those of Marx.[74] The debate was fired by the posthumous publication and reception of Rodbertus's writings and letters in national economic circles – Georg Adler's *Rodbertus, der Begründer des wissenschaftlichen Sozialismus* (Rodbertus, the founder of scientific socialism) of 1884 being a case in point.[75] Engels identified here a rival against whom he would enter the lists. Already in February 1884, he wrote to Kautsky that he would 'dispose of the myth of Rodbertus', which had 'been so widely hawked around in Germany, this country and even America, that the thing has got to be scotched once and for all'.[76] To effect this plan he used in the first place the preface – written in October 1884 and published in advance in *Die Neue Zeit* in January 1885 – to the German translation of Marx's 1847 *Misère de la philosophie* (*The Poverty of Philosophy*), which Eduard Bernstein and Karl Kautsky had been preparing since autumn 1883;[77] in the second place he took the opportunity offered by the preface to *Kapital II*.[78] In fact, he had already anticipated his offensive in the third edition of *Kapital I* (1883) by weakening the relatively positive appreciation of Rodbertus composed by Marx himself.[79] Engels took pains to acquire not only the whole gamut of Rodbertus's writings, from the early 1830s to posthumous works,[80] but also Theodore Ely's *French and German Socialism in Modern Times* (published 1883 in the United States), from which he took an excerpt which he marked in his own hand 'Rodbertus als "Gründer" des wiss. Sozialismus' (Rodbertus as 'founder' of scientific socialism).[81]

Even if Engels could confide to Kautsky that in the preface to *Das Kapital* 'I must assume an air of dignity, whereas in the preface to *Poverty* I shall be more at liberty to speak my mind', both pieces are distinctly polemical.[82] At issue is the rebuttal of an accusation of plagiarism: Rodbertus thought Marx had used him without acknowledgement in the matter of value-added theory.[83] Accusations of this kind were, in fact, common enough as a tactic for questioning an adversary's seriousness without having to confront their arguments.[84] In February 1884. Engels set up his battle lines:

I shall show, 1) that in 1850 we had had no opportunity of learning anything whatsoever from Mr Rodbertus, 2) that he was quite unknown to us, 3) that his great discoveries had already been commonplaces in 1848, 4) that the remedies he specifies for use in socialist therapy had already been criticised in the *Poverty*, *prior to* Rodbertus' discovery of them.[85]

This was a similar approach to that deployed by Kautsky in the mid-1870s discussion with followers of Rodbertus in the pages of *Die Neue Zeit*.[86] An interesting detail in this discussion comes to light in a March 1884 letter from the political economist Rudolph Meyer, an occasional contact of Engels'. Meyer saw Rodbertus as a predecessor of Marx and was one of the sources of what Engels called 'the Rodbertus cult'.[87] In his letter, he apologizes to Engels for his reading of Marx's reception of Rodbertus and explains how this arose. He expresses himself willing to accept Engels' more exact knowledge of the matter and to change the corresponding passage in the translation of his piece on emancipation.[88]

Year-end 1884 brought yet another weighty project: On 5 December the American translator and social reformer Florence Kelley Wischnewetzky had written asking Engels' permission to translate *The Condition of the Working Class* into English and have it published in the United States. It was, she wrote, 'most important that the best of the German socialist literature should be made accessible to my countrymen in the near future'. Engels was somewhat sceptical about finding a publisher but declared his readiness to write a preface sketching the principal changes that had arisen since 1845; the text would remain unchanged from that year, but he asked to see (and have the opportunity to correct) the translation before it was printed.[89] For Engels the 'English status of 1844' appeared very similar from the point of view of industrial (and especially proletarian) development to the current situation in America, and a comparison might well 'have its interest'.[90] He took up the same argument in an article he published in the American journal *The Commonweal*[91] and again in *Die Neue Zeit*,[92] in spring and summer 1885; the text was also printed as the main feature of an annex to the Wischnewetzky translation. But that publication was delayed, so Engels wrote a new preface in January 1887 (published in German in May[93]), again commenting on current developments and recommending that the various American workers' organizations should coalesce along the lines suggested in the 1848 *Communist Manifesto*[94] to form a 'National Labor Army'.[95] However, the suggestion bypassed US reality, where by far the biggest trade union organization, the 'Knights of Labor', was dedicated to campaigning for pay and bore no resemblance to a party with a programme of political socialism.[96]

In 1845 Engels had seen revolution as imminent; now, in 1887, instead of asking why none had transpired, he simply ascribed his earlier prophecy to youthful ardour. What continued to surprise him was how right he had been in so many of his forecasts – for example the regularly occurring crises and concomitant stop-and-go of the economy, the replacement of British industrial supremacy by American and German – not how wrong. The campaign of American labour for reduction of the regular working day from ten to eight hours was also in his eyes a function of economic law – specifically of laws analysed by Marx in *Kapital I*. Engels took the opportunity of the new American translation of *Condition* to repeat his assertion that capitalists simply appropriated the fruits of proletarian labour, while only a minority of the working-class, trade unionists and factory workers to a man – the 'workers' aristocracy' he called them[97] – could profit from technological and economic progress. The vast majority of working-class people, Engels maintained, still lived in the greatest insecurity.[98]

Much work went into reading and correcting the American proofs,[99] and Engels took pains to ease the over 40-year-old text back into contemporary discussion, emphasizing the topicality of its themes in prefaces and articles – a trusted procedure, especially in connection with works by Marx.[100] In the case of *Condition*, matters did not end with the American publication: in 1891 the British publisher Swan Sonnenschein brought the essay out in London,[101] and in 1892 a second German edition, for which many social democrats had been agitating for more than a decade, was issued. (The obstacle here had been less Engels' workload with the Marx manuscripts – this had not unduly held up the Wischnewetzky translation – than the Bismarckian Anti-Socialist Law, which remained in force until 1890, vitiating all political activities.)[102] Here, too, in the Swan Sonnenschein edition, Engels referred to current developments that gave hope of change – in particular the growth of new trade unions and of a British labour party – which had been further nourished by the results of that summer's parliamentary elections. These implied, he wrote in his 1892 preface, 'The superstitious belief in the "great Liberal Party" which [has] kept a hold on the English workers for nearly forty years has been destroyed.'[103] In 1863 he had rejected the idea of reissuing the essay: 'this is not a suitable moment …, now that the English proletariat's revolutionary energy has all but completely evaporated and the English proletarian has declared himself in full agreement with the dominancy of the bourgeoisie'.[104] Again in 1892, however, as in 1845, Engels' expectations failed to reflect British reality.

Revolutions interested Engels – even historical ones. In spring 1884 he was thinking of reworking his *Peasant War in Germany* (first published 1850, second and third editions in 1870 and 1874, respectively), and at the end of that year he told Adolph Sorge, 'I am completely revising my *Peasant War* and making it the pivot for my whole history of Germany'. He repeatedly put the project on his agenda (even in March 1895)[105] but never actually set pen to paper other than to sketch out some headings 'On the Peasant War'[106] and write a short piece on 'The Decline of Feudalism and the Rise of the Bourgeoisie',[107] both manuscripts dated to the end of 1884. For Engels the Reformation was 'bourgeois revolution no. 1, with the Peasant War as its critical episode'. It was 'far more European than the English, and far more rapidly European than the French [Revolution]'. In the second manuscript he traced the development of bourgeois society in the Early Modern period from its origins, especially in the cities.[108]

Finally, in 1887 Engels was working on *The Role of Force in History*, a title that suggests an extended study, but the *c.* fifty-page essay is in effect a settling of accounts with Bismarck's strong-arm policy of the previous three decades: 'We shall clearly see from this', Engels wrote, 'why the policy of blood and iron was bound to be successful for a time and why it was bound to collapse in the end'.[109] He completed only three chapters, however, and a first draft of a new section with which he was 'not at all satisfied'.[110]

Thus, we see in Engels' later years a number of projects left (at most) half done: undertakings that might each have filled half a lifetime of research. Ambition and reality increasingly parted company, and one is left wondering if all those announced writings and rewritings did not serve rather to maintain a presence in the socialist networks and the appearance of control over his own correspondence and output; in his London exile Engels was always in danger of slipping out of the inner circle of the German Social Democratic Party.

Against this background, one can also see Engels' commitment to the founding of the Second International. His main motive was to establish the primacy of Marx's approach over the so-called possibilists who held sway in France and in 1889 were about to launch an international confederation of workers' organizations. As their name suggested, they entertained the possibility of gaining a voice in political decisions and achieving improvements in the lot of workers through social reform and the extension of voting rights. Their new umbrella organization of European socialist movements took shape in congresses of 1889 and 1891. Without speaking personally at these events, Engels edited brochures and flyers and lent his structural and procedural support, not least in intensive correspondence aimed at bringing the French *Parti Ouvrier* and the German Social Democrats closer together. His interventions in the birth of the Second International were decisive.[111]

Engels was also active at the national level, notably in the German Social Democratic movement, where his impact is evident in well-documented correspondence with August Bebel, Eduard Bernstein, Karl Kautsky and Wilhelm Liebknecht. He took a clear position in inner-party disputes, for example in 1884 or between 1890 and 1892, whether these were concerned with demands for more democracy or more revolution – or, after the demise of the Anti-Socialist Law, with discussions about the new German party programme at the 1891 Erfurt Congress. He intervened, too, in the politics of the French *Parti Ouvrier*, in which Marx's son-in-law, Paul Lafargue, played a leading role. On the other hand, he had little contact with American or British organizations: virtually none with trade unions and with political parties, if at all, through Eleanor Marx Aveling. The strategies of British workers' movements differed too fundamentally from those of their confreres across the channel.[112]

Overview

After Marx's death, Engels gradually assumed a leading position among European socialists. His initial task of preparing the publication of Marx's magnum opus was soon accompanied and punctuated by other activities. But despite the fragmentary nature of Marx's literary estate, Engels was not tempted to doubt either its underlying concepts or its analysis of capitalist production methods. He held fast to the idea that the capitalist economic system and the society informed by it were a fading model. As if to avoid any problem arising from Marx's possible later insights, Engels concentrated his energies on reissuing earlier texts (and translations) they had written either singly or together and furnishing these with prefaces that took account of more recent controversies and developments.

Engels' concern in these matters was that the 'right path' should be taken, and he claimed the prerogative of defining that path for the socialist movement as such as well as for its day-to-day activities. In this respect, however, two aspects stand out: On the one hand, Engels' advocacy of parliamentary democracy, even if only as a first step towards the exercise of power by the proletariat. And he was equally insistent that democracy and freedom of discussion should prevail within the party; once the Anti-Socialist law was no longer in force, we find him writing, for example, in August 1890: 'The party is so big that complete freedom of discussion within its ranks is imperative.'[113] On the other hand, he was open-minded about the central issue of the 'right path', emphasizing that neither he nor Marx had any time for dogma: 'Our theory is not a dogma,' he wrote, 'but the exposition of a process of evolution.'[114] In response to a comment by the political economist Werner Sombart on the appearance of *Kapital III* in 1895, Engels saw Marx's achievement, apart from defining certain central points, above all in the provision of a method for investigating such evolving processes.[115] In that sense, the question still posed worldwide as to the right way out of capitalism remains open.

CHAPTER 12
WORK AND 'THE COMPANY': HISTORICAL AND CURRENT TRENDS
Norbert Koubek

In any study of the relevance of Friedrich Engels' published statements to the present and the foreseeable future, two ideas appear central. Pride of place must be given to the concept of work in all its historical and contemporary associations, as reflected in Engels' words, quoted in the opening paragraph of the Preface to this volume:

> Labour is the source of all wealth, the political economists assert. And it really is the source – next to nature, which supplies it with the material that it converts into wealth. But it is even infinitely more than this. It is the prime basic condition for all human existence, and this to such an extent that, in a sense, we have to say that labour created man himself.[1]

Secondly, an inquiry into the institutional conditions under which work processes developed during Engels' lifetime, which still prevail today and which can be expected to do so in the predictable future, must concern itself with the company or other forms of social organization framing those processes at various times and places. The two concepts are closely related, not least because their mutual relations in the period under consideration are shaped by the socioeconomic model of capitalism.

Friedrich Engels (1820–1895) – starting points and evolution

Beginning with the concept of work: Among its numerous definitions in various sciences, the following synoptic description seems in the present context particularly meaningful: 'Work is human engagement with nature for the purpose of securing a livelihood and shaping society'. Such a definition holds at all times, albeit under varying conditions and in different forms. It addresses first the individual and society; secondly, our indissoluble connection with nature and its resources; and thirdly, the tools, technologies and means of labour applied in any given situation.

Friedrich Engels (1820–1895) dealt intensively with these matters at all periods of his life and came to quite disparate conclusions and evaluations. This is especially true in his draft texts produced after 1873, most of which were not published until after his death. Between 1873 and 1883, he wrote the manuscripts which later appeared under the title *Dialectics of Nature*, including the chapter 'The Part Played by Labour in the Transition from Ape to Man', which is of particular interest in our context.[2] Of the various approaches he takes, we shall confine ourselves here to the evolutionary and through it examine the age of industrialization that increasingly shaped working and living conditions in the West from the end of the eighteenth century.

In the first decades of his practical and scientific work, both independently and in conjunction with Karl Marx, Engels took issue with the extremely onerous conditions of industrial labour in the nascent capitalist economy and society. This led to his well-known revolutionary conclusions, expressed programmatically in the *Communist Manifesto* (1848), in whose composition he and Marx both played a major role. Decades of close collaboration with Marx were to follow – years devoted to the intellectual and political elucidation of the emerging new age.

In the last two decades of his active life, Engels – motivated both by personal experience and by the evaluation of current social, economic and technological advances – became increasingly open to the principle of evolutionary change. This is evident in his collaboration with socialist organizations in general and particularly in his programmatic evaluation of the Socialist Workers' Party (SAP), founded in Germany in 1875 and renamed in 1890 (still in Engels' lifetime) as the 'Social Democratic Party of Germany' (SPD). During this period, Engels was deeply engaged in drafting the new party policies, adopted in 1891 as the 'Erfurt Programme', which included numerous suggestions and proposals from his pen.[3]

Engels also commented on other developments in the workers' movement, in some cases from a quite novel perspective, as in his preface to the first American edition of *The Condition of the Working Class in England*, a work originally published in 1845.[4] For this new edition he wrote the article 'England in 1845 and in 1885', in which he described his personal development over the preceding forty years against the background of changes in British society.[5] It becomes apparent from these texts how aware Engels was of developments in labour conditions and production processes over this period and how he became increasingly open to the possibility of an evolutionary path forward instead of – or at least in addition to – the revolutionary transformation of the economy and society he had originally advocated. The transitions he observes from small personal enterprises with a manageable labour force, few machines and little capital to big businesses and corporations with numerous plants, armies of employees and a wealth of owners, shareholders and partners already began in the late nineteenth century and have continued to define the face of capitalism to the present day. However, they have been accompanied, precisely in Germany, by a remarkably enduring complex of small and medium-sized family enterprises; indeed, the current worldwide wave of personal start-ups in connection with technological innovations may well secure the future of this twin-track economic structure.

Capitalism after Engels (1895–2020) – new forms of work and organizational frameworks

The purpose here is not to give a general historical account of capitalism, but rather to outline some distinctive changes that have taken place in the world of work and its organization. In this evaluation, on the one hand, of theoretical literature and, on the other, of real-world experience, we shall encounter various economic models, each implemented over a period of several decades in Western-dominated parliamentary societies, some of which are also to be found, with modifications, in state socialist and authoritarian societies.

In the following sections, several of these models will be briefly outlined as they have developed over time. With regulations differing in type, scope and chronology from country to country, individual, group, institutional and class interests have been accounted for in different ways at different times and places. Variants of capitalism have emerged that sometimes deviate considerably from the initial model described by Engels in the mid-nineteenth century. Defining features in this respect have been the incorporation of scientific findings relating to various forms of work and corporate structures; the institutional participation of employees in information, planning and implementation processes in plants and companies, up to and including co-determination rights; the dismantling of formal hierarchies in favour of decentralized, team-oriented organization; and the development of integrated cross-company work processes, combined with corporate networks, distinct corporate goals and, most recently, virtual organizations. These features will now be considered briefly in turn.

Taylorism and the assembly line

With ever-greater increases in the volume of production, growing demand for standardized products and growth in the number of employees in factories, scientifically based investigations into the efficiency of human labour in industrial production and how to increase it were carried out at the end of the nineteenth and beginning of the twentieth centuries, above all in the United States. The American engineer Frederick W. Taylor, in particular, conducted extensive studies and published his findings and proposals in 1911 in his classic work *The Principles of Scientific Management*.[6] The resulting model of organization, known as Taylorism, was to be advanced a few years later by Henry Ford in the American automotive industry with his introduction of assembly line production.[7]

Taylor's view of the world and humankind was characterized by the idea that people strive above all for material prosperity, with the supply of products coming about through a corresponding increase in productivity. The introduction of scientific management was intended to create the conditions for the optimization of work processes through a highly developed division of labour. This would simultaneously increase production volumes, raise profits and wages, and lower prices.

Parallel to the changes in the organization of labour, changes occurred in corporate management, with the Taylorist system of work entailing all-encompassing hierarchical structures in which scheduling and planning were exclusively determined and implemented by central management. Significant growth in pay rates was conceived as a core incentive at every level, with each worker receiving a recognizable share of profits. This, it was argued, should bring about a reduction in strike activity and related socialist demands in factories, companies and society in general.[8] Besides these numerous positive effects, however, there were considerable drawbacks in the Taylorist system. Work processes were atomized into ever smaller steps; motivation to work was based very largely on financial incentives; social contact in the work place was highly restricted and centralized hierarchies were installed, focused on detailed planning and control.

Labour, management and social psychology

The Taylorist model, with its demonstrable improvements in the physiological conditions of labour and its attendant financial incentives, reached its limit when, after the immediate material needs of the workforce had been met, criticism turned increasingly to the lack of social contact in the workplace and of opportunities to participate meaningfully in the planning and control of operational processes. Management itself recognized that job satisfaction and job performance increase when workers were more involved in work processes, at least in their given area.

A first step in the onwards development of Taylorism came with the scientific recognition of the influence of psychology on the work process. Here, the results of the Hawthorne experiments conducted in the United States in 1924 were decisive.[9] The analysis of the processes involved in work and their psychological impact on employees demonstrated that production could increase in quantity and quality even if physical conditions in the workplace – for example lighting, noise levels and the standard of technological equipment – deteriorated. The explanation for this lay in the perceived personal recognition accorded to individual workers. Readily explicable in terms of work psychology, this effect provided a key whose use has been extended through following decades to the present day, affecting aspects of operations, as well as corporate structures and cultures, and reshaping working conditions and organizational frameworks across the board.[10]

Employee participation and co-determination

A further step was to develop institutional structures that enabled subordinate employees to influence the planning, implementation and organization of the workplace and company.[11] An important step in Germany in this respect was the passing of the first Industrial Relations Act (*Betriebsverfassungsgesetz*) in 1920. This remained in force until 1934, giving employees in all companies with twenty or more staff the right to set up a works council with certain rights and duties to represent their interests.

After the Second World War, a new Industrial Relations Act was passed in 1952. Applicable at the time to all companies with five or more employees, this has since been amended and extended on several occasions. As early as 1951, the Coal, Iron and Steel Industry Codetermination Act (*Montan-Mitbestimmungsgesetz*) gave employees and their unions the right to participate in the executive and supervisory boards of joint stock corporations in this sector with more than a thousand employees. In 1976, these rights were extended in a weakened form to all corporations with more than two thousand employees. Other European countries also enacted various forms of employee participation rights during this period.¹²

Similar legislation exists in the European Economic Community [now the European Union (EU)]. For example, since 1996 there have been directives on the formation of European works councils, and since 2004, EU law has regulated the participation rights of employees in European joint stock companies. The scope and binding nature of these regulations is, however, significantly lower than that of their German equivalents. Worldwide, numerous agreements exist within the framework of the International Labour Organization (ILO) prescriptions, and some European corporations have, on a voluntary basis, introduced global participation rights for employees in collaboration with international trade unions.¹³

Kaizen and lean management

The third work and organizational model to be considered here was developed in Japan after the Second World War and first used in the Toyota automobile company. This approach essentially consists of two parts, still referred to today as *kaizen* and lean management. The term *kaizen* is made up of the words *kai* (change) and *zen* (good), while the lean management approach involves the dismantling of hierarchies in workplaces, plants and companies and the opening of organizational structures to the formation of work groups with the authority to make and implement proposals of their own.¹⁴ From 1950 onwards, these work and organizational principles were introduced first in Japan and then in the other Western countries, where they increasingly replaced Taylorism.

A particularly detailed comparison between Japan, the United States and Europe is provided in the results of a study carried out by the Massachusetts Institute of Technology (MIT) in 1991 for the automotive industry and its suppliers.¹⁵ In this study, the goals of increased quantitative, financial and qualitative efficiency in work processes were achieved via group work, the precise deployment of machines and materials and the avoidance of errors in production (or their correction directly in the workplace), thereby avoiding losses in the use of labour, materials and equipment. In the individual company these processes centred on cooperative management, automation, the replacement of individual work stations with teams, the reduction and flattening of hierarchies, increased outsourcing of aspects of the value chain and the development of various forms of cooperation with third-party companies. In conjunction with other gradually introduced innovations, this organizational approach has resulted in a permanent process of change with many positive effects on job satisfaction and the performance profile of the companies concerned.

Corporate networks and virtual organizations

With the expansion of computer-based processes in corporations and other societal institutions in recent decades, the data-based integration and networking of individual companies has greatly intensified.¹⁶ Over and above traditional supplier-customer relationships, strategic cooperations have developed between legally independent but not mutually competing companies. These networks presuppose long-term cooperation across the entire value chain, from planning and decision-making, through production and sales, to maintenance and recycling. They give rise, in appropriate circumstances, to cross-border and global forms of cooperation known respectively as 'nearshoring' and 'offshoring'.

The new tasks embraced by these forms of cooperation result from changes in strategic economic and societal objectives, exemplified in the current growth of demand in areas such as ecology, resource consumption, sustainability and qualifications. In addition to the typical fixation on the rational use of capital – or more narrowly on profitability and returns – the question of the use or abuse of resources, always present in work and production processes, but so far given too little consideration, comes here to the fore. In this context the multiple interface of economics with ecology, human resources, product design and consumer requirements[17] involves new forms of logic, complementing or even superseding mere capital rationalization. Accordingly, the increased scope of management tasks calls for varied implementation according to market conditions, legal frameworks and the objectives of the economic actors concerned.

Known in English by the abbreviations ESG (environmental social governance) and CSR (corporate social responsibility),[18] this expanded perspective demonstrates the evolution and adaptation of capitalism to new circumstances, alongside its historically dominant forms of rationalization, as diverse individuals and groups bring their heterogeneous goal sets to the table and seek to apply them.[19] At the macroeconomic level, this will predictably lead in Germany – against the backdrop of an established social market economy – to growing emphasis on ecological criteria and the corresponding development of a socio-ecological market economy.[20] The market will remain in its multifaceted coordinating function at the centre of economic activity, but it will be supported in a variety of ways by supra-capitalist objectives and directives.

Another area of transformation in classical capitalism lies in the increase in the importance of legal and ownership forms outside of joint stock corporations. This is true of the cooperatives, foundations and non-profit organizations that have long been available, but new institutions are also emerging in the production and consumption of goods and services in which producers and consumers combine into the novel entity of 'prosumers'.[21] In the renewable energy sector in particular, this is already a significant economic factor in the generation-cum-use of photovoltaic and wind-produced energy.

Global resource-related issues resulting from capitalist patterns of growth have hitherto long been neglected. This can be strikingly illustrated with the observation that in order to sustain the current Western standard of living for an expected global population reaching 10 to 11 billion by the end of the twenty-first century, three Earths would be needed instead of one. While the developed countries are primarily responsible for current methods of production and target standards of living, extreme rises in world population, both to date and in coming decades, will result from the fertility rates and population growth obtaining in the largely un- or underdeveloped states of Africa and Asia.[22]

A feature that has received little attention in the Western world in recent decades is related to the increasing skewness of wealth distribution. Here, initial discussions are emerging in an effort to give greater consideration to economic ethics and avoid destabilizing the social and economic order. It is no coincidence that Thomas Piketty's *Capital in the Twenty-First Century*, published in France in 2013 and in the United States in 2014, rapidly became a bestseller, supplemented by the thematically and historically expanded follow-up *Capital and Ideology*, which appeared in France in 2019 and in the United States in 2020.[23]

A special development based on the availability of internet networks is the creation of virtual enterprises and organizations.[24] Networks of independent companies using various IT systems can be created to engage in specific activities and fulfil orders with the aim of sharing costs, complementing each other's capabilities and exploiting market openings. The result of such ad hoc collaborations is an efficient combination of core competencies that dispenses with institutionally permanent structures. Once a commission has been fulfilled, the virtual organization dissolves and participants can cooperate in new networks with completely (or partially) different actors.

In recent years and decades, there has also been a sharp increase in the number of so-called sole traders, in which each organization consists of just one person, usually the founder. This new form of entrepreneurship, also known as crowdsourcing, is found primarily in the IT, healthcare and care sectors, as well as in trade and logistics.[25] All activities and contracts are carried out by the one person at his or her own responsibility, with all the associated risks and freedoms. In addition to greater freedom in terms of work organization, product development and the use of new forms of marketing, numerous, usually volatile, conditions and risks must be faced in regional, national and international markets. These can arise due to technological developments, variability in supply and demand, and legal regulations, as well as in qualification and health issues affecting a single person.

Conclusion – Friedrich Engels in the twenty-first century

This brief overview of significant changes in the nature of labour and its social organization over the past 125 years leads to a final question: How would today's work patterns and systemic industrial goals be evaluated if one applied the standards of Friedrich Engels, especially those of his later years?

First of all, it should be noted that technological developments and changes in employee needs, as well as in political and social structures, have greatly altered the nature and conditions of economic activity. In a globally interconnected world, different regions have different levels of development, for which different models must be applied. In the Western countries with parliamentary-democratic structures – which continue to be among the most highly developed – where industrialization began and whence it spread worldwide, processes of economic and social adaptation are demonstrably effective, while in countries at an initial stage of economic growth, the conditions described by Engels are still present to some extent. Between the two regional models lie the so-called emerging countries with influences from and options in both directions.

Numerous statements in Engels' work point to these conflicts and see unrestrained economic growth both as a central ingredient of capitalism and as a precondition of its decline. However, especially in his later years, Engels revised his earlier revolutionary and centralist positions and considered the evolutionary path of reform to contain the possibility of systemic change.

This reading of Engels allows room for the openness – also in looking to the society of the future – that he emphasized in his studies on the *Dialectics of Nature*, as well as in the several introductions he wrote to new editions of his and Marx's books. This is demonstrated with particular clarity in the following quotation from the introduction to Marx's article 'The Class Struggles in France, 1848 to 1850', which Engels published in 1895, shortly before his death:

> But history has shown us too to have been wrong, has revealed our point of view at that time as an illusion. It has done even more; it has not merely dispelled the erroneous notions we then held; it has also completely transformed the conditions under which the proletariat has to fight. The mode of struggle of 1848 is today obsolete in every respect, and this is a point which deserves closer examination on the present occasion.[26]

On the occasion of the 200th year of Friedrich Engels' birth and the 125th year of his death, the present publication seeks to pursue that closer examination.

CHAPTER 13
OVERVIEW: ENGELS IN HIS TIME
Jürgen Kocka

One usually speaks of 'Marx and Engels', and not of 'Engels and Marx', despite the fact that alphabetical order would suggest the latter. Admirers, critics and distanced observers attribute historical greatness primarily to Karl Marx, while Friedrich Engels, as he himself wrote in retrospect, liked to play 'second fiddle' in the 'partnership' conducted jointly with Marx (Nippel, this volume, 27–42). There is still a great deal to be said for such a view today, especially when one thinks of the intellectual genesis and long-term historical impact of the ideas, theories and sociopolitical strategies that have lived on in various mutations of Marxism and been so eminently influential in the history of our age. But in recent years there has been a marked revaluation of Engels relative to Marx. The essays in the present volume contribute to this process, revealing various aspects and causes, but also mapping limits, of this gradual revaluation process.

Figure 13.1 Forward to the XI SED Party Congress. Marx–Engels monument in front of the Palace of the Republic, (East) Berlin; called 'Sakko und Jacketti' (Sacco and Vanzetti) by the Berliners, 4 April 1986. © BPK.

On the one hand, Marx's iconic appeal has diminished. In addition to changes in the wider political and cultural climate, the intensive study of his life and work on the occasion of the 200th anniversary of his birth in 2018 has contributed significantly to this shift. Marx has, in effect, been historicized – that is more clearly embedded in the context of his times and hence more clearly recognizable in terms of his achievements and limitations as a figure of the nineteenth century.[1] The historicizing, contextualizing view of Marx by no means leads us away from Engels. On the contrary, it confirms their common orientation while at the same time shedding light on key differences. Engels emerges more clearly with his own unique profile; he is increasingly interesting as a historical person in his own right.

On the other hand, based on painstaking research, the new edition of the *Marx–Engels Gesamtausgabe* (*Complete Works*, aka MEGA), whose publication is by now well-advanced, has emphatically demonstrated how heterogeneous, contradictory, fragmented and unfinished Marx's written, but still largely unpublished, work was at the time of his death in 1883. It became historically effective only in the course of its posthumous publication, a process in which Engels consistently played the role not just of editor and propagator but also of original author. In the present volume, Regina Roth (this volume, 223–9) comments on this process with regard to Volumes 2 and 3 of *Das Kapital*.[2] Other chapters in the book take account of discoveries made specifically in the preparation of the new MEGA, which allow Engels' role to be appreciated more adequately than it has been in the past.[3]

If the impulses, achievements and impact of Friedrich Engels become more interesting in this way, the question of differences in his and Marx's views and attitudes also gains in importance. The present volume contains new results in this regard. Thus, Heinz Kurz (this volume, 199–221) identifies growing differences between Engels' and Marx's, above all, critical reception of the intellectual legacy of classics such as Smith, Ricardo and Malthus – differences they did not develop, but which led them to different conclusions on some basic issues of political economics. This becomes apparent, for example, with regard to the controversial thesis of a law governing the falling general rate of profit, a thesis that Marx treated with increasing scepticism, while Engels adhered to it as a key to his firm expectation of the future collapse of capitalism and sharpened corresponding passages in *Das Kapital* accordingly. That Engels' spectrum of interests and activities was much broader and more diversified than Marx's is exemplified by his military studies, a subject in which Marx had little interest 18f. and 85–100). Marx, as a trained philosopher, gave theoretical academic studies clear primacy in his thinking, as in his life, while Engels, ever the industrial merchant, spent much time and energy alongside his everyday management tasks on observing the world of work and social conditions, on practical strategic initiatives and public relations, and on his own reflections and publications. Werner Plumpe describes Marx as a person who 'for all his astuteness, was remarkably unfit for life' and who had to rely on the practical and economically successful Engels to make ends meet. His historical stature as the founder of the various Marxisms emerged only over time, in processes of widely differing reception and instrumentalization, and his image as a globally outstanding historical figure came about only through Engels' immensely committed and remarkably skilful popularization of it after Marx's death (this volume, 27–42).[4]

At times, the broader experiential background of Engels' seasoned personality also revealed itself in terms of intellectual content. Eberhard Illner shows Engels' lead over Marx in understanding and analysing the interface between machines and humans in industrial labour processes. Engels' superiority here resulted from his direct acquaintance with labour relations, especially in industrial Manchester, but also from a broader, more precise reading of the relevant literature (this volume, 63–84). It is hard to overestimate Engels' influence on Marx's turn to what was to become his life's work: the study of political economy and especially the analysis and critique of capitalism. Several essays in this volume (especially those of Hans A. Frambach and Heinz D. Kurz) trace in detail the communication between Engels and Marx in the decisive years 1843 to 1845, through which Marx, until then more philosophically oriented and practising radical critique primarily as a critique of religion, law and ideology, was won over to the critical reading of political-economic classics such as Smith, Ricardo and Malthus. With Engels' eloquent advocacy, the theoretical conviction grew that the contemporary bourgeois – and, increasingly clearly, industrial – economy determined the character of modern society, culture and politics and that, doomed by its own internal contradictions, it would necessarily give way to something new and revolutionary borne by the proletariat, be it socialism or communism.

Influenced by the massive rise of industrial capitalism and the spreading crisis of pauperism, the turn of radical-critical intellectuals to political economy – and with it to the goal of socialism or communism – was a transnational Western European phenomenon of the 'hungry', pre-revolutionary 1840s. Marx's transformation in this regard was by no means an isolated case, but it took its distinctive colouring from the combination of his philosophical – above all Hegelian – education and the powerful influence of Engels, who was already commuting between Germany and England, and whose socioeconomic knowledge and revolutionary commitment, drawn from the ideas of Moses Hess, early French socialists and radical English reformers, was profoundly reinforced by direct experience of the industrially advanced regions of England around Manchester. Engels brought Marx into direct contact with this intellectual, emotional and practical world, and their encounter from 1844 onwards developed into a rapidly deepening friendship.[5] Such aspects, among others, justify us in also speaking of 'Engels and Marx', not just of 'Marx and Engels'.

But the essays in this volume, far from putting Friedrich Engels on a pedestal – as has so often been done with Marx – seek to contribute to a critical understanding and sober evaluation of him in his historical context. They trace the admirable versatility of Engel's lifework and point to the rapid changes in his thematic emphases, which made it easier for him even in old age to absorb new aspects and at times to modify older positions (chap. 1, 3, 4, 8, 11). But the price of this was that much remained half-baked and inadequately thought through (this volume, 238f.).

The critique in these pages (this volume, 169–74; 210–21) of the one-sidedness and polemical distortion with which Engels interpreted classical English political economy in the early 1840s and passed it on to Marx is resolute and sobering. Again and again, it also becomes clear how difficult it was for Engels, shaped by the experiences and insights of the 1840s, to really understand later developments, be it in the overcoming of pauperism through successful capitalist growth in the second half of the century, the failure of the formation of a proletarian class with revolutionary potential in the United States (which both he and Marx had expected) or the survival of small and medium-sized enterprises in agriculture and commerce in Germany and Austria, whose demise both of them had confidently predicted (this volume, 59–62; 109–11; 122–4). That most of Engels' and Marx's forecasts did *not* come true was already apparent in Engels' lifetime. Engels, however, lived long enough to observe and enjoy the beginnings of the phenomenal impact that their joint achievement would have on workers' movements from the late nineteenth century onwards. The validity of their prognoses is one thing, their standing in world history quite another.

If the task of the historian is above all to contextualize a person or phenomenon in their time, then the present volume makes a significant contribution to the urgently needed historicization of Engels, especially with regard to his formative beginnings. There are two sides to this fascinating figure. On the one hand, it becomes increasingly clear how decisively Engels' ideas about capitalism and its crises were shaped by his own experiences in the West German and English textile – especially cotton – industries. He had completed the first part of his commercial apprenticeship in 1837–8 in his father's company in Barmen, where production, and to some extent the further processing, of yarns was still mainly decentralized, carried out by home workers and dependent craftsmen under the control of the merchant who distributed (or 'put out') work (already called a 'fabricant' or manufacturer). In Ermen & Engels cotton spinning mill in Manchester, however, where Friedrich Engels worked from 1842 – first as an apprentice, then as an employee on behalf of his father and finally as a co-managing partner – production was already largely centralized, that is truly factory-like. These two main conflicting forms of early industrial activity had many victims; their clash defined the structure and mindset that Engels experienced and shaped his image not only of capitalist entrepreneurship but of capitalism as such. Their inherent structural crisis was exacerbated in the 'hungry 40s' by the dire intensification of European pauperism and in Manchester by mass Irish immigration. Engels observed and personally experienced the resultant extremes of precarious working and oppressive living conditions of the workers. He described them unflinchingly in his soon famous and widely read book *The Condition of the Working Class in England* (1845) and explained them eloquently as a consequence of capitalist relations of production, without, of course, being able to classify and relativize them as a specific, even temporary phase of capitalist economic and bourgeois social history. His image of capitalism remained forever shaped by these early experiences (this volume, 120–3; 137–64).[6]

On the other hand, one can interpret Engels – in line with the present volume, albeit a step further – as a particular example of the European bourgeoisie. If, at least on the European mainland, the bourgeoisie of the nineteenth century were, for all their differences and inner contrasts, defined as socioeconomic class and culture by an often conflicting combination of forces,[7] then Friedrich Engels can be said to have lived this symbiosis in a very real and intense way. Deeply influenced by his origins in a respected bourgeois family, as well as by the not uncommon critical attitude of the bourgeoisie towards the way of life associated with such origins, the young Friedrich developed an insatiable appetite for literature through his grammar school education (which he was obliged to break off) and his temporary participation in the intellectual life of Berlin (including attending philosophical lectures at university and immersing himself in the social circles of the oppositional Young Hegelians). In this way he acquired a broad, historical, philosophical and scientific education, even if it remained imperfect and fragmentary (this volume, 169–71; 183–7).

In later years Engels continued to combine bourgeois economic and cultural interests and lifestyles. Although he scoffed at and criticized his work whether as clerk, entrepreneur or partner in Manchester, he practised it with notable success, following the rules of the hard Manchester capitalism of the day.[8] And when, with no regrets, he left this business in 1869, bourgeois economic activity by no means left his life: he supplemented his shareholder's income with earnings from investment advice and speculation on the stock exchange. That was one side of the coin; the other was his enduring respect for knowledge and science, reflected in the scope of his publications – the studies, essays and journalism through which he maintained close contact with the bourgeois cultural world of scholars and intellectuals.[9] Despite the many bohemian and other unbourgeois elements in his lifestyle and the remorseless critique of the bourgeoisie at the heart of his writings, Friedrich Engels should be seen as a product of nineteenth-century Western European bourgeois culture, with an early and viable combination of German and English dimensions. Much of his life and work can be understood from this perspective.

The present volume considers Engels decidedly, in his insights, statements and impact, as a figure of the nineteenth century.[10] This in no way diminishes the fascination emanating from this multi-layered, self-creating, dynamic and versatile personality. But, for the reception of Engels today, the historical framing in the infancy of the modern age is indispensable.

CHAPTER 14
ANNEX: NOTE ON THE EDITORIAL HISTORY OF MARX'S AND ENGELS' WRITINGS

The *Marx–Engels Gesamtausgabe* (Marx–Engels Complete Works, known as MEGA²) is the authoritative historical-critical edition of all publications, manuscripts and drafts, as well as correspondence by and to Karl Marx and Friedrich Engels, as far as these are known and have been handed down. The basis is the original manuscripts and authorized prints in their original language. Unfinished manuscripts are reproduced in accordance with the state in which they were left by the authors. Documentation of the development of the work is carried out according to modern editorial methods and is found together with a scholarly commentary in an apparatus volume, published parallel to the text volume containing the reproduction of the manuscripts or prints.

The publisher is the politically independent *Internationale Marx-Engels-Stiftung* (International Marx–Engels Foundation, IMES) founded in 1990 as a research association comprising the International Institute for Social History (IISG) in Amsterdam, where a large part of Marx's and Engels' manuscripts are held, the Berlin-Brandenburg Academy of Sciences in Berlin, the Friedrich Ebert Foundation in Bonn and the Russian State Archive for Social and Political History (RGASPI) in Moscow, which holds a third of the Marx and Engels estate. The MEGA edition, begun in Moscow and Berlin in 1975, was in its first fifteen years under political influence, expressed by the editorial commission in 1981 in the statement: 'Each volume of MEGA opens with a theoretical-historical introduction containing Marxist-Leninist assessments of the works published in the volume and situating them within the history of the development of Marxism.'[11] This changed fundamentally as a result of German Reunification and the political changes in Russia. IMES has taken up and continued the editorial work and publication as a purely academic project. In addition to the detailed work of text development, the focus is now on establishing sources and setting the texts left by Marx and Engels in their historical context.

Published by de Gruyter, the edition is divided into four sections: (I) Works, Articles, Drafts; (II) *Das Kapital* and Preliminary Works; (III) Correspondence between Marx, Engels and Third Parties; (IV) Excerpts, Notes, Marginalia. An introduction to the project, as well as an overview of the volumes so far published and in progress, can be found at: mega.bbaw.de. The digital edition of MEGA currently includes the texts of nine economics volumes from Section II, the correspondence (arranged by year, beginning with 1866) and excerpts (currently from the *Economist* and the *Money Market*

Review, 1866–7). Letters and excerpts are constantly being added. These can all be found at: megadigital.bbaw.de.

From 1927 to 1935 (or in some cases 1941), thirteen volumes of an initial *Marx–Engels Gesamtausgabe* (MEGA¹) with important early texts were published in Moscow. A total of forty-two volumes were planned. As a result of political persecution during the Stalin era, the project was, however, abandoned.

The second Russian edition of Marx–Engels' works (*Sočinenija*) – published between 1955 and 1966 in thirty-nine (main) volumes, three index volumes and eleven supplementary volumes by the Institute for Marxism–Leninism under the Central Committee of the Communist Party of the Soviet Union (CPSU) in Moscow – formed the basis for the German edition of the *Marx–Engels Werke* (Marx–Engels Works – MEW). Between 1956 and 2018 – most recently under the editorship of the Rosa Luxemburg Foundation – forty-four volumes were published in this series, along with a subject index volume and two volumes of other indexes (titles, publication data, addressees etc. of books and other writings in Vol. 1 and of letters etc. in Vol. 2). This is a widely used study edition containing all the completed and published books, articles and other writings by Marx and Engels (comprising the smaller part of the surviving estate), as well as a limited selection of manuscripts, drafts and preparatory works, and the letters of the two authors to each other and to third parties. It does not, however, aspire to 'complete publication of excerpts, rough drafts, sketches – i.e. preparatory work in general' – or 'reproduction of the texts in the original language'.[22] As a German-language variant of the second Russian edition of the works, MEW was edited according to the political guidelines of the Institutes of Marxism-Leninism at the Central Committee of the Socialist Unity Party (SED) and the CPSU equivalent in line with the political directives of the Marxist–Leninist Institutes in Moscow and Berlin. In the selection and canonization of texts, as in the prefaces, notes, commentaries and index entries, dogmatic compliance with Leninist principles is unmistakable.

The fifty-volume English-language edition *Marx–Engels Collected Works* (MECW), published by Progress Publishers Moscow between 1975 and 2004, offers a similar selection of works in chronological order (Vols 1–27), followed by Marx's works on political economy (Vols 28–37) and the letters (Vols 38–50). It is also based on the Russian edition of the works, especially in the commentaries, but in some cases goes beyond this in the selection of texts and offers English-language texts in the original.

Text references in the present volume generally follow MEGA¹ and MEGA²; only in a few exceptional cases, where the MEGA² volumes are still currently being edited (mostly correspondence from 1868 onwards), is reference made to the MEW edition. English quotations (whether original or translations) are taken wherever possible from MECW.

NOTES

PREFACE

1   MEGA² I/ 26, 540; MECW, vol. 25, 452.

CHAPTER 1

1   *Meine unsterblichen Werke*, handwritten list of writings, IISG H 142/H 73. For a comparison with the list of writings published in *Handwörterbuch der Staatswissenschaften*, see *Marx-Engels Gesamtausgabe* (Marx-Engels Complete Work, MEGA²) I/32, 517f. and 1421–5; *Marx-Engels Collected Works* (MECW), vol. 27, 614f.
2   Friedrich Engels, article in *Handwörterbuch der Staatswissenschaften*, in: MEGA² I/32, 517f., and 1421–5. See Ernst Drahn's attempt to give a complete overview of Engels' publications in *Handwörterbuch der Staatswissenschaften*, 4th ed., vol. 3 (Jena 1926), 727–30.
3   Engels and Karl Heinrich Marx, in: MEGA² I/32, 182–8 and 923–7; MECW, vol. 27, 332–43.
4   See Thomas Bauer, *Die Vereindeutigung der Welt. Über den Verlust an Mehrdeutigkeit und Vielfalt* (Ditzingen, 2018), trans. R. Livingstone, *The Decline of Complexity in the World: On the Loss of Ambiguity and Diversity*. https://www.litrix.de/en/buecher.cfm?publicationId=2983 (retrieved 29 June 2021).
5   Marx, *Ökonomisch-philosophische Manuskripte*, in: MEGA² I/2, 187–322; MECW, vol. 3, 229–346. Marx, *Historisch-ökonomische Studien (Pariser Hefte)*, in: MEGA² IV/2, 279–579.
6   MEGA² I/5; MECW, vol. 5, 19–539.
7   See Regina Roth's essay in the present volume.
8   MEGA² I/26; MECW, vol. 25, 313–588.
9   Engels, *Herrn Eugen Dührings Umwälzung der Wissenschaften*, in: MEGA² I/27; *Anti-Dühring*, MECW, vol. 25, 5–315.
10 Engels, *Briefe aus dem Wuppertal*, in: *Telegraph für Deutschland*, no. 40, March 1839, in: MEGA² I/3, 32–51 and 736ff., here 35; *Letters from Wuppertal*, MECW, vol. 2; 7–25, here 10.
11 Karl Gutzkow to Levin Schücking, 9 June 1840, cited in MEGA² I/3, 669.
12 MEGA² I/3, 192–8; MECW, vol. 2, 128–30.
13 Ibid., 139–46, here 143; MECW, vol. 2, 116–18.
14 Engels to Eduard Bernstein, 25 January 1882, and to Karl Kautsky, 15 November 1882, in *Marx-Engels Werke* (Marx-Engels Works, MEW), vol. 35, 265 and 399; MECW, vol. 46, 376f.
15 MEGA² I/3, 467–94 and 1109ff.; MECW, vol. 3, 418–43.
16 See Gareth Stedman Jones, 'Engels und die Geschichte des Marxismus', in: *Klassen, Politik und Sprache* (Münster, 1988), 231–75; original English title 'Engels and the History of Marxism', in: *The History of Marxism*, ed. Eric Hobsbawm (Brighton, 1982).
17 MEGA² I/3, 1113f.
18 Engels and Marx, *Die heilige Familie*, 191 and 186, in: MEGA¹ I/3, 294f.; *The Holy Family*, MECW, vol. 4, 5–211, here 122, 119.

Notes

19 Friedrich Engels, *Die Lage der arbeitenden Klasse in England* (Leipzig, 1845); MEGA[1] I/4, 3–286; MEW, vol. 2, 255–506; *The Condition of the Working Class in England*, MECW, vol. 4, 295–583.
20 Engels, *Condition*, in MEGA[2] I/30, 369–555, 1034ff., and 163–8 (appendix); for the preface, see MEGA[2] I/31, 29–36; MECW, vol. 4, 302–4.
21 *Frankfurter Allgemeine Zeitung*, 11 December 2007.
22 MEW, vol. 4, 459–93.
23 International Institute of Social History, Amsterdam, *Marx–Engels Nachlass* (A 22) (https://search.iisg.amsterdam/Record/ARCH00860). For a transcription of the text, see MEW, vol. 4, 610.
24 See Theo Stammen and Alexander Classen (eds), *Karl Marx: Das Manifest der kommunistischen Partei. Kommentierte Studienausgabe* (Paderborn, 2009).
25 *Die Zentralbehörde des Bundes der Kommunisten an die Kreisbehörde Brüssel* (The Central Authority of the League of Communists to the Brussels District Authority), 25 January 1848, in: MEGA[2] III/2, 384.
26 Marx and Engels, *Das Manifest der Kommunistischen Partei*, in: MEW, vol. 4, 464; trans. https://www.marxists.org/archive/marx/works/download/pdf/Manifesto.pdf (retrieved 29 June 2021).
27 See Wolfgang Meiser, *Das Manifest der Kommunistischen Partei vom February 1848: Zur Entstehung und Überlieferung der ersten Ausgabe*, in: MEGA-Studien (Amsterdam, 1996), 66–107; Thomas Kuczynski, *Das Kommunistische Manifest von Karl Marx und Friedrich Engels* (Trier, 1995); Gareth Stedman Jones, *Karl Marx and Friedrich Engels: The Communist Manifesto* (Harmondsworth, 2002).
28 See Bert Andréas, *Le Manifeste Communiste de Marx et Engels: Histoire et Bibliographie 1848–1918* (Milan, 1963).
29 Introduction to the 2012 edition of Marx and Engels' *The Communist Manifesto*. https://www.versobooks.com/blogs/1137-eric-hobsbawm-s-introduction-to-the-2012-edition-of-marx-amp-engels-the-communist-manifesto (retrieved 21 July 2021).
30 Engels, 'Progress of Social Reform on the continent', in: *The New Moral World* (London, 4 November 1843), in: MEGA[2] I/3, 495f.; MECW, vol. 3, 392–408. See *Zur publizistischen Arbeit*, 665–711.
31 MEGA[2] I/3, 554; MECW, vol. 3, 485.
32 MECW, vol. 3, 487.
33 Ibid., 187.
34 Jenny Marx, 'Kurze Umrisse eines bewegten Lebens', in: *Mohr und General: Erinnerungen an Marx und Engels* (Berlin, 1982), 186.
35 MEGA[2] I/5; MECW, vol. 5, 19–539, here 31, 38.
36 Engels to Joseph Bloch, 21–22 September 1890, in MEW, vol. 37, 463 and 464; MECW, vol. 49, 33–6; see MEGA[2] I/32, 111 and 130–48.
37 MEGA[2] I/5, 19, 20, 26, 43, 89 and 497; MECW, vol. 26, 390–1.
38 Engels, Introduction (1895) to Karl Marx's *Die Klassenkämpfe in Frankreich 1848 bis 1850*, in: MEGA[2] I/32, 330–51; *The Class Struggles in France, 1848 to 1850*, MECW, vol. 27, 506–24.
39 Engels to Marx, 15 January 1847, in: MEGA[2] III/2, 82; MECW, vol. 38, 107–9; see in detail MEGA[2] I/5, 745.
40 A copy of the document, written by Engels and distributed as a lithographed print, was first discovered in 1966 in the Hamburg State Archives (Bert Andréas (ed.), *Gründungsdokumente des Bundes der Kommunisten (Juni to September 1847)* (Hamburg, 1969)).
41 Ibid., 69; trans. https://www.marxists.org/archive/marx/works/1847/06/09.htm (retrieved 22 July 2021).

42 Engels, *Principles of Communism*, in: MEW, vol. 4, 361–80, here 372; MECW, vol. 6, 341–57, here 341f.; trans. https://www.marxists.org/archive/marx/works/1847/11/prin-com.htm (retrieved 22 July 2021).

43 'The Congress to the Confederation' (London, 15 December 1848 [1847], [signed] Secretary: J. [F.] Engels. President: Carl Schapper). https:// inlibris.at/?s=schapper&cat=6, 5&lang=en (retrieved 28 March 2020), own translation.

44 Max Nettlau, '*Marxanalekten*', in: *Archiv für die Geschichte des Sozialismus und der Arbeiterbewegung 8*, 1919, 389–99, here 396, own translation.

45 Engels, *To the Editor of the Northern Star*, in: MEGA² I/7, 6–9; MECW, vol. 6, 559–63.

46 The machine worker Alexandre Martin, called Albert.

47 Engels, *Revolution in Paris*, in: *Deutsche-Brüsseler-Zeitung*, 27 February 1848, in: MEGA² I/7, 3, 6 and 5; MECW, vol. 6, 556–8.

48 MEGA¹ I/6, 231–49; MEW, vol. 4, 40–57; MECW, vol. 6, 78–91.

49 See Dieter Langewiesche, *Der gewaltsame Lehrer: Europas Kriege in der Moderne* (Munich, 2019), ch. III/2.c.

50 Engels, 'Der preussische Pressgesetzentwurf', in: *Neue Rheinische Zeitung*, 20 July 1848, in MEGA² I/7, 367; MECW, vol. 7, 250–2.

51 Engels, 'Die auswärtige deutsche Politik und die letzten Ereignisse zu Prag', in: *Neue Rheinische Zeitung*, 12 July 1848, in: MEGA² I/7, 309; MECW, vol. 7, 212–15.

52 Engels, 'Die Niederlage der Piemontesen', in: *Neue Rheinische Zeitung*, 31 March 1849, in: MEW vol. 6, 385–7; MECW, vol. 9, 169–77.

53 Engels, 'Köln, 27 April (Erfolge in Ungarn – Aufruhr in Wien', in: *Neue Rheinische Zeitung*, 28 April 1849, MECW, vol. 9, 352.

54 MEGA² III/9, letter 201, III/8, 84; MECW, vol. 40, 105 and III/9, letter 103.

55 MEGA² I/10, 367–443 and 962ff; MECW, vol. 10, 397–482.

56 Re Engels' 1870 preliminary note; see MEGA² I/21, 167–74 and 1490ff.; MECW, vol. 21, 93–100.

57 MEGA² I/10, 37–118 and 741ff; MECW, vol. 10, 147–239.

58 Marx/Engels, *Revue. Mai bis Oktober 1850*, in: MEGA² I/10, 448, 467 and 458; MECW, vol. 10, 490–532, here 490, 510.

59 MEW, vol. 13, 225–68; MECW, vol. 16, 211–55.

60 MEW, vol. 13, 571–612; MECW, vol. 16, 567–610.

61 MEGA² I/20, 71–108 and 1024ff.; MECW, vol. 20, 37–79; see Gustav Mayer, *Friedrich Engels: Eine Biographie*, vol. 2 (Frankfurt, 1975), 134–44.

62 MEGA² I/20, 108; MECW, vol. 20, 78.

63 Engels and Marx (1892), in: MEGA² I/32, 185; MECW, vol. 27, 332–43.

64 See MEGA² I/16, 611–14 and 648–56; MECW, vol. 17, 330ff., and vol. 18.

65 MEGA² III/9, letter 46, own translation.

66 Engels to Joseph Weydemeyer, 19 June 1851, in: MEGA² III/4, 132 and 134; MECW, vol. 38, 370.

67 Engels to Hermann Engels, 15 July 1869, MEGA² III/4, 628; MECW vol. 43, 321.

68 Michael Knieriem, '*Gewinn unter Gottes Segen*'. *Ein Beitrag zu Firmengeschichte und geschäftlicher Situation von Friedrich Engels* (Neustadt an der Aisch, 1987), 108.

69 Institute for Marxism–Leninism at the Central Committee of the SED (ed.), *Mohr und General: Erinnerungen an Marx und Engels* (Berlin, 1982), 403.

70 MEGA² I/24, 3–83 and 603ff., here 39 and 57; MECW, vol. 23, 317–91, here 368.

71 MEGA² I/25, 30–45 and 565ff., here 44f.; MECW, vol. 24, 109–28, here 126. See Mayer, *Friedrich Engels*, vol. 2, 267.

72 MEGA² I/27, 541–82, 583–627 and 1249ff.; MECW, vol. 24, 281–325.

Notes

73 Engels to Karl Kautsky, 16 February 1884; Engels to Friedrich Adolph Sorge, 7 March 1884, quoted in MEGA² I/27, 591; MECW, vol. 47, 101ff. and 113ff.
74 Engels, *Der Ursprung der Familie, des Privateigentums und des Staats*. Following Lewis H. Morgan's research, in: MEGA² I/29, 7–117 and 586ff.; *The Origins of the Family*, MECW, vol. 26, 129–276.
75 MEGA² I/29, 11 and 114; MECW, vol. 26, 131 and 276, original emphasis.
76 MEGA² I/31, 179 and 612ff.; MECW, vol. 27, 11–49, here 13.
77 MEGA² I/30, 122–62 and 780ff., here 148 and 162; MECW, vol. 26, XIX, 353–98, here 398.
78 MEGA² I/31, 299–379 and 1085ff.; MECW, vol. 27, 95–176.
79 Wilfried Nippel, 'Friedrich Engels und die Politik des Prefaces', in: *Zeitschrift für Ideengeschichte* 11, 2017, 67–78, here 78. See *Der Publizist Friedrich Engels und seine Foren*, March 1891 to August 1895, in MEGA² I/32, 587–602.
80 MEGA² I/30, 27–40 and 654ff.
81 Engels, *Zur Geschichte des Bundes der Kommunisten*, in: MEGA² I/30, 89–108 and 748ff; MECW, vol. 26, 304–10.
82 MEGA² II/8, 57–61.
83 MEGA² II/9, 11–14.
84 MEGA² II/13, 5–21.
85 MEGA² I/31, 49–54 and 722ff.
86 Engels, *Wilhelm Wolff*, in: MEGA² I/25, 46–82 and 576ff., originally published in 1876 in the journal *Die Neue Welt*.
87 Engels, 'Marx und die *Neue Rheinische Zeitung* 1848–49', in: *Der Sozialdemokrat*, no. 11, 13 March 1884, in: MEGA² I/30, 14–21, here 20, own translation.
88 Engels to August Bebel, early April 1891, quoted in MEGA² I/32, 557; MECW, vol. 49, 157f.
89 Engels, *Zur Kritik des sozialdemokratischen Programmenturfs 1891*, in: MEGA² I/32, 50; MECW, vol. 27, 227, original emphasis.
90 Engels to Friedrich Adolph Sorge, 9 August 1890, and Engels to Gerson Trier, 18 December 1889, in: MEGA², vol. III/30, 395, 107 and 400; MECW, vol. 48, 423–5, and vol. 49, 10–12.
91 MEGA² I/21, 181–219 and 1506ff.; MECW, 21, 283–316; see Jürgen Herres, 'Marx und Engels über Irland', in: *Marx-Engels-Jahrbuch*, 2011, 12–27.
92 See Engels, *Notes on the War*, 1870-1, in: MEGA² I/21, 250–475, 1197ff. and 1613ff.; MECW, vol. 22, 9–258.
93 MEGA² I/26; MECW, vol. 25, 313–590; see Anneliese Griese and Gerd Pawlzig, 'Friedrich Engels' *Dialektik der Natur*, eine vergleichende Studie zur Editionsgeschichte', in: MEGA-Studien, 1995/1, Amsterdam, 1995, 33–60; Iring Fetscher, *Stalin: Über dialektischen und historischen Materialismus*. Complete text and commentary, 4th ed. (Frankfurt, 1959).
94 MEGA² I/27, 494–6, own translation.
95 See MEGA² I/26, 595f.
96 MEGA² I/24, 319–39 and 1013ff.
97 Marx and Engels, *Les prétendues scissions dans l'Internationale: Circulaire privée du Conseil Général* (Geneva, 1872); in: MEW, vol. 18, 3–5; MECW, vol. 23, 79–123.
98 Marx and Engels, *L'Alliance de la Démocratie Socialiste et l'Association Internationale des Travailleurs. Rapport et Documents*, in: MEGA² I/24, 163–283 and 776ff.; MECW, vol. 23, 471ff. and 1241ff.
99 Fritz Brupbacher, *Marx und Bakunin* (Munich, 1913), 130, own translation.
100 Mayer, *Friedrich Engels*, vol. 2, 255, own translation.
101 Engels, *Einleitung (1895) zu Karl Marx*, Die Klassenkämpfe in Frankreich 1848 bis 1850, in: MEGA² I/32, S. 330–51, 336f.; MECW, vol. 27, 506–24, here 520–1.
102 Heinrich Gemkow, *Friedrich Engels: Eine Biographie* (Berlin, 1970), 624; *Friedrich Engels: Sein Leben und Wirken* (Moscow, 1973), 561 and 567 (Russian original; Moscow, 1970).

103 Engels, *Einleitung (1895) zu Karl Marx, Die Klassenkämpfe in Frankreich 1848 bis 1850*, in: MEGA² I/32, S. 330–51, 336f.; MECW, vol. 27, 506–24, here 510.
104 Ibid., 349. See Claus D. Kernig, 'Das Verhältnis von Kriegslehre und Gesellschaftstheorie bei Engels', in: *Friedrich Engels 1820–1970. Referate, Diskussionen, Dokumente* (Hanover, 1971), 77–92.
105 Translation from the French after MEW, vol. 39, 413; MECW, vol. 50, 446–8.
106 Engels, *Einleitung zu Sigismund Borkheims Broschüre*, in: MEGA² vol. I/31, 53f., own translation.
107 Herfried Münkler, *Über den Krieg: Stationen der Kriegsgeschichte im Spiegel ihrer theoretischen Reflexion* (Weilerswist, 2002), 2nd ed. 2003, 15; Münkler, *Friedrich Engels als Theoretiker des Krieges*, 149–72.
108 MEW, vol. 37, 351; MECW, vol. 443–5, here 445; MECW, vol. 48,
109 MEGA² I/32, 209–33 and 991ff., here 209; MECW, vol. 27, 367–93, here 371.

CHAPTER 2

1 The formula Marx used in his letter to Engels of 31 July 1865 (MEGA² III/13, 509; MECW, vol. 42, 172f.) has become famous. Marx, however, intended it in a very specific sense: he was to be responsible for 'the theoretical and party work' and Engels for the financing of his family, which is the actual subject of this letter.
2 To Johann Philipp Becker, 15 October 1884, MEW, vol. 36, 218; MECW, vol. 47, 201f.
3 Preface to the 2nd ed. of *Zur Wohnungsfrage* (1887); MEGA² I/31, 21f.; *The Housing Question*, MECW, vol. 26, 424–33.
4 Karl Kautsky, 'Friedrich Engels', MEGA² I/31, 483–507, 497, 500. Engels had provided Kautsky with information but declared himself to be responsible for the facts, not their interpretation (re-genesis; see ibid., 1249–51). Kautsky emphasized his equality in stature to Marx.
5 Eduard Bernstein, 'Friedrich Engels. Ein Gedenkblatt', in: *Der wahre Jacob*, 21 September 1895, supplement, 2023–6.
6 'Marxism', 'Marxist' etc. were originally terms used polemically by adversaries. Kautsky, followed by Engels, turned them into self-descriptions.
7 That was how things were seen after the publication of *Kapital III* in 1894; only then did serious academic discussion begin. Disputes about the appropriateness of Engels' edition started only in the late twentieth century.
8 For further details, see Wilfried Nippel, 'Die Arbeit an einem Gesamtwerk von Marx: Engels, Bernstein, Kautsky', in: Martin Endress and Christian Jansen (eds), *Karl Marx im 21. Jahrhundert. Bilanz und Perspektiven* (Frankfurt, 2020), 457–510.
9 These prefaces appeared not only in party publications but also in many different translations, frequently long before the respective texts by Marx had been translated; see Wilfried Nippel, 'Friedrich Engels und die Politik des Prefaces', in: *Zeitschrift für Ideengeschichte* 11, 2017, 67–78. Engels himself checked and/or revised numerous translations of his own and Marx's works; see Renate Merkel-Melis, 'Übersetzungen im Spätwerk von Friedrich Engels', in: *Das Kapital und Vorarbeiten. Exzerpte und Entwürfe* (Hamburg, 2011), 195–208.
10 MEGA² I/31, 293–379; MECW, vol. 27, 95–176; see Wilfried Nippel, *Fussnoten, Zitate, Plagiate. Wissenschaftsgeschichtliche Streifzüge* (Heidelberg, 2014), 44–8.
11 The texts are in MEGA² I/21; see the Introduction, 1200–9.
12 MEGA² I/21, 77–82; for genesis of this sketch, see 1319–24.
13 Karl Marx to Louis Kugelmann, 30 January 1868 (MEW, vol. 32, 536f.; MECW, vol. 42, 528–30). Marx sent a somewhat more detailed list to the Russian translator of *Das Kapital*, Nikolai

Notes

F. Danielson, on 7 October 1868 (MEW, vol. 32, 563–5), but with only general reference to articles for newspapers and periodicals. As Marx kept no detailed list of his publications, even Engels had difficulty identifying anonymous publications. Newly identified articles appeared in every twentieth-century edition of the works, and false ascriptions to Marx or Engels were invariably removed or qualified as doubtful.

14 Friedrich Engels to Louis Kugelmann, 31 July 1868, MEW, vol. 32, 555; MECW, vol. 43, 77.
15 Karl Marx to Friedrich Engels, 29 July 1868, MEW, vol. 32, 128f.; MECW, vol. 43, 77f.
16 Quoted in MEGA² I/21, 1321.
17 Karl Marx to Louis Kugelmann, 26 October 1868, MEW, vol. 32, 573; MECW, vol. 43, 144.
18 All quotes in MEGA² I/21, 77f.; MECW, vol. 21, 59–64.
19 Karl Marx to Wilhelm Blos, 10 November 1877, MEW, vol. 34, 308; MECW, vol. 45, 288f. The phrase was frequently used by critics of the Lassalle cult (see Wilfried Nippel, 'Charisma, Organisation und Führung: Ferdinand Lassalle und die deutsche Arbeiterpartei', in: *Mittelweg 36*, 2018, 16–42.
20 In response to Liebknecht's request for an article about Marx and Lassalle, Engels thought of writing a popular pamphlet but in the end did not do so (Friedrich Engels to Karl Marx, 23 January 1868, MEW, vol. 32, 22; MECW, vol. 42, 525f.).
21 Wilhelm Liebknecht to Karl Marx, 17 August 1869, in: Rolf Dlubek u. a. (ed.), *Die I. Internationale in Deutschland 1864–1872: Dokumente und Materialien* (Berlin, 1964), 414. He agreed with Wilhelm Bracke and Samuel Spier (representatives of the wing of the General German Workers' Association which had joined in founding the Eisenach party) that Lassalle should not be mentioned for the time being.
22 Friedrich Engels to Karl Marx, 5 September 1869, MEW, vol. 32, 370, MECW, vol. 43, 351f. Liebknecht had 'castrated the entire biography'.
23 MEGA² I/21, 80.
24 Ibid., 81. The assertion that the (official) material used by Marx was virtually unknown in England is misleading.
25 Here and in the later texts, Engels always used Marx's autobiographical sketch from the preface to the latter's 1859 *Contribution to the Critique of Political Economy* (MEGA² II/2, 99–103; MECW, vol. 16, 472–7), as well as Marx's statements in *Herr Vogt* (1860), MECW, vol. 17, 21–329.
26 Marx claimed since 1860 that he had been invited (or recalled) to France by the provisional government and Engels repeated this claim later. In *Herr Vogt* (MEGA² I/18, 273, 330), Marx printed a document from Minister Flocon, assuring him in fulsome words of the support of the French authorities. This he dated to 1 March, when he was still in Brussels, but the date on the original is 10 March, by which time Marx was well installed in Paris (see Jacques Grandjonc, 'Eine dritte MEGA? Jacques Grandjonc im Gespräch mit Peter Schöttler', in: Doris Obschernitzki (ed.), *Frankreichs deutsche Emigranten. Texte von und Erinnerungen an Jacques Grandjonc (1933–2000)* (Teetz, 2003), 85–96, here 89. As he sent the document to his lawyer in the Vogt affair (see letter to Julius Weber, 3 March 1860, MEGA² III/10, 340; MECW, vol. 41, 92–101), the discrepancy probably reflects autosuggestion rather than any intention to deceive. That Grandjonc has been largely ignored appears from the assumption of an 'invitation' to Marx that endures even in recent literature.
27 MEGA² I/21, 80f. Engels had already stated in 1859 in a review of Marx's *Critique of Political Economy* that Marx had stayed aloof from emigrant squabbling (MEGA² II/2, 246–55, here 249; MECW, vol. 16, 470f.).
28 Friedrich Engels, 'Karl Marx (Esquisse biographique)', in: *Marx-Engels-Jahrbuch* 13, 1991, 143–56 (MEGA² I/22 supplement). Here, the erroneous assertion first appears that David Hansemann was co-founder of the *Rheinische Zeitung*, along with the rumour that Alexander von Humboldt was instrumental in Marx's expulsion from France. Engels asserted this as a

fact in his December 1881 obituary for Jenny Marx (MEGA² I/25, 291; MECW, vol. 24, 460f.). Although disproven, both errors have been repeated in twentieth-century Marx literature.
29 MEGA² I/24, 314–17, and re-genesis, 1007f. This was based on a text written in May 1873 as a preface to the French translation of *Kapital I* but not finally used as such (ibid., 295–8, and re-genesis, 967–9).
30 MEGA² I/25, 100–11; re-genesis, 638–45; MECW, vol. 24, 183–95.
31 See Marx's 1874 account, later recalled in Wilhelm Blos's *Mohr und General: Erinnerungen an Marx und Engels* (Berlin, 1982), 316f.
32 Based in London in 1850, the *Neue Rheinische Zeitung: Politisch-ökonomische Revue* 'had to be abandoned in the face of ever stronger opposition' (MEGA² I/25, 105). It failed because Marx was late with his texts and he and Engels offended some readers with their bitter personal attacks (e.g. on Gottfried Kinkel).
33 MEGA² I/25, 103.
34 Ibid. In his text on the history of the Communist League (see below), Engels wrote in 1885 that the internationality of that organization was most marked in the London Working Men's Association, which served as a basis for recruitment, albeit only for German speakers (MEGA² I/30, 94f.).
35 MEGA² I/25, 104.
36 Ibid., 106.
37 Ibid. On Marx's role in the International Working Men's Association, see in brief Wilfried Nippel, *Karl Marx* (Munich, 2018), 97–101, and in greater detail Jürgen Herres, *Marx und Engels: Porträt einer intellektuellen Freundschaft* (Stuttgart, 2018), 195–208.
38 MEGA² I/25, 107.
39 Ibid., 107ff.; for quote, see 107.
40 For background data to this paragraph, see MEGA² I/25, 642–4.
41 Ibid., 407f.; MECW, vol. 24, 463–6.
42 One may doubt whether Marx himself thought this.
43 MEGA² I/25, 415–18; MECW, vol. 24, 462–76.
44 This led to conflict with Marx's elder daughter, Laura Lafargue (see Nippel, 'Die Arbeit an einem Gesamtwerk', Die Arbeit an einem Gesamtwerk, 457–510).
45 MEGA² I/25, 418.
46 For Most, see Philip Foner, *When Karl Marx Died: Comments in 1883* (New York, 1973), 105–7; see also Engels, MEGA² I/25, 420. Marx and Engels had, at the author's request, looked over the 2nd ed. (1876) of Most's *Kapital und Arbeit*, a popularization of Marx's *Kapital*, but instead of insisting it be rewritten, Marx sent Most a list of 'the worst blunders' on condition that his name should not be associated with the work. Even if no one knew how keen Marx was on having it published (see Karl Marx to Friedrich A. Sorge, 27 September 1877, MEW, vol. 34, 294; MECW, vol. 45, 275ff.), the exchange did not shed good light on him – an aspect that in the heat of battle seems to have escaped Engels.
47 Friedrich Engels to August Bebel, 30 April 1883; Friedrich Engels to Johann Ph. Becker, 22 May 1883; Friedrich Engels to Laura Lafargue, 24 June 1883 and 14 January 1884, MEW, vol. 36, 21, 28, 43, and 85; MECW, vol. 47, 16f., 25f., 39ff., and 78f. Since the fusion of ADAV and SDAP in Gotha in 1875, the 'Sozialistische Arbeiterpartei Deutschlands' (SAP).
48 MEGA² I/30, 14–21; re-genesis, 632f.; MECW, vol. 26, 120–8.
49 Ibid., 17.
50 Ibid., 16f. The reasons given for his and Marx's going to Cologne sounds strangely apologetic, with the puzzling assertion that 'they wanted to banish us to Berlin', which has given rise to later academic speculation: see François Melis, 'Zur Gründungsgeschichte der *Neuen Rheinischen Zeitung*: Neue Dokumente und Fakten', in: *MEGA-Studien* 1998/1, 3–63, 21ff.

Notes

51 MEGA² I/30, 20f.; see also the story Kautsky published about the 'defensive Marx' and see note 96.
52 MEGA² I/30, 16.
53 Ibid., 17. Engels, *Die auswärtige Politik des russischen Zarentums* (1890): it is to Marx's credit that he has advocated the necessity of this war since 1848 (MEGA² I/31, 179).
54 MEGA² I/30, 19. The expression is Marx's: *Der 18: Brumaire des Louis Bonaparte* (1852), MEGA² I/11, 155; MECW, vol. 11, 99–197.
55 While Engels' statements have been authentically reproduced in later orthodox literature, this one has been ignored.
56 Wolff's series (March–April 1849) scathing the injustice of the tithes paid by Silesian peasant farmers to nobility and state – the most widely reprinted articles from the *NRhZ* – were reissued by the Hottingen *Volksbuchhandlung*'s 'Social-Democratic Library' in spring 1886 with Engels' (belated) obituary of Wolff (1876) as introduction (MEGA² I/25, 46–82; MECW, vol. 24, 129–71) as well as a new text from his pen: 'Zur Geschichte der preussischen Bauern' (MEGA² I/30, 112–21; MECW, vol. 26, 341–52).
57 See the 5 issues between 5 and 11 April 1849. The advertised continuation did not appear (MEW, vol. 6, 397–425; MECW, vol. 9, 197–228). The texts derive from lectures Marx had held in 1847 at the German Workers' Union in Brussels. As leading articles, especially at this juncture, they appear strangely misplaced.
58 MEW, vol. 6, 519; MECW, vol. 9, 467.
59 MEGA² I/30, 21; MECW, vol. 26, 120–8. Engels had already spread this tall story in 1850, asserting that the *NRhZ* was the only paper in which 'Rhineland workers ... saw their interests openly and decisively represented' (*Die deutsche Reichsverfassungskampagne*, MEGA² I/10, 56). With its lofty style and abundant historical and literary references, the *NRhZ* in fact appealed to an intellectual readership; its main themes concerned political developments on the European and national levels.
60 Engels had sent Bernstein an editorial copy from Marx's estate: see his letter of 5 February 1884 (MEW, vol. 36, 98; MECW, vol. 47, 90f.) and, for article details, Renate Merkel-Melis, 'Die *Neue Rheinische Zeitung* im journalistischen Spätwerk von Engels', in: *Die Journalisten Marx und Engels: Das Beispiel* Neue Rheinische Zeitung (Hamburg, 2006), 249–58, 250f.
61 Marx stood trial with Schapper and the lawyer Karl Schneider. The previous day, Marx, Engels and Hermann Korff (*NRhZ* editor) had been tried (and also acquitted) for libel in the pages of the *NRhZ*. Both trials were documented in *Zwei politische Prozesse: Verhandelt vor den Februar-Assisen in Köln* (Cologne, 1849). The 1885 booklet contains only Marx's plea in the second trial; the date in the title (9 instead of 8 February 1849) is wrong, but the error was not corrected in the 1895 reprint.
62 MEGA² I/30, 75–81; re-genesis, 726f.; MECW, vol. 26, 304–10.
63 MEGA² I/30, 79.
64 See Jürgen Herres, 'Der Kölner Kommunistenprozess von 1852', in: *Geschichte in Köln* 50, 2003, 133–55.
65 MEGA² I/30, 89–108; re-genesis, 748f.; MECW, vol. 26, 312–30.
66 Ibid., 93.
67 Ibid., 100; 'still serves today' is remarkable, given that the *Communist Manifesto* largely vanished from sight after 1850. Wilhelm Liebknecht urged its 1872 reprinting on Marx and Engels, and this was followed by various translations. From the 1880s onwards, Engels furnished new editions and translations he had authorized with prefaces celebrating the dissemination of the *Manifesto* as evidence of the worldwide triumph of Marx's teachings (see Nippel, 'Friedrich Engels und die Politik', 70–2).
68 Engels printed the text, which he did not have to hand, according to the somewhat mutilated version in Carl Wermuth and Wilhelm Stieber's *Die Communisten-Verschwörungen des*

neunzehnten Jahrhunderts (Berlin, 1853–4), vol. 1, 68f. Wermuth was a police chief in Hanover, and Stieber ran the newly established Berlin political police unit pursuing communists (with manifestly illegal methods). Initially intended for internal police use, their documentation was later made public. (Vol. 2 contains dossiers on everyone suspected of communism, with the usual mixture of fact and fiction: Marx is described as the son of an inspector of mines – a distinction repeated in many obituaries; Engels has a wrong d.o.b.) Engels dismissed his source as 'a compilation of lies and forgeries from two of the most pathetic police rogues of the century [that] continues to serve all non-communist writers as the ultimate source [of truth] about that period' (MEGA² I/30, 89; the last remark refers to Adler's book – see below). The matter was, however, not quite that simple, as Wermuth and Stieber had used papers confiscated from both wings of the Communist League that were otherwise unavailable. In the reissue of Marx's *Revelations Concerning the Communist Trial in Cologne*, Engels reprinted the March and June 1850 circulars from the London leadership of the Communist League from Wermuth and Stieber. From the second of these texts, Engels deleted the name of Johann Philipp Becker, who had also been attacked there but who later befriended Engels both politically and personally [see Herwig Förder et al. (ed.), *Der Bund der Kommunisten: Dokumente und Materialien*, vol. 2, 1849–51 (Berlin 1982), 649f.].

69 MEGA² I/30, 102. Engels had already mentioned this in his texts of 1869 and 1877 but now for the first time named the proponents, (Adelbert von) Bornstedt and (Karl) Börnstein, as well as Herwegh. His intention in doing so is, however, unclear.

70 MEGA² I/30, 102f. Engels evidently knew more about the relevant negotiations than he revealed. If the total number to be repatriated is even roughly correct, the Communist League members could not have represented a large majority.

71 MEGA² I/30, 103.

72 Ibid., 104.

73 Ibid., 106. Schapper, who later made peace with Marx, is treated more mildly.

74 Ibid., 107. Marx asserted in *Herr Vogt* (MEGA² I/18, 108 and 272; MECW, vol. 17, 21–329) that the League, at his proposal, had disbanded immediately after the Cologne trial, an account confirmed in his letter of 19 November 1852 to Engels, which the latter found later and which Marx sent to his lawyer, Julius Weber, in February 1860 (MEGA² III/10, 296; MECW, vol. 41, 59–76). Marx seems to have expected an accusation of forgery in this respect, as he pointed out both in his letter to Freiligrath and in *Herr Vogt* that the letter's authenticity was unquestionable, as it was 'sent without an *envelope* and bears *both* London and Manchester *postmarks*' (Marx to Freiligrath, 29 February 1860, MEGA² III/10, 326; MECW, vol. 41, 80–7, here 83, original emphasis). The exact content of the letter to Engels can no longer be ascertained, as we only have Marx's copy of 24 February 1860, which merely states: 'Last Wednesday [17 November 1852], at my suggestion, the League *disbanded*; similarly the continued existence of the League on the Continent was *declared* to be *no longer expedient*. In any case, since the arrest of Bürgers-Röser, it had to all intents and purposes already ceased to exist there' (MEGA² III/6, 88; MECW, vol. 41, 83, original emphasis). The decision to end the League may have been restricted to the London branch (in the original German text: 'der Bund hier'); in any case, the U.S. branches were excepted, and the extent to which the resolution applied in Germany is unclear: both organized and informal groupings, as Engels had hinted in 1869 (MEGA² I/21, 77, see above in the main text) continued to exist there [see Martin Hundt, *Geschichte des Bundes der Kommunisten 1836–1852* (Frankfurt, 1993), 766ff.]. Even recent research literature continues to speak of the dissolution of the entire League (Marx group), but Marx himself rejected the Cologne prosecution's distinction in this respect between a 'Marxian' and a 'Willich-Schapper' faction (see Marx, *Enthüllungen über den Kommunisten-Prozess*, MEGA² I/11, 371): he considered the latter a minority or 'particular league' – thereby suggesting an affinity with the league of Catholic cantons in

Switzerland whose striving for autonomy had been quashed in the 1847 'War of the Particular League'. That Willich and Schapper were in the minority held only for the meeting of the Central Committee of the League on 15 September 1850, at which the dissolution was resolved, not for the Communist Party in London as a whole (as Engels also conceded) and certainly not for the branches on the Continent (see Rolf Dlubek, 'August Willich (1810–1878). Vom preussischen Offizier zum Streiter für die Arbeiteremanzipation auf zwei Kontinenten', in: Helmut Bleiber et al. (eds), *Akteure eines Umbruchs. Männer und Frauen der Revolution von 1848–49* (Berlin, 2003), 923–1003, 956–71). Marxist historiography has viewed the 'particular league' only as a counter to the legitimate Communist League, whose history ended with its dissolution by Marx. In the absence of any (contemporary or later) accounts by its members, the group's demise after Willich's departure for the United States in 1853 can no longer be reconstructed, but many of its members later played key roles in the U.S. or European workers' movement.

75 Friedrich Engels (from Barmen) to Karl Marx, 24 April 1848, MEGA² III/2, 152f.; MECW, vol. 38, 172f.
76 Karl Marx, *Herr Vogt*, MEGA² I/18, 107: within the new legal framework, the activities of the League 'ceased of their own account'.
77 See Gerhard Becker, 'Joseph Moll: Mitglied der Zentralbehörde des Bundes der Kommunisten und Präsident des Kölner Arbeitervereins', in: Helmut Bleiber, Walter Schmidt and Rolf Weber (eds), *Männer der Revolution von 1848*, vol. 2 (Berlin, 1987), 53–83; François Melis, 'Neue Rheinische Zeitung. Organ der Demokratie. Ein Redaktionsalltag – oder mehr? Köln, 14. November 1848', in: *Jahrbuch für Forschungen zur Geschichte der Arbeiterbewegung* 2002, 85–107.
78 See Wilfried Nippel, 'Diktatur des Proletariats – Versuch einer Historisierung', in: *Zyklos. Jahrbuch für Theorie und Geschichte der Soziologie* 5, 2019, 71–130, here 100f.
79 Thus, at least Born's later recollection (1898) after knowledge of Engels' attack; Stefan Born, *Erinnerungen eines Achtundvierzigers*, Hans J. Schütz (ed.) (Berlin 1978), 102f.
80 Texts in: *Der Bund der Kommunisten*, vol. 1, 1836–49, Herwig Förder et al. (eds) (Berlin, 1983), 929f.
81 See Frolinde Balser, *Sozial-Demokratie 1848/49–1863. Die erste deutsche Arbeiterorganisation 'Allgemeine deutsche Arbeiterverbrüderung' nach der Revolution* (Stuttgart, 1962), vol. 1, 72–5.
82 In early 1848, according to central office circulars, the organization had c. 200 members (see Herres, *Marx und Engels*, 87). According to Friedrich Beck and Walter Schmidt (eds), *Dokumente aus geheimen Archiven*, vol. 5: Die Polizeikonferenzen deutscher Staaten 1851–1866 (Weimar, 1993), 44, note 40, 'at the time of its maximum outreach', the League had c. 800 members (source and temporal reference of this data are not determinable).
83 MEGA² I/30, 105. The central office circular of June 1850 notes that 'the most influential members of the Brotherhood also belong to the League' (*Der Bund der Kommunisten*, vol. 2, 1849–51, 199).
84 See Toni Offermann, 'Allgemeine deutsche Arbeiterverbrüderung, Norddeutsche Arbeitervereinigung und Bund der Kommunisten. Zu neueren DDR-Publikationen zur elementaren Arbeiterbewegung 1848–1851', in: *Archiv für Sozialgeschichte* 22, 1982, 523–43; Jürgen Schmidt, *Brüder, Bürger und Genossen. Die deutsche Arbeiterbewegung zwischen Klassenkampf und Bürgergesellschaft 1830–1870* (Bonn, 2018), 285–94. Wilhelm Haupt's letter to Karl Marx (3 December 1850) about the situation of the League in Hamburg is of interest here: the local organization has gathered a 'rag-tag-and-bobtail' (Is it a coincidence that Engels later uses the same phrase?); they think the Brotherhood is good enough – they do not need the Communist League; the only disputes are about people, not principles (MEGA² III/3, 687).

85 That at least was how Born later saw it (*Erinnerungen eines Achtundvierzigers*, 77): Engels had never forgiven him for acting 'without consulting him – the papal secretary of state in Cologne – beforehand'.
86 Engels' use of Born's originally Jewish surname 'Buttermilch' was as despicable as his titling him a 'little Swiss professor' – Born had been an extraordinary professor of literature in Basel since year-end 1879. Nor is Engels' remark exactly fair that Born participated in the Dresden May uprising in 1849 and was lucky to escape: Born had taken over command, had escaped in the last minute and was now in a desperate situation, sick and destitute in Strasbourg, the first stop in his exile.
87 Born had been expelled from the Communist League in 1850 because he had joined a 'petty bourgeois' organization in Switzerland; he then soon began to build up a middle-class existence. In 1859, when Marx sought to gain his backing in the quarrel with Carl Vogt, Born declined: he welcomed 'the approach of an old friend' and looked forward to Marx's treatise on 'national economy' but no longer shared his communist convictions and did not want to be drawn into a dispute among émigrés (letter to Jenny Marx, 23 June 1859, MEGA² III/9, 492–4). Later, too, as an editor of the *Basler Nachrichten*, Born had spoken of Marx and Engels with respect. In March 1884 he wrote in a review of Engels' *Die Entwicklung des Sozialismus von der Utopie zur Wissenschaft* that the abolition of private property was a delusion held by only one in a thousand Europeans (see Franziska Rogger, *„Wir helfen uns selbst!". Die kollektive Selbsthilfe der Arbeiterverbrüderung 1848-49 und die individuelle Selbsthilfe Stephan Borns* (Erlangen, 1986), 289–300, 331–4, 342f.). There is to my knowledge no evidence that Engels knew this review and that his attack was in response to this.
88 Friedrich Engels to Hermann Schlüter, 16 June 1885, MEW, vol. 36, 333; MECW, vol. 47, 304f.
89 Georg Adler, *Die Geschichte der ersten sozial-politischen Arbeiterbewegung in Deutschland mit besonderer Rücksicht auf die einwirkenden Theorien: Ein Beitrag zur Entwickelungsgeschichte der sozialen Frage* (Breslau [now Wrocław], 1885) (reprinted Frankfurt 1966), 157.
90 Adler, *Geschichte*, 304. In the later 1840s, Weitling and Grün were 'favourite enemies' of Marx and Engels. Engels noted in the margin of Adler's book at this point, 'Nice company!' (see Jakow Rokitjanski, 'Engels' Notizen in Georg Adlers Buch *Die Geschichte der ersten socialpolitischen Arbeiterbewegung in Deutschland*', in: *Marx-Engels-Jahrbuch* 2, 1979, 339–68, 359).
91 Friedrich Engels to Hermann Schlüter, 11 November 1885, MEW, vol. 36, 382; MECW, vol. 47, 346.
92 This appeared in *Die Neue Zeit*, February 1886, and again in: MEGA² I/30, 200–6.
93 MEGA² I/30, 201. It is one thing to correct a wrong d.o.b. for Engels and quite another to make a fuss about the publication date of Marx and Engels, *Die Heilige Familie* (*The Holy Family*), which Adler had cited, on the one hand, as 1844 and, on the other, as 1845 – a mistake Engels took as proving that Adler had never had the book in his hand. Adler had also written that Marx's grandfather had originally been called Mordechai and that his father had been a lawyer in his paternal city of Trier. The first of these points – which was correct and for which Adler had cited a nephew of Marx's – was questioned, the second corrected: Marx's father was born in Saarlouis but grew up in Trier, which could, therefore, justifiably be called his 'paternal city'.
94 The *Communist Manifesto* was dated to 1847 (MEGA² I/30, 89); that Engels had been commissioned to write this text together with Marx (ibid., 103) is at least doubtful, as the later caution by the London office was addressed to Marx alone.
95 Kautsky took over from Engels' letter of 2 December 1885 (MEW, vol. 36, 399; MECW, vol. 47, 362) the story of Marx driving away two NCOs who came to his apartment to complain about a *NRhZ* article by indicating an (unloaded) pistol under his nightgown. Engels has the two soldiers carrying sabres, Kautsky pistols in holsters. Marx did actually complain (on 3

Notes

March 1849) to the commander of the Cologne garrison about this 'visit' (MEGA² III/3, 13f., reply dated March, 277f.). The truth of the 'pistol story' (Engels) cannot be determined.

96 Adler had relied on Engels' version of the history of the *NRhZ*; he was now accused of taking over the latter's formulation as to the 'genuinely local-Cologne' character of the paper (MEGA² I/30, 16) and of having omitted Ferdinand Wolff from his list of editorial staff – a name Engels had also overlooked, along with those of Dronke, Weerth and Freiligrath, whom Adler did mention. According to Adler (*Geschichte*, 215) the *NRhZ* called in the interests of democracy for 'the immediate introduction of a dictatorship to disband and abolish the old institutions'. For this reason the paper attacked Kamphausen [sic] from the start', notably in the leading article (by Marx) of 14 September 1848 on the Prussian premier Camphausen: 'We have blamed Camphausen from the very beginning for failing to govern dictatorially, for not immediately demolishing and removing the remnants of the old institutions' (MEGA² I/7, 698: MECW, vol. 7, 431; for further detail, see Nippel, 'Diktatur des Proletariats', 80f.). Commenting on this, Kautsky (probably relying on information from Engels) wrote that the statement was not to be found in any leading article but at most in some obscure correspondence which the editors had not perused (MEGA² I/30, 204). However, Adler's summary (215–30) of the tendencies of the *NRhZ* – including the attacks (by Engels) on the Slavic peoples, whose 'lack of history' made sovereign status inadmissible – shows that he had indeed read through the whole paper.

97 See also Adler's evaluation of the *Rheinische Zeitung* and the Parisian *Vorwärts!* (1844) in his bio-bibliographical annex to *Die Grundlagen der Karl Marxschen Kritik der bestehenden Volkswirtschaft: Kritische und ökonomisch-literarische Studien* (Tübingen, 1887), 301ff. Franz Mehring, who, like Kautsky, had been engaged in various skirmishes with Adler, later reproached him for propagating a false assessment of the history of *Vorwärts!*, including Marx's expulsion from Paris, although (despite lengthy attempts and unlike Adler, who had received such a series from the former editor Heinrich Börnstein) he did not possess a complete set of the newspaper (Mehring, 'Börnsteins Memoiren', in: *Die Neue Zeit*, vol. 2, 1895, 377–80).

98 MEGA² I/30, 89f.

99 Further research is required to determine whether Engels had also used Adler in his historical text on the Communist League – for example in the passages on the impact of Weitling and others in Switzerland in the early 1840s – or whether the coincidences in their citations come from their both having used the same sources.

100 Georg Adler, *Rodbertus, der Begründer des wissenschaftlichen Sozialismus. Eine sozial-ökonomische Studie* (Leipzig, 1884); contra Adler and Karl Kautsky, 'Das Kapital von Rodbertus', in: *Die neue Zeit* 2, 1884, 337–50, 385–402; on use of references from Engels, see MEGA² I/30, 863–5. On Engels' designation of the Rodbertus cult as 'the wish of non-Communists to set up a non-Communist rival to Marx', see Friedrich Engels, letter to Eduard Bernstein, 22 August 1884 (MEW, vol. 36, 204; MECW, vol. 47, 188) and references in MEGA² I/30, 592–5 and Nippel, *Fussnoten, Zitate*, 48f.; idem, 'Friedrich Engels und die Politik', 73f.

101 Franz Mehring, *Geschichte der deutschen Sozialdemokratie*, vol. 1 (Stuttgart, 1897), 315ff. and 597. Soon afterwards, Max Quarck (ed.), *Die Arbeiterverbrüderung 1848/49: Erinnerungen an die Klassenkämpfe der ersten deutschen Revolution* (Frankfurt, 1900), with excerpts of the newspaper *Das Volk* issued under Born's editorship from May to August 1848. Born had given Quarck his copy of the issues.

102 See Jacques Grandjonc, 'Über den richtigen Gebrauch von Erinnerungen in der Geschichtsschreibung: Stephan Born über Marx und Engels, fünfzig Jahre später', in: Obschernitzki (ed.), *Frankreichs deutsche Emigranten*, 132–48.

103 MEGA² I/32, 182–8, and re-genesis, 923–9; MECW, vol. 27, 332–43. The entry was headed 'Marx, Heinrich Karl'. It is unclear who was responsible for this. Marx's birth certificate

Notes

records only one given name, 'Carl'. Two documents from his student days have 'Carl [or Karl] Heinrich', in that order. Marx never seems to have otherwise used his second given name (see MEGA² I/32, 929).

104 This contains some half dozen (mostly minor) error re-publication dates, origin unclear: Engels or editors.

105 Pointing out, among other things, Marx's expulsion from Prussia in May 1849, which had previously always borne connotations of illegality, that he had resigned his Prussian citizenship at the end of 1845.

106 In vol. III of the dictionary (text in MEGA² I/32, 517f.). Engels bibliography is preceded by a mere twelve lines of biographical data.

107 Friedrich Engels to Karl Kautsky, 26 January 1893, MEW, vol. 39, 17; MECW, vol. 50, 91.

108 His contribution to these was far greater, as first became known on publication of his correspondence with Marx in 1913.

109 The reference is to the section on ground rent in *Kapital III*. Whether Marx's late studies were aimed at continuing the book or represented a retreat from a failed project is an open question.

110 Why it should be important that Marx's draft inaugural speech and statutes sought (successfully) to quash proposals deriving from Mazzini is unclear (to me). In summer 1871 Engels asserted this in an Italian journal, after Mazzini had taken a line opposed to the IAA (see MEGA² I/22, 256–9, MEW, vol. 17, 390–2).

111 At whom this was directed (other than Adler) is uncertain. Engels had provided Marx's first biographer, Gustav Gross, *Karl Marx: Eine Studie* (Leipzig, 1885), with information, which Gross had used correctly, he confirmed, even without understanding anything of Marx's theory (see Engels to Kautsky, 13 January; to P. Lawrow, 12 February 1885; MEW, 36, 270 and 282; MECW, vol. 47, 250 and 261).

112 Marx had often been described previously as having a doctorate in law.

113 At the end of April 1895 vis-à-vis Franz Mehring, Engels appealed to his memory of conversations with Marx regarding the *Rheinische Zeitung* (MEW, vol. 39, 473f.).

114 That had happened a few years before, when he had to borrow the text from a friend – see Friedrich Engels to Pasquale Martignetti, 12 March and 18 September 1886, MEW, vol. 36, 457 and 535; MECW, vol. 47, 420 and 493.

115 Karl Marx to Friedrich Engels, 29 July 1868 (MEW, vol. 32, 128: MECW, vol. 43, 74–6); the municipal censor had been replaced by one sent from Berlin (Wilhelm von Saint Paul), and the Cologne district president had been appointed as a further authority – hence Engels' 1877 reference to a double censorship (MEGA² I/25, 100). In his letter to Mehring at the end of April 1895, he insisted, however, that there had been three levels of censorship: (1) the municipal censor; (2) von Saint Paul; and (3) the district president (MECW, vol. 50, 503f.).

116 That the obituary for Bruno Bauer (1882) appeared in the *Sozialdemokrat* already gives it a somewhat surprising claim to be an aspect of 'party history'. Engels (who later also researched and wrote on Early Christianity) emphasizes Bauer's achievement as a New Testament critic. His and Marx's polemicizing against Bauer in 1844–5 is 'forgotten' (MEGA² I/25, 299–306). Occasioned by the chance find of a poem by Weerth among Marx's papers in Engels' 1883 memoir of Georg Weerth (d. 1856), 'the first and most important poet of the German proletariat', highlights his contribution to the cultural pages of the *NRhZ* but overlooks – intentionally or out of forgetfulness – his very considerable political reporting and incidentally makes a laughing stock of Freiligrath (MEGA² I/30, 3–6). His 1886 obituary for Johann Philipp Becker acknowledges his role not only as the only German revolutionary general in the Baden Uprising of 1849 (which Engels had ignored in his portrayal of the Imperial Constitution Campaign of 1850) but also in the IAA but passes over the fact that Becker had for a while cooperated with Bakunin (MEGA² I/31, 11–18; see Rolf Dlubek, "Was kann man

Notes

denn wollen ohne die Arbeiter?' Revolutionserfahrungen im Wirken Johann Philipp Beckers 1849-1853', in: Walter Schmidt (ed.), *Demokratie, Liberalismus und Konterrevolution: Studien zur deutschen Revolution von 1848/49* (Berlin, 1998), 485-547, 501ff.; see also end of note 69).

117 See inter alia his replies to questions about the occurrences of 1848-50: Friedrich Engels to Wilhelm Liebknecht on Andreas Gottschalk in Cologne, 29 October 1889 (MEW, vol. 37, 298; MECW, vol. 48, 398f.); to Victor Adler on Marx in Vienna, 9 and 12 January 1895 (MEW, vol. 39, 372 and 376; MECW, vol. 50, 408-11 and 414); to Karl Hackenberg on Hermann Heinrich Becker and his connection with the Communist League, 16 March 1895; Inge Taubert and Bernhard Dohm, 'Engels über den roten Becker: Ein unbekannter Brief von Friedrich Engels', in: *Beiträge zur Geschichte der Arbeiterbewegung* 15, 1973, 807-14.

118 Especially Johann Philipp Becker (Friedrich Engels to Johann Philipp Becker, 5 December 1885 and 9 July 1866). but also August Bebel (8 October 1886); Eduard Bernstein (9 October 1886, MEW, vol. 36, 400, 497, 541, 544f.; MECW, vol. 47, 363f., 456f., 498f., 500-3). Becker's vast estate in the party archives was established in the 1880s in Switzerland. This also holds the estate of Moses Hess (d. 1875), with whom Marx and Engels finally broke in 1848. When August Bebel was looking for material on Weitling, Engels sent him Weitling's letter to Hess of 31 March 1846 from the party archives (which since June 1888 had been in London), containing the depiction of his excommunication by Marx and Engels in Brussels (see Moses Hess, *Briefwechsel*, Edmund Silberner (ed.) (The Hague, 1959), 150-2; see also letters of 15-31 October 1888, in: *August Bebels Briefwechsel mit Friedrich Engels*, Werner Blumenberg (ed.) (The Hague, 1965), 336-40; see Engels' letter of 25 October in MEW, vol. 37, 117-19; MECW, vol. 47, 509-11).

119 See Jürgen Rojahn, '"Er soll den beiden Alten ein Denkmal setzen": Die Entstehung der Ausgabe des Marx-Engels Briefwechsels von 1913', in: *Marx-Engels-Jahrbuch*, 2012-13, 209-85; Nippel, 'Die Arbeit an einem Gesamtwerk', 457-510.

120 'Our party archive' as Engels called it in a letter to Marx in March 1857 (MEGA² III/8, 89). Marx sent Engels all important correspondence for the 'archive', or 'to file', as he often put it, thus creating an instrument for defence against, as for attack on, opponents. In the case of the Frankfurt Mayor and later Prussian Finance Minister Johannes Miquel, the threat of publication of letters to Marx of 1850-1 was maintained over decades (see Nippel, 'Diktatur des Proletariats', 97).

121 Nevertheless, it is always worth looking closely at what is *not* explained in the abundant commentaries.

CHAPTER 3

1 Friedrich Engels, *Herrn Eugen Dühring's Umwälzung der Wissenschaft* (*Anti-Dühring*), in: MEGA² I/27, 442; MECW, vol. 25, 264 (original emphasis).
2 Karl Marx and Friedrich Engels, *Manifest der Kommunistischen Partei*, in: MEW, vol. 4, 481; *Communist Manifesto*, in: MECW, vol. 6, 533.
3 Friedrich Engels, Introduction to Marx's 'Class Struggles in France 1848 to 1850', in: MEGA² I/32, 338; MECW, vol. 27, 539.
4 MEGA² I/32; MECW, vol. 27, 547.
5 MEGA² I/32, 341; MECW, vol. 27, 542.
6 MEGA² I/32, 337.
7 MEGA² I/32, 347; MECW, vol. 27, 547.
8 Karl Marx, *Das Kapital: Kritik der Politischen Ökonomie*, vol. I (Hamburg, 1890), MEGA² II/10, 693ff.; MECW, vol. 35, 760f.

Notes

9 See Heinz D. Kurz, 'Hin zu Marx und über ihn hinaus', in: *Perspektiven der Wirtschaftspolitik* 19 (2018), issue 3.
10 For this and the following quotations from *Anti-Dühring*, see MECW, vol. 25, 264–5.
11 For his biography, see Lucian O. Meysels, *Victor Adler* (Vienna, Munich, 1997).
12 The house belonging to Adler's father later made way for a new one which would become world famous as Sigmund Freud's house.
13 *Friedrich Engels' Briefwechsel mit Karl Kautsky*, ed. Benedikt Kautsky (Vienna, 1953), 80.
14 'Die Fabrikinspektion, insbesondere in England und in der Schweiz', first published in the *Jahrbücher für Nationalökonomie und Statistik* (new series), vol. 8 (1884), reprinted in *Victor Adler's Aufsätze, Reden und Briefe*, ed. Party Executive of the Social Democratic Workers' Party of German Austria, 1922ff., issue 5, 19–66. During his study trip, Adler met the leaders of German social democracy, Wilhelm Liebknecht and August Bebel, and in Switzerland Eduard Bernstein.
15 See *Adlers Aufsätze*, issue 4, 11ff.
16 Engels, *Briefwechsel mit Karl Kautsky*, 84; MECW, vol. 47, 57.
17 Victor Adler, *Briefwechsel mit August Bebel und Karl Kautsky*, ed. Friedrich Adler (Vienna, 1954), 26.
18 Engels, *Briefwechsel mit Karl Kautsky*, 219.
19 Ibid., 214.
20 *Die österreichische Sozialdemokratie im Spiegel ihrer Programme*, with an introduction by Ernst Winkler (Vienna, 1964), 29.
21 Friedrich Adler in the introduction to the correspondence between Engels and Adler, in: *Adlers Aufsätze*, issue 1, VII.
22 According to the new edition of the correspondence, ed. Gerd Callesen (Berlin 2011), fifty-nine letters (not counting greeting cards) have been preserved, of which twenty-nine are from Engels and thirty from Adler, plus three letters from Emma Adler to Engels. All the important letters are already included in *Adlers Aufsätze*, issue 1.
23 *Adlers Aufsätze*, issue 1, 131.
24 Gustav Mayer, *Friedrich Engels* (Frankfurt, Berlin, Vienna, 1975), vol. II, 414.
25 The *Arbeiter-Zeitung* appeared in place of *Die Gleichheit* from 1889, initially as a weekly and from 1895 as a daily until it ceased publication in 1991; MECW, vol. 27, 61.
26 Ibid.
27 Mayer, *Friedrich Engels*, 503.
28 See Helmut Rumpler, *Österreichische Geschichte 1804–1914 Eine Chance für Mitteleuropa* (Vienna, 1997), 496f.
29 See Adler, *Briefwechsel mit August Bebel und Karl Kautsky*, 120.
30 Ibid., 124f.
31 *Adlers Aufsätze*, issue 1, 88.
32 *Briefwechsel Engels mit Kautsky*, 388.
33 Ibid., 391f; MECW, vol. 50, 225.
34 On the issue of nationality in the Habsburg Monarchy, see Helmut Konrad, *Nationalismus und Internationalismus* (Vienna, 1976) and the specialist literature cited therein.
35 Otto Bauer, *Die Nationalitätenfrage und die Sozialdemokratie*, Marx-Studien, vol. 2 (Vienna, 1907), 304.
36 Friedrich Engels, *Den tschechischen Genossen zu ihrer Maifeier eine Erinnerung aus dem Jahr 1848*, 8 April 1893, in: MEGA² I/32, 239; MECW, vol. 27, 425.
37 *Sozialdemokratie im Spiegel ihrer Programme*, 29.
38 Adler, *Briefwechsel mit August Bebel und Karl Kautsky*, 221.
39 Konrad, *Nationalismus and Internationalismus*, 63.
40 Published under the pseudonym 'Synopticus'.

Notes

41 Konrad, *Nationalismus and Internationalismus*, 207.
42 Published under the pseudonym 'Rudolf Springer'.
43 Stalin, who 'until the end of his life regarded the national question as one of his special fields', wrote his work *Marxism and the National Question* during a stay in Vienna in 1912–13. Franz Marek, *Was Stalin wirklich sagte* (Vienna, 1970), 99.
44 See Mayer, *Friedrich Engels,* vol. 2, 385.
45 Engels' correspondence with Kautsky, 301; MECW, vol. 49, 200.
46 Mayer, *Friedrich Engels*, vol. 2, 490.
47 Ibid., 366.
48 'You are in a rising political movement', Engels wrote to Adler in July 1894, 'you are on the offensive. … Whereas in France, Germany, Italy, our people are on the defensive, not even always hopeful' (*Adlers Aufsätze*, issue 1, 102). Engels also praised the *Arbeiter-Zeitung*: 'It is really necessary that the insufferable *Vorwärts* be given an example of how to do it' (ibid., 102).
49 On the history of trade unions in Austria, see Fritz Klenner, *Die österreichischen Gewerkschaften* (Vienna, 1974).
50 For example Victor Adler's speeches on the Marx commemorations in 1893 and 1903, reprinted in *Adlers Aufsätze*, issue 1.
51 *Briefwechsel Engels mit Kautsky*, 391; MECW, vol. 50, 224.
52 Friedrich Engels, *Nachwort* (1894) to *Soziales aus Russland*, in: MEGA² I/32, 249; *Postscript*, MECW, vol. 27, 433.
53 Friedrich Engels, 'The Peasant Question in France and Germany', MEGA² I/32, 308–27; MECW, vol. 27, 481–502.
54 Georg von Vollmar, 'Über Staatssozialismus' (1892), in: *Materialien zum politischen Richtungsstreit in der deutschen Sozialdemokratie*, ed. Peter Friedemann (Berlin, Vienna, 1978), vol. I, 170f.
55 In a letter to Kautsky in April 1898, in: Adler, *Briefwechsel mit August Bebel und Karl Kautsky*, 242.
56 Ibid., 266.
57 Ibid., 287f.
58 Adler's report on the Stuttgart Party Congress in the *Arbeiter-Zeitung*, in: *Adlers Aufsätze*, issue 6, 225.
59 See the section 'The Final Crisis of Capitalism'.
60 *Adlers Aufsätze*, issue 6, 231.
61 Norbert Leser, *Zwischen Reformismus und Bolschewismus* (Vienna, 1968), 221.
62 *Die österreichische Sozialdemokratie im Spiegel ihrer Programme*, 23 and 33.
63 On Pernerstorfer and Ellenbogen, see the articles by Günther Steinbach and Norbert Leser in: *Werk und Widerhall: Grosse Gestalten des österreichischen Sozialismus*, ed. Norbert Leser (Vienna, 1964).
64 With regard to Rosa Luxemburg, whose positions Adler sharply criticized, Adler nevertheless hoped that she would 'yet learn, and from the relentlessly fermenting grape juice it is to be hoped that in time a few drops of good wine will be obtained' (*Adlers Aufsätze*, issue 6, 228f.).
65 Leser, *Zwischen Reformismus und Bolschewismus*, 184.
66 'Gedenkrede zur Marx-Feier 1903', in: *Adlers Aufsätze*, issue 1, 167.
67 See the quotations in Leser, *Zwischen Reformismus und Bolschewismus*, 212ff.
68 *Adlers Aufsätze*, issue 6, 242.
69 Rudolf Hilferding, *Das Finanzkapital. Eine Studie zur jüngsten Entwicklung des Kapitalismus* (Vienna, 1910; cited here from the new edition, Frankfurt, 1973).
70 The argument of this comprehensive study cannot be further discussed here; see Heinz Kurz, 'Rudolf Hilferdings *Das Finanzkapital*', in: *Rudolf Hilferding: Finanzkapital und organisierter Kapitalismus*, ed. Gunther Chaloupek, Heinz D. Kurz and William Smaldone (Graz, 2011).

71 Hilferding, *Das Finanzkapital*, 322f.
72 Ibid., 507.
73 Otto Bauer, 'Die Akkumulation des Kapitals', in: *Die Neue Zeit*, year 31, vol. I (1912–13), reprinted in: Karl Marx, *Kapital II*, ed. Rudolf Hickel (Berlin, 1970), 772–93.
74 Ibid., 791ff.
75 Apart from the fundamental work of Norbert Leser, Gerald Mozetic's *Die Gesellschaftstheorie des Austromarxismus* (Darmstadt, 1984) should be mentioned here.
76 See Leser, 'Max Adler', in: Leser, *Werk und Widerhall*, 36ff.
77 Mozetic, *Die Gesellschaftstheorie*, 72ff.
78 See Leser, *Zwischen Reformismus und Bolschewismus*, 183.
79 This applies at least to Bauer and Max Adler, while Renner repeatedly points out problematic aspects.
80 On Bauer's attitude to Bolshevism, which he rejected for Western European countries but saw as a transitional phase until a hoped-for later democratic catharsis, see Leser, *Zwischen Reformismus und Bolschewismus*, 120ff.
81 Initially under the name *Deutsch-Österreich* in the widely shared hope of a pan-Germanic unification with Germany – an aspect which cannot be dealt with here.
82 See Karl Pribram, 'Die Sozialpolitik im neuen Österreich', in: *Archiv für Sozialwissenschaft und Sozialpolitik* 48 (1921), 615–80.
83 Otto Bauer, *Die österreichische Revolution* (Vienna, 1923), 284.
84 *Sozialdemokratie im Spiegel ihrer Programme*, 43.
85 *Adlers Aufsätze*, issue 6, 233.
86 This also applies to the value of labour theory, now viewed as untenable in economic theory, which – whether justifiably or not is not the issue here – served as legitimization for the moral claim 'to the entire yield of labour'.
87 See Günther Chaloupek, 'Karl Renners Konzeption des "demokratischen Wirtschaftsstaats"', in: Chaloupek et al., *Rudolf Hilferding*, 73–104.

CHAPTER 4

1 For an overview, see Akos Paulinyi and Ulrich Troitsch, *Mechanisierung und Maschinisierung* (Berlin, 1991); Akos Paulinyi and Karl von Delhaes, *Technik und Wirtschaft in der Industrialisierung* (Düsseldorf, 2012); Joel Mokyr, *The Lever of Riches: Technological Creativity and Economic Progress* (New York, Oxford, 1990), 81–148; and Maurice Daumas, 'Introduction', in: Marguerite Dubuisson, *L'Expansion du Machinisme, Histoire générale des Techniques*, vol. 3 (Paris, 1968), 7–24.
2 On dating the period, see, for example, Phyllis Deane, *The First Industrial Revolution* (Cambridge, 1965), 1–19, for beginnings around 1750 and 254–75 for end of the first stage with the Great Exhibition of 1851.
3 The long-held uniqueness of British developments is evidently being softened by intensive discussion of special developments in certain regions and sectors. From the point of view of recent global and universal historical considerations, spatial and temporal delimitations are now being set, albeit with a certain loss of conceptual clarity. For examples in the cotton industry, see Giorgio Riello, *Cotton: The Fabric That Made the Modern World* (Cambridge, 2013), and Sven Beckert, *Empire of Cotton: A Global History* (New York, 2014).
4 At the end of 1843, Engels wrote the *Outlines of a Critique of National Economy* and the series 'Die Lage Englands' (The Condition of England, an extended review of Thomas Carlyle's *England Past and Present*) for the *Deutsch-Französische Jahrbücher*. When Marx, after almost

Notes

ten years' study of his own, still referred to Engels' overheated theoretical essay – which to a large extent followed the critique of British national economists made by early French socialists, especially Charles Fourier – as a 'brilliant essay', then this was probably meant as a *captatio benevolentiae* towards his *compagnon* (see Marx, *Vorwort* Zur Kritik der Politischen Ökonomie, January 1859, in: MEW, vol. 13, 10; preface to *A Contribution to the Critique of Political Economy*, MECW, vol. 29, 264). Still instructive on the precursors, the reception and impact of Marx and Engels' critique of the consequences of the Industrial Revolution is Ernst Nolte, *Marxismus und Industrielle Revolution* (Stuttgart, 1983), and still controversial is Theo Pirker, Hans-Peter Müller and Rainer Winkelmann (eds), *Technik und Industrielle Revolution: Vom Ende eines sozialwissenschaftlichen Paradigmas* (Opladen, 1987).

5   Friedrich Engels, *Die Lage der arbeitenden Klasse in England*, MEGA^1 I/4, Berlin 1932, 10–286; *The Condition of the Working Class in England*, MECW, vol. 4, 295–596, here 333.

6   Printed and published by Otto Wigand, Leipzig. On new editions and translations, see Walter Kumpmann (ed.), *Friedrich Engels, Die Lage der arbeitenden Klasse in England* (Munich, 1973), 395–7; on its contemporary reception, see Wolfgang Mönke, *Das literarische Echo in Deutschland auf Friedrich Engels's Werk 'Die Lage der arbeitenden Klasse in England'*, Deutsche Akademie der Wissenschaften (Berlin, 1965).

7   Engels, *Lage*, 27; *Condition*, 325.

8   Adolphe J. Blanqui, *Histoire de l'économie politique en Europe depuis les Anciens jusqu'à nos jours* (Paris, 1837); *History of Political Economy in Europe*, translated by Emily J. Leonard (New York, London, 1885). For Blanqui's biography, see Richard Arena, 'Adolphe-Jerome Blanqui, un historien de l'économie aux préoccupations sociales', in: *L'économie politique en France au XIXe siècle* (Paris, 1991), 163–83.

9   Blanqui, *Histoire*, vol. 2, 144; *History of Political Economy in Europe*, 472.

10 Engels based his exposition on Porter, *Progress of the Nation*, 3 vols (London, 1836 and 1843).

11 Engels considered Richard Arkwright's spinning throstle (waterframe) and James Watt's steam engine 'the most important mechanical invention of the eighteenth century. It was calculated from the beginning for mechanical motive power and was based upon wholly new principles'. Despite being terminologically somewhat awkward, Engels here recognized the novel, functional quality of the waterframe and the constructions that followed it and saw 'the victory of machine-work over hand-work' as being finally realized in Crompton's mule around 1804; see Engels, *Lage*, 15ff.; *Condition*, 312.

12 Engels, *Lage*, 131ff.; *Condition*, 429.

13 In the third edition of his *Principles of Political Economy and Taxation* (1821), David Ricardo had departed from his original view of possible market-based compensation and possibly for this reason remained unmentioned in Engels' *Condition of the Working Class in England*. Engels was particularly critical of the conservative chemist Andrew Ure, whose overview of textile production, for example in *The Philosophy of Manufactures* (1835), was well-informed on the provenance of cotton but clearly behind the times in terms of manufacturing technology and, as far as working conditions were concerned, was transparently on the side of the factory owners. Ure was thus easy prey for Engels. The mathematician and inventor Charles Babbage, in his study *On the Economy of Machinery and Manufactures* (London, 1832), also postulated possible market-based compensation for jobs lost to rationalization but at least developed the concept of piece-rate wages as an alternative, which – applied later – ensured greater wage transparency in times of economic upswing. On the question whether Engels consulted the French literature of the time, including Eugène Buret, *La misère des classes labourieuses en Angleterre et en France* (1840), see Gustav Mayer, *Friedrich Engels*, vol. 1, 2nd ed. (Cologne, 1971), 195.

14 Engels admitted in the preface to the second German edition (1892) of *The Condition of the Working Class in England* that the book bore 'the stamp of the author's youth' and that the

excesses had also been mitigated in the course of the immense industrial growth that had taken place in the meantime, because 'the petty accessory extortions' stood in the way of 'large-scale business', MEGA² I/32, 152; MECW, vol. 27, 311.

15 N. N. Stoskowa's *Friedrich Engels über die Technik: Zu ihrer Rolle in der Entwicklung der Gesellschaft* (Leipzig, 1971) is limited to a collection of references.

16 Marx first studied the basic economic works of Ricardo, Say, Sismondi, Mill and MacCulloch in the summer of 1844 in Paris and from 1845 in Brussels. He read the works of the English authors, however, in French translation and – as far as Ricardo's work *On the Principles of Political Economy and Taxation* was concerned – adopted the judgements of the bibliography of economic literature by John Ramsay MacCulloch (1789–1864), who had commented only cursorily on Ricardo's theory of value.

17 Paulinyi identified three periods (1845–6, 1851 and 1862–3) in which Marx was concerned with questions of technology; see Akos Paulinyi, *Karl Marx und die Technik seiner Zeit*, LTA-Forschung, no. 26/1997 (Mannheim, 1998), 7ff. The work by A. A. Kusin, *Karl Marx und Probleme der Technik* (Leipzig, 1970), is an uncritical collection of references. The most recent contributions by Ágnes Heller and Kurt Bayertz do not go beyond a conventional reconstruction of Marx's ideas on the role of technology in capitalism. Although Marx did not develop a philosophy of technology of his own, he nevertheless believed that technology, after being detached from its bondage to capitalism, 'can be freely and comprehensively applied in the service of humanity. How this change of function will take place, however, remains in the dark' (own translation); cf: Kurt Bayertz, 'Technik bei Marx', in: Michael Quante and Erzsébet Rózsa, *Anthropologie und Technik* (Munich, 2012), 57–70, here 70, and Ágnes Heller, *Marx und die Frage der Technik*, 45–56.

18 Johann Heinrich Moritz von Poppe (1776–1854), *Die Mechanik des 18: Jahrhunderts* (Pyrmont, 1807); *Lehrbuch der allgemeinen Technologie* (Frankfurt, 1809); *Die Physik vorzüglich in Anwendung auf Künste* (Tübingen, 1830); *Die Geschichte der Mathematik* (Tübingen, 1828) and *Geschichte der Technologie* (Göttingen, 1807–11) were all historical-theoretical works by a German professorial engineer, with no practical applications. The comprehensive and many-volume standard work by Robertson Buchanan, *Practical Essays on Mill-Work and Other Machinery* (Edinburgh, 1841), with its empirical-practical approach of hypothesis and practical testing, would have given Marx an insight into the typical approach of British 'craftsmen engineers' in the early period.

19 Babbage had referred several times in his book to the importance of the *slide rest* in connection with the reduction of production costs. Since Marx only excerpted individual chapters, he overlooked this important insight in his later argumentation, which Babbage had already arrived at in the early 1830s (see Paulinyi, *Karl Marx*, 21).

20 This is vividly described in the catalogue of the exhibition of the secret state archives of the Stiftung Preussischer Kulturbesitz (Prussian Cultural Heritage Foundation) in Berlin, *Klosterstrasse 36: Sammeln, Ausstellen, Patentieren – Zu den Anfängen Preussens als Industriestaat* (Berlin GSTA, 2014). The *History of the Cotton Manufacture in Great Britain* by Edward Baines was translated by Christoph Bernoulli and published as early as 1836 by Cotta, Stuttgart. The *Polytechnisches Journal* continuously reported on the latest technical developments at home and abroad and was published from 1820 to 1874, thereafter as *Dingler's polytechnisches Journal*. In addition, the trade association also published travel reports such as Friedrich Nottebohm's *Auszug aus dem Tagebuche eines Reisenden durch Grossbritannien und Belgien* (1841), *Verhandlungen des Vereins für Gewerbefleisses in Preussen* (Berlin, 1842). The Paris Ecole Polytechnique also kept abreast of developments in England and the United States, see: Yves Deforge, *Le Graphisme technique: Son Histoire et son Enseignement* (Seyssel, 1986), 101ff.

Notes

21 See Karl Marx, *Skizze einer einfach wirkenden atmosphärischen Dampfmaschine nach Thomas Newcomen ca. 1720, nach Andrew Ure (1835)* (c. 1851), in: IISG Marx Engels Archive, B 56, 41; transcription of the excerpt in Hans-Peter Müller (ed.), *Karl Marx, Die technologisch-historischen Exzerpte* (Frankfurt, Berlin, Vienna, 1981), 154–61. Marx's sketch is often erroneously referred to in the literature as a drawing of a 'Watt's steam engine'. James Watt's single-acting steam engine was built as a prototype in 1788 (see Daumas, 'Introduction', 1968, 41).

22 Paulinyi, *Karl Marx*, 11ff.

23 James Nasmyth, 'Remarks on the introduction of the slide principle in tools and machines employed in the production of machinery', in: Robertson Buchanan, *Practical Essays*, 393–418. Marx was unaware of the 1841 article by the London engineer, who was already famous by 1850. Only indirectly, via the later evaluation of the popular scientific work *The Industry of Nations, Part II. A Survey of the Existing State of Arts, Machines and Manufactures* (London, 1855), in which the basics of the machine tool according to Nasmyth were outlined, did Marx learn of the pioneering effect of the slide principle. See the textual comparison in Paulinyi, *Karl Marx*, 32.

24 In 1851 the industrial statistics in Britain listed 76,500 machine builders, 55 per cent of them in London, Lancashire and the West Riding. Twenty thousand were active in Lancashire, the centre of the cotton industry. There were 115 engineering firms there by 1841, with 17,000 workers and a capital stock of £1.5 million.

25 The English bourgeoisie was calling 'all its vassals from France to China to a great examination, at which they are to prove how they have used their time'. Karl Marx, *Revue*, May–October 1850, in: MEGA² I/10, 448–88, here 457; MECW, vol. 10, 500.

26 Marx's mention of the Boulton and Watt steam engine at the 1851 World's Fair (MEGA² II/8, 369) as well as his long-winded remarks on the American envelope machine at the 1861 World's Fair (MEGA² II/8, 370) suggest that he had only indirect knowledge from descriptions by others, including *The Industry of Nations, as Exemplified in the Great Exhibition of 1851: The Materials of Industry* (London, 1852) (MECW, vol. 33, 449ff.). Neither in his writings nor in the letters that have survived are there any indications that Marx ever personally visited a World's Fair.

27 For excerpts and manuscripts, see MEGA² II/3.6; see also with comments by Hans-Peter Müller (ed.), *Karl Marx*, as well as Rainer Winkelmann (ed.), *Exzerpte über Arbeitsteilung, Maschinerie und Industrie* (Frankfurt, Berlin, Vienna, 1982). Between 1861 and 1863 Marx produced compilations of these 1851 excerpts on machinery, MECW, vol. 33, 372ff.

28 In detail Paulinyi, *Karl Marx*, 24ff.

29 Karl Marx to Friedrich Engels, 28 January 1863, in: MEGA² III/12, 323f.; MECW, vol. 41, 449. Alongside William Whewell with his textbook *The Mechanics of Engineering* (Cambridge, 1841), Robert Willis was one of the teachers at Cambridge University competent in mechanics and especially in the training of mechanical engineers (see Paulinyi, *Karl Marx*, 26ff.). Marx's participation in a six-hour lecture for workers will at best have sufficed for an introduction to mechanics.

30 Karl Marx, *Kapital I* (Hamburg, 1890), MEGA² II/10, 161–80; MECW, vol. 35, 374–508. On the transmission of the economic manuscripts and *Das Kapital* in the second section of MEGA² (with content overviews), see Regina Roth, 'Marx on technical change in the critical edition', *European Journal of the History of Economic Thought* (December 2010), 1223–51. Amy E. Wendling's *Karl Marx on Technology and Alienation* (London, 2009), 136–73, seeks to reconstruct Marx's understanding of technology from MECW purely on its own terms, without taking into account the context of the history of technology.

31 For the following, see Oliver Müller, 'Marx und die Philosophie der Technik', *Allgemeine Zeitschrift für Philosophie*, issue 3 (2018), 323–51.

32 MEGA² II/10, 163; MECW, vol. 35, 189.
33 Hegel already emphasized the enduring functional value of the tool: 'the *plough* is more honourable than are the immediate pleasures which are prepared by it, or its ends. The *tool* remains when the immediate pleasures pass and are forgotten. In his tools man possesses power over external nature, even though according to his purposes he is rather subject to it' [Hegel, *Science of Logic* II, Works in 20 Volumes, ed. Eva Moldenhauer and Karl Marcus Michel, vol. 6 (Frankfurt, 1986), 453 (own translation, original emphasis)].
34 MEW, supplementary Vol. 1, 513.
35 Karl Marx, *A Contribution to the Critique of Political Economy* (186163), MEGA² II/3/6, 2058; MECW, vol. 34, 30.
36 MEGA² II/3/6, 2059; MECW, vol. 34, 31.
37 MEGA² II/10, 377; MECW, vol. 33, 497.
38 MEW, supplementary vol. 1, 515.
39 See Donald MacKenzie, 'Marx and the Machine', in *Technology and Culture*, 25 (1984), 473–502; most recently, Tiago Mata and Robert van Horn, 'Capitalist threads: Engels the businessman and Marx's *Capital*', *History of Political Economy*, vol. 49, issue 2 (2017) – their arguments, drawn intrinsically from Marx's work, submit to Marx's logic and mistake business questions he addressed to Engels for technological questions.
40 See Friedrich Engels (senior) to Friedrich Engels, 12 August 1854, in MEGA² III/7, 394ff.; Friedrich Engels to Emil Engels, 16 November 1859, MEGA² III/10, 85f.; MECW, vol. 40, 528; Friedrich Engels (senior) to Friedrich Engels, 6 January 1860, MEGA² III/10, 147–9.
41 Because of its linguistic proximity to German, Marx translated the English term 'machinery' as *Maschinerie*. Both terms referred predominantly to the technological side of a semi- or fully automatic water- or steam-driven machine tool. In German, however, the definitions were narrower, because manually driven devices were classified as *Gerät* or 'apparatus'. In his argumentation, which covered economic aspects in particular, Marx used the broader French conceptual field of 'l'industrie', which included social components such as the use of the natural sciences or the reorganization of work as a result of the use of machines. On the French understanding of industry, machines and mechanics, see Maurice Daumas, *Histoire générale des techniques*, vol. 3, *L'expansion du machinisme*: 1725–1860, Introduction (Paris, 1996), XIIff.
42 See MEGA² II/10, 334; MECW, vol. 35, 376.
43 The classification made by Marx is found in this way only in the area of accident prevention, which provided for area-wide and regular inspections of boiler plants and pressure vessels and provided relatively reliable data on the performance and age of the plant. In accordance with the mandate of the inspections, focus was laid only on steam-carrying plant components; mechanical power transmissions were not examined. The statistics collected since the 1840s in England, France and Germany distinguished 'steam engines' (i.e. prime movers) and working and machine tools (partly pressure- or steam-driven) from transmissions (power transmission via belts, rods or gearwheels); see Ernst Engel, *Das Zeitalter des Dampfes in technisch-statistischer Beleuchtung*, 2nd ed. (Berlin, 1881).
44 Thus, while a 'transmission mechanism', however complicated it may seem, cannot be identified as a distinct type of machine, since it is only a means for the transmission and transformation of power, Marx saw in the *Werkzeugsmaschine* (lit. 'machine tool') 'a mechanism which, after being set in motion, performs with its tools the same operations that were formerly performed by the workman with similar tools' (MEGA² II/10, 335; MECW vol. 35, 377). This general definition can also be applied to an *Arbeitsmaschine* (lit. work machine), and Marx thus often uses *Arbeitsmaschine* and *Werkzeugmaschine* synonymously, a fact reflected in the standard English translation, where *Werkzeugmaschine* is variously translated as 'tool or working machine' or 'working machine' (often simply shortened to 'machine')

Notes

or dropped altogether when used by Marx in combination with the word *Arbeitsmaschine*. Thus, 'Sehn wir uns nun die Werkzeugmaschine oder eigentliche Arbeitsmaschine näher an,' reads in the recognized English version: 'On a closer examination of the *working machine proper*' (MEGA² II/10, 335; MECW, vol. 35, 376) and 'an die Stelle eines Werkzeugs eine Werkzeugmaschine getreten ist' reads: 'a machine has taken the place of his tool' (MEGA² II/10, 337; MECW, vol. 35, 379), with similar formulations on following pages.

45 MEGA² II/10, 345ff.; MECW, vol. 35, 386ff.
46 MEGA² II/10, 347; MECW, vol. 35, 389.
47 'As soon as a machine executes, without man's help, all the movements requisite to elaborate the raw material, needing only attendance from him, we have an automatic system of machinery' (MEGA² II/10, 342; MECW, vol. 35, 384).
48 MEGA² II/10, 378; MECW, vol. 35, 422.
49 MEGA² II/10, 354; MECW, vol. 35, 398.
50 Here, Marx quoted from Friedrich Engels, *Lage*, 217; see MEGA² II/10, 380. *Condition*, MECW, vol. 35, 425.
51 MEGA² II/10, 81.
52 MEGA² II/10, 343; MECW, vol. 35, 384.
53 MEGA² II/10, 345; MECW, vol. 35, 387.
54 To interpret the monster metaphor as Marx's personal phobia of technology and identify Engels as its author, Amy E. Wendling's *Karl Marx on Technology*, 146ff, overlooks Marx's lack of technological expertise and knowledge, which he sought to compensate with metaphors, as well as Engels' thoroughly positivist belief in technological progress.
55 For example, G. Gregory Olinthus, *A Treatise of Mechanics*, 3 vols (London, 1806); David Scott, *The Engineer and Machinist's Assistant: A series of plans, sections and elevations, of stationary, marine, and locomotive engines, water wheels, spinning machines, tools, etc., taken from machines of approved construction, with detailed descriptions, and practical essays on various departments of machinery* (Glasgow, Edinburgh, London, 1856). More recent literature – for example Ken Baynes and Francis Pugh, *The Art of the Engineer* (Guildford, 1981), as well as Jean-Marc Combe and Bernard Escudie, *L'Aventure scientifique et technique de la Vapeur* (Paris, 1986), 31–149 – provides impressive evidence of how the decisive principles of systematic and industrial mechanical engineering were developed, particularly in railway and locomotive construction and shipbuilding, from the 1820s onwards in Britain and a little later in the United States.
56 Ernst Kapp, *Grundlinien einer Philosophie der Technik: Zur Entstehungsgeschichte der Cultur aus neuen Gesichtspunkten* (Braunschweig, 1877), V; reprinted Düsseldorf 1978 with introduction by Hans-Martin Sass; reprinted Hamburg 2015 with annotations by Harun Maye and Leander Scholz. *Elements of a Philosophy of Technology: On the Evolutionary History of Culture* (Minnesota, 2018), 51.
57 See Eduard Korte, *Der anthropologische Massstab: Die Philosophie Ernst Kapps vor ihrem kulturphilosophischen und geistesgeschichtlichen Hintergrund* (Düsseldorf, 1991), 155.
58 Ernst Kapp, *Grundlinien*, 172; reprint, 159; *Elements*, 185 (own translation, original emphasis).
59 Departing from Feuerbach's critique of Hegel, Marx saw the world of work as a place of self-alienation. Idealism, he argued, offered only pseudo-solutions regarding our relation with reality: the focus must lie on the concrete and particular, and the instruments and types of organization used in capitalist commodity production contributed causally to social alienation. Only by eliminating such alienation could work once again assume a dimension of freedom.
60 See Eduard Korte, *Der anthropologische Massstab*, 167ff.; Harald Leinenbach, *Die Körperlichkeit der Technik. Zur Organprojektionstheorie Ernst Kapps* (Essen, 1990), criticizes the 'rapidly fading magic of analogy' of Kapp's organ-projection theory. Even though

later exponents of the philosophy of technology mostly rejected Kapp's theory of the self-perfection of man, Leinenbach sought to identify productive aspects of his work with the help of Heidegger's philosophy.

61 Ernst Kapp, *Grundlinien*, 241ff.; reprint, 216ff.; *Elements*, 230.
62 Ibid., 154; reprint, 144; *Elements*, 152.
63 Ibid., 74; reprint, 79; *Elements*, 119.
64 See Michael Deege, 'Ernst Kapp, Bemerkungen zur Philosophie der Organprojektionstheorie', *Prima Philosophia*, vol. 14, issue 1 (2001), 51–68, here 64.
65 Ernst Kapp, *Grundlinien*, 74; reprint, 100; *Elements*, 136.
66 Ibid., 100; reprint, 100; *Elements*, 136.
67 Ibid., 103ff.; reprint, 103; *Elements*, 138. Marx placed the clockwork automatons of Jacques de Vaucanson on a par with the inventions of Arkwright and Watt; see MEGA² II/6, 373; MECW, vol. 35, 385.
68 Ibid., 131; reprint, 125; *Elements*, 157.
69 Ibid., 132; reprint, 126; *Elements*, 158.
70 Ibid., 126; reprint, 121; *Elements*, 154.
71 Ibid., 133; reprint, 127; *Elements*, 159.
72 Friedrich Engels, *Der Anteil der Arbeit an der Menschwerdung des Affen* (Eng: *The Part Played by Labour in the Transition from Ape to Man*). The manuscript was written around June 1876 and remained unfinished. The text was first printed after Engels' death in: *Die Neue Zeit*, Jg. XIV, 1896, 545–54; MEGA² I/26, 88–99; MECW, vol. 25, 452–64.
73 Engels took up Charles Darwin's intensively discussed theses of the 1870s from *The Descent of Man and Selection in Relation to Sex* (London, 1871), here vol. 1, 444.
74 MEGA² I/26, 93; MECW, vol. 25, 457.
75 Friedrich Engels, *Dialectics of Nature, Introduction*, MEGA² I/26, 82ff; MECW, vol. 25, 318ff.
76 Friedrich Engels, *Anteil der Arbeit*, MEGA² I/26, 89ff.; MECW, vol. 25, 453–4.
77 Even the steam engine, so far his most powerful tool for the transformation of nature, depends, because it is a tool, based in the last resort on the hand. But, step by step, with the development of the hand went that of the brain; first of all came consciousness of the conditions for separate practically useful actions, and later, among the more favoured peoples, and arising from that consciousness, insight into the natural laws governing them. And with the rapidly growing knowledge of the laws of nature the means for reacting on nature also grew; the hand alone would never have achieved the steam-engine if, along with the parallel to the hand, and partly owing to it, the brain of man had not correspondingly developed (Friedrich Engels, *Dialectic*, MEGA² I/26, 83; MECW, vol. 25, 330).
78 Ibid., 83; MECW, vol. 25, 331.
79 The German engineer Franz Reuleaux (1829–1905), who initially worked as a constructor at Baehrens Engineering Works, Cologne, published the textbook *Constructionslehre für den Maschinenbau* (Braunschweig, 1854), together with Carl Ludwig Moll. As a professor at Zurich Polytechnic, Reuleaux published the standard textbook *Der Constructeur: Ein Handbuch zum Gebrauch beim Maschinen-Entwerfen* (Braunschweig, 1861, French translation Paris, 1875). Reuleaux was a judge at the 1862 and 1867 World's Fairs in London and provided numerous reports on new developments in mechanical engineering. As a professor of mechanical engineering at the Technische Hochschule Berlin-Charlottenburg and an influential advisor, he was one of the leading figures in technology in the German Empire. For biographical information, see Hans-Joachim Braun, 'Franz Reuleaux', in: Wilhelm Treue and Wolfgang König (eds), *Berlinische Lebensbilder*, vol. 6 (Berlin, 1990), 279–92.
80 Franz Reuleaux, *Theoretische Kinematik: Grundzüge einer Theorie des Maschinenwesens* (Braunschweig, 1875). Although Reuleaux's theory of kinematics dealt with a central subfield

Notes

of mechanical engineering, his theory contributed little to the development of cutting-edge technology in the chemical and electrotechnical industries; see Jochen Schneider, 'Franz Reuleaux und die Theorie der Maschinen', in: Tilmann Buddensieg, Kurt Düwell and Klaus-Jürgen Sembach (eds), *Wissenschaften in Berlin, Gedanken* (Berlin, 1987), 173–7.

81 Ernst Kapp, *Grundlinien*, 184; reprint, 168; *Elements*, 159.
82 Franz Reuleaux, *Theoretische Kinematik*, 492.
83 Quoted in Ernst Kapp, *Grundlinien*, 199; reprint, 181; *Elements*, 203; see also Franz Reuleaux, 'Die Maschine und die Arbeiterfrage', in: *Soziale Zeitfragen* (Minden, 1895).
84 Ernst Kapp, *Grundlinien*, 199; reprint, 181; *Elements*, 203.
85 On what follows, see Ernst Kapp, *Grundlinien*, 316ff.; reprint, 281ff.
86 These considerations already appear in Kapp's pamphlet *Der constituirte Despotismus und die constitutionelle Freiheit* (Hamburg, 1849). In 1877, his concept of the state (Chapter XIII) forms the conclusion of his philosophy of technology. His critical reception – which did not begin until some 100 years later with the rediscovery of his book by Ernst-Martin Sass – has a fiercely debated offspring in Marshall McLuhan's *Understanding Media: The Extensions of Man* (New York, 1964 – German *Die magischen Kanäle*, Düsseldorf, Vienna, 1968). McLuhan understands technical artefacts as 'extensions' of man; see Gerald Emanuel Stearn (ed.), *McLuhan, Für und Wider* (Düsseldorf, Vienna, 1969).
87 Friedrich Engels, *Dialectics of Nature* (1873–1882), MEGA² I/26 gathers Engels' attempts to come to terms with the immensely increased scientific knowledge of his time. Whether these drafts and flashes of thought on the most diverse disciplines reflect the current state of research at the time is another matter. Nevertheless, his more in-depth remarks on the understanding of electrical engineering research in the 1880s attest to his special interest in this field; see Friedrich Engels, '*Elektrizität*', 236–83; MECW, vol. 25, 368ff.
88 For an overview, see Dieter Schott, 'Das Zeitalter der Elektrizität: Visionen – Potentiale – Realitäten', *Jahrbuch für Wirtschaftsgeschichte*, vol. 40, issue 2 (1999), 31–50.
89 The engineer Marcel Deprez from Sceaux (Seine) had connected two electric dynamos with direct current over 50 km with a telegraph wire, description in: *Catalog der Internationalen Elektrizitäts-Ausstellung 1882* (Munich), 18.
90 Friedrich Engels to Eduard Bernstein, 1 March 1883, MEW, vol. 36, 444f.; MECW, vol. 46, 445–50, here 449. For detailed background information, see Wolfgang König, Friedrich Engels und die 'Elektrotechnische Revolution', *Technikgeschichte*, vol. 56, issue 1 (1989), 9–38. Eberhard Illner, 'Friedrich Engels and Electricity', in: Jürgen G. Backhaus, Günther Chaloupek, Hans A. Frambach (eds), *200 Years of Friedrich Engels. A Critical Assessment of His Life and Scholarship. The European Heritage in Economics and Social Sciences* 25 (Cham, Swizerland 2022), 153–66.
91 Friedrich Engels, Introduction (1895) to Karl Marx's *The Class Struggles in France 1848 to 1850*, in: MEGA² I/32, 338; MECW, vol. 27, 506–24.
92 Ibid., 340ff.; MECW, vol. 27, 521.
93 For an overview of the economics discussion, see Heiner Ganssmann, 'Das Ende des Kapitalismus als Technikfolge?', in: Theo Pirker, Hans-Peter Müller and Rainer Winkelmann (eds), *Technik und Industrielle Revolution: Vom Ende eines sozialwissenschaftlichen Paradigmas* (Opladen, 1987), 290–314.

CHAPTER 5

1 Friedrich Engels to Karl Marx, 23 May 1851, in: MEGA² III/4, 124; MECW, vol. 38, 361–4.

Notes

2   George Ripley and Charles A. Dana (eds) (New York, 1858–63). Engels published articles there under the name of Karl Marx, see: MEGA² I/16–I/18; MECW, vol. 18.
3   For greater detail on Engels' military expertise, see more recently Herfried Münkler, *Über den Krieg, Stationen der Kriegsgeschichte im Spiegel ihrer theoretischen Reflexionen* (Weilerswist, 2002), 149–72.
4   Jenny Marx to Louis Kugelmann, 19 November 1870, in Bert Andreas, 'Briefe und Dokumente der Familie Marx aus den Jahren 1862–1873 nebst zwei unbekannten Aufsätzen von Friedrich Engels', *Archiv für Sozialgeschichte*, vol. 167 (1962), 231. On Engels' military articles, see Jürgen Herres, *Marx und Engels, Portrait einer intellektuellen Freundschaft* (Ditzingen, 2018), 231ff.
5   Friedrich Engels, 'Der Amerikanische Bürgerkrieg und die Panzer- und Widderschiffe', *Die Presse*, no. 181 (3 July 1862), MEW, vol. 15, 511–13, here 511; MECW, vol. 19, 213ff.
6   The concept was initially restricted to the technological impulses from the ICT of the day but can usefully be applied to the analysis of naval structures between 1850 and 1890: see Max Boot, *War Made New: Technology, Warfare, and the Course of History, 1500 to Today* (New York, 2006), 8.
7   Emil O. Huning, *Die Entwicklung der Schiffs- und Küstenartillerie bis zur Gegenwart* (Berlin, Leipzig, 1912), 15ff.
8   Jacques Mordal, *25 Jahrhunderte Seekrieg* (Munich, 1963); Lawrence Sondhaus, *Naval Warfare, 1815–1914* (London, 2001), 57f.
9   On the significance of the Crimean War for the genesis of modern naval fleets, especially for the modernization of the French fleet, see Wilhelm Treue, *Der Krimkrieg und die Entstehung der modernen Flotten* (Göttingen, 1951), 135–45, 142f.
10 'They bombarded Odessa and discovered that the most miserable coastal battery was indisputably superior to their seaborne artillery – an experience the allies were to repeat on numerous occasions, accompanied by severe losses, in the course of the war' (Wilhelm Treue, *Krimkrieg*, 19f.).
11 Friedrich Engels, 'Navy', c. 22 November 1860, *New American Cyclopaedia*, in: MEGA² I/18, 567–75, German translation: MEW, vol. 14, 368–80, here 377; MECW, vol. 18, 364–78.
12 Ibid., 376f.
13 Ships designed for engagement with non-armoured enemy vessels – as were the typical new warships of the 1870s – carried both types of artillery.
14 Emil Huning, *Entwicklung*, 31.
15 Ulrich Israel and Jürgen Gebauer, *Panzerschiffe* (Berlin, 1998), 72. 'The British victims were caused by Satsuma gunnery as well as accidents due to the imperfect breech-loading guns developed by the English engineer William George Armstrong' https://en.wikipedia.org/wiki/Namamugi_Incident (retrieved 15 February 2020).
16 Emil Huning, *Entwicklung*, 31.
17 John F. Beeler, *British Naval Policy in the Gladstone-Disraeli Era, 1866–1880* (Stanford, 1997), 71.
18 Friedrich Engels, *Artilleristisches aus Amerika*, 18–26 September 1863 (unpublished manuscript for the *Allgemeine Militärzeitung* transcribed and commented at length in Heinz-Lutger Borgert, *Die Marineplanungen in Deutschland 1860–1867 und Friedrich Engels* (Frankfurt, Bern, 1977), 31ff.; see also Werner Hahlweg, 'Sozialismus und Militärwissenschaft bei Friedrich Engels', in: Hans Pelger, *Friedrich Engels 1820–1970* (Hanover, 1971), 63–72.
19 Wilhelm Treue, *Krimkrieg*, 137f.
20 Friedrich Engels, *Artilleristisches*, 32.
21 Arnold A. Putnam: 'Rolf Krake, Europe's first turreted ironclad', *Mariner's Mirror*, vol. 84, issue 1, February 1998, 56–63.

Notes

22 Roger Chesneau and Eugene M. Kolesnik (eds), *Conway's All the World's Fighting Ships 1860-1905* (Greenwich, 1979); *Geschiedenis van de techniek in Nederland: De wording van een moderne samenleving 1800–1890*, Deel IV, 1993, 90–93.

23 At the time of his essay (*c.* 22 November 1860), Engels knew nothing of these new ships: the Rolf Krake went into service only half a year later, on 1 June 1863, and the Dutch vessel only several years later.

24 James Phinney Baxter, *The Introduction of the Ironclad Warship* (Bel Air, 1968).

25 Kurt Möser, *Turmschiff Captain: Neue Grauzonen der Technikgeschichte* (Karlsruhe, 2018 = *Technikdiskurse 14*), 71–81.

26 This included, for example, Jules Verne's bestseller *From the Earth to the Moon*, which celebrated the achievements of Baltimore Cannon Club in producing large calibre cannon and ironically noted records in numbers killed.

27 Kurt Möser, *Turmschiff Captain*.

28 John F. Beeler, *Birth of the Battleship, British Capital Ship Design 1960–1881* (London, 2004), 92f.

29 The Royal Navy's Committee of Designs stated in 1871: 'A perfect ship of war is a desideratum which has never yet been attained and is now further than ever removed from our reach. Any near approach to perfection in one direction inevitably brings with it disadvantages in another'; see *Encyclopaedia Britannica*, 9th ed., vol. 17, 285.

30 Peter Hore, *The Ironclads: An Illustrated History of Battleships from 1860 to the First World War* (London, 2006).

31 See Beatrice Heuser, 'Naval History Down to Our Own Day Is Filled with Instances of Wrong Deductions from Observed Occurrences', *The Evolution of Strategy: Thinking War from Antiquity to the Present* (Cambridge, 2010), 226.

32 Rudolf Brommy and Heinrich von Littrow, *Die Marine. Gemeinfassliche Darstellung des gesammten Seewesens* (Vienna, Pest, Leipzig, 1878, repr. Leipzig, 1982), 309f.

33 Cited in ibid., 263.

34 Friedrich Engels, *Der Amerikanische Bürgerkrieg und die Panzer- und Widderschiffe*. Engels was mistaken about the armaments of the two ram ships he mentions, the USS *Queen* and USS *Monarch*, both of which had been armed by General Ellet with cannon as well as marksmen.

35 Friedrich Engels, article on 'The Fleet'.

36 Ibid.

37 Emil Wilde, *The Development of Sailing Ship Tactics Compared to That of Steam Tactics, with a Glance into the Future*, 1911. https://tandfonline.com/doi/abs/10.1080/03071841209435 550?journalCode=rusi19 (retrieved 7 June 2020).

38 Matthew Allen, 'The Deployment of Untried Technology: British Naval Tactics in the Ironclad Era', *War in History*, vol. 15 (2008), 269–93.

39 Nicolas A. M. Rodger, 'Die Entwicklung der Vorstellung von Seekriegsstrategie in Grossbritannien im 18. und 19. Jahrhundert', in: Jörg Duppler (ed.), *Seemacht und Seestrategie im 19. und 20. Jahrhundert* (Hamburg, 1999), 84–103, here 100.

40 Friedrich Engels, 'On Rifled Cannon', *New York Daily Tribune*, 7 April, 21 April and 5 May 1860, in: MEGA^2 I/18, 401–11, German translation: MEW, vol. 14, 27–38; MECW, vol. 17, 354–66.

41 Friedrich Engels, 'Artillery', October–November 1857, *New American Cyclopaedia*, in: MEGA^2 I/16, 80–100, German translation: MEW, vol. 14, 187–212, on the development of naval artillery 206f.; MECW, vol. 18, 188–210.

42 William N. Still, *Iron Afloat: The Story of the Confederate Armorclads* (Columbia, 1985), 136f.

43 Ibid., 129.

44 Alfred Thayer Mahan, *The Influence of Sea Power Upon History, 1660–1783* (New York, 1890), German translation: *Der Einfluss der Seemacht auf die Geschichte*, vol. 2, 1783–1812 (Berlin, 1899). The book – ostensibly a history of the high-seas fleets in the seventeenth and

eighteenth centuries – recommended the construction of a globally operating high-seas fleet as an instrument of sovereign power. Widely read, it was used to legitimize the naval arms race around 1900 – a prime example of political historiography.

45 Volkmar Bueb, *Die* Junge Schule *der französischen Marine: Strategie und Politik 1875–1900* (Boppard, 1971). See also Paul Dislére, *La guerre d'escadre et la guerre des cotes* (Paris, 1876) – an important primary text.
46 'By one of the sharpest ironies of the Ironclad Age, which saw the emergence of the doctrine of sea command and the dogma of its achievement by decisive fleet action, there were very few battles between fleets, and of the few that did occur by no means all were decisive'; Richard Hill, *War at Sea in the Ironclad Age* (London, 2002), 178.
47 See Heinz-Lutger Borgert, *Marineplanungen*, 245ff.
48 'Battlefleet deployments, in short, were dictated by technological limitations' (see John F. Beeler, *Birth of the Battleship*, 21).
49 Ibid., 24.
50 Beeler, *British Naval Policy*, 24; Heuser, *The Evolution of Strategy*, 217f.; Donald M. Schurman, *Imperial Defence 1868–1887* (London, 2014); Robert Gardiner, *Steam, Steel and Shellfire: The Steam Warship 1815–1905* (London, 1992).
51 In 1871, the Royal Navy's Committee of Designs recommended coastal defence vessels at least for the country's overseas possessions:

> At present we find ourselves compelled to regard the attainment of a very high degree of offensive and defensive power united with real efficiency under sail as an insoluble problem; and we believe that our transmarine possessions and other important interests in distant parts of the world, will be more efficiently protected by the establishment, where requisite, of centres of naval power, from which vessels of the 'Devastation' class may operate, than by relying upon cruising ships. (*Encyclopaedia Britannica*, s.v. 'Navy', 9th ed. vol. 17 (1884), 287–301; here 286

52 'Much of the seemingly defensive employment was a consequence of technological factors' (Beeler, *British Naval Policy*, 22).
53 See Heuser, *The Evolution of Strategy*, 226f.
54 Beeler, *British Naval Policy*, 18ff.
55 Friedrich Engels, 'British Defences', *New York Daily Tribune*, 10 August 1860, in: MEGA² I/18, 468–71, German translation: MEW, vol. 15, 93–97; MECW, vol. 17, 425–8; Friedrich Engels, 'Could the French Sack London?', *New York Daily Tribune*, 11 August 1860, in: MEGA² I/18, 472–5, German translation: MEW, vol. 15, 103–8; MECW, vol. 17, 434–8.
56 Friedrich Engels, *Die britische Verteidigung*, 93.
57 Ibid., 95.
58 Ibid.

CHAPTER 6

1 Friedrich Engels to August Bebel, 20–23 January 1886, in: MEW, vol. 36, 428; MECW, vol. 47, 386–91, 391.
2 Friedrich Engels to Laura Marx Lafargue, 24 November 1886, in: MEW, vol. 36, 570; MECW, vol. 47, 524–7, 525.
3 Friedrich Engels to August Bebel, 20–23 January 1886, in: MEW, vol. 36, 428; MECW, vol. 47, 386–91, 391.
4 Stefan Link and Noam Maggor, 'The United States as a Developing Nation: Revisiting the Peculiarities of American History', *Past and Present*, vol. 246 (2020), 269–306. In this regard,

Notes

other developing non-European economies, for example Canada, Argentina, Mexico, Chile, Brazil, South Africa and India, lacked America's balanced economy of agriculture, industry and supplier of raw materials.

5 Karl Marx, *Das Elend der Philosophie. Antwort auf Proudhons 'Philosophie des Elends'*, in: MEW, vol. 4, 132; MECW, vol. 6, 105–212, 167.
6 Friedrich Engels to Conrad Schmidt, 8 October 1888, in: MEW, vol. 37, 103; MECW, vol. 48, 220–1.
7 Friedrich Engels, *Die Lage der arbeitenden Klasse in England*, in: MEGA¹ I/4 (Berlin, 1932), 279; MECW, vol. 4, 295–596, 579–80.
8 Jonathan Sperber, *Karl Marx: A Nineteenth-Century Life* (New York, 2013), 19.
9 Karl Marx, 'Zur Judenfrage' (1844), in: MEW, vol. 1, 352; MECW, vol. 3, 146–74; J. P. Mayer, 'Alexis de Tocqueville und Karl Marx: Affinitäten und Gegensätze', *Zeitschrift für Politik*, vol. 13 (1966), 4.
10 'Zirkular gegen Kriege', in: MEW, vol. 4, 3–17; for criticism of the Free Soil Movement, 8–11; MECW, vol. 6, 35–51.
11 Karl Marx and Friedrich Engels, *Deutsche Ideologie: Manuskripte und Drucke* (1845/46), Kap. 'Das Leipziger Konzil', III. Sankt Max in: MEGA² I/5, 271; MECW, vol. 5, 117ff.; cf. August H. Nimtz, *Marx, Tocqueville and Race in America: The 'Absolute Democracy' or the 'Defiled Republic'* (Lanham, MD, 2003), 49.
12 Amy Bridges, 'Becoming American: The Working Classes in the United States before the Civil War', in: Ira Katznelson and Aristide R. Zolberg (eds), *Working-Class Formation: Nineteenth-Century Patterns in Western Europe and the United States* (Princeton, 1986), 162, 165, 185–9, 191–6.
13 Karl Marx and Friedrich Engels, 'Revue', in: *Neue Rheinische Zeitung: Politisch-Ökonomische Revue*, 2. Ausgabe, January–February 1850, in: MEGA² I/10, 218; MECW, vol. 10, 257–70, 265.
14 Cf. MEGA² I/10, 218ff.
15 Karl Marx to Friedrich Engels, 20 October 1857, in: MEGA² III/8, 184; MECW, vol. 40, 191–4, 191.
16 Karl Marx, *Das Kapital*, vol. 1, Kap. 3, Sek. 4, Der Arbeitstag, in: MEGA² II/5, 239ff.; MECW, vol. 35, 239ff., 305.
17 Ibid.; Vorwort, 13; MECW, vol. 35, 9. In 1861, Marx anticipated the world-historical significance of abolishing unfree labour in Russia and the United States: Karl Marx to Friedrich Engels, 11 January 1860, in: MEGA² III/10, 153; MECW, vol. 41, 3ff.
18 Karl Marx to Friedrich Engels, 7 August 1862, in: MEGA² III/12, 186–7; MECW, vol. 41, 399ff.; Karl Marx to Friedrich Engels, 29 October 1862, in: MEGA² III/12, 256–8; MECW, vol. 41, 419ff.; Karl Marx to Friedrich Engels, 23 April 1866, in: MEGA² III/12, 256–8; MECW, vol. 42, 268.
19 Friedrich Engels to Karl Marx, 5 November 1862, in: MEGA² III/19, 282; MECW, vol. 41, 422–3, 423.
20 Friedrich Engels to Karl Marx, 30 July 1862, in: MEGA² III/19, 169; MECW, vol. 41, 386–88, 388.
21 Friedrich Engels to Karl Marx, 9 September 1862, in: MEGA² III/12, 230; MECW, vol. 41, 414–15, 415.
22 Friedrich Engels to Karl Marx, 5 November 1862, in: MEGA² III/12, 262; MECW, vol. 41, 422–3, 423.
23 Friedrich Engels to Joseph Weydemeyer, 24 November 1864, in: MEGA² III/13, 72; MECW, vol. 42, 37.
24 Ibid.
25 Karl Marx to Lion Philips, 29 November 1864, in: MEGA² III/13, 90; MECW, vol. 42, 48.

Notes

26 Karl Marx to Nicolai Franzewitsch Danielson, 15 November 1878, in: MEW, vol. 34, 359; MECW, vol. 45, 344. The term 'wage slavery' was frequently used in this time period.

27 See MEGA² II/5, 240; MECW, vol. 35, 305.

28 Marx judged Britain's second Reform Act in 1867 also in positive terms: MEGA² III/13, 429; cf. Jürgen Herres, 'Einführung', in: MEGA² 1/21, 1131, 1136.

29 Karl Marx, 'Zu den Ereignissen in America', in: *Die Presse*, Nr. 281, 12 October 1862, in: MEW, vol. 15, 553; MECW, vol. 19, 248–51, 250.

30 Martin Shefter, 'Trade Unions and Political Machines: The Organization and Disorganization of the American Working Class in the Late Nineteenth Century', in: Ira Katznelson and Aristide R. Zolberg (eds), *Working-Class Formation: Nineteenth-Century Patterns in Western Europe and the United States* (Princeton, 1986), 199–200, 204.

31 Karl Marx to Nikolai Franzewitsch Danielson, 15 November 1878, in: MEW, vol. 34, 359; MECW, vol. 45, 344 (author's emphasis).

32 Karl Marx to Nikolai Franzewitsch Danielson, 10 April 1879, in: MEW, vol. 34, 374ff.; MECW, vol. 45, 357–8.

33 Friedrich Engels to August Bebel, 10–11 May 1883, in: MEW, vol. 36, 27; MECW, vol. 47, 23.

34 For statistics on labour markets, see MEGA² IV/32: Ohio (1879–80), New Jersey (1878–9), New York (1886–91) and Pennsylvania (1876–80), 110–13; for national statistics (1876–81, 1886, 1886–94), 112, 271; for Iowa (1884–5), 334; for Massachusetts (1870–82), 545; for Missouri (1881), 596; for Massachusetts (1875), 602; Karl Marx to Friedrich Engels, 25 August 1879, in: MEW, vol. 34, 97; MECW, vol. 45, 376ff. For European statistics, see MEGA² IV/26, 826–8.

35 Karl Marx to Friedrich Adolph Sorge, 5 November 1880, in: MEW, vol. 34, 478; MECW, vol. 42–46.

36 John Swinton, 'Account of an Interview with Karl Marx Published in the "Sun"', in: MEGA² I/25, 443; Carl-Erich Vollgraf, '"Marx's Arbeit" am dritten Buch des Kapital in den 1870/80er Jahren', in: *In memoriam Wolfgang Jahn: Der ganze Marx. Alles Verfasste veröffentlichen, erforschen und den 'ungeschriebenen Marx' rekonstruieren* (Hamburg, 2002), 33–56, 53.

37 Gerald Hubman and Regina Roth, 'Die "Kapital-Abteilung" der MEGA. Einleitung und Überblick', *Marx-Engels Jahrbuch* 2012/13, 64.

38 Friedrich Engels to Friedrich Adolph Sorge, 29 June 1883, in: MEW, vol. 36, 46; MECW, vol. 47, 42–3, 43. For a more exhaustive analysis of Marx's delays with *Capital*, see Regina Roth, 'Karl Marx's Original Manuscripts in the Marx-Engels-Gesamtausgabe (MEGA): Another View on Capital', in: Riccardo Bellofiore (ed.), *Re-reading Marx: New Perspectives after the New Edition* (Basingstoke, 2009), 38; see too Andrew Dawson, 'Reassessing Henry Carey (1793–1879): The Problems of Writing Political Economy in Nineteenth-Century America', *Journal of American Studies*, vol. 34 (2000), 465–85.

39 Carl-Erich Vollgraf, 'Marx' Arbeit', 52; Regina Roth, 'Karl Marx's Original Manuscripts', 40ff. Because Marx did not draft his own thoughts in his own language on the material that he excerpted and took notes on, Engels could not divine what conclusions Marx reached. For a list of Marx's surviving materials, see Roth, 'Karl Marx's Original Manuscripts', 31ff. According to Roth, Engels pursued a 'solution-oriented' work program. He was concerned about not only quickly publishing a readable work but also presenting a study that offered answers to the burning questions on surplus value and profit rates.

40 Friedrich Engels to Eduard Bernstein, 3 May 1882, in: MEW, vol. 35, 315; MECW, vol. 46, 250–1, 251.

41 Friedrich Engels, 'Über die Konzentration des Kapitals in den Vereinigten Staaten', in: *Der Sozialdemokrat*, Nr. 21, 18 May 1882, in: MEW, vol. 19, 306–8, 307.

42 Karl Marx to Friedrich Engels, 25 July 1877, in: MEW, vol. 34, 59; MECW, vol. 45, 250ff.

Notes

43 Friedrich Engels to Karl Kautsky, 1 February 1881, in: MEW, vol. 35, 150ff.; MECW, vol. 46, 56–58, 57.
44 Ibid., 151; MECW, vol. 46, 57.
45 Friedrich Engels, 'Vorwort zur vierten Ausgabe (1890) des Manifests der Kommunistischen Partei', in: MEGA² I/31, 255; MECW, vol. 27, 53–60, 54.
46 Friedrich Engels, 'Über die Konzentration des Kapitals in den Vereinigten Staaten', in: *Der Sozialdemokrat*, Nr. 21, 18 May 1882, in: MEW, vol. 19, 306–8, 307.
47 See MEGA² I/31, Apparat, 879; Joanne R. Reitano, *The Tariff Question in the Gilded Age: The Great Debate of 1888* (Philadelphia, 1994), 129.
48 Friedrich Engels to Nikolai Franzewitsch Danielson, 29 October 1891, in: MEW, vol. 38, 195; MECW, vol. 49, 278ff.
49 https://history.house.gov/Historical-Highlights/1851-1900/The-McKinley-Tariff-of-1890/ (accessed 28 June 2021).
50 Friedrich Engels to Florence Kelley-Wischnewetzky, 3 February 1886, in: MEW vol. 36, 432ff.; MECW, vol. 47, 395–7.
51 Friedrich Engels to Nikolai Franzewitsch Danielson, 8 February 1886, in: MEW, vol. 36, 438ff.; MECW, vol. 47, 400–2, 402.
52 Friedrich Engels to Nikolai Franzewitsch Danielson, 24 February 1893, in: MEW, vol. 39, 37ff.; MECW, vol. 50, 109–12, 111.
53 Friedrich Engels to August Bebel, 18 March 1886, in: MEW, vol. 36, 465; MECW, vol. 47, 426–9.
54 Friedrich Engels to Florence Kelley-Wischnewetzky, 11 April 1888, in: MEW, vol. 37, 48; MECW, vol. 48, 172.
55 Friedrich Engels, 'Die Arbeiterbewegung in Amerika: Vorwort zur amerikanischen Ausgabe der Lage der arbeitenden Klasse in England', in: MEGA² I/31, 29ff.; MECW, vol. 26, 399–405; Henry David, *The History of the Hay Market Affair: A Study of the American Social-Revolutionary and Labour Movements* (New York, 1963); James R. Green, *Death in the Haymarket: A Story of Chicago, the First Labor Movement, and the Bombing That Divided Gilded Age America* (New York, 2006); Timothy Messer Kruse, *The Trial of the Hay Market Anarchists: Terrorism and Justice in the Gilded Age* (London, 2011).
56 Friedrich Engels to Friedrich Adolph Sorge, 29 November 1886, in: MEW, vol. 36, 579; MECW, vol. 47, 531–4. For a concise overview of organized workers' politics, see Walter Licht, *Industrializing America: The Nineteenth Century* (Baltimore, 1995), 166–96.
57 Friedrich Engels to Florence Kelley-Wischnewetzky, 28 December 1886, MEW, vol. 36, 589; MECW, vol. 47, 540ff; idem, 3 June 1886, MEW, vol. 36, 490; MECW, vol. 47, 451–2, 452.
58 Ibid., 452.
59 Friedrich Engels, 'Die Arbeiterbewegung in Amerika', 42.
60 Friedrich Engels to Friedrich Adolph Sorge, 31 August 1888, MECW, vol. 48, 207.
61 Friedrich Engels to Florence Kelley-Wischnewetzky, 3 June 1886, in: MEW, vol. 36, 490f.; MECW, vol. 47, 451ff., 452.
62 Friedrich Engels to Friedrich Adolph Sorge, 29 November 1886, in: MEW, vol. 36, 580; MECW, vol. 47, 531–4, 533.
63 Friedrich Engels, 'Vorwort zur vierten Ausgabe (1890) des Manifests der Kommunistischen Partei', in: MEGA² I/31, 257; MECW, vol. 27, 53–60.
64 Friedrich Engels to Friedrich Adolph Sorge, 16 September 1887, in: MEW, vol. 36, 704; MECW, vol. 48, 103–4, 103.
65 Walter Licht, *Industrializing America*, 173.
66 Friedrich Engels to Laura Marx Lafargue, 23 May 1886, in: MEW, vol. 36, 489; MECW, vol. 47, 450–1.

67 Friedrich Engels to Friedrich Adolph Sorge, 7 March 1884, in: MEW, vol. 36, 123; MECW, vol. 47, 113-15.
68 Friedrich Engels to August Bebel, 11 October 1884, in: MEW, vol. 36, 215; MECW, vol. 47, 197ff.; Friedrich Engels to Friedrich Adolph Sorge, 2 December 1893, in: MEW, vol. 39, 173; MECW, vol. 50, 235ff.
69 Friedrich Engels to Friedrich Adolph Sorge, 29 April 1886, in: MEW, vol. 36, 478; MECW, vol. 47, 439-43.
70 Friedrich Engels and Eduard Bernstein, 22 May 1886, in: MEW, vol. 36, 487; MECW, vol. 47, 448-9.
71 Friedrich Engels to Friedrich Adolph Sorge, 29 June 1883, in: MEW, vol. 36, 47; MECW, vol. 47, 42-4.
72 Friedrich Engels to Friedrich Adolph Sorge, 29 January 1886, in: MEW, vol. 36, 431; MECW, vol. 47, 393-5.
73 Friedrich Engels to Friedrich Adolph Sorge, 16 September 1887, in: MEW, vol. 36, 304; MECW, vol. 48, 103-4.
74 Friedrich Engels to Florence Kelley-Wischnewetzky, 28 December 1886, in: MEW, vol. 36, 589; MECW, vol. 47, 540-2.
75 Friedrich Engels to Florence Kelley-Wischnewetzky, 27 January 1887, in: MEW, vol. 36, 597; MECW, vol. 48, 8-9; here 8.
76 Friedrich Engels, 'Preface to the American Edition of *The Condition of the Working Class in England in 1844*' (1887), in: MEGA² I/31, 46; MECW, vol. 26, 434-42, 440.
77 Friedrich Engels to Friedrich Adolph Sorge, 31 December 1892, in: MEW, vol. 38, 560; MECW, vol. 50, 73-76, 74.
78 David Montgomery, 'Labor in the Industrial Era', in: Richard B. Morrs (ed.), *The US Department of Labor Bicentennial History of the American Worker* (Washington, 1976), 117ff.
79 Friedrich Engels to Friedrich Adolph Sorge, 8 August 1887, in: MEW, vol. 36, 689; MECW, vol. 48, 90-2.
80 Friedrich Engels to Friedrich Adolph Sorge, 31 December 1892, in: MEW, vol. 38, 560; MECW, vol. 50, 73-6.
81 Walter Licht, *Industrializing America*, 173-5; for European strike waves, see Friedhelm Boll, *Arbeitskämpfe und Gewerkschaften in Deutschland, England und Frankreich: Ihre Entwicklung vom 19. zum 20. Jahrhundert* (Bonn, 1992).
82 A similar debate about pragmatic union aims also arose in Germany between the SPD and the unions; see Carl E. Schorske, *German Social Democracy, 1905-1917: The Development of the Great Schism* (Cambridge, 1955).
83 The American Federation of Labor nonetheless called for international solidarity in 1886, invoking universal forms of class conflict: Martin Shefter, 'Trade Unions and Political Machines', 225.
84 Edwin Lawrence Godkin, 'The Labor Crisis', in: *North American Review*, vol. 105, issue 216 (July 1867), 178.
85 Seth Cotlar, *Tom Paine's America: The Rise and Fall of Transatlantic Radicalism in the Early Republic* (Charlottesville, 2011).
86 David Montgomery, *The Fall of the House of Labor: The Workplace, the State, and American Labor Activism, 1865-1925* (Cambridge, 1987); Montgomery, *Citizen Worker: The Experience of Workers in the United States with Democracy and the Free Market During the Nineteenth Century* (Cambridge, 1993); Harold Livesay, *Samuel Gompers and Organized Labor in America* (Boston, 1978); William H. Harris, *The Harder We Run: Black Workers Since the Civil War* (New York, 1982); Robert E. Weir, *Beyond Labor's Veil: The Culture of the Knights of Labor* (University Park, 1996); Linda Gordon, *The Great Arizona Orphan Abduction* (Cambridge, 2001).

Notes

87   Timothy Messer-Kruse, *The Yankee International: Marxism and the American Reform Tradition, 1848–1876* (Chapel Hill, 2000), 157–86; for a positive assessment of Marx's position on the role of race in the United States, see August H. Nimtz Jr, *Marx, Tocqueville, and Race in America*, 227ff.
88   Friedrich Engels to Friedrich Adolph Sorge, 16 January 1895, MEW, vol. 39, 385ff.; MECW, vol. 50, 421–3.
89   Friedrich Engels to Friedrich Adolph Sorge, 31 December 1892, MEW, vol. 38, 560; MECW, vol. 50, 73–76.
90   Friedrich Engels to Friedrich Adolph Sorge, 24 October 1891, MEW, vol. 38, 182; MECW, vol. 49, 264–6.

CHAPTER 7

1   Jürgen Osterhammel, *Die Verwandlung der Welt. Eine Geschichte des 19. Jahrhunderts* (Munich, 2009); English translation: *The Transformation of the World: A Global History of the Nineteenth Century* (Princeton, 2014).
2   On techno-economic transformation, see Hugh Thomas, *A History of the World*, revised ed. (New York, 1984); on global interconnectedness, see R. Bin Wong, 'Möglicher Überfluss, beharrliche Armut. Industrialisierung und Welthandel im 19. Jahrhundert', in: Sebastian Conrad and Jürgen Osterhammel (eds), *Wege zur modernen Welt 1750–1870, Geschichte der Welt*, vol. 4 (Munich, 2016), 255–410.
3   Roland Wenzlhuemer, *Connecting the Nineteenth-Century World: The Telegraph and Globalization* (Cambridge, 2013).
4   Christopher Bayly, *The Birth of the Modern World 1780–1914: Global Connections and Comparisons* (Oxford, 2004). See also the essays in Friedrich Jaeger, Wolfgang Knöbl and Ute Schneider (eds), *Handbuch Moderneforschung* (Stuttgart, 2015).
5   Arthur Schopenhauer, 'Zur Rechtslehre und Politik' (1851), in: *Parerga und Paralipomena: Kleine philosophische Schriften*, vol. 2 (Zurich, 1988), 224ff.; English translation: *The Essays of Arthur Schopenhauer: On Human Nature*, trans. T. Bailey Saunders (London, [1897] 2019).
6   See Gareth Stedman Jones, Karl Marx and Friedrich Engels, *The Communist Manifesto* (Harmondsworth, 2002); German translation: *Das Kommunistische Manifest von Karl Marx und Friedrich Engels* (Munich, 2012).
7   See for example Heinz-Gerhard Haupt, Konsum und Handel. Europa im 19. und 20. Jahrhundert (Göttingen, 2003); Wolfgang König, Geschichte der Konsumgesellschaft (Stuttgart, 2000).
8   Carl Jantke and Dietrich Hilger, *Die Eigentumslosen. Der deutsche Pauperismus und die Emanzipationskrise in Darstellungen und Deutungen der zeitgenössischen Literatur* (Freiburg, Munich, 1965).
9   See, for example, Patrick Eiden-Offe, *Die Poesie der Klasse: Romantischer Antikapitalismus und die Erfindung des Proletariats* (Berlin, 2017).
10 Thomas Welskopp, *Das Banner der Brüderlichkeit: Die deutsche Sozialdemokratie vom Vormärz bis zum Sozialistengesetz* (Bonn, 2000).
11 Friedrich Engels, *Die Lage der arbeitenden Klasse in England: Nach eigner Anschauung und authentischen Quellen*, 1st edn 1845, in: MEGA¹ I/4 (Berlin, 1932), 10–286; *The Condition of the Working Class in England*, MECW, vol. 4, 295–596.

12 For example, Charles Dickens, *Hard Times* (1854). In addition to Dickens, the works of Elizabeth Gaskell, Charles Kingsley, Charles Reade or Elizabeth Barrett-Browning and Thomas Hood should be mentioned.
13 Eugène Sue, *The Mysteries of Paris* (Paris, 1843). English translation (London, 2015).
14 Ilsedore Rarisch, *Das Unternehmerbild in der deutschen Erzählliteratur der ersten Hälfte des 19. Jahrhunderts. Ein Beitrag zur Rezeption der frühen Industrialisierung in der belletristischen Literatur* (Berlin, 1977).
15 Friedrich Engels, 'Briefe aus dem Wuppertal', *Telegraph für Deutschland*, no. 49 (March and April 1839), in: MEGA² I/3, 32–51; 'Letters from Wuppertal', MECW, vol. 2, 7–25.
16 Jürgen Kocka, *Arbeitsverhältnisse und Arbeiterexistenzen. Grundlagen der Klassenbildung im 19. Jahrhundert* (Bonn, 1990).
17 Jürgen Reulecke, *Sozialer Frieden durch soziale Reform: Der Centralverein für das Wohl der arbeitenden Klassen in der Frühindustrialisierung* (Wuppertal, 1983).
18 On the background to the revolution, see Hans-Ulrich Wehler, *Deutsche Gesellschaftsgeschichte*, vol. 2, 1815–45/9 (Munich, 1987).
19 Ulrike Laufer and Hans Ottomeyer (eds), *Gründerzeit 1848–1871. Industrie und Lebensräume zwischen Vormärz und Kaiserreich* (Dresden, 2008); Werner Plumpe, 'Realistische Zeiten: Ökonomischer Aufschwung und gesellschaftliche Selbstbilder in den Gründerjahren 1852–1873', in: Laurenz Lütteken (ed., *Das Jahr 1868: Musik zwischen Realismus und Gründerzeit* (Kassel, 2019), 17–38.
20 Friedrich Engels to Karl Marx, 23 September 1851, in: MEGA² III/4, 213; MECW, vol. 38, 463–7, here 460.
21 Hans Rosenberg, *Die Weltwirtschaftskrise 1857–1859: Mit einem Vorbericht* (Göttingen, 1974).
22 Rudolf Berthold and Hans-Heinrich Müller (eds), *Geschichte der Produktivkräfte in Deutschland von 1800 bis 1945*, vol. 2 (Berlin, 1985).
23 For an overview, see Werner Plumpe, 'Unternehmensgeschichte im 19. und 20 Jahrhundert', *Enzyklopädie Deutscher Geschichte* (Berlin, 2018), 94.
24 For a detailed description, see Gerhard A. Ritter and Klaus Tenfelde, *Arbeiter im Deutschen Kaiserreich 1871–1914* (Bonn, 1992).
25 Marcus Gräser, *Wohlfahrtsgesellschaft und Wohlfahrtsstaat: Bürgerliche Sozialreform und 'Welfare State Building' in den USA und in Deutschland 1880–1940* (Göttingen, 2009).
26 See for example David F. Crew, *Bochum: Sozialgeschichte einer Industriestadt 1860–1914* (Frankfurt, 1980).
27 Jürgen Reulecke, *Geschichte der Urbanisierung in Deutschland* (Frankfurt, 1985); Joachim Schlör, *Nachts in der grossen Stadt. Paris, Berlin, London 1840–1930* (Munich, 1991); for a contemporary report, see Georg Simmel, 'Die Grossstädte und das Geistesleben (1903)', in: *Simmel, Gesamtausgabe*, vol. 7 (Frankfurt, 2006).
28 For a typical view, see Ludwig August von Rochau, *Grundsätze der Realpolitik: Angewendet auf die staatlichen Zustände Deutschlands (1853/1859)*, ed. and introduced by Hans-Ulrich Wehler (Frankfurt, 1972).
29 Hermann Lübbe, *Politische Philosophie in Deutschland: Studien zu ihrer Geschichte* (Munich, 1974).
30 Erik Grimmer-Solem, *The Rise of Historical Economics and Social Reform in Germany, 1864–1894* (Oxford, 2003).
31 Karl Marx, *Friedrich Engels: Preface* [to the 'Manifesto of the Communist Party' (to the German edition of 1872)], in: MEW, vol. 4, 573; MECW, vol. 23, 174.
32 Friedrich Engels, 'England 1845 and 1885', in: *Die Neue Zeit, June 1885*, in: MEGA² I/30, 67–73, here 71; MECW, vol. 26, 295–301, here 299.

Notes

33 Werner Plumpe, 'Vom Supranaturalisten zum Kommunisten: Der Weg des jungen Friedrich Engels zur Ökonomie', in: Rainer Lucas, Reinhard Pfriem and Hans-Dieter Westhoff (eds), *Arbeiten am Widerspruch: Friedrich Engels zum 200. Geburtstag* (Marburg, 2020), 213–48.
34 Friedrich Engels to Arnold Ruge, 26 July 1842, in: MEGA² III/ 1, 235; MECW, vol. 2, 545.
35 Friedrich Engels to Joseph Weydemeyer, 19 June 1851, in: MEGA² III/4, 132; MECW, vol. 38, 370ff.
36 See particularly the relevant texts from England, beginning with the first reports for the *Rheinische Zeitung* of December 1842 and ending with Friedrich Engels, 'Umrisse zu einer Kritik der Nationalökonomie', in: Arnold Ruge and Karl Marx (eds), *Deutsch-Französische Jahrbücher 1844* (Paris, 1844), 86–114, in: MEGA² I/3, 467–94; *Outlines of a Critique of Political Economy*, MECW, vol. 3, 418–43; and Friedrich Engels, *Lage/Condition*, MECW, vol. 4, 295–596.
37 Engels, *Lage*, 262; *Condition*, MECW, vol. 4, 563.
38 Engels, *Lage*, 261; *Condition*, MECW, vol. 4, 562.
39 Friedrich Wilhelm Krummacher, the first Reformed preacher in Elberfeld at the time of Engels' youth, Engels' favourite hate figure, he was as pietistically stubborn as he was rhetorically brilliant, according to Engels, Briefe, 36–41.
40 See Werner Plumpe, '"Dies ewig unfertigige Ding" – Das Kapital und seine Entstehungsgeschichte', in: *Aus Politik und Zeitgeschichte*, vol. 67, issue 19–20 (2017), 10–16.
41 See especially Friedrich Engels, 'Letters from London I', in: *Schweizerischer Republikaner*, 16 May 1839, in: MEGA² I/3, 449–66; MECW, vol. 3, 379–91.
42 Friedrich Engels, 'Progress of Social Reform on the Continent', in: *The New Moral World*, 4 November 1843, in: MEGA² I/3, 495–510; MECW, vol. 3, 392–408.
43 Friedrich Engels, 'Die innern Krisen', in: *Rheinische Zeitung*, 9 December 1842, in: MEGA² I/3, 442; MECW, vol. 2, 373.
44 Friedrich Engels, 'Lage der arbeitenden Klasse in England', in: *Rheinische Zeitung*, 25 December 1842, in: MEGA² I, 3, 447; MECW, vol. 2, 378.
45 Ibid.
46 MEGA² I, 3, 448; MECW, vol. 2, 379.
47 See Heinz D. Kurz, 'Der junge Engels über die "Bereicherungswissenschaft", die "Unsittlichkeit" von Privateigentum und Konkurrenz und die "Heuchelei der Oekonomen"', in: Lucas, Pfriem and Westhoff (eds), *Arbeiten am Widerspruch*, 65–120.
48 Plumpe, 'Dies ewig unfertige Ding'.
49 Stedman Jones, *Manifesto*.
50 Preface to Zur Kritik der politischen Ökonomie of 1859, Karl Marx, Ökonomische Manuskripte und Schriften, 1858–1861, in: MEGA² II/2, 100f.; Preface to *A Contribution to the Critique of Political Economy* MECW, vol. 29, 263.
51 MEGA² II/2, 101, MECW, vol. 29, 263.
52 Michael Krätke, 'Friedrich Engels und die grossen Transformationen des Kapitalismus', in: Lucas, Pfriem and Westhoff (eds), *Arbeiten am Widerspruch*, 121–59, here 154.
53 Richard Tilly, *Vom Zollverein zum Industriestaat: Die wirtschaftlich-soziale Entwicklung Deutschlands 1834–1914* (Munich, 1990).
54 For example, in Sven Beckert, *Empire of Cotton: A New History of Global Capitalism* (New York, 2014).
55 Friedrich Engels, 'Cotton and Iron', *The Labour Standard*, 30 July 1881, in: MEGA² I/25, 281–3, here 281; MECW, vol. 24, 411; German translation: *Baumwolle und Eisen*, in: MEW, vol. 19, 283.
56 Friedrich Engels, 'The French Commercial Treaty', *The Labour Standard*, 18 June 1881, in: MEGA² I/25, 260–3, here 263; German translation: *Der Handelsvertrag mit Frankreich* (1881), in: MEW, vol. 19, 264; MECW, vol. 24, 392.

57　Ibid.
58　Ibid., 393.
59　Ibid.
60　On this, especially on the observations made by Engels in the context of his work on volumes 2 and 3 of *Das Kapital*, see Krätke, *Friedrich Engels*.
61　Engels, *Condition of the Working Class*, passim.
62　Marx, *Ökonomische Manuskripte*, 102; MECW, vol. 29, 263.
63　Friedrich Engels, *Anti-Dühring*, in: MEGA² I/27; MECW, vol. 25, 5–312.
64　Friedrich Engels, *Die Entwicklung des Sozialismus von der Utopie zur Wissenschaft*, in: MEGA² I/27, 581–627. English translation by Edward Aveling (1892), *Socialism Utopian and Scientific*, in: MECW, vol. 24, 281–325.
65　Ibid., 609.
66　MEGA² I/27, 614; MECW, vol. 24, 313, original emphasis.
67　MEGA² I/27, 615; MECW, vol. 24, 314.
68　MEGA² I/27, 615; MECW, vol. 24, 314–15.
69　Ibid.
70　Friedrich Engels, *Anti-Dühring*, 3rd ed., II. Theoretical, in: MEGA² I/27, 532; MECW, vol. 24, 316.
71　Engels, *Die Entwicklung des Sozialismus*, 617ff., see also MEW, vol. 19, 220ff.; MECW, vol. 24, 317–18.
72　Engels, *Die Entwicklung des Sozialismus*, 622; MECW, vol. 24, 322.
73　Ibid., 322–3.
74　Friedrich Engels, 'Discours prononcé lors des obsèques de Karl Marx', in: *La Justice*, 20 March 1883, in: MEGA² I/25, 405ff. German translation: *Entwurf zur Grabrede von Karl Marx*, in: MEW, vol. 19, 333ff.; MECW, vol. 24, 463–6.
75　See Vladimir Ilyich Lenin, 'Der Imperialismus als höchstes Stadium des Kapitalismus. Gemeinverständlicher Abriss' (1917), in: Vladimir I. Lenin, *Ausgewählte Werke*, vol. II (Frankfurt, 1970), 643–770. English edition: *Imperialism, the Highest Stage of Capitalism* (London, 2010); Rosa Luxemburg, 'Die Akkumulation des Kapitals: Ein Beitrag zur ökonomischen Erklärung des Imperialismus' (1913), in: *Gesammelte Werke*, vol. 5 (Berlin, 1985), 5–412. English edition: *The Accumulation of Capital: A Contribution to an Economic Explanation of Imperialism* (Abingdon, 2003).
76　Friedrich Engels, 'Elektricität', in: *Dialektik der Natur (1873–1882)*, in: MEGA² I/26, 471–516; MECW, vol. 25, 402–51.
77　Ulrich Ruschig, 'Über den Marxismus der kritischen Theorie: Horkheimers Aufnahme und Weiterführung von Engels' Die Entwicklung des Sozialismus von der Utopie zur Wissenschaft', *Zeitschrift für Kritische Theorie*, vol. 22 (2016), 76–96.

CHAPTER 8

1　Friedrich Engels, *Briefe aus dem Wuppertal*, in: *Telegraph für Deutschland*, March and April 1839, in: MEGA² I/3, 32–51, here 34; *Letters from Wuppertal*, MECW, vol. 2, 9.
2　Ibid., 7.
3　Angus Bethune Reach, *Manchester and the Textile Districts in 1849*, C. Aspin (ed.) (Helmshore, 1972), 1.
4　Quoted in Asa Briggs, *Victorian Cities* (New York, 1963), 89.
5　'The purple waves of the narrow river flow sometimes swiftly, sometimes sluggishly between smoky factory buildings and yarn-strewn bleaching-yards. Its bright red colour, however,

Notes

is due not to some bloody battle ... but simply and solely to the numerous dye-works using Turkey red' (Engels, *Letters*, MECW, vol. 2, 7).

6   Roger Lloyd-Jones and M. J. Lewis, *Manchester and the Age of the Factory: The Business Structure of Cottonopolis in the Industrial Revolution* (London, 1988), 33. There were by then two large firms there, each employing more than 1,000 workers (ibid.).

7   Catherine Bowler and Peter Brimblecome, 'Control of Air Pollution Prior to the Public Health Act of 1875', *Environment and History* 6 (2000), 71–98, here 76; Hans J. Teuteberg, 'Zeitgenössische deutsche Reflexionen über die Rolle des Faktors Arbeit in den frühen Phasen der britischen Industrialisierung (1750–1850)', in: Hermann Kellenbenz (ed.), *Wirtschaftspolitik und Arbeitsmarkt* (Munich, 1974), 238–70, here 260.

8   Lloyd-Jones and Evans, *Manchester*, 111.

9   Hans J. Teuteberg, *Zeitgenössische deutsche Reflexionen*, 260.

10 Duncan Bythell, *The Sweated Trades: Outwork in Nineteenth-Century Britain* (London, 1978), 36ff.

11 Beginning in the mid-1820s, several severe crises shook the cotton trade (1826, 1829, 1837–8 and 1841), caused by cotton speculation in England and the United States, the collapse of some American banks in 1837–8 and several poor harvests – the last in 1841.

12 Georg Weerth, *Sämtliche Werke*, vol. 3: *Die englischen Arbeiter* (Berlin, 1957), 210; own translation.

13 Joyce Burnette, *Gender, Work and Wages in the Industrial Revolution* (Cambridge, 2008), 265; J. L. Hammond and Barbara Hammond, *The Skilled Labourer 1760–1832* (reprint New York, 1967), 149.

14 Michael Knieriem, 'Die Firma Ermen & Engels in Manchester und Engelskirchen im 19. Jahrhundert', *Marx-Engels-Jahrbuch* 10 (1987), 211–34, here 219.

15 Reach, *Manchester*, 12.

16 Burnette, *Gender*, 265.

17 In the crisis years of 1829–30, wage cuts led to a series of strikes among the spinners; see R. G. Kirby and A. E. Musson, *The Voice of the People: John Doherty (1798–1854) Trade Unionist, Radical and Factory Reformer* (Manchester, 1975), 85.

18 Friedrich Engels, *Die Lage der arbeitenden Klasse in England*, 1st ed. 1845, in: MEGA^1 I/4, Berlin 1932, 10–286, here 134; *The Condition of the Working Class in England*, MECW, vol. 4, 295–596.

19 Reach, *Manchester*, 14. The coinage abbreviations here and below are: s = shilling, d = penny (plural pence – 12d = 1s); ha'penny = half a penny, farthing = quarter of a penny.

20 Ibid., 21, 51.

21 Ibid., 21, 48ff.

22 See also Engels, who refers to a proportion of women as 50–70 per cent, based on the data of Lord Ashley in 1844, Engels, *Lage*, 143; *Condition*, MECW, 436.

23 The payroll of Courtauld's Factory [http://www.womeninworldhistory.com/textile.html (retrieved 24 February 2020)] shows 114 men and 899 women as working there; see also Carol Adams, Paula Bartley, Judy Lown and Cathy Loxton, *Under Control: Life in a Nineteenth-Century Silk Factory* (Cambridge, 1983), 17; for 1861, Courtauld's gives the number of women as 901 and of men as 114.

24 Knieriem, 219. In the associated bleachery, Ermen & Engels employed another twenty-seven men and fifty-eight women. Only men and a few boys worked in the dye works.

25 Nicola Verdon, *Rural Women Workers in Nineteenth-Century England: Gender, Work and Wages* (Woodbridge, 2002), 11ff.

26 Erich Richards, 'Women and the British Economy since about 1700: An interpretation', *History* 59 (1974), 337–57; for a discussion, see also Burnette, *Gender*, 306–11.

Notes

27 H. M. Boot and J. H. Maindonald, 'New Estimates, of Age- and Sex-Specific Earnings and the Male: Female Earnings Gap in the British Cotton Industry', 1833–1906, in: *The Economic History Review* 61 (2008), 380–404, here 399–403.
28 Engels, *Lage*, 137; *Condition*, 432: He cites average weekly wages of 8s to 9s for women.
29 Reach, *Manchester*, 76, 89; see also Paul Minoletti, '"The Importance of Ideology:" The Shift to Factory Production and Its Effect on Women's Employment Opportunities in the English Textile Industries", *Discussion Papers in Economic and Social History* 87 (February 2011), 1 (http://www.nuff.ox.ac.uk/Economics/History).
30 Minoletti, 'The importance of ideology'.
31 Ibid., 7.
32 Engels, *Lage*, 138; *Condition*, MECW, vol. 4, 435.
33 Courtauld's factory payroll [http://www.womeninworldhistory.com/textile.html (retrieved 24 February 2020)]; D. C. Coleman, *Courtaulds: An Economic and Social History* (Oxford, 1969), 232.
34 Minoletti, 'Importance', 18.
35 Burnette, *Gender*, 3.
36 Minoletti, 'Importance', 5ff.
37 Joyce Burnette, *Women Workers in the British Industrial Revolution*, EH Net, 6.
38 Boot and Maindonald, *New Estimates*, 395.
39 Burnette, *Women Workers*, 9.
40 Ibid.; see also Burnette, 'An Investigation of the Female-Male Wage Gap during the Industrial Revolution', *Economic History Review* 59 (1999), 257–81, 268f.
41 Burnette, *Gender*, 327.
42 See for example ibid., 306; Friedrich Engels, *Der Ursprung der Familie, des Privateigentums und des Staats*, in: MEGA² I/29, 41; *The Origin of the Family, Private Property and the State*, MECW, vol. 26, 129–276.
43 Engels, *Lage*, 140; *Condition*, MECW, vol. 4, 436.
44 Engels' moral reservations and his concern about the dissolution of family structures through women's factory work can be seen as characteristic of many contemporaries; see ibid., 137ff.
45 Burnette, *Gender*, 326.
46 See Gisela Mettele, 'Mary and Lizzy Burns, the life companions of Friedrich Engels', *Marx-Engels Jahrbuch* (2011), 130–49; see also W. O. Henderson, *Marx and Engels and the English Workers and Other Essays* (London, 1989), 37, where he describes Mary as an 'Irish millhand' who lived in Ancoats, the industrial quarter of Manchester.
47 Mettele, *Burns*, 131. Mary Burns is described as a maid in the tax lists of the 1840s and as a cotton spinner on her death certificate.
48 Seasonal harvest labourers were not a specifically Irish-English phenomenon. Cross-border unskilled agricultural seasonal workers and harvest labourers also existed in Germany, such as the so-called *Hollandgänger* from north-west Germany; see Horst Rössler, 'Hollandgänger, Zuckerbäcker, Amerikaauswanderer. Grenzüberschreitende Fernwanderungen aus dem Elbe-Weser-Dreieck (ca. 1650–1914)', *Niedersächsisches Jahrbuch für Landesgeschichte* 81 (2009), 31–55.
49 See Engels, 'Die irische Einwanderung': 'These Irishmen Who Migrate for Fourpence to England'; Engels, *Lage*, 91; *Condition*, MECW, vol.4, 390.
50 Donald MacRaild, *Irish Migrants in Modern Britain 1750–1922* (London, 1999), 45; see also Arthur Redford, *Labour Migration in England 1800–1850*, 2nd ed. W. H. Chaloner (ed.) (Manchester, 1964), 141–9.
51 John Belchem, *Irish, Catholic and Scouse: The History of the Liverpool Irish, 1800–1939* (Liverpool, 2007), 31ff.
52 Engels, *Lage*, 93; *Condition*, MECW, vol. 4, 392.

Notes

53 MacRaild, *Irish Migrants*, 51.
54 Mervyn A. Busteed and Rob I. Hodgson, 'Irish Migrant Responses to Urban Life in Early Nineteenth-Century Manchester', *The Geographical Journal* 162 (1996), 139–52, here 145.
55 Redford, *Labour Migration*, 151ff.; F. J. Williams, 'Irish in the East Cheshire Silk Industry 1851–1861', *The Historic Society of Lancashire & Cheshire* 136 (1986) [https://www.hslc.org.uk/wp-content/up-loads/2017/11/136-7-Williams.pdf (retrieved 12 March 2020)]. Although the majority of Irish were unskilled workers, in some cities there was a significant proportion of semi-skilled or low-skilled Irish; see MacRaild, *Irish Migrants*, 70. In Birmingham the proportion of skilled Irish was relatively higher; see Roger Swift (ed.), *Irish Migrants in Britain, 1815–1914* (Cork, 2002), Doc. 8.6, *The Irish in Birmingham 1872*, 45.
56 Belchem, *Irish Liverpool*, 1.
57 Jakob Venedey, *England* (Leipzig, 1845), 249 [http://mdz-nbn-resolving.de/urn:nbn:de:bvb:12-bsb10282154-1 (retrieved 20 February 2020)]; own translation.
58 MacRaild, *Irish Migrants*, 55; Busteed and Hodgson, 'Irish migrant responses', 139–53.
59 MacRaild, *Irish Migrants*, 59ff.
60 Busteed and Hodgson, 'Irish Migrant Responses', 145ff.
61 Engels, *Lage*, 63; *Condition*, MECW, vol. 4, 361.
62 Venedey, *England*, 5 May 1844, 264; Graham Davis, 'The Irish in Nineteenth Century Britain', *Saothar* 16 (1991), 130–5, 134. J. P. Kay, *The Moral and Physical Condition of the Working Classes in the Cotton Manufacture in Manchester* (Manchester, 1832); Kay also strongly influenced Engels' views.
63 Davis, 'The Irish in Nineteenth Century Britain', 131; F. J. Williams, *Irish in the Cheshire Silk Industry*, 108. [https://www.hslc.org.uk/wp-content/uploads/2017/11/136-7-Williams.pdf (retrieved 24 February 2020)].
64 British Parliamentary Papers Report on the State of the Irish Poor 1836, VII–IX; –XXX–XXXI, quoted in Williams, *The Irish in the Cheshire Silk Industry*, 101; MacRaild, *Irish Migrants*, 56f.
65 Engels, *Lage*, 90–93; *Condition*, MECW, vol. 4, 392; similar remarks can be found in Weerth, *Die englischen Arbeiter*, 200ff.
66 Robert L. Boyd, 'Competition and Coexistence in the Urban Economy: Native Whites, European Immigrants, and the Retail Trade in the Late Nineteenth Century United States', *Sociological Focus* 44 (2011), 37–54.
67 MacRaild, *Irish Migrants*, 167.
68 Samuel Holme before the Royal Commission on the Conditions of the Poorer Classes in Ireland, Appendix G: Report on the Irish Poor in Britain, 36, quoted in: MacRaild, *Irish Migrants*, 52, 56.
69 Henry Mayhew, *The Morning Chronicle Survey of Labour and the Poor: The Metropolitan Districts*, vol. 6, Caliban Books (ed.) (Horsham, 1982), 172ff. The division of labour was more advanced in the London tanneries than in Germany; see Reinhold Reith (ed.), *Lexikon des alten Handwerks. Vom späten Mittelalter bis ins 20. Jahrhundert* (Munich, 1991), esp. 84–91, on tanners. The only skilled workers in the manufacture of leather in London were the leather finishers. They formed a separate occupational group with a powerful trade union.
70 Swift (ed.), *Irish Migrants*, Doc 9.2, 54.
71 The wage gap between Germany and London made it attractive for North German workers who came from agriculture to go into the sugar industry in London, especially considering the associated prospect of an improvement in living conditions; see Horst Rössler, '"Die Zuckerbäcker waren vornehmlich Hannoveraner": Zur Geschichte der Wanderung aus dem Elbe-Weser-Dreieck in die britische Zuckerindustrie', in: *Jahrbuch der Männer vom Morgenstern* (Bremerhaven, 2003), 137–236.
72 Redford, *Labour Migration*, 150–4.

73 Engels speaks in *Lage*, 29, of 'dritthalb Millionen'; *Condition* (MECW, vol. 4, 328) translates accurately 'two and a half millions of human beings'. According to Wrigley and Schofield, London had a population of just under 2 million in 1841 and more than 2.3 million in 1851; see Edward A. Wrigley and Roger Schofield, *The Population History of England 1541–1871: A Reconstruction* (London, 1981).
74 Francis Sheppard, *London 1808–1870: The Infernal Wen* (London, 1971).
75 Weerth, 'London', in: *Sämtliche Werke*, vol. 3, 44; own translation.
76 Engels, *Lage*, 29ff.; *Condition*, MECW, vol. 4, 328.
77 Reach, *Manchester*, 3.
78 Engels, *Lage*, 33ff.; *Condition*, MECW, vol. 4, 332.
79 David R. Green, *From Artisans to Paupers: Economic Change and Poverty in London, 1790–1870* (Aldershot, 1995), 183; on the Irish in London, see also L. H. Lees, *Exiles of Erin: Irish Migrants in Victorian London* (Manchester, 1979).
80 See also Engels, who reports that the city had begun to cut wide roads through St Giles, *Lage*, 32.
81 Gareth Stedman Jones, *Outcast London: A Study in the Relationship Between Classes in Victorian Society* (Oxford, 1971), 216ff.
82 Panikos Panayi, *German Immigrants in Britain During the 19th Century, 1815–1914* (Oxford, 1995), 97; see also Christiane Swinbank, '"Love ye the stranger": Public and private assistance to the German poor in nineteenth-century London', PhD thesis, Reading, 2007.
83 See Iorwerth J. Prothero, *Artisans and Politics in Early Nineteenth-Century London* (Folkstone, 1979), 2; M. Dorothy George, *London Life in the Eighteenth Century* (Harmondsworth, 1965), 15; see also David Barnett, *London, Hub of the Industrial Revolution: A Revisionary History 1775–1825* (London, 1998), 2.
84 See in detail on the example of tailoring Andrew Godley, 'Immigrant Entrepreneurs and the Emergence of London's East End as an Industrial District', *The London Journal* 21 (1996), 38–45; Barnett, *London*, loc. cit.
85 On his biography, see Edward P. Thompson, 'Mayhew and the *Morning Chronicle*', and Eileen Yeo, 'Mayhew as a Social Investigator', in: *The Unknown Mayhew: Selection from the Morning Chronicle 1849–1850*, Thompson and Yeo (eds) (London, 1971), 11–50 and 51–95, here 81.
86 He developed a new journalistic method of investigation, letting interviewees speak for themselves. Today, his reportage is a treasure trove for research into London's lower classes; for detail, see Yeo, *Unknown Mayhew*, 54–58.
87 J. L. Hammond and Barbara Hammond, *The Skilled Labourer 1760–1832* (reprint New York, 1967), 209; on strikes and violence, see Margrit Schulte Beerbühl, *Vom Gesellenverein zur Gewerkschaft. Entwicklung, Struktur und Politik der Londoner Gesellenorganisationen 1550–1825* (Göttingen, 1991), 246ff.
88 See on this and the following R. H. Jones, 'Technology, Transaction Costs and the Transition to Factory Production in the British Silk Industry 1700–1870', *The Journal of Economic History* 47 (1987), 71–96, 78–80.
89 Jones, 'Technology', 82.
90 Ibid., 84, footnote 64.
91 Ibid., 85.
92 Jones, *Outcast London*, 101.
93 Engels, *Lage*, 188; *Condition*, MECW, vol. 4, 488.
94 Yeo, *Unkown Mayhew*, 111ff. Average working hours had been ten hours a day at an average wage of 14s 6d a week by 1824; by 1850, working hours were fourteen hours a day at an average weekly wage of 4s 9d.
95 Jones, *Outcast London*, 101.
96 Jones, 'Technology', 90.

Notes

97 Ibid., 88.
98 Ibid., 93.
99 On the decline of shipbuilding and its impact on many trades, see Jones, *Outcast London*.
100 Engels, *Lage*, 85ff; *Condition*, MECW, vol. 4, 385.
101 Ibid., 33; MECW, vol. 4, 332.
102 Henry Mayhew, *London Labour and the London Poor*, 4 vols. (London, 1861–2), vol. 1, 104.
103 Ibid., vol. 1, 104, 114.
104 Ibid., 104ff.
105 Mayhew compared the difference between a regular street trader (costermonger) and an Irish apple seller to that between a craftsman and a day labourer (see ibid., 105).
106 Georg Weerth, *Die englischen Arbeiter* [http://www.zeno.org/nid/20005876877 (retrieved 25 March 2020)].
107 Mayhew, *London Labour*, vol. 2, 136f.; own translation.
108 Ibid., vol. 1, 117ff.
109 Ibid., 130–9.
110 Ibid., 468–72.
111 Ibid., 135.
112 Ibid., 472.
113 Ibid., 106ff.
114 Ibid., vol. 2, 121.
115 Ibid., 119ff.
116 Lloyd P. Gartner, *The Jewish Immigrant in England 1870–1914* (London, 1960), 283; Bernard Gainer, *The Alien Invasion: The Origins of the Aliens Act of 1905* (London, 1972), 3.
117 Gainer, *Alien Invasion*, 3, 5.
118 Bill Williams, *The Making of the Manchester Jewry, 1740–1875* (Manchester, 1985), 57, 268.
119 Panayi, *German Immigrants*, 97ff. New centres for Germans emerged further east in London in Canning Town and the Victoria Docks, and west in Battersea; Swift, *Irish Migrants*, Doc. 10.7, 'The Economic Condition of the Irish in late-Victorian Liverpool', 62.
120 According to Gainer, *Alien Invasion*, 20.
121 Ibid., 20ff.
122 Ibid., 17.
123 Georg Weerth, *Die englischen Arbeiter* [http:// www.zeno.org/nid/20005876877 (retrieved 25 March 2020)].
124 MacRaild, *Irish Migrants*, 65ff., 72; Lees, *Exiles of Erin*, 117–22.
125 Heinrich Heine, *Lutetia*, Teil 2, Artikel LVII, Paris, 5 May 1843 [http://www.heinrich-heine-denkmal.de/heine-texte/lutetia57.html (retrieved 27 January 2018)]; William Fardely, *Der electrische Telegraph, mit bes. Berücksichtigung seiner praktischen Anwendung für den Betrieb von Eisenbahnen etc.* (Mannheim, 1844), 62.
126 Strikes, protests and violence were expressions of the absence of modern labour relations. These had to be painstakingly won at first.
127 MacRaild, *Irish Immigrants*, 42ff.
128 See Barnett, *London*, 161, 163, on the rise in assured wealth of shoemakers and clothing retailers.

CHAPTER 9

1 See Gregory Claeys, 'Engels' Outlines of a Critique of Political Economy (1843) and the Origins of the Marxist Critique of Capitalism', *History of Political Economy* 16(2), 1984,

207-32; Claeys, 'The Political Ideas of the Young Engels, 1842-1845: Owenism, Chartism, and the Question of Violent Revolution in the Transition from "Utopian" to "Scientific" Socialism', *History of Political Thought* 6, 1986, 455-78; Terence W. Hutchison, 'Friedrich Engels and Marxist Economic Theory', *Journal of Political Economy* 86(2), 1978, 303-19; Gareth Stedman Jones, 'Engels and the Genesis of Marxism', *New Left Review* 106, 1977, 79-104; Stedtman Jones, 'Engels, Friedrich (1820-1895)', *The New Palgrave* 2, 1987, 144-6; Harry Schmidtgall, *Friedrich Engels' Manchester-Aufenthalt 1842-1844. Soziale Bewegungen und politische Diskussionen* with excerpts from Jakob Venedey's book on England (1845) and unknown documents of Friedrich Engels' (Schriften aus dem Karl-Marx-Haus, no. 25, Trier 1981); Keith Tribe, *The Economy of the Word: Language, History, and Economics* (Oxford, 2015), ch. 6. For general background, see also the major Engels biographies by Gustav Mayer, *Friedrich Engels. Eine Biographie, vol. 1: Friedrich Engels in seiner Frühzeit 1820 bis 1851* (Berlin, 1920), and Tristram Hunt, *The Frock-Coated Communist: The Life and Times of the Original Champagne Socialist* (London, 2009). And see especially the recent article by Heinz D. Kurz, 'Der junge Engels über die "Bereicherungswissenschaft", die "Unsittlichkeit" von Privateigentum und Konkurrenz und die "Heuchelei der Oekonomen"', in: Reiner Lucas, Reinhard Pfriem and Dieter Westhoff (eds), *Arbeiten am Widerspruch – Friedrich Engels zum 200. Geburtstag* (Marburg, 2020), 65-121, as well as Kurz's essay 'This Frederick! This Frederick!' in the present volume, XXX, which critically scrutinizes the remarks Engels makes in his foundational *Outlines* on Smith, Ricardo, Marx and Say. The initial critical reception of Engels' essay (and esp. of his *Condition of the Working Class in England*) in Germany, exemplified in Bruno Hildebrand's *Die Nationalökonomie der Gegenwart und Zukunft* (Frankfurt, 1848) – after Hildebrand had himself visited the English manufacturing centres in 1846 – should not be overlooked either (see Mayer, *Friedrich Engels*, 208).

2 On 'revolution from above', see for example Paul Nolte, *Staatsbildung als Gesellschaftsreform: Politische Reformen in Preussen und den süddeutschen Staaten 1800-1820* (Frankfurt, New York, 1990), 32; Georg Winter, *Die Reorganisation des Preussischen Staates unter Stein und Hardenberg, erster Teil: Allgemeine Verwaltungs- und Behördenreform*, vol. 1. (Leipzig, 1931), 306. On the continuation of the reforms after the end of the Napoleonic Empire, see for example Elisabeth Fehrenbach, *Vom Ancien Régime zum Wiener Kongress* (Munich, 2001), 115; Friedrich Lütge, 'Über die Auswirkungen der Bauernbefreiung in Deutschland', *Jahrbücher für Nationalökonomie und Statistik* 157, 1943, 353-404, here 361; Thomas Nipperdey, *Deutsche Geschichte 1800-1866: Bürgerwelt und starker Staat* (Munich, 1998), 21, 33; Wolfgang Treue, 'Die preussische Agrarreform zwischen Romantik und Rationalismus', *Rheinische Vierteljahrs-Blätter* 20, no. 1/4, 1955, 337-57, here 337.

3 With the transition of formerly royal and princely property into the possession of the state, court and state exchequers were separated. The monarch received compensation in terms of a fixed annual allowance sufficient for an appropriate lifestyle as well as for representational purposes.

4 August Hennings, *Historisch-Moralische Schilderung des Einflusses der Hofhaltungen auf das Verderben der Staaten* (Altona), reprint from *Schleswigsches Journal* 5, 1782, 46, 389.

5 Volker Bauer, *Hofökonomie: Der Diskurs über den Fürstenhof in Zeremonialwissenschaft, Hausväterliteratur und Kameralismus* (Vienna, 1997), 267f.; Friedrich Wilhelm Rudolf Zimmermann, 'Die Zivilliste in den deutschen Staaten', in: Georg Schanz and Julius Wolf (eds), *Finanz- und volkswirtschaftliche Zeitfragen*, issue 60 (Stuttgart, 1919), 48ff.

6 For example Joseph v. Sonnenfels, *Grundsätze der Polizey, Handlung und Finanz*, vol. I (Vienna, 1787), 20f.

7 Gottlieb Hufeland, *Neue Grundlegung der Staatswirthschaftskunst durch Prüfung und Berichtigung ihrer Hauptbegriffe von Gut, Werth, Preis, Geld und Volksvermögen, mit un unterbrochener Rücksicht auf die bisherigen Systeme*, vol. I (Giessen, Wetzlar, 1807), 14.

Notes

8   See Kurz, 'Der junge Engels', 71.
9   The historian James Sheehan, *German History 1770–1866* (Oxford, 1989), 194, speaks of cameralism in this context as the 'science of political management'.
10 Hans Frambach, 'The Decline of Cameralism in Germany at the Turn of the Nineteenth Century', in: Keith Tribe and Marten Seppel (eds), *Cameralism in Practice: The Principles of Early Modern State Administration and Economy* (Martlesham, 2017), 239–61, here 239, 257.
11 Wilhelm Roscher, *Geschichte der National-Oekonomik in Deutschland* (Munich, 1874), 231, 473, 533ff., 593f., 635, 843; Joseph Alois Schumpeter, *Geschichte der ökonomischen Analyse*, vol. 1 (Göttingen, 1965), 229ff.
12 Examples of such views can be found in Christian J. Kraus, *Staatswirthschaft* (1811), Johann Georg Büsch, *Schriften über Staatswirtschaft und Handlung*, Gottlieb Hufeland, *Neue Grundlegung der Staatswirthschaftskunst*, Georg Friedrich Sartorius, *Handbuch der Staatswirthschaft zum Gebrauche bey akademischen Vorlesungen nach Adam Smith's Grundsätzen ausgearbeitet*, or Friedrich Benedict Weber, *Handbuch der Staatswirthschaft* (1804); see also Keith Tribe, 'Cameralism and the science of government', *Journal of Modern History* 56, (June 1984), 263–84, 278ff.; Tribe, *Governing Economy: The Reformation of German Economic Discourse, 1750–1840* (Cambridge, New York, Sydney, 1988), ch. 7, 147f.
13 See, for example, Johann Heinrich Gottlob v. Justi, *Gesammelte politische und Finanz-Schriften. Über wichtige Gegenstände der Staatskunst, der Kriegswissenschaften und des Kameral- und Finanzwesens*, vol. I, 1761/91 (Aalen, 1970), 524; Justi, *Die Grundfeste zu der Macht und Glückseligkeit der Staaten oder ausführliche Vorstellung der gesamten Polizeywissenschaft*, vol. I, 1760/61 (Aalen 1965), 701f.; Justi, *Staatswirthschaft oder systematische Abhandlung aller Oekonomischen und Cameralwissenschaften, die zur Regierung eines Landes erfordert werden*, vol. I, 1755/8 (Aalen, 1963), 152ff.; Justi, *System des Finanzwesens. Nach vernünftigen, aus dem Endzweck der bürgerlichen Gesellschaften und aus der Natur aller Quellen der Einkünfte des Staats hergeleiteten Grundsätze und Regeln abgehandelt*, repr. of first ed. 1766 (Aalen, 1969), 5; Sonnenfels, *Grundsätze der Polizey*, 22ff.
14 Keith Tribe's thesis that by the end of the eighteenth century the work of the German physiocrats rather than *The Wealth of Nations* represented the only substantial alternative to cameralism is also questionable (see Tribe, 'Cameralism and the science', 279). In basic positions, the leading German physiocrat Johann August Schlettwein (1731–1802), for example, agreed with the classical political economists; see Schlettwein, *Grundfeste der Staaten oder die politische Ökonomie* (Giessen, 1779), 1ff., 94ff., 111ff., 287ff.; Schlettwein, *Die Rechte der Menschheit oder der einzige wahre Grund aller Gesetze, Ordnungen und Verfassungen* (Giessen, 1784), 52ff., 69ff., 90ff., 161ff.
15 Andre Wakefield, *The Disordered Police State: German Cameralism as Science and Practice* (Chicago, London, 2009), 5.
16 Frambach, 'The Decline of Cameralism', 259; Klaus Hinrich Hennings, *Aspekte der Institutionalisierung der Ökonomie an deutschen Universitäten: Die Institutionalisierung der Nationalökonomie an deutschen Universitäten* (St. Katharinen, 1988), 46f.
17 Karl Heinrich Rau, *Grundsätze der Volkswirthschaftspflege mit anhaltender Rücksicht auf bestehende Staatseinrichtungen* (*Lehrbuch der politischen Oekonomie*, vol. II) (Heidelberg, 1828), 1.
18 Friedrich Julius Heinrich Reichsgraf von Soden, *Die Nazional-Oekonomie: Ein philosophischer Versuch, über die Quellen des Nazional-Reichthums, und über die Mittel zu dessen Beförderung* (Leipzig, 1805), 24.
19 Sartorius, *Handbuch der Staatswirthschaft*, 92, 98ff.
20 Heinrich Luden, *Handbuch der Staatsweisheit oder der Politik. Ein wissenschaftlicher Versuch* (Jena, 1811), 4f.

21 Friedrich Engels, *Umrisse zu einer Kritik der Nationalökonomie*, in: Arnold Ruge and Karl Marx (eds), *Deutsch-Französische Jahrbücher* (Paris, 1844), 86–114, in: MEGA² I/3, 467–94, 467; English translation: *Outlines of a Critique of Political Economy*, MECW, vol. 3, 418–43, here 418, and see also Martin Milligan's 1996 translation at https://www.marxists.org/archive/marx/works/1844/df-jahrbucher/outlines.htm (retrieved 18 June 2021).
22 See, for example, Friedrich Engels, *Briefe aus dem Wuppertal*, in: *Telegraph für Deutschland*, no. 49, March and April 1839, in: MEGA² I/3, 32–51, esp. 32, 34f.; *Letters from Wuppertal*, MECW, vol. 2, 7–25; Engels, *Die Lage der arbeitenden Klasse in England. Nach eigner Anschauung und authentischen Quellen*, 1845, in: MEGA¹ I/4, Berlin 1932, 10–286, 29ff.; *The Condition of the Working Class in England*, MECW, vol. 4, 295–596; Engels, 'Preussischer Schnaps im deutschen Reichstag', in: *Der Volksstaat*, no. 23, 25 February 1876, in: MEGA² I/25, 30–46, 35; 'Prussian Schnapps in the German Reichstag', MECW, vol. 24, 109–28.
23 William Otto Henderson, *The Life of Friedrich Engels* (London, 1976), 7; Mayer, *Friedrich Engels*, 22f.
24 Hunt, *The Frock-Coated Communist*, 39.
25 Engels, *Briefe aus dem Wuppertal*, 43, 47, 49; *Letters from Wuppertal*, MECW, vol. 2, 7–25.
26 For further details, see Kurz, 'Der junge Engels'.
27 Engels, *Umrisse*, 471; *Outlines*, MECW, vol. 3, 420.
28 Ibid., 472.
29 Johann Gottlieb Fichte, *Der geschlossne Handelsstaat: Ein philosophischer Entwurf als Anhang zur Rechtslehre, und Probe einer künftig zu liefernden Politik mit einem bisher unbekannten Manuskript Fichtes 'Ueber StaatsWirthschaft'*, 1800 (Hamburg, 1979), 36f.
30 Georg Wilhelm Friedrich Hegel, *Jenaer Realphilosophie. Vorlesungsmanuskripte zur Philosophie der Natur und des Geistes von 1805–1806*, reprinted from Johannes Hoffmeister's 1931 ed. of *Jenenser Realphilosophie II 1805–06* (Hamburg, 1969), 232.
31 Hans Frambach, *Arbeit im ökonomischen Denken: Zum Wandel des Arbeitsverständnisses von der Antike bis zur Gegenwart* (Marburg, 1999), ch. 5.
32 Franz v. Baader, *Schriften zur Gesellschaftsphilosophie*, 1835 (Jena, 1925), 325.
33 Adam H. Müller, *Die Elemente der Staatskunst*, 1809 (Vienna, Leipzig, 1922), vol. I, 357, 376, 380.
34 Friedrich List, *Das nationale System der Politischen Oekonomie*, 1840 (Jena, 1904), 220ff.
35 Hildebrand, *Die Nationalökonomie*, 27ff.
36 Bruno Hildebrand, 'Die gegenwärtige Aufgabe der Wissenschaft der Nationalökonomie', in: idem, *Die Nationalökonomie der Gegenwart und Zukunft und andere gesammelte Schriften I*, 1848 (Jena, 1922), 268–96, here 284.
37 Werner Conze, s.v. 'Arbeit', in: Otto Brunner, Werner Conze and Reinhart Koselleck (eds), *Geschichtliche Grundbegriffe. Historisches Lexikon zur politisch-sozialen Sprache in Deutschland* (Stuttgart, 1972), 154–215, here 191f.
38 Hermann Wagener, 'Arbeit, Arbeiter, Arbeitszeit', in: *Staats- und Gesellschaftslexikon*, vol. II (Berlin, 1859), 478–89, 479f., here 486.
39 Friedrich Lange, *Die Arbeiterfrage: Ihre Bedeutung für Gegenwart und Zukunft*, 1865 (Leipzig, 1910), 16.
40 Gustav von Schmoller, *Zur Social- und Gewerbepolitik der Gegenwart. Reden und Aufsätze* (Leipzig, 1890), 2.
41 Schmoller, 'Die Arbeiterfrage', in: *Preussische Jahrbücher*, vols 14 and 15, 393–424 (Part I), 395; 523–47 (Part II) (Berlin, 1864).
42 Schmoller, *Grundriss der Allgemeinen Volkswirtschaftslehre*, 1900/23 (Berlin, 1978), 366.
43 Ibid., 362.
44 Schmoller, *Zur Social- und Gewerbepolitik*, 9, 12.

Notes

45 Wilhelm Roscher, *Die Grundlagen der Nationalökonomie. Ein Hand- und Lesebuch für Geschäftsmänner und Studierende*, vol. 1 (Stuttgart, 1854), 112ff., 122ff.
46 Karl Marx, z. B. in *Das Kapital I*, 1867, in: MEGA² II/5, 58, 113, 154, 163; MECW, vol. 35.
47 Karl Marx, *Ökonomische Manuskripte 1863-67*, in: MEGA² II/4.1, 50; *Das Kapital II, Manuskripte 1868-81*, in: MEGA² II/11, 712; MECW, vol. 36.
48 Engels, *Umrisse*, 483; *Outlines*, MECW, vol. 3, 431.
49 Ibid., 473; *Outlines*, ibid., 421-2.
50 Ibid.; *Outlines*, ibid., 422.
51 Ibid., 473f.; *Outlines*, ibid.
52 Ibid., 475; *Outlines*, ibid., 423.
53 Kurz, 'Der junge Engels', 81f.
54 Engels, *Umrisse*, 476; *Outlines*, ibid., 424f.
55 Ibid., 477; *Outlines*, ibid., 426.
56 Ibid.; *Outlines*, ibid.
57 Ibid., 478; *Outlines*, ibid., 427.
58 Ibid.; *Outlines*, ibid.
59 Ibid., 478f.; *Outlines*, ibid., 427f.
60 Adam Smith, *An Inquiry into the Nature and Causes of the Wealth of Nations* 1776, Edwin Cannan (ed.) (Chicago, London, 1952), 143.
61 John Stuart Mill, *Principles of Economics* (London, 1848/71); German translation: *Grundsätze der politischen Ökonomie mit einigen ihrer Anwendungen auf die Sozialphilosophie* (Jena, 1913/24), 66f.; Jean-Baptiste Say, *Traité d'économie politique* 1803/1826; German translation: *Ausführliche Darstellung der Nationalökonomie oder der Staatswirtschaft*, vol. 1 (Stuttgart, 1833), 47ff., 88ff.
62 Engels, *Umrisse*, 479; *Outlines*, MECW, vol. 3, 428.
63 Ibid., 480; *Outlines*, ibid., 429.
64 Ibid.; *Outlines*, ibid.
65 See also ibid., 482; *Outlines*, ibid., 431.
66 Ibid., 481; *Outlines*, ibid., 430.
67 Ibid.; *Outlines*, ibid.
68 Ibid., 482; *Outlines*, ibid., 431.
69 Ibid.; *Outlines*, ibid.
70 Ibid.; *Outlines*, ibid.
71 Ibid.; *Outlines*, ibid.
72 Ibid., 483; *Outlines*, ibid., 432.
73 Ibid.; *Outlines*, ibid.
74 Ibid.; *Outlines*, ibid.
75 Ibid., 483f.; *Outlines*, ibid., 433f.
76 Ibid., 484; *Outlines*, ibid.
77 Ibid.; *Outlines*, ibid., 434.
78 Ibid.; *Outlines*, ibid.
79 Ibid., 485; *Outlines*, ibid.
80 Ibid., 487; *Outlines*, ibid., 436.
81 Ibid., 485; *Outlines*, ibid., 434.
82 Ibid.; *Outlines*, ibid.
83 Ibid., 486; *Outlines*, ibid.
84 Ibid., 485; *Outlines*, ibid., 435.
85 Kurz, 'Der junge Engels', 73f.
86 Of particular interest here is the repetition of passages from the *Théorie des quatre mouvements* (draft of section 'On Three External Factors') printed in *Phalange* in 1845 after Fourier's death.

Engels had translated the first seven chapters, which he published in 1846 (with preface and afterword) as 'A Fragment of Fourier's on Trade' in H. Püttmann's *Deutsches Bürgerbuch*.

87 Charles Fourier, *Ein Fragment über den Handel*, with translation, introduction and afterword by Friedrich Engels, 1846 (Duisburg, Istanbul, 2018), 10f., 14; *A Fragment of Fourier's on Trade*, MECW, vol. 4, 613–44.
88 Engels, *Umrisse*, 487f.; *Outlines*, MECW, vol. 3, 437f.
89 Ibid., 487; *Outlines*, ibid., 437.
90 Ibid., 488; *Outlines*, ibid.
91 Friedrich Engels, *Briefe aus London* (I–IV), in: *Schweizerischer Republikaner*, no. 39, 16 May 1843 (I), no. 41, 23 May 1843 (II), no. 46, 9 June 1843 (III), no. 51, 27 June 1843 (IV), in: MEGA² I/3, 451–66; *Letters from London*, MECW, vol. 3, 379–91.
92 Ibid., 452.
93 Thomas Robert Malthus, *An Essay on the Principle of Population*, 1798; German translation: *Eine Abhandlung über das Bevölkerungsgesetz*, 1798/1826 (Jena, 1905), vol. I, 466ff.
94 Ibid., vol. II, 254ff.
95 Adolphe Blanqui, *Histoire de l'économie politique en Europe*, 1837; German translation: *Geschichte der politischen Ökonomie in Europa*, vol. 2, 1841 (Glashütten im Taunus, 1971), 105f.
96 Engels, *Briefe aus London*, 452; *Letters from London*.
97 William J. Brazill, *The Young Hegelians* (New Haven, London, 1970), 179, 194.
98 Ibid., 194.
99 Stephan Born, *Erinnerungen eines Achtundvierzigers* (Leipzig, 1898; Berlin, Bonn, 1978), 19, see also 26ff.
100 Mayer, *Friedrich Engels*, 67ff.
101 Hegel's idea of dialectical development understood history as a movement from affirmation, through negation, to negation of negation and the final triumph of reason and freedom, embodied in the Prussian state under Friedrich Wilhelm III. At the same time, Hegel saw the narrow Prussian Protestantism of the 1820s as the *summum bonum* of spirituality – a combination of ideas that presented the Young Hegelians (including Engels) with eminent reason for rebellion. For them the Prussian state was merely a stage on the way to the self-realization of the spirit and by no means the highest fulfilment of rationality.
102 Friedrich Engels Senior, 'Friedrich Engels (sen.) an Karl Wilhelm Moritz Snethlage in Berlin', Barmen, 5 October 1842, in: Michael Knieriem (ed.), *Die Herkunft des Friedrich Engels. Briefe aus der Verwandtschaft 1791–1847* (Trier, 1992), Schriften aus dem Karl-Marx-Haus, no. 42, 590–1, here 590f.
103 Hunt, *The Frock-Coated Communist*, 64ff.
104 Friedrich Engels, 'Progress on Social Reform on the Continent', *The New Moral World*, no. 19 (4 November 1843) and no. 21 (18 November 1843), in: MEGA² I/3, 495–510, 509; MECW, vol. 3, 392–408.
105 Moses Hess, *Sozialismus und Kommunismus. Einundzwanzig Bogen aus der Schweiz*, Georg Herwegh (ed.) (Zurich, Winterthur 1842), 74–91, here 77.
106 Ibid., 78.
107 Engels, 'Progress on Social Reform on the Continent', 509f.
108 See the essay by Eberhard Illner, 'Man and Machine', in the present volume, XXX.
109 In an article in the *Rheinische Zeitung*, no. 343 (9 December 1842), titled 'Die innern Krisen', Engels posed what he saw as the key question for the future of Great Britain: 'Is revolution in England possible or even probable?' (see MEGA² I/3, 439–43, 493; *The Internal Crises*, MECW, vol. 2, 370–4). The article was continued on the following day (*Rheinische Zeitung*, no. 344). In a further short article titled 'Lage der arbeitenden Klasse in England' for the

Notes

same newspaper on 25 December 1842 (*Rheinische Zeitung*, no. 359; MEGA² I/3, 447–8, 447; *The Condition of the Working Class in England*, MECW, vol. 2, 378–9), he poignantly described the workers' lot in Manchester and the ignorance of the state, which succeeded only in turning people without bread into people without morals.

110 Engels, *Die innern Krisen*, 443; *The Internal Crises*.
111 Henderson, *The Life of Friedrich Engels*, 40, footnotes 124 and 125; for the influence of James Leach, leader of the Manchester Chartists, on Engels, see Illner, ibid., XXX; see also Stedman Jones, 'Engels, Friedrich (1820–1895)', 145; Tribe, *The Economy of the Word*, 187.
112 Gregory Claeys, *Machinery, Money and the Millennium: From Moral Economy to Socialism 1815–60* (Cambridge, 1987), 169ff.; Tribe, *The Economy of the Word*, 187.
113 Engels, *Umrisse*, 467; *Outlines*, MECW, vol. 3, 418.
114 John Watts, *The Facts and Fictions of Political Economists: Being a Review of the Principles of the Science, Separating the True from the False* (Manchester, 1842), 6.
115 Ibid., 5f., 11ff., 21f., 28ff., 35f., 42, 48, 57f.
116 Engels, *Briefe aus London*, 455, 458; *Letters from London*.
117 Tribe, *The Economy of the Word*, 182.
118 Hermann Pechan, *Louis Blanc als Wegbereiter des modernen Sozialismus* (Jena, 1929), 91.
119 Louis Blanc, *Organisation du Travail*, first ed. 1840 (Brussels, 1848), 57ff.
120 Ibid., 117ff.
121 Ibid., 120.
122 Tribe, *The Economy of the Word*, 187.
123 Engels, *Progress on Social Reform*, 503.
124 Karl Diehl, *Pierre Joseph Proudhon: Seine Lehre und sein Leben*, 1888 (Aalen, 1968), 65, 99, 109.
125 Hess, *Sozialismus und Kommunismus*, 78.
126 Ibid., 78.
127 Ibid., 89f.
128 Engels, *Progress on Social Reform*, 495.
129 Engels, *Umrisse*, 492; *Outlines*, MECW, vol. 3, 439.
130 Engels, *Die Lage der arbeitenden Klasse*, 280; *Condition*, MECW, vol. 4, 581.
131 For example Albert Lindemann, *A History of European Socialism* (New Haven, London, 1983), 38; Schumpeter, *Geschichte der ökonomischen Analyse*, 271, 564.
132 Friedrich Engels, *Die Entwicklung des Sozialismus von der Utopie zur Wissenschaft*, 1882 (French original 1880), in: MEGA² I/27, 587–672, 593; *Socialism Utopian and Scientific*, MECW, vol. 24, 282–325.
133 Roscher, *Geschichte der National-Oekonomik*, 1020.
134 Karl Marx and Friedrich Engels, *Deutsche Ideologie: Manuskripte und Drucke* (1845–6), in: MEGA² I/5, 3–646, 552ff.; MECW, vol. 5, 19–539.
135 Ibid., 552.
136 Friedrich Engels, 'A Fragment of Fourier's on Trade', first published in the annual *Deutsches Bürgerbuch für 1846*, in: MECW, vol. 4, pp. 613–44, here 613–14, 641–4.
137 Ibid., 614.
138 Lorenz von Stein, *Geschichte der sozialen Bewegung in Frankreich von 1789 bis auf unsere Tage*, vol. I, 1850/Munich 1921 (Darmstadt, 1972), 117.
139 Ibid., 135f.
140 Ibid., 118.
141 Lorenz von Stein, 'Die soziale Bewegung und der Sozialismus in England', in: *Die Gegenwart* (Leipzig, 1849), 464–87, here 469.
142 Friedrich Engels, *Cola di Rienzi: Ein unbekannter dramatischer Entwurf* (1840–1), in: MEGA² I/3, 157–91; MECW, vol. 3, 537–68.

Notes

143 Letter to his school friend, the pastor's son and theology student Friedrich Graeber, late April 1839. *Friedrich Engels an Friedrich Graeber* (Bremen, about 23 April–1 May 1839), in: MEGA² III/1, 114–26, 114; MECW, vol. 2, 425–7.
144 Friedrich Engels, *Engels an Friedrich Graeber in Berlin* (Bremen, 12–27 July 1839), in: MEGA² III/1, 145–50, 149; MECW, vol. 2, 457–63.
145 Friedrich Engels, *Engels an Wilhelm Graeber in Berlin*, Bremen, 8 October 1839, in: MEGA² III/1, 160–2, 160; MECW, vol. 2, 471–4.
146 David Friedrich Strauss, *Das Leben Jesu, kritisch bearbeitet*, 1, vol. 1 (Tübingen, 1835), for example 50.
147 Stephen Henry Rigby, *Engels and the Formation of Marxism: History, Dialectics and Revolution* (Manchester, New York, 1992), 63.
148 Karl Marx and Friedrich Engels, *Manifest der Kommunistischen Partei*, 1848, in: MEW, vol. 4 (Berlin, 1972), 459–93, 462, 473ff., 481f., 493; *Manifesto of the Communist Party*, MECW, vol. 6, 477–519.
149 Joseph L. Bower and Clayton M. Christensen, 'Disruptive technologies: Catching the wave', in: *Harvard Business Review* 73, no. 1 (January–February 1995), 43–53.
150 Joseph Alois Schumpeter, *Capitalism, Socialism, and Democracy*, 1942 (New York, 2008), Cap. VII and VIII.
151 Joseph Alois Schumpeter, *Theorie der wirtschaftlichen Entwicklung*, 1912/34 (Berlin, 1997), 99ff., 207ff.
152 Schumpeter, *Geschichte der ökonomischen Analyse*, 34f.; see Alexander Ebner, 'Joseph A. Schumpeter und die Geschichte der ökonomischen Analyse', in: *Schumpeter, Geschichte der ökonomischen Analyse*, IX–XLI, XXff.; Hans Frambach, 'Der Schumpetersche Unternehmer in der Geschichte der ökonomischen Analyse', in: Hans Frambach, Norbert Koubek, Heinz D. Kurz and Reinhard Pfriem (eds), *Schöpferische Zerstörung und der Wandel des Unternehmertums* (Marburg, 2019), 213–28, here 213, 219f.
153 Werner Sombart, *Krieg und Kapitalismus* (Munich, Leipzig, 1913), 207.
154 Hugo Reinert and Erik Reinert, 'Creative Destruction in Economics: Nietzsche, Sombart, Schumpeter', in: Jürgen Backhaus and Wolfgang Drechsler (eds), *Friedrich Nietzsche (1844–1900): Economy and Society* (Boston, 2006), 55–85, here 58.
155 Friedrich Nietzsche, *Also sprach Zarathustra: Ein Buch für alle und keinen*, following the first ed. 1891 (Munich, 1980), 20; own trans.; see *Thus Spoke Zarathustra: A Book for All and None*, trans. A. Del Caro (Cambridge, 2006), 14.
156 Ibid., 50; own trans.; see ibid., 43.
157 Ibid., 54; own trans.; see ibid., 47.
158 Ibid., 95; own trans.; see ibid., 90.
159 Friedrich Nietzsche, *Ecce homo: Wie man wird, was man ist*, written 1888/9, first ed. 1908 (Berlin, 2013), 71; own trans.; see *Ecce Homo: How One Becomes What One Is*, trans. R. J. Hollingdale (Harmondsworth, 1979), 59.
160 Arno J. Mayer, *Adelsmacht und Bürgertum: Die Krise der europäischen Gesellschaft 1848–1914* (Munich, 1984), 286.
161 Reinert and Reinert, 'Creative Destruction', 56.
162 Eduard März, *Joseph Alois Schumpeter – Forscher, Lehrer und Politiker* (Munich, 1983), 99.
163 Friedrich Nietzsche, *Unzeitgemässe Betrachtungen* (1893/1954/Berlin, 2014), 292; own trans.; see *Thoughts out of Season*, trans. A. Collins (Edinburgh, London, 1909), 111.
164 Reinert and Reinert, 'Creative Destruction', 58.
165 Lars Immerthal, 'Dionysische Störungen: Ein Kommentar zur Her- und Zukunft der Metapher der "schöpferischen Zerstörung"', in: Frambach et al. (eds), *Schöpferische Zerstörung*, 455–80, 456ff.

Notes

166 Ibid., 457; Vivetta Vivarelli, 'Bacchus und die Titanenkämpfe als Gründungsmythen bei Hölderlin und Horaz', in: Anja Ernst and Paul Geyer (eds), *Die Romantik: ein Gründungsmythos der Europäischen Moderne* (Göttingen, 2010), 225–46, here 226.
167 Immerthal, 'Dionysische Störungen', 460.
168 Friedrich Hölderlin, 'Das Werden im Vergehen', in: Hölderlin, *Theoretische Schriften* (c. 1800), first printed in *Gesammelte Werke* (Jena, 1911/Berlin, 2013), 42–5, here 42.
169 Hunt, *The Frock-Coated Communist*, 18.
170 See for example the young Engels' poem 'Mir dämmert in der Ferne' of 1836, in: MEGA² I/3, 4; 'The evening sky grows dimmer', MECW, vol. 2, 554.
171 Engels, *Briefe aus dem Wuppertal*, 417; *Letters from Wuppertal*.
172 Friedrich Engels, *Die deutschen Volksbücher*, in: *Telegraph für Deutschland*, no. 186, November 1839, in: MEGA² III/1, 65–72, 65; MECW, vol. 2, 32–40.
173 Karl Marx and Friedrich Engels, *Manifest der Kommunistischen Partei*, 464, 472; *Manifesto of the Communist Party*, MECW, vol. 6, 477–519, here 486, 495.
174 See Henderson, *The Life of Friedrich Engels*; Hunt, *The Frock-Coated Communist*; Mayer, *Friedrich Engels*.
175 Hunt, *The Frock-Coated Communist*, 243.
176 Friedrich Engels to Eduard Bernstein, London, 8 February 1883, in: Eduard Bernstein (ed.), *Die Briefe von Friedrich Engels an Eduard Bernstein: Mit Briefen von Karl Kautsky an ebendenselben* (Berlin, 1883), 109–11, 110; MECW, vol. 46, 432ff.
177 Engels, Friedrich, *Dialektik der Natur* (1873–82), in: MEGA² I/26, chronological ordering, 5–288, 175; systematic ordering, 293–553; *Dialectics of Nature*, MECW, vol. 25, 313–590, here 356.
178 Ibid., 173f.; see also Hans Frambach, 'Zur Erklärung von wirtschaftlicher Entwicklung bei Karl Marx', in: Rainer Lucas, Reinhard Pfriem and Claus Thomasberger (eds), *Auf der Suche nach dem Ökonomischen – Karl Marx zum 200. Geburtstag* (Marburg, 2018), 23–41, here 27.
179 Friedrich Engels, *Herrn Eugen Dührings Umwälzung der Wissenschaft* (Anti-Dühring), written 1876–8, in: MEGA² I/27, 217–483, 331f.; MECW, vol. 25, 5–312.
180 Ibid., 332.
181 Henderson, *The Life of Friedrich Engels*, 681, 742, footnote 146; Hutchison, 'Friedrich Engels', 317.
182 Engels, preface to *Das Kapital*, vol. III, Friedrich Engels (ed.) (Hamburg, 1894), in: MEGA² II/15, 5–23, here 13; MECW, vol. 37, 13.
183 Engels, *Dialektik der Natur* (*Dialectics of Nature*), 49f.
184 Ibid., 50.
185 Ibid.
186 Here, in contrast to the earlier section of this chapter on 'Engels' perception of economic theory: II. The young moralist of *Outlines*' – reference is made especially to Engels' later writings. The young Engels had no theory of economic crisis in the strict sense. Fluctuations in economic development had been recognized as such since at least the seventeenth century and had been extensively described by mercantilists and classical political economists like Smith, Say, Malthus, Ricardo and Simonde de Sismondi, albeit (as is to be expected) with no (or scarce) explicit use of such concepts as 'crisis' or 'cycle'. Here, the young Engels is a true pioneer. Thus, the theories of economic development presented by Malthus – whose population theory, for example, to a great extent 'merely' summarized the economic thought of his day – and Simonde de Sismondi are in their economic analysis superior to the (frequently nonsensical) arguments of the young Engels, who confined his remarks to the critical description of gluts, dearths, stoppages etc. in the economic process (see Fourier, *Ein Fragment*, 24ff.; *A Fragment of Fourier's on Trade*). The later Engels, on the other hand, developed (in collaboration with, and indeed dependence on, Marx) a genuine theory of

crisis in the form of the 'law of the tendentially falling rate of profit' – one of the greatest of all crisis theories. Today, a confusing facet of this discussion is the widespread restriction of such terminology to the Marxist tradition: modern economic theories prefer to speak of cycles of expansion and contraction, cyclical growth, cyclical setbacks etc.
187 Engels, *Dialektik der Natur* (*Dialectics of Nature*), 50.
188 Karl Marx, *Zur Kritik der Hegelschen Rechtsphilosophie* (1844), in: MEGA^2 I/2, 5–138, 79; *Contribution to the Critique of Hegel's Philosophy of Law*: MECW, vol. 3, 175–87.
189 Engels, *Die Entwicklung*, 608; *Socialism Utopian and Scientific*.
190 Engels, *Umrisse*, 48; *Outlines*, MECW, vol. 3, 439.
191 See Hildebrand, *Die Nationalökonomie*, 155ff., 168ff., 196f., 202, 211ff., 226; Kurz, *Der junge Engels*, 69ff., 75, 81ff., 90ff., 105ff., 114ff.; Schumpeter, *Geschichte der ökonomischen Analyse*, 484.

CHAPTER 10

1 Gareth Stedman Jones, *Karl Marx: Greatness and Illusion* (Cambridge, MA, 2016), 569, speaks of 'noticeable changes in the character of his theory as a whole'.
2 Ibid., 711f.
3 Regina Roth, 'Marx on Technical Change in the Critical Edition', *European Journal of the History of Economic Thought*, 17(5), 2010, 1223–51, paid tribute to Engels' editorial achievement and to his skill in weaving the various manuscript sections and fragments in Marx's estate into a coherent whole.
4 John King raised these questions in private correspondence with me after reading my essay 'Der junge Engels' (65–120). It is an interesting question, to which the following paragraph can offer only a few fragments in terms of an answer.
5 In the preface to his *Zur Kritik der politischen Ökonomie* (*Contribution to the Critique of Political Economy*) of 1859, Marx wrote: 'Frederick Engels, with whom I maintained a constant exchange of ideas by correspondence since the publication of his brilliant essay on the critique of economic categories (printed in the *Deutsch-Französische Jahrbücher*), arrived by another road (compare his *Condition of the Working-Class in England*) at the same result as I'; Karl Marx, *Ökonomische Manuskripte und Schriften*, 1858–61, in: MEGA^2 II/2, 101/2; MECW, vol. 29, 264.
6 In response to Engels' essay, Marx buried himself from March to August 1844 in the works of Smith, Ricardo, Say etc.; see Stedman Jones, *Karl Marx*, 161.
7 Gareth Stedman Jones, 'Engels and the Genesis of Marxism', in: *New Left Review*, 106, 1977, 79–104; Terence W. Hutchison, 'Friedrich Engels and Marxist economic theory', in: *Journal of Political Economy*, 86, 1978, 303–19; Gregory Claeys, 'Engels' Outlines of a Critique of Political Economy (1844) and the Origins of the Marxist Critique of Capitalism', in: *History of Political Economy*, 16(2), 1984, 207–32; Claeys, 'The Political Ideas of the Young Engels. 1842–1845: Owen, Chartism and the Question of Violence in the Transition from "Utopian" to "Scientific" Socialism', in: *History of Political Thought*, 6, 1986, 454–78; Claeys, *Machinery, Money and the Millennium: From Moral Economy to Socialism, 1815–1860* (Princeton, 1987); Keith Tribe, *The Economy of the Word: Language, History, and Economics* (Oxford, 2015), Ch. 6. The biographies of Engels and Marx by Gustav Mayer, *Friedrich Engels: Eine Biographie*, vol. I and supplement (Berlin, 1920); Tristram Hunt, *Marx's General: The Revolutionary Life of Friedrich Engels* (New York, 2009); and Stedman Jones, *Karl Marx*, provide greater detail on Engels' intellectual formation and his debt to early French and English (utopian) socialists.
8 Mayer, *Friedrich Engels*, 139.

Notes

9 Friedrich Engels, *Die Lage der arbeitenden Klasse in England. Nach eigner Anschauung und authentischen Quellen* (Leipzig, 1845), MEGA¹ I/4, 5–286; *The Condition of the Working Class in England*, MECW, vol. 4, 295–596.
10 As they also do for example in public speeches given by Engels in Elberfeld in 1845 after his return from Manchester.
11 Adam Smith's *An Inquiry into the Nature and Causes of the Wealth of Nations* (1776) states unequivocally in the chapter 'On the Wages of Labour' that higher wages can increase productivity: 'Where wages are high, accordingly, we shall always find the workmen more active, diligent, and expeditious than where they are low.' Engels used Smith in the edition introduced by John Ramsay McCulloch (Edinburgh, 1828) [see: https://www.marxists.org/reference/archive/smith-adam/works/wealth-of-nations/book01/ch08.htm (retrieved 27 October 2021)].
12 For Engels, political economy came into being as a direct result of the expansion of trade in the mercantile period and its development followed the model of pre-Christian religion and theology. In this sense Smith was, for him, the '*Economic Luther*' (Engels, *Umrisse*, 474; *Outlines*, MECW, vol. 3, 422, original emphasis) whose doctrine of free trade sought to give a more just and human face to the violent and anarchic procedures of the mercantile period, replacing in Engels' view Catholic openness with Protestant hypocrisy.
13 Engels, *Umrisse*, 475; *Outlines*, MECW, vol. 3, 424.
14 I am indebted here to Regina Roth for her comments on an earlier version of the manuscript.
15 Between 1875 and 1883, Engels also wrote numerous articles on economic, political and social questions for newspapers and journals; see MEGA² I/25.
16 Engels confirmed this after Marx's death.
17 See MEGA² II/3; MECW, vol. 29.
18 See his numerous references to this opposition in MEGA² II/3 critical apparatus, 3215.
19 MEGA² II/4.2, 333; MECW, vol. 37, 258; original emphasis.
20 MEGA² II/1.2, 622; own translation.
21 MEGA² II/15, 227; own translation.
22 The exceptions are the questions of how to determine value (costs vs. needs) and the Malthusian law of population.
23 Engels, *Umrisse*, 467; *Outlines*, MECW, vol. 3, 418.
24 Ibid., 473; *Outlines*, ibid., 422.
25 Adam Smith, *Wealth of Nations*; see Note 11 above.
26 John Ramsay McCulloch, *A Discourse on the Rise, Progress, Peculiar Objects, and Importance of Political Economy* (Edinburgh, 1824).
27 Adam Smith, *Wealth of Nations*, IV, 1; see also Heinz D. Kurz, 'Adam Smith über das Merkantil- und das Agrikultursystem', in: Hendrik Hansen and Tim Kraski (eds), *Das Staatsverständnis von Adam Smith*, 67–92.
28 The orator John Watts, a follower of Owen's greatly esteemed by the young Engels, argued that no distinction could be made between the economic, the purpose-oriented and the moral and therefore spoke of the 'moral' rather than political economy; see John Watts, *The Facts and Fictions of Political Economists: Being a Review of the Principles of the Science, Separating the True from the False* (Manchester, 1842), iv and 60.
29 Engels, *Umrisse*, 491; *Outlines*, MECW, vol. 3, 441.
30 What Engels has to say here about the growing inequality of distribution of incomes and wealth is interesting in itself and anticipates in broad outline reflections of modern writers like Thomas Piketty.
31 Engels, *Umrisse*, 485; *Outlines*, MECW, vol. 3, 434.
32 Here is perhaps a suitable place to refer to Piero Sraffa, whose first phase of critical and constructive work, leading up to his book *Production of Commodities by Means of Commodities*

(Cambridge, 1960), took place between 1927 and 1930 (see Heinz D. Kurz, 'Don't Treat Ttoo Ill My Piero! Interpreting Sraffa's Papers', in: *Cambridge Journal of Economics*, 36, 2012, 1535–69). Sraffa's reconstruction of classical value and distribution theory distinguishes precisely between a system without and one with social production surplus. The former describes the realm of 'social need' in which everything produced is indispensable for the reproduction of society: Sraffa speaks here of a 'natural economy' in which every product, whether it be a means of subsistence or of production, is involved directly or indirectly in the production of the sum of all products, including itself. He shows clearly that the exchange rate of products that guarantee reproduction is determined only by the real physical costs of production and can be calculated by solving a set of simultaneous production equations. Only when a surplus occurs does the question of its distribution – whether for purposes of consumption or investment – really arise and with it the question of societal institutions regulating such distribution. Engels, however, implies that even early ethically ordered societies already produced a surplus without institutional regulation – a view incompatible with Sraffa's analysis. The problem of an ethically ordered society free from regulatory institutions will recur in the following pages.

33 Engels, *Umrisse*, 477, original emphasis; *Outlines*, MECW, vol. 3, 426.
34 Ibid., original emphasis; *Outlines*, ibid.
35 Ibid.; *Outlines*, ibid.
36 Ibid., 472, original emphasis; *Outlines*, ibid., 420.
37 Ibid., 478; *Outlines*, ibid., 427.
38 Ibid., 488; *Outlines*, ibid., 437.
39 Ibid.; *Outlines*, ibid.
40 Ibid., 486; *Outlines*, ibid., 436.
41 Ibid., 488; *Outlines*, ibid., 438.
42 Ibid., 490f.; *Outlines*, ibid., 440.
43 Stedman Jones, *Karl Marx*, 173.
44 Tribe, *The Economy of the Word*, 186f.
45 For an overview of the history of economic thought, see Heinz D. Kurz, *Economic Thought: A Brief History* (New York, 2016).
46 Stedman Jones, *Karl Marx*, 174.
47 However, as the German economist Herrmann Heinrich Gossen has emphasized, even in cloud-cuckoo land there is one economic problem to be solved: the allocation of the scarce resource of time for indulgence in alternative pleasures. In *Consumption Takes Time: Implications for Economic Theory. The Graz Schumpeter Lectures* (London, 2001), Ian Steedman addressed the rather neglected role of time in modern economics and showed how it clashes with numerous principles of conventional microeconomics.
48 As can also be seen in his *Der Ursprung der Familie, des Privateigenthums und des Staats*, in: MEGA² I/29; *The Origin of the Family, Private Property and the State*, MECW, vol. 26, 129–276.
49 Engels, *Umrisse*, 483; *Outlines*, MECW, vol. 3, 433.
50 Ibid.; *Outlines*, ibid. As Engels sees recent economic development as characterized by a stream of innovations, the 'advance' of which he speaks here cannot be technological, nor, in view of the dynamic energy of the socioeconomic system, is his concept of 'goal' at all clear. The same holds *mutatis mutandis* for the ethical order of society, which according to Engels is not stationary but in constant development.
51 Engels, *Umrisse*, 484; *Outlines*, ibid.
52 Ibid., 483; *Outlines*, ibid., 432, original emphasis.
53 Ibid., original emphasis; *Outlines*, ibid.
54 Ibid.; *Outlines*, ibid., 432–3.

Notes

55 The classical concept of monopoly should not be confused with the marginalistic concept developed by Antoine-Augustin Cournot. A classical monopoly arises when the market price of a good can be sustainably held above its natural level, and other prices accordingly sink below their natural level. Thus, such a monopoly is conceived in relation to the whole system of production not in relation to one specific market.
56 See Heinz D. Kurz, 'Adam Smith', loc. cit., 67–92.
57 Smith, *Wealth of Nations*, IV, ii, 21.
58 Joseph A. Schumpeter criticized Smith with respect to the (temporary) monopoly created by innovations. Smith, however, was concerned not with that case but with monopolies granted by the government, for example to the East India Company. Peter Thiel, a hedge-fund manager, suggested cynically in the September 2014 *Wall Street Journal* that 'competition is for losers'.
59 Smith, *Wealth of Nations*, I, xi, b.5.
60 John Stuart Mill, *Principles of Political Economy: With Some of Their Applications to Social Philosophy* (London, 1848, reprinted New York, 1973), vol. II, 242.
61 Karl Marx, *Das Kapital, Vol. I* (Hamburg, 1890), MEGA² II/10, 530; MECW, vol. 35, 588.
62 For what follows, see Heinz D. Kurz and Neri Salvadori, *Theory of Production: A Long-Period Analysis* (Cambridge, 1995, rev. ed. 1997), ch. 1, which surveys the early classical authors from William Petty through Cantillon and Smith to Ricardo, as well as Marx and the early Marginalists from William Stanley Jevons to Alfred Marshall.
63 Smith, *Wealth of Nations*, I, vi, 1.
64 The scale used for this purpose by the classical authors and Marx is the prevailing wage structure. In his theory of wage differentials (*Wealth of Nations*, I, x), Smith distinguishes five dimensions of heterogeneity of labour based on differences in: 1. Training costs (today called 'human capital'); 2. Talents; 3. Stability of employment; 4. Trust in employees required for work with expensive tools and materials; 5. Health and mortality risks connected with specific work processes. Kurz and Salvadori, *Theory of Production*, ch. 11, provide an analytic treatment of the considerations proposed by Smith – and following him by Ricardo and Marx – on the heterogeneity of labour as a factor of value theory.
65 Engels, *Umrisse*, 482, original emphasis; *Outlines*, MECW, vol. 3, 431.
66 The conviction that the value of labour theory adequately explains exchange relations between utility values in primitive societies, and hence would have prevailed 'historically', is not expressed clearly in *Outlines* but was clarified by Engels in later writings composed either on his own or together with Marx – before Engels, several other authors, most prominently Adam Smith and Robert Torrens (1780–1864), had taken the same position. Based on the work of anthropologists and ethnologists, Piero Sraffa has pointed out that in primitive societies, materials were of paramount value; the time spent working on an object was of little concern for determining its value, for in such societies, 'waiting is the rule', as an observer put it. Time started to become valuable, according to Sraffa, only with the advent of a positive rate of interest: 'It is interest on money that hammers into the head of man the notion that time is valuable, as valuable as material' – quoted from Kurz and Salvadori, 'Sraffa and the labour theory of value: A few observations', in: J. Vint, J. Metcalfe, H. D. Kurz, N. Salvadori and P. A. Samuelson (eds), *Economic Theory and Economic Thought: Essays in Honour of Ian Steedman* (London, 2010), 187–213, 199.
67 Engels, *Umrisse*, 476; *Outlines*, MECW, vol. 3, 425.
68 Prescinding here, for the sake of simplicity, from both renewable and exhaustible natural resources and hence from differential profit margins and royalties.
69 Engels, *Umrisse*, 485, original emphasis; *Outlines*, MECW, vol. 3, 434.
70 Smith, *Wealth of Nations*, I, vii, 72. Smith was in this respect overly optimistic. We know today that markets are less stable than he assumed. On the problem of 'gravitation' in *Wealth*

of Nations, see the summary presentation in Heinz D. Kurz, 'Zur Politischen Ökonomie des homo mercans: Adam Smith über Märkte', Deutsches Jahrbuch Philosophie, 7, 2016, 23–48, section 4.
71 Engels, Umrisse, 485; Outlines, MECW, vol. 3, 434.
72 Ibid., 484; Outlines, ibid., 433. Another reason assumed by Engels for price fluctuations was changes in the distribution of income reflecting a shift in the balance of power among the different social classes – though in the short term, this generally plays only a minor role. Stedman Jones (Karl Marx, 175) writes that Ricardo's 'inclusion of capital in the value of a commodity introduced instability into the relationship between value and price'. But this can mean at most that real wages, production costs and rate of profit are interdependent quantities and that a change in real wages affects the other elements, not that it generates instability in the sense described above.
73 Engels, Umrisse, 484; Outlines, ibid.
74 According to Smith, this does not apply to financial markets, whose positive feedback mechanisms create an inherent tendency to instability, which consequently needs regulation. For a summary of Smith's position, see Kurz, Zur Politischen Ökonomie, section 6.
75 Engels, Umrisse, 484; Outlines, ibid., 434.
76 After these lines were written, the COVID-19 pandemic brought impressive confirmation.
77 Engels, Umrisse, 484; Outlines, MECW, vol. 3, 433.
78 Ibid.; Outlines, ibid.
79 Ibid.; Outlines, ibid., 434.
80 Apart from some early indications in the relevant literature, the reason had to wait almost a century before authors like Michal Kalecki and John Maynard Keynes established the principle of effective demand. This posits that investments determine savings, not vice versa, inasmuch as they govern the level of effective demand in the economy as a whole and hence also the level of GDP and employment.
81 Engels, Umrisse, 484; Outlines, MECW, vol. 3, 434.
82 Ibid., 486; Outlines, ibid., 436.
83 Ibid., 488; Outlines, ibid., 437.
84 Ibid.; Outlines, ibid.
85 Ibid., 490; Outlines, ibid., 439.
86 Ibid.; Outlines, ibid., 440.
87 Ibid., 493; Outlines, ibid., 442.
88 Ibid., 486f.; Outlines, ibid., 436.
89 Marx, Kapital 1890, MEGA² II/10, 383f., and Karl Marx, Das Kapital: Kritik der Politischen Ökonomie, Vol. I (Hamburg, 1867), MEGA² II/5, 505; MECW, vol. 35, 622.
90 Marx, Kapital 1890, MEGA² II/10, 288; see also Friedrich Engels, editor's preface to Karl Marx, Capital: A Critical Analysis of Capitalist Production, Vol. I, trans. Samuel Moore and Edward Aveling, ed. Frederick Engels (London, 1887), MEGA² II/9, 14; MECW, vol. 35, 30–36, and Engels' commentary no. 37 to Karl Marx, Das Kapital: Kritik der Politischen Ökonomie, Vol. III, ed. Friedrich Engels (Hamburg, 1894), MEGA² II/15, 257–9; MECW, vol. 37, 261 (see also 393f.).
91 Karl Marx, Ökonomische Manuskripte 1863–1867, MEGA² II/4.2, 333, own translation.
92 See Engels, Umrisse, 493; Outlines, MECW, vol. 3, 442.
93 See Heinz D. Kurz, 'Technical progress, capital accumulation and income distribution in Classical economics: Adam Smith, David Ricardo and Karl Marx', European Journal of the History of Economic Thought, 17(5), 2010, 1183–222, here sections 4 and 5; Heinz D. Kurz, 'David Ricardo: On the art of "elucidating economic principles" in the face of a "labyrinth of difficulties"', European Journal of the History of Economic Thought, 22(5), 2015, 818–51, here Section 7.

Notes

94. See Heinz D. Kurz, 'Hin zu Marx und über ihn hinaus: Zum 200. Geburtstag eines deutschen politischen Ökonomen von historischem Rang', *Perspektiven der Wirtschaftspolitik*, 13(3), 2018, 245–65.
95. Engels, *Umrisse*, 489; *Outlines*, MECW, vol. 3, 439.
96. Ibid., 491; *Outlines*, ibid., 441.
97. See David Ricardo, *Collected Works and Correspondence of David Ricardo*, ed. Piero Sraffa with the collaboration of Maurice H. Dobb (Cambridge, 1951), vol. VIII, 194.
98. See Piero Sraffa, *Production of Commodities by Means of Commodities* (Cambridge, 1960), Ch. III.
99. Marx had to work hard to free himself from Engels' prejudices against the classical economists in order both to allow them a modicum of justice and to build on their achievement.

CHAPTER 11

1. Friedrich Engels to Laura Lafargue, 8 March 1885, MEW, vol. 36, 286; MECW, vol. 47, 264f.; Friedrich Engels to Johann Philipp Becker, 2 April 1885, ibid., 290; MECW, vol. 47, 267f.; Friedrich Engels to August Bebel, 4 April 1885, ibid., 293; MECW, vol. 47, 269ff.; see also Friedrich Engels to Nikolai Franzewitsch Danielson, 23 April 1885, ibid., 301f.; MECW, vol. 47, 277f.; see also Carl-Erich Vollgraf and Regina Roth, 'Einführung' (Introduction), in: Karl Marx and Friedrich Engels, M*anuskripte und redaktionelle Texte zum dritten Buch des* Kapitals *1871 bis 1895* (Berlin, 2003), in: MEGA² II/14, 391f.
2. Friedrich Engels to August Bebel, 4 April 1885, MEW, vol. 36, 294; MECW, vol. 47, 269ff. On the other hand, Engels does not think at all highly of *Kapital II*: 'It contains virtually nothing but rigorously scientific, very minute examinations of things that take place within the capitalist class itself, and nothing at all out of which to fabricate catch-words and orations', Friedrich Engels to Karl Kautsky, 18 September 1883, MEW, vol. 36, 61; MECW, vol. 47, 55ff.
3. Friedrich Engels to Laura Lafargue, 24 June 1883, MEW, vol. 36, 44; MECW, vol. 47, 39f.; on the discussion about a monument to Marx, see also August Bebel to Friedrich Engels, 17 March 1883, and Engels' reply of 30 April 1883, ibid., 22; MECW, vol. 47, 16f.
4. Friedrich Engels, 'Preface', in: Karl Marx, *Das Kapital III*, ed. Friedrich Engels (1894) (Berlin, 2004), in: MEGA² II/15, 6; MECW, vol. 37, 5–26, here 6.
5. See the essay in this volume by Jürgen Herres, 'My Immortal Works', p. XXX, note 4.
6. Karl Marx, *Ökonomische Manuskripte 1863–1867*, Part 1 (Berlin, 1988), in: MEGA² II/4.1, 137–381; Karl Marx, *Ökonomische Manuskripte 1863–1867*, Part 3 (Berlin, 2012), in: MEGA² II/4.3, 32–56, 285–382; Karl Marx, *Manuskripte zum zweiten Buch des* Kapitals *1868 bis 1881* (Berlin, 2008), in: MEGA² II/11; MECW, vol. 36, V–VIII, 31–523.
7. Friedrich Engels, 'Preface', in: Karl Marx, *Kapital II/Capital. A Critique of Political Economy, Vol. II*, ed. Friedrich Engels (1885) (Berlin, 2008), in: MEGA² II/13, 8; MECW, vol. 36, 5–23, here 9.
8. MEGA² II/4.1, 381.
9. Karl Marx, *Das Kapital I/Capital. A Critique of Political Economy, Vol. I* (1867) (Berlin, 1983), in: MEGA² II/5, S. 479; cf. MECW, vol. 35, 591 (vol. 35 contains the fourth edition of 1890).
10. MEGA² II/11, 814; MECW, vol. 36, 315.
11. Engels, on the other hand, saw the mistake and replaced Marx's working with better examples; hence, the break in the print version appears unnecessary (see MEGA² II/13, 477f.). On Engels' alterations and their impact on reception, see also Kenji Mori, 'Einführung', ibid., 545.
12. MEGA² II/11, 816ff., 826.
13. Karl Marx to Friedrich Engels, 31 May 1858, MEGA² III/9, 157; MECW, vol. 40, 317f.

Notes

14 MEGA² II/11, 818f.; re-genesis, see ibid., 1611.
15 For 'accumulation, or reproduction in extended steps', see MEGA² II/4.1, 381.
16 MEGA² II/11, 790.
17 On unsolved problems of accumulation in Marx's *Kapital II*, see Teinosuke Otani, Ljudmila Vasina and Carl-Erich Vollgraf, 'Einführung', MEGA² II/11, 873–81.
18 Karl Marx, *Ökonomische Manuskripte 1863–1867*, Part 2 (Berlin, 1992), in: MEGA² II/4.2, 7–110. *Marx's Economic Manuscripts of 1864–1865* (Historical Materialism, vol. 100), ed. Fred Moseley, trans. Ben Fowkes (Leiden, Boston, 2015).
19 MEGA² II/14, 19–150.
20 MEGA² II/4.3, 2–4, 7–9, 10–31, 383–96; see also Carl-Erich Vollgraf, 'Einführung', 427f.
21 MECW, vol. 37, 432. Examples can be found, for example, throughout chapters 21–32 of *Kapital III* Part 5 (MECW, vol. 37, 336–517).
22 Karl Marx to Friedrich Engels, 14 November 1868, MEW, vol. 32, 204; MECW, vol. 43, 160.
23 John Swinton, 'Account of an Interview with Karl Marx Published in *The Sun*', in: MEGA² I/25, 443; MECW, vol. 24, 583–5.
24 For Marx's work on *Kapital III*, see MEGA² II/14, 446ff.; see also Carl-Erich Vollgraf, '"Marx" Arbeit am dritten Buch des *Kapital* in den 1870/80er Jahren', in: *In memoriam Wolfgang Jahn: Der ganze Marx* (Hamburg, 2002), 33–66.
25 Karl Marx to Friedrich Engels, 13 February 1866, in: MEGA² *Letters 1866*; MECW, vol. 42, 227: 'The treatise on ground rent alone, … is in its present form almost long enough to be a book in itself.'
26 MEGA² II/4.2, 690, 816f.
27 In the scope of their Russian material, for example, these bear witness to the regional breadth of Marx's interests, as does a series of excerpts on chemical and geological subjects to his concern for agricultural production and ground rent. The significance of these aspects for Marx's economic theory has not yet been thoroughly researched. See Marx's heading 'Agricultur + Bodenpreis, Rent' above excerpts of 1878 from Johann Gottlieb Koppe, Ernst Erhard Schmid and Friedrich Schoedler, in: *Karl Marx, Exzerpte und Notizen zur Geologie, Mineralogie und Agrikulturchemie, März bis September 1878* (Berlin, 2011, MEGA² IV/26, 123); see also various excerpts on 'Relations of geology to agriculture' from James F. W. Johnston, *Elements of Agricultural Chemistry and Geology*, in: MEGA² IV/26, 70–94; on the excerpts from the late 1860s, see Kohei Saito, *Natur gegen Kapital: Marx' Ökologie in seiner unvollendeten Kritik des Kapitalismus* (Frankfurt, 2016).
28 Among themes suggested by these manuscripts are the circulation of money, crises and a cyclical economic model for money and goods similar to the *Tableau Economique* of the physiocrat François Quesnay. See Michael R. Krätke, "Hier bricht das Manuskript ab' (Engels): Hat das *Kapital* einen Schluss?', Part 1, 2, in: *Beiträge zur Marx-Engels-Forschung* (new series) 2001, 7–43; 2002, 211–62.
29 Friedrich Engels to Pjotr Lawrowitsch Lawrow, 28 January and 5 February 1884, MEW, vol. 36, 94, 99; MECW, vol. 47, 87f., 92f.
30 Friedrich Engels to Karl Kautsky, 24 March 1884, ibid., 129; MECW, vol. 47, 120; Friedrich Engels to Laura Lafargue, 31 March 1884, ibid., 131; MECW, vol. 47, 121f.; see also Engels' edition of *Kapital III*, MEGA² II/14, 461.
31 Friedrich Engels to Johann Philipp Becker, 20 June 1884, MEW, vol. 36, 162; MECW, vol. 47, 151f.
32 Friedrich Engels to Hermann Schlüter, 22 February 1885, ibid., 285; MECW, vol. 47, 263f.; Friedrich Engels to Laura Lafargue, 8 March 1885, ibid., 287; MECW, vol. 47, 264f.
33 Friedrich Engels to Laura Lafargue, 4 July 1885, ibid., 339: 'what can be dictated' (MECW, vol. 47, 310); see also Engels' edition, MEGA² II/14, 465.

Notes

34 Friedrich Engels to Karl Kautsky, 21–22 June 1884, MEW, vol. 36, 164; MECW, vol. 47, 153f.; Friedrich Engels to Laura Lafargue, 13 December 1883, ibid., 75; MECW, vol. 47, 70f.; Friedrich Engels to August Bebel, 11 October 1884, ibid., 214; MECW, vol. 47, 197ff; see also Engels' edition, MEGA² II/14, 461ff.
35 Friedrich Engels to August Bebel, 30 April 1883, MEW, vol. 36, 21; MECW, vol. 47, 16f.; see also Renate Merkel-Melis, 'Einführung', in: *Friedrich Engels, Werke, Artikel, Entwürfe Mai 1883 bis September 1886* (Berlin, 2011), in: MEGA² I/30, 577.
36 Friedrich Engels to Karl Marx, 20 January 1845, MEGA² III/1, 262; MECW, vol. 38, 20.
37 On his longing for release, see Friedrich Engels to Karl Marx, 27 April 1867, MEGA² *Letters 1867* (https://megadigital.bbaw.de/briefe/detail.xql?id=B00256); MECW, vol. 42, 362–5. On his leaving the business in 1869, see Friedrich Engels to Karl Marx and to Elisabeth Engels, 1 July 1869, MEW, vol. 32, 329, 615–17; MECW, vol. 43, 299ff.; Jürgen Herres, *Marx und Engels: Porträt einer intellektuellen Freundschaft* (Leipzig, 2018), 217f.
38 Keizo Hayasaka, 'Oscar Eisengarten – Eine Lebensskizze', in: *Beiträge zur Marx-Engels-Forschung* (new series) 2001, 83–110, here 85ff.
39 Friedrich Engels to August Bebel, 24 July 1885, MEW, vol. 36, 348; MECW, vol. 47, 315ff. On *Kapital II*, see Friedrich Engels to Karl Kautsky, 21–22 June 1884, ibid., 164; MECW, vol. 47, 153f.
40 Friedrich Engels to August Bebel, 30 August 1883, ibid., 53: 'Besides that there is the handwriting which certainly cannot be deciphered by anyone but *me,* and then only with difficulty'; see also Friedrich Engels to Pjotr Lawrowitsch Lawrow, 5 February 1884, ibid., 99; MECW, vol. 47, 92f.
41 Friedrich Engels to August Bebel, 24 July 1885, ibid., 348; MECW, vol. 47, 315ff.; see also 'Einführung', MEGA² II/14, 398.
42 MEGA² II/4.3, 2–4, 7–9, 10–31, 383–96; see also 'Einführung', ibid., 427f.
43 Engels' trip to the United States from 7 August to 29 September 1888 is recorded in his notes and numerous letters; see *Friedrich Engels, Werke, Artikel, Entwürfe Oktober 1886 bis Februar 1891* (Berlin, 2002) in: MEGA² I/31, 159ff.; on its preparation, see ibid., 914, MECW, vol. 26, 581–8; Malcolm Sylvers, 'Marx, Engels und die USA – ein Forschungsprojekt über ein wenig beachtetes Thema', in: *Marx-Engels-Jahrbuch 2004*, 48–50. His route and programme show that Engels travelled primarily as a private person, but he observed economic and technological developments closely, including the growth of workers' organizations, on which he had already commented in the preface to the 1887 American edition of *Condition*; see Frederick Engels, 'Preface to the American edition of "The Condition of the Working Class"', MEGA² I/31, 35. See also Tristram Hunt, *The Frock-Coated Communist* (London, 2009), 316ff.
44 Friedrich Engels to Laura Lafargue. 15–16 March 1886, MEW, vol. 36, 460; MECW, vol. 47, 423.
45 Friedrich Engels to Laura Lafargue, 21 March 1887, ibid., 637; MECW, vol. 48, 40f.; Engels was allowed to work only for two to three daylight hours. In both 1892 and 1894 he had health problems; on Engels' editorial activities, see MEGA² II/14, 468, 473, 475f., 488.
46 MEGA² II/14, 19–150.
47 'Einführung', ibid., 359.
48 For the genesis of *Kapital III*, see ibid., 511f.
49 Ibid., 185–213.
50 MEGA² II/15, 29–143; on the detailed stages of Engels' editorial activities, see MEGA² II/14, 466ff; MECW, vol. 37, V–IX.
51 MEGA² II/15, 70. See also Regina Roth, 'Marx's Vorlagen und Engels' Redaktion: Anmerkungen zum Ersten Abschnitt des dritten Buchs des Kapitals', in: *MEGA-Studien 2001*, 127–41.
52 MEGA² II/15, 237; MECW, vol. 37, VII.

Notes

53 Ibid., 243, lines 13–15 and comment in MEGA² II/4.2, 315, lines 17–19; MECW, vol. 37, 245.
54 MEGA² II/15, 227; see MEGA² II/4.2, 319; MECW, vol. 37, 228. On this and Engels' interventions, see also 'Einführung', MEGA² II/14, 407ff.; Regina Roth, 'Die Herausgabe von Band 2 und 3 des *Kapital* durch Engels', in: *Marx-Engels-Jahrbuch 2012/13*, 168–82.
55 Friedrich Engels to Laura Lafargue, 11 February 1889, MEW, vol. 37, 151; MECW, vol. 48, 264.
56 MEGA² II/4.2, 469; MECW, vol. 37, 397.
57 MEGA² II/15, 386.
58 Engels' letter of 4 July 1889 to his and Marx's longstanding correspondence partner in St. Petersburg, Nikolai Franzewitsch Danielson, banker and translator of *Kapital I* into Russian, indicates that he had long cherished the desire to issue *Kapital III*: 'This crowning volume is such a splendid and unanswerable work' that he sought 'to bring it out in a shape in which the whole line of argument stands forth clearly and in bold relief' (4 July 1889, MEW, vol. 37, 244; MECW, vol. 48, 346).
59 On Engels' editorial interventions, see also 'Einführung', MEGA² II/14, 402ff; MECW, vol. 3.
60 For Engels' preface to *Kapital III*, see MECW, vol. 37, 8–9.
61 For further interpretations, see Michael R. Krätke, 'Geld, Kredit und verrückte Formen', in: *MEGA-Studien 2000/1*, 64–99; Michael Heinrich, *Die Wissenschaft vom Wert* (Hamburg, 2014), 284ff.
62 On Engels' editorial activities, see MEGA² II/14, 477ff.; for re-genesis, see MEGA² II/15, 931f.
63 See the essay by Heinz D. Kurz in this volume and Carl-Erich Vollgraf, 'Engels' Kapitalismus-Bild und seine Zusätze zum 3. Band des *Kapitals*', in: *Beiträge zur Marx-Engels-Forschung* (new series) 2004, 7–53.
64 Friedrich Engels to Johann Philipp Becker, 20 June 1884, MEW, vol. 36, 163; MECW, vol. 47, 152; on Engels' editorial activities, see also MEGA² II/14, 460f.
65 Friedrich Engels to August Bebel, 30 April 1883, MEW, vol. 36, 21; MECW, vol. 47, 16f. On the further task of writing a biography of Marx, see also the essay by Wilfried Nippel in this volume.
66 See Christina Morina, *Die Erfindung des Marxismus: Wie eine Idee die Welt eroberte* (Munich, 2017), 203ff., 218ff.
67 Karl Marx, *Das Kapital I*, 3rd ed. 1883 (Berlin, 1989), in: MEGA² II/8; MECW, vol. 35; for re-genesis, see ibid., 850.
68 MEGA² II/8, 347, footnote 50a and commentary; MECW, vol. 35, 356, footnote 2.
69 'The man seized the reins in the house ... the woman was degraded, enthralled, became the slave of the man's lust, a mere instrument for breeding children. This humiliated position of women ... has become gradually embellished and dissembled and, in part, clothed in a milder form, but by no means abolished' [Friedrich Engels, *Der Ursprung der Familie* (1884) (Berlin, 1990), in: MEGA² I/29, 33; *Origin of the Family*, MECW, vol. 26, 129–276, here 165]. See also Friedrich Engels to Friedrich Adolph Sorge, 7 March 1884, MEW, vol. 36, 124; MECW, vol. 47, 113ff.; Hunt, *The Frock-Coated Communist*, 310f.
70 Thus Eduard Bernstein's 1918 memory (cited in MEGA² I/29, 591); see Lawrence Krader, *Ethnologie und Anthropologie bei Marx* (The Ethnological Notebooks of Karl Marx) (Frankfurt, 1976), 231. Editors of MEGA, however, set the composition of the text in mid-April, after Engels' receipt of Morgan's work (ibid., 591f.).
71 Friedrich Engels to Karl Kautsky, 24 March 1884, MEW, vol. 36, 129; MECW, vol. 47, 120. The suggestion came from Kautsky; see *Friedrich Engels' Briefwechsel mit Karl Kautsky*, ed. Benedikt Kautsky (Vienna, 1955), 103.
72 Friedrich Engels to Karl Kautsky, 26 April 1884, MEW, vol. 36, 142; MECW, vol. 47, 132, original emphasis; Krader, *Ethnologie*, 231f.; MEGA² I/29, 590ff.

Notes

73 Friedrich Engels to Karl Kautsky, 19 July 1884, MEW, vol. 36, 176; MECW, vol. 47, 164f., 204; for re-genesis, see MEGA² I/29, 606ff.
74 Regarded as an advocate of state socialism, Rodbertus (1805–75) considered liberal trade policies to be a cause of the scandalous immiseration of the nineteenth-century working class. For his radical ideas on state reform of this system on the basis of work-value theory, see *Geschichte der sozialen Ideen in Deutschland: Sozialismus – Katholische Soziallehre – Protestantische Sozialethik. Ein Handbuch*, ed. Walter Euchner et al. (Heidelberg, 2005), 57ff.
75 For re-genesis, see MEGA² II/13, 561f. Engels supported Karl Kautsky's critical review of Georg Adler's 1885 account of the beginnings of German social democracy (see MEGA² I/30, 200ff.); for re-genesis, see ibid., 886ff.; on the controversy with Georg Adler (at the time a young political economist, later a social politician), see also the essay by Wilfried Nippel in this volume.
76 Friedrich Engels to Karl Kautsky, 16 February 1884, MEW, vol. 36, 108.; MECW, vol. 47, 101.
77 Eduard Bernstein to Friedrich Engels, 10 and 23 November 1883, 31 January 1884, in: *Eduard Bernsteins Briefwechsel mit Friedrich Engels*, ed. Helmut Hirsch (Assen, 1970), 230, 233, 241; for re-genesis, see also MEGA² I/30, 656, 660; for preface text, see ibid., 28–40. The book itself appeared in early 1885 (ibid., 929f.).
78 Friedrich Engels to Kautsky, 22 August 1884, MEW, vol. 36, 204; MECW, vol. 47, 186ff.; for re-genesis, see MEGA² I/30, 659, and MEGA² II/13, 563ff.; for preface text, see ibid., 5–21.
79 MEGA² II/8, 503; Marx's versions in 1867 and 1872 editions: MEGA² II/5, 430, footnote 17; MEGA² II/6, 495.
80 For re-genesis, see MEGA² I/30, 658f.
81 IISG, Marx–Engels Collection (J 37); for re-genesis, see MEGA² I/30, 657.
82 Friedrich Engels to Karl Kautsky, 22 August 1884, in: MEW, vol. 36, 202; MECW, vol. 47, 186ff.
83 Engels, 'Preface' (1885), in: MEGA² II/13, 9 and commentary.
84 Marx took this line, for example, in a draft article of 1845 on Friedrich List's book *Das nationale System der politischen Oekonomie*; see 'Ein neues Manuskript von Karl Marx', in: *Beiträge zur Geschichte der Arbeiterbewegung* 14 (1972), 423–46; MECW, vol. 4, 265–93; see also Karl Marx, 'Plagiarismus' (12 December 1867), in: Karl Marx and Friedrich Engels, *Werke, Artikel, Entwürfe September 1867 bis März 1871* (Berlin, 2009), in: MEGA² I/21, 33ff.; for re-genesis, see ibid., 1272ff. For another accusation of plagiarism, see Karl Marx, 'Mein Plagiat to F. Bastiat' (draft 1868), ibid., 75f.; for re-genesis, see ibid., 1314ff.
85 Friedrich Engels to Karl Kautsky, 16 February 1884, MEW, vol. 36, 108; MECW, vol. 47, 101f., original emphasis; MEGA² I/30, 28ff.; MEGA² II/13, 9ff.
86 For re-genesis, see MEGA² II/13, 564f.; 'Einführung', MEGA² II/14, 442.
87 Friedrich Engels to Eduard Bernstein, 22 August 1884, in: MEW, vol. 36, 204; MECW, vol. 47, 188.
88 IISG, Marx–Engels Collection (L 4973); for Engels' opinion on Meyer, see his letter to Karl Kautsky, 23 May 1884, MEW, vol. 36, 149; MECW, vol. 47, 137f.; Engels, 'Preface' (1885), in: MEGA² II/13, 9f.
89 For quote and genesis, see MEGA² I/30, 1034f.
90 Friedrich Engels to Florence Kelley Wischnewetzky, 10 February 1885, MEW, vol. 36, 280; MECW, vol. 47, 259.
91 Friedrich Engels, 'England in 1845 and in 1885', in: *The Commonweal*, nos 1 and 2 (1885), in: MEGA² I/30, 61–66; for re-genesis, see ibid., 706–13; MECW, vol. 26, 295–301.
92 Friedrich Engels, 'England 1845 und 1885', in: *Die Neue Zeit* (1885), in: MEGA² I/30, 67–73; for re-genesis, see ibid., 714–23.
93 Friedrich Engels, 'Die Arbeiterbewegung in Amerika', in: *Der Sozialdemokrat* (1887), in: MEGA² I/31, 40–8, for re-genesis, see ibid., 707–21; MECW, vol. 26, 434–42.

94 In his 'Preface to the American Edition' (dated 26 January 1887), Engels wrote 'The *Communist Manifesto* of 1847', perhaps merely for the sake of an exact 40-year gap between the two publications; see MEGA² I/31, 35; MECW, vol. 26, 512-18.
95 Ibid.
96 On the situation in the United States, see also the essay by James M. Brophy in this volume.
97 Engels, 'England in 1845 and in 1885', in: MEGA² I/30, 64. He coined the phrase 'workers' aristocracy' in Hermann Schlüter's 'Chartistenbewegung in England' (1887); see MEGA² I/31, 453-545; for re-genesis, see ibid., 615.
98 Frederick Engels, 'Appendix to the American edition of *The Condition of the Working Class*' (1886), in: MEGA² I/30, 164ff.; MECW, vol. 26, 399-405.
99 For re-genesis, see MEGA² I/30, 1038ff.
100 'Einführung', MEGA² I/30, 581; MEGA² I/31, 616ff.; MEGA² I/32, 592ff. See also Wilfried Nippel, 'Friedrich Engels und die Politik des Vorworts', in: *Zeitschrift für Ideengeschichte* 11, 2017, no. 3, 67-78.
101 For re-genesis, see MEGA² I/30, 1055f.
102 See for example Wilhelm Liebknecht to Friedrich Engels, 25 March 1865, MEGA² III/13, 357; Friedrich Engels to Karl Kautsky, 16 February 1884, MEW, vol. 36, 109; MECW, vol. 47, 101f.; Hermann Schlüter to Friedrich Engels, 10 December 1884, IISG, Marx-Engels Collection (L 5514). For re-genesis of 2nd German ed., see MEGA² I/32, 871ff.
103 MEGA² I/32, 152-66, here 164ff.; MECW, vol. 27, 322.
104 Friedrich Engels to Karl Marx, 8 April 1863, MEGA² III/12, 354; MECW, vol. 41, 464f.
105 Friedrich Engels to Friedrich Adolph Sorge, 31 December 1884, MEW, vol. 36, 264; MECW, vol. 47, 244ff.; Friedrich Engels to Karl Kautsky, 25 March 1895, MEW, vol. 39, 447; MECW, vol. 50, 480ff.
106 MEGA² I/30, 41f.
107 MEGA² I/30, 43-53.
108 MEGA² I/30, 41. Eduard Bernstein had asked about a new edition in March 1884; see 'Einführung' MEGA² I/30, 585ff.; for re-genesis, see ibid., 673ff., 681ff.
109 MEGA² I/31, 66; MECW vol. 26, 455.
110 Friedrich Engels to Hermann Schlüter, 12 February 1888, MEW, vol. 37, 22. See also MEGA² I/31, 55-116; for re-genesis, see ibid., 610ff., 732ff.; MECW, vol. 48, 147f.
111 For Engels' documentation, see MEGA² I/30, 167f., 171f., 274-8; 'Einführung', ibid., 511-21, 526-39; for re-genesis, see ibid., 621f.; on related correspondence, see Gerd Callesen and Svetlana Gavrilčenko, 'Einführung', in: MEGA² III/30, 694f. and letters cited there. See also Markus Bürgi, *Die Anfänge der II: Internationale. Positionen und Auseinandersetzungen 1889-1893* (Frankfurt, New York, 1996).
112 See 'Einführung', MEGA² I/30, 595ff.; MEGA² I/31, 622f.; MEGA² III/30, 681ff.; on British perspective, see also Hunt, *The Frock-Coated Communist*, 324ff.
113 Engels to Friedrich Adolph Sorge, 9 August 1890, MEGA² III/30, 395f.; MECW, vol. 49, 11; see also 'Einführung', ibid., 687f.
114 Engels to Florence Kelley Wischnewetzky, 28 December 1886, MEW, vol. 36, 589; MECW, vol. 47, 541; see also 'Einführung', MEGA² I/30, 595.
115 Friedrich Engels to Werner Sombart, 11 March 1895: 'But Marx's whole way of thinking [Auffassungsweise] is not so much a doctrine as a method. It provides, not so much ready-made dogmas, as aids to further investigation and the method *for* such investigation' (MECW, vol. 50, 461).

Notes

CHAPTER 12

1. Friedrich Engels, 'The Part Played by Labour in the Transition from Ape to Man', in: MEGA² I/27, 88; Preface, Note 1 (MEGA² I/ 26, 540; MECW, vol. 25, 452).
2. Ibid.
3. Friedrich Engels, 'Zur Kritik des sozialdemokratischen Programmentwurfs 1891', in: MEGA² I/32, 42–54; *A Critique of the Draft Social-Democratic Programme of 1891*, MECW, vol. 27, 217–50.
4. See Friedrich Engels, *Die Lage der arbeitenden Klasse in England: Nach eigner Anschauung und authentischen Quellen*, 2. ed. 1892, orig. 1845, in: MEGA¹ I/4, Berlin 1932, 10–286; *The Condition of the Working Class in England*, MECW, vol. 4, 295–596.
5. See Friedrich Engels, 'England 1845 und 1885', *Die Neue Zeit*, vol. 3, issue 6, June 1885, in: MEGA² I/30, 67–73; 'England in 1845 and in 1885', MECW, vol. 26, 295–301. In his extensive biography of Engels, *Marx's General: The Revolutionary Life of Friedrich Engels* (New York, 2009), Tristram Hunt makes frequent reference to these changes in perspective.
6. Frederick W. Taylor, *The Principles of Scientific Management* (1911).
7. Werner Pfeiffer and Enno Weiss, *Lean Management: Grundlagen und Organisation industrieller Unternehmen* (Berlin, 1992), 20–41. The development of Fordism over the decades has led to a distinction being made between 'pure' and 'modern' Fordism.
8. See Taylor, *Principles*, 37ff.
9. See Pfeiffer and Weiss, *Lean Management*, 43ff.; see also Lutz von Rosenstiel, *Grundlagen der Organisationspsychologie* (Stuttgart, 2003), 11, 271ff.
10. See Walter A. Oechler, *Personal und Arbeit: Grundlagen des Human Resource Management und der Arbeitgeber-Arbeitnehmer-Beziehungen* (Munich, Vienna, 2000).
11. See Michael Kittner, *Arbeits- und Sozialordnung. Ausgewählte und eingeleitete Gesetzestexte* (Frankfurt, 2020).
12. See Heinz Gester, Norbert Koubek and Gerd R. Wiedemeyer (eds), *Unternehmensverfassung und Mitbestimmung in Europa* (Wiesbaden, 1991).
13. See International Labour Organization, *Tripartie Declaration of Principles concerning Multinational Enterprises and Social Policy* (Geneva, 2017).
14. See Pfeiffer and Weiss, *Lean Management*, 43ff.
15. See James P. Womack, Daniel T. Jones and Daniel Roos, *Die zweite Revolution in der Autoindustrie* (Frankfurt, 1991).
16. See Arnold Picot, Ralf Reichwald, Rolf T. Wigand et al., *Die grenzenlose Unternehmung: Information, Organisation & Führung* (Heidelberg, 2020).
17. See Norbert Koubek, *Jenseits und Diesseits der Betriebswirtschaftslehre: Institutionen – Unternehmenstheorien – Globale Strukturen* (Wiesbaden, 2010).
18. See Birgit Spieshöfer, *Unternehmerische Verantwortung zur Entstehung einer globalen Wirtschaftsordnung* (Baden-Baden, 2017).
19. See Bob Hancké (ed.), *Debating Varieties of Capitalism* (Oxford, 2009).
20. See Reinhard Pfriem, Uwe Schneidewind, Jonathan Barth, Silja Graupe and Thomas Korbun (eds), *Transformative Wirtschaftswissenschaft im Kontext nachhaltiger Entwicklung* (Marburg, 2017).
21. Hans-Gerd Servatius, Uwe Schneidewind and Dirk Rohlfink (eds), *Smart Energy: Wandel zu einem nachhaltigen Energiesystem* (Berlin, Heidelberg, 2012).
22. Report: *The State of World Population 2018* (Geneva, 2018).
23. Thomas Piketty, *Capital in the Twenty-First Century* (Cambridge, MA, 2014); *Capital and Ideology* (Cambridge, MA, 2020).
24. See Picot, Reichwald, Wigand et al., *Die grenzenlose Unternehmung*, end of chapter on 'Virtual Enterprises'.

25 See Jan Marco Leimeister, Shkodran Zogaj, David Durward and Ulrich Bretschneider, 'Neue Geschäftsfelder durch Crowdsourcing: Crowd-basierte Start-ups als Arbeitsmodell der Zukunft', in: Reiner Hoffmann and Claudia Bogedan (eds), *Arbeit der Zukunft* (Frankfurt, New York, 2015), 141–58.
26 Friedrich Engels, 'Introduction to Karl Marx's *The Class Struggles in France*, 1848 to 1850, in: MEGA² I/32, 336; MECW, vol. 27, 510.

CHAPTER 13

1 See Marin Endress and Christian Jansen (eds), *Karl Marx im 21. Jahrhundert. Bilanz und Perspektiven* (Frankfurt, New York, 2020). Two recent, intensively researched biographies have opened new vistas: Jonathan Sperber, *Karl Marx: A Nineteenth-Century Life* (New York, London, 2013); and Gareth Stedman Jones, *Karl Marx: Greatness and Illusion* (Cambridge, MA, 2016).
2 Much of the work published as Volumes II and III of *Das Kapital* was *in statu nascendi* at the time of Marx's death, his project of 'scientific socialism' still unachieved. Engels ordered, linked and completed much that he had left in fragments, making not a few changes in the process.
3 See for example XXXf. above on Engels' only recently discovered (co-)authorship of publications for the *New York Tribune* (1851–1862) long thought to have been written by Marx alone.
4 Wilfried Nippel, 'Friedrich Engels und die Politik des Vorworts', *Zeitschrift für Ideengeschichte* 11, 2017, 67–78; Christina Morina, *Die Erfindung des Marxismus: Wie eine Idee die Welt erobert* (Munich, 2017).
5 Engels' early publications *Umrisse einer Kritik der Nationalökonomie* (1844)/*Outlines of a Critique of Political Economy* (MECW, vol. 3, 418–43) and *Die Lage der arbeitenden Klasse in England* (1845)/*The Condition of the Working Class in England* (MECW, vol. 4, 295–583) played an important role in the genesis of this friendship; see in general Jürgen Herres, *Marx und Engels: Das Portrait einer intellektuellen Freundschaft* (Ditzingen, 2018).
6 On connections (and comparisons) between Barmen, Engelskirchen and Manchester, see Eberhard Illner, 'Das Textilunternehmen Engels in Manchester: Wirtschaftsbeziehungen und Arbeitsverhältnisse', *Marx-Engels-Jahrbuch* 2011, 94–112.
7 For greater detail, see Jürgen Kocka, *Das lange 19: Jahrhundert. Arbeit, Nation und bürgerliche Gesellschaft* (Stuttgart, 2001 - also publishd in Gebhardt, *Handbuch der deutschen Geschichte* 13, 115–19).
8 See Tristram Hunt, *Marx's General: The Revolutionary Life of Friedrich Engels* (New York, 2009)/*Friedrich Engels: Der Mann, der den Marxismus erfand* (Berlin, 2017), 253–8; Klaus Körner, '*Wir zwei betreiben ein Compagniegeschäft': Karl Marx und Friedrich Engels. Eine aussergewöhnliche Freundschaft* (Hamburg, 2009), 115–17; Illner, 'Das Textilunternehmen', 111f.; Engels died a wealthy man.
9 On the marked heterogeneity of Germany' educated middle classes, see Jürgen Kocka (ed.), *Bildungsbürgertum im 19: Jahrhundert. Teil IV: Politischer Einfluss und gesellschaftliche Formation* (Stuttgart, 1989).
10 On the intellectual history of the pairing 'creative destruction', common in nineteenth-century thought, and its role in Engels, see Frambach (→XXX–XXX).

CHAPTER 14

1. Erich Kundel and Alexander Malysch, 'Bilanz und Perspektiven. Ein Bericht der Sekretäre der Redaktionskommission über die Herausgabe der Marx-Engels-Gesamtausgabe nach dem Erscheinen der ersten 10 Bände'.
2. MEW, vol. 2, IX–X.

BIBLIOGRAPHY

Carol Adams, Paula Bartley, Judy Lown and Cathy Loxton, *Under Control: Life in a Nineteenth-Century Silk Factory*. Cambridge, 1983.
Georg Adler, *Rodbertus, der Begründer des wissenschaftlichen Sozialismus: Eine sozialökonomische Studie*. Leipzig, 1884.
Georg Adler, *Die Geschichte der ersten sozialpolitischen Arbeiterbewegung in Deutschland mit besonderer Rücksicht auf die einwirkenden Theorien: Ein Beitrag zur Entwickelungsgeschichte der sozialen Frage*. Breslau, 1885, repr. Frankfurt a.M. 1966.
Georg Adler, *Die Grundlagen der Karl Marxschen Kritik der bestehenden Volkswirtschaft: Kritische und ökonomisch-literarische Studien*. Tübingen, 1887.
Matthew Allen, 'The Deployment of Untried Technology: British Naval Tactics in the Ironclad Era', *War in History* 15, 2008, 269-3.
Bert Andréas, 'Briefe und Dokumente der Familie Marx aus den Jahren 1862-1873 nebst zwei unbekannten Aufsätzen von Friedrich Engels', *Archiv für Sozialgeschichte* 167, 1962: 167-293.
Bert Andréas, *Le Manifeste Communiste de Marx et Engels. Histoire et Bibliographie 1848-1918*. Milano, 1963.
Bert Andréas, ed., *Gründungsdokumente des Bundes der Kommunisten (Juni bis September 1847)*. Hamburg, 1969.
Richard Arena, 'Adolphe-Jerome Blanqui, un historien de l'économie aux préoccupations sociales'. In Yves Breton and Michel Lutfall (eds), *L'économie politique en France au XIXe siècle*, 163-83. Paris, 1991.
Frolinde Balser, *Sozial-Demokratie 1848/49-1863. Die erste deutsche Arbeiterorganisation „Allgemeine deutsche Arbeiterverbrüderung" nach der Revolution*. Stuttgart, 1962.
David Barnett, *London, Hub of the Industrial Revolution: A Revisionary History 1775-1825*. London, 1998.
Thomas Bauer, *Die Vereindeutigung der Welt. Über den Verlust an Mehrdeutigkeit und Vielfalt*. Ditzingen, 2018.
Otto Bauer, *Die Nationalitätenfrage und die Sozialdemokratie*, Marx-Studien, vol. 2. Vienna, 1907.
Otto Bauer, 'Die Akkumulation des Kapitals', *Die Neue Zeit* I(31), 1912/13: 831-8.
Otto Bauer, *Die österreichische Revolution*. Vienna, 1923.
Volker Bauer, *Hofökonomie. Der Diskurs über den Fürstenhof in Zeremonialwissenschaft, Hausväterliteratur und Kameralismus*. Vienna, 1997.
James Phinney Baxter, *The Introduction of the Ironclad Warship*. Cambridge (MA), 1968.
Kurt Bayertz, 'Technik bei Marx'. In: Michael Quante and Erzsébet Rózsa (eds): *Anthropologie und Technik*. Munich, 2012, 57-70.
Christopher Bayly, *Die Geburt der modernen Welt*. Frankfurt a. M., 2006.
Ken Baynes and Francis Pugh, *The Art of the Engineer*. Guildford, 1981.
Gerhard Becker, 'Joseph Moll: Mitglied der Zentralbehörde des Bundes der Kommunisten und Präsident des Kölner Arbeitervereins'. In: Helmut Bleiber, Walter Schmidt and Rolf Weber (eds): *Männer der Revolution von 1848*, vol. 2. Berlin, 1987, 53-83.
Sven Beckert, *Empire of Cotton: A Global History*. New York, 2014.
Germ.: *King Cotton. Eine Globalgeschichte des Kapitalismus*. Munich, 2014.
John F. Beeler, *British Naval Policy in the Gladstone-Disraeli Era, 1866-1880*. Stanford, 1997.
John F. Beeler, *Birth of the Battleship: British Capital Ship Design 1960-1881*. London, 2004.

Bibliography

John Belchem, *Irish, Catholic and Scouse: The History of the Liverpool-Irish, 1800–1939.* Liverpool, 2007.

Eduard Bernstein, 'Friedrich Engels: Ein Gedenkblatt', *Der wahre Jacob* 21(Suppl 239), September 1895, 2023–6.

Rudolf Berthold and Hans-Heinrich Müller (eds), *Geschichte der Produktivkräfte in Deutschland von 1800 bis 1945* (3 vols), vol. 2: *Produktivkräfte in Deutschland 1870 bis 1917/18.* Berlin, 1985.

Friedhelm Boll, *Arbeitskämpfe und Gewerkschaften in Deutschland, England und Frankreich: Ihre Entwicklung vom 19. Zum 20. Jahrhundert.* Bonn, 1992.

H. M. Boot and J. H. Maindonald, 'New Estimates, of Age- and Sex-Specific Earnings and the Male:Female Earnings Gap in the British Cotton Industry', 1833–1906, *The Economic History Review* 61, 2008, 380–404.

Max Boot, *War Made New Technology, Warfare, and the Course of History, 1500 to Today.* New York, 2006.

Heinz-Lutger Borgert, *Die Marineplanungen in Deutschland 1860–1867 und Friedrich Engels.* Frankfurt a. M., Bern, 1977.

Joseph L. Bower and Clayton M. Christensen, 'Disruptive Technologies: Catching the Wave', *Harvard Business Review* 73(1), January–February 1995, 43–53.

Catherine Bowler and Peter Brimblecome, 'Control of Air Pollution prior to the Public Health Act of 1875', *Environment and History* 6, 2000, 71–98.

Robert L. Boyd, 'Competition and Coexistence in the Urban Economy: Native Whites, European Immigrants, and the Retail Trade in the Late Nineteenth Century United States', *Sociological Focus* 44, 2011, 37–54.

Hans-Joachim Braun, 'Franz Reuleaux'. In: Wilhelm Treue and Wolfgang König (eds): *Berlinische Lebensbilder*, vol. 6: *Techniker*, 279–92, Berlin, 1990.

William J. Brazill, *The Young Hegelians.* New Haven, London, 1970.

Amy Bridges, 'Becoming American: The Working Classes in the United States before the Civil War'. In: Ira Katznelson and Aristide R. Zolberg (eds): *Working-Class Formation: Nineteenth-Century Patterns in Western Europe and the United States.* Princeton, 1986.

Rudolf Brommy and Heinrich von Littrow, *Die Marine: Gemeinfassliche Darstellung des gesammten Seewesens.* Vienna, Pest, Leipzig 1878, repr. Leipzig, 1982.

Fritz Brupbacher, *Marx und Bakunin*, Munich, 1913.

Volkmar Bueb, *Die „Junge Schule" der französischen Marine. Strategie und Politik 1875–1900.* Boppard am Rhein, 1971.

Joyce Burnette, *Gender, Work and Wages in Industrial Revolution.* Cambridge, 2008.

Joyce Burnette, 'An Investigation of the Female–Male Wage Gap During the Industrial Revolution', *Economic History Review* 59, 1999, 257–81.

Mervyn A. Busteed and Rob I. Hodgson, 'Irish Migrant Responses to Urban Life in Early Nineteenth-Century Manchester', *The Geographical Journal* 162, 1996, 139–52.

Duncan Bythell, *The Sweated Trades: Outwork in Nineteenth-Century Britain.* London, 1978.

Günther Chaloupek, '*Karl Renners Konzeption des „demokratischen Wirtschaftsstaats"*'. In: Günther Chaloupek, Heinz D. Kurz and William Smaldone (eds): *Rudolf Hilferding: Finanzkapital und organisierter Kapitalismus.* Graz, 2011, 73–104.

Roger Chesneau and Eugene M. Kolesnik (eds), *Conway's All the World's Fighting Ships 1860–1905.* Greenwich, 1979.

Gregory Claeys, 'Engels' Outlines of a Critique of Political Economy (1843) and the Origins of the Marxist Critique of Capitalism', *History of Political Economy* 16(2), 1984, 207–32.

Gregory Claeys, 'The Political Ideas of the Young Engels, 1842–1845: Owenism, Chartism, and the Question of Violent Revolution in the Transition from "Utopian" to "Scientific" Socialism', *History of Political Thought* 6, 1986, 455–78.

Gregory Claeys, *Machinery, Money and the Millennium: From Moral Economy to Socialism 1815–60*. Princeton, 1987.

Donald C. Coleman, *Courtaulds: An Economic and Social History*. Oxford, 1969.

Jean-Marc Combe and Bernard Escudie, *L'Aventure scientifique et technique de la Vapeur*. Paris, 1986.

Werner Conze, 'Arbeit'. In: Otto Brunner, Werner Conze and Reinhart Koselleck (eds): *Geschichtliche Grundbegriffe: Historisches Lexikon zur politisch-sozialen Sprache in Deutschland*. Stuttgart, 1972, 154–215.

Seth Cotlar, *Tom Paine's America: The Rise and Fall of Transatlantic Radicalism in the Early Republic*. Charlottesville, 2011.

David F. Crew, *Bochum: Sozialgeschichte einer Industriestadt 1860–1914*. Frankfurt a. M., 1980.

Maurice Daumas, 'Introduction'. In: Marguerite Dubuisson (ed.): *L'Expansion du Machinisme, Histoire générale des Techniques*, vol. 3. Paris, 1968, VII–XXIV.

Charles Darwin, *The Descent of Man, and Selection in Relation to Sex*. London, 1871.

Henry David, *The History of the Hay Market Affair: A Study of the American Social-Revolutionary and Labour Movements*, 3rd ed. New York, 1963.

Graham Davis, 'The Irish in Nineteenth Century Britain', *Soathar* 16, 1991, 130–5.

Andrew Dawson, 'Reassessing Henry Carey (1793–1879): The Problems of Writing Political Economy in Nineteenth-Century America', *Journal of American Studies* 34(3), 2000, 465–85.

Phyllis Deane, *The First Industrial Revolution*. Cambridge, 1965.

Michael Deege, 'Ernst Kapp, Bemerkungen zur Philosophie der Organprojektionstheorie', *Prima Philosophia* 14(1), 2001, 51–68.

Yves Deforge, *Le Graphisme technique: Son Histoire et son Enseignement*. Seyssel, 1986.

Karl Diehl, *Pierre Joseph Proudhon: Seine Lehre und sein Leben*, 1st part (Die Eigentums- und Wertlehre), 1st ed. 1888. Aalen, 1968.

Rolf Dlubek, 'August Willich (1810–1878): Vom preußischen Offizier zum Streiter für die Arbeiteremanzipation auf zwei Kontinenten'. In: Helmut Bleiber, Walter Schmidt, Susanne Schötz et al. (eds): *Akteure eines Umbruchs: Männer und Frauen der Revolution von 1848/49*. Berlin, 2003, 923–1003.

Rolf Dlubek, '"Was kann man denn wollen ohne die Arbeiter": Revolutionserfahrungen im Wirken Johann Philipp Beckers 1849–1853'. In: Walter Schmidt (ed.): *Demokratie, Liberalismus und Konterrevolution: Studien zur deutschen Revolution von 1848/49*. Berlin, 1998, 485–547.

Patrick Eiden-Offe, *Die Poesie der Klasse: Romantischer Antikapitalismus und die Erfindung des Proletariats*. Berlin, 2017.

Leonid Fjodorowitsch Iljitschow, *Friedrich Engels: Sein Leben und Wirken*. Moscow, 1973 (Russian orig., Moscow, 1970).

Elisabeth Fehrenbach, *Vom Ancien Régime zum Wiener Kongress*. Munich, 2001.

Iring Fetscher, *Stalin: Über dialektischen und historischen Materialismus,* complete text and critical comment, 4th ed. Frankfurt a. M., 1959.

Philip S. Foner, *When Karl Marx Died: Comments in 1883*. New York, 1973.

Hans Frambach, 'The Decline of Cameralism in Germany at the Turn of the Nineteenth Century'. In: Keith Tribe and Marten Seppel (eds): *Cameralism in Practice: The Principles of Early Modern State Administration and Economy*. Martlesham, 2017, 239–61.

Hans Frambach, *Arbeit im ökonomischen Denken: Zum Wandel des Arbeitsverständnisses von der Antike bis zur Gegenwart*. Marburg, 1999.

Hans Frambach, 'Zur Erklärung von wirtschaftlicher Entwicklung bei Karl Marx'. In: Rainer Lucas, Reinhard Pfriem and Claus Thomasberger (eds): *Auf der Suche nach dem Ökonomischen – Karl Marx zum 200. Geburtstag*. Marburg, 2018, 23–41.

Bibliography

Hans Frambach, 'Der Schumpetersche Unternehmer in der Geschichte der ökonomischen Analyse'. In: Hans Frambach, Norbert Koubek, Heinz D. Kurz and Reinhard Pfriem (eds): *Schöpferische Zerstörung und der Wandel des Unternehmertums*. Marburg, 2019, 213-28.

Bernard Gainer, *The Alien Invasion: The Origins of the Aliens Act of 1905*. London, 1972.

Heiner Ganßmann, 'Das Ende des Kapitalismus als Technikfolge?' In: Theo Pirker, Hans-Peter Müller and Rainer Winkelmann (eds): *Technik und Industrielle Revolution: Vom Ende eines sozialwissenschaftlichen Paradigmas*. Opladen, 1987, 290-314.

Robert Gardiner, *Steam, Steel and Shellfire: The Steam Warship 1815-1905*. London, 1992.

Lloyd P. Gartner, *The Jewish Immigrant in England 1870-1914*. London, 1960.

Heinrich Gemkow, *Friedrich Engels: Eine Biographie*. Berlin, 1970.

M. Dorothy George, *London Life in the Eighteenth Century*. Harmondsworth, 1965.

Jan M. Dirkzwager, *Geschiedenis van de techniek in Nederland: De wording van een moderne samenleving 1800-1890*. Deel IV, Harry Lintsen (ed.), Zutphen, 177-213, 1993.

Heinz Gester, Norbert Koubek and Gerd R. Wiedemeyer (eds), *Unternehmensverfassung und Mitbestimmung in Europa*. Wiesbaden, 1991.

Edwin Lawrence Godkin, 'The Labor Crisis', *North American Review* 105(216), 1867.

Andrew Godley, 'Immigrant Entrepreneurs and the Emergence of London's East End as an Industrial District', *The London Journal* 21, 1996, 38-45.

Linda Gordon, *The Great Arizona Orphan Abduction*, Cambridge (MA), 2001.

Marcus Gräser, *Wohlfahrtsgesellschaft und Wohlfahrtsstaat. Bürgerliche Sozialreform und „Welfare State Building" in den USA und in Deutschland 1880-1940*. Göttingen, 2009.

Jacques Grandjonc, 'Eine dritte MEGA? Jacques Grandjonc im Gespräch mit Peter Schöttler'. In: Doris Obschernitzki (ed.): *Frankreichs deutsche Emigranten: Texte von und Erinnerungen an Jacques Grandjonc (1933-2000)*. Teetz, 2003, 85-96.

Jacques Grandjonc, 'Über den richtigen Gebrauch von Erinnerungen in der Geschichtsschreibung: Stephan Born über Marx und Engels, fünfzig Jahre später'. In: Doris Obschernitzki (ed.): *Frankreichs deutsche Emigranten*, 132-48, Hentrich & Hentrich, 2003.

David R. Green, *From Artisans to Paupers: Economic Change and Poverty in London, 1790-1870*. Aldershot, 1995.

James R. Green, *Death in the Haymarket: A Story of Chicago, the First Labor Movement, and the Bombing That Divided Gilded Age America*. New York, 2006.

Anneliese Griese and Gerd Pawlzig, *Friedrich Engels' „Dialektik der Natur", eine vergleichende Studie zur Editionsgeschichte*. In: MEGA-Studien, 1995/1. Amsterdam, 1995, 33-60.

Erik Grimmer-Solem, *The Rise of Historical Economics and Social Reform in Germany, 1864-1894*. Oxford, 2003.

Gustav Groß, *Karl Marx: Eine Studie*. Leipzig, 1885.

Werner Hahlweg, 'Sozialismus und Militärwissenschaft bei Friedrich Engels'. In: Hans Pelger (ed.): *Friedrich Engels 1820-1970*. Hannover, 1971, 63-72.

John Lawrence Hammond and Barbara Hammond, *The Skilled Labourer 1760-1832*, 1st ed. 1912. New York, 1967.

Bob Hancké (ed.), *Debating Varieties of Capitalism*. Oxford, 2009.

William H. Harris, *The Harder We Run: Black Workers since the Civil War*. New York, 1982.

Terence W. Hutchison, 'Friedrich Engels and Marxist Economic Theory', *Journal of Political Economy* 86(2), 1978, 303-19.

Heinz-Gerhard Haupt, *Konsum und Handel: Europa im 19. und 20. Jahrhundert*. Göttingen, 2003.

Ágnes Heller, 'Marx und die Frage der Technik'. In: Michael Quante and Erzsébet Rózsa (eds): *Anthropologie und Technik*. Munich, 2012, 45-56.

William Otto Henderson, *Marx and Engels and the English Workers and Other Essays*. London, 1989.

William Otto Henderson, *The Life of Friedrich Engels*. London, 1976.
Klaus Hinrich Hennings, *Aspekte der Institutionalisierung der Ökonomie an deutschen Universitäten: Die Institutionalisierung der Nationalökonomie an deutschen Universitäten*. St Katharinen, 1988.
Jürgen Herres, 'Der Kölner Kommunistenprozess von 1852', *Geschichte in Köln* 50, 2003, 133–55.
Jürgen Herres, 'Marx und Engels über Irland', *Marx-Engels-Jahrbuch 2011*, 12–27, Berlin 2012.
Jürgen Herres, *Marx und Engels: Porträt einer intellektuellen Freundschaft*. Stuttgart, 2018.
Beatrice Heuser, *The Evolution of Strategy: Thinking War from Antiquity to the Present*. Cambridge, 2010.
Rudolf Hilferding, *Das Finanzkapital: Eine Studie zur jüngsten Entwicklung des Kapitalismus*, Vienna, 1910, new ed. Frankfurt a. M., 1973.
Richard Hill, *War at Sea in the Ironclad Age*. London, 2002.
Eric Hobsbawm, 'Einleitung'. In: *Karl Marx: Das kommunistische Manifest*. Eine moderne ed, Hamburg, 1999, 7–38.
Peter Hore, *The Ironclads: An Illustrated History of Battleships from 1860 to the First World War*. London, 2006.
Gerald Hubman and Regina Roth, 'Die "Kapital-Abteilung" der MEGA. Einleitung und Überblick', in: *Marx-Engels Jahrbuch*, 2012/13, Berlin 2013.
Martin Hundt, *Geschichte des Bundes der Kommunisten 1836–1852*. Frankfurt a. M., 1993.
Emil O. Huning, *Die Entwicklung der Schiffs- und Küstenartillerie bis zur Gegenwart*. Berlin, Leipzig, 1912.
Tristram Hunt, *Marx's General: The Revolutionary Life of Friedrich Engels*, New York, 2009. German: *Friedrich Engels. Der Mann, der den Marxismus erfand*, 3. ed., Berlin, 2013.
Terence W. Hutchison, 'Friedrich Engels and Marxist Economic Theory', *Journal of Political Economy* 86, 1978, 303–19.
Institut für Marxismus-Leninismus beim ZK der SED (ed.), *Mohr und General: Erinnerungen an Marx und Engels*. Berlin, 1982.
Ulrich Israel and Jürgen Gebauer, *Panzerschiffe*. Berlin, 1998.
Friedrich Jäger, Wolfgang Knöbl and Ute Schneider (eds), *Handbuch Moderneforschung*. Stuttgart, 2015.
Carl Jantke and Dietrich Hilger, *Die Eigentumslosen: Der deutsche Pauperismus und die Emanzipationskrise in Deutungen und Darstellungen der zeitgenössischen Literatur*. Freiburg, Munich, 1965.
S. R. H. Jones, 'Technology, Transaction Costs and the Transition to Factory Production in the British Silk Industry 1700–1870', *Journal of Economic History* 47, 1987, 71–96.
Karl Kautsky, 'Das Kapital von Rodbertus', *Die neue Zeit* 2, 1884, 337–50.
Claus D. Kernig, 'Das Verhältnis von Kriegslehre und Gesellschaftstheorie bei Engels'. In: *Friedrich Engels 1820–1970: Referate, Diskussionen, Dokumente*. Hannover, 1971, 77–92.
Raymond George Kirby, Rosina Greene Kirby and Albert Edward Musson, *The Voice of the People: John Doherty (1798–1854) Trade Unionist, Radical and Factory Reformer*. Manchester, 1975.
Michael Kittner, *Arbeits- und Sozialordnung: Ausgewählte und eingeleitete Gesetzestexte*, 45th ed. Frankfurt a. M., 2020.
Fritz Klenner, *Die österreichischen Gewerkschaften*. Vienna, 1974.
Michael Knieriem, *„Gewinn unter Gottes Segen": Ein Beitrag zu Firmengeschichte und geschäftlicher Situation von Friedrich Engels*. Neustadt an der Aisch, 1987.
Michael Knieriem, 'Die Firma "Ermen & Engels" in Manchester und Engelskirchen im 19.Jahrhundert', *Marx-Engels-Jahrbuch* 10, 1987, 211–34.
Michael Knieriem (ed.), *Die Herkunft des Friedrich Engels: Briefe aus der Verwandtschaft 1791–1847*, Schriften aus dem Karl-Marx-Haus, no. 42. Trier, 1991.

Bibliography

Jürgen Kocka, *Arbeitsverhältnisse und Arbeiterexistenzen: Grundlagen der Klassenbildung im 19. Jahrhundert*. Bonn, 1990.

Wolfgang König, 'Friedrich Engels und die "Elektrotechnische Revolution"', *Technikgeschichte* 56(1), 1989, 9–38.

Wolfgang König, *Geschichte der Konsumgesellschaft*. Stuttgart, 2000.

Helmut Konrad, *Nationalismus und Internationalismus*. Vienna, 1976.

Eduard Korte, *Der anthropologische Maßstab: Die Philosophie Ernst Kapps vor ihrem kulturphilosophischen und geistesgeschichtlichen Hintergrund*. Düsseldorf, 1991.

Norbert Koubek, *Jenseits und Diesseits der Betriebswirtschaftslehre: Institutionen – Unternehmenstheorien – Globale Strukturen*. Wiesbaden, 2010.

Michael Krätke, 'Friedrich Engels und die großen Transformationen des Kapitalismus'. In: Reiner Lucas, Reinhard Pfriem and Dieter Westhoff (eds): *Arbeiten am Widerspruch – Friedrich Engels zum 200. Geburtstag*. Marburg, 2020, 121–59.

Thomas Kuczynski, *Das Kommunistische Manifest (Manifest der Kommunistischen Partei) von Karl Marx und Friedrich Engels. Von der Erstausgabe zur Leseausgabe. Mit einem Editionsbericht*. Trier, 1995.

Walter Kumpmann (ed.), *Friedrich Engels, Die Lage der arbeitenden Klasse in England*. Munich, 1973.

Heinz D. Kurz and Neri Salvadori, *Theory of Production: A Long-Period Analysis*. Cambridge, 1995, rev. paperback ed. 1997.

Heinz D. Kurz and Neri Salvadori, 'Sraffa and the Labour Theory of Value: A Few Observations'. In: John Vint, J. Stanley Metcalfe, Heinz D. Kurz, Neri Salvadori and Paul A. Samuelson (eds): *Economic Theory and Economic Thought: Essays in Honour of Ian Steedman*. London, 2010, 187–213.

Heinz Kurz, 'Rudolf Hilferdings Das Finanzkapital'. In: Günther Chaloupek, Heinz D. Kurz and William Smaldone, *Rudolf Hilferding: Finanzkapital und organisierter Kapitalismus*. Graz, 2011, 11–51.

Heinz Kurz, 'Don't Treat Too Ill My Piero! Interpreting Sraffa's Papers', *Cambridge Journal of Economics* 36, 2012, 1535–69.

Heinz Kurz, *Economic Thought: A Brief History*. New York, 2016.

Heinz Kurz, 'Zur Politischen Ökonomie des homo mercans: Adam Smith über Märkte', *Deutsches Jahrbuch Philosophie* 7, 2016, 23–48.

Heinz Kurz, 'Technical Progress, Capital Accumulation and Income Distribution in Classical Economics: Adam Smith, David Ricardo and Karl Marx', *European Journal of the History of Economic Thought* 17(5), 2010, 1183–222.

Heinz Kurz, 'David Ricardo: On the Art of "Elucidating Economic Principles" in the Face of a "labyrinth of Difficulties"', *European Journal of the History of Economic Thought* 22(5), 2015, 818–51.

Heinz Kurz, 'Hin zu Marx und über ihn hinaus: Zum 200.Geburtstag eines deutschen politischen Ökonomen von historischem Rang', *Perspektiven der Wirtschaftspolitik* 13(3), 2018, 245–65.

Heinz Kurz, 'Adam Smith über das Merkantil- und das Agrikultursystem'. In: Hendrik Hansen and Tim Kraski (eds): *Politischer und wirtschaftlicher Liberalismus: Das Staatsverständnis von Adam Smith (Staatsverständnisse)*. 67–92, Baden Baden, 2019.

Heinz Kurz, 'Der junge Engels über die „Bereicherungswissenschaft", die „Unsittlichkeit" von Privateigentum und Konkurrenz und die „Heuchelei der Oekonomen"'. In: Reiner Lucas, Reinhard Pfriem and Dieter Westhoff (eds): *Arbeiten am Widerspruch – Friedrich Engels zum 200. Geburtstag*. Marburg, 2020, 65–120.

International Labour Organization (ILO), *Tripartie Declaration of Principles Concerning Multinational Enterprises and Social Policy*, 5th ed. Geneva, 2017.

Dieter Langewiesche, *Der gewaltsame Lehrer. Europas Kriege in der Moderne*. Munich, 2019.

Bibliography

Ulrike Laufer and Hans Ottomeyer (eds), *Gründerzeit 1848–1871: Industrie und Lebensträume zwischen Vormärz und Kaiserreich*. Dresden, 2008.

L. H. Lees, *Exiles of Erin: Irish Migrants in Victorian London*. Manchester, 1979.

Jan Marco Leimeister, Shkodran Zogaj, David Durward and Ulrich Bretschneider, 'Neue Geschäftsfelder durch Crowdsourcing: Crowd-basierte Start-ups als Arbeitsmodell der Zukunft'. In: Reiner Hoffmann and Claudia Bogedan (eds): *Arbeit der Zukunft*. Frankfurt a. M., New York, 2015, 141–58.

Harald Leinenbach, *Die Körperlichkeit der Technik: Zur Organprojektionstheorie Ernst Kapps*. Essen, 1990.

Wladimir Iljitsch Lenin(ed.), 'Der Imperialismus als höchstes Stadium des Kapitalismus: Gemeinverständlicher Abriss' (1916). In: *Ausgewählte Werke*, vol. II. Frankfurt a. M., 1970, 643–770.

Norbert Leser (ed.), *Werk und Widerhall: Große Gestalten des österreichischen Sozialismus*. Vienna, 1964.

Norbert Leser, *Zwischen Reformismus und Bolschewismus*. Vienna, 1968.

Walter Licht, *Industrializing America: The Nineteenth Century*. Baltimore, 1995.

Albert S. Lindemann, *A History of European Socialism*. New Haven, London, 1983.

Stefan Link and Noam Maggor, 'The United States as a Developing Nation: Revisiting the Peculiarities of American History', *Past and Present* 246, February 2020, 269–306.

Harold Livesay, *Samuel Gompers and Organized Labor in America*. Boston, 1978.

Roger Lloyd-Jones and M. J. Lewis, *Manchester and the Age of the Factory: The Business Structure of Cottonopolis in the Industrial Revolution*. London, 1988.

Reiner Lucas, Reinhard Pfriem and Dieter Westhoff (eds), *Arbeiten am Widerspruch – Friedrich Engels zum 200. Geburtstag*. Marburg, 2020.

Hermann Lübbe, *Politische Philosophie in Deutschland: Studien zu ihrer Geschichte*. Munich, 1974.

Friedrich Lütge, 'Über die Auswirkungen der Bauernbefreiung in Deutschland', *Jahrbücher für Nationalökonomie uns Statistik* 157, 1943, 353–404.

Rosa Luxemburg, 'Die Akkumulation des Kapitals: Ein Beitrag zur ökonomischen Erklärung des Imperialismus (1913)'. In: *Gesammelte Werke*, vol. 5: *Ökonomische Schriften*. Berlin, 1985, 5–412.

Donald MacKenzie, 'Marx and the Machine', *Technology and Culture* 25, 1984, 473–502.

Marshall MacLuhan, *Die magischen Kanäle*. Düsseldorf, Vienna, 1968.

Donald MacRaild, *Irish Migrants in Modern Britain 1750–1922*. London, 1999.

Eduard März, *Joseph Alois Schumpeter – Forscher, Lehrer und Politiker*. Munich, 1983.

Alfred Thayer Mahan, *The Influence of Sea Power upon History, 1660–1783*. New York 1890. German: *Der Einfluss der Seemacht auf die Geschichte*, vol. 2, *1783–1812: Die Zeit der Französischen Revolution und des Kaiserreichs auf Veranlassung des Kaiserlichen Ober-Kommandos der Marine*, transl. Karl Ferdinand Batsch and Karl Paschen. Berlin, 1899.

Franz Marek, *Was Stalin wirklich sagte*. Vienna, 1970.

Tiago Mata and Robert van Horn, 'Capitalist Threads: Engels the Businessman and Marx's Capital', *History of political Economy* 49(2), 2017, 207–32.

Arno J. Mayer, *Adelsmacht und Bürgertum: Die Krise der europäischen Gesellschaft 1848–1914*. Munich, 1984.

Gustav Mayer, *Friedrich Engels: Eine Biographie, Erster Band: Friedrich Engels in seiner Frühzeit 1820 bis 1851*, and supplementary vol. Berlin, 1920, 2 vols. Frankfurt a. M., 1975.

Franz Mehring, 'Börnsteins Memoiren', *Die Neue Zeit* 13(2), 1895, 377–80.

Franz Mehring, *Geschichte der deutschen Sozialdemokratie*, vol. 1: *Von der Julirevolution bis zum preußischen Verfassungsstreite 1830 bis 1863*. Stuttgart, 1897.

Bibliography

Wolfgang Meiser, 'Das Manifest der Kommunistischen Partei vom Februar 1848: Zur Entstehung und Überlieferung der ersten Ausgabe', in: *MEGA-Studien*, 1996/1, 66–107.

François Melis, 'Zur Gründungsgeschichte der Neuen Rheinischen Zeitung. Neue Dokumente und Fakten', in: *MEGA-Studien* 1998/1, 3–63.

François Melis, 'Neue Rheinische Zeitung. Organ der Demokratie. Ein Redaktionsalltag – oder mehr? Köln, 14 November 1848', *Jahrbuch für Forschungen zur Geschichte der Arbeiterbewegung* 2(2002), 85–107.

Renate Merkel-Melis, 'Die Neue Rheinische Zeitung im journalistischen Spätwerk von Engels'. In: *Die Journalisten Marx und Engels: Das Beispiel Neue Rheinische Zeitung*. Hamburg, 2006, 249–58.

Renate Merkel-Melis, 'Übersetzungen im Spätwerk von Friedrich Engels'. In: *Das Kapital und Vorarbeiten: Exzerpte und Entwürfe*. Hamburg, 2011, 195–208.

Timothy Messer-Kruse, *The Trial of the Hay Market Anarchists: Terrorism and Justice in the Gilden Age*. London, 2011.

Timothy Messer-Kruse, *The Yankee International: Marxism and the American Reform Tradition, 1848–1876*. Chapel Hill, 1998.

Gisela Mettele, 'Mary und Lizzy Burns, die Lebensgefährtinnen von Friedrich Engels', in: *Marx-Engels Jahrbuch 2011*, 130–49.

Lucian O. Meysels, *Victor Adler*. Vienna, Munich, 1997.

Paul Minoletti, 'The Importance of Ideology: The Shift to Factory Production and Its Effect on Women's Employment Opportunities in the English Textile Industries', *Discussion Papers in Economic and Social History* 87, February 2011. http://www.nuff.ox.ac.uk/Economics/History.

David Montgomery, 'Labor in the Industrial Era'. In: Richard B. Morrs (ed.), *The U.S. Department of Labor Bicentennial History of the American Worker*. Washington, 1976.

David Montgomery, *The Fall of the House of Labor: The Workplace, the State, and American Labor Activism, 1865–1925*. Cambridge, 1987.

David Montgomery, *Citizen Worker: The Experience of Workers in the United States with Democracy and the Free Market During the Nineteenth Century*. Cambridge, 1993.

Wolfgang Mönke, *Das literarische Echo in Deutschland auf Friedrich Engels's Werk 'Die Lage der arbeitenden Klasse in England'*, Deutsche Akademie der Wissenschaften zu Berlin, Vorträge und Schriften 92. Berlin, 1965.

Kurt Möser, 'Turmschiff Captain'. In: *Neue Grauzonen der Technikgeschichte*, Technikdiskurse 14. Karlsruhe, 2018, 71–81.

Jacques Mordal, *25 Jahrhunderte Seekrieg*. Munich, 1963.

Joel Mokyr, *The Lever of Riches: Technological Creativity and Economical Progress*. New York, Oxford, 1990.

Gerald Mozetic, *Die Gesellschaftstheorie des Austromarxismus*. Darmstadt, 1984.

Oliver Müller, 'Marx und die Philosophie der Technik', *Allgemeine Zeitschrift für Philosophie* 3, 2018, 323–51.

Herfried Münkler, *Über den Krieg: Stationen der Kriegsgeschichte im Spiegel ihrer theoretischen Reflexion*. Weilerswist, 2002.

Max Nettlau, 'Marxanalekten'. In: *Archiv für die Geschichte des Sozialismus und der Arbeiterbewegung*, 8 vols. Leipzig, 1919, 389–99.

August H. Nimtz, *Marx, Tocqueville and Race in America: The "Absolute Democracy" or the "Defiled Republic"*. Lanham, 2003.

Wilfried Nippel, *Fußnoten, Zitate, Plagiate: Wissenschaftsgeschichtliche Streifzüge*. Heidelberg, 2014.

Wilfried Nippel, 'Friedrich Engels und die Politik des Vorworts', in: *Zeitschrift für Ideengeschichte* 3, 2017, 67–78.

Wilfried Nippel, 'Charisma, Organisation und Führung. Ferdinand Lassalle und die deutsche Arbeiterpartei', *Mittelweg 36* 27(6), 2018, 16–42.
Wilfried Nippel, 'Diktatur des Proletariats – Versuch einer Historisierung', *Zyklos. Jahrbuch für Theorie und Geschichte der Soziologie* 5, 2019, 71–130.
Wilfried Nippel, 'Die Arbeit an einem Gesamtwerk von Marx: Engels, Bernstein, Kautsky'. In: Martin Endreß and Christian Jansen (eds): *Karl Marx im 21: Jahrhundert. Bilanz und Perspektiven*. Frankfurt a. M., 2020, 457–510.
Thomas Nipperdey, *Deutsche Geschichte 1800–1866. Bürgerwelt und starker Staat*. Munich, 1998.
Ernst Nolte, *Marxismus und Industrielle Revolution*. Stuttgart, 1983.
Paul Nolte, *Staatsbildung als Gesellschaftsreform: Politische Reformen in Preußen und den süddeutschen Staaten 1800–1820*. Frankfurt a. M., New York, 1990.
Walter A. Oechler, *Personal und Arbeit: Grundlagen des Human Resource Management und der Arbeitgeber-Arbeitnehmer-Beziehungen*, 7th ed. Munich, Vienna, 2000.
Toni Offermann, 'Allgemeine deutsche Arbeiterverbrüderung, Norddeutsche Arbeitervereinigung und Bund der Kommunisten: Zu neueren DDR-Publikationen zur elementaren Arbeiterbewegung 1848–1851', *Archiv für Sozialgeschichte* 22, 1982, 523–43.
Jürgen Osterhammel, *Die Verwandlung der Welt: Eine Geschichte des 19. Jahrhunderts*. Munich, 2009.
Panikos Panayi, *German Immigrants in Britain during the 19th Century, 1815–1914*. Oxford, 1995.
Akos Paulinyi and Ulrich Troitsch, *Mechanisierung und Maschinisierung*. Berlin, 1991.
Akos Paulinyi, *Karl Marx und die Technik seiner Zeit*, LTA-Forschung, 0940-2748, issue 26/1997. Mannheim, 1998.
Akos Paulinyi and Karl von Delhaes, *Technik und Wirtschaft in der Industrialisierung*. Düsseldorf, 2012.
Hermann Pechan, *Louis Blanc als Wegbereiter des modernen Sozialismus*. Jena, 1929.
Werner Pfeiffer and Enno Weiß, *Lean Management: Grundlagen und Organisation industrieller Unternehmen*. Berlin, 1992.
Reinhard Pfriem, Uwe Schneidewind, Jonathan Barth, Silja Graupe and Thomas Korbun (eds), *Transformative Wirtschaftswissenschaft im Kontext nachhaltiger Entwicklung*. Marburg, 2017.
Arnold Picot, Ralf Reichwald and Rolf T. Wigand, *Die grenzenlose Unternehmung: Information, Organisation & Führung*, 7th ed. Heidelberg, 2020.
Thomas Piketty, *Das Kapital im 21: Jahrhundert*. Munich, 2014.
Thomas Piketty, *Kapital und Ideologie*. Munich, 2020.
Theo Pirker, Hans-Peter Müller and Rainer Winkelmann (eds), *Technik und Industrielle Revolution: Vom Ende eines sozialwissenschaftlichen Paradigmas*. Opladen, 1987.
Werner Plumpe, '„Dies ewig unfertige Ding" – Das „Kapital" und seine Entstehungsgeschichte', *Aus Politik und Zeitgeschichte* 67(19–20), 2017, 10–16.
Werner Plumpe, *Unternehmensgeschichte im 19. und 20. Jahrhundert*, Enzyklopädie Deutscher Geschichte 94. Munich, 2018.
Werner Plumpe, 'Realistische Zeiten: Ökonomischer Aufschwung und gesellschaftliche Selbstbilder in den Gründerjahren 1852–1873'. In: Laurenz Lütteken (ed.): *Das Jahr 1868: Musik zwischen Realismus und Gründerzeit*. Kassel, 2019, 17–38.
Werner Plumpe, 'Vom Supranaturalisten zum Kommunisten: Der Weg des jungen Friedrich Engels zur Ökonomie'. In: Rainer Lucas, Reinhard Pfriem and Hans-Dieter Westhoff (eds): *Arbeiten am Widerspruch: Friedrich Engels zum 200. Geburtstag*. Marburg, 2020, 213–48.
Karl Pribram, 'Die Sozialpolitik im neuen Österreich', *Archiv für Sozialwissenschaft und Sozialpolitik* 48, 1921, 615–80.
Iorwerth J. Prothero, *Artisans and Politics in Early Nineteenth-Century London*. Folkstone, 1979.

Bibliography

Arnold A. Putnam, 'Rolf Krake, Europe's First Turreted Ironclad', *Mariner's Mirror* 84(1), February 1998, 56–63.

Max Quarck (ed.), *Die Arbeiterverbrüderung 1848/49: Erinnerungen an die Klassenkämpfe der ersten deutschen Revolution*. Frankfurt a. M., 1900.

Ilsedore Rarisch, *Das Unternehmerbild in der deutschen Erzählliteratur der ersten Hälfte des 19. Jahrhunderts. Ein Beitrag zur Rezeption der Industrialisierung in der frühen belletristischen Literatur*. Berlin, 1977.

Erich Richards, 'Women and the British Economy since about 1700: An Interpretation', *History* 59, 1974, 337–57.

Arthur Redford, *Labour Migration in England 1800–1850*, 2nd ed. Manchester, 1964.

Joanne R. Reitano, *The Tariff Question in the Gilded Age: The Great Debate of 1888*. Philadelphia, 1994.

Reinhold Reith (ed.), *Lexikon des alten Handwerks: Vom späten Mittelalter bis in 20. Jahrhundert*. Munich, 1991.

Jürgen Reulecke, *Sozialer Frieden durch soziale Reform: Der Centralverein für das Wohl der arbeitenden Klassen in der Frühindustrialisierung*. Wuppertal, 1983.

Jürgen Reulecke, *Geschichte der Urbanisierung in Deutschland*. Frankfurt a. M., 1985.

Giorgio Riello, *Cotton: The Fabric That Made the Modern World*. New York, 2013.

Stephen Henry Rigby, *Engels and the Formation of Marxism: History, Dialectics and Revolution*. Manchester, New York, 1992.

Gerhard A. Ritter and Klaus Tenfelde, *Arbeiter im Deutschen Kaiserreich 1871–1914*. Bonn, 1992.

Hugo Reinert and Erik S. Reinert, 'Creative Destruction in Economics: Nietzsche, Sombart, Schumpeter'. In: Jürgen Backhaus and Wolfgang Drechsler (eds): *Friedrich Nietzsche (1844–1900): Economy and Society*, The European Heritage in Economics and the Social Sciences 3. Boston, 2006, 55–85.

Nicolas A. M. Rodger, 'Die Entwicklung der Vorstellung von Seekriegsstrategie in Großbritannien im 18. und 19. Jahrhundert'. In: Jörg Duppler (ed.): *Seemacht und Seestrategie im 19. und 20. Jahrhundert*. Hamburg, 1999, 84–103.

Horst Rössler, '„Die Zuckerbäcker waren vornehmlich Hannoveraner": Zur Geschichte der Wanderung aus dem Elbe-Weser-Dreieck in die britische Zuckerindustrie'. In: *Jahrbuch der Männer vom Morgenstern*. Bremerhaven, 2003, 137–236.

Horst Rössler, 'Hollandgänger, Zuckerbäcker, Amerikaauswanderer. Grenzüberschreitende Fernwanderungen aus dem Elbe-Weser-Dreieck (ca. 1650–1914)', *Niedersächsisches Jahrbuch für Landesgeschichte* 81, 2009, 31–55.

Franziska Rogger, *„Wir helfen uns selbst!". Die kollektive Selbsthilfe der Arbeiterverbrüderung 1848/49 und die individuelle Selbsthilfe Stephan Borns*. Erlangen, 1986.

Jürgen Rojahn, '„Er soll den beiden Alten ein Denkmal setzen": Die Entstehung der Ausgabe des Marx-Engels Briefwechsels von 1913', in: *Marx-Engels-Jahrbuch* 2012/13, 209–85.

Jakow Rokitjanski, 'Engels' Notizen in Georg Adlers Buch „Die Geschichte der ersten socialpolitischen Arbeiterbewegung in Deutschland"', in: *Marx-Engels-Jahrbuch* 2, 1979, 339–68.

Hans Rosenberg, *Die Weltwirtschaftskrise 1857–1859: Mit einem Vorbericht*. Göttingen, 1974.

Lutz von Rosenstiel, *Grundlagen der Organisationspsychologie*, 5th ed. Stuttgart, 2003.

Regina Roth, 'Karl Marx's Original Manuscripts in the Marx-Engels-Gesamtausgabe (MEGA): Another View on Capital'. In: Riccardo Bellofiore (ed.): *Re-reading Marx: New Perspective after the New Edition*. Basingstoke, 2009.

Regina Roth, 'Marx on Technical Change in the Critical Edition', *European Journal History of Economic Thought* 17(5), December 2010, 1223–51.

Ulrich Ruschig, 'Über den Marxismus der kritischen Theorie: Horkheimers Aufnahme und Weiterführung von Engels' „Die Entwicklung des Sozialismus von der Utopie zur Wissenschaft"', *Zeitschrift für Kritische Theorie* 22, 2016, 76–96.
Joachim Schlör, *Nachts in der großen Stadt, Paris, Berlin, London 1840–1930*. Munich, 1991.
Jürgen Schmidt, *Brüder, Bürger und Genossen: Die deutsche Arbeiterbewegung zwischen Klassenkampf und Bürgergesellschaft 1830–1870*. Bonn, 2018.
Harry Schmidtgall, *Friedrich Engels' Manchester-Aufenthalt 1842–1844: Soziale Bewegungen und politische Diskussionen*. Mit Auszügen aus Jakob Venedeys England-Buch (1845) und unbekannten Engels-Dokumenten, Trier, Schriften aus dem Karl-Marx-Haus, n.o 25, 1981.
Jochen Schneider, 'Franz Reuleaux und die Theorie der Maschinen'. In: Tilmann Buddensieg, Kurt Düwell and Klaus-Jürgen Sembach (eds): *Wissenschaften in Berlin, Gedanken*. Berlin, 1987, 173–7.
Carl E. Schorske, *German Social Democracy, 1905–1917: The Development of the Great Schism*. Cambridge (MA), 1955.
Dieter Schott, 'Das Zeitalter der Elektrizität: Visionen – Potentiale – Realitäten', *Jahrbuch für Wirtschaftsgeschichte* 40(2), 1999, 31–50.
Margrit Schulte Beerbühl, *Vom Gesellenverein zur Gewerkschaft: Entwicklung, Struktur und Politik der Londoner Gesellenorganisationen 1550–1825*. Göttingen, 1991.
Joseph Aloys Schumpeter, *Capitalism, Socialism, and Democracy*, 1st ed. 1942. New York, 2008.
Joseph Aloys Schumpeter, *Geschichte der ökonomischen Analyse*, vol. 1 (2 vols). Göttingen, 1965.
Joseph Aloys Schumpeter, *Theorie der wirtschaftlichen Entwicklung*, repr. of ed. 1934, 1st ed. 1912. Berlin, 1997.
Donald M. Schurman, *Imperial Defence 1868–1887*. London, 2014.
Hans-Gerd Servatius, Uwe Schneidewind and Dirk Rohlfink (eds), *Smart Energy. Wandel zu einem nachhaltigen Energiesystem*. Berlin, Heidelberg, 2012.
James Sheehan, *German History 1770–1866*. Oxford, 1989.
Martin Shefter, 'Trade Unions and Political Machines: The Organization and Disorganization of the American Working Class in the Late Nineteenth Century'. In: Ira Katznelson and Aristide R. Zolberg (eds): *Working-Class Formation: Nineteenth-Century Patterns in Western Europe and the United States*. Princeton, 1986.
Georg Simmel, 'Die Großstädte und das Geistesleben (1903)'. In: *Gesamtausgabe*, vol. 7. Frankfurt a. M., 2006.
Werner Sombart, *Krieg und Kapitalismus*. Munich, Leipzig, 1913.
Lawrence Sondhaus, *Naval Warfare, 1815–1914*. London, 2001.
Die österreichische Sozialdemokratie im Spiegel ihrer Programme, introd. by Ernst Winkler. Vienna, 1964.
Jonathan Sperber, *Karl Marx: A Nineteenth-Century Life*. New York, 2013.
Birgit Spieshöfer, *Unternehmerische Verantwortung zur Entstehung einer globalen Wirtschaftsordnung*. Baden-Baden, 2017.
Piero Sraffas, *Production of Commodities by Means of Commodities*. Cambridge, 1960.
William N. Still, *Iron Afloat: The Story of the Confederate Armorclads*. Columbia, 1985.
Theo Stammen and Alexander Classen (eds), *Karl Marx: Das Manifest der kommunistischen Partei*. Kommentierte Studienausgabe. Paderborn, 2009.
Gareth Stedman Jones, 'Engels and the Genesis of Marxism', *New Left Review* 106, 1977, 79–104.
Gareth Stedman Jones, 'Engels und die Geschichte des Marxismus'. In: *Klassen, Politik und Sprache*. Münster, 1988, 231–75.
Gareth Stedman Jones, *Outcast London: A Study in the Relationship between Classes in Victorian Society*. Oxford, 1971.
Gareth Stedman Jones, 'Engels and the Genesis of Marxism', *New Left Review* 106, 1977, 79–104.
Gareth Stedman Jones, 'Engels, Friedrich (1820–1895)', *The New Palgrave* 2, 1987, 144–6.

Bibliography

Gareth Stedman Jones, *Das kommunistische Manifest von Karl Marx und Friedrich Engels.* Einführung, Text, Kommentar, Munich 2012 (Engl. original 2002).
Gareth Stedman Jones, *Karl Marx: Greatness and Illusion.* Cambridge (MA), 2016.
Ian Steedman, *Consumption Takes Time: Implications for Economic Theory. The Graz Schumpeter Lectures.* London, 2001.
Nina Nikolaevna Stoskowa, *Friedrich Engels über die Technik. Zu ihrer Rolle in der Entwicklung der Gesellschaft.* Leipzig, 1971.
Roger Swift (ed.), *Irish Migrants in Britain, 1815–1914.* Cork, 2002.
Christiane Swinbank, *Love ye the Stranger: Public and Private Assistance to the German Poor in Nineteenth-Century London.* Reading, 2007.
Inge Taubert and Bernhard Dohm, 'Engels über den „roten" Becker: Ein unbekannter Brief von Friedrich Engels', *Beiträge zur Geschichte der Arbeiterbewegung* 15, 1973, 807–14.
Frederick W. Taylor, *The Principles of Scientific Management*, repr. ed. 1913, 1st ed. 1911. Weinheim, 1977.
Hans J. Teuteberg, 'Zeitgenössische deutsche Reflexionen über die Rolle des Faktors Arbeit in den frühen Phasen der britischen Industrialisierung (1750–1850)'. In: Hermann Kellenbenz (ed.): *Wirtschaftspolitik und Arbeitsmarkt: Bericht über die 4. Arbeitstagung der Gesellschaft für Sozial- und Wirtschaftsgeschichte in Wien am 14. und 15. April 1971.* Munich 1974, 238–70.
Hugh Thomas, *Geschichte der Welt.* Stuttgart, 1984.
Richard Tilly, *Vom Zollverein zum Industriestaat: Die wirtschaftlich-soziale Entwicklung Deutschlands 1834–1914.* Munich, 1990.
Edward P. Thompson, 'Mayhew and the Morning Chronicle'. In: Eileen Yeo (ed.): *The Unknown Mayhew: Selection from the Morning Chronicle 1849–1850.* London, 1971, 11–50.
Wilhelm Treue, *Der Krimkrieg und die Entstehung der modernen Flotten.* Göttingen, 1951.
Wilhelm Treue, 'Die preußische Agrarreform zwischen Romantik und Rationalismus', *Rheinische Vierteljahrs-Blätter* 20(1/4), 1955, 337–57.
Keith Tribe, 'Cameralism and the Science of Government', *Journal of Modern History* 56, June 1984, 263–84.
Keith Tribe, *Governing Economy: The Reformation of German Economic Discourse, 1750–1840.* Cambridge, New York, New Rochelle, Melbourne, Sydney, 1988.
Keith Tribe, *The Economy of the Word: Language, History, and Economics.* Oxford, 2015.
UNO-Weltbevölkerungsbericht 2018, Genf 2018.
Nicola Verdon, *Rural Women Workers in Nineteenth-Century England: Gender, Work and Wages.* Woodbridge, 2002.
Vivetta Vivarelli, 'Bacchus und die Titanenkämpfe als Gründungsmythen bei Hölderlin und Horaz'. In: Anja Ernst and Paul Geyer (eds.): *Die Romantik: ein Gründungsmythos der Europäischen Moderne.* Göttingen, 2010, 225–46.
Erich Vollgraf, 'Marx' Arbeit am dritten Buch des Kapital in den 1870/80er Jahren'. In: *In memoriam Wolfgang Jahn: Der ganze Marx. Alles Verfasste veröffentlichen, erforschen und den 'ungeschriebenen Marx' rekonstruieren.* Hamburg, 2002, 33–66.
Georg von Vollmar, 'Über Staatssozialismus (1892)'. In: Peter Friedemann (ed.): *Materialien zum politischen Richtungsstreit in der deutschen Sozialdemokratie*, vol. 1. Frankfurt a. M. Berlin, Vienna, 1978.
Andre Wakefield, *The Disordered Police State: German Cameralism as Science and Practice.* Chicago, London, 2009.
Hans-Ulrich Wehler, *Deutsche Gesellschaftsgeschichte*, vol. 2: *1815–1845/9.* Munich, 1987.
Robert E. Weir, *Beyond Labor's Veil: The Culture of the Knights of Labor.* University Park (Pennsylvania State University), 1996.
Thomas Welskopp, *Das Banner der Brüderlichkeit: Die deutsche Sozialdemokratie vom Vormärz bis zum Sozialistengesetz.* Bonn, 2000.

Emil Wilde, *The Development of Sailing Ship Tactics Compared to That of Steam Tactics, with a Glance into the Future*, 1911 (https://tandfonline.com/doi/abs/10.1080/03071841209435550?journalCode=rusi19).
Bill Williams, *The Making of the Manchester Jewry, 1740-1875*. Manchester, 1985.
Rainer Winkelmann (ed.), *Exzerpte über Arbeitsteilung, Maschinerie und Industrie*. Frankfurt, Berlin, Vienna, 1982.
Georg Winter, *Die Reorganisation des Preußischen Staates unter Stein und Hardenberg, erster Teil: Allgemeine Verwaltungs- und Behördenreform*, vol. 1. Leipzig, 1931.
Amy E. Wendling, *Karl Marx on Technology and Alienation*. London, 2009.
Roland Wenzlhuemer, *Connecting the Nineteenth-Century World: The Telegraph and Globalization*. Cambridge, 2013.
F. J. Williams, 'Irish in the East Cheshire Silk Industry 1851-1861', *The Historic Society of Lancashire & Cheshire* 136, 1986. https://www.hslc.org.uk/wp-content/uploads/2017/11/136-7-Williams.pdf.
James P. Womack, Daniel T. Jones and Daniel Roos, *Die zweite Revolution in der Autoindustrie*. Frankfurt a. M., 1991.
R. Bin Wong, 'Möglicher Überfluss, beharrliche Armut: Industrialisierung und Welthandel im 19.Jahrhundert'. In: Sebastian Conrad and Jürgen Osterhammel (eds): *Wege zur modernen Welt 1750-1870, Geschichte der Welt*, vol. 4. Munich, 2016, 255-410.
Edward A. Wrigley and Roger S. Schofield, *The Population History of England 1541-1871: A Reconstruction*. London, 1981.
Eileen Yeo, 'Mayhew as a Social Investigator'. In: Eileen Yeo (ed.): *The Unknown Mayhew: Selection from the Morning Chronicle 1849-1850*. London, 1971, 51-95.
Friedrich Wilhelm Rudolf Zimmermann, 'Die Zivilliste in den deutschen Staaten'. In: Georg Schanz and Julius Wolf (eds): *Finanz- und volkswirtschaftliche Zeitfragen*, issue 60. Stuttgart, 1919.

Historical texts

Victor Adler, 'Die Fabrikinspektion, insbesondere in England und in der Schweiz', first published in *Jahrbüchern für Nationalökonomie und Statistik N.F. 8*, 1884, reprinted in Victor Adlers Aufsätze, Reden und Briefe, ed. Parteivorstand der Sozialdemokratischen Arbeiterpartei Deutschösterreichs, issue 5. Vienna, 1922ff., 19-66.
Victor Adler, *Briefwechsel mit August Bebel und Karl Kautsky*, ed. Friedrich Adler. Vienna, 1954.
Victor Adler and Friedrich Engels, *Briefwechsel*, ed. Gerd Callesen and Wolfgang Maderthaner. Berlin, 2011.
Franz v. Baader, *Schriften zur Gesellschaftsphilosophie*, 1st ed. 1835. Jena, 1925.
Charles Babbage, *On the Economy of Machinery and Manufactures*. London, 1832.
Edward Baines, *Geschichte der britischen Baumwollindustrie*, transl. Christoph Bernoulli. Stuttgart, Tübingen, 1836.
August Bebels, *Briefwechsel mit Friedrich Engels*, ed. Werner Blumenberg, *Quellen und Untersuchungen zur Geschichte der deutschen und österreichischen Arbeiterbewegung*, vol. 6. Mouton, London, the Hague, 1965.
Friedrich Beck and Walter Schmidt (eds), *Dokumente aus geheimen Archiven, Bd. 5: Die Polizeikonferenzen deutscher Staaten 1851-1866. Präliminardokumente, Protokolle und Anlagen*. Weimar, 1993.
Louis Blanc, *Organisation du Travail*, 5th ed., 1st ed. 1840. Brussels, 1848.
Adolph J. Blanqui, *Geschichte der politischen Oekonomie in Europa vom Alterthume an bis auf unsere Tage, nebst einer kritischen Bibliographie der Hauptwerke über die politische Oekonomie*,

Bibliography

vol. 2 (2. vols), transl. of *Histoire de l'économie politique en Europe depuis les Anciens jusqu'à nos jours*, ed. and transl. Franz Joseph Buß, Paris 1837, repr. of the ed. 1841. Glashütten im Taunus, 1971.

Stephan Born, *Erinnerungen eines Achtundvierzigers*, ed. Hans J. Schütz, 3rd ed. Leipzig 1898. Berlin, Bonn, 1978.

Robertson Buchanan, *Practical Essays on Mill-Work and Other Machinery*. Edinburgh, 1841.

Johann Georg Büsch, *Schriften über Staatswirtschaft und Handlung: Der Bund der Kommunisten. Dokumente und Materialien, Bd. 2, 1849–1851*, ed. Herwig Förder et al. Berlin, 1982.

Eugène Buret, *La misère des classes laborieuses en Angleterre et en France, Paris*. Leipzig, 1840.

Catalog der Internationalen Elektrizitäts-Ausstellung. Munich, 1882.

Charles Darwin, *The Descent of Man, and Selection in Relation to Sex*. London, 1871.

Charles Dickens, *Harte Zeiten (1854)*. Berlin, 1984.

Disléré, *La guerre d'escadre et la guerre des cotes*. Paris, 1876.

Ernst Engel, *Das Zeitalter des Dampfes in technisch-statistischer Beleuchtung*, 2nd ed.. Berlin, 1881.

Die Briefe von Friedrich Engels an Eduard Bernstein. Mit Briefen von Karl Kautsky an ebendenselben, ed. Eduard Bernstein. Berlin, 1883.

Friedrich Engels' Briefwechsel mit Karl Kautsky, ed. Benedikt Kautsky. Vienna, 1953.

William Fardely, *Der electrische Telegraph, mit bes. Berücksichtigung seiner praktischen Anwendung für den Betrieb von Eisenbahnen etc.* Mannheim, 1844.

Johann Gottlieb Fichte, *Der geschloßne Handelsstaat: Ein philosophischer Entwurf als Anhang zur Rechtslehre, und Probe einer künftig zu liefernden Politik mit einem bisher unbekannten Manuskript Fichtes „Ueber StaatsWirthschaft"*, 3rd rev. ed., 1st ed. 1800. Hamburg, 1979.

Georg Wilhelm Friedrich Hegel, *Jenaer Realphilosophie: Vorlesungsmanuskripte zur Philosophie der Natur und des Geistes von 1805–1806*, repr. of „Jenenser Realphilosophie II", ed. Johannes Hoffmeister 1931, 1st ed. 1805/6. Hamburg, 1969.

Georg Wilhelm Friedrich Hegel, *Wissenschaft der Logik II, Werke in 20 Bänden auf der Grundlage der Werke von 1832–1845*, vol. 6, ed. Eva Moldenhauer and Karl Marcus Michel. Frankfurt, 1986.

Heinrich Heine, 'Lutetia, 2. Teil, article LVII, Paris 5. May 1843'. In: *Sämtliche Schriften*, vol. 5, ed. Klaus Briegleb, repr. of 2nd rev. ed. 1984. Munich, 2005.

Moses Heß, *Sozialismus und Kommunismus. Einundzwanzig Bogen aus der Schweiz*, ed. Georg Herwegh. Zürich, Winterthur 1842.

Moses Heß, *Briefwechsel*, edby Edmund Silberner. The Hague, 1959.

Bruno Hildebrand, 'Die gegenwärtige Aufgabe der Wissenschaft der Nationalökonomie'. In: *Die Nationalökonomie der Gegenwart und Zukunft und andere gesammelte Schriften I*, 1st ed. 1848. Jena, 1922.

Bruno Hildebrand, *Die Nationalökonomie der Gegenwart und Zukunft*. Frankfurt a. M., 1848.

Friedrich Hölderlin, 'Das Werden im Vergehen'. In: *Theoretische Schriften (um 1800), 1. print in Collected Works*. Jena, 1911; Berlin, 2013.

Gottlieb Hufeland, *Neue Grundlegung der Staatswirthschaftskunst durch Prüfung und Berichtigung ihrer Hauptbegriffe von Gut, Werth, Preis, Geld und Volksvermögen, mit ununterbrochener Rücksicht auf die bisherigen Systeme*, vol. I. Gießen. Wetzlar, 1807.

The Industry of Nations, as Exemplified in the Great Exhibition of 1851. The Materials of Industry. London, 1852.

The Industry of Nations, Part II. A Surwey of the Existing State of Arts, Machines and Manufactures. London, 1855.

Die I. Internationale in Deutschland 1864–1872. Dokumente und Materialien, ed. Rolf Dlubek et al. Berlin, 1964.

Bibliography

Johann Heinrich Gottlob v. Justi, *Gesammelte politische und Finanz-Schriften: Über wichtige Gegenstände der Staatskunst, der Kriegswissenschaften und des Kameral- und Finanzwesens*, vol. I (3 vols), ed. 1791, 1st ed. 1761. Aalen, 1970.

Johann Heinrich Gottlob v. Justi, *Die Grundfeste zu der Macht und Glückseligkeit der Staaten oder ausführliche Vorstellung der gesamten Polizeywissenschaft*, vol. I (2 vols), ed. 1760/1. Aalen, 1965.

Johann Heinrich Gottlob v. Justi, *Staatswirthschaft oder systematische Abhandlung aller Oekonomischen und Cameralwissenschaften, die zur Regierung eines Landes erfordert werden*, vol. I (2 vols), 2nd ed. 1758, 1st ed. 1755. Aalen, 1963.

Johann Heinrich Gottlob v. Justi, *System des Finanzwesens: Nach vernünftigen, aus dem Endzweck der bürgerlichen Gesellschaften und aus der Natur aller Quellen der Einkünfte des Staats hergeleiteten Grundsätze und Regeln abgehandelt*, repr. 1766 of the 1st ed. Aalen, 1969.

Ernst Kapp, *Der constituirte Despotismus und die constitutionelle Freiheit*. Hamburg, 1849.

Ernst Kapp, *Grundlinien einer Philosophie der Technik: Zur Entstehungsgeschichte der Cultur aus neuen Gesichtspunkten*. Braunschweig, 1877; repr. Hamburg, 2015.

James Phillips Kay, *The Moral and Physical Condition of the Working Classes Employed in the Cotton Manufacture in Manchester*. London, 1832.

Friedrich Albert Lange, *Die Arbeiterfrage: Ihre Bedeutung für Gegenwart und Zukunft*, 1st ed. 1865, rev. and ed. Adolf Grabowsky. Leipzig, 1910.

Friedrich List, *Das nationale System der Politischen Oekonomie*, 1st ed. 1840. Jena, 1904.

Heinrich Luden, *Handbuch der Staatsweisheit oder der Politik: Ein wissenschaftlicher Versuch*. Jena, 1811.

John Ramsay McCulloch, *A Discourse on the Rise, Progress, Peculiar Objects, and Importance of Political Economy*. Edinburgh, 1824.

Thomas Robert Malthus, *Eine Abhandlung über das Bevölkerungsgesetz oder eine Untersuchung seiner Bedeutung für die menschliche Wohlfahrt in Vergangenheit und Zukunft, nebst einer Prüfung unserer Aussichten auf eine künftige Beseitigung oder Linderung der Übel, die es verursacht*, transl. of *An Essay on the Principle of Population*, 6th ed. (2 vols) 1826, 1st ed. 1798. Jena, 1905.

Karl Marx and Friedrich Engels, *Historisch-Kritische Gesamtausgabe (MEGA[1])*, published on behalf of the Marx-Engels-Lenin-Institut Moscow by David Borisovic Rjazanov and Vladimir V. Adoratskij. Berlin, 1927.

Karl Marx and Friedrich Engels, *Gesamtausgabe (MEGA[2])*, ed. Internationale Marx-Engels-Stiftung (IMES) (International Institute of Social History, IISH). Berlin, 1975.

Marx-Engels-Werke (MEW), 44 vols. Berlin, 1956.

Karl Marx, *Die technologisch-historischen Exzerpte*, ed. Hans-Peter Müller. Frankfurt, Berlin, Vienna, 1981.

Karl Marx, *Exzerpte über Arbeitsteilung, Maschinerie und Industrie*, ed. Rainer Winkelmann. Frankfurt, Berlin, Vienna, 1982.

Gareth Stedman Jones, *Das kommunistische Manifest von Karl Marx und Friedrich Engels: Introduction, Text, Comment*. Munich, 2012.

Henry Mayhew, *The Morning Chronicle Survey of Labour and the Poor: The Metropolitan Districts*, vol. 6. Horsham, 1982.

Henry Mayhew, *London Labour and the London Poor*, 4 vols. London, 1861–2.

John Stuart Mill, *Principles of Political Economy: With Some of Their Applications to Social Philosophy*, London 1848, repr. ed. New York, 1973.

John Stuart Mill, *Grundsätze der politischen Ökonomie mit einigen ihrer Anwendungen auf die Sozialphilosophie*, 2nd German ed. Jena 1913, 7th ed. London 1871, vol. 1, books I–III, 1st ed. 1848. Jena, 1924.

Adam H. Müller, *Die Elemente der Staatskunst*, 2 vols, repr. 1st ed. 1809. Vienna, Leipzig, 1922.

Bibliography

Friedrich Nietzsche, *Also sprach Zarathustra: Ein Buch für alle und keinen*, ed. 1891, 1st ed. 1883. Munich, 1980.

Friedrich Nietzsche, *Ecce homo: Wie man wird, was man ist, entstanden, 1888/89*, 1st ed. 1908. Berlin, 2013.

Friedrich Nietzsche, *Unzeitgemäße Betrachtungen*, 3rd ed., vol. I (3 vols), 1954, 1st ed. 1893. Berlin, 2014.

Friedrich Nottebohm, *Auszug aus dem Tagebuche eines Reisenden durch Großbritannien und Belgien, im Jahre 1841, Verhandlungen des Vereins für Gewerbefleißes in Preußen*, issue 21. Berlin, 1842.

G. Gregory Olinthus, *A Treatise of Mechanics*, 3 vols. London, 1806.

Johann Heinrich Moritz von Poppe, *Die Mechanik des 18. Jahrhunderts*. Pyrmont, 1807.

Johann Heinrich Moritz von Poppe, *Lehrbuch der allgemeinen Technologie*. Frankfurt, 1809.

Johann Heinrich Moritz von Poppe, *Die Physik vorzüglich in Anwendung auf Künste*. Tübingen, 1830.

Johann Heinrich Moritz von Poppe, *Die Geschichte der Mathematik*. Tübingen, 1828.

Johann Heinrich Moritz von Poppe, *Geschichte der Technologie*, 3 vols. Göttingen, 1807–11.

Pierre Joseph Proudhon, *Qu'est-ce que la propriété? ou Recherches sur le principe du Droit et du Gouvernement*. Paris, 1840.

Karl Heinrich Rau, *Grundsätze der Volkswirthschaftspflege mit anhaltender Rücksicht auf bestehende Staatseinrichtungen (Lehrbuch der politischen Oekonomie, vol. II)*. Heidelberg, 1828.

Franz Reuleaux and Carl Ludwig Moll, *Lehrbuch Constructionslehre für den Maschinenbau*. Braunschweig, 1854.

Franz Reuleaux and Carl Ludwig Moll, *Der Constructeur: Ein Handbuch zum Gebrauch beim Maschinen-Entwerfen. Für Maschinen- und Bau-Ingenieure, Fabrikanten und technische Lehranstalten*. Braunschweig, 1861.

Franz Reuleaux and Carl Ludwig Moll, *Le Constructeur Aide-Mémoire a l'usage des Ingénieurs, Constructeurs, Architectes, Mécaniciens, etc*. Paris, 1875.

Franz Reuleaux and Carl Ludwig Moll, *Theoretische Kinematik. Grundzüge einer Theorie des Maschinenwesens*. Braunschweig, 1875.

Franz Reuleaux and Carl Ludwig Moll, 'Die Maschine und die Arbeiterfrage'. In: *Soziale Zeitfragen 2*. Minden, 1895.

David Ricardo, *On the Principles of Political Economy, and Taxation*, 1st ed. 1817, 3rd ed. 1821, vol. 1 of the *Collected Works and Correspondence of David Ricardo*, ed. Piero Sraffa and Maurice H. Dobb, Cambridge 1951, German ed. by Heinz D. Kurz and Christian Gehrke, *Über die Grundsätze der Politischen Ökonomie und der Besteuerung*, 2nd ed. Marburg, 2006.

Angus Bethune Reach, *Manchester and the Textile Districts in 1849*, ed. C. Aspin. Helmshore, 1972.

Ludwig August von Rochau, *Grundsätze der Realpolitik: Angewendet auf die staatlichen Zustände Deutschlands (1853/9)*, ed. and introd. Hans-Ulrich Wehler. Frankfurt a. M., 1972.

Wilhelm Roscher, *Die Grundlagen der Nationalökonomie: Ein Hand- und Lesebuch für Geschäftsmänner und Studierende*, vol. 1: *Ein Hand- und Lesebuch für Geschäftsmänner und Studierende*. Stuttgart, 1854.

Wilhelm Roscher, *Geschichte der National-Oekonomik in Deutschland*. Munich, 1874.

Georg Friedrich Sartorius, *Handbuch der Staatswirthschaft zum Gebrauche bey akademischen Vorlesungen nach Adam Smith's Grundsätzen ausgearbeitet*. Berlin, 1796.

Jean-Babtiste Say, *Ausführliche Darstellung der Nationalökonomie oder der Staatswirtschaft*, transl. of the 5th ed. of *Traité d'économie politique von 1826*, 1st ed. 1803, vol. 1 (3 vols). Stuttgart, 1833.

Johann August Schlettwein, *Grundfeste der Staaten oder die politische Ökonomie*. Gießen, 1779.
Johann August Schlettwein, *Die Rechte der Menschheit oder der einzige wahre Grund aller Gesetze, Ordnungen und Verfassungen*. Gießen, 1784.
Gustav v. Schmoller, *Zur Social- und Gewerbepolitik der Gegenwart: Speeches and Essays*. Leipzig, 1890.
Gustav v. Schmoller, 'Die Arbeiterfrage'. In: *Preußische Jahrbücher* 14 u. 15, 393–424 (part I), 395; 523–47 (part II). Berlin, 1864.
Gustav v. Schmoller, *Grundriß der Allgemeinen Volkswirtschaftslehre*, 2 vols, repr. 1923 of the 1st ed. 1900. Berlin, 1978.
Arthur Schopenhauer, 'Zur Rechtslehre und Politik' (first published 1851). In: *Parerga und Paralipomena: Kleine Schriften 2*. Zurich, 1988.
David Scott, *The Engineer and Machinist's Assistant: A Series of Plans, Sections and Elevations, of Stationary, Marine, and Locomotive Engines, Water Wheels, Spinning Machines, Tools, etc., Taken from Machines of Approved Construction, with Detailed Descriptions, and Practical Essays on Various Departments of Machinery*. Glasgow, Edinburgh, London, 1856.
Adam Smith, *An Inquiry into the Nature and Causes of the Wealth of Nations*, 1st ed. 1776, ed. Richard H. Campbell and Andrew S. Skinner in *The Glasgow Edition of the Collected Writings of Adam Smith*, 2 vols. Oxford, 1976.
Adam Smith, *An Inquiry into the Nature and Causes of the Wealth of Nations*, 1st ed. 1776, introd. John Ramsay McCulloch, 4 vols. Edinburgh, 1828.
Adam Smith, *Untersuchung über Wesen und Ursachen des Reichtums der Völker*, ed. and introd. Erich Streissler, transl. Monika Streissler. Düsseldorf, 1999.
Joseph v. Sonnenfels, *Grundsätze der Polizey, Handlung und Finanz*, vol. I, 5th ed., 1st ed. 1765. Vienna, 1787.
Friedrich Julius Heinrich v. Soden, *Die Nazional-Oekonomie: Ein philosophischer Versuch, über die Quellen des Nazional-Reichthums, und über die Mittel zu dessen Beförderung*. Leipzig, 1805.
Lorenz v. Stein, *Geschichte der sozialen Bewegung in Frankreich von 1789 bis auf unsere Tage*, 3 vols, 1st ed. 1850, repr. of the ed. Munich 1921. Darmstadt, 1972.
Lorenz v. Stein, 'Die soziale Bewegung und der Sozialismus in England'. In: *Die Gegenwart*. Leipzig, 1849, 464–87.
David Friedrich Strauss, *Das Leben Jesu, kritisch bearbeitet*, 2 vols. Tübingen, 1835.
Eugene Sue, *Die Geheimnisse von Paris (1843)*. Berlin, 1843.
Andrew Ure, *The Philosophy of Manufactures: Or, An Exposition of the Scientific, Moral and Commercial Economy of the Factory System of Great Britain*. London, 1835.
Jakob Venedey, *England*. Leipzig, 1845.
Hermann Wagener, 'Arbeit, Arbeiter, Arbeitszeit'. In: *Staats- und Gesellschaftslexikon*, vol. II: *Almquist bis Atthalin*. Berlin, 1859.
John Watts, *The Facts and Fictions of Political Economists: Being a Review of the Principles of the Science, Separating the True from the False*. Manchester, 1842.
Friedrich Benedict Weber, *Systematisches Handbuch der Staatswirthschaft mit vorzüglicher Rücksicht auf die Literatur derselben*. Berlin, 1804.
Georg Weerth, *Sämtliche Werke*, vol. 3: *Die englischen Arbeiter*. Berlin, 1957.
Carl Wermuth and Wilhelm Stieber, *Die Communisten-Verschwörungen des neunzehnten Jahrhunderts*. Berlin, 1853/4.
William Whewell, *The Mechanics of Engeniering*. Cambridge, 1841.
Zwei politische Prozesse: Verhandelt vor den Februar-Assisen in Köln. Cologne, 1849.

INDEX

Note: Figures are indicated by page number followed by "f". Endnotes are indicated by the page number followed by "n" and the endnote number e.g., 20 n.1 refers to endnote 1 on page 20.

Adler, Georg 40, 235, 267 n.89, n.90, 268 n.96, n.97, n.100, 314 n.75
Adler, Max 57, 58
Adler, Victor 2, 43, 271 n.17, 272 n.50
  and Austromarxism 43, 57–59
  childhood 46
  final crisis of capitalism 56–57
  first May Day 49–50
  Friedrich Engels' friendship with 43, 48
  to Marxist socialism 47
  nationalities question 51
  political involvement 46
  profession 46
  reformism and revisionism 53–56
  road to socialism 44–45
  Social Democratic Movement in 1886 46
  suffrage movement 50
Altersbriefe (Engels, Friedrich) 10
America 64
  Irish immigration in 144–145
  Socialist Labour Party 114
American Civil War (1861–5) 19, 86, 89, 90, 96, 98, 103, 105, 109, 116
American Federation of Labour (AFL) 111, 117
Amsterdam 119, 255
Ancient Society (Morgan, Lewis Henry 1877) 20, 21, 234
Anti-Duhring (Engels, Friedrich) 10, 45, 203, 227
Anti-Slavery war 106
anti-socialist law 22, 24, 36–40, 46, 48, 55, 237, 238–239
Aristotle 64, 77, 82
Arkwright, Richard 65, 139, 219, 274 n.11
armoured ships 87, 88
  types of 99f
Austria 2, 17, 61, 252
  Social Democratic Party 43, 46, 47, 52–53
  Socialist International 48
  socialist movement in 46–48
  Unification Party Congress of 1888–9 46
Austromarxism 43, 51
  theory and politics 57–59
'automaton' 73, 74
Aveling, Edward 230, 291 n.64, 309 n.90

Aveling, Eleanor Marx 230, 238
von Baader, Franz Xaver 171
Babbage, Charles 68, 70, 72, 81, 219, 274 n.13, 275 n.19
Bakunin, Mikhail Alexandrovich 23, 34, 35f, 41, 117
Barmen 11, 66, 65, 137, 167, 182, 193, 200, 220, 252
Battle of Lissa 94, 96, 97
Battle of Trafalgar 94
Bauer, Bruno 182, 269 n.116
Bauer, Heinrich 38
Bauer, Otto 51, 56, 57, 59, 273 n.73
Bauer, Thomas 10, 257 n.4
Bayly, Christopher 119, 288 n.4
Bebel, August 25, 85, 101, 111, 238, 52, 263 n.47, 271 n.14, 310 n.2
Beerbühl, Margrit Schulte 4, 295 n.87
Belgium 30, 32, 193
Berlin 17, 20, 37, 39, 41, 70, 124, 182, 253, 255
Bernstein, Eduard 21, 24, 27, 36, 54, 55, 234, 235, 238, 257 n.14, 261 n.5, 264 n.60, 270 n.118, 271 n.14, 304 n.176, 313 n.70, 314 n.77
Berthollet, Claude-Luis 219
Blanc, Louis 39, 184–185, 202
Blanqui, Jérôme-Adolphe 65–66, 181, 274 n.8, 301 n.95
blue water schools 96–99
Bohemia, Czechs in 17, 51
Bolshevik Communism 58
Boot, H. M. 87, 141, 143, 293 n.27
Booth, Charles 152
Borkheim, Sigismund 22
Born, Stephan 39, 40, 182
Boulton, Mathew 68, 276 n.26
'bourgeoisie' 14, 49, 51, 52
Boyd, Robert 145, 294 n.66
Bracke, Wilhelm 32, 262 n.21
Brentano, Lujo 21, 27
Britain 64, 83, 234
  coast versus capital 98–100
  cotton market 18
The British Bee Hive, (Cruikshank, George 1840) 155f
Brno Nationalities Programme 51

Index

Brockhaus encyclopaedia 173
Brophy, James M. 3, 315 n.96
Buret, Eugène 274 n.13
Burnette, Joyce 142, 143, 292 n.13
Burns, Lizzy 19, 228, 293 n.46
Burns, Mary Ellen 19, 67, 293 n.47
Busteed, Mervyn A. 144, 294 n.54
Bythell, Duncan 139, 292 n.10

Cameralism 1, 167, 170
Canada
    Irish immigration in 144–145
Cantillon, Richard 213
Capital and Ideology (Piketty, Thomas) 247
Capital in the Twenty-First Century (Piketty, Thomas) 247
capital 177
    accumulation of 1, 45
    theory of 25
capitalism 1, 3, 5, 10, 14, 15, 22, 29, 34, 44, 53, 59, 60, 197
    after Engels 242
    final crisis of 56–57
Capitalism, Socialism, and Democracy (Schumpeter, Joseph Aloys) 190
Carlyle, Thomas 210, 273 n.4
Cartwright, Edmund 139, 219
Chaloupek, Günther 2
child labour 141, 151
Christensen, Clayton 303 n.149
    theory of disruptive innovation 190
'classical bourgeois' 204
classical
    economics 175
    economists 184, 204, 206
    national economic theory 171–175
Coles, Cowper captain 92, 93
communism 12, 15, 58, 124, 126, 183, 187, 189, 251
Communist Manifesto (Marx and Engels) 15, 39, 44, 105, 109, 120, 123, 128, 190, 193, 236, 242, 267 n.94
competition 56, 59, 79, 82, 88, 109, 128, 130, 146, 171, 178, 197, 202, 211–213
The Condition of the Working Class in England (Engels, Friedrich) 2, 4, 12, 143, 189, 252
consumption 1, 197, 246
A Contribution to the Critique of Political Economy (Marx, Karl 1859) 41, 204, 262 n.25, 305 n.5
Corliss Steam Engine 112f
corporate networks and virtual organizations 243, 245–247
Cournot, Antoine-Augustin 308 n.55
creation and destruction
    in economic thought 190
    in Egyptian mythology 192

German philosophy 192
    in Hinduism 192
creative destruction 65, 165, 190, 214
    laws of 195
Crimean War (1853–6) 19, 85, 89, 98
Critique (1844) 199, 210
Crompton, Samuel 139, 219
crowdsourcing 247
Cruikshank, George 155f
CSR (corporate social responsibility) 246
CSS *Atlanta* 97f

Darwin, Charles 20, 79, 134, 195, 199
Das Kapital 213, 220, 227–228, 229f
    Engels as 'editor' 228
    Volumes II and III of 2, 3, 5, 10, 22, 27, 29, 30, 32, 36, 41, 199, 205
Das Zollvereinsblatt (Bulletin of the German Customs Union) 172f
Davis, Graham 145
Davy, Humphry 219
Denmark
    marine innovations 91–92
Deprez, Marcel 83
Der Kampf (journal) 52
Deutsche Fortschrittspartei (German Progress Party) 46
Deutsche-Brüsseler-Zeitung (Brussels German News) 16
Dialectics of Nature (Engels, Friedrich) (1873–82) 10, 194
Dickens, Charles 121
digitization 5
Dionysus 192
Discourse of Political Economy (Smith, Adam 1824) 206
'dismal science' 210
division of labour 148, 175
Docks, Millwall 72
Doré, Gustave 156f–164f
Dühring, Eugen 20

Eastern European Jews 151–152
    from Poland and Russia 152
Ecce Homo (Nietzsche, Friedrich) 190
economic liberalism 171
economic revolution 25
economic theory
    at beginning of nineteenth century 166–169
economies of scale 4
On the Economy of Machinery and Manufactures (Babbage, Charles 1832) 219–220, 274 n.13
Edison, Thomas 83
von Eichhorn, Friedrich 31f

Index

Einstein, Albert 23
Eisengarten, Oscar 228
Elkan, David Levi 31f
Elster, Ludwig 7, 41
employee participation and co-determination 244–245
Engels, Friedrich 1, 3, 40, 63, 102f, 120, 137, 165, 187, 199, 201f, 206, 225f, 249, 257 n.2, n.9, n.10
   articles 19
   for Austrian social democracy 52–53
   attack on Malthus population theory 180–182
   balance sheet, with errors 40–41
   capitalism after 242
   classical national economic theory 171–174
   economic thought 196
   employee participation and co-determination 244–245
   in Ermen & Engels, Manchester 183
   essay in public relations 29–32
   funeral oration for Marx 35–36
   human–machine interface in early writings 65–68
   and ideas of *jeune école* 96–98
   intellectual transformation 12
   as journalist and publicist 7
   Kaizen and lean management 245
   knowledge of economic theory 165
   labour 244
   Letters from Wuppertal (1839) 193
   Malthus and population question 180–182
   management 244
   My Immortal Works (Engels, Friedrich) 7, 8–9f
   on Marx 27
   on military science and technology 3
   and naval warfare debate 85
   perception of economic theory 169–170
   political journalist in 19–24
   political refugee and 'cotton-lord' in Manchester 17–19
   social psychology 244
   starting points and evolution 241–242
   Taylorism and assembly line 243–244
   territorial principle 51
   as textile industrialist 11
   in twenty-first century 247–248
   volumes II and III 223
   work in Manchester and London 137
   young moralist of Outlines 174–180
Engels, Friedrich Sr 140
England 14, 16, 32, 43, 144
   textile industry 68
Erfurt programme 53, 242
Ericsson, John 92
Ermen & Engels 194, 252
Ermen, Gottfried 194

ESG (environmental social governance) 246
The Essence of Christianity (Feuerbach, Ludwig 1841) 183
Europe 1, 18, 245
European Revolution of 1848–9 16–17
European social democracy 43
European Union (EU) 245
exploitation
   of labour 4

Facts and Fictions of Political Economy (Watts, John 1842) 184
Fairie, Thomas 146
Fardely, William 153
Feuerbach, Ludwig 21, 183
Fichte, Johann Gottlieb 171
finance capital 57
Ford, Henry 243
Fordism 5
Fourier, Charles 65, 180, 187, 200
   Des trois unités externs 187
Frambach, Hans A. 4, 251
France 14, 16, 32, 43, 115, 234, 247
Franco-Prussian War of 1870 7, 22–23
Franklin, Benjamin 72
French Revolution of 1789 12, 22, 26, 63, 68, 166
French socialism 187
Freud, Sigmund 271 n.12

Geikie, James 224
gender discrimination
   in textile industry 142
German Communist Party 24, 38
The German Ideology (Engels and Marx) 14, 203
German March Revolution 16
German Revolution of 1848–9 104, 203
German Socialist Party (SPD) 44
Germany 14, 16, 39, 43, 46, 52, 115, 122, 234, 252
   Anti-Socialist Law 235
   Industrial Relations Act in 1920 244
   Coal, Iron and Steel Industry Codetermination Act 244
global capitalism 101
globalization 5, 26
Godwin, Edwin L. 116
von Goethe, Johann Wolfgang 192
Gompers, Samuel 117
Gossen, Hermann Heinrich 175, 307 n.47
Gotha Party Congress in 1875 46
Graeber, Friedrich 189
Great Britain 120
Great Depression of 1930 61
Grün, Karl 40
Gutzkow, Karl 10, 257 n.11

339

Index

Hainfeld Programme 46, 51, 53, 55, 56
Handwörterbuch der Sozialwissenschaften (Concise Dictionary of the Social Sciences) 7
Handwörterbuch der Staatswissenschaften (Concise Dictionary of Political Science) 7, 40
Handwörterbuch der Wirtschaftswissenschaft en (Concise Dictionary of Economics) 7
von Hardenberg 166
Hargreaves, James 219
Harrison, Benjamin 109
Hegel 64, 77, 124, 197, 277 n.33, 301n.101
Heine, Heinrich 153
Heinzen, Karl 113
Helmholtz, Hermann 78
Herder, Johann Gottfried 192
Herres, Jürgen 2, 264 n.64
Herwegh, Georg 38, 301 n.105
Hess, Moses 183, 186, 196, 200, 251
Hildebrand, Bruno 173, 296-7 n.1
Hilferding, Rudolf 56, 57, 272 n.69
historical materialism 14
HMS *Warrior* 88f
Hobbes, Thomas 211
Hobsbawm, Eric 14
Hodgson, Rob I. 144
Hölderlin, Friedrich 192
Holmes, Samuel 146
The Holy Family or Critique of Critical Criticism: Against Bruno Bauer and Company (Engels and Marx 1845) 11, 190
Horkheimer, Max 135
Hufeland, Gottlieb 167
Hungary 17, 19
Hutcheson, Francis 206
Huxley, Thomas 195

Illner, Eberhard 3, 250
imperialism theory 56
Indian uprising of 1857-8 19
Industrial Revolution 1, 13, 14, 63, 67
industrialization 26
International Labour Organization (ILO) 245
International Working Men's Association 43
Internationale Arbeiter-Assoziation (International Working Men's Association) 32
Internationale Marx-Engels-Stiftung (International Marx-Engels Foundation, IMES) 255
investment 1
Ireland 66
Irish
  men and women 144
  people immigration 144
  mass immigration of 153-154
Italian revolution 17
Italian War of Independence of 1859 18, 19

Italy 17, 19

von Jakob, Ludwig Heinrich 167
Japan 245
Jerrold, Blanchard 156f
Jevons, William Stanley 175, 195, 308 n.62
Jews
  mass immigration of 153-154
Jones, Gareth Stedman 147, 199
Jones, Stedman 210

Kaizen and lean management 245
Kalecki, Michal 309 n.80
Kapp, Ernst 3, 63, 64
  philosophy of technology 75-84, 76f
  publications 78
Kautsky, Karl 21, 27, 43, 46, 108, 204, 234, 235, 236, 238, 257 n.14, 260 n.73, 267 n.95, 269 n.107
Kay, James Phillips 67, 184
Kelley-Wischnewetzky, Florence 110
Keynes, John Maynard 309 n.80
Kocka, Jürgen 5
Köppen, Karl Friedrich 182
Koubek, Norbert 5
Krieg und Kapitalismus (War and Capitalism, Sombart, Werner 1913) 190
Kriege, Hermann 104
Kugelmann, Ludwig (Louis) 29, 261 n.13, n.14
Kurz, Heinz D. 4, 175, 250, 251, 271 n.9, 272 n.70

labour 1, 3, 20, 34, 177, 241, 244
  exploitation of 4
labour unions 117
Lafague, Paul 25, 35, 238
land
  rent 177-178
Lange, Friedrich Albert 173
Lassalle, Ferdinand 29-30, 113
  model of state socialism 61
Leach, James 67
lean management 5
Lenin 35
Lessner, Friedrich 35
Leupold, Heinrich 169
liberal economic system 181
von Liebig, Justus 204, 219f
Liebknecht, Wilhelm 20, 29, 35, 52, 85, 238, 262 n.21, 264 n.67, 270 n.117, 271 n.14
Liebmann, Otto 78
The Life of Jesus Critically Examined (Strauss, David Friedrich 1835-6) 189
Lincoln, Abraham 105, 107
List, Friedrich 168f, 171, 190, 206
Liverpool

Index

Irish immigration in 144–145
German immigrants in 146
Locke, John 211
London: A Pilgrimage, 1872 156f–164f
London 4, 17, 18, 43
  economic migrants 147
  political refugees of Europe 147
  social differentiation 151
  street people 150–151
Loria, Achille 36
Lübbe, Hermann 122
Luden, Heinrich 169
Luxemburg, Rosa 24, 57, 272 n.64
Lyell, Charles 195

MacRaild, Donald 153, 144–145
Mahan, Alfred Thayer 97
Majer, Friedrich 192
Malthus, Thomas R. 67, 165, 170, 184, 202, 210, 218, 250, 251
  population theory 4, 180–182, 218
man and machine 63
management 244
Manchester 19
  cotton city of 139
  Irish immigration in 144–145
  Stock Exchange 18
Manifesto of the Communist Party 12, 13f
  impact in European continent 14
marginalists 216
Marx and Engels 42
  into active politics 15
  Communist Manifesto 15
  criticism of religion and philosophy 14
  Das Kapital, Volumes II and III of 2
  formative years for 14
  The German Ideology 10
Marx Engels Collected Works (MECW) 199
Marx, Eleanor 34–35
Marx, Jenny 14, 258 n.34
Marx, Karl 1, 3, 11, 29, 33f, 37, 40, 63, 69f, 120, 126, 165, 183, 199, 209, 220, 226f, 242, 257 n.5
  autodidactic course in technology 68, 70
  The Class Struggle in France 1848–1850 24
  conception of history, creating 32–36
  Das Elend der Philosophie (The Poverty of Philosophy) 22
  Das Kapital 22
  Economic and Philosophic Manuscripts of 1844 10
  expulsion from Prussia 269 n.105
  intellectual transformation 12
  Kapital I 224
  manuscripts of 233f, 237
  money and capital 82
  monument 249f
  publisher 237
  Revelations Concerning the Communist Trial in Cologne (1885) 22
  second Russian edition of 256
  topics and argumentation 232, 234
Marx–Engels Collected Works (MECW) 199, 256
Marx–Engels Gesamtausgabe (MEGA) 42, 232, 250, 255, 256
Mayer, Gustav 24, 200, 271 n.24, 274 n.13
Mayhew, Henry 148, 151–152
McCormick 109
McCulloch, John Ramsay 175, 184, 206, 306 n.11
Mehring, Franz 40, 268 n.97, n.101
Menger, Carl 175, 176f
Meyer, Rudolph 236
Meysels, Lucian O. 271 n.11
Mill, John Stuart 177, 184, 213
  Principles of Economics (1848) 177
Minoletti, Paul 142
Misère de la philosophie (*The Poverty of Philosophy*, Marx, Karl) 235
'modern scientific socialism' 34
Moll, Joseph 38
monopoly 213, 308 n.55
Moore, Samuel 230
More, Thomas 190
Morgan, Lewis Henry 20, 234
Moscow 42, 255, 256
Möser, Kurt 3
Müller, Adam 171
Münkler, Herfried 25, 260 n.107

'naïve cosmopolitanism' 51
Napoleonic Wars in 1815 149
'national economy' 174, 206
natural prices 216
nature 5, 30, 36
  theory of 23
naval engagements
  close combat and ramming 93–94
  Gun placement 91–93
  long-range combat 95
  precision versus contingency 95–96
  strategy 93–95
  in time of transition 89–91
nearshoring 246
neoclassical economics 175
the Netherlands
  marine innovations 91–92
Neue Rheinische Zeitung (New Rhenish Newspaper) 16, 39, 193
Die Neue Zeit (The New Age) journal 12, 56, 235, 267 n.92
New American Cyclopaedia 19

341

Index

New York Tribune 18–19
Nietzsche, Friedrich 190, 192
Nippel, Wilfried 2, 21, 249, 260 n.79, 261 n.8, 263 n.37, 266 n.78

offshoring 246
On the Origin of Species (Darwin, Charles 1859) 195
Oswald, Friedrich 121, 193
Outlines of a Critique of Political Economy (Engels, Friedrich) 4, 187, 202, 206
Outlines of a Philosophy of the History of Man (Herder, Johann Gottfried 1784–91) 192
Owen, Robert 14, 184, 185f, 200, 202, 211

The Pall Mall Gazette (Newspaper) 7
Paine, Thomas 104
Paixhans, Henri-Joseph 87
Panayi, Panikos 152
Paris 16
Paris February Revolution 1848 16
participative management 5
Philippe, Louis French King 16
The Philosophy of Manufactures (Ure, Andrew 1835) 274 n.13
Piketty, Thomas 247
Plumpe, Werner 3, 250
Po and Rhine (Engels, Friedrich 1859) 18
political economics 186, 199, 206, 250
Pope Benedict XVI 12
population theory 180–182
Prague 46
pre-classical economics 175
Die Presse (Viennese daily newspaper) 19
price
    fluctuations 216–217
    true value versus 214–216
Principles of Political Economy (Mill, John Stuart 1848) 213
Principles of Political Economy and Taxation (Ricardo, David 1821) 274 n.13
The Principles of Scientific Management (Taylor, Frederick W.) 243
'private economy' 174
private property 211
production factors
    classical division of 177
professorial socialism 122
'proletariat' 14
Proudhon, Pierre-Joseph 15, 39, 103, 186, 200, 202, 212f
Prussia 16, 53, 97

Qu'est ce que la propriété? (What Is Property?, 1840) 186

Rau, Karl Heinrich 169
Reach, Angus Bethune 137, 140, 142
Reed, Edward 93
reformism and revisionism 53–56
Renner, Karl 51, 57, 58, 61
Reuleaux, Franz 79, 81
revolution 2, 10, 36, 38
    anticipation of 11–15
revolutionizing of labour 137
Rheinische Zeitung (Rhenish News) 32, 183
Ricardo, David 5, 111, 165, 170, 175, 202, 204, 209, 218, 220, 250, 251
    Principles of Political Economy and Taxation (1821) 274 n.13
Richards, Eric 141
Rodbertus, Johann Karl 40, 235
Roscher, Wilhelm 167, 174, 187
Roth, Regina 5, 250, 257 n.7
Ruge, Arnold 11, 124, 182
Russia 19

Saint-Simon 187
de Saint-Simon, Henri 200
Sardinian War, 1859 95
Sartorius, Georg Friedrich 169
Savoy, Nice and the Rhine (Engels, Friedrich 1860) 18
Say, Jean Baptiste 65, 165, 175, 202, 209
    Traité d'économie politique (1803) 177
Schapper, Karl 38, 264 n.61, 265 n.73
von Schlegel, Friedrich 171
Schelling, Friedrich Wilhelm 182
Schleiermacher, Friedrich 124, 189
First Schleswig War 17
Schlüter, Hermann 36, 37, 38, 40, 235, 267 n.88, n.91
Schmoller, Gustav 173
Schopenhauer, Arthur 120, 192
Schumpeter, Joseph A. 4, 65, 165, 167, 190, 191f, 214, 308 n.58
science and social productive powers 218–220
'scientific socialism' 4, 40, 42, 117, 187, 189, 202
Scotland 144
Sheppard, Francis 147
Siebel, Carl 29
von Siemens, Werner 83
silk industry
    manufacturers of England 149–150
    of Spitalfields 148–150
de Sismondi, Charles Simonde 65, 184
Smeaton, John 70
Smith, Adam 5, 165, 166, 167, 170, 200, 202, 206, 207f, 209, 211, 250, 251, 306 n.11, 308 n.64, n.66, n.70, 309 n.74
    division of labour 175

Index

Der Sozialdemokrat (The Social Democrat) 21
'Social Democratic Party of Germany' (SPD) 46, 61, 101, 242
social psychology 244
socialism 4, 12, 20, 27, 181, 197, 251
Socialist Unity Party (SED) 256
Socialist Workers' Party (SAP) 242
von Soden, Friedrich Julius 167
Sombart, Werner 190, 239
Sorge, Friedrich Adolph 103
specialization 79
Spitalfields Act 148–149
Stalin 21
'state socialism' 53
  and Marxist socialism 54
von Stein, Lorenz 4, 187, 188f
Stirner, Max 182
Strauss, David Friedrich 124, 189
Sue, Eugène 121
sustainability 5
Switzerland 16, 17, 32, 46, 193, 271 n.14

Taaffe, Count 50
Taylor, Frederick W. 243
Taylorism 5
  and assembly line 243–244
technology 1, 3, 4, 25
Telegraph 193
Tesla, Nikola 84
Teuteberg, Hans J. 139
textile mills
  men and women in 142
Theories of Surplus Value (Kautsky, Karl 1905–10) 204
Theory of Economic Development (Schumpeter, Joseph Alois 1912) 190
theory of marginal utility 175
Thoughts out of Season (Nietzsche, Friedrich) 192
von Thünen, Johann Heinrich 175
de Tocqueville, Alexis 104
trade unions 117
transformation of world 119
  capitalism as dead end 130–132
  social protest and communist principles 126–128
  socialism as a way out 132–133
  technological progress and revolutionary expectations 128–130
Turgot, Anne Robert Jacques 213

UNESCO
  Index Translationum (Index of Translations) 2
  World Documentary Heritage list 12
Unification Party Congress of 1888–9 43, 46

'Declaration of Principles' 47
United States 83, 122, 231, 234, 245, 247
  capital and free trade 107–111
  and future of capitalism 101
  giant steps and civil war 103–107
  workers' movement 111–118
  unskilled immigrants 148
Ure, Andrew 68, 71f, 73, 274 n.13
USS *Monitor* 92f

Vanderbilt, Cornelius 108
Venedey, Jakob 144, 145
Verne, Jules 119
Volksbuchhandlung (People's Press) 235
Volks-Kalender (People's Calendar) 32
Der Volksstaat (The People's State) (Newspaper) 20
von Vollmar, Georg 52, 53, 272 n.54
'vulgar economists' 204

wage discrimination 142
  in textile industry 142
Wagener, Hermann W. 173
Walras, Léon 175
Watt, James 65, 68, 219, 274 n.11
Watts, John 65, 66, 184, 196, 197, 200, 209
The Wealth of Nations (Smith, Adam 1776) 166, 206, 207f, 210, 213, 306 n.11
Weerth, Georg 67, 139, 147, 150–151
Weitling, Wilhelm 38, 40
Weydemeyer, Joseph 106
white water schools 96
Wilhelm, Friedrich III 182
Wilhelm, Friedrich IV 183
Williams, Bill 152
Williams, F. J. 145
Willich, August 38, 85
Wischnewetzky, Florence Kelley 236
Wolff, Wilhelm 22, 37, 264 n.56
women
  age-specific differences 142–143
  in agriculture 143
  gender discrimination 142
  in industry 141
  and men in textile mills 142
  wage discrimination 142
workers' movement 18, 39
  in Europe 21, 22, 25
  in German 29, 30, 34
  international 40, 42

Zarathustra (Nietzsche, Friedrich) 190
Zur Wohnungsfrage (On the Housing Question) of 1872 20